THE COMPLETE POEMS

OF

LOUIS DANIEL

BRODSKY

VOLUME FOUR, 1981–1985

Books by LOUIS DANIEL BRODSKY

Poetry

Five Facets of Myself   (1967)* (1995)
The Easy Philosopher   (1967)* (1995)
"A Hard Coming of It" and Other Poems   (1967)* (1995)
The Foul Rag-and-Bone Shop   (1967)* (1969, exp.)* (1995, exp.)
Points in Time   (1971)* (1995) (1996)
Taking the Back Road Home   (1972)* (1997) (2000)
Trip to Tipton and Other Compulsions   (1973)* (1997)
"The Talking Machine" and Other Poems   (1974)* (1997)
Tiffany Shade   (1974)* (1997)
Trilogy: A Birth Cycle   (1974) (1998)
Cold Companionable Streams   (1975)* (1999)
Monday's Child   (1975) (1998)
Preparing for Incarnations   (1975)* (1976, exp.) (1999) (1999, exp.)
The Kingdom of Gewgaw   (1976) (2000)
Point of Americas II   (1976) (1998)
La Preciosa   (1977) (2001)
Stranded in the Land of Transients   (1978) (2000)
The Uncelebrated Ceremony of Pants-Factory Fatso   (1978) (2001)
Birds in Passage   (1980) (2001)
Résumé of a Scrapegoat   (1980) (2001)
Mississippi Vistas: Volume One of *A Mississippi Trilogy*   (1983) (1990)
You Can't Go Back, Exactly   (1988, two eds.) (1989) (2003, exp.)
The Thorough Earth   (1989)
Four and Twenty Blackbirds Soaring   (1989)
Falling from Heaven: Holocaust Poems of a Jew and a Gentile *(with William Heyen)*   (1991)
Forever, for Now: Poems for a Later Love   (1991)
Mistress Mississippi: Volume Three of *A Mississippi Trilogy*   (1992)
A Gleam in the Eye: Poems for a First Baby   (1992)
Gestapo Crows: Holocaust Poems   (1992)
The Capital Café: Poems of Redneck, U.S.A.   (1993)
Disappearing in Mississippi Latitudes: Volume Two of *A Mississippi Trilogy*   (1994)
A Mississippi Trilogy: A Poetic Saga of the South   (1995)*
Paper-Whites for Lady Jane: Poems of a Midlife Love Affair   (1995)
The Complete Poems of Louis Daniel Brodsky: Volume One, 1963–1967
   (edited by Sheri L. Vandermolen)   (1996)
Three Early Books of Poems by Louis Daniel Brodsky, 1967–1969: *The Easy Philosopher*,
   "A Hard Coming of It" and Other Poems, and *The Foul Rag-and-Bone Shop*
   (edited by Sheri L. Vandermolen)   (1997)
The Eleventh Lost Tribe: Poems of the Holocaust   (1998)
Toward the Torah, Soaring: Poems of the Renascence of Faith   (1998)
Voice Within the Void: Poems of *Homo supinus*   (2000)
Rabbi Auschwitz: Poems Touching the Shoah   (2000)*
The Swastika Clock: Endlösung Poems   (2001)*
Shadow War: A Poetic Chronicle of September 11 and Beyond, Volume One   (2001) (2004)
The Complete Poems of Louis Daniel Brodsky: Volume Two, 1967–1976
   (edited by Sheri L. Vandermolen)   (2002)
Shadow War: A Poetic Chronicle of September 11 and Beyond, Volume Two   (2002) (2004)
Shadow War: A Poetic Chronicle of September 11 and Beyond, Volume Three   (2002) (2004)
Shadow War: A Poetic Chronicle of September 11 and Beyond, Volume Four   (2002) (2004)
Shadow War: A Poetic Chronicle of September 11 and Beyond, Volume Five   (2002) (2004)
Heavenward   (2003)*
Regime Change: Poems of America's Showdown with Iraq, Volume One   (2003)*

Regime Change: Poems of America's Showdown with Iraq, Volume Two   (2003)*
Regime Change: Poems of America's Showdown with Iraq, Volume Three   (2003)*
The Complete Poems of Louis Daniel Brodsky: Volume Three, 1976–1980
   (edited by Sheri L. Vandermolen)   (2004)
Peddler on the Road: Days in the Life of Willy Sypher   (2005)
Combing Florida's Shores: Poems of Two Lifetimes   (2006)
Showdown with a Cactus: Poems Chronicling the Prickly Struggle Between the Forces of
   Dubya-ness and Enlightenment, 2003–2006   (2006)
A Transcendental Almanac: Poems of Nature   (2006)
Once upon a Small-Town Time: Poems of America's Heartland   (2007)
Still Wandering in the Wilderness: Poems of the Jewish Diaspora   (2007)
The Location of the Unknown: Shoah Poems   (2008)*
The World Waiting to Be: Poems About the Creative Process   (2008)
The Complete Poems of Louis Daniel Brodsky: Volume Four, 1981–1985
   (edited by Sheri L. Vandermolen)   (2008)

Bibliography *(coedited with Robert Hamblin)*

Selections from the William Faulkner Collection of Louis Daniel Brodsky: A Descriptive
   Catalogue   (1979)
Faulkner: A Comprehensive Guide to the Brodsky Collection, Volume I: The Biobibliography   (1982)
Faulkner: A Comprehensive Guide to the Brodsky Collection, Volume II: The Letters   (1984)
Faulkner: A Comprehensive Guide to the Brodsky Collection, Volume III: *The De Gaulle Story*   (1984)
Faulkner: A Comprehensive Guide to the Brodsky Collection, Volume IV: *Battle Cry*   (1985)
Faulkner: A Comprehensive Guide to the Brodsky Collection, Volume V: Manuscripts
   and Documents   (1989)
Country Lawyer and Other Stories for the Screen by William Faulkner   (1987)
Stallion Road: A Screenplay by William Faulkner   (1989)

Biography

William Faulkner, Life Glimpses   (1990)

Fiction

Between Grief and Nothing *(novel)*   (1964)*
Between the Heron and the Wren *(novel)*   (1965)*
"Dink Phlager's Alligator" and Other Stories   (1966)*
The Drift of Things *(novel)*   (1966)*
Vineyard's Toys *(novel)*   (1967)*
The Bindle Stiffs *(novel)*   (1968)*
Yellow Bricks *(short fictions)*   (1999)
Catchin' the Drift o' the Draft *(short fictions)*   (1999)
This Here's a Merica *(short fictions)*   (1999)
Leaky Tubs *(short fictions)*   (2001)
Rated Xmas *(short fictions)*   (2003)
Nuts to You! *(short fictions)*   (2004)
Pigskinizations *(short fictions)*   (2005)

Memoir

The Adventures of the Night Riders, Better Known as the Terrible Trio *(with Richard Milsten)*   (1961)*

* *Unpublished*

Louis Daniel Brodsky and Robert Hamblin
(circa 1984)

The Complete Poems

of

Louis Daniel

BRODSKY

Volume Four, 1981–1985

Edited by

Sheri L. Vandermolen

TIME BEING BOOKS
POETRY IN SIGHT AND SOUND

An imprint of Time Being Press
St. Louis, Missouri

Time Being Books®
10411 Clayton Road
St. Louis, Missouri 63131

Time Being Books® is an imprint of Time Being Press®, St. Louis, Missouri.

Time Being Press® is a 501(c)(3) not-for-profit corporation.

Time Being Books® volumes are printed on acid-free paper, and binding materials are chosen for strength and durability.

ISBN 9781568091242 (Paperback)

Library of Congress Cataloging-in-Publication Data:

Brodsky, Louis Daniel.
    The complete poems of Louis Daniel Brodsky / edited by Sheri L. Vandermolen.
    [Poems]
    St. Louis, Mo. : Time Being Books, c1996–<c2004>
    Related Names: Vandermolen, Sheri L.
        v. <1–3> : ill. ; 24 cm.
    ISBN 1568090196 (v. 1); 156809020X (v. 1 : pbk.); 1568090730 (v. 2);
    1568090749 (v. 2 : pbk.); 156809101X (v. 3); 1568091028 (v. 3 : pbk.);
    9781568091242 (v. 4 : pbk.)
    Incomplete Contents: v. 1. 1963–1967 — v. 2. 1967–1976 — v. 3. 1976–1980
    — v. 4. 1981–1985
    Includes index.
    PS3552.R623 A17   1996
    811'.54—dc20   96017149

Cover picture (Brodsky, circa 1982) photographed by an unknown source, at
    Rowan Oak, Faulkner's estate, in Oxford, Mississippi
Frontispiece picture (Brodsky and Dr. Robert Hamblin, circa 1984) photo-
    graphed by Paul Leuders
Cover design by Jeff Hirsch
Book design and typesetting by Sheri L. Vandermolen
Manufactured in the United States of America

First Edition, first printing (2008)

ACKNOWLEDGMENTS

My gratitude for Time Being Books's Editor in Chief, Sheri Vandermolen, is immense. Without the attention she's paid to accurately rendering each poem in my oeuvre, this fourth volume would not stand as the definitive record of this period in my career. In addition, she's brought to the editorial process sage oversight as well as critical skill.

Jerry Call, Managing Editor of Time Being Books, has sat by my side, every day of the four years it's taken to prepare this volume, giving to me his studied and candid consultation, which has led to an infinitely more balanced presentation of this material. Thank you.

I wish to give due mention to the following publications, in which certain of my poems from January 1981 through December 1985 were published, some in different forms: *Amelia* ("Tipton's 'Hidden' Treasures," as "Hidden Treasures"); *Anthology of Magazine Verse and Yearbook of American Poetry*, 1984 edition ("A Day in the Life of Willy Sypher"); *Anthology of Magazine Verse and Yearbook of American Poetry*, 1985 edition ("Inundation" and "Willy's Southern Route"); *Anthology of Magazine Verse and Yearbook of American Poetry*, 1986–1988 edition ("A Renewal of Faith" and "Young Willy Is Chosen to Work an Important Account," as "Young Willy Services Two Major Accounts"); *Ariel* ("Tied to Our Tides," as "Changing in Midstream"); *Big Muddy* ("Going to a Colloquium at Ole Miss," as "Going to a Colloquium at Ole Miss, 1982," and "A Renewal of Faith"); *Cape Rock* ("Inundation," "Street Cleaner," and "The Thorough Earth"); *Columbia Missourian Magazine* ("Boxcars"); *Confrontation* ("Intimations in Spring"); *Contemporary American Voices* ("An Autumnal," "A Failure to Exorcise Demons," "An Ode to the Westerly Wind," and "Resurrection"); *Cumberland Poetry Review* ("Committed"); *Dalhousie Review* ("An Old Road Peddler Grows Sullen, over Supper"); *First Time* ("Mizpah," "On the Demise of an Egyptian King of the First Dynasty, in His Infancy," "Tamer of Wild Beasties," "A Toss of the Coin," and "Traveling Home, in a Hearse"); *Forum* ("Cracow Now," "Earthly Rewards," "Of Fishes and Bears: An Elegy," as "Of Fishes and Bears," and "A Renewal of Faith"); *Georgia State University Review* ("The Motion of Heavenly Bodies" and "Small-Town Origins"); *Iconoclast* ("Cosmic Consolations"); *Images* ("A Devotee of the Southern Way of Making Love," as "A Devotee of the Southern Way of Lovemaking," "Implacable Impasse," and "Jogging Bailey's Woods"); *Jewish Spectator* ("An Exotic Species"); *Kentucky Poetry Review* ("A Christmas Card for My Parents"); *Limestone: A Literary Journal* ("Yearnings of a Taciturn Man," as "Moe Sings of Cabbages and Kings"); *Literati Chicago* ("Cracow Now"); *Mattoid* ("Choosing a New Place to Die"); *Meridian Anthology of Contemporary Poetry* ("Hardening of the Arteries"); *Midwest Poetry Review* ("Disenchanted," "Reinstating Claims," and "An Unaborted Distortion"); *Nassau Review* ("Working the Promised Land"); *New Welsh Review* ("[Even as I enter the Capital Café]," as "Triskaidekaphobiacs," "Prizefight," as "Moe Fischer: A Latter-Day Maxie Rosenbloom," "A Solitary Lemming," as "Casting the First Stone," and "Watching for Snakes, in the Forest," as "Watching for Snakes"); *Other Poetry* ("Mizpah"); *Parnassus Literary Journal* ("The Tall Convict"); *Peckerwood* ("Arrested"); *Phase and Cycle* ("Acid Rain," as

"Victim of the Liberation"); *Plainsongs* ("Saying No, Again"); *Porcupine Literary Arts Magazine* ("Bardic Apostle" and "*The Birth of Venus*"); *Portland Review* ("[Day dwindles like a Chardonnay bouquet]," as "Goat-Poet's Agony"); *Publications of the Missouri Philological Association* ("Blown off Course"); *Pudding Magazine* ("Amicable Separation" and "Not Returning Together"); *Pulpsmith* ("Boxcars"); *Red Hawk Review* ("Paradox"); *Seattle Review* ("Morning Flight"); *Sepia Poetry Magazine* ("Traveling Home, in a Hearse"); *Small Pond* ("Amicable Separation," "Form Follows Function," "The Peabody," and "Rep for the Mid-South," as "Commuting over the Wilderness Route"); *South Carolina Review* ("Collision Course"); *Southern Review* ("Between Seasons," "A Day in the Life of Willy Sypher," "Guilty Until Proven Innocent," "Willy's Southern Route," and "Young Willy Is Chosen to Work an Important Account," as "Young Willy Services Two Major Accounts"); *Trinity Review* ("A Devotee of the Southern Way of Making Love," as "A Devotee of the Southern Way of Lovemaking," "The Fawns," and "Under the River's Stern Surveillance," as "Under the River's Surveillance"); *TriQuarterly Magazine* ("Ritual Disappearance"); *Whetstone* ("The Arctic Heart"); and *Zilla* ("Extravagant Fancies of an H.M.S. *Bounty* Deck Hand").

"Author of the Pentateuch," "Boxcars," "Cracow Now," "A Day in the Life of Willy Sypher," "Gone Fishing," "Log-Thoughts South," "Willy: Fisher of Men," and "Willy's Southern Route" appear in the unpublished pamphlet *Selections from the Ash Keeper's Everlasting Passion Week* (1986).

"The Birds and the Trees," "Intimations in Spring," and "An Ode to the Westerly Wind" appear in the unpublished pamphlet *Rooted to the Earth and the Sky: A Transcendental Almanac* (1987).

"Hiatus" (as "Rites of Way"), "[I leave Farmington, at 5:55.]" (as "Obsession"), "Of Fishes and Bears: An Elegy" (as "Of Fishes and Bears"), and "You Can't Go Back, Exactly" appear in *You Can't Go Back, Exactly*, released as first and second editions, by Timeless Press (now Time Being Books), in 1988 and 1989, and as a third edition, by Time Being Books, in 2003; they also appear in a compilation translation of that text (Paris: Éditions Gallimard, 1994).

"Black Hole-ocaust," "Boxcars," "Chelmno Rain," "Cracow Now," "A Day in the Life of Willy Sypher," "Log-Thoughts South," "One Out of Six Million," "Palindrome" (as "Ghetto-Echoes"), "The Thorough Earth," "Willy: Fisher of Men," "Willy's Southern Route," and "Young Willy Is Chosen to Work an Important Account" (as "Young Willy Services Two Major Accounts") appear in *The Thorough Earth* (Timeless Press, 1989) and in a compilation translation of that text (Paris: Éditions Gallimard, 1992).

"Author of the Pentateuch," "Breezes, Birds, and Bees" (as "Birds, Breezes, and Bees"), "Conception on the Road," "Crucifishion," "Guilty Until Proven Innocent," "Intimations in Spring," "The Motion of Heavenly Bodies," "Mystical Union: An Adoration" (as "Mystical Union"), "Outpatient," "The Physics of Love," "Practitioners of the Vernacular," "Roads Lined with Wind-Trees," "Small-Town Origins," "Something," "Tipton's 'Hidden' Treasures" (as "Tipton's Hidden Treasures"), and "Total Eclipse of the Vulcan Sun" (as "Total Eclipse") appear in *Four and Twenty Black-*

birds Soaring, published by Timeless Press, in 1989, and in a compilation translation of that text (Paris: Éditions Gallimard, 1992).

"Incarnations of the Pawnbroker" (as "Incarnations of a Pawnbroker") and "Waiting for Connecting Trains, at Katy Station" (as "Waiting for Connecting Trains, 1983") appear in *Falling from Heaven: Holocaust Poems of a Jew and a Gentile* (with William Heyen; Time Being Books, 1991).

"Foregone Illusions" (as "Foregone Delusions, Germany, 1937"), "Franz" (as "Franz, Prague, 1919"), "Frau Victoria" (as "Race Defilers"), "Premonitions" (as "The Gathering Storm, Europe, 1938"), "A Toast to the Forties" (as "A Toast to the Forties, 1985"), and "Warring Fantasies" (as "Inherited Characteristics") appear in *Gestapo Crows: Holocaust Poems* (Time Being Books, 1992).

"Cracow Now" and "The Thorough Earth" appear in *Telling the Tale: A Tribute to Elie Wiesel on the Occasion of His 65th Birthday — Essays, Reflections, and Poems*, edited by Harry James Cargas (Time Being Books, 1993).

"The Aldermen of Sodom and Gomorrah," "The Battle of the Books: Ancients vs. Moderns" (as "Icarus in Lapinga"), "A Belated Gift" (as "An Unopened Gift"), "Break-Fast" (as "Moe's Package Vacation"), "[Breakfast at the Capital is not exactly]" (as "Travels into Several Remote Nations"), "Café des Beaux-Arts" (as "Clayton Ladue at the Café des Beaux-Arts"), "[From my stiff-back booth seat]" (as "Vinnie Polenta Makes Two Service Calls"), "Last Day in the Old Capital Café," "May Day" (as "Emancipation Proclamation"), "Messianic Vestiges," "Near Helicon" (as "Rioting Heathens"), "On the Lecture Circuit: A Poet's Auto-da-Fé" (as "Under Laputa: Poet, Pass By), "Our Town: An Acrid Approximation," "Recorder of Deeds, Pro Tem" (as "Recorder of Deeds"), "The Visigoth," "[With euphemistic subterfuge]" (as "City of Traditional Progress"), and "Yearnings of a Taciturn Man" (as "Moe Sings of Cabbages and Kings") appear in *The Capital Café: Poems of Redneck, U.S.A.* (Time Being Books, 1993).

The following poems appear in *Mississippi Vistas: Volume One of A Mississippi Trilogy*, which was originally published as a first edition, with no subtitle, by the University Press of Mississippi, in 1983, and was then issued as a second, revised edition by Timeless Press, in 1990; the poems also appear in the compilation translation of the Time Being Books text (Paris: Éditions Gallimard, 1994) and in the unpublished book *A Mississippi Trilogy: A Poetic Saga of the South* (1995): "Elegy South," "Gone Fishing," "Hanging Out the Wash," "Homeward Looking" (as "Oxford"), "Ineffectual Spectator" (as "Spectator"), "Reverend Whitfield's Apostasy," "Rummaging in the Attic," "The Tall Convict," and "Time's Harvest."

"Abnegating Fate," "Admiration for the Man Who Admired Faulkner" (as "Admiration for a Man Who Admired Faulkner"), "Attending a Lecture" (as "Out of My Element"), "Autobiographia Literaria," "Awakening Sleeping Dragons" (as "Waking Sleeping Demons"), "Backlash" (as "White Backlash"), "Blown off Course," "Byhalia," "A Chance Encounter" (as "Chance Encounter"), "A Day at the Races" (as "Daydreaming of Night-Mares"), "Dozing Off," "Even the Highway Is My Crucifix," "Faulkner's Unravished Brides of Quietness" (as "Faulkner's Ravished Brides of Quietness"), "5:30

Picnic at Rowan Oak" (as "Picnic at Rowan Oak"), "For Willie, in Oxford" (as "Counts No-Count"), "Ghost House," "Going Home" (as "Educational Miscegenation"), "Going to a Colloquium at Ole Miss" (as "Going to a Colloquium at Ole Miss, 1982"), "Hammurabian Reprisals" (as "Getting Butterflies"), "[I hear them. I hear them so near,]" (as "Haunting Voices"), "Implacable Impasse," "In Flood Time," "Intimations of Dante at Rowan Oak," "Intimations of Immortality, in Spring," "Inundation," "Jogging Bailey's Woods," "Killer Sun," "Legacies," "Limbo Now" (as "Making Another Desert Trek"), "May Stocktaking," "A Night in the Burying Place," "One Final Run" (as "Isolated at the Oasis"), "Recent Divorcé" (as "The Profligate Jew Returns"), "Rehearsing in Mississippi" (as "Rehearsing in Purgatory"), "Rep for the Mid-South" (as "Commuting over the Wilderness Route"), "Ritual Disappearance," "Saturday-Morning Auguries" (as "Ku Klux Kudzu"), "Seeking a Change of Venue," "Strangulation," "Street Cleaner," "Taking a Bad Fall" (as "Valedictory for a Jogger"), "Tours de Force," "Traveling to the State Capital (as "Innisfree, Mississippi, 1983"), "West Helena's West Side," and "Working the Promised Land" appear in *Disappearing in Mississippi Latitudes: Volume Two of A Mississippi Trilogy* (Time Being Books, 1994) and in the unpublished book *A Mississippi Trilogy: A Poetic Saga of the South* (1995).

"Aubade," "Browning and Barrett: A Meeting South" (as "Vapors and Apparitions"), "Cloven-Hoofed Goat," "Collision Course," "Cosmic Consolations," "[Day dwindles like a Chardonnay bouquet]" (as "Goat-Poet's Agony"), "The Defrocking of Rudy Toothacre, Itinerant Minister of the Universal Gospel of the Synod for All Churches of the What's Happenin' Now" (as "Defrocked"), "A Devotee of the Southern Way of Making Love" (as "A Devotee of the Southern Way of Lovemaking"), "The Dioscuri" (as "Star-Crossed"), "Earthly Rewards," "Exhortation in Praise of Spontaneity," "Extravagant Fanices of an H.M.S. *Bounty* Deck Hand," "The Fawns," "Following the River South," "A Gift of Time," "Goldenrods," "[I enter your house, not a stranger]" (as "Sweet Ruination"), "In Defense of Physical Manifestations," "[It is an evening of serene honeysuckle.]" (as "My Heart's Darling"), "It Was the Summer of the Snakes, and She Ran," "Keats's Urn-Turning Lovers" (as "Leaving Home"), "A Latter-Day de León" (as "Rasselas"), "Making Berth at Oxford," "Matriarchy" (as "Diana"), "Mistress Mississippi," "Mizpah," "Naming the Muse" (as "Caving In"), "Night Vipers," "Of Elegies and Renascence" (as "Of Elegies and Elegies"), "On the Virtues of Being a Man of Action," "The Peabody," "Poetic Vectoring," "The Profligate," "A Renewal of Faith," "Running Scared," "Sir Galwyn of Arthgyl," "Skimming Mississippi's Urn" (as "Skimming Mississippi's Rim," in *Mistress Mississipi*), "Sparks Jumping the Gap," "Tied to Our Tides" (as "Changing in Midstream"), "To His Distant Mistress: A Loose Persuasion, After Marvell" (as "To His Distant Mistress"), "Under the River's Stern Surveillance" (as "Under the River's Surveillance"), "Unexpected Awakening," "Vague Lady from Holly Springs," "The Warehouse, Friday Night," "Wind Devils," and "Wisteria" appear in *Mistress Mississippi: Volume Three of A Mississippi Trilogy* (Time Being Books, 1992) and in the unpublished book *A Mississippi Trilogy: A Poetic Saga of the South* (1995).

"Acid Rain" (as "Victim of the Liberation"), "A Curse on My Father's Successors" (as "A Curse on His Father's Successors"), "Daddies' Girls," "Feinstein the Clothier," "Rosh Hashanah for One Fallen from Grace" (as "Rosh Hashanah for a Survivor"), and "Turkey Truck" appear in *The Eleventh Lost Tribe: Poems of the Holocaust* (Time Being Books, 1998).

"Brailling the Sun" and "Inquiry into the Essence of Existence and Divinity" appear in *Toward the Torah, Soaring: Poems of the Renascence of Faith* (Time Being Books, 1998).

"['Bastards!' Willy chastises invisible fates]" (as "What a Bitch!"), "Between Seasons," "A Break in the Routine"* (1/18/84 — [1], as "Tomorrow's Fish-Wrap"), "Catering to the Ethnic Trade" (as "Spring/Summer Sales Meeting: Catering to the Trade"), "A Day in the Life of Willy Sypher," "Nigger in the Woodpile" (as "Interloper"), "One Long Road," "Our Credo, Spring '84" (as "Spring/Summer Sales Meeting: Our Credo"), "Spring '84 Sales Meeting: Presentation of the Tailored-Suit Line" (as "Spring/Summer Sales Meeting: Presentation of the Tailored-Suit Line"), "Two Days in the Life of Willy Sypher, Purveyor" (as "Fall/Winter Sales Meeting: A Credit to the Profession"), "Willy Declines His Hard-Earned Promotion" (as "Hard-Earned 'Promotion'"), "Willy: Fisher of Men" (as "Fisher of Men"), "Willy Suffers a Loss of Heart" (as "A Loss of Heart"), "Willy Sypher: A Company Man" (as "A Company Man"), "Willy's Day of Reckoning" (as "Day of Reckoning"), "Willy's Last Season" (as "Final Season"), "Willy's Southern Route," and "Young Willy Is Chosen to Work an Important Account" (as "Young Willy Services Two Major Accounts") appear in *Peddler on the Road: Days in the Life of Willy Sypher* (Time Being Books, 2005).

"[For two days and nights straight,]" (as "Raging Winds")," "[Just now, the moment contains us]" (as "Awaiting Takeoff"), and "Sand Crab" appear in *Combing Florida's Shores: Poems of Two Lifetimes* (Time Being Books, 2006).

"The Birds and the Trees," "Coexistence," "Ice Storm," "A Nonconforming Easter Sonnet" (as "Easter Green"), "Trinitarians," and "Where Snow Comes From" appear in *A Transcendental Almanac: Poems of Nature* (Time Being Books, 2006).

"Change of Hands," *Morte d'Arthur* (as "Glory's Hour"), "Prairie Town — Jacksonville, Illinois: Looking West, Along Morton" (as "Looking Both Ways, Along West Morton"), "628 West Columbia," and "Tipton's 'Hidden' Treasures" (as "Hidden Treasures") appear in *Once upon a Small-Town Time: Poems of America's Heartland* (Time Being Books, 2007).

"Postmodern Noah" and "Secular Rabbi" (as "Secular Sofer") appear in *Still Wandering in the Wilderness: Poems of the Jewish Diaspora* (Time Being Books, 2007).

"Artisan" (as "The White Rose"), "[Driving home, alone,]" (as "Forwarding Address"), "Fancy's Flight" (as "Ascending"), "Fashioning Word-Chimes" (as "Internal Rhymes"), "Fisher Poet," "Keeper of the Word-Hoard," "Polar Poet," and "Whitmanesque Confession" (as "Wide Drive") appear in *The World Waiting to Be: Poems About the Creative Process* (Time Being Books, 2008).

"[At 7:16 a.m.,]" (as "Running Late"), "Bespelling the Speller," "Between Snows," "Conflict of Interest" (as "The Next Three Days"), "The 'Dude' Introduces His Boy, Troika, to Katy Station" (as "Dude Introduces His Boy, Troika, to Katy Station"), "Freeing Genies" (as "Connecting Dots"), "Gentle Revolutionaries," "Getting Our Tree," "Her First Bunking Party," "Hopgrassers and Flutterbies," "In the Name of All That's Sacred" (as "The Bedouins"), "'It Seems like Fall,'" "Lion Day," "Ministering to the Fish," "*Morte d'Arthur*" (as "Glory's Hour"), "New Snow," "One-Room School," "Outsmarted," "Paean to Joshua Lionel Cowen," "Portrait of a Painter and Poet, on a Snowy Morning," "Post-Giraffic," "The Punishment," "Spectator at the Games," "Supermen," "Thanksgiving 1981," "Trilogy is Eight, Today," "Trilogy Solos," "Trilogy's Seventh Birthday," "Troika's Dad, the Pants Peddler," and "Who Holds Our Children Up, If the World's Hope Is on Their Shoulders?" (as "Visions") are scheduled to appear in volume four of *The Seasons of Youth*, a series to be published by Time Being Books, and "The Day After Labor Day," "Happy Accidents," "Latchkey Children" (as "Nervous Morning"), and "On Her Beginning Her Second Decade" (as "Trilogy Begins Her Second Decade") are slated for volume five of that series.

*Because two poems bear this title, within volume four, the date of creation is listed, to indicate the appropriate text.

For Robert Hamblin,

who, for thirty years,
has shared, with me, his intellect and wisdom,
his humble humanity,
and who has graced me with friendship and generosity
that have made us brothers

I believe that man will not merely endure: he will prevail. He is immortal, not because he alone among creatures has an inexhaustible voice, but because he has a soul, a spirit capable of compassion and sacrifice and endurance. The poet's, the writer's, duty is to write about these things. It is his privilege to help man endure by lifting his heart, by reminding him of the courage and honor and hope and pride and compassion and pity and sacrifice which have been the glory of his past. The poet's voice need not merely be the record of man, it can be one of the props, the pillars to help him endure and prevail.

— William Faulkner, from his Nobel Prize acceptance speech, 1950

CONTENTS

EDITOR'S GUIDE

"The South is my anointing."

These prophetic words, penned, by Louis Daniel Brodsky, in his aptly titled poem "Mistress Mississippi" (October 1981), speak to the degree to which the writer had been absorbed into that region's culture and climate, by the early 1980s, and transformed into a dutiful, yet daring, novitiate enthralled by his own obsessions.

Although his roles as a husband, father, and businessman remained priorities, Brodsky had become an impassioned William Faulkner scholar, immersing himself in the author's Mississippi realms — both the real (Oxford, in Lafayette County) and the fictional (Jefferson, in Yoknapatawpha County). Seemingly light-years away from his early days as a young Faulkner enthusiast (when Yale professor R. W. B. Lewis kindled his initial interest, leading Brodsky to seek out New Haven book dealer Henry Wenning, who would instruct him in purchasing the first of many rare tomes), Brodsky had, by 1981, amassed a preeminent Faulkner collection that was garnering international praise.

Aware that organizing such vast holdings was well beyond the scope of one man's capabilities, Brodsky continued to collaborate with his dear friend Dr. Robert Hamblin, an English professor at Southeast Missouri State University, to bring bibliographic order to the collection, highlights of which had been the feature of a three-month exhibition, held, in 1979, at the museum on that campus. Having received global recognition for that event and acclaim for the printing of *Selections from the William Faulkner Collection of Louis Daniel Brodsky: A Descriptive Catalogue* (University of Virginia Press, 1979), a hardcover volume listing all the pieces in the exhibition, the two were inspired to forge ahead with their project, to assess and document the rest of Brodsky's acquisitions.

Because most of those items were stored in Farmington, Missouri, Hamblin frequently traveled to the small rural community, about eighty miles north of his own residence, staying overnight at the Brodsky family home, where the pair labored away, many a late evening and weekend, identifying and dating each artifact and then establishing bibliographic annotation for its place within the immense collection. Other days, they carried out their studies in a conference room at Farmington's Mercantile Bank or in a small writing office (adjoining his old bedroom) in Brodsky's parents' house, in St. Louis, depending on which overflowing box's stacks were to be tackled next.

When he wasn't working with Hamblin, either at home or in St. Louis or Cape Girardeau, Brodsky was typically conducting business throughout the Midwest and the South, in his role as manager of factory-outlet stores, for his father's company, Biltwell. He clocked countless hours, heading to those stores' locations, in the Missouri towns of Tipton, Salisbury, and Sullivan (and, in 1983–84, Jefferson City and Rolla), as well as in New Athens, Illinois, but only his treks to West Helena, Arkansas, where his father had purchased a garment factory, in 1976, and where Brodsky had opened yet another flourishing outlet store, offered him the chance to ease his frenetic mind, with side trips to Oxford.

West Helena's proximity to that small Mississippi town enabled Brodsky to make repeated visits to Faulkner's estate, Rowan Oak. There, he would commune with the essence of "Bill's" spirit, hoping to "press up against low-flying ghosts" and penetrate "Mississippi's chrysalis" ("For Willie, in Oxford," March 1985). As he walked the surrounding grounds or jogged through the mazy depths of Bailey's Woods, each wandering step, each breath of humid, thick-scented air, brought him in touch with Faulkner and the ragged Yoknapatawpha panoply Brodsky hoped to assimilate into his very being ("Jogging Bailey's Woods," August 1982; "Tours de Force," August 1982; "Faulkner's Unravished Brides of Quietness," December 1982; "Seeking a Change of Venue," April 1983; "Wisteria," April 1983; "Intimations of Dante at Rowan Oak," March 1985; "Ghost House," October 1985).

His visits to Oxford often brought him to the University of Mississippi (Ole Miss), as well. As a regular attendee and lecturer at the school's annual Faulkner and Yoknapatawpha Conference, he participated in a variety of events, at each seminar, and it was during the 1981 gathering's farewell celebration that he met a Jackson native whose subtle grace and beauty he found irresistible. Undone by her attentiveness and gentle sensuality, he felt urgently compelled to be with her, both physically and emotionally.

Casting aside guilt over betraying his wife, Jan, he allowed himself to revel in this woman's appreciation of his intellect, his wit, his talents as a writer. No concerns of being a negligent husband or absentee father could prevent his withered ego from eagerly soaking up the affection lavished upon him by this wonderfully vibrant lady, a gifted artist in her own right. Surprised by his own willingness to indulge in such "unintentioned intimacy," he wrote the poem "The Fawns," on his melancholic way home from the conference, lamenting having to leave behind, in Mississippi, the "acceptance, / So total and unabashedly passionate" she had shown him and wondering when, again, he might take comfort in her "sheltering gaze" (August 1981).

In the coming months, Brodsky scheduled additional work trips to West Helena, permitting for brief trysts, in Oxford or Jackson, with his new lover. Recorded in three sequences of achingly tender poems (starting with "Poetic Vectoring," September 1981, and ending with "Even the Highway Is My Crucifix," October 1981), their days together brought Brodsky tranquillity, as if his union with her were inviolable, granting them the power to "Transcend the sweetest metaphysical liquefactions, / And defy time," despite their knowing that, soon enough, his commitment to his family — the stable upbringing of his seven-year-old daughter, Trilogy, and four-year-old boy, Troika — would force this budding relationship to be "irrevocably jettisoned / And forever lost to the winds of chaos" ("[I enter your house, not a stranger]," October 1981).

Inextricably mixed into the decision to end the liaison was the fact that even this paramour, with her persuasive charms, could not unseat Brodsky's preoccupation with his principal mistress, Mississippi, regardless of his increasing awareness of its illusory ways. Irrevocably drawn to the land and its inhabitants, he was, nonetheless, exasperated by how long he'd been chasing a seemingly unattainable dream — of finding a path to greatness, matching Faulkner's — and he astutely called Oxford "the green light on my Gatsbyed youth's dock, / Flashing, erratically, in middle age, / Faulknerian emanations I still crave / Despite premature senility / And an irretrievable innocence," labeling the town, at once, a "princely frog" and an "unclothed toad" ("Homeward Looking," December 1981).

Still, he considered his trips to the South more than mere digressions, emphatically feeling that they were unavoidable extensions of his vocation, both as a representative of Biltwell and as a zealous Faulkner scholar. His most significant endeavors, for the latter, involved pursuing connections with dozens of Faulkner's family members and associates, including agents, editors, and lawyers. While these contacts were typically reluctant to grant a stranger — especially a Northern outlander — admittance to their private domains, Brodsky's resolve to forge relationships over a period of months, or even years, never wavered; he slowly earned the trust of each individual, by demonstrating that augmenting his collection was not his only goal. Indeed, his foremost interest, in each instance, remained being made privy to the animated personal accounts of those who knew, firsthand, Faulkner's "brooding moods," "demon-laced sullenness," and "deeply disguised sentimentality" ("Faulkner's Unravished Brides of Quietness," December 1982). Although this mission required endless wells of resilience and determination, Brodsky was sincere in his attempts to form lasting ties with those who, like him, so profoundly admired William Faulkner.

Such had certainly been the case with Ben Wasson, Faulkner's first New York agent and subsequent editor (for *Sartoris*), with whom Brodsky had become acquainted, in 1980, after months of correspondence. Following their initial meeting, in Greenville, Mississippi, Wasson had opened up, sharing his unique Faulkner stories with "non-Southerner" Brodsky (and eventually contributing personal keepsakes to the collection). To show his thanks and further prove himself as a Faulkner devotee, Brodsky had gifted Wasson, in May 1980, with a small keepsake entitled *Mississippi Vistas: 5 Poems by Louis Daniel Brodsky*, which Brodsky then expanded into a seventeen-piece pamphlet, simply entitled *Mississippi Vistas*, to distribute as a signed limited run of fifty copies, at a poetry reading on the Ole Miss campus, in November of that year.

Brodsky saw the potential for a full-length book, in that grouping's poems, and in fleshing out the concept, he sought the input of some of the most well-respected luminaries of Southern criticism, including Malcolm Cowley, Lewis P. Simpson, Cleanth Brooks, and Robert Penn Warren, all of whom understood his efforts as a labor of love. Enthused by the positive response he received from these prominent men of letters, Brodsky decided to pursue the manuscript's development. Thus, when Brodsky and Hamblin were offered a contract, with the University Press of Mississippi, at Jackson, for the series *Faulkner: A Comprehensive Guide to the Brodsky Collection*, the first volume of which (*The Biobibliography*) would be issued in 1982, Brodsky opted to take advantage of his associations with the university, to see if he might secure an agreement for the release of *Mississippi Vistas* as well. His approach paid off, with the press proposing a 1983 publication of that book.

Although Brodsky's concerns ranged far beyond having his Southern verse reach a wider audience, his short-lived attempt, in the summer of 1981, to keep pace with revising his other current work was not successful. Originally typing out manuscripts for many new pieces (not just Southern poems) shortly after composing them in his notebook, he soon found that assignment unmanageable and chose, instead, to focus almost exclusively on editing pieces that he felt could fill out his series of Mississippi poems, which he was now envisioning as a trilogy.

However, despite having had to scale back revision efforts on his new work, Brodsky remained insistent that the immediacy of his day-to-day creative process not take a back burner to the production of the Southern trilogy. Thus, preparing *Mississippi Vistas* for print never took precedence over creating new poems — stretching to find a new form, voice, image, with every composition, remained his primary goal. Utilizing skills honed over the nearly twenty years he'd spent devoted to his craft, Brodsky delved into increasingly surreal motifs (meditations, nightmares, images of soaring) that revealed his mystic propensity, and his lines of verse, though convoluted, had an unmatched clarity and level of control, an inspired fluidity. At the age of forty, he had truly found his stride.

But even before reaching that milestone birthday — April 17, 1981— Brodsky had been mulling over the advancing years and their meaning to him. At times, those ruminations took an upbeat approach, declaring him a poet anticipating "undreamed outposts / Blossoming with exotic possibilities / For my aging soul's growth" ("Sailing Toward Ararat," April 1981). Some carried a spiritual essence as well, disclosing a determined poet too busy for death, who wishes to "Assert his refusal to give up the ghost" ("Saying No, Again," February 1981) and remind himself that "Neither tomorrow nor yesterday count. / Now is my appointed hour, eternity" ("Salvation on a Per Diem Basis," March 1981). And even occasional grandiose paeans made their way to his page, as he would "implore the lesser deities that be / To transport me to the Land of Poetry, / Where I might find, in sundering abundance, / Invocations to *Paradise Lost* and *The Divine Comedy*, / That my ink might sing the twilight to sleep tonight" ("Registration in Purple and Pink," March 1981).

More often, though, these poems echoed Brodsky's feelings of failure and disenchantment, his "recent awareness, on reaching forty, / That time accepts no excuses," as well as intimations that "No longer does the lure of self-discovery / In the mind's Klondike / Hold out excitement, motivate the heart" ("A Change of Dreams," February 1981). While Brodsky logged these words during another evening alone, in Columbia, Missouri, simply dismissing such sentiments as the late-night ramblings of a melancholic poet is to diminish their accuracy. Particularly telling are these fatalistic lines from "Looking Ahead" (February 1981): "Now, he can't even remember / When trying to outdistance, keep abreast, / Merely stay in the race, / Chasing his intractable opponent, / Gave way to abject defeat, depression, / Despondency assuaged by Chablis / And ephemeral infidelities."

These feelings of anguish were not mere false misgivings generated by inward reflection. In reality, his family life had been deteriorating for several years, and Brodsky's fleeing allowed him to avoid direct confrontation over the marital dissatisfaction he and Jan both felt. And, now, those problems were compounded by the anger and sadness welling in his children, since Trilogy and Troika had grown old enough to register their father's frequent absences and express their own disdain and grief ("Calling Home," April 1981; "Fractionating Atoms," July 1981). Brodsky habitually pondered his sorrow and theirs, even while trying to "Neutralize the truth / That lies behind my voluntary exile" ("Who Holds Our Children Up, If the World's Hope Is on Their Shoulders?," September 1981). The guilt could be overwhelming, ironically pushing him even further from home, but never, while away, did he cease to hear his little ones' voices "Beseeching me, between the lines, / To quit my desultory occupations / And resume my position in our family shrine" ("It Seems like Fall," July 1981).

Still, being in Farmington had its joyous moments, spent bonding with his children. From waking Trilogy and taking her to school ("[At 7:16 a.m.,]," December 1981; "Between Snows," January 1982; "Lion Day," March 1982) to playing with preschooler Troika ("Paean to Joshua Lionel Cowen," January 1982; "Post-Giraffic," April 1982; "Outsmarted," September 1982), Brodsky did his best to make up for lost time, become involved in his kids' lives. In fact, the simplest family activities, such as watching movies ("Supermen," December 1981) or catching fireflies ("Freeing Genies," June 1982), held heightened significance for Brodsky, who tried never to take such precious hours for granted. Nor did he leave grander celebrations unrecognized, always recording holidays and birthdays, in verse ("Thanksgiving 1981," November 1981; "Trilogy Is Eight, Today," May 1982; "Getting Our Tree," December 1982).

But the constrictions of residing, with his family, in a small, rural town weighed heavily on both Brodsky and his wife. While they could shield their children from crime, pollution, drugs, and urban blight, by living there, Farmington had its limitations. In return for safe streets, fresh air, and a simpler way of life, the Brodskys had become culturally and socially landlocked in the community's "migraine desolateness" ("The Lesser of the Evils," June 1981). Worse, they were exposed to bigotry and narrow-mindedness they had not faced, so directly, during their early adulthood, spent in major metropolitan areas, such as St. Louis, San Francisco, New York, and Miami. The fact that they had formulated their own beliefs during the free-thinking equal-rights era of the 1960s made it particularly difficult for the two of them to tolerate the "jingoistic Americanism" and "Christian morality / With an old-rugged-cross bias / Toward Baptist exclusivity" they encountered in Farmington ("[With euphemistic subterfuge]," April 1981).

While the locals accepted them and appreciated Brodsky, for expanding Biltwell's enterprise there, he still could not help but feel that the town stewards tended to "Lobby against new industry — / Progress in any form —," and he was particularly self-conscious, knowing that they always regarded him as an outsider, the odd Jew poet, who, during breakfasts at the local café, would shrink "into a convenient booth, / To listen to their impugning conversations, / Waiting for inevitable allusions to his Judaism" ("Feinstein the Clothier," May 1981).

But Brodsky used such fodder as substance for his poems, fashioning a variety of poetic vignettes featuring the "characters" he had observed in the town café and other local haunts ("The Aldermen of Sodom and Gomorrah," February 1981; "Messianic Vestiges," February 1981; "Near Helicon," December 1981; "The Battle of the Books: Ancients vs. Moderns," January 1982). And he did the same while visiting the entire Midwestern range of his outlet stores, fully aware that one of the biggest advantages of having extracted himself from the insularity of academia was his ability to keep in touch with the raw energy and hands-on experience needed for dynamic composition. Instead of writing in the compact, erudite, ambiguity-laden manner of his peers, Brodsky let his verse flow unrestrained, achieving everything from eloquently lyrical odes to fully narrative pieces brimming with "local flavor," never seeing a poem as an abstract, unknowable entity but as a concrete work to be read, touched, felt, understood, by his audience.

While not wanting to commit to a role as a professor at a large university, which he believed would remove him from active participation in the "real world," Brodsky did wish to cultivate the thrill of exploring writing and literary techniques, in hope of avoiding artistic inertia. Living in Farmington made it possible for Brodsky to seek out a small, local school, where he could limit his duties and yet reap the benefits of working with students. As a result, he took a position teaching creative writing and short fiction, at Mineral Area Junior College, in nearby Flat River, Missouri, one evening a week. Instructing his class (a slightly older, nontraditional night-school group) about the building blocks of composition put him on notice that he, too, should be mindful of those elements. As a poet always obsessed with moving ahead, this task of analyzing the actual creative process, not just the result of that process, enhanced his own skills and gave him a rare opportunity to interact with others sharing his interests. Appreciative of this mental stimulation and the opportunity to contribute to his community, he would continue, with this sideline, for a full decade.

Another benefit of residing in Farmington was its low cost of living, which allowed Brodsky to lease a sizable office near the town square. A converted apartment on the second floor of a building not half a block from the courthouse, the space offered him the solitude he needed in order to concentrate fully on his scholarly writing and his poetry revision. Each time he ascended those stairs, his mind would assume a single focus, without the distractions of home or the factory intervening; ensconced in his desk chair, he could seal himself off from the world, become "Oblivious to existence beyond this cosmos" ("The Surprise," February 1982).

Although occasionally enjoying the office as a retreat, where he could open the French doors, step out onto the balcony, and take in the entire square, all the while contemplating his place in small-town America, more often Brodsky would spend his time, in that quiet workplace, performing Faulkner research and constructing bibliographic pieces. Having experienced extreme humiliation, in his graduate days, when Washington University granted him a master's degree but denied him the chance to finish ten additional credit hours and earn his Ph.D. (the board claiming that his thesis was adequate but lacked proper form and citation), Brodsky had become a resilient Thomas Sutpen, picking himself up, amidst rejection, determined to persevere and make a name for himself, in the very arena that had snubbed him. Thus, while that initial rebuff had an immediate benefit — crystallizing his realization that he should become a writer, not a teacher — it also served, in the 1980s, as a driving force behind his desire to prove himself academically.

His vindication arrived swiftly, as he received widespread praise for his bibliographic work. His textual-scholarship articles were published time and again, by the prestigious *Studies in Bibliography* (1980–1981, 1983–1988), to the acclaim of the illustrious Fredson Bowers, and Brodsky's interviews and long critical essays appeared in notable publications such as *Southern Review* (1982, 1985), *California* (1985), and *Faulkner Journal* (1985–1987). Even shorter articles, such as that printed in *Faulkner Newsletter and Yoknapatawpha Review* (1982), received notice, as did his papers presented at the Faulkner and Yoknapatawpha Conferences, which were incorporated into the popular compilation books from those events (1981, 1983–1984). He also assembled catalogues (and typically wrote their introductions), for various exhibitions of his collection, including those hosted at Ole Miss (1980, 1982–1983), the University of Tulsa (1983), and Southeast Missouri State University (1984).

As a result, scholars nationwide not only came to know Brodsky's name but to hold it in high esteem, aware that Brodsky was not compelled by the "publish or perish" standards of any university but, instead, thrived simply on sharing his collection with the public, his writing fired by his artist's soul and infused with the excitement of presenting, to the Faulkner community, original materials never before seen in print. Academia's appreciation of the in-depth studies he executed (which rivaled the work required for multiple Ph.D.'s) helped Brodsky sweep aside his painful memories from his days as a young graduate student, so he might relish his newfound fame.

But Brodsky wasn't one to bask, long, in any particular accomplishment, and although busy with Faulkner scholarship, he also continued with the preparation of the *Mississippi Vistas* manuscript. With full-scale revision of the text underway throughout 1982, he again sought the guidance of Malcolm Cowley as well as that of Lewis P. Simpson, who also facilitated the publication of three of Brodsky's poems ("Between Connections," June 1976; "Joseph K.," July 1975; and "Manager of Outlet Stores," July 1975) in the *Southern Review*, that same year. Corresponding regularly, with them, about his Southern poems and about the Faulkner collection, Brodsky valued their authoritative comments and developed an abiding friendship with both men, carrying on an engaging epistolary dialogue with Cowley, who would later contribute a number of significant items to

Brodsky's Faulkner holdings. Robert Penn Warren and Cleanth Brooks also made suggestions to fine-tune *Mississippi Vistas*, and Brodsky fostered friendships with them as well (Brooks ultimately permitting Brodsky to acquire his entire Faulkner library).

By 1983, Brodsky had finished *Mississippi Vistas*. It was issued by University Press of Mississippi, for the Center for the Study of Southern Culture, in April, and was the first of Brodsky's poetry texts to be printed as in a large-quantity run. Despite the book's impressive sales and its having been conceived as part of a trilogy, the press eventually had to rescind its offer to publish the following two volumes, due to financial pressures. This cancellation proved to be a blessing in disguise, for Brodsky, who had received criticism, from both Cowley and Simpson, that the voices and narrative lines, in volumes two and three, were too disparate and needed to be united. Dejected and unable to devote the time it would take to resolve such issues, Brodsky put the project on hold indefinitely, not addressing those complexities for nearly a decade (until the 1992 publication of *Mistress Mississippi: Volume Three of A Mississippi Trilogy* and the 1994 publication of *Disappearing in Mississippi Latitudes: Volume Two of A Mississippi Trilogy*, by Time Being Books).

Relieved of that burden, Brodsky could now funnel more of his energy into writing new poems, with much of his inspiration springing from his responsibilities at Biltwell and his observations of the salesmen, who were the true drive behind the company's success. Like them, in a manner of speaking, he too serviced accounts, regularly calling on his four to seven outlet stores and shuffling merchandise, from warehouse to store, in his station wagon, but Brodsky still remained an outsider, since his true capacity was as assistant manager of Biltwell's Farmington factory and manager of the outlets.

Nonetheless, he attended the company's semiannual sales meetings, in St. Louis, as well as the parties hosted, by his parents, for the salesmen and their wives, and he came to know those "road peddlers" on a personal level. His father, typically busy directing the meetings with the salesmen, paid little mind to Brodsky, who would simply fade into the background, to jot notes and even compose poems, on the spot, logging the essence of the gatherings, as both participant and detached spectator ("Catering to the Ethnic Trade," January 1981; "Two Days in the Life of Willy Sypher, Purveyor," June 1981; "Spring '84 Sales Meeting: Presentation of the Tailored-Suit Line," June 1983; "Our Credo: Spring '84," June 1983).

Utilizing his role within his father's company, Brodsky found that his presence at such gatherings gave the poems both authenticity and perspective. He had perfected this skill, of quietly functioning as an interloper within an inner circle, not only during his years as a member of the Biltwell sales force but as an outlander in Oxford, where he felt connected to the community's tight-knit social cliques and yet sensed that he never truly belonged. In both situations, Brodsky was admitted into the fold but maintained the writer's omniscient vantage.

The notion of such willing dislocation was nowhere more apparent than in Brodsky's Jewish traveling-salesman character, Willy Sypher. In conceiving of Willy, Brodsky's intention was for him to be a unique entity, not based on a specific Biltwell representative, Brodsky's father, or even Brodsky himself. Certainly, he did draw on his own highs and lows in the industry — especially those times when he was out on the road, alone, hauling his goods and being his own boss. Yet Brodsky tried to stay attuned, as he composed, to those flights of imagination specifically giving rise to Willy's singular spirit, infusing the character with a life all his own, such as in the poems "Willy's Day of Reckoning" (June 1982), "Between Seasons" (May 1983), "Willy: Fisher of Men" (July 1983), "Willy's Southern Route" (July 1983), "A Break in the Routine" (January 1984), "Willy's Last Season" (July 1984), "Young Willy Is Chosen to Serve an Important Account" (November 1984), "Willy Declines His Hard-Earned Promotion" (January 1985), "['Bastards!' Willy chastises invisible fates]" (January 1985), "One Long Road" (June 1985), and many more.

There were, however, instances when Brodsky attempted to summon Willy but failed. The poem's imagery might be too abstract, such as in "Blown into a Snow Zone" (February 1983), to be a true "Willy" piece. Another might veer too heavily into the semiautobiographical, right down to describing Brodsky's seeing, in the rearview mirror, his own "gold-rimmed profile," "strange handlebar mustache, large bulb nose," and "Brillo hair" ("Willy Loses His Sense of Direction," May 1982).

At other times, he depicted the true essence of Willy but did not keep the character's biographical circumstances in check with preceding poems. Brodsky was not, however, concerned with stopping to fix those contradicting elements. Instead, he allowed the details to remain fluid (changing Willy's familial status or accounts of his career at the fictional Acme-Zenith clothing company) and let Willy evolve, knowing, all the while, that he would someday sort his hundreds of salesman poems and bring consistency to Willy's personal background, when shaping a retrospective book spanning the character's entire adult life (which came to pass in 2005, when Time Being Books published *Peddler on the Road: Days in the Life of Willy Sypher*).

While the "Willy" pieces dealt with bigotry and pariahdom as seen through the eyes of a persistent but weary — and often persecuted — Jewish salesman, divulging loneliness, sadness, and angst, Brodsky also explored the Jews' legacy on a wholly darker level, penning a number of Holocaust pieces. His interest in the subject (which had been sparked as early as the 1960s but had not taken flight, as a regular theme of his work, until the 1980s) was triggered, in part, by his reading, in 1982, Thomas Keneally's *Schindler's List*, which inspired him to delve into that sacred territory, typically reserved for historians or those who actually lived the horror, survived the ghettos and camps. In certain pieces, including "Boxcars" (August 1982), "Cracow Now" (April 1983), "Palindrome" (April 1985), "Acid Rain" (June 1985), "Chelmno Rain" (June 1985), and "Black Hole-ocaust" (June 1985), he approached the topic in a first-person voice, daring to assess the past's haunting presence in the modern-day and even envisioning himself in a "destinationless *Güterwagen*" ("A Toast to the Forties," September 1985). In other poems, such as "The Thorough Earth"

(June 1981), "One Out of Six Million" (April 1983), and "Rosh Hashanah for One Fallen from Grace" (September 1984), he was so bold as to invent, from a third-person perspective, Holocaust refugees and survivors.

Unthinkable to some, Brodsky considered it essential to let art coalesce with truth, making the experience of the Holocaust and its aftermath accessible, on a deeply personal, emotional level, to readers. And although most writers would not have made the leap, Brodsky saw, in the stark reality of the Jews' plight, the potential for a strikingly bold point of comparison with his character Willy. It was that concept — of juxtaposing "Willy" poems and Holocaust poems — that would lead, in 1986, to a pamphlet entitled "The Ash Keeper's Everlasting Passion Week," and, in 1989, to the Timeless Press volume *The Thorough Earth*.

With his imagination regularly seeking out such intense topics, it's no wonder that Brodsky often found himself unable to pull back, compose humorous or loving pieces, especially given that his relationship with Jan had grown increasingly volatile. Much of his writing now dealt with the concept of a displaced family man, uncertain how to cope with the withdrawal of a spouse who "for five years, has sequestered herself / Within the solitude of a valetudinarian's convalescence" ("[He rises, robotically, from his bed,]," January 1983). Aware of their personal flaws and impatience with each other's limitations, he could not help but know that "he and his mate nurtured the ruse, / Abused their mutual self-respect, / With subterfuge, lying, unfulfilled promises," leaving each stranded, alone, at "the iceberg's apex" ("Miscellaneous Man," February 1983). And while he had yet to apply such formal terms as "codependence" to their situation, which had dwindled to a state in which he perceived they might "drown in . . . profound unhappiness," he obliquely labeled their relationship as such, stating, "Why we persist in loving one another / Is destiny's guess. Our separation would devastate the universe" ("[Who has ever shared another's solitude?]," May 1983).

Incapable of supporting his family solely through his undertakings as a writer, Brodsky continued in his capacity as a manager at Biltwell, which only amplified his frustration and despair. Isolation, during his travels to the remote outposts of his stores, afforded him ample time in which to compose new poems but also swallowed him in lacunae of silence — moments spent "knowing that being a poet is the loneliest incarnation of all" ("Incarnations," June 1983). Feeling indentured to his incredibly successful father only made matters worse, since it was impossible for him not to compare himself to his dad and judge himself, as he felt his father continually did to him, for not following more precisely in his father's footsteps. While Brodsky had a keen business sense, he was undeniably plagued with guilt for having taken "to reading, pondering, criticizing, / Writing adolescent verse, instead of apprenticing / To his dad, the self-made Baruch" ("The Self-Made Son of a Self-Made Man," June 1983).

To bolster his sense of pride, overcome his perception that he would never live up to the image of who his wife and his father wanted him to be, Brodsky occasionally withdrew into the comfort of romantic fantasy, especially when in Oxford, where he was free to imagine himself an uninhibited man, a "rabidly passionate cloven-hoofed goat" ("Sir Galwyn of Arthgyl," May 1984). The Warehouse, a restaurant/bar, in Oxford, bustling with college students, offered refuge, for Brodsky, who would sit, for hours, composing poems, drinking wine, and dreaming of his submission, "Without hesitation," to the first casual smile or wink that might come his way, "knowing local Loreleis can't resist foreign exhibitionists" ("Making Berth at Oxford," June 1984).

It was in this vulnerable frame of mind that Brodsky was introduced, by a mutual Oxford friend, during the summer of 1984, to a young lady who would cause him, once again, to stray from his vow of fidelity to Jan. Finding this woman tantalizingly seductive, he was instantly smitten and began a liaison that would last through the end of the year. From luxuriating in the "secret heat" of their union ("Night Vipers," July 1984) to harboring anxiety about "being found out" for the "fruition of . . . misdeeds" ("Under the River's Stern Surveillance," November 1984), Brodsky considered their relationship exhilarating but too unpredictable. Passionate and exciting, this lady also seemed emotionally unbalanced, making Brodsky fear for her safety and his own. He quickly ended the affair and vowed to stay true to Jan from that time forward, which he did.

Yet, he found little stability back at home, either. Believing that Farmington could not provide adequate education for their growing children, Brodsky and his wife had moved, in the summer of 1984, from their beloved Victorian mansion in Farmington, to a rented house in St. Louis. Although that relocation did, in fact, help them expose Trilogy and Troika to greater diversity and better schooling, it also presented them with new uneasiness, in a "less neighborly" urban environment, and brought them into more direct contact with Brodsky's parents.

Unable to dismiss his "father's abusive disrespect / For the person he nurtured, if not in his image, / As a businessman, at least as one / Conversant with sustaining the work ethic / As a purposive means to reasonably effective success," Brodsky considered himself "A son, poet, longing so for his dad's words of praise" ("Bearing Grudges," August 1984) — words that would never come. And so it remained, that Brodsky kept paying his dues, at Biltwell, but not earning approval, from his father. Calling it what it was — "grasping at straws, being at odds, loggerheads" — he acquiesced to this truth: "The fact remains unchanged: he and I / Have always seen completely eye to eye, / Without ever having agreed" ("Oedipus," June 1985).

He also resigned himself to the idea that he and Jan had squandered their best years, with futile, passive-aggressive fighting, and had now settled in a city that felt very little like home, "their only possessions their very uprootedness" ("Discontinuing Passenger Service," June 1984). Whereas, in Farmington, days filled with familial joy could supersede moments of sadness, they found that, in St. Louis, the balance shifted, revealing "the extent of her desperation / And mine, the vacuum absence imposes on the heart / When lovers let their blood, from neglect, / Forgetting, or petty rejection, cause its flow / To clog" ("The Irretrievable," September 1984).

Denying his wife's allegations that she and their children were never Brodsky's priority, he professed his love for Jan and the family but realized there were strains of truth to her comments, admitting, if to no one but himself, that writing was the only way he had of saying he *existed*, any given day. His poems had been and would always be, in his artist's mind, a tangible and true measure of his value as a human being. In essence, a day without his creating a poem, creating something, held no justification for living, as confessed in these lines from "A Lost Tribe's Latter-Day Scribe" (June 1984): "If there be any greatness in my paltry psyche, / It must be my capacity to cajole the mediocre / Into nobility, refine, from cacophony, melody, unmask chaos, / By naming stars, insects, unborn babies." So too did he profess that writers "thrive on shimmering images / Derived of Shakespearean antecedents, / Rendering, from negligibles, provocative essences, / Ultimately our most coveted possessions" ("[Those of us — poets, dreamers, winos,]," August 1985).

Jan found herself competing not only with Brodsky's muse, and his primal need to create, but also with William Faulkner and Brodsky's mythical mistress, Mississippi. Obsessed with fulfilling obligations, Brodsky continually strived to meet his commitments regarding his Faulkner collection. By 1985, he and Hamblin had completed three additional books in the series *Faulkner: A Comprehensive Guide to the Brodsky Collection* (*Volume II: The Letters*, 1984; *Volume III: The De Gaulle Story*, 1984; and *Volume IV: Battle Cry*, 1985), and Brodsky had added to his holdings a wealth of additional materials, including thousands of pages of manuscripts and correspondence, legal documents, movie scripts, photographs, and artwork, making his one of the finest Faulkner collections in the world, behind only those of the Alderman Library (University of Virginia), the Harry Ransom Humanities Research Center (University of Texas at Austin), and the Department of Archives and Special Collections and the Center for the Study of Southern Culture (both at the University of Mississippi at Oxford). In fact, despite those centers' substantial assets, Brodsky's collection — already distinctive, for representing the work of a private individual, without the support of institutional budgets of staffing — was considered to have the most inscribed books, the best trove of film matter and legal documents, and one of the most significant selections of Faulkner's letters and early poetry. To ensure the safekeeping of such precious pieces, Brodsky agreed to deposit the bulk of the collection in the rare-book room of the Kent Library, at Southeast Missouri State University, thus guaranteeing its proper storage and maintenance and facilitating his scholarly work with Hamblin.

In the summer of 1985, Brodsky also attended the Faulkner and Yoknapatawpha Conference, again positioning himself amidst the elite of Southern studies. Even at casual gatherings on the grounds of the Faulkner estate, egotistic jockeying was the norm, with attendees there to "register our various ambitions, / Note one another's tedious vocations / Within academe or slightly to the left or right of life, . . . / Proclaim that each of us is similarly gifted," during that "curious Eucharist, shabby communion with our Lord, Billy" ("5:30 Picnic at Rowan Oak," July 1985). And it was precisely the pretensions of such rituals that cultivated his growing disenchantment with the Faulkner community, leaving him to ponder "what conceivably could have brought him back / To this brackish desolation" ("One Final Run," July 1985). He had always recoiled from such posturing, and yet he had actively been "courting approval of others / Into whose arbitrary custody I remanded my shadow — / Academicians, mainly, whose aims and motivations / Are fundamentally inimical to mine, / Enemies of freedom and creativity, / Except as those elusive concepts fit their theses" ("Going Home," August 1985).

Disillusioned, he couldn't help but wonder what he was doing, how he had strayed so far from home. And where was "home" — St. Louis? Oxford? St. Louis had no quaintness, no small-town charm, and the beguilement of Mississippi was certainly wearing thin. He missed the simplicities that had so enraptured his poet's eye, in Farmington, and he regularly made brief stops or stayed the night, at his old house, to wander about the "drowsing premises," taking into account "each change that might have alchemized / Since we four, an intact, sane, happy family, / Vacated this somnolent Pompeii" ("Quincunxes in Everything," August 1985).

Even at this emotional crossroads, though, Brodsky did not capture such sentiments, in verse, as a mechanism for catharsis. His writing, though sometimes wistful or reflective, was still truly a means of propulsion, of arresting and exploding a moment in time, through image and metaphor, and then moving forward. Stalling in self-analysis, to transform himself or dissect the past, would have halted the process, put the emphasis on purging Brodsky of his demons, distilling his emotional responses, instead of advancing his art. Rejecting such stasis, he always sought to cast the quotidian in a fresh light.

Approaching his mid-forties made such progress ever more attainable, for Brodsky. His increasing maturity allowed him to reach beyond first-person confessional tones, to explore broader themes. Beginning to take on politics ("*Kryptopterus bicirrhis*," June 1984) and current events ("[Exiting southwest, out of Gopher Prairie,]," October 1985; "Blind Leading the Blind," November 1985; "Apocalypse Then and Now, and Right Now!," November 1985), he expanded his use of omniscient, third-person, and first-person-plural voices, and he developed his narrative forms as well, especially in his local-interest pieces ("The Black Pariah," March 1985; "The Visigoth," April 1985) and his modern-day takes on traditional conceits ("Donne's 'Meditation XVII': An Oblique Reprise," October 1985).

Another form that Brodsky employed in 1985 (for the first time since his apprentice years) was the suite composed purely of poetry, with no prose insertions. Although uncommon at this stage of his writing, he constructed "New Orleans Suite," in January of that year, with four poems from November 1984: "Transfiguring Silence," "Young Willy Services Two Major Accounts" (originally titled "Young Willy Is Chosen to Work an Important Account"), "Under the River's Surveillance" (originally titled "Under the River's Stern Surveillance"), and "Star-Crossed." Unlike "The Farmington Altarpiece: A Renaissance Triptych" (February 1977), a suite-like work created within days of the individual poems' composition but blended with a prose introduction, Brodsky crafted the "New Orleans" suite two months after writing the poems, in an effort to have the work published in *Southern Review*. He subsequently retooled it, in December 1985, so it comprised only "Following the River South" (October 1984), "Under the River's Surveillance," and "Star-Crossed," and then submitted it to *Xavier Review*.

While this particular suite was perhaps more contrived than his later ones, due to Brodsky's motivation of having the suite published, the mode of conceiving of such a compilation after the act of composition would remain his standard for years to come. (In fact, it was not until the 1990s that Brodsky became aware that he was consciously conceiving of a suite while writing the poems it would eventually include, contemporaneously devising the suite and keeping its overall intent in mind as he wrote each of the individual pieces.) And even as the process evolved, Brodsky found that the intention was always the same — preserving the integrity of each suite as its own poetic entity, a unit unto itself, beyond that of the poems it comprises. As a result, each suite is shown, within the *Complete Poems* volumes, in its own form, bearing the date upon which the suite itself was created and the tracking number assigned to it within the master database maintained by Time Being Books.

Likewise, the other pieces in this book bear their creation dates and tracking numbers, at the bottom of each poem, and they have been arranged according to their dates of creation, which represent the time of their original composition, not their revision. If a poem has more than one creation date (i.e., if it was started on one day and not finished until another, with extra stanzas, closure, or the title coming at that later time), it is situated, in this volume, by its first date, because Brodsky's poems typically have their intent, as well as the majority of their content, in place at that point. If two or more poems were produced in one day, each of those poems bears a bracketed numeral, after the creation date, indicating the sequence of composition.

If a creation date could not be verified, a question mark follows the unconfirmed portion, which may be the month, the day, or the year. On rare occasions, the entire date may be in doubt (in which case it is bracketed and followed by a question mark), indicating either that it could represent revision instead of composition or that the drafts were undated but were found near other material written at that time. Also, the date may appear twice for the same poem, once with a question mark and once without, signifying that it is accurate for at least a portion of the text but may or may not apply to the whole piece.

The dates and tracking numbers will eventually serve as cross references between the standard *Complete Poems* volumes and the two concluding books of this series: the index of the Time Being Books database tracking records and the volume of ultimate, later revised versions. The index, to be arranged chronologically, will detail where each poem was composed, provide its publication data, and supply, if relevant, notes about the poem's history. This information, in turn, will link the standard set with the final volume, which will show the corrected, most recent version of every poem drastically revised after its final early version was in place (such as a poem edited to fit the context of a new publication). Any poem, in this book, that will have its later form printed in the concluding volume — either because it has already undergone such revision or because it has been assigned to a future Time Being Books text and will, presumably, undergo such revision — bears a delta symbol (Δ) after its title.

Thus, in the *Complete Poems* set, the standard volumes will present the text of each poem, in its corrected original form, the penultimate volume will chronicle its creation data and its publishing history, and the final volume will show its subsequent, revised version, if applicable.

To retain the poems' original authorial voice from the period of composition, the editorial staff of Time Being Books has not fully revised any of the pieces in this volume (except when generating later versions of those poems that have been culled for new publications). For instance, poems with incorrect stanza lengths have typically been preserved in their original form and simply bear a note, in the tracking system, stating that a particular stanza is one line short or long. Even unfinished poems have not been edited stylistically, because they illustrate the evolution of Brodsky's writing, in juxtaposition with his completed pieces. To alert the reader to such verse, fragmental poems, which are typically ten lines or fewer, carry a dagger symbol (†) after the title, and incomplete poems, which are normally well developed but without the thrust to move toward closure, bear a double-dagger symbol (‡).

Brodsky did, however, revise most of his poems, after writing them, with the intention of refining their grammatical form. To help him achieve that goal, the editorial staff of Time Being Books has worked with Brodsky to make all pieces in this series meet the company's current guidelines for language usage and mechanics, correcting spelling, punctuation, grammar, and syntax as needed, in accordance with *The Chicago Manual of Style* and Edward D. Johnson's *Handbook of Good English*. In instances where dedications or certain details were consciously excised from the original manuscript (such as given names of female companions) but can be deduced, from the context, Brodsky has attempted to restore that wording to those poems, adding his estimation, in brackets. Bold and italic typefaces have also been applied, as appropriate, and preferred spellings (as listed in *Random House Webster's Unabridged Dictionary*) have been utilized as well. While Brodsky's use of neologisms and compound words has been preserved throughout, hyphens have generally been inserted in them, in this volume (unlike volume one), to prevent ambiguity and make the usage more uniform.

These editorial changes are meant to standardize the work and enhance its readability, without any relineation or substantive revision, and they have been made only under Brodsky's direct supervision, bringing clarity and order to the pieces presented here, in volume four of *The Complete Poems of Louis Daniel Brodsky*.

Sheri L. Vandermolen
5/9 . . . 6/3/2008
Peoria, Illinois

INTRODUCTION

In 1981, I turned forty and, in many respects, felt as though I were in the prime of my life, physically and intellectually. Jan and I, married for just over a decade, had a seven- and four-year-old, and we were well ensconced in one of the most beautiful edifices in Farmington, Missouri: a white-clapboard wedding cake of a house, built in 1896, boasting a wrap-around porch, with gingerbread motifs, and a colossal attic surmounted by three spires and a widow's walk.

We were so proud of our residence at 628 West Columbia, replete with a freestanding cookhouse and a four-stall stable, on three acres. I reveled in being a landowner, a homeowner, a provider for my wife and two kids. I loved coming home from the factory, not five minutes away.

Our Victorian mansion was a living museum, displaying an eclectic array of American antiques, which I'd been collecting since graduating from Yale, in 1963. We didn't have one traditional piece of furniture in the house. We did our formal dining at an 1890s roulette table with claw-and-ball feet, decorated green felt, and a smooth-spinning wheel; around it were two highly ornate 1870s McDannold optometrist chairs and four white-porcelain Koken barber chairs. The dining room was so large that it also boasted two six-foot, turn-of-the-century Mills quartersawed golden-oak console slot machines (the Owl and the Dewey) and comfortably held a Mutoscope, Holcomb & Hoke Sunkist Popcorn Machine, an oak-encased Watling upright scale, a six-foot-tall Sidney advertising clock, and a Cremona Style 2 nickelodeon. But the highlight of the room was a nine-foot-tall, seven-instrument 1912 Wurlitzer Model C orchestrion with three art-glass front-panel doors and a "wonder light." We fondly referred to this exquisite mechanical piano as "Winnie" and "The Big Music." I cherished those moments when I'd hold my children in my arms, dancing to the ten-tune paper rolls, whose spirited sounds would lift the roof off the house.

During those years, I composed many poems referencing these antiques and others I'd acquired. Our house was central to our existence. My eyes had memorized each inch of its insides; so had Jan's.

That storybook setting framed our existence and became the ultimate symbol of the life we'd built together, in Farmington (as notably detailed in "628 West Columbia"). Still longing to preserve the devotion and domesticity we'd shared, there, for so long, I expressed my adoration of Jan, in poems I'd dedicate to her not just for her birthdays and our anniversaries but for no reason other than needing to show my love, such as in "Keeping the Vows," "Mystical Union: An Adoration," "Stargazers," "The Seven Senses," "Botticelli's *Birth of Venus*," "Total Eclipse," and "Silkscreen."

Inside and out, the domain seemed a place of easy tranquillity. From early spring to late fall, I would start up my ancient, rusted, red Wheel Horse riding mower and, with wineglass in hand, navigate our estate. On my mufflerless machine, I was fearless Don Quixote atop Rocinante, or Captain Ahab at the helm of the *Pequod*. I knew every bush and tree by heart, every adventitious clump of onions, every swath of blue- and ryegrass.

At least three evenings a week, I would barbecue steaks or chicken breasts. It was a ritual I looked forward to whether it was ninety or twenty degrees out. The grill was my sacred retreat, cooking on it an opportunity to commune with nature and myself. "Dude," as my kids called me — and as I called myself — would "do the honors." All too often, indulging, to excess, in wine, as the meat, above the lowest possible flame, cooked and cooked, I would burn the chicken to crisps indistinguishable from the briquettes, turn our thick-cut steaks into shriveled shoe leather. Although, for a long time, my predictable culinary disasters were occasions for laughter and gentle censure, it eventually became apparent to my family that barbecuing was just my excuse for drinking. The stress of trying to make something of myself, not only as a family man and businessman but as a poet, was eating away at me.

All the while, I was writing my poems, chronicling my life. I never relaxed. Everything I did, from inspecting my factory-outlet stores, in Missouri, Illinois, and Arkansas, to visiting Bob Hamblin, in Cape Girardeau, where we'd busy ourselves with documenting artifacts in the Brodsky Faulkner Collection, took me more and more frequently from my family.

In those years, I became a citizen of impersonal motels, cafés, restaurants with busy bars, hotel music rooms featuring amateurish bands — all of them serving as sanctuaries from my travels, where I'd unwind, after work, with glasses of wine, my trusty pen in hand, recording my anguish and occasional joy, in poem after poem. I was adrift in an archipelago of Tipton, Salisbury, New Athens, West Helena, and Sullivan (and, later, Jefferson City and Rolla), each a destination on my three-state map, each a home to one of my slack-factory-outlet stores. And, of course, there was Oxford, Mississippi, to which I gravitated every few months, to immerse myself in Faulkner's Yoknapatawpha.

Sadly, even my time in Farmington began to feel like time away from home. Nights with Jan grew into mere occasions of marital frustration. I'm sure her dissatisfaction was every bit equal to mine, or even greater. Our small Missouri town had no cultural outlets, no fine dining, no movies, just a twice-weekly newspaper, which often arrived *once* a week. Farmington had its assets (no traffic jams, little crime, a low cost of living, friendly people), but its liabilities far outweighed them. To revitalize ourselves, Jan and I would frequently leave for St. Louis, to visit my parents, or for Jacksonville, Illinois, where her mother and father were always eager to entertain us, in their home and at the town's one country club. And there were occasional weekends when we'd import friends to our house, for parties.

At this time, I began teaching a three-hour evening class (creative writing or short stories, given the semester), one night a week, at Mineral Area Junior College, in Flat River, five miles away. I felt that by doing so, I was giving something back to the community. And in some respects, my position at the school was the fulfillment of my original plan in 1968, when I went to Miami-Dade Junior College, to pursue a career as an instructor. I found that teaching people for whom higher education was an exception, not an escape from the real world and a postponement of work (as I'm sure the case was in affluent Coral Gables), was a privilege. Their appreciation of my efforts was enough to sustain my enthusiasm. More so, cut off as I was from academia (other than for the scholarly work I was doing with Bob Hamblin and for the friendships I'd made within the Faulkner and Yoknapatawpha Conference community), teaching kept my critical and analytical faculties honed.

For all the satisfaction of the classroom, home had begun to offer little respite. Jan and I tried our best to hold our marriage together, but arguing had become our language, and we diminished each other with our barbs, our carping, our fighting. Though young, our children must have registered our turmoil, without being able to intervene on their own behalf or ours. Things got progressively more embittered between Jan and me. She was venting her frustration with my abrupt departures from Farmington. I was constantly defending myself, arguing that my traveling for Biltwell was our sole source of income, although, in truth, some of my trips were not necessary, rather excuses for me to escape domestic stress. Our marriage had become a tribulation. Our gentleness had hardened into ugliness. Our time together was perfunctory. And our intimacy ceased to exist.

Dejectedly, I drove to Oxford, Mississippi, in August 1981, to attend my sixth Faulkner and Yoknapatawpha Conference. It had been a year since I stumbled into marital indiscretion, a year since I had looked at any woman other than Jan. I believed I had learned a painful, humiliating lesson and that I had atoned for, mitigated, if not absolved myself of, my sin.

Faulkner's hometown had become as familiar to me as Farmington. I felt comfortable in its sleepy purlieus, from South Lamar to St. Peter's Cemetery, Old Taylor Road to the courthouse square, the Ole Miss campus (especially the John Davis Williams Library and the Alumni House — the hotel where I'd stay) to Bailey's Woods and Rowan Oak. And I knew its fictional counterparts by heart. Faulkner's novels were my scriptures, his protagonists apostles I worshiped.

The last evening of the conference, attending a party at Square Books, in downtown Oxford, I met a young lady, a Mississippian with a beguiling smile and sensual drawl. She was so respectful, polite, and accepting of me. That night, we initiated what would become a frenzied love affair and a deeply intimate friendship. "The Fawns," which I wrote the following morning, between Memphis and Farmington, on my drive home, describes my enchantment.

One month later, using a scheduled trip to my outlet store in West Helena, Arkansas, as a disguise for my real motives, I met my new lover, in Oxford. My sexual liberation was ecstasy. I believed that her appreciation of me as a poet was typical of Mississippians, whom I felt revered their artists.

On September 12, 1981, I composed three poems in my notebook, while driving the 333 miles from Oxford to Farmington. "Of Elegies and Renascence" and "Sparks Jumping the Gap" express my complete admiration for my Southern belle. During that seven-hour drive, I also wrote

"The Defrocking of Rudy Toothacre, Itinerant Minister of the Universal Gospel of the Synod for All Churches of the What's Happenin' Now," which, like "Guilt-Throes," from the year before, bespoke my self-loathing for having again defiled my marriage with Jan.

But the pain was not as great as the longing for my new "fawn" from Jackson, Mississippi. And as fate would have it, the manuscript for *Faulkner: A Comprehensive Guide to the Brodsky Collection, Volume I: The Biobibliography*, which Bob Hamblin and I had worked on for almost two years, was due at the University Press of Mississippi, in Jackson, at the beginning of October. (This initial volume of a seven-book series that Bob and I would eventually produce was published the next year.) Even though I had only been home a month, from Oxford, I knew that delivering our four-hundred-page manuscript, in person, to Barney McKee, director of the press, would not only allow me to discuss critical design issues with him but also to meet my lover.

I recorded my liaison with her in a sequence of five extremely sensual and highly emotional poems: "Mistress Mississippi," "Running Scared," "[I enter your house, not a stranger]," "Wind Devils," and "Goldenrods." So captivated was I, by this woman, that I dreamed of throwing everything away and moving to Jackson, to stay with her for the rest of my life. Mine was a desperate ecstasy, at best, as was hers. For our few days together, we were kindred Mississippians — I an adopted native, she a latter-day Scarlet O'Hara, living by her resourcefulness, mystique, and guile.

The romance we shared was unlike any I had experienced in years. In her kitchen, while she cooked dinner, I wrote "[I enter your house, not a stranger]" for her. She became my Southern muse, my mistress Mississippi.

At the far end of that same month, we met again, in Oxford. Like the previous trip, this one also yielded a sequence of love poems: "In Defense of Physical Manifestations," "Exhortation in Praise of Spontaneity," "Cosmic Consolations," "Even the Highway Is My Crucifix," and "Rummaging in the Attic," a lament for Jan, expressing my sad sense of longing for her amidst all the chaos of our lives.

Despite our need for each other, this woman and I knew that our relationship was ephemeral, doomed to lapse into silence. She had committed herself to me completely; she had no other attachments. I was married, with two children.

Over the next ten months, I returned to Oxford five times but only saw her once more, in March 1982, when I told her that I had decided not to leave Jan and my kids, not to move to Oxford or Jackson, not to devote myself to her. With melancholy, I confessed my fear of cutting loose from what I had come to accept as familiar, if not fulfilling. To leave it all behind — two children, especially — for someone I'd known less than a year, been with fewer than half a dozen times, was too risky, foolhardy.

In two poems, I penned my disgust with the licentiousness that had once again wormed its way into my heart: "The Profligate" and "Cloven-Hoofed Goat."

In April 1982, I turned forty-one and vowed, for a second time, to recommit my apostate soul to Jan. My daughter, Trilogy, was almost eight, and my son, Troika, was about to turn five. If Jan and I weren't compatible as lovers, husband and wife, at least we were able to share satisfaction in being parents, as reflected in "Post-Giraffic," "Connecting Dots," "Getting Our Tree," "One-Room School," and "Gentle Revolutionaries."

And we enjoyed our separate pursuits. She'd made an affiliation with the YMCA in St. Louis, to create a branch in Farmington and serve as the lead instructor for the new aerobics program. As she got into shape, I became more sedentary, continuing not only to write my poems but also mine my Faulkner materials, with Bob Hamblin (preparing *Faulkner: A Comprehensive Guide to the Brodsky Collection, Volume II: The Letters* [1984]; *Volume III: The De Gaulle Story* [1984]; and *Volume IV: Battle Cry* [1985]), and pen a variety of articles and essays on William Faulkner, which were published in *Studies in Bibliography*, the *Southern Review*, and the *Faulkner Journal*, as well as in several collections of the annual Faulkner and Yoknapatawpha Conference lectures.

Jan was also taking flying lessons at the Farmington Municipal Airport, practicing in a Piper Cherokee. I had vast misgivings, but she felt at ease with her training. She invited me to fly with her on her first "cross-country," from Farmington to Perryville. She made a perfect landing, in a massive cross wind, with me in the backseat, vomiting. She stepped out of the cockpit like Amelia Earhart. She loved her new avocation.

Yet, despite our activities, life in Farmington was stuck in a time warp. Things refused to change. The town's official logo, glaring from the water tower, was "City of Traditional Progress" (corrected, some years later, to "City of Tradition and Progress"). Everything happened in quarter-time. While Jan continued to feel imprisoned by Farmington's sluggish ambiance, I enjoyed the slow pace, marking the progress of my family, in poem after poem. Trilogy's and Troika's antics were so delightful that I couldn't resist capturing them. I preserved those years in the fourth of my unpublished books of poems about our days at 628 West Columbia (*Hopgrassers and Flutterbies: Volume Four of The Seasons of Youth*) — vignettes depicting adoring parents nurturing their two children. I did this even as I was spending more and more time on the road.

Even when I was home, my daytime hours were often spent in my writing office, editing my first book of Southern poems. It was a highlight of my career when, in 1983, the University Press of Mississippi published *Mississippi Vistas*, selling all fifteen hundred hardback copies, within the first six months. Immediately, I began working on sequels to that edition, to fulfill my vision of creating an ambitious trilogy of the South. University Press of Mississippi tacitly committed to publishing volumes two and three.

By the middle of 1984, I had completed first drafts of *Mistress Mississippi* and *Disappearing in Mississippi Latitudes*, though I had no idea that they were conceived in reverse order. (Fortunately, the University Press of Mississippi's board of directors decided to discontinue publishing poetry; otherwise, I would have issued books two and three out of sequence.) Their further development was delayed until 1992 and 1994, when the problem was resolved, under the guidance of Time Being Books' first Editor in Chief, Jane Goldberg, with *Mistress Mississippi* correctly published as the trilogy's concluding volume.

During that period, a tormented persona appeared to me, haunted me, inhabited my imagination, compelled me to flesh him out, in the form of many characters from the Holocaust — victims, survivors, and perpetrators. Most of the Holocaust poems from this time would not find their way into a book until 1989 (*The Thorough Earth*), but the appearance of poems such as "Cracow Now" and "One Out of Six Million" signaled to me another side of the unhappiness I was feeling in my marriage. If my Willy Sypher traveling-salesman poems (which derived from my experience with managing Biltwell's outlet stores) reflected my uprootedness and solitude, and the Southern poems exposed me, in the guise of a Northern outlander, as a moral reprobate and a drunk, the Holocaust poems presented me as a victim. My victimization, I realized, was metaphorical and certainly not to be confused with the devastating obliteration of human lives in the Nazi scourge. Nonetheless, my psyche's torment was unrelenting.

To ameliorate my pain, I found myself gravitating to Oxford, Mississippi, as often as possible, where I could steep myself in the Faulkner mythos. People there respected me as one of the world's premier Faulkner collectors and scholars. Though uncomfortable with celebrity, I did find it flattering to have strangers want to shake my hand, introduce themselves, talk with me about Faulkner.

But mine was, by choice, a lonely quest. When in Oxford, I'd end my days at the Warehouse, a restaurant converted from a cotton-storage facility, just off the square. Despite the bustling atmosphere, I blended into this easygoing, stained-glass setting. It was a favorite watering hole for Ole Miss students. I would sit in the dining room, drinking carafes of Mouton Cadet white, writing poems, sometimes past midnight. There, it was easy for me to imagine myself a reclusive Faulkner. And in the solitude of that crowded place, I was free from the disappointment and pervasive sense of personal failure in my relationship with Jan, free to commune with my imagination.

One night, while sitting in the Warehouse, fantasizing about making love with any one of the many Temple Drakes in the place (Ole Miss co-eds who might have stepped from the pages of Faulkner's *Sanctuary*), I was introduced, by a university friend, to a tall, slim, young woman with long blond hair. I was mesmerized; she arrested my breath. When my friend excused himself from our company, she whispered to me that she hoped we could get together. The next afternoon, I picked her up, and we drove off to her hometown, Holly Springs, to visit her father and go swimming at a friend's house, tour the town, and mingle with the ghosts in Hillcrest Cemetery, which contains the history of that quaint antebellum Mississippi town.

Nothing about her was deliberate; she was all nuances, textures, suggestiveness. I'd never seen such physical beauty combined with such ravishing openness. She was primal.

The beginning of our affair coincided with the 1984 Faulkner and Yoknapatawpha Conference. "Night Vipers," "Vague Lady from Holly Springs," "Skimming Mississippi's Urn," and "The Peabody" came out of our departing Oxford, for our first tryst, in Memphis's legendary hotel, The Peabody, an institution Faulkner so loved, and, thereafter, poems about our long-distance relationship exploded from my psyche.

A month later, I headed back to Oxford; she traveled up from Jackson, where she lived with her young daughter. We were so good together, so happy during that transitory encounter. After I returned to Farmington, I wrote "Tied to Our Tides," a lament on leaving her in Memphis, "Matriarchy," about hearing her voice on the phone, "Aubade," a paean to her intellect and sexual energy, and "Byhalia," about our visit, at my behest, to Dr. Wright's sanitarium, in a small Mississippi town, where Faulkner was last sent to dry out and where he died of coronary thrombosis.

Four weeks after that, we met again, in Memphis. "Following the River South," "Mizpah," and "Unexpected Awakening" captured this rendezvous.

In November 1984, we drove to New Orleans, indulged ourselves — Commander's Palace, Court of Two Sisters, jazz, the atmosphere of the Vieux Carre, Cabildo, Pirates' Alley (where Faulkner shared an upstairs room with the artist William Spratling, in 1925), and Ignatius J. Reilly's weenies (both of us admired John Kennedy Toole's *A Confederacy of Dunces*).

But our trip got strange. What I didn't know was that my "vague lady from Holly Springs" had a dark side. While in New Orleans, she had a manic episode, and I grew terrified for my well-being and hers. I hadn't imagined that she could be self-destructive. Lying in bed with her, on our first night there, I began to wonder where I was, just how far I had roamed from home.

Suddenly, all I wanted to do was leave the Crescent City, rewind the clock, bring myself home safe, to Jan and my children, to all that was predictable.

I ended my flight from reality with two poems, "The Dioscuri" and "Under the River's Stern Surveillance," which I composed in an attempt to put closure to that misguided period. Though I had considered, during the past year, starting a new life, I couldn't. The history Jan and I had written, the traditions and rituals and myths we'd carved out of our time together, and Trilogy and Troika, who carried our mutual imprint so deeply, had kept me from leaving Jan.

But even having ended that volatile relationship did not lessen the tumult I was experiencing, now that my family and I had relocated to St. Louis. Although Jan and I had determined that our children needed a better education, it was still with immense regret that, during the summer of 1984, we had closed our beautiful Victorian mansion in Farmington, moved to a rented house on busy, tree-lined Wydown Boulevard, in Clayton, an affluent suburb of St. Louis, and enrolled our two children in Glenridge Elementary School.

For the next few years, I traveled between St. Louis and Farmington, working in the factory, by day, and driving home at night. Occasionally, suffering bouts of nostalgia, or after teaching my Monday-night class at Mineral Area Junior College, I'd stay over, at our old house, alone with fifteen years of memories. Some evenings, sitting outside on the back patio, I'd barbecue, drink wine, and write poems such as "September Moon Through the Elms: A Nocturne" and "Dad in His Empty Country Castle." The first of these poems expresses my hopeful attitude toward the future: "Sitting amidst these mellifluous crickets, / I wish not that we might be as before / But as we are, that we might yet explore / What's left of love's metaphoric Horae, / Scavenge the sky's floor, for doubloons and other moons / Repoussé with our faces, search the earth, for signs of our newest designs."

But in "Dad in His Empty Country Castle," this nostalgia and optimism are tainted by melancholy over our having so completely uprooted ourselves: "I discover myself marooned, / A derelict stranded in isolated inebriation, / Lonely old man bereft of wife, children, friends, / Inventing jack rabbits that roamed these acres, / Years ago, when all of us were just growing." Inherent in this mood of loss is a vast uncertainty as to the wisdom of our move to St. Louis. Sadly, the next five years would justify my misgivings.

Louis Daniel Brodsky
11/17–18/00
5/9 . . . 7/11/01
7/13–14/05
5/21/08
St. Louis, Missouri

THE COMPLETE POEMS

OF

LOUIS DANIEL

BRODSKY

VOLUME FOUR, 1981–1985

Catering to the Ethnic Trade ^Δ

Each man's swatches,
Segregated and bound, by ranges,
Between brown, rubber-banded boards,
Clutter the U-shaped table
Like sliced corned beef
Piled on a delicatessen countertop.

Periodically,
The salesmen reach for a new stack.
Their sensitive fingers and thumbs,
Testing texture — "hand" —
Are circular knives
Cutting through new, pinked fabrics

Emblematic of food to be worn:
Joseph-coats,
Moses-robes, Pharaoh's stretch togas —
A feast of raiment
Prepared for a pharisaical public,
To which these experts will cater,

Over the next few months,
Like sophisticated waiters taking orders
Off menus they carry in cases
And on hangers, for eager customers.
Today, they sample their samples,
Epicureans keeping a kosher house.

1/3/81 — [1] (02393)

Hellfire

For the last three days,
Fever has obscured processes
By which thought rises to the moon,
Through cumulative illumination.

The scourge has transformed my psyche
Into a dry fountain,
A volcano, imploding magma,
Without release, an empty sky.

Only my corpulent body
Confines me to its earthly routines.
Eating, sleep, defecation
Are fetishistic rituals aborigines practice —

Not recessive features of my being
Silently forming by-products,
Rather distracting primary functions
Keeping me from my godly chores

Of translating Masoretic texts
Written of kissing lips,
Telling the heart's changeless time,
Alchemizing poetry from monkey dung.

The eyes blur. My nostrils and throat
Are roaring crematoriums.
All ideation turns to white ash,
As I pass back and forth, in bed,

Between eternity and right now,
When dying
Seems so far less final
Than surviving even another hour

And living is a poor alternative
To the essential wisdom of sleep,
Impregnable to dreams and demons,
Forgetfulness laced with sepulchral austerity.

I toss from exhaustion and stiffness
Too much rest causes,
Suspecting that neither death
Nor recovery will rescue my soul —

Not yet, anyway.
My ears have deciphered hell-whispers,
My eyes masked facial agonies.
They know the "slow ghost" has taken hold.

1/3/81 — [2] (00865)

Tiger, Tiger

Jesus,
          someone let the striped feline free,
     *

This bright-burning,
                    Blakeian morningtime,
Crowded the horizon with gyrfalcons
        wheeling in dapple-dazed
                                gyrations,
Rotating on absolutely impossible planes,
Preposterous
                by standards humanistic man
Has come to accept
        as too exacting to tolerate
                existentially . . .

Someone
                exonerated me of limitations
Imposed by waking, walking, working,
        talking back to echoless shadows
Stalking my genes with guilt and
        libidinous contempt for the ten dictates
Etched on my Mosaical gonads.
Jesus, I, like tiger, bright-blazing
                tiger,
Am both prey and predator,
Within the forest of metaphors
        Imagination preserves against interlopers,
Who might otherwise trespass,
        hunt me into extinction
Through too much curiosity-seeking.

Whichever direction I may take,
My destination, today,
Will be waiting at highway's end,
Looming, as always,
In the shape of a Gaudí church,
Outrageous and ramshackle
Yet sacred in that its myriad chambers
        contain my images,
A colossal reliquary rising in the air,
        through whose sleek convolutions
I soar,
        each glorious morning and eve.

Ah, the blessed metamorphosis!
Jesus,
        transportations,
        *

ecstasies,
epiphanic transubstantiations!
Ahead, an inscrutable gate opens,
Admitting my entranced mind
down a passageway lined with bones,
Whole skeletons.
Now, I know I've arrived.
The tiger has eaten himself alive and died.

1/8/81   (05737)

A Morning Convergence

Just behind the blue-tinted glass,
Like a torpid fish
Hovering, bug-eyed, inside its tank,
I stare abstractedly
At the bulbous red- and white-striped nacelle,
The plane's twin pendant pods,
Attached to slender, elongated pylons,
At opposite sides of a singular wingspan,
And three strutted ganglia of rubber feet.

My eyes scrutinize this idle machine
With increasing fright
And obvious apprehension,
As though even now,
In its silent benignity,
Aware of my presence,
It might be monitoring me as an alien,
A threat to its integrity,
Programming ways to dematerialize my immediacy.

Safety, whether airborne
Or landlocked, is an unstable construct
The mind invents repeatedly,
To spare itself the agonies of knowledge
Incomplete and endlessly mutable.
I realize this but resist uncertainty,
Persisting in gossamer prophecies
That I shall remain indomitable
Against fate's vagaries and machinations.

Yet, as I sit here, gazing out,
A shapeless premonition
Crashes through the stratosphere
Protecting my imagination from demons and fear,
Penetrates my brain,
Exploding into possibilities of doom
That scatter doubts about my future.
Confusion turns solemnity to burning rubble.
Soon, even my nerves are ashes.

Suddenly, an anonymous voice
Arouses me from sleepy lassitude,
With cryptic insistence, forces my body
Toward the door whose corridor
Connects earth to air.
Our confrontation is at hand.
I enter and am entered by its spirit.
For the moment, we must trust each other.

1/14/81 — [1] (05738)

Sinking Sensation

The eyes capsize in this gigantic ocean,
Whose undulating waves
Are people breaking, with murmurous echolalia,
Against each other,
Arriving, by accident, simultaneously,
At the same vortex.

Escape is the unfinished symphony's coda,
The name its composer
Would have chosen had he known
That all waves, even waves,
End in momentary silence
Somewhere far away from their conception,

Flowing in a final, seething silence
Before starting back home,
Achieving liberation,
If only on shores
Where no natives wait
To record their transitory roar.

My eyes, sinking caravels
Once captained by my mind's heroes,
Pitch and roll out of control
In this desolation,
Floated with mad and lonely souls,
And blur into murky opacity,

Below the ever-multiplying waves
Of people chasing people
Regenerating prolifically as sea bass.
Briefly, the storm subsides.
Sleep's soothing tides
Obliterate the tempest, dilute its fury,

Override my requirement
To navigate by dead reckoning.
Yet, in my cabin, absolutely blind,
I feel the eyes growing heavy with barnacles,
Going permanently shut.
Tomorrow morning, I'll be driftwood.

1/14/81 — [2] (05739)

Survival of the Fittest

The pen stutters above the paper.
Its point hovers like a snake's head
Poised to strike unsuspecting prey.
The hiatus its hesitation causes
Is unmistakably breathtaking.
Neither blank page
Nor single-fanged face moves,
Yet changes occur
In the space connecting them.
Without knowing, both objects know
That, too soon,
Each will subsume the other
In one all-consuming flash,
As though God were reenacting Creation
In the vaporous firmament
Above and beneath their separation.

Suddenly, on intuitional cue,
The snake releases itself from stasis,
Like an overwound clock spring snapping.
The white flesh bleeds.
Inky blue drips from its wounds,
As the indomitable viper,
Locked tightly, rips and twists
Its buried head,
Refuses to let loose its grip
Until certain its victim is vanquished,
Its mission finished,
The distance not merely diminished
But dematerialized,
Body, spirit, and soul assimilated,
Snake and page having become poem,
Whole, irreversible, redeemed from mere predation.

1/15/81 — [1] (05740)

Saying No: Expatiations in Chablis

Sweet sounds . . . dissolution abounds . . .
    life is unwinding
        without interruption,
Despite hyperbole, honorifics, corruption
    in the private and public sectors.

No reinterpretation of the Scriptures
    can change the basic truth
        or possibly undo the absolute fact
            that death prevails
For all humans,
    no matter their status, their station.

All dematerializes sooner or sooner,
    regardless of favors savored,
        nepotism, or primogenitary succession.

For now, the music staves off the end,
    mitigates inordinate paranoias,
Soothes the awful, sinking awareness
    that the old, fat bastard
Waits . . . is waiting . . . will remain patient

For whatever time it takes
    to convert flesh to dust motes
Floating in the eyes of Beelzebub and Satan,
    eradicate all traces of bone
And brain and that slender breath

The imagination exhales, making itself known
               to the living,
    groping in the dark, dank terrain
Separating silence from creativity.

For now, the sweet sounds confound me
    sufficiently to remove my cowering,
Inflate my ego and pride
To such haughty degrees
    I no longer care whether death
Intervenes or hides.

I have become the overriding factor,
    the spoiler, whose delusions
Neutralize all premonitions.
    The music surrounds my spirit
In a protective halo. . . .

        Inside this sensuality, I thrive,
Oblivious to time, space, finality.
    I climb the Jacob's ladder
That ends higher than the sky,

    higher than the inner eye reaches
As it flies out of its shell —
    the butterfly rising through ethers,
Into pure unorthodox soaring.

The sounds deliver me from myself,
Return my awkward intellect
        to the source where pure melody rises
From fountains spewing sweet sounds.

    Redemption is so terribly palpable
I cry. My weeping is eternal.
    What voice my words record
Ripples through man's passional chronicle.
    The eons register my appeal
As the earth's slow groaning.

Even the unformed genes of my offspring
Sing themselves alive tonight.
    I am the only hope for their survival.
Yet without them,
    my chances for self-perpetuation
Would be merely accidental, nearly impossible.

I need those uncreated scions
    to substantiate my present articulation.
If they fail to recognize my presence tonight,
    even my specter won't last
Past this scribbling. All my writing will die
    with my casket squeaking into its hole.

Whether this incredible mellifluousness
    will project me ahead,
While sustaining my hummingbird spirit,
    remains not only for tomorrow to tell
But the future to sell.

                    I touch the hand
    that clutches the pen, spans the pages,
And know, in a flash,
    that death doesn't even have a chance
Against my idiosyncratic capacity
                    for spontaneous expatiation.

Slowly, the lights dissipate;
                    vocals drift into silence;
Vibrations from guitar, piano, traps collapse,
    until I am left to my wiles,
Realizing past and future are identical,
    in that they belong to me,

Who, without choice, must continue,
    for the simple reason
That quitting signals signal defeat.

Ah, sweet sounds . . .
                    you'll accompany me
    to sleep, this evening.
Whatever imminent consequences
        might be assigned to my fate,
Tonight, I know, my existence is safe
        from unutterable annihilation.

I am the forebear, the strange one
        who's had to devise lyrics
To make the silence resonate. God,
    let me penetrate this halo
And arrive at tonight's other side,
Capable of navigating daylight alone . . . alone.

1/15/81 — [2] (01343)

Plea Before Boarding ^Δ

Five days away from my blessed babies,
My wife, the familiar landscape
Stippled with known shadows,
Suns, moons, dusks, and the house
Ancient carpenters fashioned manually

Have made my lonely passage unbearable.
I share with winter
A frozen barrenness, a slowing in the veins,
As though they were tributaries,
Solid as obsidian, beneath Siberian skies.

My heart stutters like a Model T.
It backfires from pressure
Sadness imposes on its overworked motor.
Time is a highway
Going deathward at rush-hour speed.

What I fly, seated here,
In this eerie airdrome,
Is a phantom sampan,
Phantasmagorical spore,
Rather than a sleek, soaring machine.

I require retrieval, redemption,
A physical resurrection,
Protection from alien creatures
That would assassinate my passion,
For gratuitous satisfaction,

Attack my imagination, with madness,
Leave me for lost, in a morass
*

Defoliated by Agent Orange,
Grasping at straw partners,

To cast my proxy vote for survival.
Return me, please,
To my port of origin, my offspring.
Spirit me home
Before my spirit forgets its direction.

1/18/81 — [1] (00687)

In Flight

Just now,
As dusk touches us,
The gypsy in me leaves the earth,
Enters the frigid ethers,
On an odyssey to the end of memory,
Where, once again,
My spirit will have outdistanced its shadow.

But my core remains,
Radiating love
Like a lodestone in the middle of nowhere,
Keeping memory alive
Despite entropy and natural attrition.
Those I've recently bespelled
Tell themselves my heart is their pillow.

Being in two places
Simultaneously
Is as easily conceived as reincarnation,
Easier yet
For those upon whom the poetic intellect
Bestows a belief in creation
Exempt from reason's limitations.

Slowly, night dissolves.
My senses grope, in locating home
Amidst the shimmer below.
Although imminent,
Arrival continues to be postponed.
Something, it seems, would have me suspended
Between forever and never,

Everywhere within the circumference
Described by the diameter
Connecting *here* and *there*,
When and *then*, *can* and *can't*.
Suddenly, immortality embraces my genes;
Traveler and settler unite
In a voice the future recognizes as its own.

1/18/81 — [2] (05741)

Crusades: The Return Journey

For three days and two nights,
I've stayed in Periclean Athens, Alexandria,
Constantinople, Jerusalem, old Rome,
And spoken with their august emissaries,
Been exposed to hammered gold
Intuition and insight into the human condition
Hold out to those with scruples,
Decency, reminded of kindness, compassion,
Love for the less gifted intellectually,
The bereft and dispossessed.

For three days, I've waded through oceans
Floated with free-spirited ideas,
Wandered down streets and alleyways
Crowded with concerns about individual freedom,
Diluted education, political corruption,
And the soul's Mephistophelean compromise
With things religious . . . things material . . . things.
I've listened to the clearest bell notes
Lifting at vespers and matins,
Whose tongues kiss the ears with inspiration,

And now, I've returned home,
To this desolation so far removed
From society it seems primordial.
Everywhere, fleshed skeletons
Clothed in motley and slang and bigotry
Approach and diminish from focus —
Spectral ghosts marking time on earth.
I live alone, behind their invisibility:
*

Jerome in the desert, Pharaohed Moses,
A poet stranded in the buffer zone.

1/19/81   (00592)

Ancient Dwellers

The blurry eyes guide me
Through sleep's labyrinthian caverns,
Toward outside light
Beyond the yawning inrush of oxygen.

My fetal thoughts escape as primal ideas,
Enter consciousness,
Get dressed in robes
Those in my society recognize.

The silhouette my shape projects
Enters the café
And is immediately penetrated by voices
Seething like a thousand newborn vipers.

Snorting noise unites us
In a common language.
We speak by hand, facial gesture,
Grunting an animated demotic,

As we discuss prospects for war,
Abundance of food and water,
When our next move might be required,
And who will assume leadership for the tribe.

Now, it has begun to snow.
We disband erratically,
Slowly returning to our separate caves,
To sleep, drowse in hibernal stupors.

A few might even paint their walls
With bison, reindeer, tapirs,
While I alone retire to conceive
Cathedrals, castles, and a Gutenberg Bible.

1/20/81   (02063)

Café des Beaux-Arts [Δ]

No Botticellian *La Primavera*, this lithograph,
Or sprawling scene
From prematurely surreal Bosch
Or serene fifteenth-century Flemish rendering
With placid stream
Meandering to its vanishing point
In the mythical distance gyved by a castle
Probing divinely skyward;

Rather two four-by-four-foot posters,
Redolent of Woolworth's five and dime,
Decorate the Capitol Café's booth-lined wall,
Their puckered vertical seams
Obviously mismatched
At the juncture where separate horizons
Run past each other
On endlessly bending parallel tracks.

The time of day is dusk,
Emblazoned mauve, fuchsia, and gaudy shades
Cast in hazy yellow and orange gradations.
The sleazy scene repeats a timeless cliché:
A smooth, primordial ocean
Surmounted by an even more tranquil sky,
The whole enclosed, on the left side,
By a lone palm

Growing out of an unseen beach,
Climbing, in slender, gentle sinuosity,
Toward the upper border,
Its frond tops lopped off.
Momentarily, my eyes
Superimpose a Renaissance maiden
Rising out of the water,
Thighs, belly, nipples dripping eternally.

My intellect populates the nonexistent sands,
Just below the lower frame,
With Hieronymus's myriad bodies
Bathing in bikinied obeisance to the sun,
To the great god lust.
Fleetingly, fancy persuades me
*

I can actually reach fabled Cathay,
If only focus can be maintained.

Suddenly, a plain, brainless waitress,
Undistinguished save for her pleasant smile,
Disturbs my reverie, politely apologizes
As she places eggs and toast on the table.
Later, on paying, I turn once more
And, viewing the incongruous scape,
Realize how it saved me, for an hour,
From life's even shabbier reproductions.

1/22/81   (00591)

Pariah

Passing effortlessly
From one plane to another,
Leaping eons each eye-blink,
Thinking dreams into existence
At every quiet street corner
And tree along the way
Is both vocation and divertissement for him.

The man whose two children,
Troika and Trilogy,
Call him "Dude"
And to whom the small town
In which he's resided twelve years
Alludes, in its inarticulate suspiciousness,
As eccentric Jew, interloper, fool,

Finds almost total repose,
The perfect incubator for his poetry,
Here in Gomorrah.
Speciousness, bigotry, stunted grammar,
Lack of ambition, impoverished intellects
Only serve to reinforce his ego,
Remind him of his gifts

And the mandate to seek Canaan daily
In this arid desolation.
Paradoxically, his rhythms, music, ideas
*

Have blossomed like cacti,
Suspending the most delicate, precious flowers
Above the treacherous desert soil;
His soul has broken from its calyx and blossomed.

How the future will assay his passage,
His brief stay
In this ephemeral and anomalous way station,
Remains for belated discoveries
To recover from stray trunks,
Bags, cardboard boxes, bank vaults,
His prodigious, prolific manuscripts.

For the moments he yet owns,
His chief concern is satisfaction he gets,
Capturing, from oblivious matter
Scattered in the life-force haloing his existence,
Whole chains of original chaos,
Actual shards of the celestial creation
He translates into poems singed with divinity.

Now, walking alone, lost in thought,
He approaches the pants factory.
The ladies peer, laugh, claw the glass,
Without realizing they are his people
And that he's been leading them
Through the wilderness for years.
Their jeers shiver his meek heart to compassion.

1/23/81   (05462)

The Punishment △

Few of us have ever known,
Firsthand,
Famine, tortures of war, pestilence,
Or oppression by megalomaniacal leaders
Of the Khomeini and Pahlavi persuasion.

Fewer have directly felt physical pain,
Alimental deprivation,
Dehumanizing verbal abuse
Associated with territorial occupation
By alien powers.

Having driven Trilogy to school, this morning,
Without our usual joyous music
And, more important,
Deprived her of breakfast
As an alternative to her being tardy,

Watching her disconsolate, defeated shape
Enter that temple of learning
Without a solitary backward glance,
I sensed, for the first time,
The degree of cruelty to which man can accede.

Had my little girl
Turned to glimpse her daddy behind the wheel,
Waiting as though a blink
Might reverse morning's motion,
She would have seen a totally deflated king.

If only my eyes possessed insight,
They would have arrested her
At her desk, crying into a book,
And intuited her worship had not diminished,
That we'd suffered a common defeat.

1/26/81   (01452)

Oedipal Regressions

I am no Tiresias;
No blind Oedipus trudging home
Illuminates my deepest suspicions
With insight into my destiny.

Instead, I rely on dead reckoning,
Consult with spectral selectmen,
To vector myself closer, each day,
Toward my vessel's final destination.

Friendly enemies, distant relatives,
Dispassionate contemporaries
Proffer specious advice
Disguised in the robes of diplomacy and reason,

While fantasies, delusive and extravagant,
Hover just above my eyes,
Like houseflies swarming over garbage.
I hear invisible maggots multiplying in my brain.

Neither moon nor pulsing stars
Crowd my night skies;
Rather, forebodings cloud my psyche
With migraine tremors,

Whenever it appears
Experience might be clearing the way
For intuition to deliver me
To the future's temple gates,

Where youth, my deceased father,
And gentleness, blessed mother,
Who guided me through adolescence,
Wait to own me again.

Briefly, I glimpse them
Enshrined side by side,
Partaking of a silence so frangible
Butterflies fluttering could disturb their tranquillity.

But the vision shatters like an optic glass
Falling from the wall
Separating my retinas from reality.
I stall at a dusty crossroads,

While my shadow regains its breath,
Memory its composure,
Lingering until all my senses
Have had a chance to locate themselves,

Recognize this juncture
As the place they've set up tent
A thousand times before.
This four-way cul-de-sac,

Death's nexus to the netherish terrain,
Bears witness to my presence.
Suddenly, a distant chorus swells,
Compelling me to rise, grope,

Go back to my last introspection,
As though a clue from the past,
Unheeded previously,
Might be inviting me to a private audience.

The music grows louder,
Metamorphoses into the combined voices
Of mother and wife. Slowly, I enter them,
A child again and lover, inviolable.

1/27/81   (05742)

The "Victims"

I've watched, amazed, bemused, stupefied,
As the "Iranian Crisis"
Has uncoiled like a striking cobra,

Hitting me, in the mind's eye,
With its pernicious hype —
Agitation spat dead center by the vicious viper

(Whose spine seems to consist of religious fanatics
Lining up, thick, behind a head
Named Khomeini),

To distinguish it from nonvenomous types.
For months, I've convalesced
Within a stuporous languor, restive,

Suspicious that the original snake
Might have been less to blame
Than originally assessed.

And now that the "prisoners of war,"
"Hostages," to some,
Have come home under ticker tape,

Surrendering themselves voluntarily
To dour psychiatrists
And endless questioning and persiflage

By media eager to exploit,
On otherwise numbing airtime,
"Heroes" created, on this specific occasion,

For calculated effect,
To remind an entire people
That post-Nixonian patriotism is still conceivable

In a country reeling yet
From the combined wounds inflicted by
Morally bankrupt politicians,

Academicians, businessmen, J.D.'s,
Doctors, and food-coupon recipients . . .
Now that they've had accolades lavished on them,

Gained our undivided attention
And blind praise, for having met the enemy
On foreign soil

And maintained the irrefragable integrity
Of the American Way,
The missionary ethos inherent in democracy

And Christianity,
The dignity of the Western World
And its great Maker's chosen people . . .

Now that these fifty-two "victims"
Have sifted back into the woodwork,
To make room for newer bemusements

Promised us by the Reagan administration
And universal dissension,
I am better able to classify the other creature

Who slithered out of hiding:
A two-headed serpent was he,
Named Pahlavi and CIA.

1/28/81 (05743)

Designing to Scale

At a certain juncture,
The focal point which defines human existence
By separating youth
From aging's point of no return,
*

Bisecting ambition, enthusiasm, power,
And athletic prowess,
Grows hazy, indistinct.

That cryptic lifeline,
The divider against which physical time
Gets measured in limitations
Placed on mentality and flesh,
Fades like skywriting,
Leaving delusive memory and forgetting
To feud over the remains.

In the final stages,
Foreground and back
Merge into a dimensionless perspective
Lacking dynamism, animation.
A static portrait materializes.
Face, hands, stomach, legs, and feet
Fuse in a flat plane

Akin to a limner's primitive tavern sign
Swinging, from rusting chains,
Above an abandoned door,
Deteriorating from within,
Its features flaking by rainy degrees,
Until, ultimately, all that's left
Is an invisible rectangle suspended in space.

1/29/81   (05744)

[From my stiff-back booth seat] △

From my stiff-back booth seat
In the smoke-drenched Capital Café,
I envision daring courtiers
Scaling privy courtyard walls,
To connect, by night,
With nubile Melibeas and convent-bound Juliets
Dressed to the neck in lust's lacy disguise.

I see a hundred Tom Jones
Tumbling, half-naked,
From loft windows, past iron grates
*

Covering basement openings
Just above castle moats,
Escaping scrupulously, with their dubious intentions intact,
Their active libidos unscathed.

My rampant fancy
Dances to the celebration of mating rites
Lifting across the ages,
Wafting past my ears, on their way home
To be regenerated
In the shimmering dynamo
God fires to perpetuate the life-force.

Yet when my eyes lift from the paper
On which mental images exist
In cryptic hieroglyphics
(A record of my ephemeral visit this morning?),
Disengaged from ideation
Long enough to distract a fleet waitress,
Petition her for the favor of her coffeepot,

They find a vasectomized nobility
Partaking of ribaldry,
Sedentary gossip, garrulity of a nature,
And calumniation
Of all institutions, administrators, and future goals —
A group glutted on cattle and poultry fatteners,
Satisfied with status quo impotence,

Infatuated by the notion of a "moral majority"
And hypocrisy's ultimate obliteration
By patriotism and a Reaganized American way.
Suddenly, a vague suspicion
That I'm being stared at awakens me
To the shapely, slender girl

Haloing my absent-mindedness,
Waiting for me to acknowledge her presence.
At such close range,
Her Modigliani face, visibly erect nipples,
And flushed breasts
Whisper my raging blood alive.
My blush invites her to pour.

Her smile bites me in the penis.
I sense my body being repossessed
By the spirit of Don Juan Tenorio.
She creams my coffee with lascivious thoughts
And a musky aroma.
Later today, we'll consummate breakfast,
With the lust of upland apes.

2/3/81   (00590)

Toward a Newer Humanism

Not infrequently, the social elite,
Academic factotums,
And Kafkaesque clerks
Pursued obliquely by agents of the state

Threaten my conception
Of a humane universe ruled harmoniously
By providence, fate, godly ordination.
They disrupt my blind concentration

On divine phenomena in nature,
Distract my better-intentioned verse
From its singular task:
To compress essence to its quintessence.

These interruptions,
Ostensibly to conduct business,
Discuss politics, or argue religion,
Inevitably postpone or terminate the process

By which visions,
Through symbol, simile, syncopation,
Get translated into recognizable images
And shapes the unpossessed can yet arrest,

With their ears and mind-eyes,
In moments approximating apotheosis:
Scrutinizing blue jays fighting their shadows;
Listening to grass growing;

Tasting the ripe tomato's raspy aroma
Lingering on the fingertips
*

Long after harvest lapses into frost;
Inching across a recently frozen stream

And myriad unfathomable paths
The curious heart and spontaneous intellect take,
In selecting, from nonexistence,
Connecters acting as lenses and tympanums

That transmute reality,
Render the looker susceptible to "seeing,"
The eager listener
Receptive to hearing previously silent stimuli.

Privately, I curse their intrusions,
Vehemently denounce them
As subversive merchants from Porlock,
Members of Satan's crew,

Who, in one fell swoop,
With considerable verbal flourishes,
I hurl past limbo, into forgetting,
To burn in eternal pandemonium.

Yet in my soul, I know these people
Are the harbingers and gypsies,
The prophets, philosophers, and charlatans,
Verse requires to keep alive its dream

Of becoming nutriment for man's sensibilities,
Food for the psyche,
The gruel that sticks to the body's bones,
On days too cold for the spirit to rise

From its repose among the centuries
Buried beneath a mound
Recently dug up and recovered
With the remains of the latest generation's poets,

A dream of one day being the Esperanto
With which mankind will speak
A peaceful dialogue among his multitudinous self.
For now, then, I surrender my ego

To the possibilities this postulation evokes,
Resolve to allow skeptics
*

As well as those who praise my efforts,
Obvious detractors and patrons alike,

Into the zone where I've lived alone
For so many years.
Hopefully, we'll discover, in this intercourse,
A human metaphor for blessedness.

2/5/81   (00589)

Saying No, Again

The better part of his days on earth,
Early a.m.'s, anyway,
Has been spent in unfamiliar cafés,
Writing cryptic verse,
In capricious, hieroglyphic cursive script,
Between blue notebook lines.

Though it's a hapless avocation at best,
He yet pursues his craft
Fastidiously as a war correspondent
Whose deadline, ever imminent, is his life,
Hoping to expose an old goal,
A forgotten ambition

Conceived by the ghost he once believed
Would deliver his underachieving intellect
To the pinnacle of Mount Sinai,
From which he might transmit his own passion:
The youth his past keeps hidden
In the closet stuffed with his brittle manuscripts.

For all his eavesdropping,
Daydreams, his fantastical fugues
And transmutations of truth,
He's never succeeded at finding his identity
Among creations his writing isolates
Or ever located a soul mate

In the shadows that ferry him
From café to smoky café,
Someone, a confidant, female or male,
*

He might read his poetry to
And excite the most elemental feedback,
A basis for communication,

The feeblest excuse for human intercourse,
Perhaps just the beginning
Of an ephemeral relationship to teach him
About taking people at face value
Rather than always changing them
To fit his imagination's requirements.

Still, he continues to scribble in his book
As though ceasing
Would create a vacuum in the future
He could never hope to negotiate or bridge,
A hole in the vast silence,
Through whose vapors his psyche has passed,

From adolescence to this present moment,
By having adapted its expectations
To crave anonymity and loneliness.
The words, at least, like urine, feces, sweat,
Say his apparatus yet works,
Assert his refusal to give up the ghost.

2/6/81   (02062)

Morty Horowitz, Field Rep: A Family Man

His astigmatic eyes ache
As though magma were bubbling in craters
Below their closed lids.
They contain twin phobias instead of lenses,
Whose viscid humors are floated with demons,
Vestiges of last night's dreams,
Spectral visages risen from the crematoriums
His apocalyptic visions fueled:

Men and boys blind, tongueless,
Lacking penises, testicles bleeding,
Whose brief, arsenical breathing,
Veiled in green screaming,
Awakened the dead to their impending advent;
*

Ladies with sutured vaginas, severed breasts;
Nubile, smooth-skinned girls
Begging sodomy from eunuchs.

His eyes open slowly,
Tentative as clams sensing interlopers
Trespassing in their beds,
Cautiously avoiding the fugitive daylight
Penetrating his rented room,
Whose adventitious trappings remember him
From a thousand previous trips
In a hundred other towns along his route.

Finding no immediate enemy
In the visible, living world, they focus,
Hoping to capture a passing image,
A redolence, a trace of the nightmare
That plagued their master.
Purblind, dazed, he showers, shaves,
Staggers from the motel. They alone have noticed
Nylons crumpled in the corner, like shaggy winos.

2/10/81   (02392)

The Aldermen of Sodom and Gomorrah △

On this coldest of snow-cold days,
Only the most stalwart
Capital Café regulars venture out,
Attend their daily convocation at the back table.

Naturally, their conversations dovetail,
Interweaving, in contrapuntal fashion,
Metaphysical considerations, predictions
For summer drought, power outages,

The common drama of busted pipes,
Dead batteries, isolated cases of death
By hypothermia and frostbite —
A potpourri laced with select expletives

Underscoring the heavy-duty respect
These aldermanic city fathers,
*

In nonacademic acquiescence
And patriotic modesty, have for acts of God

And other unforeseeable natural disasters
Outlined, in fine print,
On individual homeowner's-insurance policies.
Responsibility to the constituency

That narrowly elected them
Over indistinguishably lesser malingerers
Desirous of adding to meager incomes
The hundred-dollar monthly dole,

To sift and sort
Fortuitous gossip from truth,
Has forced them to hold their meetings
In this conspicuously public location,

Where they hope to enhance their reputations
For taking their duties to heart. This morning,
However, their insights and exhortations
Have failed to change fate's course,

Remove the frigid gray gloom from a sky
Obviously laden with more snow,
Or postpone, indefinitely, personal obligations
To show up at a place of "bidness."

Slowly, each cringes into his winter coat,
Reluctant to leave, be swallowed alive
By a ten-below-zero beast
Crouching outside, everywhere,

Wondering, now, why he even bothered
To seek wise counsel,
Take nature under advisement,
And boast a future conclusion to the present dilemma.

Once outside, assaying his futility
In the face of this vicious freeze,
Each glances back at the café
And changes into a block of feedlot salt.

2/12/81 (00588)

Coincidences

A valentine for Jan

Too damn many superstitions
Are colliding, today,
For me to maintain my equanimity and faith
In nature's basic regard for humankind.

As I debark from my parked car,
This Friday the thirteenth,
My eyes perceive a penny in the gutter
And command my senses to pick it up,

Drop its crusty, wet shape
In my pocket before I head inside
To buy Valentine's cards
For the trinity that gently dominates my life.

Surely, within these blatant antagonisms,
A harmonious design looms,
Whose talismanic scheme relies on reason
Rather than magic or divination,

Demands obeisance not from fear
But because contrarieties
Excite the intellect to wonderment and joy,
By their sheer circumstantiality.

I pause before the Wishing Well,
To assess my silhouette,
Floating, like a golden fish,
Amidst copious window displays,

And watch its shadowy visage
Shift with each movement I make,
To gain clearer perspective
On the changes continually taking place

Behind and in front of the glass,
As I pace anxiously,
Waiting for some sort of spontaneous clue
To illuminate my condition,

Motivate me to escape the stasis
That has enslaved my mood
*

To the foolish, schizophrenic delusion
That invisible agents have marked me today,

Doomed me to question my emotions,
Doubt my own soul's notion
That fate is totally fortuitous anyway,
Regardless of caution and planning.

Finally, I break the magnetic spell
My compelling gaze
Has exercised over my curiosity
And enter the store,

Where I discover my children and wife
Browsing among the greeting cards,
In search, so they say,
Of nothing, shopping for nobody in particular.

Suddenly, all my anxieties dematerialize —
Good luck and evil scattered in the whirlwind
My purgative laughter stirs.
Against love, superstition hasn't got a chance.

2/13/81 (04182)

Metamorphosis

This morning, he is irredeemably lost
In a maze, in an altarpiece,
Tunneled centuries deep
By termites and worms oblivious to ethics and dreams.
He's one with lesser creatures,
Approximating the microscopic,
Caught up inside the workings of parasites
Busy dismantling, an idea at a time,
His delicate intellect's complex paradigms.

He crawls deeper into the labyrinth,
Having cast off musty sheets,
Sleep's mummy shrouds,
Above the bier on which rest vestiges
Of what once was his skeleton
Dressed in fleshy accouterment of affluence,
*

Platonic aesthetics, Medicean acquisitiveness.
Slowly, as he goes,
His earthly shadow is left in the dust.

The darkness is so compacted with silence,
Filling the tight space
Through which his migration progresses,
That his spirit surrenders itself to dead reckoning.
Dissolution is a sweet, swift amnesia
Erasing memory's shimmering, magnetic halo,
Until the spirit climbs, weightless,
To a height above the lowest firmament
Between death and forever,

Searching, like an imago,
For an opening in the cocoon, the chrysalis,
Butterfly or moth inconsequential
Compared to the potential for soaring free.
As the minister finishes his consecration,
Reminding the mourners that their dearly departed
Has gone the way of all flesh,
The altarpiece begins to reverberate,
Swelling the air with inaudible fluttering.

2/16/81 (05745)

Rushing to Conclusions

Alone, his flown spirit,
Dressed in repressive clothing,
Confined inside the speeding vessel
Which, on so many prior journeys,
Has provided escape
From zones of greater density
To those whose lesser pressure
Has offered temporary respite from his foe, time,
Soars far from home.

Yet this occasion feels different.
His clogged ears
Hear extraterrestrial communications.
An anomalous February sun
*

Sears his eyes to near blindness,
Causing the highway and its vehicles
To blend, resembling budding willow limbs
Swaying continually in a bending breeze.
Even his sense of direction is skewed,

And time, which he can usually suspend
In a solution of undiluted repose,
During which he composes poetry
While the road guides him
Toward his assigned destination, without incident,
Refuses to let his contemplation
Arrest the passing moments,
Collect them, like fireflies in a jar.
Uninspired silence envelops his driving.

Soaring becomes unyielding turbulence.
The sky changes from blue to slate.
Unannounced, his cargo shifts,
Canting his car to the left,
In a violent, unnavigable yaw.
Suddenly, he crosses the median,
Veers into the oncoming lane,
And, lost in thoughtlessness, disappears,
Leaving one survivor: the other driver, fate.

2/17/81 — [1] (05746)

The Drift of Things

This inordinately warm afternoon
In mid-February,
Coming so soon after a week
Besieged by sub-zero temperatures,
Mitigates seasonal gloom,
Petty desperations, explodes despondencies.

My joyous spirit flourishes like jonquils
Stirring prematurely in the earth,
Or forsythias, inchoate and dormant,
Urgently wishing to break into yellow singing.
My veins tingle with sap freeing up,
Stretching, like ink blotted from my heart, out.

I am a participant in the celebration
That has awakened me
To my potential being, that part of essence
Which never sleeps, for fear
It might miss even a single minute
Of life's perpetual divine comedy.

My treachery, this outrageous day,
Is nothing less than radical treason.
Having chosen to escape,
I rush from my disheveled desk,
Leaving no address or number, with my secretary,
Where I might be reached,

No time when I plan to return.
With coat in hand,
My body, its trappings, and its shadowy outline
Exit the office, drive away.
Already, my jubilant intellect, my senses
Are miles ahead of winter's procession for the dead.

2/17/81 — [2] (05747)

Sun-Crazed

The flaming day descends,
Whose sun is a portentous spider
Suspended pendularly from a nimbus-web.
It lets itself down my vision,
By invisible inches. Looking directly ahead,
Into its colossal presence,
I cringe and squint, reckoning west
By sheer incomprehensible intuition.

Yet as I go, neck sweaty,
Shoulders taut from stretching backward,
To keep my head hidden behind the visor,
A reckless lethargy subdues my intellect,
As though I've been penetrated by venom,
Been made crazy, gone numb.
In a daze, I watch the spider touch down
And crawl away, to seek other prey.

2/17/81 — [3] (05748)

Hopgrassers and Flutterbies ^Δ

For my Trilogy and for my Troika;
I love you both so much
I could be happy dying
this particular moment.
You are too beautiful.

From this distance, halfway across the state,
Within the amberous sanctity
Of an antique railroad station, sipping Chablis,
I sense images of you two,
My beautiful children, flooding my bloodstream
With cravings for your sweet bouquet.
Reverentially, I toast you and drink you in,
Grow slowly intoxicated,
As effervescent visions of you, my scions,
Dance across the screen behind my eyes,
On which you weave Isadora-choreography,
Unself-consciously,
Before rising to the surface of this glass's liquid,
Shimmering in sympathy
With my imperceptibly trembling fingers.

As I sit here, oblivious to ambition, tradition,
Politics, philosophy, and religion,
The poetry of old age recites rhymes
At a level I recognize even in this daze,
Which tends to heighten forgetting.
I sing your blessed *inocencia*,
Measure the depth and breadth of your intellects,
In fears that possess me,
Anxieties that you will both grow away
From the metaphor your parents conceived,
By which you might each softly fly
On flutterby wings or soar like wild geese,
Fleeing their own shadows, on a freedom-course,
And leap with abandon, on hopgrasser legs,
Through Elysian fields of Queen Anne's lace.

I suspect my inordinate concern
Is the unavoidable permutation worked through
By an overly doting,
Far too possessive father, who shares
*

With an equally introspective wife
An obsessiveness so weighted with compassion
And gentle sentimentality and love
That no amount of pretended unconcern
Could dislodge Snow White's poison apple,
Undream the wolf from the piggies' chimney,
Or beg *Starsky and Hutch* and *CHiPs*
To quit their shitty Hollywood shtick
And retire to the melodrama of connubial bliss.
Yet I know my phobias are warranted . . .
Demons slither on the far horizon.

Fifteen years from right this moment,
You, my gorgeous, sensitive Trilogy,
Might be in the Gorgon's jaws,
Writhing beneath Valentino's empty head
And ingenuine body, and you, sweet Troika,
Will just be entering the scorpion's sensuous zone,
Crowded with easy cunt and accessible drugs,
Where funky fucking is another jungle disease
In the thesaurus of societal malignities.
Now, I realize that I, like both of you,
Am helpless. None of us can dissuade fate
From his arbitrariness, his cruel, vindictive ways,
Nor can we predict our ultimate estates.
All I know, at this sacrosanct moment,
Is that I pray for you, blessed babies of mine:
May God bless, with all His omniscience, your preciousness.

2/17/81 — [4] (02572)

Exhortation

O God, let me be famous!
Let me tell the kids to be faithful
To those they love,
That infidelity is a Biblical sacrilege,
A travesty of the most enormous proportions,
A sin of the gravest import.

   I want, more than anything, to read
      my poetry,
   *

Written in total seriousness, with honesty,
   to those who will not only listen
     but decipher what they hear,
Regard the words as incisions chiseled
     in the two stones of Moses.

I beg you, with all that You have seeded
   in my modest mentality,
To let my inauspicious surface flower,
   make my tiny plot flourish
With blooms worthy of the finest intellects.

   Above all, invite me to read
At the official presentations of the gods.
   Permit my verse to have audience
     and ultimate acceptance with You,
   the One who tells fate how to behave
     and whose explanations,
   at any given moment in a specific millennium,
   are accepted as mandate.

   More than anything, I pray
That all my words will have sway
   in the great Sanhedrin of the Final Mind,
   which arbitrates all differences
And decides every suit against the state.

Let my case adjudicate those
Who've been accused of being fat, flat bastards,
Retards, eunuchs, Gregor Samsa
Devoid of compassion, and *l'étranger*
Accused of using mistress and mother — fuckers.
Let my reputation vindicate those
Who've lived in Siberia, alone,
Without the benefit of a doubt or a serious poet.

Acquitted by virtue of having fabricated
The smoking gun by which Nixon
Might have been acquitted
Were it not that Rosemary Woods
Erased eighteen minutes, I agree
That foul play has occurred,
Butterfield was in error in having disclosed
The White House tapes in the first place.

And now, I return to my original thesis:
    I pray You teach me how
To tell the kids that fidelity
    is the most relevant reality —
Love one, once, and never again, only!

2/17/81 — [5] (02606)

Warring Fantasies [△]

Dreams weave an insidious spell,
Like a constricting halo,
About my pulsating brain,
As though an egomaniacal Draco
Had determined to make me his slave,

Confine my energies to creating manuscripts
He might offer to foreign powers,
In exchange for jet fighters and replacement parts,
Tanks and nuclear missiles.
Hallucinations barter me for entire arsenals,

While nightmares sell me callously
At whatever rate of exchange exists
At any given moment,
Dependent merely on whim or excessive speculation —
I'm worth at least two radar units,

Three World War II destroyers
Yet in mothballs,
Five AT-6s or Corsairs
Anchored to the decks
Of one of ten *Flying Enterprise*s;

My life is worth at least two assaults
On Kwajalein or Corregidor.
My mind is, at any time of the day,
An unprepared Pearl Harbor,
Ripe for utter destruction and chaos.

Even in a waking state, I am anxious
About the potential dilemma
That might arise from my acquiescence
To the nearest bartender,
Hoping no one will invite me to celebrate

The end of the most recent war
Between nations ill at ease with each other,
At odds with their distinctive PR.
I fear social obligations,
Parties held in honor of Howard Cosell,

Muhammad Ali, and Jefferson Davis.
Whatever the occasion, I prefer the privacy
Inherent in ultimate celebrity.
Now, I retire to sleep's isolated beachheads,
On which all my public insecurities fight,

And I discover myself on a dog tag
Hanging from Yoko Ono's neck.
The outrageous vagaries increase,
One by two by three to the tenth power,
Like an exaggerated Polack joke,

And suddenly, I recognize myself as the butt
Of a slowly burning cigarette.
My indefinite personal location comes into focus
Near Berlin. In a concrete bunker
Peopled by Goebbels and his family, Bormann,

Eva Braun, and various others,
I discover myself as the one
With the cropped mustache — the paperhanger,
Malevolent Schicklgruber himself,
Selling propaganda, by the whaleboat,

To eager idiots, nymphomaniacs, and Aryans
Imbued with Jewaphobia. Nightmares pale
Before such stark surrealities. I die,
Contemplating the immediacy of such possibilities.
The spell dreams have woven is irrevocably broken.

2/17/81 — [6] (01347)

O Ye Eidolons!

I am the ending day's descendant,
This night's newest generation,
Whose forebears have birthmarked my genes,
*

Speech, my unmistakable features,
With all the idiosyncrasies and unorthodoxies
Of their fading, forgotten past.
What determines my future moves
Is the subtly unspoken press of their collective history.
The dead hoist me to their bony shoulders,
From whose unreliable height
I try to fathom the path that leads
From sleep, toward morning's prothalamion,
Into the marriage ceremony of my undisclosed hours.

I am the son of the father of cycles
Endlessly permutating, daybreak's child,
The scintillating product of star sparking star,
Night's swain, afternoon's suitor,
Mating and mated, sun and gibbous moon
In a Paolo-Francesca race through eternity.
My mother is the fertile earth,
From whose womb I have risen
And to which my spiritless flesh has returned
On at least a thousand thousand occasions.
My own son I am and will be,
Nonincestuously, as my soul recreates itself
Through superfetation of its ageless intellect.

2/18/81 — [1] (02573)

A Change of Dreams

Lately, I've had a change of dreams.
Youth's golden hopes, conquistadors' goals,
Have not so much been jettisoned
As oxidized in the corrosive ethers of growing old.

Compromise with fear's conspiratorial agents
And greed have diluted the pure solution,
Caused the resilient bones to go brittle,
Necessitated unnatural prosthetics,

To repair the spirit's many breaks
And hairline fissures. Regret thrives
On the languid mind's increasing ineptitudes,
While senescence infiltrates Birnam Wood,

Surrounding the defunct fortress,
In whose highest tower
Cowers the unexercised imagination,
A flabby captive, exiled to anonymity.

No longer does the lure of self-discovery
In the mind's Klondike
Hold out excitement, motivate the heart
To brave the snowy loneliness of self-sacrifice

And silence required to write Upanishads,
Psalms, and letters to Corinthians and Thessalonians
In newer, more communicable poetries
Capable of resonating the clitoris and penis.

Perhaps it's my recent awareness, on reaching forty,
That time accepts no excuses,
No matter how seemingly valid and empirical,
And that success has little to do with excellence,

Rather the finesse with which one is able
To perform cunnilingus,
Give blow jobs on a moment's notice,
Which has changed my dreams to rusted nails

Buried in unopened kegs in barnacled holds
In sunken sailing ships
Listing precipitously in deep-sea crevasses,
Nails originally destined for Tyre

And Nineveh and Cathay, to help assemble
The world's most fantastical pleasure domes;
Not nails, exactly, but metaphors
Heading toward immortality,

Shipwrecked before they could touch shore
With the promise of absolute perfection.
Now, all that remains of the original inspiration
Is fate's shadowy, contractual promise,

That brittle document, signed in blind faith,
By which the recipient agrees
To release his soul from its birthright forever,
In exchange for instantaneous celebrity.

At forty, all that's left for me
Is a sleazy conception of resurrection
*

For the earthly unredeemed, heavenly perfection
To correct the dream's imprecise magnetic heading,

And, for having squandered promise,
The meager punishment of life eternal,
Spent wondering just how golden
Youth's hopes really might have been.

2/18/81 — [2] (02571)

Satirist

Crystal-quick, solipsistic philippics
Flick vitriolically from his pen,
Like a frog's tongue picking off insects,
Out of infested air,
Hovering just above its sullied bog.

The objects of his outrage, indignation,
And public disapprobation
Over botched obligations and responsibilities,
Political, religious, economic, and militaristic,
In which his country's leaders are engaged

Are victims of their own naive obtuseness
And overwhelming vanity.
They read him without realizing
His barbs have gigged them
Clean through to the heart. They bleed,

Yet only their rhetoric gushes.
They remain oblivious to the numbing,
Rarely feel radical surgery being performed,
Amputation of the gangrenous parts
Deformed by greed, pedantry, and venal deceit.

For all his deep-throated croaking,
Shot through with too-subtle hope,
The old bull has never come close
To shortening his strokes,
Purposely missing a low-flying altruist

Misguidedly posing as a soaring "reformer"
Or right-wing "humanist,"
*

Nor has he ever disclosed
The identity beneath his amphibian disguise,
By kissing ass of any princess in distress,

Rather chosen to go pseudonymously
From pond to pond,
As each dries up,
While two new ones materialize,
He surviving on gnats, mosquitoes, and dragonflies.

2/19/81 — [1] (05749)

Assessing Failure

I

Emblems, symbols, and dim-lit images
Shimmer, like northern lights,
In the zone where his poetry flourishes.

Yet each entrancement ends in suspicions
And worrisome concerns that he's not illumined
Any new truth about himself

Or successfully arrested, in universal measures,
Scents of axle grease and lilacs,
Colors of ghetto squalor,

Sounds of grass growing,
Volcanoes blowing ash into the air,
The pain and shame rape victims inherit.

He fears that the "voices" he hears
And transcribes with fidelity to craft,
Through his perfect ear for metaphor and lyricism,

Belong to frauds and charlatans
Selling Kickapoo Juice for a sideline,
Instead of muses stroking his erect intellect.

II

For dead sure, he knows
He's never once honestly approached
The poetry of tracer bullets and exploding napalm

Or recorded the slow, seething meters
Cells permeated by Agent Orange,
Sprayed with Zyklon B

In Auschwitz showers, or irradiated
By Three Mile Island "hot" water
Demand, as scapegoats for man's presumptuousness.

It's his crass, middle-class disinclination
For politics, his refusal to heed
Fascism and religious fanaticism

That have rendered his verses impersonal to him.
For all their introspective Zen
And ego-testimonials, they are defunct.

Now, he realizes how he's cheated his idolaters,
In seeking their patronage. God alone is witness
To the ultimate insignificance of his minimal assessments.

2/19/81 — [2] (02570)

Katy Station's Poet-in-Residence

So obsessive is his need to express himself,
So compulsive his overt drive to write,
He never has time for pleasures or recreation;
Rather, he seeks no-man's-lands
Where hundreds congregate
To swill beer and screwdrivers and wine,
For composing his sacred verses.

Such paradoxical aloneness
Suffices for him to resurrect inventions
Lonely men and women unfamiliar with solitude
Might hardly hope to utilize,
Much less convert into a burning furnace

From which words lift like phoenixes
And realign themselves in divine exhortations
Meant to convert profligates and degenerates
Into penitential preachers and teachers and poets.

In truth, these gathering places,
Oases for students initiated in the Kama Sutra
*

And aging, undisciplined professors,
Have a positive, cathartic effect on his heart
And intellect. He gets to see, firsthand,
The future parents of his ultimate audience
Before they bear their offspring,

As they inebriate their untrained bodies
To the flash point at which sex
No longer is a colossal Cyclops
But a diminished angel craving attention
And gentle sentimentality and love.

It is during these evanescent hiatuses
That the poet leaves his mind's confines,
Where whatever is alive is set free
And that which was meant to die falls away,

As he begins to move his pen
With a furiousness bordering on madness,
Displaying a strange calligraphy
Whose cryptic script
Contains that magical formulation
By which amputees learn to dance
And alcoholics discover abstinence is divinity.

In this raging zone, where aloneness
Flourishes like Renaissance painting,
He is a newer Michelangelo,
Determined to outlive the eighty-nine years
His peer somehow connived from God.

He recreates his subtle guts on paper,
Hoping that out of this regurgitation of verses
Dictated by God, he will discover one
Worthy of turning his muse into a nubile prostitute.

2/19/81 — [3] (02569)

Looking Ahead

Sheer time
And the exigencies of survival and responsibility
(A line to show, two seasons annually,
*

For eight to ten weeks,
On and off the nymphomaniacal road,
Two young children,
A wife dissatisfied by her isolation,
Immobility, and lack of sexual desire
For anyone other than TV's
Most duplicitous Lotharios)
Have metamorphosed his most recent ambitions
To succeed, retire wealthy, by the ocean,
In a neat, trouble-free condominium.

For a decade, at least, he's not awakened
To green dreams
Photosynthesized by youth's delusive belief
In the efficacy,
The hierarchial superiority, of anarchy,
Self-reliance, and individuality
Practiced for its own sake only,
Nor have golden hopes
For discovering the code to cancer,
Creating unique poetic strophes,
Composing the score for the Second Coming
Hovered about tuned-out antennas
That once probed the life-force for inspiration.

Domesticity,
That vast abstraction he used to debate
In university coffee lounges
As though it carried Socratic weight,
And inflationary forces flamed by politics
None of them, in those days,
Could have fantasized or, in their most radical posturings,
Rhetorically hyperbolized
Have conspired to reduce his illusions to ciphers,
Digits, inconsequential phonetics
Issuing hourly from computerized input
Calculated to keep track
Of his bowel movements, brain waves, location

Relative to where his radar and sonar blips
Appeared the same hour
Each day, every year prior,
On the screen monitoring his existential beat.
*

Now, he can't even remember
When trying to outdistance, keep abreast,
Merely stay in the race,
Chasing his intractable opponent,
Gave way to abject defeat, depression,
Despondency assuaged by Chablis
And ephemeral infidelities with waitresses,
Barmaids, college girls on the make,
In nameless towns along his trade route.

Neither his early romantic notions
Of wandering in Wordsworthian solitudes,
Apotheosizing prose eccentricities
Like Faulkner playing to a gullible public,
Nor lesser middle-age expectations
Of resettling in Cape Coral,
On a plot beside a planned channel,
Where sand-plants grow
And skin wizens overnight, have materialized.
No coalescence of hopes and dreams
Has blessed his unceremonious sojourn.
His only potential recourse, he knows,
Is to outlast the aftershock of his failures.

2/24/81 (04181)

Messianic Vestiges ^Δ

Once again, Farmington's gentry
Has been exonerated, made the recipient
Of a mid-February mid-Missouri reprieve.

The stay of execution, by freezing and gloom,
Is in glistening evidence,
This 8 a.m., on the plate glass,

Through whose smoke-smudged fenestration
Regulars glimpse the prismatic day,
Measure its potential intensity

In shadows rising, like window shades
Lifted by invisible hands,
On the facades of stores not yet open

And against the monolithic courthouse,
Whose anomalous Greek redolence
Is a look of amazement on a quizzical face.

One by one, prewound voices enter
And seek their own level,
At tables separated according to tribes.

At one are seated county sheriff,
Presbyterian minister,
High-school agribusiness teacher,

Who doubles as driver's-ed instructor
To augment his self-image and adequate income,
And the head of City Light & Water.

Each is a Whitman's Sampler of expertise
On local, state, and federal politics,
The most current quotes

On July and September beans and corn,
Hogs and barrows on and off
The hoof, recent slayings, accidents,

God's latest manifestations of grace,
The cost of power bought for resale
To a small anorectic town.

Two tables away,
The owner of the local roller-skating rink
Argues with the Chevrolet dealer,

Over the decontrol of fuel
And public transportation,
As though both had a vested interest in lobbying

Or were privy to inside information
By which they might influence
The nation's future. A third, the city comptroller,

Regards his silence as a valuable contribution
To the discussion. He times his nods
To coincide like applause, as each pauses briefly

While his friendly opponent
Unleashes Demosthenes-chat from his slingshot
Without taking time to aim.

Toward the rear, where two tables
Have been permanently coupled
Like mating dogs stuck after copulation,

A quorum of the city's aldermen gathers.
Their lofty demeanor, the rhetoric
That issues forth with gravity,

And the furtive surreptitiousness
Of their occasional collective whispering
Set them apart, elevate them on a stage,

Endow them, somehow,
With a vague yet plausible resemblance
To the supping disciples.

Depending upon through whose eyes
They're viewed, they all resemble Christ
Or Judas, the mendacious one.

Regardless the perspective taken by their audience,
They represent ends of the continuum,
Antimonies, antipodes. No in-between exists

For these servants to assume. Martyrdom
Hovers above them,
In the guise of sublime, pellucid cigarette smoke.

The café, an embodiment of its former soul,
Is a cathedral almost Gothic,
A breathing reincarnation

Echoing with Old World guffaws,
Ancients' laughter, catcalls, hilarity
Amidst intermittent sado-pseudoseriousness.

Suddenly yet with mystical prestidigitation,
The proprietor, robed in white
Except for breakfast egg-stains and grease,

Opens the front door, to let morning
Pass through the hallowed portal.
Fresh warm air, like floodwater,

Rushes in, labors to insinuate itself
In tiny lacunae of the room's lungs
Possibly unviolated by pollution.

The transformation is slow to occur.
Even more reluctant is the metamorphosis
That begins to purge the inner sphere,

Clear away diaphanous vapors,
And permit light to unsuffocate the dimness.
One by one, the regulars pay

Their token dime for two-hour coffee
And leave as though driven out
By rumor of nearby invaders.

Empty, at last, by half past ten,
The café lapses into quietude.
With less than an hour to prepare for lunch,

Recover, those who run the establishment
And those who've disappeared
Behind their nests, desks, pulpits

Attempt to conclude routine matters,
Knot loose ends, so that, at noon,
They might resume more consequential duties.

2/25/81 (00587)

The Bereaving

Whether his brain can actually translate
The tempestuous coursing of blood
Through his sclerotic veins
Or merely calculate the changing seasons
Behind and ahead of his stasis
As forebodings, omens,
Retrospective premonitions weighted with decay
Is difficult to assay, these days,
Especially esoteric and frustrating to contemplate
Now that she's in the ground
And both of them have gone home,
Closed the trapdoor on their past,
Leaving him to do battle, alone,
With pernicious old age.

He still wanders, for hours,
Through hazy vapor-fields
Seeded in reveries profuse as dim,
Trying to fathom where and how and when
The butterfly colors, ginger-cinnamon visions,
And dulcet scents of lilac
Dropped off their flowers in the instant
It took a solitary, eye-blinking breath
To reach its predestined shore
And make way for the next today,
The next yesterday, tomorrow.
Yet senescence keeps its secret
Too discreetly. Winter stubble and summer weeds
Speak to his shoes, with inscrutable screeching.

On alternating fortnights,
His two grown children phone,
Spend ten minutes
Inquiring into his eating habits, his health,
Exhorting him to seek nursing care,
Which they euphemistically refer to as "assistance,"
And assure him that on a moment's notice,
They'll race to his side
Whenever he should need them or wish,
Each knowing stubborn pride
Would never permit his tongue to cry uncle.
Solitude and forgetting have taken their places,
As he empties himself of memory, goes forward,
Closing the separation between him and his wife.

2/26/81   (05750)

Intimations of Teufelsdröckh

Row upon row of men's dress clothing —
Suits, sportscoats, "quad-robes" —
Fill my vision, this slow morning,
With ghostly notions, omens of doom.

As my eyes scan the vast expanse
Under one roof,
*

This distribution center, from which
Hundreds of cartons are shipped daily,

I can't help fantasizing,
Formulating images: each hangered garment
Is a dead man dangling from a hook;
Some are psychotics in straitjackets;

Others appear merely to be resting
In attitudes of ecclesiastical repose,
Like priests, rabbis, poets;
Still others are vested lawyers,

Accountants, doctors,
Crumpled salesmen, humble schoolteachers.
All wear a funereal irreality,
Beneath the fluorescent glare

Within this airless necropolis,
Where the quick pick them
Not with arbitrary indifference
But according to strict, specific procedure,

Pack and ship them out
As if by higher ordination,
So that none among the living
Might ever be accused of violating graves.

Transmogrifications of this nature
Occur so frequently
No one even stops to consider
Just what lasting toll

These flowing souls might eventually exact
From those assigned to route them.
Suddenly, the racks begin to shimmer.
I sense the clothes preparing to take flight.

Frightened that I might have been invited
To attend death's formal reception,
I bolt before an empty black suit
Locates me and tries me on for size.

2/27/81 (02391)

Be Still

For Mitt,
eternally lost,
with love

If only I could permit myself leisure
With which to luxuriate in daydreams,
Contemplating the cohesiveness of atoms, marriages, and poetry,
And penetrate being's core,
By being focused invisibly on the inner eye's lens,
Then every implausibility, all absurd hyperboles,
Might assume infinity's ineffable shape.

My name would resound down the ageless corridors
That connect satellite souls,
Floating endlessly home, with those yet earthbound.
Its designation among the stellar reaches
Would be endowed with supernumerary powers,
By agents capable of exploding entire planets
In a single cosmic exhalation.

Love, which I've husbanded and lavished
On only one lady, two children, and my parents —
Blessed objects fated to solace my lonely quest —
Would shuttle me through gossamer light shafts
Inherently timeless. Love's coadjutant, compassion,
Would deliver my speeding essence
To its destination, for celestial fueling and rejuvenation.

But I can't seem to be still,
Can't stand or luxuriate long enough in a place
To shake the opprobrious shadows
Mystery, mortality, and anonymity cast over me.
Registering cloven hoofs etching their tympanums,
My ears alert whitewater veins
To accelerate the pace. Silence ignites, disintegrates.

3/3 & 3/5/81 (04180)

Moses Meursault

I

The years have helped create a degenerative condition
Known in high psychiatric circles
*

As the "inescapable rat-maze syndrome."
His shrinking memory, like a vast lake
Located over a collapsing salt dome,
Exempt from reading, letter-writing, speaking,
Has been expunged, effaced,
Liquidated into its preliterate stage.
Not a solitary trace of recognition
Ripples his face, his placid gaze,
When the radio or phosphorescences of television
Momentarily recreate scenes
Charged with potential evocations,
Nor do occasional communiqués from "lost persons"
Penetrate his sticky nets.
From waking, through narcoleptic snoozes,
Into sleep, he keeps busy
Being absolutely catatonic, not dreaming,
Speculating, allowing even a solitary gesture
Redolent of satisfaction or ease
To creep out, or acknowledging his bodily needs.
Indeed, although, in the beginning phases,
He almost sought professional help,
Felt it might be prudent
To have rational explanations for why his bowels
Didn't require evacuation,
Why his alimentary canal, its juices,
And myriad hormones seemed to function
Exclusive of routine feeding,
He finally determined not to disturb providence,
Opted to leave well enough be.

II

Now, at thirty-nine,
Having witnessed fifteen thousand homicides
On TV, flown twenty million miles,
Personally sold,
Without even receiving commission
On accounts serviced by the central office,
65,000,000 men's dress trousers,
300,000 sportscoats,
195,000 suits,
Having averaged two hundred days each year,
For the past twelve, in motels,
Three different women a month,
*

In addition to regulars,
Listed by phone number first,
Followed, in descending importance, by age,
Address, and cost, where appropriate,
And a minimum of two new invisible neighbors
Moving into his condominium building
Every six months or so,
He senses there are no Canaans ahead,
No Mount Sinais or burning-bush signs,
No tribes for him to begin,
No temples to rebuild,
In which to deny idle worship of bodies
His womb-bound youth knew
In orphanages and teenage houses of detention.
Still, in vested polyester suits,
Tone-on-tone dress shirts,
Tasseled shoes, he perpetuates the image
God fashioned when choosing him,
Moses Meursault, for the wilderness shtick.

3/6/81 (01024)

Points of No Return

His day begins later than usual,
An exceptional rule whose game he would play
Were it not for the press
Survival has placed on him,
Between shoulder blades and solar plexus,
Providing for his brood of two and a wife,
Maintaining appearances
In the face of an escalating identity crisis,
Which, on his approaching forty,
Grows increasingly more acute for him,
A bacchanal for furies and demons infesting his psyche,
Mind-parasites gnawing away at pia mater
That once contained, in embryonic configurations,
Unique components resembling original Creation,
Capable of exploding into future painting and music,
Poetry known only to the Heliconian gods.

He would arrive at work late daily,
Later, lace the weeks with calculated truancies,
Until, ultimately, his duties
Might be covered by eight others,
His functions performed perfunctorily,
With him assuming an honorary position
Of absentee landlord over his paper domain,
Invisibility,
His check arriving punctually as dividends;
He would pursue this Mittyish profligacy
Were it not for prudence and cowardice
His overly fastidious superego manifests
In dealing with such ephemeral deviations
As today's, which has resulted in his pay being docked
One hour, for an unavoidable visit to the hospital,
For x-rays . . . he's detected blood in his urine.

3/10/81 — [1] (05751)

A Lowly Provider's Last Ride

Shadows passing in rapid succession
Ricochet off the glass
That keeps vision mummified in this speeding casket.

Images and dissolving landscapes
Are those seen by a breathing dead man
Retreating, inexorably, from a past incarnation

Recently jettisoned,
An existence thriving in a terrarium,
Among other terribly delicate sprigs

Classified, by phylum, genus, and species,
As "Wife," "Children," "Parents," "Relatives," "Friends"
And recorded in the universal book of seasons.

The road he travels is not of his choosing,
Nor does it go anywhere
That might lead him safely home;

Rather, he pursues, with insatiable curiosity,
Its inscrutable meandering,
As if, wearing translucent shades over his eyes,

He were being guided, by intuition,
Toward a destination behind the horizon,
An oasis, a nation of Canaans, New Jerusalems.

But over each concrete incline
Rises no colossal city on the plains,
No vast, new, fecund civilization.

Instead, his dead, opaque eyes
Are greeted with sinister apparitions
Disguised as memories from his last cycle:

His boy and girl, their grieving mother
Form a desperate trinity,
From whose gaze he cannot escape,

No matter how powerfully he concentrates
On highway signs. He realizes, now,
Just how premature he was,

Setting out in quest of a new homestead
Where, isolated from humanity,
He might discover solemnity, decency, and solitude

For himself and his blessed family,
Provide each of them
With gentle breeding, mercy, and loving

Unsusceptible to sundering and collapse
By possessiveness, greed,
Licentiousness, or natural restlessness.

As his casket moves closer to dusk,
Its shadows blend with others
Moving fast past him.

Suddenly, a scudding, cloudlike vapor
Captures his traveling soul.
His ashes whisper their own scattered eulogy.

3/10/81 — [2] (04179)

Succubus

For years, he'd endured, of his own volition,
An asceticism so severe
*

Even the most devout monk,
Fearing for his sanity,
Would have interceded, through superiors,
To mitigate the relentless abstemiousness
And loneliness he must surely have been suffering.

But such was the orthodoxy
Imposed upon him, by a Catholic heritage
Dating back centuries,
That he'd considered his fidelity and reverence
Minuscule recompense for his birthright,
Less indebtedness than he might have expected,
Being priest of a cathedral so resplendent.

Then, one evening, while drowsing in the rectory,
Laboring to weed clichés
From his Saturday morning Mass sermon,
He was visited by a young lady,
Naked as the Scriptures, beneath a white shawl
Draped her slender body's full length —
An earthly manifestation of God's blessedness.

Knowing not how to refuse her request
For admittance, he gave her leave
To enter his sanctum, undefiled, until now,
By female nudity. He trembled,
Unable to take his eyes off the stranger,
Whose smooth flesh against the crocheted garment
Resembled Queen Anne's lace.

Silence owned the dialogue they spoke
With their blinkless gazes,
Until the lady began to cry, whimper,
Rise from the couch, pausing before him
As if waiting for his recognition.
When she finally said his name aloud,
It was that certain proud, nervous quality

He'd loved from another attitude
That whispered his past into existence,
Brought their shared affair crowding back
On all he'd voluntarily buried
When asked to marry the Church forever.
Uncontrollably, he took her,
His robes muffling her orgastic moaning,

And ravished her with an inextricable embrace
That made his veins pulsate
So loudly the coursing blood drained his ears
Of all sounds other than those
Emanating from their combined physical climax.
Soon, her torn shawl, his frock
Lay strewn over them, on the carpet,
Like an etching set in a frame,

Where, for hours, they alternated laughter
With insatiable lovemaking,
Moving, fuguelike, from playful moods,
Through guilt, shame, defiance,
To less somber interludes, and back,
Into hilarious, seriocomic posturings,
As night gave way to lavender dawn
And gaiety faded and spontaneity lapsed

Into fitful self-consciousness, upon his waking
To find himself absolutely naked,
On the floor of his chambers,
Not amnesic but at a complete loss
To explain the nature of his intemperance
And the degenerate behavior that occasioned it.
Fearful of being discovered
By he knew not whom,

Lest it be the all-seeing One Himself,
He hastened to shower, dress,
Repress his robes, which he did just in time
To make his inspirational entrance, deliver the Mass
With uncommon eloquence, and administer Communion,
Not once glancing out at the congregation.

3/10/81 — [3] (05752)

Registration in Purple and Pink

Twilight speaks to me
In Chablis-tinged liquescences
Sifting through a stained-glass eventide,
Whose shimmering shafts complete the dialogue
My lonely heart initiates with the sky.

I perpetuate this blessed conversation
By reenacting a secular eucharist
In the presence of strangers,
Among whom I've chosen to come, tonight,
To pray, to write, to commune with the Blessed One,

Who hovers somewhere just above,
In the zone where imagination ceases
And inspiration catches fire,
Waiting to make personal acquaintance
With His diminutive offspring.

My palms caress and stroke
The wineglass's full-blown shape,
Whose dovelike belly contains golden ichor.
My lips taste wafers plied with cheese,
Embodiments of His flesh and blood,

And record ecstasies undreamed while one's alive
Inside the waking day,
Where detail and reason and easy syllogisms,
Patterned after Plato and Socrates,
Dominate and life fails to approximate climax.

Slowly, communion resolves itself into shadows
Winging westward, toward the Kingdom,
Where all ideas, once released from anonymity,
Fly, to be judged on their potential for immortality.
I imbibe between stanzas, lines, caesuras,

Depending upon my dependence on Him,
My trepidation, angst, ennui, and lassitude.
I sip nervously,
Trying to accelerate the courage required to create,
Hoping to make a favorable impression,

Persuade my Mentor that I comprehend
Dusk's unbending implications,
By echoing, in my lines, its incredible light
And by translating the tacit, seemingly passive sky
Into rhymes worthy of lavender and blurry purple.

In this artificial, inside environment,
I exhort my quivering fingers,
Grasping their pen-extension as if for survival,
To inscribe the celebration at hand,
Proclaim my fealty to my Lord,

And implore the lesser deities that be
To transport me to the Land of Poetry,
Where I might find, in sundering abundance,
Invocations to *Paradise Lost* and *The Divine Comedy*,
That my ink might sing the twilight to sleep tonight.

3/10/81 — [4] (02568)

Lazarus

OK! So what?
Who gives a shit whether night's
Advance guard has located the enemy
Or not? It's all so immaterial, anyway,
When you consider man's ephemeral span.
Whether you're born Richard Speck,
John Wilkes Booth, John Fitzgerald Kennedy,
Or Emil Horowitz is of insignificant concern,
Since, lose or win, death succeeds
At preempting all comers.

I concede to his demonic mastery,
His salutary jubilation,
Knowing, from experience, that the end
Is an identical double play
From short to first base,
Celebrity to instant anonymity and obsolescence,
Regardless whether the body
Is destined to be buried in Manhattan,
Cremated and scattered over the Aegean Sea,
Or donated to Mount Zion Hospital.

I must agree that dying
Is indeed an occupational hazard
All human beings must eventually admit exists.
Immortality is the propagation of a lie
So preposterous that even Richard Nixon
And John Mitchell couldn't hope to perpetuate it,
Despite the enormity of its implications
Or the propriety of their sacred offices.
Ultimately, each of us is required to confess
That death ain't all that big a deal

Or living, with all its sacrosanct rituals,
That spectacular; that in the final analysis,
What counts is the degree of compassion
One generates for flood victims in Haiti
As well as for one's own daughter or son
Who doesn't make the grade, win first place
In the personality contest . . . we must confess
That being the best at anything,
Failing at everything, amount to the same.
Blessed are those who die in their sleep.

And yet I must still refuse to accept
An attitude as profoundly nihilistic as this.
I say nay to anyone
Who so agreeably gives in to the obvious,
Without a fight or the slightest altercation
Provoked for its own sake only.
Where the fuck is your anarchic spirit,
That individual freedom that refuses to acknowledge
The inevitable, on general principles?
Where are you, sombitch?

Why aren't you out tending your flock,
In your modest garb,
When I need you to reinforce my disagreeableness,
Instead of playing fate's slot machines
In abject resignation? Bastard!
How could you possibly have let death
Back you into his painted corner?
He's a fucking Mr. Phony-Baloney!
I know! I beat him at his own game.
I'm alive, who died blaspheming his name.

3/10/81 — [5] (02611)

The *Rachel*'s Captain

Setting myself adrift
At unpredictable intervals,
Without requiring another's permission,
Has become my single condition for existence,
The one certain release
*

From all that is trivial or critical or vital
For survival. My tiny ship
Has such a shallow draft
That escape, day or night, from the busy harbor
Where, for prolonged yawns,
My lines strain against their taut moorings
Is a negligible dissolution.
It makes almost no ripples at all.
Never has my intended destination been disclosed
Or my cargo surcharged on loading.

Once I'm out of land's sight,
Tensions, like tenacious leeches
Sprinkled with salt, relinquish their hold,
Shrivel, and disappear in the saline ocean air
Surrounding my free-floating vessel.
I alone decide who shall climb the masts,
Unfurl the sails, man the wheel,
Guide me through alien waters
By charting the far-strewn stars.
I am my own crew of one,
Whose entire allegiance is to me, right or wrong.
Navigation is a product of neither astrolabe
Nor computer, rather metaphor
Capable of penetrating the hurricane's eye,
Soaring, astride the tsunami, safely to shore.

What motivates me to leave home,
Bolt, periodically, from the pervasive innocence
My children provide, the tender, secure acceptance
My wife engenders, despite her skepticism, her fright,
Remains unanswered. I confess
To being slightly mad, unquestionably obsessed
With the tempestuous quest for freedom
And the need to locate the child
Who washed overboard as I grew older,
The lost youth, once so close,
Whose creative core was that of a great poet.
For him I search with raging fury,
My boat the poem, the ocean on which it floats
Ink continuously flowing, my mission
To rescue my own drowning spirit from the fishes.

3/11/81 — [1] (02612)

Edifice *Rex*

My intricate, delicate intellect is the fragile castle
I call home. No one can enter
Until the bridge over my moat is lowered,
The portcullis raised, and soldiers
Whose constant surveillance protects me from interlopers
Are permitted to escort him into my presence.

The kingdom over which I rule
Stretches decades deep and metaphors wide,
Beneath a horizon arrested, at twilight,
To correct whatever myopia
Reality might suffer me to develop over time.
It extends past night, to day's beginning,

Into the no-man's-land
Inhabited by strange voices and silhouettes
Redolent of sourceless thoughts, images, and ideas
Generated by gland-creatures,
Lotus-eaters bent on destroying sensibility,
Subverting reason and measure to their venal ends.

Occasionally, an alien in the shape of a maiden,
Sensual, subservient, and profoundly disconcerting,
Slips through my fastidious defenses.
More commonly, my privacy is sundered
By inordinate imbibing of wine,
Which arrives disguised as relaxation.

My thresholds crumble
Under such persuasive, concupiscent temptations.
My house is defiled by nakedness and inebriation,
While I lie defenseless in my bed,
A victim of my own pleasure-seeking instincts,
Infiltrated by a head-enemy of my own making.

At such junctures, all cognition ceases.
Ideation and image-making
Give way to writhing flesh and dazed sensations
In which the gonads require release
And volcanic headaches rock the brain.
The foundations creak.

Water from the moat seeps into the basement.
Mind-furniture shifts,
Breaks loose from its glued seams, cracks.
Imagination fails to register changes,
Even while the mountains supporting the castle
Begin to disintegrate.

After the blast has finally subsided,
Disappointments and frustrations dissolve, like ice,
In the heat resulting from refurbishing the castle.
Basic bodily routines resume.
Forgetting sets up its stolid defenses again.
The intellect begins picking up its scattered facets,

Turning them into figurative artifacts
That fill the brain's myriad convolutions
With luminosity and distinctiveness.
And suddenly, I feel receptive, eager to entertain
The next Quixote, Sancho, and Dulcinea
Hollering for me to lower my drawbridge.

3/11/81 — [2] (02613)

Nigger in the Woodpile △

I arise at 5:45,
In Tipton's Twin Pine Motel,
To the clacking matins of diesel pistons at idle
Inside the engine of an eighteen-wheeler
Stammering at roadside while its driver
Makes ready to move camp
Another eight hundred miles.

Like a stallion wind ripping door seals,
The truck's lusty exhaust
Pries open the modular box
That has suffered me for an evening,
As if bent on suffocating me.
I rush into soiled clothing,
Escape without brushing hair, teeth, shaving,

My paranoia intact. Hysteria chases me
Right onto the dark highway,
Which fails to materialize, immediately,
*

Through opaque fog on my windshield.
Something about entering the universe again,
In the middle of nowhere,
Scares the shit out of me,

Sends my inventive apparatus spinning —
Black holes, hurricane eyes,
Judges' chambers, strange hospital rooms
Loaded with scanning and x-ray machines.
Suddenly, the four-way junction
Rushes up, assails vision,
Demands the brain make a decision. I stop,

Park on the ominous lot
Bolted to the earth by pickup trucks,
And am caught up in shadows
Scaling the Crystal Café's sides like water
Dripping, in reverse, up a cave's wall.
Inside, my eyes scan rapidly
For a familiar landmark,

Guide me to an unobtrusive booth
Beyond the pale the two tables
Crowded with jeering, raucous regulars cast,
And I slink down, hoping to hide
In my furtive silence. Like frightened snakes,
Their voices coil and test the air,
Then slither sideways, toward me.

My ears avoid their biting strikes
For a while, dodging slander
Obviously meant to poison me into submission.
The scent of cooking eggs and ham,
Gravy, and heated doughnuts and cakes is sullied
By the acrid odor bigotry emits.
Fangs spewing "Jew," "Jew," "Jew"

Shred the dead, stale air to tatters,
As I cower behind my coffee,
Knowing, now, that they've recognized me
In their posted forest — an enemy,
The interloper, Nate Lieberman,
Men's clothing representative,
Bringing Manhattan's latest to the Ozarks, wholesale.

3/13/81 — [1] (02390)

[They say he's a superstitious son-of-a-bitch,]

They say he's a superstitious son-of-a-bitch,
Who suffers from a polysyllabic malady
Known as triskaidekaphobia.
This being another of those fated thirteens
That occurs on accidentally-on-purpose Fridays,
He's nervous as an assault force
Nearing a mined beachhead
And couldn't give less of a shit
What others think about his idiosyncrasies.

He's his own self-created victim,
Whose inordinate fear
Of certain digits and days,
Arranged in apocalyptic configurations,
Is his fetishistic concern, his alone to endure,
In a universe he perceives as impersonal and evil.
Just now, his chief worry is not
A severe chest pain, the gas gauge
Inching past empty, or the fact that he's late

For a compulsory interview in St. Louis,
With the IRS,
Rather that he was awakened by a blackbird
Squawking from a tree beneath his window
As if screeching details of his autopsy.
Suddenly seized by twelve other interpretations,
He realizes his ultimate bad luck
In not having been summoned from bed
By a turtledove cooing, instead.

3/13/81 — [2] (05753)

[If you didn't know] †

If you didn't know

3/14/81 (08089)

Sundogs and Moondogs

The days load up with chaos,
Like gray landscapes filling with snow.
Everywhere I go is a slogging,
A slow sloshing toward the City of Poetry,

Through blizzards exploding like mines
In my face, shattering expectations, dreams
Of writing perfectly crystal verse.
Flakes floating earthward, daily,

Change to comets refusing to dis-
Integrate as they enter my space, like hot cinders
Flying from the cosmic grinding wheel.
Blindness guides my senses inward,

From the base of two flaming volcanoes
Erupting below the eyes' mountainside.
I dive beneath its roaring core,
Whose magma-metaphors and symbol-images and tropes,

Imploding with phantasmagorical force,
Absorb my soul's energy, its genetic identity.
The psyche rises like glowing snow,
Loading the horizon with whiteness momentarily,

Before dissolving into fiery water
Drying to death-dust on the eyeing retinas.
Home is nowhere close.
Getting there is how the poem is made.

3/17/81 (05754)

Flying Fish

Its engines whine, shimmer, resonate,
As the jet taxis,
Dolphining, over uneven concrete,
Toward runway's into-the-wind end.

Within this whale's churning belly,
We are adventitious polyps,
*

Diatoms, and plankton
Swishing around inside its sounds.

Abruptly, it, we, lift,
Rotating on an upward-thrusting axis,
Leaving the dusty floor beneath us.
The air-ocean opens,

Accepting our swift, slender penetration
As if this vessel
Were a colossal white marlin
Breaching the sea's surface,

Soaring above the breaking waves,
Which, below our flight,
Are broken clouds blotching the horizon.
We hang in glistening arrest,

Floating with gentle, undulatory motions
Like those of a manta ray
Slowly making its way
To one of a hundred destinations,

Before metamorphosing into shark
Voraciously circling,
Focusing its homing apparatus
On patterns emanating from anxious splashing

Concentrated in a very specific space
Below the ocean's waves,
Its vaporous, hazy depths,
Just beyond a great Pangaea-like shelf.

With amazing force, it strikes, shudders.
Its rubber teeth bite,
Take hold, as its engines, whining in reverse,
Climax into torpid silence,

And we issue from the fish, unmolested,
Our spirits only slightly soiled
For having been transported so miraculously —
Oceangoing disciples of Jonah and Pinocchio.

3/20/81 (05755)

Salvation on a Per Diem Basis

The mere act of awakening amazes me.
There's such a precarious space to navigate,
Going from abyss to surface,
Negotiating those straits
Barnacled with nightmares, phobic accretions
That, like a giant narwhal tusk,
Could rip a vessel's keel and sides to shreds.

What makes for safe passages eludes me.
I do know it has little to do
With volition, goals, ambition
To circumvent, one day more,
Time's physical subjugation of the intellect,
Premature senescence, forgetting,
Latent insanity, or fleshly dissolution.

Somehow, I sense,
Awakening depends on a force greater,
Infinitely more abundant and wiser
In its insight, an attendant spirit
With an overview so expansive
As to encompass, and render inessential, magic,
The occult, necromancy, accident, faith.

Whether yawning is a by-product,
Catalyst, or an actual godly slap
That sets the newborn apparatus in motion
Is irrelevant to the constancy of its existence.
Perhaps those strange shapes
The mouth makes in gasping for additional oxygen
Are masks we assume, to repulse demons,

Facial stage sets to hide behind
When death, myriadly disguised, approaches
In hope of making a fresh selection
From among the earth's sleeping auditionees.
Whatever these extra breaths
Might represent, they let me celebrate
Another return from the oneiric depths

Without regretting the solitariness of my quest
Or fearing the destination,
*

Which, ever nearing, seems to recede
By illusory degrees, until sleep becomes
The one anodyne, out of all elixirs,
Capable of placating human restiveness.
I'm an addict in need of a nightly fix.

Each evening, I freely submit
To the hours between ten and six,
Lie down in their soft-sheeted coffin,
And pray for resurrection and deliverance.
Each morning is my reanointment.
Neither tomorrow nor yesterday count.
Now is my appointed hour, eternity.

3/23/81 — [1] (01028)

A Get-Well/Birthday Card

For Janny,
my love

What an auspicious way to salute a ceremony of this magnitude.
        I only wish, mistress most blessed, you were
A little less sick, more like your effervescent, jubilant self,
        Ready and willing to do battle with unicorns
And other such horny creatures, in whose category I am included.

        Instead, we sit at 15th Street Fisheries,
Not exactly melancholic, despite the fact that you cannot swallow,
        Taste the smooth, cool Chablis, oysters,
And erotically exotic, aphrodisiacal cuisine and pastries,
        By which to drift away into sensual dimensions,

So much as lackluster, uninspired, frustrated, and disgusted
        At not being able to rise to the occasion,
Celebrate your thirty-seventh birthday with uninhibited devilment.
        Yet let us forget the "might have been"s and regrets
And praise having spent tonight in such splendid, friendly company.

        You do realize, I suspect, dear Lady Jan,
That our vows to take each other in sickness as well as in health
        Were not gestures made by posturing fools
But promises to be kept. So tonight, I toast your infectious germs:
        L'chaim! And may you have many, many more.

3/23/81 — [2] (02061)

[Just now, the moment contains us] △

Just now, the moment contains us
In suspended hiatus. We wait
For the preordained takeoff to eventuate.
Inside this plane,
Machinery spins in neutral, holds steady;
Bodily functions get queasy
As flight time rapidly approaches.

And I can't contain my amazement
At realizing we're leaving,
Returning to commitments we eagerly left,
Secretly dreaming, then, that our trip
Might be permanent, that our destination
Might make mythical paradise
Seem like an appetizer before the feast.

Soon, the air will ferry us home.
We shall be safely ensconced
In our known space, isolated, again,
From the preposterously colossal ocean,
With all its idiosyncratic shapes
And sounds and constantly changing colors.
Already, I can hear the absence of waves

Crashing against our small-town clapboards,
The violent winds not lashing
And swirling about the peaks and eaves
Of our gingerbread mansion. Already,
I miss the broad, sandy expanses
Over which we ran to reach the Indies
And eat at the fabled hot-dog stand.

It's true,
Everything could have been different.
We might easily have decided
Never to travel to the farthest reaches,
Where leisure and timelessness converge.
We might have stayed inside our buzz-hive
Of trivialities. We might have died

Without realizing the world outside exists
And remained naive to the fears
*

Now climbing our spines like thick ivy.
We might have avoided this anxiety,
Taxiing to runway's end. But then,
What advantage would we have gained by hiding
From the destinies that already own us?

3/29/81 (05461)

Making the Trip, Alone

In this green-screaming solitude
Through which my speeding vehicle moves,
A withheld truth,
Disguised in April's most beguiling clothes,
Slowly unfolds.

It intrudes on my quietest moments,
First as purple magnolias,
Whose clitoral buds
Are bursting into perfectly turned goblets
Containing godly fragrance,

Then as two smooth children
Tumbling through space,
Into my outstretched gaze,
Like ivory moons
Or dove feathers released, in silence, from above,

Soft, supple children
Possessed of a diamond cutter's touch,
Mounting dusk's pastel-faceted lavenders
And radiant red-orange hues
In my eyes' settings, with absolute precision.

Finally, it arrives
As ubiquitous drooping leaf clusters
Tingeing the horizon, in every direction,
With Monet-strokes
Dripping, dripping, still dripping dry,

The cruel, indefensible truth
That my visions are mine alone,
My images, disassociated from time,
*

Are unshared lives,
Poetry's bones buried in a stoneless grave.

4/1/81   (05756)

[With euphemistic subterfuge] ‡ ∆

With euphemistic subterfuge
Befitting the most Merlinish pretender to the throne,
They refer to this small town,
Cradled in the Ozark foothills of Missouri,
As a "bedroom community,"
"A nice place to retire to,"
A "five star" city,
Whose motto, "Tradition and Progress,"
Can be readily seen,
From vehicles speeding south to Arkansas,
On the solitary ten-by-forty-foot billboard
Stranded back off Highway 67,
In a cornfield, like an abandoned manure spreader.

Demographers ranging out
To take soundings, drill cores,
Need go no farther
Than the Capital Café to glean statistics
On how easily excitable
Is public contempt for such old saws
As bigotry, smugness, complacence,
Chauvinism, hypocrisy,
And inflexible fanatical religiosity.
Each citizen is an exemplar of jingoistic Americanism,
Christian morality
With an old-rugged-cross bias
Toward Baptist exclusivity.

"A nice place to raise children"
Permeates the rhetoric,
The Chamber of Commerce antiphons and litanies;
It sifts to the streets, like confetti
And ticker tape at a parade,
Off the tongues of everyone afraid to extricate his head
From the ostrich hole he's dug, over the decades,
*

Until "ain't"s and "don't"s,
Fornicating in fifth and sixth grades,
Eschewing a junior-college education
Replace present-day expectations,
Become the significant qualifications
For maintaining their community's own self-image.

4/6/81 (00586)

Cataracts

I

Destinies, Furies, Eumenides, and Valkyries
Swirl in the twin whirlpools
His desperate eyes stir up,
Gazing insanely at the face containing them.

Vision is Milton's satanic hell-pit,
Filled with grizzly, hissing demi-Gorgons,
Chimeras, and scaly lizards
Clawing his reflection to bleeding tatters.

Focus goes from pain to pounding,
In and out of sequence
Neither can memory recollect
Nor the intellect arrest in a clear image

Long enough for recognition to occur.
The profile in the optic glass
Both pupils keep pressed
Against intuition's collective retinas shatters.

Mole, cheeks, chapped lips,
And grotesque handlebar moustache,
Pasted in antic frieze,
Below the Jew nose, by a graffiti artist,

Fly out of the thickly misted mirror,
Like bees rushing from a hive
Threatened by curious invaders
And disappearing inside their vaporized buzzing.

II

When his eyes finally locate themselves —
Contiguous algae-crested pools
Oozing in primordial lassitude
At the dead center of an abandoned ossuary —

They are void of all sight.
Occasionally, they blink at stray clouds
Passing through lanes just above.
Otherwise, nothing but rain,

Turbulent winds, and misguided insects
Hovering too near
Their murky surface disturb their purblindness.
Even radiant suns

Fail to penetrate the dense dimensions
Sealed beneath a bleak soul
Resigned to obdurate cynicism and doubt
About humanity's future.

Sundered under tons of glassy opacity,
They remain abstracted,
Blinkless, no longer refractive,
As lachrymal days stagnate
Along their lidded, lashy banks.

Now and then, children skim rocks,
Drop baited hooks into the viscid waters,
And lovers tryst on nearby hills,
Oblivious to his wizened, invisible spirit, below.

4/7/81 — [1] (00864)

Keeping the Vows

For my one love,
Jan

This morning, as I leave town,
We gift each other
With delicately faceted crystal kisses,
Set, one by one,
*

With masterly precision,
In the imperceptibly raised settings
On our glistening lips.

All day and evening,
We wear these precious pieces,
Sharing our creations,
Cherishing their mutual design,
As if they were matched wedding rings
Binding us inextricably
During this brief separation.

4/7/81 — [2] (04178)

Hunting Rabbits and Rabbits ^Δ

Whoever has pressed against bitter cold,
Snapping glassy, brittle icicles
In passing through fields,
Shotgun shouldered, listening to his breath
Fashion frozen languages in lifting smoke,

Waiting for bassets and beagles
To flush rabbits, scented with fear,
From warm nests, send them flashing past,
As they begin their widening arc,
Knows habit's reputation for predictability.

Tonight, I am both hunter and prey,
Returned to this desolation
Where chase and waiting ultimately converge
On memory. Alone, in patient amazement,
I watch for first signs

Of an idea or image, hiding in shadows,
To break from silence, rush into open terrain,
Where my trained eye,
Lining up the speeding essence
In sights mounted to my slender pen,

Might make clean contact,
Stab the leaping life in midstride,
Dead-center through the heart.
But nothing stirs in the frigid dimension
To which I've returned. I wait,

Hoping something magical
Will awaken the landscape to my presence.
Neither familiar face nor metaphor
Materializes out of the stale air,
Where, always, in the past, I've bagged my limit,

Returned home with a catch
Worthy of the craftiest practitioners.
Suddenly, the wine I've imbibed,
To keep me heated for versing, and the music
My listening ears have filtered

Go dry. The severe silence is dynamite
Blasting an entire mountainside.
My poised gun shakes from the reverberation,
Scribbles senseless scattershot
Like a child urinating in its diaper.

Looking out through vertiginous eyes,
I catch a glimpse of the prize
Scooting over the horizon, out of sight.
The ineluctable, elusive inspiration,
Finally flushed, escapes with its precarious life,

While I, a poet who had hoped to equal
Former feats, freeze beneath snow
Forming over my spoken and written verses,
Which will drip into icicles and dissipate in the first sun.

4/8/81 — [1] (03489)

Calling Home

Tonight, from this galactic distance
Beyond mortal existence,
I phoned home, hoping to make contact
With both children I own
By virtue of love, lust, and sheer fucking.

Having disclosed my vital statistics
To a voice indecipherable and totally alone,
Located somewhere out there,
Between dead air and the net below,
I was allowed to speak, to express my joy.

But when my blessed daughter
Finally assumed the invisible mouthpiece,
All she could form was a negative echo,
Miming her unconscious hatred of me
For traveling, leaving her and her brother.

When I tried to persuade Trilogy
To speak, she slammed the phone
Against all my desire to communicate.
Momentarily, I sat on the bed,
Listening to the dial tone drifting into repetition,

As my mind assimilated its position
Relative to that galactic distance
It had caused to accrete over time.
As the apparatus abruptly short-circuited,
My numb ear filled to tears, with buzzing,

From such an unexpected rejection.
Now, I sit here wondering what I've done
To create such inutterable pandemonium
Among my gentle offspring,
Why my children might spurn their father.

In this stark, dark room,
My eyes dart from the black phone
To the blank walls. One by one,
They start counting Haydite blocks
Enclosing me in my own stoniness.

4/8–10/81 — [2] on 4/8 & [1] on 4/10   (01453)

Hammurabian Reprisals [Δ]

Already, the thick Mississippi air
Is astir with April's first flush
Of butterflies.
They drift and hover
Like dreams riding slipstreams
Toward certain finalities.
We converge. The silent crash
Of insects impacting grille and bumper
Sets up a painful thudding
*

So loud inside my head
I might be taking ak-ak flak
To the vital psyche.
Sinister premonitions explode,
Vaporize around me like black holes,
Honeycombed anxieties,
Then dissolve. Queasy, I tremble with guilt,
For inescapably maiming and annihilating
Nature's gentlest creatures.
All the way home,
As though suffering a nervous tic,
My eyes flick from the road
To rearview mirror.
My head continually shifts
Back over its shoulders,
Possibly to catch a split-second re-
Flection of a juggernaut
Fate might be guiding toward me,
Unperceived,
On whose grille or bumper
I will be squashed and splattered.

4/10/81 — [2] (03488)

Prevail, Prevail

His eyes emit crystal mystifications,
Invisible, cryptic signals
That whisper him from tongue
To place simultaneously,
As if the entire universe,
Through which he paces and struts,
Were plugged into his spine's base,
Wired to his racing heart.

Each inspiration he takes
Turns his lungs to volcanoes,
From whose rims, every other second, he plunges,
Into their collapsing craters,
Driven, by sheer exhilaration,
To expunge his excessive, wasted energy
And keep from hyperventilating.

Even during sleep,
He swims just under the surface,
Skimming off the best dreams
By which to achieve his purposes
In the waking world,
Gathering elusive colors and shapes
For each new day's book of hours.

Not exactly a magician or gypsy,
Neither is he a seer,
Pragmatist, completely organized
And reasonable philosopher and father,
Rather something of a juggler,
All of whose flying balls and pins
Fall occasionally but never touch the ground.

Once in a great, wide while,
He becomes disconnected from the wire
Attaching him to the dynamo
That electrifies the sky, oceans, and land.
Momentarily, he dies,
Forgets the name and body
God loaned him,

Before remembering his mystical business
Of surviving to time's end.
Instantly, his breathing revives,
Firing the eyes to crystal mystifications.
Through a misty effluvium,
He looks out on a new Creation
And sees Eve approaching with birds of paradise.

4/10/81 — [3] (05757)

Turning Forty

Forty is a violent white rhino
Rumbling toward me
As though my mere existence were contemptible,
A threat to be bluffed into retreat
Or met head-on and defeated.

Standing out here, alone,
Stranded at the absolute epicenter
Of this creature's rage,
Unarmed, naked, frozen,
I wait for the fateful convergence to annihilate me.

Suddenly, disguised as dust,
I'm running toward day's edge,
To get behind night's retaining wall,
And the stampeding beast
Dissolves, like dye, into the twilight.

Now, out of curiosity, I return to the arena,
To see if anything remains
From that confrontation just yesterday.
Right where I stood,
The white rhino grazes, unfazed by my presence.

4/10/81 — [4] (05758)

Recorder of Deeds, Pro Tem ^Δ

The men enter the café
Like minnows darting, from coverts,
To a crumb-strewn surface,
Overeducated tongues
Guzzling bottles
Filled with intoxicating word-wine,
Mice creeping, surreptitiously,
Toward spring-loaded peanut butter
Or cheese planted, inconspicuously,
Between monolithic pots and pans.

Each morning, they arrive by droves,
One at a time,
To register their living franchise,
Vote their identity into voluble existence,
Announce themselves
Well-equipped to solve the Sphinx's riddles,
Advise wise Solomon,
Confine, through their own puissance,
Hadrian, Draco, and Savonarola
To lip-service posturings.

Having long ago discovered the secret
To transforming myself, on a moment's notice,
From a first-person participant
Into an omniscient third-person entity,
Identityless, ubiquitous,
I sit, each morning,
Invisible within my nimbus,
Listening to wisdom recreate itself
Exponentially, trying to copy, exactly,
Each progeny's birth date and origin.

Transcribing such impressive rhetoric,
So many impromptu speeches and diatribes,
Tracts, harangues, and sermons
Redolent of those delivered on Areopagus,
From podiums in Swiftian academies
And Matherish pulpits,
Is not easy for a humble amanuensis
Not yet all that flexible of wrist
Or proficient in capturing flawed testimony
And unbowdlerized speaking in tongues.

Yet I've done it in the past,
Been assigned tasks by God's apostles.
In fact, I am the author
Not only of Deuteronomy and the Psalms
But Corinthians, Thessalonians,
And the epistles to the Galatians and Ephesians.
Furthermore, it was my hand
That translated the Koran, Rig-Veda,
Kama Sutra, Rosetta stone,
And those brittle Dead Sea Scrolls.

Why, then, this particular morning,
My pen refuses to chase them
Through their deft histrionics —
These men representing civilization
Reaching beyond apotheosis, toward zenith —
Despite my realizing each static moment
Will register, one day, as a devastating lapse
In the golden book, I can't say.
I hope it's only narcolepsy
And not the poet in me growing senescent.

4/14/81   (00585)

Sailing Toward Ararat

For my mother and my father,
who fashioned my vessel
from their bones and flesh

In two days, I shall have reached
Ararat's peak,
From whose sacred altitude,
Equidistant from its terrestrial base
And the lowest tinged fringes of eternity,
I should be able to scan
Vast sands of a passed civilization
And locate abandoned decades
Which cradled my youth's celebration.

Once landed,
I would also expect to see, through mist,
Pervading plains to the west,
Resplendent new communities
And undreamed outposts
Blossoming with exotic possibilities
For my aging soul's growth.
Then I would search and locate
The only path down the mountainside

And be delivered of all former ties,
A free, apostolic spirit,
The heart's peripatetic bard,
Singing sweet-sad threnodies
And lullabies to unborn children,
Naiads, and beggars not yet arrived
To that mystical wilderness,
A poet weaving wind-strands into bridges
Spanning the abyss between *now* and *forever*.

These vagaries my vessel churns up,
As it surges through mid-April's
Cool morning seas, and leaves in its wake
Are elusive as music not yet scored.
Two days remain
Before coordinates converge at forty.
By then, I might have veered
Too far, setting my sights on siren stars
Shimmering, like pyrite, in an unchartable sky.

For now, I hold the wheel
As though it were wired
With nitroglycerin,
Praying my destination will appear
On the horizon, without fate's interference,
Hoping to touch shore safely,
Kiss the sand,
And commence my inland trek
To the first day of my second childhood.

4/15/81   (02060)

[We synthesize our inextricable lives] ^Δ

We synthesize our inextricable lives
Each time we smile,
Touch, kiss, hug,
Or gaze, in abstracted amazement,
At each other, proclaiming ourselves
Keepers of the family's pride,
Its collective reputation
For fiercely uncompromising indignation
Over acts and deeds
Lacking compassion, partaking of ignominy.

We anoint each other king and queen,
Princess and prince,
Over the fragile dream we share
Of ultimately accomplishing celestial synthesis
Of all gone souls
Who ever belonged to this extended family,
That man might be granted another chance
To discover his kindredness
By advancing from Creation, through love,
To an understanding of God's mysterious ways.

4/16/81   (01019)

Shadowboxing

I awakened, this cold April morning,
Naked and aching
*

Like a boxer surfacing slowly
From having been knocked through a hole
In the ropes separating consciousness
From blessed comatose arrest.

Moments in which focus
Refused to settle on a specific pose,
For objects crowding its field,
Telescoped into years
Hovering, like dandelion seeds,
Above memory's weedy backyard.

Dislocating, wallpaper I'd glued
Not ten years ago
And lithographs, coded to my psyche,
I'd purchased in San Francisco,
In my coming-of-age student days,
Fused into a hallucinogenic salmagundi.

My eyes filled with chaos,
As though invisible children or gnomes
Were splattering them with finger paint,
Conforming to sinister designs
Conceived by twin Rabelaisian cartoonists
Dante and Milton.

Finally, the vague, flatulent shadow
Containing my brittle frame
Escaped the weight sleep's sheet
Had draped over me,
And drained, like spilled tea,
Down the bed's side, to the gritty rug.

Once ambulatory, my wobbly spirit
Began to seize objects
In its immediate path, hoping recognition
By sheer touch might lead it
To a familiar sound, aroma, coax vision
To home in on its own frequency.

Suddenly, vertiginous reeling ceased.
The foreboding, twisted staircase
Leading, from nowhere,
To the thirteenth floor of nightmare,
Straightened before my teetering shape,
Beckoned me descend.

Gripping the smooth rail, with sweaty hand,
I sensed the elevation diminishing,
Air thinning, my bones becoming limber,
As one step closed
And the next opened, like reciprocal valves
In an iron lung supporting my life.

Then it was that my senses discovered
The nature of the oppressive essence
Whose acrid effluvium
Had embalmed my dreaming in caustic fluids
All weekend,
Shriveled my soul to the prune's confinement.

I alone, the creature's keeper,
The machine's mechanic,
The shadow's black packing,
Which kept its flabby silhouette inflated,
Had been flattened by an unknown opponent
During the night, dropped to the floor,

In the squared-off, roped-in ring
Forming the dimensions of my earthly performance.
Evidently, I'd taken the count,
Been carried out on a stretcher and buried
In dawn's potter's field,
To revive inside morning's lavender quietude.

Now, I rise. My legs and stomach
Respond to stretching, flexing muscles,
Running blood. A tepid shower
Animates my unbaptized body.
Coffee revivifies the clearing hemispheres.
In the mirror, I see my sparring partner

Still reveling under the high-decibel cheering
Of a faceless crowd of jurors,
Who generally attend the court of Joseph K.
He doesn't see me staring
As I pass him on my way out the door, to work,
My attaché filled with fight plans and strategies.

4/20/81 (05759)

Something ^Δ

For Bob Hamblin;
another way of saying no
to death

Something there is
Preternaturally compelling,
In the essential genes controlling my mind,
That provokes its cortical Sanhedrin
To mandate my hand to take up pen
And write; something unexplainable,
In lay translation, that might describe
Why my insatiable psyche
Never seems satisfied with its prolificness
Or considers its signature,
Affixed in rhythmic mellifluousness,
Sufficient proof of its sole authorship;

Something mystical, magical,
That would have me rhyme the universe
Into a divine pattern
Indivisible by mere human comprehension,
Which, like sheet lightning,
Might play out the entire range of sky
Before discovering its own design;
Something informing my recorded chronicle
With my tiny spirit's grandeur;
Something, approximating godliness,
That reminds me, ultimately, my dying
Shall not be squandered on cosmic silence.

4/21/81 (00131)

Poetical Geometrics

For Jan,
who dances all over my soul

The shortest distance between our bodies
Is an eye-blink,
A leap of the imagination,
Flashes of heat,
*

Daydreaming, whose metaphorical thrust
Surpasses that of a rocket
Blasting off its pad,
The sigh of relief
Each of us makes as a wide yawn
Edges toward death,
Then falls back into synchronous beat.

The shortest distance between our hearts
Is poetry I write
And recite, occasionally,
Before we rush toward separate sleeps.
It alone needs no coaxing
Or specialized training in divination
To disclose the celebration of our souls.
It lets us touch,
Listen to, and focus on each other's love,
By recirculating our blood
Along its lines of least resistance.

4/22/81   (02059)

Intimations in Spring ^Δ

I yawn. My spirit stretches
Beneath its taut flesh
As if in the incipient stages of molting.

Indeed, on this warm morning,
Lush and fecund as teenage girls
Flaunting full pink breasts,

I realize how precious yet precarious
Is my connection to the quick
And those souls no longer existent.

It must have something to do
With the rhythmic stichomythia birds echo
In the outrageously thick twigs,

Be something about wet grass
That outglistens cut glass
And multifaceted diamonds,

Something in the ecstasy
My young daughter, Trilogy, exudes
Arcing recklessly

Through the too-humid April air,
Before we leave for school
(Her blessed innocence of finalities, perhaps,

As she asks me why the trees
Aren't loading up
With all the colors, "besept" green,

As, in fall, they do, unloading),
That brings me so early
To the brink of thinking's magical pool,

To drink in its mystical truth
And get drugged . . . and get crazy
On the pure, pristine perfection of beauty

That has nothing to do
With human formulation, rather waits
To be seen, to be heard, to be entered

By the most brainless creature,
Let alone receptive poet,
In order to complete its own metamorphosis

And be possessed by those few
Who would get close enough to the core
To see God watching them.

Something, this morning, convinces me
My spirit has already outgrown its mortality
And is about to soar.

4/23/81 (00145)

In Retreat

I feel and hear the pumping lungs
Thumping in wrists, the neck,
My tense chest,
As though I've abruptly stopped running
*

Instead of just awakened
From malevolent premonitions of disaster,
Chasing me out of sleep.

Sitting up beneath crumpled sheets,
Startled as a possum
Freezing in the eerie aura
Of a charging car's headbeams,
Unable to locate thoughts and dreams
I placed under my pillow,
On surrendering to repose, late last night,

I grope through somniferous debris
That washed ashore with me.
My eyes scavenge ocean-vestiges
For shell-shaped messages
Containing my final recorded roaring,
Hoping to authenticate my identity,
Proclaim myself king,

Rather than sleazy bastard pretender,
In the natural succession
Accorded all daily-changing creatures.
No clues materialize within the gloom
My bedroom engenders,
Nothing except rusty blood,
Encrusted, like barnacles, along one leg,

Emanating enigmatically
From two tiny punctures below my groin,
As though a shadow-spider or succubus
Might have taken advantage,
Entered my temple during vesper hours
And stolen bell, book, and candle,
Blown out my lambent votives.

Suddenly, I recognize both symptom
And etiology of my drowsiness,
My dislocation: I've been victimized
By demons trepanning my psyche,
Letting the air out of my brain chamber,
Deflating my self-esteem,
As day turns to year, to decade, nightly,

Demons possessing my features,
Death-breaths setting off klaxon-screeching
Along the cardiovascular avenues,
Warning me to run from the invading enemy,
Old age, run for my life.
But I can't penetrate the body's barricades
Or escape. Waking is perpetual retreat.

4/24/81   (05760)

Departures

So far, the hardest assignment I've had
Has been adjusting to departures,
Keeping head and heart whole
While in flux, dislocated, alone,
Heeding Lilith's siren smile with caution.

This morning, the road-whore I've known
So many dissolute years
Has a haggard voice. Her whine
Reminds me we're both getting older.
She's no longer nubile and smooth,

Rather tending toward arthritic.
We lunge and weave
Like two rough beasts tightly locked
In impossible copulative stride.
I should never have left,

Except that volition wasn't consulted
When plans were formulated,
Nor, for that matter,
Was I warned, until hours before,
That I'd be expected to sally forth,

Enter the evanescent slipstream
All gone souls
Have left in their wakeless wake,
Take to the highway,
And fly, on a yawn, toward inspiration.

Now, dawn splinters.
Crimson vapors scream in the distance,
As though aliens with a syringe
Had run the sun through.
My eyes cringe,

Begin to leak vitreous humors,
Until vision is a grieving stream
In which naked penitents bathe,
Hoping to hide inside my blindness.
My profile won't wash from their faces.

Suddenly, the road narrows.
Drowning seems a less shabby alternative
Than tracing my shadow's steps,
From home to horizon
And back, just to keep from being caught

In static backwash
Caused by circumstances controlled by me.
Up ahead, the city rises.
My soul is impaled on its glistening spires.
I suffer such crucifixions frequently.

4/28/81 — [1] (05761)

Spatial Clichés

Here today, gone tomorrow,
As the clichéd saying would have it,
Save that yesterday and now
Were and are both sooner or later,
Depending on when death
Decides to set in or delay its onset.

There tomorrow, gone today,
Inside a magical illusion time performs
When it rends the brain in twain
And revives superstition,
To convince infidels that survival depends
On believing the spirit is immortal.

Gone now, nowhere yesterday,
I surrender to surreality
Unfurling like a tidal wave on the beach
Where my naked psyche has lain
All the waking days of its early retirement
From life and burns eternally.

Here, as recently as an hour ago,
Within the sweet aura
Your wet lips described around my eyes,
Like Raphael-halos,
I sense my senses hovering yet,
Though you have changed to vapors

And I have flown, alone, from here
To there, wherever tomorrow is located,
Gone, now, as a lost metaphor
Or sandblasted visage on a defunct Sphinx,
Gone as Abishag's beauty,
Already catapulting toward oblivion.

Here today, gone tomorrow,
As the old saying so sagaciously puts it
For those conversant with lay terminology.
There yesterday, here again in memory,
Who loved his friends,
Closely touched his children and wife.

A wisp in the breeze, dandelion seeds,
The springbound bird-sounds,
And squirrels scampering around tree trunks
Are all components of my soul,
The spirit's residue, scattered atoms
Trying desperately to simulate my former shape.

Arrived, I am here, am here,
Nevermore, forever, to be there,
From where gone is the absence of now
And poetry is death's counterweight.
Here I am, in a dimensionless paradise,
Ready to begin the endless sojourn through space.

4/28/81 — [2] (05762)

Speaking in Tongues

I

Sitting in this bar in the Hilton's lobby,
So far from home
And family, partaking of dry Chablis,
Listening to the after-work persiflage
Of accountants, lawyers, junior executives,
And bankers in training, all on the make,
My most profound thoughts focus on you,
Jan, blessed wife,
Maiden of my heart's bold quest,
Queen in modest clothing.

And as my eyes scan the voluble crowd
And my ears record their gobbling,
I can't contain a wild cynicism
That would normally stay quiet
Beneath the sarcophagus lid of my existence.
I hear my chambers resonating with laughter
At all this dissimulation
And bawdy, lust-provoked stimulation,
Realizing that every man's objective
Is to fornicate, commit adultery — fuck.

They are all so strange,
In their something-less-than-classic poses,
Their prepared sophistications
And bilingual, swinging-singles charades.
Each reminds me of a shadow puppet
Swaying from Piranesian chains,
Behind scrim curtains,
Tarzan rushing in to save his Jane
From being raped by an orangutan
Or fantastical, mystic-colored rubber snake.

II

Even the piano's dulcet, effeminate notes
Have that quality of being evoked,
From thin nothingness, by Dali brush strokes.
The wine soothes and smoothes out
*

Rough edges that keep roaring in
Against the shore, dialects so foreign
That no amount of on-the-scene translation
Can interpret the meaning of interlopers
Invading our coasts. I try to decipher
The Pearl Harbor code, without success,

Suspecting that the enemy is surrounding us
Without our knowing it,
Planning to bomb us with import goods
Of all manner, from microwaves
To compact sports cars to "smart machines."
All I know for certain is that this bar
Is no more indigenous to my heritage
Than a samovar nor less reprehensible
Than an internment camp in San Francisco
To Second World War Japanese-Americans.

Suddenly, the music ceases.
I become noticeably uneasy amidst the silence
Perforated by mile-a-minute tongues
Conversing in tactics, logistics, and modes.
I imagine my gentle, unsuspecting wife
And blond children reposing in the heartland,
Waiting for their savior to return
From reconnoitering the front. I hasten to my room,
To phone long-distance, reassure them
I'm safe, though the mainland is under siege.

4/28/81 — [3] (04177)

On Visiting "Do" Commins

I sit here, with piqued anticipation,
In this stifling station,
Breathing the incantatory ichor
Of the quest. I am the last crusader,
Mad as Ahab,
Crazed as a screaming meteor
Blasting through space. It's the chase
That makes the blood race,
Not through the veins
*

But along their outside walls,
And keeps the brain exercised,
Ready, on a moment's notice,
For fight or flight or sequestration.

The minutes are pinpricks
Stabbing me systematically. Anxiety
Bleeds invisibly from all my closed pores,
As my destination magnetizes me
And I am drawn toward the precipice,
Ready to master the mystic abyss.

4/29/81   (02290)

"Do"

Like ancient Nile inhabitants
Dragging, floating, sliding quarried blocks
Inestimable distances,
To stack them in pyramidal oblation to gods
Needing insatiable appeasement,

She transports her people's Talmudic wisdom
From deep, oblique recesses
Aging ceaselessly tries to conceal,
To her remembering tongue,
Whose teacher's instinct beseeches her speak

To me . . . ah, yes, to me alone,
And I listen as though eavesdropping on God
Singing to Moses, Jesus,
And their gentle prophets and apostles.
She whispers, "Never stop growing!

"You must forever guard your integrity,
That, like polished moonstone,
It will shine even in night's blindness."
My heart weeps; it weeps,
Assimilating such simplicity,

And I know now, leaving her,
Returning to my own blessed children,
My wife, that I've been sanctified;
*

My lifeline has deviated slightly.
A temple rises on my eyes' horizon.

"Do" (pronounced "dough"): the nickname of Dorothy B. Commins, wife of
William Faulkner's Random House editor, Saxe Commins

5/3/81 (02058)

Hardening of the Arteries

I am the endlessly elongating highway
That drives me
Forever farther away from the place
Where I started,
In the heartland that nurtured my soft bones.

For years, my past
Has been unable to glimpse shadows
My forward momentum casts backward —
A fleet, spectral meteor
Disintegrating, ash by ash, in its passage.

Everything up ahead
Reminds me of what was behind,
As if the road and I
Were a seamless nickelodeon roll
Repeating itself indefinitely.

Suddenly, my destination materializes.
The concrete narrows,
Changes to gravel, to rutted mud.
An open, empty grave
Waits to transport me the final way home.

5/6/81 — [1] (05763)

Crack Salesman

Just now, the spinning top widens its circle,
Wobbles centrifugally.
The dynamo slows to an innocuous hum.
*

His apparatus finally comes to a numbing halt,
As his lips succumb
To the tart, aphrodisiacal fix
He's become addicted to over the years.

Anonymous as a Times Square whore,
In this heartland college bar,
Buzzing with enchanted conversations,
Subtle intimacies, touching,
Treaties entered into between lovers,
And gestures redolent of Nobel Prize speeches,
He sifts the living shadows,

Searches each animated face
For the slightest hint of a recognition.
He would engage the Modigliani lady
In red dress, tight white sweater,
Sipping wine, from a brandy snifter,
By herself, were it not for fear
Of initiating nuclear fission,

Disappearing inside an instantaneous explosion
Of uncontrollable passion.
He knows his own idiosyncrasies
All too well,
Has precipitated, on numerous occasions,
Infidelities
In which his semen has seeded offspring

Destined to vague transformations,
Urgent abortions,
For which he's been forced, sub rosa,
To supply funds, to have performed.
He's a master of dissimulation,
Subterfuge, clandestine artifice,
In which the greatest loser is always his spirit,

For having to make full account to his heart,
Suffer silent guilt,
Slink unnoticed into convenient synagogues,
On Friday nights, and confessionals, on Saturdays,
When the green light burns
Against ancient carved oak,
To absolve himself of gross abominations.

He would approach her and violate her
With his viperine tongue, his satanic lechery
Steeped in Moral Majority rhetoric,
Were it not for dubiety
Regarding his energy. He remembers vividly
Last evening's debauchery,
His all-night revelry with a lonely divorcée

He met in a town a hundred miles distant
From now. He'd approach her;
He'd make pointed overtures. Suddenly,
He discovers he's standing over his table,
Pressing toward the solitary lady
Locked in her elongated Modigliani shape,
Fashioning his opening remarks,
Preparing to parry her feigned rebuffs.

Within a matter of steps,
He's described a circle about his prey,
Like an undersea monster
Approaching a helpless crustacean.
She cringes, then bends forward,
Into his gentleness. She surrenders rapidly
To his tentacled vernacular.

Without knowing why, where, when,
He ends up in her bed,
Not so much lamenting his profligacy
As defending the essence of his mortal purpose,
The ethics which have guided him,
So often, to such climaxes,
From which his only release is disappearance

Into the great wide frontier,
Stretching from college town to major city,
Through which his route takes him
Every six months,
As one new line succeeds the last
And the past is recorded in his company's ledgers.
Now, the sun illuminates last night.

He rises beside a naked lady,
Whose name is as vague as her slender body.
She looks over at him. He shimmers,
*

As if something sacred were forming a halo
Over the two of them,
Then enters her silky, lathery silence
One more time, before leaving.

Day cascades through clouds.
Blue spring sampans float past,
While his vision recuperates,
Excuses him from whatever indiscretions
He might have committed out of loneliness,
Justifying his misdeeds
In the name of Willy . . . Willy Loman,

That avatar, that symbol of degeneracy
He's carried with him forever,
To remind him of the potential danger
To which he's exposed his soul,
All these years of his traveling.
Tentatively, he enters the new day,
In soiled shirt and wrinkled blue blazer,

Contemplating breakfast and his first appointment.
Before the day has ended,
He will have spent eight loud hours
With three buyers, vying for their preference,
Deferential as a monk, a millionaire's chauffeur.
By dusk, he'll be dying, once again,
For the chilled, aphrodisiacal fix of tart Chablis.

5/6/81 — [2] (02614)

Scrollwork ^Δ

Zigzag fragments
From my imagination's jigsaw
Fall to the floor of its workshop,
As I fashion, with fastidious precision,
The design aesthetic decision outlines on my psyche.

I am a craftsman, an artisan,
Who cuts, from a monolithic block,
The tabula rasa, semblances of perfection,
Furniture to ornament the intellect,
Metaphors neatly mortised and glued.

All day and night, I labor,
Planing, straining, smoothing each to a high gloss,
That its surface might reflect,
Not betray, the deep-textured grain
Contained, like compassion, at its core,

Until I know it's ready for display.
Then, without invitations being sent,
People attend my opening show,
Partaking of the gentle artwork,
Whose shapes are the sounds inspiration creates.

5/8/81 (02258)

Sea Captain's Valedictory

The passing days,
Each and every undeviating one,
Are barnacles. My hull
Is an irregular accretion of memories.
My vessel's speed has slowed considerably.
Even in pacific seas,
It creaks with sluggish unmaneuverability.
A torpid psyche guides its intellect
Toward shore,
Without ever penetrating the atoll barrier
Reefing the safe harbor
Where the king's sleek fleet is berthed.

For years, in fact,
A slack wind has held my tiny ship
In agonizing calm. No waves
Have scratched themselves to bleeding,
On my bulwarks. The ocean's roll,
To which my equilibrium has grown accustomed,
Has not disturbed my motionlessness,
Let alone sparked hope
Of one day getting under way,
Sailing to Byzantium, via Piraeus and Tyre.
Lately, I've heard time's water line
Climbing my bow, gurgling like quicksand.

5/11/81 (02057)

Trilogy's Seventh Birthday $^\Delta$

Blond-headed, resplendent
In her figured, long party dress,
Bedecked with white gloves,
High pink socks,
Blue tennis shoes, knitted sweater
Draped over her shoulders,
Buttoned just at the neck,
She resembles a delicate figurine,
An essence arrested
In hand-painted bone china,
A presence more perfect
Than even God might have tried to create.

She takes with her to school
The sacred, ritualistic accouterment
That she's grown used to:
Her ribboned tote bag,
Brimming with papers and "secrets,"
The most recent in a sequence of readers,
A purse — her reliquary —
Containing youth's perpetual mysteries.
But today,
It's the invisible ecstasy
Her specialness generates
That sets her apart from the rest,

Who squeal and buzz
As she makes her regal entrance
Into the classroom.
The imminent celebration
Has translated itself to each face;
Even her teacher beams
With jubilation Trilogy's spirit radiates.
All day belongs to her alone,
Who anticipates cupcakes, lemonade
Made by her mom, a reading from Dr. Seuss,
By her dad, later in the afternoon,
To ceremonialize her years, among peers.

How these magical passages work,
What motivates existence
*

To perpetuate itself, defy stasis,
Gain momentum, grow from embryo,
Through pupa, imago,
Floating flutterby, to love object
So reverential and abiding
That not even dying can dissolve her spell
Over the enchanted hearts of parents,
No matter how old
Or ancient they become,
Intrigues me as I focus on Trilogy today.

And I know that adoration, love,
Is a function of shared blood,
Kinship affinities formed in the womb,
Seeded out of respect and desire,
Leading to shared pleasure.
Reflecting on our child,
I suddenly realize she's starting eight,
Completed seven.
By imaginative prestidigitation,
I nudge the numeral 8 onto its side
And weep.
Already, she's arrived at infinity's beginning.

5/13/81 (02106)

When the Old Spark Is Gone

I listen fastidiously
To my glistening words listening to me
Speaking to them, in oblique tongues.
I'm surprised they recognize whispers
Of "The Phoenix and the Turtle,"
The Prelude, "Out of the Cradle Endlessly Rocking,"
Stunned to find such relics
Still lurking behind the mind's palate,
Yet trying, after all these years,
To influence my poetics,
Provide guides by which my lost spirit
Might return to its first senses,
Youth's metaphors,
Which bore brilliant children,
*

Who rode inside Greek horses, for fun,
Defeated Egypt's Pharaohs,
By mastering metamorphosis,
Changed da Vinci's brainstorms
Into generic terms and household words,
Symbols shimmering with hummingbird eloquence.

But as I listen to echoing echoes
Being magnified in the space between paper and brain,
I realize the words evoked
Are children of the children who adopted me
As their surrogate father,
To be their translator, promoter, and bard.
Although they glisten like their forebears,
No passion burns my lips,
Singes my ears. I am a poet
Writing verse for deaf-mutes to recite.

5/15/81 (02105)

Family Ties

Each time I leave you,
My sweet, loving mother and father,
I am assailed by chimeras
And sepulcher-shaped doom-clouds,
As if our most recent good-bye
Were also our last. All the way home,
I grieve, though no one has departed,
Commit myself to premature lonesomeness
So total no music or memories
Can wake me from my waking somnambulism.

Amniocentesis of my fecund imagination
Reveals serious defects.
My identity is in jeopardy. I weep,
As if you two,
Who have nurtured all that I am,
Were called from the delivery room
Unexpectedly,
Abandoning my fledgling soul
To an excruciating breech birth.
I'm forced to suture my own wounds.

A child again, at forty,
I clamber and grope and stumble
Through antiseptic hallucinations,
Hoping to locate my rightful place,
Secure my own patrimony
In a life leased, by the room,
By the minute, by the day, to the prince
Whose inhuman demons and ghosts
Would keep me from the truth.
I'm a scion of Saul's tribe, a king.

Nearing my destination,
I realize something other than heritage
Informs our living, with loving oneness.
Suddenly, doom-clouds lift,
Chimeras take flight, and you,
Mom and Dad, materialize in the doorway,
To welcome me home,
On my return from paranoia's womb.
What a surprise, finding you again,
All these years after my demise.

5/19–20/81 — [2] on 5/20   (02104)

The Ascension

Waking into this bright, bright day,
After having languished in rain's incarceration
For nearly a fortnight,
Is cause for celebration. My jubilant soul
Swims a water strider's frenzy
Through thin sun-streams
Punctuating the air, pirouettes extravagantly,
Fancying itself a dancing bear
Rather than inhabitant
Of an ungainly weather vane of a man
Who fluctuates with every minute mood change,
Recording vicissitudes,
Filing his reports in cryptic verse,
By which future meteorologists
Might decipher the climate of the times,
*

Through which he flies faster than atoms,
Whose sonic blast will merely awaken them
To his passing, before their birth.

Waking into this celestial day,
I gaze earthward,
Peer through a clear stratosphere
Without detecting thermal mushrooms
Blossoming, with sinister malignancy, on its surface,
And assume nothing irrefragably tragic
Has occurred to disturb my old haunts.
With supreme naiveté, I pray,
Hoping that my spirit, alive down there,
Is busy defending its eccentricity,
Exemplifying, for torpid, disbelieving cynics,
The importance of taking time
To count all the tiles
Inlaid in a Byzantine mosaic halo,
Stopping, awhile, by a New England woods
Just to listen to it filling up with snow,
Smelling roses growing wild
Between cracks in Manhattan sidewalks.

Yet as I concentrate, my focus blurs.
Even being resurrected
Doesn't necessarily guarantee perfect omniscience.
I see frenzied people
Banging into mirrors, shattering their illusions,
Worshiping white dust, opiate vapors,
Staring at eclipses, baring their bodies, to Goths,
On beaches, surrendering reason to preachers
Promising miracles, redemption, eternity,
For a weekly premium on holy insurance.
Nowhere can I isolate
Gentle souls engaged in writing poetry,
Painting, composing music, each for its own sake,
Unmotivated by instantaneous fame,
Immediate fortune,
And a claim on posterity's good graces.
Suddenly, rain obscures vision.
I turn heavenward and resume my journey.

5/20/81 — [1] (02103)

The Poet Ponders His Parents' Departure

So infrequently does he stop to ponder
Cosmic loneliness
Inherent in possibilities of becoming fatherless,
Unmothered, a son cut loose,
Drifting through distant cities
Invisibly as the wind,
That when brief separations arise,
His nerves ignite a prairie fire
Burning his insides to a char.

This morning, he envisions himself
A Prufrockian speck,
Feckless, inessential, a maggot, fly,
A red ant, redundant as feces, in a colony,
A poet reduced, from his lofty naiveté,
To perpetual writer's block,
By doom-rumors beyond his perspective,
Conspiring to arrest his parents' ongoingness,
On their present westerly flight east.

He sits, motionless as a hypnotist's robot,
In a booth in a café
Situated at the hub of a slovenly little town
To which he exiled himself,
His Elba, thirteen years prior,
In a community deserted as Machu Picchu —
Waif, pariah, hermit,
Contemplating, with alexic ratiocination,
His profound dislocation, his screaming anonymity.

For hours, he stares into the glare
Streaming through plate glass
Facing the courthouse, which squats on the square
Like a defecating polar bear,
And gazes past unfamiliar faces
Entering, loitering, emigrating from the place,
To higher land, greater responsibilities
Dotting day's widening horizon.
He malingers, as if staying were ordained by God,

As though, somehow, this café
Were Gethsemane and Golgotha, his Calvary,
*

The reclamation depot
For aging, dissociated souls,
Waiting for a change of venue,
To beg merciful release from their emptiness.
No one sees him scribbling valedictories,
Evoking soaring horses, with foundered metaphors,
To lift his spirit out and over the abyss.

None realizes the Jesus-like genius in his midst,
The anguished little artist
Cringing behind taut, wizened frown,
Ostentatious handlebar mustache,
Gold-rimmed glasses, and Semitic ringlets.
Not even he can fathom fully
These self-inflicted crucifixions,
Which occur whenever he suspects the enemy
Lurking in his heart's sacred purlieus.

5/22/81   (02102)

Still Growing ^Δ

I awaken to another steamy, somnolent day
Under the invisible bell jar,
A still, silent philodendron
Confined to its split-leafed freedom,
Whose paradoxical expansiveness
Deceives the myopic eye,
By psychic restrictions
And the size of its physical container.

Although normal vision
Fails to detect the stifling condition
My roots have assumed beneath the surface,
Above which I seem to flourish,
I sense it pervasively.
The pain of being smothered from below
Indicates impotence, decay.
One tug could unloose my whole shape.

The slightest deprivation
Would wither me,
Cause my waxy, lustrous design to shrivel,
*

A leaf and stem at a time,
Like bacon crisping in a skillet.
Such precariousness as this
Is the occupational hazard that accompanies wisdom,
Consciousness, domesticity.

Alone, this morning, in my stately radiance,
Among less sensitive intellects,
I sense change in the air.
The interface connecting *now* with *tomorrow*
Is wet and warm as a womb.
Though I'm crowded to death, in this terrarium,
There is yet room, apparently,
For one more sprouting leaf in my creation.

5/26/81 (02101)

Feinstein the Clothier ^Δ

Driving to work early,
Coursing down streets desolate and wet,
As though he's been preceded by a medieval plague,
He ponders his own loneliness,
Attempts to relate it to essential elements
That constitute his spare cosmos.

The changeless town changes, daily,
His basic attitude toward dying and death.
Both he and it are twin insects,
Blending into themselves and the environment
That supports their symbiotic natures.
Each conceals the other from the enemy: life.

Stasis is sovereign, whose reciprocal ukase
Demands of its minions compromise,
Equivocation, greed. Neglect and forgetting,
Rather than impeding competition,
Speed up the process,
Risk being cited for conflict of interest,

As faction pits itself against cabal,
To restrain trade in pornography,
Controlled substances, door-to-door solicitors,
*

Impious morality, whores.
They bonfire the books, with Hitlerian zeal,
Jam radio and television waves,

Lobby against new industry —
Progress in any form — from deep fear
That something might give,
Destroy the "quality of life" they've enjoyed
Since before century's turn.
They teach their children faith in Braille,

Convinced that the greatest good
Is translated by chapter and verse,
A line, a word at a time.
As he nears the Capital Café, parks his car,
And approaches its opening, a stark shiver
Whispers his bones to a high pitch.

Self-consciousness betrays his physiognomy.
His flushed face heats up,
Burns his forced smile to a tight scar.
No matter how he tries
To evade their penetrating eyes,
His thoughts are impaled, suspicions speared.

Suddenly, he's naked as a rapist
Caught by a female police decoy.
Neither criminal nor victim exactly,
He shrivels into a convenient booth,
To listen to their impugning conversations,
Waiting for inevitable allusions to his Judaism.

Soon, he'll throw open the doors
To his wholesale emporium,
Attend their wives' bovine wiles
Solicitously, help the town fathers
Fit into flawed bargains, with altruistic enthusiasm,
And momentarily forget breakfast,

Lose sight of his ambiguous position
In the town's golden chain of being.
Soon, measuring inseams, seat-seam outlets,
Waists, sleeve lengths, neck sizes
Will arrest and replace calumniation and jealousy.
Depressing the cash-register buttons

Will anesthetize him to the truth of his dislocation.
For now, his bony fingers
Caress the chipped china coffee cup
As if it were a chalice from which Moses sipped.
Gazing straight ahead,
He focuses on the courthouse, across the street,

Watching its ubiquitous pigeons hover and scurry
In a continuous flurry of loose feathers
And blurred hues. He can almost hear them,
Feel their idiotic murmurs
Rising in his throat, their shit evacuating his tract,
Splattering on the sacrosanct marble.

5/27/81 (02203)

Saying No

Auguries and oracles,
Garrulous as sparrows and chattering monkeys,
Dominate the space surrounding me.

Morning is an aviary, a cage.
Off to one side,
Next to the partition separating outside

From within, I gaze,
A stranded spectator, amazed,
Groping to understand

The phonetics and gestures of metaphors
And symbols embodied by creatures
Flying and leaping

Without concern that anyone
Might be spying, trying to decipher secrets
Emanating from them.

Suddenly, a three-legged monkey
Drops to my neck;
A one-eyed bird lights in my ear.

Emerging from hiding,
My reflection rises before and behind
Morning's murky plate glass,

Converges on itself as shadow, echo,
Superimposed ghost.
In a flash, I know the origin,

Destination, and meaning
Of these foreign oracles and auguries:
They are agents of my caged imagination,

Begging escape,
Trying to break free
By riding my wide fear of dying

From its source, deep in the glands,
Through orifices inspiration uses
To penetrate the mind's eyes,

Out into daylight,
Where no phobias exist
And immortality thrives in a perpetual *now*.

A single blink dissolves me.
Rude cacophonies,
Which, moments before, were monkeys and sparrows,

Become singing verse,
Agile, swinging, winged words
Converging above gardens of sweet alyssum,

Near Arcadia and Delphi.
Today, my heart is safe;
Tomorrow is too far away to hear.

5/29–30/81   (02100)

Galactic Explorer

For "Dr. Al" Karraker

The infinitesimal silhouette his verse describes,
Bouncing off farthest galaxies,
Tacking, like phantom catamarans,
Back across time's black lake,
Reentering his eyes' minute orbits,
Is that of a colossus,
*

Cloaked in gossamer robes,
Stalking the deepest reaches of his mind-sky,
Questing the cosmic needle
In eternity's haystack,
That he might stitch his ambitious metaphors
Into a magical chart-book
Stargazers can use to locate him
When his schizoid spirit quits its soaring.

6/1/81   (02099)

The Thorough Earth ^Δ

He moves ahead by fits,
Suffers amnesic fugues and dislocations
Every few weeks,
Stutters, halts, falls forward, balks,
Like a needle of an EKG machine,
Whenever he hears sirens
Or sees police. They arrest his thoughts,
Remind him of the Nazi-time
Before he fled Germany, for Amsterdam,
Then St. Louis, his heart's exile.

Although more years than forty
Have worn away the details
Of the horrendously gargoyled paranoia
That cathedraled his meek spirit
In those gothic seasons
When that latter-day Wagner
Stabbed and perforated the world's eardrums
With his necromantic baton,
He still detects, in his mirrored crow's-feet
And eyes, fear's lacy rose windows,

Yet suspects that beneath the smooth facade
His desired anonymity projects,
The old disease festers.
Today, he appears inordinately upset.
Whether it's graffiti
Splattered on the side-street wall of his sleep,
Cops pervading his TV screen,
*

Surrounding a shot president,
Or swastikas taped to his shop windows,
He can't say, this morning.

Perhaps the weight of sheer accretion
Is crushing his skull,
Exploding his brains, squashing his soul,
Like a dog run over by a semitrailer.
He collapses to the sidewalk before his store,
Blood seeping from his nostrils like lava,
His vested suit and gold watch fob
Forming a convenient shroud.
More than an hour elapses
Before anyone identifies his corpse.

Another forty-five minutes dissolve
While police, city coroner, and ambulance
Conclude their routine scrutiny
And eucharistic rituals of removing evidence
That might suggest death arrived and left,
Placing padlock on the door,
Quarantine cards on the windows.
Now, silence descends. The still earth,
Belatedly having satisfied its claim
On an escaped victim, begins its search again.

6/2/81 (00093)

Programmer

He sifts and, as they say today,
Processes all the data his dreams generate,
That he might know in a flash
And locate his destiny on a coded printout.

Each morning, over coffee and toast,
He conceives new images and ideas
That symbolize civilizations moribund and rising,
Synthesize theology, philosophy,

And the inevitable political rhetoric of survival.
Instead of typing onto a screen,
Via computer keyboard,
He pens his input into a notebook

That illuminates his energized psyche
From dawn, through yawning, to sweet sleep.
Its pages conform to his abbreviations only.
His visions are both the medium and the message.

Obsessed by loneliness,
The occupational hazard every operator knows,
Who spends awake time deciphering stimuli
Impinging on consciousness, he enters it,

Not in its palpably agonizing form,
Rather in metaphorical guise,
That his apparatus won't reject it, on sight,
As an inimical force capable of exploding his circuitry.

Having recorded all source material
Accumulated since last transmission,
He scrutinizes its appearance
Before sending it off to the heart's core,

For final updating, collating,
Eventual readout as completed poem.
Then, pressing forgetting's "Delete" key,
He turns to the next empty page and waits.

6/3/81   (02053)

Resurrection

My dormant, torpid body
Stirs from sleep's vague opiate vapors
And lifts into daylight,
Like a heavier-than-air weather balloon
Struggling to overcome gravity
And gather the most recent readings
On the human condition.

Through my eyes' portals,
Vision enters, oblique and translucent,
As though passing through alabaster corneas.
Unable to rectify the distortions,
My sensors collect raw data
And feed it to computers
Heated for squeezing meaning from sunspots

And aberrations in the atmosphere.
Soaring, now, through fog,
Rising, on invisible thermals, into a sky
Whose anodized patina consists of clouds,
My precarious flying vessel
Arrives at its predestined setting.
Breathing at this height is completely futile.

I am thrall; all decisions, choices
Are subordinate to an inordinate force
Attaching its apparatus to jacks
Wired psychically to my head and heart.
I float in eternity's ocean,
A sweet, ambrosial Ishmael-seed
Hoping a hospitable shore will stop me,

Plant me in its galactic sand,
And let me grow, through fantasy,
Into a bloom fruiting among other blooms,
In Edenic serenity. Suddenly, I know
Why this altitude is so total:
Dying is 360 degrees;
Forever is the gone soul being drawn home.

6/4/81 — [1] (02051)

Aging Troubadour

The road home isn't even paved.
Neither proverbial gold
Nor good intentions hold incentive
For my metaphorizing mind
To forget the distance remaining
Or the miles already traveled.

Fatigue has defeated creativity,
Drained my major resource: energy.
No words flow as I go ahead,
Forced to focus on myself
Rather than allowing poetical divertissement
To guide me safely home.

This solitary moment,
In which I sense my own presence,
*

Is so wide, ten locomotives
Could scream through it, side by side,
Belching pure cocaine smoke,
And I doubt I'd notice them,

Let alone perceive they were meant
To remind me the psyche
Must never resign itself to introspection,
That insight most penetrant
Resides in seeing the world
Through all other eyes except my own,

And that invention is the crucial clue
To discovering human magic
In the universal rubric,
Whose paradigm is made of perpetual *now*.
Suddenly, I catch myself gazing at my face,
In the rearview mirror —

A cow afraid of its own shadow —
And draw back hastily,
To avoid detecting the monumental emptiness
My tired eyes suggest.
Up ahead, the highway divides.
I hesitate, then guess at my destined direction.

6/4/81 — [2] (02052)

Paradox

For David Braun,
who is the dream he articulates

For years, he despaired
Over not dreaming nocturnally
Or being able to wake and share with himself
Blueprints to futuristic cities,
Medieval altarpieces
Exhumed from forgetting's extravagant cathedrals,
Awards received for his verse,
Valor in wars,
Glorious medical and scientific discoveries,
Strides toward peace. He despaired incessantly,

Convinced that various chemical imbalances
And genetic aberrations were to blame
For his shameful inadequacy.
Deprived of night dreams,
He believed his intellect incapable of reaching
The psyche's northernmost slopes,
Recording the soaring roar of metaphors
Fueled by the heart's dark passions,
Imploding miles below his soul's volcano,
At its flaming crater's core.

When he died, an entire nation grieved.
Disciples of his writing
Viewed his presence lying in state. His eulogy,
Manipulated by wire services,
To fit space, praised his stoicism
In refusing to retreat from personal demons,
Dreaming his dreams in broad daylight,
And converting them, whole, into poetry,
Instead of reducing shadows to half-truth —
The quintessence of his restive genius.

6/6/81   (02050)

The Lesser of the Evils

The distinguishing thing
I detect about this Monday morning
Which links it to all days spent
In this rural-mid-Missouri
Five-star "bedroom community"
Is its migraine desolateness.

To my eyes and psyche,
It feels like a Dreiserian sentence
Fumbling desperately to crawl free from briars
Or a buzzard trying to light
In a tight red locust tree —
One of a hundred million Mondays.

Sometimes, I wonder what has kept me here,
Let me expose my children
To Orwellian education among pigs and cattle,
Whose hog-trough talk
*

Harks back to preliterate sages
And whose ambitions rarely transcend the glands,

Why I hired on as a factory hand,
When all my advanced training
Suggested prestigious accolades in academe,
A sedentariness rivaled by the Greeks',
For its lofty self-aggrandizement,
Cum guarantees of early retirement, to write books,

Tracts, treatises, encyclopedias,
Oblique and erudite,
On the carnal hallucinations of Thomas Aquinas
And St. Francis of Assisi,
Or psychobiographies on the lives of Gulliver,
Diogenes Teufelsdröckh, Ike Snopes' inamorata.

I don't know yet what wild notion
Or providential design might have inspired me
To reside more than thirteen years
In this impoverished enclave,
Convinced me to submit my fertile brain
To its slave trade,

Where accomplishment is measured in inches
Of rainfall and in minutes required
To incite good old boys to riot.
I have no answers, only surmises,
As to why I exiled us
To an archipelago of such stark depravity.

Most likely, the pursuit of peace
And personal liberty and freedom of speech
Had some bearing on my original decision
To abandon civilization's cradle,
Reroot my family tree in sand,
Take a stand, in anonymity,

Against the most pernicious inhumanity of all:
Calling uniqueness heresy.
I suspect we came and stayed
Because here, at least, dishonesty and wickedness
Can't easily be misconstrued for truth,
And the enemy is a snake, not a rose.

6/8/81 (02049)

Ephemeralities

I refuse to contemplate the consequences
Of Israel's latest foray
Into Saudi Arabia,
To obliterate an atomic reactor,
Or America's oblique threat
To make a neutron bomb,
Nor do I anxiously await reactions from Britain,
Peking, Moscow, and Kuwait.

My psyche regards news, current and obsolete,
As fabricated feces, offal dropped
By fanatics, zealots, and the masses
Frightened by lightning,
Famine, plagues, firestorms, typhoons,
Evacuations that take the shape of trees
In a petrified forest — man's frantic antics,
Cast in scybala.

There is something terribly tautological
About trying to "stay current,"
"Keep abreast" of topical events,
Since they merely represent the daily pap
Spoon-fed to teachers and heads of state.
Determining one's destiny is an absurdity
Perpetrated, on meek, weak people,
By lunatics who seize power for a few hours,

Then relinquish it to cyanide
Or hang upside down, in naked effigy,
While a rabble passes in amnesic disbelief,
Squeezing penis and gonads superstitiously,
To reconfirm its own human neutrality.
Participating in fate's decision-making
Is a Mephistophelean process
The very rich cherish,

While the rest of us, poets included,
Are haphazard straw, ash,
Gaily colored confetti raining down,
Through the eddying winds.
Nothing can save us from the crush
Of impinging events nudging us over the edge,
*

Into history's abyss,
Like dust settling from a twisting gristmill.

6/9/81   (02048)

Sculptor and Sculptress

We spent so many years and hopes
Fastidiously chipping and chiseling away
At the mountain which lay before us,
Surrounded our lives,

Trying to liberate, from monolithic time,
A singular image of us both,
By which the world might know our love
As one of total devotion — a Grecian frieze

Arresting, weaving us mystically
In a great immemorial chase —
We possessed of Keatsian mellifluence,
Oblivious to religious zealots, feverish duces

Who might object to our nakedness,
Complain such perfection
Is attainable only in nature,
Skeptics uninitiated into the aesthetics of Eros.

But long before we completed the sculpture
Resulting from our collaboration,
Its life-size features
Began to erode invisibly from within.

Painless fissures issued from the heart,
Then burst to the surface,
As though the mountain we'd worked
Were a furrowed field, a frowning countenance.

Now, we two,
Who have abandoned all pretenses
Of creating godly art with our meager tools,
Spend tedious days of implacable toil

Removing rubble, assisting each other
Only when obstacles threaten existence,
*

Hoping to maintain minimal separate shelter
At the base of our collapsed dream.

6/10/81   (02047)

[The whole notion of growing up,] ^Δ

For Camp Nebagamon

The whole notion of growing up,
Getting older,
Changing noticeably,
Slowing down,
Is so vexatious to my enthusiastic soul
That I've never really taken time
To stop,
Turn back, and pass a whole moment,
Alone,
Focusing on all of forgetting's blur,
Never considered worthwhile
Locating the chubby little boy
Who, dreaming of becoming a man,
A poet and lover,
A romantic, roaming bohemian soul,
Tumbled out of youth's hibernal cave,
Into the world at large.

Perhaps it has been pernicious fear
Of discovering disparities
Between memory and fact
That has always effaced every temptation
To look backward.
Possibly, the lesson of Lot's wife's fate
Has kept me intact,
By discouraging curiosity and passion.
Regardless, I realize, today,
Why a sudden, vague sadness
Has spread its diaphanous, shadowy net
Over my forgetful brain: it's my child,
My own chubby little boy,
Getting ready to leave for the summer,
To attend camp in the same Wisconsin
Where I spent my boyhood . . . my child,
*

Preparing to leave his preciousness forever,
Enter twilight, die into life.
All at once, I know for certain
What has always mitigated
Against lingering on the past, reminiscing,
Mythicizing the actual,
Apotheosizing that which never really existed:
Death. To beat him,
One has got to marshal immediacy,
Conscript and enlist volunteers born now.
Only the most palpable *now*
Can defeat him.
Nostalgia weakens the spirit,
Devours the most venerable spirits,
Vitiates energy.
      I guess what has always guided me
Is the necessity to survive
By myself.
Doomed to hack new paths
Rather than lapsing into old routines,
I've declined to return.
Even now, my child must fly away
On his own. I refuse to weep
For what was,
No matter how bittersweet,
How incompletely perfect. Those moments,
Though beatific in retrospect,
Can't compare with the gentle remorse
I feel this very morning.
Ecstasy is me. I celebrate myself,
A spontaneous agent,
Ageless in my capacity to be excited,
Moved,
      to write the truth, as I feel it,
Through words.

6/11/81 (01358)

Monday Mornings Are for Shit

Monday morning is a real whore,
Crafty old clairvoyant,
*

A muse-witch who sees through my ploys
To buoy life by writing verse,
Attempting to invent purpose,
From fictive nothingness, by backing into truth
Accidentally. She's witnessed me,
Too frequently, emerging from weekends,
Into the fluid discontinuity,
Not to realize my need for self-fulfillment
By creating compensatory experience.

Although she'd never discourage me from searching,
I've sensed far too many omens,
Arriving as rain-laden clouds, snow,
Even blazing sun, some days,
Scratching my eyes like circular sandpaper,
Not to know that she promises neither relief
Nor success. At best,
She might provide access to the corridor
Leading toward Tuesday. More likely,
She'll regale in seeing me transmute truth
Into fool's gold, word-guano.

6/12/81   (02046)

Beware: Turtle Crossing

Turtles, seemingly static in their torpor,
Mark fortuitous passage
Across the precarious highway I travel.
The paradox shocks me to curiosity,

But June's humidity stifles my imagination.
Even capricious analogies
Droop like weeping cherry trees.
The brain dies from silence,

Which, just a few days prior,
When the season was profuse with seedlings
Exploding into delicate white petals
Shaped, silhouetted, and scented like my children

And fragile, blessed wife,
Ripened at the center of my spice fields,
*

Miles from the nearest intruder,
Liberating oblivion of its undisclosed poetries.

Now, no matter how I try
To elaborate the image of migrating turtles
Braving, with outrageous aloofness,
Instantaneous annihilation,

Searching interminably, intractably,
For the familiar, scratchy high grasses,
Where the opposite edge commences,
I'm unable to relate my situation to theirs.

Suddenly, the road I drive,
Stretching in measureless rectitude,
Refocuses itself in my perspective.
It's not long at all, rather wide.

Actually, this trip is a crossing
Between home and my unknown destination.
I pray my own speed is slow enough
For fate to avoid obliterating me.

6/15/81 — [1] (02045)

Tree House

Yesterday, we climbed a tree house
And, for a fleet eternity,
Transcended *now*, then entered a dimension
Neither divine nor timeless,
Rather measured in mind-suspensions,
Where ten-legged caterpillars,
Dangling from argentiferous branches,
Smoking opium, blew golden halos —
Love-essences — in our faces
And speckled butterflies wove reveries
Into a carpet sustaining our magical disbelief.

For hours, we ecstasied, drowsed,
Then descended into the immediate *now*
And rendezvoused with our two blond children,
Who, all the while we'd been gone,
*

Entertained themselves, playing games
Neither fabled nor bespelled,
Partaking of adulthood. Since then,
We've made only mediocre adjustments
To our old known world.
Discovering the Above, together,
Has left us alone, bereft, exiled forever.

6/15/81 — [2] (02044)

Ineffectual Spectator [△]

As I go south, in the river's parallel aura,
Traversing the verdant Delta,
From West Helena to Greenville,
My eyes sieve the steamy humidity,
To discern meaning from the land's design:

Combines winding their amber harvest
Out of the fields, onto spools
Revolving before them;
Groups of blacks, with hoes,
Weeding beneath the ferocious sun;

Tractors maneuvering through young cotton,
Spraying for owners
Who can't afford to pay for dusting planes.
All this activity presages the season
Which distinguishes this region,

Gives reasonable justification for its existence,
Whose economy owes its survival
Not so much to feudal ways
As to natural accidents and acts of God —
An abandoned Euphrates, forgotten Tigris,

A Nile-like civilization defiled by the few
Who would seek to squeeze poverty dry,
Conceive, in tenancy, the means
To riches and security,
By denying equality of opportunity to the rest,

Oppressed forever in legal servitude.
Driving south, I'm staggered by the abundance
*

Of poverty: ramshackle cabins
Outnumbering prefabricated "plantation houses"
Ten thousand to one;

Country stores and gas stations
Boarded up, defunct,
Other than for birds, snakes, and mice,
Derelict cars, idle biplanes
Parked beside trailers;

And, ubiquitously, the triumphant heat,
Proclaiming defeat of the enemy,
Man, in this doomed Dead Sea.
Relief is inconceivable except to me.
I'm destined to leave,

A free agent retaining my insular dignity
By having come and seen,
Reporting my findings, with poetical rhetoric —
Old Ike McCaslin
Repudiating his responsibility to life.

6/16/81 — [1] (00039)

Moses Unloosed

Having come so far,
Blowing the ancient shofar
Like a nomad or peripatetic tribesman
Crossing myriad wildernesses,
I finally settle in this encampment
And inquire after the wife of a Midianite,
To succor and quiet me
During the interminable lapses between journeys
To the edges and margins and peripheries
Where the mind's reason ceases
And the psyche's fantasies leap free
And reach for the limitless stars.

Nothing suffices, in this temporary oasis,
To render my surrender complete,
Which relies on total defeat,
Absolute retreat from the enemy, doubt,
*

Who would parade me, naked,
In barred pageant wagons, from country fair
To city circus, as a freak of nature,
A charlatan, fakir, a poseur
Skilled in the fine art of dissimulation.
I decline all offers to perform
Before the king and queen of sweet and sour
Hearts. I refuse to run nude,

When the rest of the world is content to hide
Behind and inside its flesh —
Ace of spades flying from the tight deck,
To connect with the reckless joker,
And the universe deals itself a fresh hand,
To rectify the cosmic mistake.
I slump into my fine white wine
And drown, while the tribe reassembles
In the tents of Dagon, discussing Goshen and Sheol.
Suddenly, I awaken from my soaring madness,
A broken poet, gazing homeward,
Hoping one day to quit my wandering.

6/16/81 — [2] (03573)

Shipwreck

All cargo shifts. The giant waves
Chew my vessel's decks
As though they were teeth of mighty Leviathan,
Eating through everything in their path.

I am wrenched overboard.
The ocean assimilates the ghost I disclose,
Like plankton washing into a whale.
I tread in the cold element,

Hoping for a phantom ship to slip past
And haul me aboard;
Only, no boats ply these lanes,
And the darkness refuses to relent,

Open, before sunlight stretches,
Breaking night's shackles.
*

I float in the vicious foam, minuscule,
Spawned of disaster and discontent,

Alone in this cold, silent zone
Inhabited by sleek, fluting creatures,
Sharks, and undulating mantas and eels
Hovering just above the floor

Covered with urchins, barnacles, and coral.
The sheer weight of murky volumes
Seals my silence. I am the ocean's ghost,
The broken poet, floating into shore, alone.

6/16/81 — [3] (03574)

Doomsayer

Day dwindles, diminishing, by inches,
Against the beady window
Separating air-conditioned inside winds
From fire-belching dragons held at bay
Just beyond night's twilight.

Demons just beyond ear's reach
Whisper banshee dialects
Meant to communicate their dissatisfaction with me
For staring at them. Actually,
My abstract gaze races past their auras,

Aiming at a far more sinister image,
Lifting along the glass
Not as shadow, rather black jaws
Locked in a wide yawn,
As though, any moment, they might close on the earth

And consume man's entire notion of progress.
Why I've been plagued
By nuclear hallucinations at a time like this,
And in such remote confines,
Remains unequivocally mystifying and vexatious.

Possibly, the total lack of physical activity
Required to entrance the imaginative spirit,
Let it resurrect itself from living death
*

And die into life, writing itself awake,
Takes apocalyptic energies

Whose very existence threatens the psyche and soul
With potential dementia,
Causes the host to set loose
Too many Medusas,
Producing Faustian Catch-22s

In which victim and victimizer exist
Within a simultaneous limbo
Whose myriad ambiguous exits
Lead to infernal regions at the brain's base —
Silos containing steaming atomic missiles

Aimed at my face and groin and feet.
I freeze, a breathing corpse
Anesthetized by fear, here in Oxford,
Where the same sun disappears by degrees
And starry darkness envelops half the universe.

As I drown in a sea of the sweetest Chablis,
Intimations of doom overcome me.
Something about my peaceful obliviousness
To forces rising in the silent east
Makes me suspect tonight's sleep might be eternal.

6/17/81 — [1] (03487)

Wishful Thinking

Before my brief life deteriorates
And succumbs to the voracious nematodes,
I would like to reverse civilization's projector
And watch and savor and revel
In the Hiroshima mushroom
Sucking itself up into diminishment.

My eyes would cherish the opportunity
To participate in signing the treaty
Concluding the War Between the States,
Return to Kitty Hawk, Titusville,
Sutter's Mill, Edison's East Orange,
Uninvent John Wilkes Booth.

Conceivably, history can recreate itself,
So that shameful assassinations,
Wanton assignations between revered politicos
And blissful lovers, and impeachments of presidents
Won't occur with such frequency
Or predictable attribution to human error.

Possibly, the course of man's events
Will deviate from lascivious entrapments and trysts
Long enough for him to isolate pernicious bacilli
And viruses responsible for cancer,
Devise alternatives to polluting drinking water
With DDT, Agent Orange, Zyklon B.

Maybe I'll outlive overwhelming probabilities
Of disintegrating in an atomic flash,
Wasting away in a hospital bed,
Or dying behind the collapsed steering wheel
Of a ninety-mile-per-gallon vehicle
Made of tissue paper, tinfoil,

And model airplane dope, maybe,
Provided inimical forces
Sponsored by the Moral Majority,
Professional golf, and the all-volunteer army
Don't discourage further search for solutions,
Tuck us too comfortably into bed

En masse. Maybe I'll survive
Despite the bleak prognosis for the disease
Which has descended as a plague
Neither medieval nor contemporary,
Rather pervasive, the chronic debilitation
Suffered by man: fascination with sameness.

For now, I must satisfy my desire to exist
Outside society's pale, as a pariah,
By remaining a writer of mystical poems,
A bum uninterested in clothing,
Money, or coveted interviews
On the *Mike Donahue*, *Phil Douglas* shows,

Hoping, nonetheless, the day may come
When making verse will be considered the epitome
*

To which people might aspire
And afterwards succumb to the worms,
Knowing they're being eaten
By even baser creatures than themselves.

6/17/81 — [2] (02043)

Writing in Flight

Cruising along this highway, north,
Like a forlorn goose flying smoothly and silently
Against day's haze-shimmering horizon,
I aim homeward, alone,
Leaving the mid-South in siege,
Its harvested fields burning infernos
And city streets rivers of oozing magma,

A hero victorious while in retreat
From permanence, a soldier of fortune
Already off to his next campaign
Before the spoils are divided,
A spirit not wholly nomadic
Yet given to roaming, consorting with the road,
Whose heritage is the varying seasons

And destination ten thousand places
Exactly like this nowhere zone
Over which I'm soaring right now.
For too many years, I've commuted
Between life and death,
A cipher whose statistic is still viable,
An unexpired probability

Willing to submit, daily, to circumstance,
For the sole chance of surviving forever.
Such grandiose presumptuousness,
Although absurd to a fault,
Sustains my immitigable ambitiousness,
My obsession with immortality,
Leaving navigable shadows behind,

Creating visible slipstreams
Wherever I've flown in search of verse,
*

That those who never knew my voice
Might hear, in the winds,
My musical mellifluences, word-notes,
And sing themselves safely home
To mistress, mother, children, wife, muse.

I'm a tatterdemalion goose,
Neither footloose nor fancy-free,
Rather wild as raging Ahab,
Crazed like wandering Ulysses,
Flying my destiny in every direction
It's willing to take me,
Scribbling insights and prophecies

Like a skywriter designing lines,
In pure white, over the troposphere,
Hoping that those who can't hear me
Might at least see my passage,
Written longhand, in flight,
Printed on oblivion's page —
My travelogue illuminated for the ages.

6/18/81   (03575)

Invisible Man

I pass into the gray rain and through it,
Penetrating day
Without leaving a trace.

My chalky pastels smudge.
Facial features fuzz, merge nervously
Into indistinguishable effacement, then dissolve

Like water guttering off a pitched roof.
Now, I'm completely invisible
To the naked eye,

Myself a naked manifestation of a ghost.
Nobody in this local café
Knows that what he sees is not me

But the persistence of memory,
Which substantiates myriad preconceptions
Each has fashioned by which to perceive my presence,

Imagine my inconceivable intricacies.
Even I feel lighter than usual today,
Not so much weightless as empty,

The ultimate halving half-life
Of the last eviscerating atom in the universe,
Not dust, cosmic ash,

Rather silence tightened down
To its final notch,
The complete cessation of being's apparatus.

As I sit here, sipping liquid,
Listening, through the absolute galactic distance,
To spherical music, voices,

Noise void and indecipherable,
Rising, like heady balloons, into space
Before exploding inessentially,

I realize, this time,
The rain may have washed me clean,
Succeeded in absolving me of mortality.

On leaving, I notice all heads
Gazing in my direction, with abstract stupefaction,
As if witnessing a dead man waking.

6/19/81 (02042)

God in Three Persons: Ahab, Ishmael, and Me

This Monday-oriented morning
Is a Melvillean odyssey
Materializing through disparate reflections
Lifting from my coffee cup.
Genies, phoenixes, and demons,
Disguised as insights, rise to my eyes,
Penetrate their murky humors,
And burrow obliquely into consciousness,
Partaking of a strange, diaphanous attenuation,
Like a protracted carcinoma.

I am both Ahab and the whale,
Imbibing myself a tentative sip at a time,
As if each hallucination
Swirling up out of the steam
Were awash with mind-diatoms,
A voracious leviathan
Consuming itself not for food
But reassurance that it's still alive,
Corporeal, mortal, amphibious,
A monster unnoticed in the cosmic ocean.

I swim in two seas simultaneously,
Driving deep to the cup's bottom
Whenever I intuit vision's harpoons
Flying through the silence,
Breaching when my lips grip the edge,
Tip the universe heavenward,
To let the hot liquid containing my image
Cascade into the body electric,
Waiting to alchemize its constituents
Into unimagined reciprocals of its original.

Suddenly, we reach impasse.
Cessation results not from satiety,
Rather natural consequence.
Neither stomach nor brain
Can tolerate the constant caffeine barrage
To which my raging spirit
Has subjected each, on its desperate quest
After the perfect catch:
The sleek, shimmering semblance of perfection,
Apotheosis of demon/truth — the poem.

Once again, barbed gaffs
And sharpened harpoons are clean,
Bleached ropes unbloodied;
Even the metaphor-nets, although wet,
Are empty of conceptions.
Now, the vessel and its watery parts disappear.
I, the only survivor, am left
To write whatever forgetting might remember
Of transmuted half-truths,
Fractured approximations of godliness.

6/22/81 (05765)

Fashioning Word-Chimes ^Δ

Getting started is the hardest part,
Being drawn into the spawn, gone,
Surrounded by profound sound, drowning,
The senses surrendered to endless invention,
Slaves to quavering waves
Straining to drain off the brain's complaints.

Once I'm resigned to the redefined design
Materializing in the mesmerized eyes' miasmas,
The rest — questing suggestiveness,
Recording the origins of metaphors,
Harvesting the farthest, darkest star-gardens —
Is as easy as squeezing meaning from freezing reason.

6/24/81   (05766)

Willy's Terminal Condition

Sometimes, I actually believe
That this lassitude, which subdues me daily,
Is a passing phase,
A malaise evanescent, if not ephemeral,
Meant to awaken me to the distance
Existing between my present position
And my ambitious, wish-driven capriciousness,
Which would dissociate me from my mortality,
Committing my spirit to living history.

But rationalizations of this magnitude
Serve a flatulent purpose:
Inflating my empty self-esteem with vaporous gas,
Causing very temporary digressions
From the banal routines of breathing,
Defecating, the ineluctable disengagement of brain.
Even I recognize truth
Leering at me, with gargoyle sneer,
From the rearview mirror we share,

Realize that ennui and I are coevals,
Symbiotically inextricable.
Together, we survive life's blatant alternative —
*

Breathless sleep —
Sleeping in a constant state of wakefulness,
As days located along the highways
I choose to take
Fade into each other, with outrageous sameness,
And years rust like derelict tractors.

Sometimes I actually believe
Nothing at all can assuage my distress
And that this contemptible lassitude
Is my providential punishment
For the sin I committed by allowing myself
To be conceived and born —
A graceless, insensate deformity
Placed here to take up precious space
Both living and when buried,

A walking exclamation point
Emphasizing the world's most eloquent expletive,
"Fuck" . . . or is it "shit"?
My existence, resigned to repetition,
Is all too palpable, too certain.
Tonight, I'll draw the curtains
In another motel, recite the Lord's Prayer,
And submit to immitigable demonizations,
Before returning to hell, to serve my time.

6/25/81 — [1] (02389)

Tamer of Wild Beasties

The empty pages in this notebook
Are a prestidigitator's circus cages,
Waiting for the first wave of his mystical wand
Before rolling to center ring,
Filled with whatever fabulous creatures
His capricious will conceives. These cages rattle
Even when no shapes stir or pace
In the spaces between their horizontal bars,
As though ghosts from ancient incarnations
Were crowded invisibly within,
Eager for another chance to materialize
And prance to his muscular wrist,
*

Dance before the whiplike tip he brandishes,
Leap from platform to precarious perch,
Fly through rings on fire,
Rise to pinnacles of physical eloquence,
Reveling in their own apotheoses,
The act climaxing in a roar of disappearing metaphors,
As the magically acrobatic tamer
Turns the page and, racing away
To prepare for his next demonstration,
Stares ahead, at the empty main-ring cage,
Amazed at being saved again from a ghastly fate.
He's always feared being eaten alive by silence.

6/25/81 — [2] (02615)

Katy Station

The stained-glass fanlights in this place
Etch dusk on my impressionable brain.
My eyes surrender to rainbows
Stretching, at clerestory level,
The entire length of this renovated station
From Victorian days, when steam prevailed
All along the railways
And people believed in the efficacy of progress
And peace, no matter what price
Or sacrifice. My ears strain to hear echoes
From ghosts these old bricks remember.
My bones reverberate,
Although no trains berth here
And the passengers who cross these portals
Depart with full bellies, inebriated,
Ready for youthful lovemaking.

I frequent this anachronistic depot
Neither deceived nor disappointed by changes
This "historic monument" has undergone
But, rather, pleased to be able to relax,
Sip chilled Chablis
In air-conditioned ease, and release tensions
Observing, writing poesies, being absolutely anonymous,
For the press of myriad "travelers"
*

Passing through. I admire my privacy,
The exiled status my existence has achieved
Among all those who don't know me
Or might even imagine me the next genius
In the panoply their unborn children will read
And apotheosize in college. Meanwhile,
I flash on the stained-glass fanlights,
Pretending the rainbow's end begins here.

6/25/81 — [3] (02616)

Alfresco

Having run three miles,
At the local high-school track, and showered
In my motel room, I now relax
Outdoors, under a diminishing sun,
Below a Cinzano umbrella, sipping Chablis,
Marveling at the smooth, pewter dusk
Softly rusting the horizon,
Reveling in lesbian ladies smoking, drinking,
Conversing about their imaginary lovers,
And dream of being acceptably goatish,
Reciting Omar Khayyám, Keats, and Shelley
To very unvirgin maidens.

The late afternoon fuses into evening
Unnoticeably, as I record my emotions
In rhyme-tones, trying to fashion verse
From terse twilight rhapsodies,
Create glorious insights from shadows
Insinuating themselves, like subtle arguments,
Into night's myriad dialogue.
Slowly, the wine finds its inevitable level
In my psyche. I begin writing
Colors, textures, glints, and gentle scents,
As if my senses were attached,
By a stethoscope, to God's pulse,

As though my entire being were connected,
By a mystical umbilical cord, to a fetus
Growing from heaven's eye.
*

I see deeply into musical night,
Intuit the essence of everlasting pleasure
Brightening evanescently across the horizon,
While I sit here speculating on days
Not yet arrived and those already accomplished
And realize that *now* is forever
As long as I am willing to accept myself
As a latter-day savior
And life as a magic trick worth memorizing.

6/25/81 — [4] (02617)

Mystical Fix ^Δ

The empty page awakens to my touch.
No matter how much
I might wish to neglect its beckoning,
Its white promise urges me out of hiding.

I abide with its clandestine silence,
Ride its smooth waves into shore,
Before realizing that its destructive element
Is my own inhibited imagination.

Slowly, I climb night's mountainside,
Rise to the pinnacle of excitement,
Then plummet in the violent rock slide
Aggravated by changes of climate in the psyche,

A pioneer lost in the distant wilderness,
Caught up in the heights,
Destined to experience extraterrestrial delights,
Northern lights reaching inwardly,

Beyond night, into the eyes I use
To see through the emptiness,
Imagine symbols and metaphorical mirages
Capable of evoking universal truths.

Suddenly, the page fills up with writing
Internally rhymed, divided into stanzas,
Verse emoting compassionate word-courage,
Singing of things unearthly,

Bringing into synthesis diverse prophecies
Gathered from foreign sources.
I gaze, with unutterable amazement,
On what I've made without trying: this poem.

6/25/81 — [5] (01346)

If Youth Knew and Age Could

Whoever conceived and cast into clichéd statue
The apothegm "Youth is wasted on the young"
Was an unschooled sculptor,
Ignorant of the proper tools and their use
For chipping, from ignorance, truth and beauty.

The children we were and become
Or bequeath the world, from our older selves,
Are eternal figments of the vernal equinox,
The east-rising, orange, screaming sun,
Lovers first discovering each other's blush.

Not one blunder, exasperated gasp,
Or sigh of ineluctable wonderment
Has ever shattered the newness youth reflects
In its looking glass or rendered useless
Myriad illusions of boundless hope

Inherent in the extended summer that comes once
To each of us, then lapses irrevocably.
Never has any spirit forfeited its franchise
On suppleness, muscularity, and enthusiasm
Or the inchoate soul refused to grow.

The fool who believed he'd isolated truth,
Pontificating, from envy or perverse solitude,
On the questionable virtue of not squandering spring
While winter still lurks surreptitiously,
Waiting to annihilate crocuses, forsythias, and fruit trees,

Surely must have circumvented childhood
Or forgotten all he'd ever learned
About invention, caprice, whimsy, imagination.
Only a fool or an uninspired sculptor
Could possibly wish to deny his birthright

By trying to appropriate those qualities
Which belong solely to another time
And, thus, produce a hybrid, a monstrosity,
Michelangelo's abandoned slaves, Don Juan
Forced to submit to a prostate operation annually.

Youth *is*, and age assumes its duties
Systematically. Nothing is squandered or gained,
Save according to fate or predestination.
If, indeed, regrets are germane,
It might rightly be said that death must inevitably intervene.

6/26/81 — [1] (02618)

Stalled in Columbia: Friday Night

Having opted to pass this Friday night
On the road rather than pressing toward home,
With fatigue's necromantic bag of tricks
Riding in the front seat, beside me,
I now languish in Columbia's oasis,
Swilling wine, like beer, from oversize glasses,
Eyeing the naiads dressed to kill, in tight fashions,
Writing seminal (or are they semenlike?) poems
In the notebook I carry everywhere with me —
My Linus-blanket, the atavistic womb
That satisfies my cosmic loneliness, my doom,
Whenever intimations of sadness intrude.

Sitting here, surrounded by happiness and laughter,
Aware that these myriad people
Share the distinct advantage of being connected,
Attached to each other, while my umbilical cord
Floats off in space — a severed hose
Providing no fresh breaths, no support —
I begin to hallucinate, fantasize.
The adroit ladies, so blondly enticing,
Darting in and out of tables, like gold carp,
Stimulate my primal instincts,
Transfigure my mild, retiring demeanor
Into Clark Kent's coeval, a flying freak,

Whose blood, commingled with chilled Chablis,
Bubbles. I reach out timidly
*

To the nearest unsuspecting Lois Lane
Who might rearrange me into the unknown poet
Whose cryptic attributes might obliquely suggest
A special human being beneath my glasses.
But none of the ladies pays attention
To my quiet dementia or makes the effort
To investigate my eccentric silence.
I neither wait nor deliberate
The possibilities, rather regard my chances,
For making a liaison, almost totally baseless.

Without warning, three college girls,
Unable to find a berth in this crowded port,
Beg respite at my table.
Naturally, I acquiesce. My senses boil
As I listen to their innocence,
Imbibe their naiveté, trying ineffectually
To empathize with the urgency of their cosmology.
Suddenly, the one closest to me,
Whose bone-thin arms, Modigliani face,
Perfectly formed, sandaled toes,
And subtly sculpted, restless breasts
Arouse me to indescribable heights,

Leans into the formerly unassailable privacy
I've maintained around me, like a moat,
And dislodges the perfect symmetry of my vigilance.
I not only allow her to enter
But make the penetration painless. . . .
Looking back now, I never would have guessed
That my suffering was so total,
Lacking, inutterably, that simplistic compassion
She was able, so naturally, to provide
Merely by taking my hand, a stranger's,
Kissing my parched lips, inviting me
To participate in the beginning of a relationship

That would take flight high into the night,
Light in her Spartan room, her delicate bed
Strewn with gardenia petals
And the scents of orchids delicately suspended in space.
But the progression was accomplished,
Haloed in ecstasy engendering from inexplicable whim
She had pursued. To this day,
*

I am unable to adequately explain how it occurred
Or why she might have volunteered me
To be her accomplice to such fantasy,
When all I pretended to be, from the outset,
Was a poet commissioned, by God, to witness and record this scene.

Nonetheless, she captivated me,
Unbalanced my counterweights, changed my time
To daylight savings, in which touching and tasting
Displaced the unsophisticated fears I'd known
All the years of my inhibitions.
To this day, I have no idea why
She took me to husband her wifedom,
Pretend I might protect her, that singular night,
From the oppressive demons Satan sent
To defeat her as she indulged her blessed pleasures.
Yet she singled me out of that madness.
Undoubtedly, she was the muse assigned to my decline.

6/26/81 — [2] (02619)

Ghost Writer

Despite this late hour,
Words still urgently devour me,
In their importunacy. I cower,
Praying their appetite isn't so voracious
That to satisfy their carnivorousness,
They will require my soul.

I'm so tired, the very thought of sacrifice
And taking energetic flight
Is beyond my imagination, my creative scope,
Yet I've never declined the chance
To record circumstance in verse,
Invent stars for uncharted galaxies.

The music insinuates my ears with spears
That provoke me to evocation,
Stir my hearing to new acuity.
Slowly, metaphors ignite,
Blaze into prairie fires, spewing volcanoes.
From the ashes, spoken smoke rises.

Now, even my eyes can't follow the lines
Filling up, for their shimmer.
Focus contains images in its strict grasp,
Although the pen trips mystically across the page,
Moving to some invisible rhythm,
Forming letters at the speed of sound and light.

Why this perverse curse dogs me
Whenever I travel, I can't fathom,
Except to suspect that my own ghosts
Motivate me to scribble my signature freely
On any space, hoping to communicate with me,
Express their displeasure with my facility for confession.

6/26/81 — [3] (01345)

Two Days in the Life of Willy Sypher, Purveyor ^Δ

Again, the men gather for two days,
To breathe in the hype, be inspired,
Imbibe the host of new clothing
Emanating from the head table. They banter
Like high-court judges, disciples of Christ —
A stadium of nameless faces, faceless names,
Their clichés for sales techniques
Ricocheting like basketballs off backboards.
They apotheosize vernacular and nomenclature
For tailored suits and slacks,
Fashion-import sportscoats. They chatter
Between transitions, like frenetic chimpanzees,

While I sit, shivering, back in the corner
Of an air-conditioned sanctum
Pinnacling this Midwestern city,
Exiled to my own private despair,
Not exactly pariah,
Rather road peddler, old pro
No longer motivated by pride or ambition
To exceed my previous year's bookings,
Compete for additional commission points,
Mule sample lines and swatch cards
*

From stall to stall, woeful and brokenhearted
Over not being able to quit,

Fearful of having my associates expose my apostasy,
In their trial by fiery rhetoric
And flatulent eloquence, to which I can't rise,
Embracing new fabrications,
Uniquely recycled designs,
Entirely resigned to my decline
Yet unable to forget the inevitability
Of having to make a living
With the only tools I've utilized for decades
(Dissimulation, horse trading, cajolery,
Sycophantish fastidiousness) — in short,
A total sell-job of soul and body.

The meeting gains zealous momentum.
Previously dissenting voices fuse.
Thinking coalesces into a common gospel
Each can take to his customers.
Isolated in my despondency, I resist commitment.
Discomfiture and squeamishness
Barely remain quiet inside their disguise
Of public equanimity and easy equability.
Suddenly, blood rushes to my brain;
Dizziness sunders equilibrium.
I grow faint, collapse in my seat,
My head slamming to the table.

Awakening is a surfacing through murky volumes,
A ranging back, through a sticky maze,
To conscious recognition of familiar faces
Focusing nervous concern,
Like gentle, warm rain, over me.
For the remainder of the meeting,
My presence provides a catalyst.
I seem to have achieved martyrdom —
The heroic old pro devoted to his vocation,
A credit to the profession, a road peddler
Among less dedicated men, a giant
Flying home to be greeted by universal admirers.

6/29–30/81 — [1] on 6/30 (02388)

[Balding and gray-haired,] ‡

Balding and gray-haired,
The majority bespectacled, chain-smokers,
All imbued with the aura of Oriental purveyors,
Whose camels are laden
With precious, delicate gold-laced fabrics,
Soft, lush damasks and velvets and brocades,
Whose treasure chests contain fashions
Coveted by kings, emperors, and shahs,
They convene to standardize their public image,
Reassess their position within the trade,
Forecast potential achievable targets,
Attainable market shares.
An ancient OPEC,
Mysterious, extravagant, exotic,
Boasting inordinate possibilities
For multinational unilateral agreements
Struck, in the name of secretive cohesion,
Among allies and enemies, alike,
This Sephardic cartel,
Having arrogated to itself special powers,
Meets to

6/30 — [2] & 7/2/81 (02387)

Mixed Addictions

A constant smooth swishing chews my ears.
It's not ordinary music
My instincts hear but a low moaning,
Like a foreboding banshee's distant droning
Or an old man snoring toward death,
Forlorn and alone in a rented tenement room
Adjacent to the groaning el.

Something funereal about the revolving tires
Sets up a sympathetic vibration in my bones.
I'm vaguely conscious of flying home
In a spectral vessel,
Insulated from all recognizable landmarks.
Forgetting settles into my cells
Like waters flooding seeded Delta fields.

Abruptly, I awaken from my mistaken identity
As the car screws through weeds,
Strewn in screaming blue and purple blurs,
Off to the right. Fear grasps the wheel.
Adrenaline guides me back
Onto the highway, as unrelated metaphors
Continue orbiting in their foreign courses.

Driving westerly, I ponder the process
Which, in its hypnotic swishing,
Nearly arrested my unsuspecting spirit,
This anesthetized morning. Whatever spell
Squeezed visions of broken levees
And screeching Chicago trains
From my brain's mesentery,

Forcing such disparate images into existence
By evacuating them out imagination's anus,
Must have emanated from a resident sorcerer
Or wayward alchemist,
Who, apprehending my death-oriented express,
Tried to waylay my destiny,
Change me into eternity's spokesman,

A mystical poet capable of explaining God's mysteries
In mortal strains. Yea or nay,
I've somehow survived fate's wiliness,
Eluded the hairy legs
And grotesquely expanding fangs
Time's spider flashes from its netted lair.
Maybe it's the mixed metaphors that keep me alive.

7/6/81   (05767)

628 West Columbia ^Δ

> *For my beloved Janny,*
> *on our eleventh anniversary,*
> *7/8/81*

On the occasion of your extended absence,
I've taken to gazing at our house.
The enchantment with which its curved facade,
Eaves, gingerbread, widow's walk,
Turrets, and peaks captivate me is fantastical.
*

It is intricately carved orient ivory,
Pieces inside pieces, my eyes' touchstone,
A white, shimmering crystal palace,
A meteor brightening the daytime sky.

It is also a metaphor quite Victorian,
Slightly Gothic in its imagistic eloquence,
Partaking of Elizabethan exaggeration,
A castle that keeps my mortality warm,
My tiny princess, prince,
And queen safe from invaders and plagues,
A museum our shared heritage decorates
With Gobelin-woven hopes
Tapestried into gardenia-scented dreams
Of, one day, bequeathing to people,
Through our poems, paintings, gentle teaching,
The secret of saying to each other
(Oh, those echoing articulations!),
"I love you!"
And "I love you, too!"
Such sweet simplicities as these
Elicit so much jubilation
Nothing can sway us from our basic natures.

We are one of the chosen families,
A frangible cluster He cast into a galaxy
Too vast to categorize
Other than by arbitrary naming: man.
This house, on which I gaze today,
Although temporarily empty,
Is the edifice He assigned to our ancestral destinies,
Eternity's earthly home,
Waiting for its blessed residents to return.

7/7/81   (02271)

Mystical Union: An Adoration ^Δ

> *For loving Jan,*
> *on the eleventh revolution*
> *of our wedding*

Eleven years ago this moment,
Ocean and land joined hands,
*

The sky held its breath,
While you and I, Jan,
Celebrated our own fusion of soul and bone,
In San Francisco's misty Sutro Park.

That cornflower morning,
You, draped in antique crocheted lace —
A nymph born of that glorious day —
And I, in workshirt, jeans, and boots,
Both swigging Chianti,
Pinching hunks of raisin bread

From a freshly baked loaf,
Exchanged "forever after"s, with our eyes
And nervous laughter. We tasted grace!
Ah, that irretrievable "just yesterday"
Seems so terribly recent
Yet so impalpably far, far away

From where we are this very moment,
Sipping Chablis, alfresco,
In midtown St. Louis, at noon,
Reminiscing, in gentle, dizzy whispers,
About that sacred act
And its rituals, fashioned to fit our idiosyncrasies.

The hiatus between now and then
Is an endless instant
Measured agains two blessed children,
Poetry, paintings, home, goals, a purpose —
A blend of private personal accomplishments
Meant to complement each other

Rather than indenture us to conventions
Aging nets over one's head and heart.
With invisible grief rising to exultation,
We toast that mystical moment and this,
Knowing ocean and land and sky
Still reverberate with our abiding love.

7/8/81 (00111)

Les fleurs du mal

Mimosas, hibiscuses, and lilacs
Soften and preen against morning's acetylene fog,
Hover in gentle suspensions
As if hung from invisible strings —
Such delicate, singing things, these blossoms!

I hardly deserve such exotic figments
Fingering my eyelids,
Pink mimosa blooms, especially,
Approximating sea anemones pulsing, pulsing,
Undulant creatures ignorant of their own beauty,

Hibiscuses, too — so arterial purple!
I dive headfirst, slowly flowing
Into the tender Zen of their glazed openings,
Hoping to reverse growth,
Appropriate their languorous vaginal scent.

But the opiates, illusory female perfume,
Lose poignancy as my olfactories
Extract and savor them,
Try transmuting them into hallucinatory shapes
Capable of consuming my waking days with bemusement.

Soon, I withdraw from the soft fog,
Retreat indoors, for coffee,
Before exiling myself to the world of sounds,
Where human tongues — flowering kudzu —
Choke themselves and everything else around.

7/9/81 (02040)

[Each sentence gyved to this page,] † Δ

Each sentence gyved to this page,
In endless horizontals,
Is a fence separating one breath
From the next, image from idea.
Each is an invisible guy wire,
A net, each contiguous pair of lines
Forming a channel of the maze
Through which my thoughts run helter-skelter;

7/10/81 (02039)

Charlotte's Comet

For my mother,
on her special birthday:
sixty-six

We celebrate your orbiting progressions,
Each July 17,
Witness your comet's light show
As it passes rapidly through eclipse,
Emerges just west of us,
And resumes its harmonious, flowing trajectory,
Toward its own unknown destination.

With every new year,
You're supposed to grow older,
Appear different, change holistically,
Yet none of us
Who has studied your celestial fluctuations,
With scientific curiosity,
Can either detect cosmic deterioration

Or project potential deviation from patterns
Whose idiosyncratic characteristics
We've come to expect and regard with awe
And profoundly deep inspiration.
Our affection, respect, and love for you
Are Saturn-rings revolving about your sphere,
Halos attracted to your angel-glow.

Although periodically we lose sight of you,
We've never doubted
Your phenomenal light is any less bright
Through whatever heavenly sector
You might be flying. We've had faith
In the inextinguishability of your flame,
Your self-perpetuating core.

Just now, gazing in silent abstraction,
We see you coming into view,
Illuminating the horizon of our combined years,
Setting our shadows free, momentarily,
As we kneel in obeisance,
To pray for your safe passage through our galaxy
Today, next year, unagingly.

7/14/81 (02038)

Mr. Ladd

In commemoration of eighty years

If ever my best conceptions of Walt Whitman
Materialized in reincarnated eyes,
Sinewy body, quick, articulate intellect,
And anecdotic wit,
Surely they would coalesce in the guise
Of G. Carleton Ladd,

Who, in strength, Biblical wisdom, humor,
Is more man at eighty
Than any I've met
Half, nay one quarter, his age,
A man raised out of the earth,
Who chose to remain close to it

And still regards the sweet loam his home.
His sweaty vocation has pleasured him,
Let him linger among scents
Of mowed grass, mimosa blooms in summer —
Friend of pine cone, mole's foe,
Coeval of squirrels, birds, trees,

A communer with all God's children and creatures,
Quoter and composer of poetry
Redolent of Whitcomb Riley, Longfellow,
Oliver Wendell Holmes.
Wanderer in winter's cold and snow, also,
He bespells each day with private hopes

And public proclamations
Directed to all who fall into his audience
By accident or purposely,
Singeing them with flameless fire,
Rendering them inspired,
Rekindling their faith in self-reliance.

What ineradicable impressions
His being has made on my dreams and visions,
I will never completely fathom.
Still, his bottomless Ozark laughter,
Stoical Sunday demeanor,
Posturings as preacher, teacher, keeper of gardens

Have fashioned a unique image
Of an American individual
Whose likes, most likely,
Will not animate my life and spirit again.
You, Mr. Ladd, at eighty,
Loom gigantic in a land of antiheroes.

7/15/81 (02037)

The Natural Progression of Kings

For my blessed father

Saul's soul is a hallowed vessel,
Whose fantastical plants,
Flowering hourly,
Disclose a cornucopia of rainbows
Shaped like myriad halos
Above those whom he reaches, with merciful concern,
Each time he breathes or speaks.

His sweet, eternally compassionate wisdom
Is the flint-glint sunlight strikes
In an old lion's eyes,
A sagacity tempered by time trials.
He's a survivor of Cyclopean invasions,
Political intrigues, betrayals
By Tiresias's crew, disguised as Dante and Einstein.

Now, this scion of ancestral kings
Slips into retirement,
Relinquishing, with raging resignation,
Title, retainers, entourage,
And earthly throne — his desk —
Though not pride in the reputation
Integrity has taken fifty-two years to create.

Slowly, he goes in quest of familial ecstasy,
Dedicated to lavishing caprice
And whim on his wife and four children —
Rainbows he seeded and set in the earth,
Out of his flesh and blood,
Whose fruition confirms his original purpose:
To conceive handles by which God might move the planet.

7/17/81 (02036)

Willy in the Wilderness ^Δ

Upheaval keeps me from growing stagnant,
Slowing to putrescent humors,
Having ideas pulverized and blown away
In mind-typhoons and cyclones
One hundred and fifty miles deep.

Uprootedness perpetuates the destiny
Bequeathed me by the tribe.
I'm a Semitic Ulysses,
Moling his way homeward, daily,
Just below knowing's surface.

The howling owl, stranded in sunlight,
Ululant loon, rank buzzard
Approximate my soul,
In their loneliness,
Their unscrupled refusal to take wing

And soar despite endless movement
From one conquest to the next,
In their predacious peregrinations.
Beaked and beady-eyed,
We wear the same arrogant disguise,

Share the very same imperative to survive
By blending into our environment,
Camouflaged by silence.
Just now, my sense of direction is muddled.
Descending and rising are indistinguishable,

Under this hooded mantle.
Driving south, away from my wife and children,
Has confused my gyros and gauges.
I've navigated this unfamiliar terrain
A thousand times, forgotten why I'm alive

And the reason for my leaving hiding,
Earlier this morning.
Inexorably, upheaval gives way
To a weakening in the knees and solar plexus.
Breathing thins to fast gasping,

As where I've been
And my impending destination
*

Prepare to collide in violent chaos.
Somewhere ahead, my next victim
Waits to ply me with wine, bread, and bed.

7/20/81 — [1] (02035)

Idle Impressions

Dispossession is such an expressionless exercise,
I could die giving birth
To my feckless poesies, yet they sustain me
When all else fails to satisfy the psyche.

My destiny predates the Virginia settlers
And those the cold Massachusetts winters
Accepted provisionally.
I am the reincarnation of Increase Mather,

Edward Taylor, sermons decrying vermin
And apostasy against Christ's vision.
My mission in the New World
Is to proselytize freedom and free will,

The redemptive essence of preaching self-reliance
And individuality. I am Emily Dickinson,
Walt Whitman, Thomas Cole, and Mathew Brady,
Recording gore and bloody war scenes.

I recoil under history's extreme weight,
A Romantic tatterdemalion
Belonging not to Hamlin Garland, Mark Twain,
William Dean Howells, Henry James,

Rather to Stephen Crane, Theodore Dreiser,
Climbing inexorably toward modernity,
The spider's prey, history's victim,
The open boat's survivor,

Drouet's classy whore, Carrie —
Brooke Shields, Suzanne Somers,
Loni Anderson, Morgan Fairchild,
And a thousand other forgettable bodies and faces.

Soon, time will have superseded me, too,
Just as it has passed and forgotten the rest,
*

Without brooding. I'll grow fat,
Torpid as cataleptic worms,

Such that all my training and tutored study
Will be squandered on audiences
Disinterested and bored, supplanted by music
Conceived in studios, to harvest money.

Slowly, I fade as the sounds amplify.
Increase Mather gathers his cult;
Emily draws her devotees,
While Stephen Crane magnetizes his readers.

My poetry reaches deep into the heart,
To weld believers to its cause.
Together, we resonate in echoing melody,
As the past drifts into focus,

Appears, ghostlike, in our eyes and ears.
Slowly, the whole panorama of poets
Discloses its most closely guarded secrets.
We gasp, realizing truth and reason

Are the embodiments of treasonous free will.
We recoil, dreaming ourselves
Toward night's horizon, begging a ride
To day's edge, where metaphor ends.

7/20/81 — [2] (05768)

Navigating by the Stars

On this drive, my eyes forage the sky
For propitious signs.
Against a cloudless blue ocean
Washing the treetops' irregular shoreline,
An opaque moon, or its illusionary consort,
Arrested in three-quarter phase,
Floats like a boat under full sail,
A phantom sampan,
Edward Teach's caravel raised from the deep.

I gaze through portholes
Protruding from the hull of the cruise ship
*

Daydreams power
Like a flying carpet on which I've booked passage,
To be transported from mood to mood
Whenever I need to leave my dark harbor.
Momentarily, she dematerializes,
Lost to vision, beneath a tossing trough
Off to my left, in a valley.

As my vessel mounts an elongated crest,
I catch sight of her again,
Fading, fusing, about to efface
All remaining traces of her diaphanous shape.
Something about her lingering appearance
Causes me to speculate
On the nature of memory, death, and birth.
She is mother to all three,
My progenitor as well.

Nearing the city, I notice the ocean
Loading up with polluted vapors,
Like a vast eye hosting a growing cataract.
The sky ceases engaging my imagination,
Rather distracts me
With malevolent omens. As I enter
The outer reefs of hell's inner harbor,
Eunuch sun, the moon's suitor,
Slaps me. Seeing stars, I faint.

7/21/81 (02034)

A Day in the Life of Willy Sypher △

No Huckleberry Findelbaum am I
But Willy Sypher,
Peddler to the Midwestern territory
Serviced by Acme-Zenith Clothing,
Lighting out again, this lonely morning,
Not even hoping to open new accounts,
Just hold my own
Against competition and a limp economy.

The road has come to own me,
Dreams and soul, body, spirit, volition
*

(Synonyms line up at my heart's gate,
To gain audience with my popish tongue).
I've known so many homes,
These past twenty-five centuries:
Bedouin tents, nomadic oases, posadas,
Hostels, motels, boardinghouses.

Gas-station attendants, reservationists,
Waitresses, union musicians,
Bartenders are the ephemera
In my unchanging equation for transience.
Uprootedness is crucial to erosion.
The topsoil in the cradle
Through which I commute is constantly removed,
Replaced by newer sediments,

Yet I remain untouched
By each upheaval,
As I hustle overstocks and thirds,
Garments not quite perfect,
For mill flaws, manufacturing defects,
And hawk merchandise from swatch books,
Samples locked in my trunk,
Pushing worsteds and corduroys in July,

Cotton tropicals and whisper flannels in February.
Unfazed by such paradoxes,
I've grown accustomed to existence
Lived upside down, inside out.
Despite my marrying a Midianite wife,
Who raised two kids in my hiatus,
My entire life
Has been a night shift bereft of family ties.

Just now, I press westward,
Hurrying to arrive in time for lunch
With the buyer for Quicksilver's, in Tipton,
A mom-and-pop shop
I've called on for thirty-five years.
As I approach and park,
Signs splayed on the plate glass curse me:
GONE OUT OF BUSINESS — PERMANENTLY.

7/22/81 (00077)

On the Lecture Circuit: A Poet's Auto-da-Fé [Δ]

The parking lot is a potluck supper,
Whose spread consists of tourist vans,
Horse trailers, campers,
A solitary semi with its engine snoring,
Three bedizened motorcycles,
And the local armada of pickup trucks.

I've not been here in nearly a year,
Yet everything is just as I left it,
A time capsule containing memorabilia
Of Tipton's Crystal Café,
A Walker Evans documentary photo,
An arrested metaphor.

From indigenous Virgils, Homers,
And myriad Cincinnatuses
Gathering repast, sharing social repose
And moral succor, for the moment,
Over biscuits and red-eye gravy,
Smoked ham steaks, molten coffee,

Deliberating, debating, pontificating on milo
And rain, grain and swine prices,
The shameful state of slaughter cattle and hogs,
To eighteen-year-old waitress
Isolde Jones,
Disporting her perfectly juggled breasts

In a see-through blouse
And nubile butt in too-tight jeans,
Magnetizing the men's eyes like metal filings;
From the nondimensional full-length mural,
Depicting the Sierra Madres' snowy slopes,
To the neon-rimmed advertising clock,

Not a single item has shifted position
Nor any player quit the stage,
Changed roles in this daily psychodrama,
With one obvious exception, that is —
I no longer seem connected, affected,
Provoked to compose paeans and odes

To the mythic-proportioned Crystal Café,
With its Christian and Greco-Roman protagonists.
Perhaps time has dulled the eye
That filters blood of the Lamb and silk purses
From reality's sow-ears and turnips.
Possibly this place is still the gas station

Where I used to fill up
On my trips to Tipton and other remote regions,
Untouched by my volatile imagination.
Whatever the case,
I lament my inability to transmute truth,
Perform legerdemain on my psyche,

And lose myself, in a hallucinatory fugue,
Long enough to forget
My obligation to lecture on semiotics and prosody,
At the university, this afternoon.
Soon, I won't even remember how
To redeem drowsing dreams from my waking sleep.

7/23/81 — [1] (00584)

Inquiry into the Essence of Existence and Divinity ^Δ

For the last three days,
I've been circumventing God's wrath,
Barely escaping His physical anathemas,
Passing through this Midwest,
Cursed with disastrous flash flooding,
Power outages from lightning
Biting through wires, like shark teeth,
Collapsed shelters
Chewed and spit out of tornadic mouths.

Temporarily I relax with a glass of Chablis,
Pondering the accidental nature
Inherent in both survival and dying,
Wondering why I've been allowed to continue
My lifelong inquiry into existence
At a safe distance from the fathomless abyss.
*

Amazed by the profound naiveté
My poetical vocation has nurtured and perpetuated,
These forty years,
I set pen to paper and prepare to investigate

The religious implications of my seeming inviolability.
This way station embraces me,
Encourages metaphors to spawn and surface
With unhesitating poise — phosphorescent fish
Leaping over the Ancient Mariner's deck.
Providence and final cause
Witness the marriage of my visionary spirit
Groping to grab hold of the ladder
Reaching to heaven's trapdoor.

I climb time's stalactite-hung cave,
Then enter the endless dimension
Of indentured adventurers
Who sought the mystical elixir of immortality,
In youth and old age,
Failed, and were punished for their arrogance,
By being stranded halfway home,
Alone in crowded detention,
Their eyes sewn shut, lips stitched.

Traversing this lugubrious plain,
My flying mind finally arrives
At the celestial seat of all-knowing and mercy.
"Maker, I beseech Thee,
Tell me, please,
What distinguishes my soul from those who suffer
And, in suffering, know Your disapprobation?
Why have You granted me amnesty
From the lightning and floods, the killing storms?"

Soon, I sense the Sea of Silence part.
My shadow enters its lubricous path
And is bathed in celestial wetness,
Taken beyond its most rational threshold,
To the edge of ultimate insight.
My eyes record His message,
Whose blind revivification is the essence of life
Everlasting.
Suddenly, I shiver with His compassionate mercy,

A non-Christian born again,
In the Hebraic image of blessed Elohim.
Never have I known such peace
As in this haloed moment I comprehend and accept
As the justification for my inquiry into the Lord.
Suddenly, I grasp the reason for His leniency:
"In seeking shall ye find your reward."
This ceaseless refrain, translating His wisdom,
Reverberates in the words I write.

Now that the wine has penetrated my brain,
There can be no complaints.
All constraints have surrendered to inebriation,
And I rest my case,
With this rather unoriginal peroration:
"My innocence is appreciated, dear God.
In gratitude for Your having given me the freedom
To create, I am obliged to reciprocate,
By never defiling Your name

"Or deprecating Your gentle intentions
Before all those who will read my verse
Out of perverse curiosity
Or for diversion from loneliness.
I comprehend why my life has been spared
Despoliation, depravity, molestation
By forces that might distract me from Your word:
I am the poet of touch and taste,
Your blessed, perpetual son."

7/23/81 — [2] (02620)

Infatuation

Light still fills my eyes' pools
With stained-glass inspirations,
Tiffany-type phenomena,
Phantasmagoria related to the aurora borealis,

Whose musical fluctuations and vicissitudes
Set intellectual prairies afire,
Burn dry plains with astral inspiration.
Chablis creates an atmosphere

In which nubile female breasts and buttocks
And mythic faces grace my brain
With potential conquests, exaggerated profiles
Deliberately beautiful beyond belief.

I lapse into intransigent infatuations
With bodies floating on the air,
Imagining lush, writhing thighs
And wet nipples dripping godly milk,

Sleeping in sensual, gentle embrace,
Refusing to surrender to loneliness and solitude.
Startlingly, the young lady across the way
Rises, lunges toward me,

Accompanies her planned amazed leap,
Completely "spontaneous," into my stratosphere,
With her half-drunk glass of Chablis,
And lands in my lap and face.

Instantaneously, I experience love
For the first and ultimate time,
Open-armed, ready to accept acceptance
On whatever terms it sets forth,

An exile, a prisoner of war
Behind enemy lines.
I respond with the passion of Jezebel's consort,
A mere poet, blown away, obliterated

In the cyclones that race through space.
When I gaze over,
Her eyes are locked on mine.
Supine, annihilated, I surrender,

Her slave, ancient lover, motherfucker,
Anxious to subdue
And free her from all those cerebral demons
That have kept her captive to her willpower,

Devour her in the hour of her flowering.
Now, I announce myself,
Pronounce my male power over her meek femaleness.
Together, we immerse ourselves in elements

Phenomenal and destructive and essential
To animal nature.
In public, I undress her
And appropriate whatever she's been protecting,

All these years of her inexpressiveness.
Suddenly, the two of us
Shudder under the implications of our innocence.
We have found, in each other, blessedness.

7/23/81 — [3] (02621)

Fractionating Atoms

My leave-takings are so frequent
That our times together
Have assumed the status of visitation rights.

My wife no longer questions why
Or even grieves,
Except in the deepest recesses of privacy,

While my vexed boy, Troika,
And desperately insatiable daughter, Trilogy,
Express their disgust

And unassuageable reluctance to touch me,
Kiss and hug me,
On learning I'm returning to the road.

This particular morning,
I slip out of the house unperceived,
For their fragile breathing,

And enter the silence anonymity radiates,
As vulnerable to ridicule
As an original idea, tiny as a solitary firefly

Trying to illuminate the universe
By outshining the sun. Only memories of them,
Simulacra, persist,

As my physical self diminishes
And the prospect of dying alone increases
With distance. The miles are graves.

For hours, I rehearse my family's consternation
On waking — three little lives
Deprived of their tribal guide,

A displaced trinity of disbelieving survivors,
Seeds exposed, by erosion,
To the foul air. Suddenly, I realize

My feelings of guilt are not excuses
Brooding engenders or dispensations
Lugubriousness grants on long journeys

But, rather, irrefutable truths.
Whether at home or roaring away,
My heart is either orphaned or divorced.

7/29/81 (02033)

"It Seems like Fall" △

*For Trilogy Brodsky,
from Daddy*

As I drive south,
My thoughts, idle as dynamos at rest
Except those focusing on you,
Blessed Trilogy, and the phone call you made
Before motors and engines began to spin,
Fly in separate directions, like fire
Fanned by a gale, then fix
On your precious voice and its love message.

I consecrate this paean to you
With the title you specially requested,
Whose words refer to the anomalous air,
This late July,
Pervaded by too-cool Canadian breezes
Streaming down from Minnesota and Wisconsin.
Now, your whisperous conversation
Reverberates in my memory-caves.
I shimmer with residual amazement

And sympathetic compassion,
Remembering how you delineated
Waking before the others,
Determined, by your own prompting alone,
*

To phone me. I reflect on that act,
Knowing ineluctably
That you and I, my daughter,
Share, intact, an invisible umbilical cord
That nourishes our symbiotic temperaments.

Together, we spoke
While your mother and baby brother slept,
Just we two,
Discussing the nature of stone paperweights
Covered in purple "fur,"
Your final gymnastics class,
Which you didn't even get to attend,
And how many are the days remaining
Before school reopens,

So that you might calculate
When the roller-skating rink will commence —
Nine, seventeen days? Twenty-nine?
"Soon, dear one."
"How soon is soon, Dude?"
"Quick as mad, rabid rabbits mating,
Faster than Afghanistani mountain goats
Scaling the Matterhorn."
"Be serious, Daddy; I mean it!"

Driving south,
So totally out of earshot,
I still hear your fragile, groping voice
Beseeching me, between the lines,
To quit my desultory occupations
And resume my position in our family shrine.
Sensing the heart's grief,
My throat tightens, chokes off a whimper.
Mine is a tribe of lost, loving survivors.

7/31/81 — [1] (01454)

Practitioners of the Vernacular

Anyone who, with a straight face, can say,
"I ain't got but one"
And not suffer the slightest trace of anguish
Or guilt, for perpetrating, on the language,
*

Heinous effrontery,
Should be struck dumb
By some higher denomination of angels

Or at least publicly stoned
For condoning metaphorical rape, plunder,
And Visigothic molestation,
Instead of revered mimetically
By all who would emulate this very pattern
In daily speech, legal disputation,
And pulpit harangue. Now, ain't that so?

7/31/81 — [2] (00124)

The Fawns ^Δ

[For Jane Rule]

To have had your acceptance,
So total and unabashedly passionate,
Is to know that in your absence,
Long before memory commences
And forgetting lapses into occasional desperate groping
Through dark, drafty corridors,
Toward the shadowed shores of your hospitable eyes,
There will yet remain an unslakable tension
Between dying and ecstasy,
To sustain hope of again nesting in your sheltering gaze,
Redefining those soft-shaped contours
We kneaded out of a common clay,
Recapturing that fascination
So primal, kind, and defenselessly intense.

Might I have taken you away with me
Or, certainly worse,
Never engendered the courage,
That very first evening, in Oxford,
To converge on your mesmeric radiance,
Dare rearrange the spaces in our strangeness,
My somnolent heart doubtless
Never would have known such perfect irregularity
Or my dreams, born of chimeras,
Been transformed into soaring orient herons,
*

Nor, just now, would either of us
Possess such sweet preoccupation
Over the details of our inconvenienced destinies
Or savor the raging pain of our sequestration.

Ah, but indeed, dear and dearest friend,
Ivory child of my descending years,
Whom I retrieved from that forest-night
When porphyry sleep enclosed us
In deliquescent twilight
And forest and lovers became one entanglement,
From which neither desired extrication . . .
You and I must preserve and extend
Our unintentioned intimacy
Or else accept reprisals for self-denial
And futile remorse.
How pathetically regrettable it will be
If ever either one of us forgets
We are both dappled children of the same blessed doe.

8/8/81   (00156)

Desert Stirrings ^Δ

For the time we have
Together, today/tonight,
How can I,
Like an inscrutable cat
Seeking absolute attention,
Leap into your lap
And get you
To complete my leap to freedom,
By petting me,
Translating my purring words
Into something more
Than feline sensualities
Yet something less than
Leonine roaring,
Whose reverberations might
Quake the forest of the night,
Awaken you
To my forceful performance?

Perhaps by insisting you listen
And, listening, imagine me
Neither domestic cat
Nor maned lion,
Rather creature
Crouching in the sand,
Verging on lunging
Toward your straining ears,
A vital shape,
Evocation of dreams
You've stroked in previous sleeps,
About to bite,
Make your psyche bleed
And, bleeding, beg
My heart inflate your veins
With answers to my riddles,
A merciful Sphinx
Whispering plaintive refrains.

8/13/81   (02095)

[The sheer vacuum in which I fly]

The sheer vacuum in which I fly
Is incandescent light
Supercharged to the speed
At which memories of the future
Collide with Lethe's backward-rushing flood.

Within this brief immediacy,
All visions and dreams are submerged
Beneath the surface,
Just above which my psyche hydroplanes.
I don't even own my own direction,

Let alone know why I've been chosen
To outrace time
To its funereal destination.
Perhaps this morning is a corpse,
Intoxicated with embalming fluid,

Into whose cooling vat
My spirit has been gratuitously injected
By a maniacal Dr. Mengele,
*

In a demented attempt
To unite me with the prehistoric force,

The unicellular ooze and viral slime
Out of which I arose,
To reweave my DNA
Into a creature more metaphorical,
Responsive to things unseen,

Undreamed, inconceivably enlightening,
Instead of dead, deadly,
Deadening as topical sprays.
Maybe I was meant to simply disappear
Without a trace, be buried in the air

Before anyone who might identify me
Awakens. Possibly,
I'm neither slave nor victim
Of my own fiendish machinations and vagaries,
Rather a celestial speck

Orbiting my next projected reincarnation,
Preparing to be drawn home,
Through intuition's centripetal field,
Where all that I've assimilated
Will assume destiny's newest shape.

Suddenly, all motion ceases.
My eyes swim toward my brain's shore,
For safety, dig frantically in the sand,
And bury themselves just before the sun
Explodes hope for a painless escape from life.

8/18/81   (00863)

Author of the Pentateuch $^\Delta$

Alone, as always,
I heed my solitudinous calling,
By reaching for pen and notebook,
In which to record the momentary stirrings
My words create,
Giving birth to, nursing,
Weaning their progeny, poetry.

No matter where I sojourn,
Forebears and scions
Find me resigned to timeless contemplation,
Recognize, in me, their songmaker,
Composing sky and trees into rhapsodies,
Exploding odes from lullabies —
Mystical whispers of kissing gods.

Patriarch, baby, middle-aged,
Father and Son, simultaneously One,
I sign my name in lamb's blood,
Rediscovering, daily,
My reason for reigning over,
While remaining subservient to, the senses.
I am the tribal scribe,

Whose earthly curse,
Transubstantiating, into verse,
Expiations my unholy soul rehearses,
Is also the hallmark of my paltriness,
The ecstasy that dignifies dying.
Why else would I write
With such merciful, worshipful determination?

8/20 & 8/25/81   (00133)

Documentary ^Δ

I sit before the TV screen,
Witnessing London,
Stalwart, intractable, heroic,
Riding out the cataclysmic German blitz,

With stern upper lip,
Watching the meticulous chivalry
Of Spitfire fliers
Striking back,
Sticking the Luftwaffe
In its most conspicuous part,
Its arrogance,

Admiring a united populace
Organized, to the man
And child, by habit,
*

By the blackout block,
By a common desire to survive
Nightly Armageddon.

As I view the luminous screen
Shadowing my bedroom walls
With intermittent triumph and gloom,
Gaze in complacent isolation,

Safe as blessed Jesus in His tomb,
Inside my inviolable house,
My little boy, Troika,
Invades my privacy,
With importunate cries for help.
A bleeding nose
Has flooded his sweet dreaming.

His presence dismantles stupefaction,
Blurs my focus on death's locus.
My convenient lullabies
Comfort his three years,
Finally clot the red demons
Streaming out one nostril.

"But I can't sleep," he whimpers.
"The rain is scary."
"It's not raining, little one," I feign.
"Look out the window, Daddy."

I place my head next to his,
Monitor his breathing
As it ranges cautiously toward slumber,
Then leave,
Taking one more glance at the storm
Beyond the shade,
To reconfirm its immediacy.

An eerie mercury-vapor street lamp's glaze
Exposes parachute-mines,
Bomb clusters, raging fire-grapes.
A conflagration of frothing August water
Lights my way to nightmare.
Yesterday's siege is again underway.

8/28–30/81 (02073)

Going to the City, to Shop

As I come across country, this dawn,
The land is awash with fog.
Sun funneling down slanted tunnels
Etches my retinas. The heavens are furrowed.
The road over which I travel
Is a blind man's tentative shuffle.
Even this vehicle balks,
Coughs like a B-29
Flying in the eye of a cyclonic sandstorm.

My resolve to navigate fate's frustration
Forces me on. I grope,
Hoping the internal mechanism,
Gyros, and gauges controlling dead reckoning
Won't fail or the ropes
Holding my brain's counterweights in place
Give way under the strain,
Allow my nerve-workers to suffocate
From a break in the occluded veins.

My eyes register the digital clock,
Arrayed in eerie green diodes,
Changing configurations at changeless intervals,
Like lips shaping conversations
From invisible ideation. They can't hear
The mind's time,
The spirit's nearness to winding down,
For the universal electric impulse,
Or fathom the heart's frightened anxieties,

As they try to envision a divination,
On the display,
That might guide them to safety.
Each silent alteration
Burns a raw design on my impatience.
Minutes and decades are indistinguishable,
For the pain. Not even the radio,
Unable to stay fixed on a single signal,
Discloses a location, call letters.

I'm a barge floating on the River Lethe,
Charon rowing across Styx,
*

Pharaoh trapped between the Red Sea's
Labial waves, Jonah, Ahab, Geppetto
Following/swallowed by Leviathan,
A hapless bastard
Doomed to ply open waters,
Whose life precludes furloughs, sabbaticals,
Hiatuses, shores, brief peace.

Suddenly, the fog lifts.
I break loose, enter, freewheeling,
As the sinuous road divides into highway
And I mix with myriad travelers
Going in the same direction,
Decidedly toward a given destination,
The citadel rising in the distance,
Like a futuristic Carcassonne,
This civilization's necropolis: the shopping mall.

9/5/81 — [1] (05769)

[Driving home, alone,] △

Driving home, alone,
Having spent my precious energies
Proclaiming the intellect's suzerainty over lethargy,
I allow cool September air
Entry into my ears' temples.
It blesses me with sweet benedictions,
Bathes forehead and cranium
With scents engendering from Missouri's fields.
A gentle inebriation seizes me.
I am a hibiscus bloom
Perfectly at peace with my earthly turn.

Undisturbed by my precarious attachment to the sky,
My vertiginous fix above the earth,
I sip of the sanctified elixir, life,
Whose draught bespells the spirit,
Enchants me. I dance on the tip
Of an invisible magician's stick,
Commanding images to quit their hiding,
Materialize as nymphs, trees,
*

Demons, centipedes, butterflies,
The child whose husk I precipitously discarded,
On molting my mothered adolescence.

Now, I speed home, impelled as hell
By an eagerness to discover
Who might be waiting at the door, to greet me,
Especially since it's been ten years
That I've been gone,
A decade spent racing toward
The forwarding address I gave my soul,
On leaving my senses
Just to see if I could arrive whole
Before they exploded, my destination
The City of Poetry, my goal to die alive.

9/5/81 — [2] (04176)

Conception on the Road [△]

The road over which I float
Is a fallopian tube
Coercing me, coaxing,
Guiding my intellect inexorably higher
Into its sinuous conduit.
I am a motile sperm
Traveling miles to reach my destination
Somewhere up ahead.

The fluid moving my senses
Is flagellant music
Undulating in rhythmic sympathy,
This concupiscent morning.
Whether metaphor awaiting fertilization
Or symbolic enigma
Quivering with euphoric anticipation
Of being penetrated,

The core toward whose shore I soar
With furious determination
Is a vaginal firmament
Capable of creation and regeneration.
Suddenly, in one ecstatic ejaculation,
I drive into the sun,
*

Arrive home with a newborn poem —
Father to the child I've just become.

9/8/81 — [1] (00132)

Intimations of Autumn

Although the truth keeps changing,
My heart will know when it's time to die.
The trick is learning to determine
Whose truth we're using, today,
And how much credence
Its mutability ultimately deserves.

I, for one,
Decline to accept abstract platitudes
And absolutes as fact.
Life has a way of remembering us
By our last names first,
So that birth and death converge
In seamless circles —
Saturn-rings gracing our faces
With God-patterns, Satan-halos
Shadowing each generation in shrouds.

Just now, geese flying south
Attract me, by their holy crusade,
To my own need to be leaving again.
I can almost feel their honking
Freeing me from gravity,
Peremptorily setting my heart's wings beating.

9/8/81 — [2] (02030)

A Pastoral ᐃ

This glory-torn September morning,
His pen is a nervous shepherd
Wending through obscure undergrowth,
Over oblique slopes,
In quest of one missing member
Of his blessed flock.

Having spent hours
Inventing disastrous fates
Alternating with ecstasies,
On imagining ululations
And bells sifting through the sky's neck —
Mere siren plaints —

He prepares to abort his search.
Just now, in a clearing,
Peaceable as a sleeping fay-child,
The lost sheep materializes,
A wet lamb suckling beneath her.
Both know he'll lead them safely home.

9/8/81 — [3] (02031)

On Rocks and Other Inanimate Objects

My silence is so total, so deep,
I can almost hear,
In the absence of all falling sounds,
The internal earth's workings,

Those eerie, mysteriously hissing furnaces,
Myriad spinning gears
Interminably intermeshed,
Geysers and cantankerous volcanoes

Erupting at unpredictably abrupt intervals,
Ceasing unreasonably.
I can almost hear hellhounds
Chasing naked Satan

Through regions where vegetation
Is barbed laughter and guffaws,
Raucous screeching, wailing, growling,
Whose inhabitants slither and claw . . .

Almost hear the planet, in its ellipse,
Spinning, the gaseous sun
Crackling in constantly expanding
And contracting flatulent spasms . . .

Almost hear my own groaning voice
Trying to teach its tongue
To shape expiatory benedictions
And prayers on the forgiving air.

But the silence causes chaos
That frustrates confession,
And I slide back into total deafness,
Resigned to bliss, to blessed ignorance.

9/8/81 — [4] (02032)

Poetic Vectoring △

As I enter this land, of my own volition,
My ears hear, in the distance,
Your whisperous voice
Redeeming, from desperation and loneliness,
My choice to leave home alone.

My eyes strain to locate the source
From which your transmissions emanate.
Intuition sets up vectors
My imagination selects,
In plotting a flight plan and landing,

Yet my guidance systems
Fail to focus your elusive shape,
On the eyes' computerized screens.
I wait for omens,
Superstitious rituals to signal your existence

In this mystical air space,
Three hundred miles due south,
And invite me to climb
High inside your tree house,
Rest from my agonizing odyssey,

Sip chilled Chablis, kiss warm lips,
And get celestially blitzed.
After a statical lapse,
I suddenly catch sight of your voice, again,
Racing naked across my wrist,

Making my magical pen
Compose your heart's verse,
Guiding me to the picnic cemetery,
On a frequency your breathing creates
As you sing me softly home, inside my poem.

9/8/81 — [5] (00152)

On Recapturing Youth

At precisely one hour before noon,
I order my ghost crew
To hoist anchor, raise jib, mizzen,
And main sails into place.
Without fanfare, I scramble, fleet-footed,
To the crow's-nest, breathe deeply
From this scintillant day's rife sea breeze,
Screaming leeward, to no one particularly,
Screaming out exuberantly,
For the prepossessing freedom seizing me,
Screaming, "Be done with thee, land,
And a good riddance, too!"

Soon, my vessel is out of human sight,
A floating fossil
Moving, through watery strata,
Without timewound constraints,
Preserving a wayward-gypsy life form.
Like Gulliver and Cristóbal Colón,
I press ahead, guiding by hope and dream,
For measurements of latitude and degree,
Surmise and inductive reason,
For longitude, ellipse, azimuth, stars, and moon.
This caravel, with me at the wheel,
Is full equal to the whole swollen ocean,

Adequate match for any finned fish
Or leviathan. "Watch out, sun!
Get in my way just once,
And I snatch you from the sky,
In my bare hand! Do you hear me?"
Now, cruising in tepid climes
South of the equator, I sail toward you,
*

Muse, whose concupiscent siren cries
Have tantalized me, all these years
Of my cloistered terrestrial exile.
As I near, phosphorescent leaping fish
Form sundogs across the horizon.

Such refracted brilliance blinds my eyes.
I peer through my excitement,
Trying to avoid singeing fantasy's screens
While looking for a safe cove
Deep enough to let me land.
Suddenly, you appear on the sandy beach,
Naked as a magnolia bloom unfolding,
Motioning me to come ashore,
Quit my tortuous journey, travel no more.
Before I can act, a brainstorm
Washes me back out to sea —
A warning not to trespass on ancient remains.

9/9/81 (03576)

Of Elegies and Renascence ^Δ

Now, as I leave Oxford,
Weaving through an unusually cool 9 a.m.,
Into silence, flying past kudzu
And stolid loblollies,
The miles dissolve into minutes clicking away
Like diodes in a pacemaker.

I watch them, with quizzical disbelief,
As they cycle in nonrepeating inevitabilities,
While thronging sunflowers,
Peering out from swollen roadside coverts,
Whisper mystical concupiscences,
Shoot scintillant inarticulations at my diminishment.

I weep into the colossal valley
Your absence spreads before my eyes.
Images festooned in Steely Dan music,
Pouilly-Fuissé, a fleet, lake-green Mercedes,
Crisp, garlic-tinged toast
Lift, in shimmer-mist, off morning's pool.

The valley deepens, widens to an immeasurable abyss
Echoing with the amplified roar
Each invisible tear that drips from my pen
Scribbles as it hits bottom,
Splitting into dismal strophes
Recording my own lonely dissolution.

Separation is such an amorphous place.
My heart's hour is now,
But its blood stutters, sputters,
Back-floods before making atrial escape
Into the body's undisclosed tributaries,
To arbitrate our most precious differences

With its pulsating rush, then soothe,
Kiss smooth a past we never shared
And replace it with uncommon caring, patience,
Gently spontaneous lovemaking,
Mutual acceptance of each other's demons
And prodigious artistic gifts.

I hold my breath all the way home,
Hoping the slowing process
Might let my thoughts uncreate the miles,
Dismantle time's hierarchy
One sunflower, pine, and kudzu vine at a time,
Allow my grief to subside,

My lugubrious spirit to resume old duties
Implicit in coexistent survival.
But it won't. From now on, if I am to prevail,
You must be, always, out there somewhere,
Keeping vigil over my hibernating soul,
Until sleep breathes us whole again.

9/12/81 — [1] (03535)

Sparks Jumping the Gap △

Why, when you gently squeeze your eyes,
Do I materialize,
Sit beside your most precious keepsakes,
*

Gewgaws of the unbought kind,
Each so meticulously chosen,
From a prior life,
For its unique imperfections,
Flaws which render it a gem,
Each a reflection of your Southern pride
And tastefully sophisticated grace?

Why do I arise, genie-eager, behind your eyes,
Anxious to do your gentle bidding,
Infuse your entire body into mine,
As a sculptor pours heated bronze into a casting
He's fashioned, with his hands,
From an outsize imagination,
And fly into sleep's peaceable kingdom,
Your cheek resting on my chest,
To keep the black dogs off your head,
Your slender body my spirit's reciprocal wing?

And why, merely by closing your lids,
Do I feel obliged to recite odes
To the azure winds, fling elegies
Across the silent abyss, whose distance
Is the astigmatic out-of-roundness
Your seeing accommodates and rectifies
Whenever you desire to focus me home,
Bringing my colors into clearer registration,
My poetries into truer resolution
With your own intuitions?

Why, if not that yours is a magical passion
Capable of sustaining me in our absence,
Resurrecting me from desperation,
Allowing me to be seen through Maine mists
And Mississippi Delta humidities?
I appreciate you not only close
But from this inhospitable distance.
You give my invisibility dignity and dimension
Whenever I sense you dreaming me alive . . .
And I always know when you're closing your eyes.

9/12/81 — [2] (00177)

The Defrocking of Rudy Toothacre, Itinerant Minister of the Universal Gospel of the Synod for All Churches of the What's Happenin' Now ^Δ

Having stopped, on this headlong trek home,
This raucous juggernaut
Out of honeyed Canaan,
To reenergize the caffeine
Streaming through my artificially excited system,
I now resume my final leg,
Hoping to make an inconspicuous approach
And unscandalous landing.

Neurotically reviewing calculations,
Statistical figures, alibis,
In case my delay warrants justification,
I rehearse possibilities,
Fabricate convenient viable obstacles
That might easily have threatened my safety,
Caused sufficient consternation
To keep me from leaving sooner.

Although driving I-55
For six consecutive hours, I fly,
A migrating aviator, going paradoxically north,
Into irreversibly colding climes.
As I enter the geography
Which spawned my profound distaste for mediocrity
And bland ambitions,
My eyes recognize not one familiar sign.

Instead, my ears clog;
The stomach becomes an ever-knot;
Vision is an asthmatic attack.
Severe throbbing pain, accompanied by fear
That these grievous symptoms
Are an occupational hazard of existence
In Newer Laputa and St. Louis,
Announces my presence in the old air zone.

Now, as I cruise, downwind, to my house,
Surveying the land-lay,
My ears detect an urgent groaning
*

Emanating from the motor.
Five miles out, I lose full power,
Slide into a steep dive,
Lose my wits,
Forgetting all emergency procedures, and crash.

Anesthetized by chilled Chablis
My shattered visage requires to keep itself alive,
I mumble salutations,
Feigned sighs of relief,
Preoccupy myself with needless details
About my mission, to the hinterland,
To proselytize recruits for my next crusade to Mecca,
And pray sleep will not exact my confession.

9/12/81 — [3] (03484)

The Morning of an Orphan's Birth

Even now,
Although I've been driving for miles,
My sleep-sundered eyes
Decline to rise to the occasional environment
Surrounding them like fecal stench,
Penetrate and enter this accidental place,
In which they find themselves captive slaves,
Chattel, second-class apparatus
Assigned the Renaissance task
Of guiding my lassitudinous spirit home,
Through an incipient, autumnal Septembering,
When, already, the greening boughs
Are slipping, ineluctably, into faint penumbrae,
That unmistakable, immemorial stasis,
Death-breath waning fast.

Slowly, the eyes accommodate,
Advance, moment to moment, opening slowly,
As they stray from night's maze, into day —
Strangers, lambent candle flames,
Two coals glowing preternaturally
(Their white heat ice-cold),
Unpumiced Lake Superior agates,
Geodes containing, in their lacunae,
*

Pirates' caches, fabulous caverns.
My constricting pupils suck in the sky,
Their meshed screens sieving it
For elusive metaphors and favorable portents
That might disclose celestial road signs
By which my paltry spirit
Can locate its providential way home.

But clouds coalescing on the horizon
Confuse vision,
Stymie my determination to press ahead,
Remain of this world
While seeking surreal redemption
Through poetical transportation,
Courting oblivion with blind faith.
Words desert me.
My eyes' slurred parts of speech blur insight.
Wisdom accretes an opaque film,
Through whose horny layer
Even annihilation appears inviting, golden.
Suddenly, silence announces my arrival.
I step out of my trance,
An orphaned phantasm abandoned at death's door.

9/17/81 — [1] (05770)

Transmigrations

This evening sky is alive with butterflies'
Crazy mating,
A chaotic, frenzied fluttering
Of clustered monarchs
Rushing to complete floral fornications.

Dusk's crepuscular pastels
Undulate like northern lights
Across a crisp July Wisconsin night,
As these migrating *mariposas*
Soar and hover in transcendent epiphany.

Oh, for just a moment's knowing,
One brief ride
On those ecstasy-driven wings,
*

To come inside their heated, orgasmic spiraling
And sense such vibrancy

And irrational freedom just prior to dying!
If only my eyes could fly,
My inspirations whisk me to heights
Where sight and what's seen collide,
I, too, might expire

With a flourish of wordless pirouettes,
End my days as they began,
In blessed jubilation.
I watch as they pass from shape to shadow,
Backlit against the moon,

Then dissolve into autumnal phonetics
Throbbing beyond sleep.
Later, in vertiginous dreams,
I emerge just as the butterflies cease,
Each a falling leaf, a season,

Another eternity
Come and gone, caught and lost
In an evening's thoughts and brief glimpses,
Whose release releases me from any uncertainty
That even dying is a celebration of Creation.

9/17/81 — [2] (05771)

In Time's Nick

The radio's music,
Screwed to the deafening, galactic crackling
An avalanche in space makes
As an entire asteroid belt breaks up,
Cuts through my brain,
In reiterating, ear-shattering waves.

Thought, imagination, and memory collapse,
As I drive ahead,
Tumbling within this miasmic chasm
While maintaining seeming equilibrium,
Keeping the highway beneath my haphazard speed,
Avoiding collisions with disaster.

City concrete, glass, and asphaltic rationality
Suddenly give way to hillsides
Stippled in saplings, evergreens,
And dappled, spawn-drawn bumble-honeys.
I twist the dissonant sounds down,
Like turning off a faucet.

The sky behind my outbound passage
Bulges like a rubber pipe,
Groans from having to hold back
Such devastating pressure,
While I escape, with my sanity intact.
In my rearview mirror, I see it explode.

Rain vapors chase me all the way out,
Never quite catching up
With my concentrated pace.
The relief silence provides is an elixir imbibed.
Intoxicated, I drive home,
Knowing, by now, Hiroshima is in windless cinders.

9/17/81 — [3] (05772)

A Member of the Road Company

There just must be someone
Chasing me,
To make me perpetuate this madness
On a daily basis,
The mindless dislocation constant traveling
Defines in concrete lines.

Perhaps it's a phantasm,
Programmed to effect my annihilation
By computerized contract,
Or carcinomatous spores,
Trying to contract my disease,
That frighten me into forever leaving,

Executing emigrations, even in my dreams,
Stirring my adrenalized blood
With anxieties shaped like divining rods
Squirming erratically as weather vanes
*

Anticipating a hurricane.
Maybe it's only my timorous silhouette,

Filling fast, of late, with bilious fluid,
My brain, pulsating
Like a thousand contradictory neon signs
Simultaneously flashing,
That drive me, so intensely,
To such irreconcilably neurotic uprootings.

Whatever the reason,
It seems painfully obvious, to those
Who claim they know me,
That mind-parasites have invaded and possessed
My stable senses, controlled my thoughts,
Changed me into a demonic stranger

Incapable of communicating with friends,
My own wife and children.
And here I go again,
Ranging out from my life's hub,
Along another ancillary spoke,
Hoping to ascertain a destination

Before I discover the wheel
Onto which I hold in desperate dread
Of letting go and being flung far into space,
On an unchartable trajectory,
Broken into unidentifiable pieces
Indistinguishable from my shattered psyche.

Suddenly, my straining ears
Are assailed by a carnival barker's rhetorical
"Round and round she goes,
And where she stops, nobody knows."
Vision limns my blind spirit with insight.
I see myself tied to an oversized wheel,

Knives flying in at me, from all directions,
Spinning myself, through sheer fear of bleeding,
In endless reverse/forward rotation,
As I perform a circus act
To gore-oriented packed stands,
All along my heart's back roads and arteries.

9/18/81 (02386)

Sacerdotal Misgivings

Antonio Gaudí haunts me,
This sun-brazed day. His cathedral
De la Familia Sagrada adumbrates my thoughts,
Washes me in perforated penumbrae.

My inebriated spirit reels and stutters,
Weaving through Barcelona streets
Without leaving my landlocked desk.
Something inevictably portentous

Has set about accomplishing my restiveness,
As though to desecrate routine,
Which has convenienced me, all these years
Of my solitary novitiate.

I squirm in my seat, swivel,
And, peering out, across the room,
At fifty other faces peering at screens,
Processing orders on keyboards,

Begin to realize why
One photograph, on a TWA calendar
Hanging slightly askew,
In Christlike tranquillity, on the wall,

Might excite my quiet, compliant blood to riot.
In those grotesque pinnacles,
Frightening for their absurd, irregular designs,
My eyes recognize their trinitied enemy:
Hypocrisy, arrogance, and indifference.

Suddenly, I vividly see myself
Coming upon that church for the first time,
As a college boy touring Europe,
Dumbstruck, discovering that a house of God

Could be all facade, a colossal desolation
Lacking walls, apse, nave,
(The sky for its roof), God, myself —
An adventitious creation, incomplete and empty.

9/21/81 (05773)

Who Holds Our Children Up, If the World's Hope Is on Their Shoulders? ^Δ

Approaching four years of age
With eager resoluteness,
My boy, Troika, entertains himself
In fanciful alternations. Momentarily,
He imagines himself a full-blown Dracula,
"But not with the teeth."
Presto — he is chief pilot of his Tonka
Twin-engine jet airplane,
Whose triggered handle,
Attached to the fuselage's underbelly,
He squeezes, to activate the propellers.
"This is TWA, Delta,
Both — did'ja know?"
"Can you fly me to Nineveh and Tyre?" I ask.
"Right away. Climb in."

Now, as I diminish from his presence
By a day, a night,
One hundred miles, that sweet, unassuming innocence
Shimmers through my isolation
Like escaping aromas of baking cookies.
Visions of this inquisitive little fella,
So gifted with inventiveness
And wit, who admitted, not five minutes
After having been spanked
For a justly punishable misdemeanor,
"I apurse-see-ate you anyway,"
Which he riveted home
With a ten-kiss tattoo on my cheek . . .
Visions of his blessed face arrest me,
Distract me, as I drive west,

Cause me temporarily to forget death,
Attached to my spirit lampreylike,
Inexorably draining me, weighing me down.
The visions suspend my solitudinous brooding
Over conclusions postponed too long,
A future woven of painful separations.
This morning, I choose to focus on him,
Neutralize the truth
*

That lies behind my voluntary exile. My weeping
Is the whine this vehicle's tires
Stroke from the road's smooth surface,
As I enter alien terrain,
Alone, not for the first time, certainly,
But possibly the last, that valley
Where the heart's sadness runs on to the sea.

9/22/81 — [1] (01455)

The Laureate of Katy Station

I sit here, alone,
In this commodious antique atmosphere,
Peering into the nearest materializing vision,
In hope of locating my wayward soul,

Recording images as they appear before me,
Like a priest dispensing wafers
To communicants petitioning Eucharistic feast,
And behold each object, God-like,

In my own private Creation:
A Vesuvian popcorn machine,
Spewing its delectables
At unpredictable intervals; a whole caboose,

Completely reconstructed, with fastidious authenticity,
Within this lounge; stained-glass fanlights,
Surmounting each fenestration
In this brick Victorian railroad station;

Cast-iron-based, laminated tables,
Occupied not by drummers making connections,
Rather tight-jeaned collegiate ladies
On the make and confetti-headed fraternity brothers

Postponing classroom assignments,
For another chance to prove themselves priapic.
Just now, late afternoon dissolves
Into prismatic refractions; the sun is a peacock

Preening, spreading its eyeleted tail feathers.
My location and identity remain unknown
Even to the waitress who does my bidding,
Continually serving chilled golden Chablis.

If this is indeed an Edenic garden,
To which I occasionally return
For succor and mellow release, then why
Must I always confront such ecstasy solitudinously,

Unable to share my nerves' uncoupling,
My wild spirit's biting free of its muzzle,
My pen's uninhibited groping
Over notepaper, the eyes' total mystification?

What design might I divine
From this volitionless routine of mine,
Whose mensal predictability is in phase with the moon?
What draws me to this impersonal oasis,

To create my solipsistic verse,
Search for the missing link in my relationship
With existence? Is it the paranoia
Connected with dying in utter anonymity

Or the uncertainty of expiring
Without having explored every avenue to immortality
That drives me to circle back
To write my exploratory, tentative lyrics?

Even my bones don't know the answer or care.
All that matters is I am here, alive,
Celebrating my brain's twitching cerebrations,
Telling my heart's irrelevant time.

9/22/81 — [2] (02624)

Lady Magic

You, lady, bother me!
Such inexpressibly passionate aggravations
Rumble my bones to avalanche,
Cause my pen to experience orgasmic spasm.

I sit here, completely immobilized,
Focusing on your writhing thighs, your breasts
Swelling beneath the spell
My body, pivoting on your clitoral fulcrum, exerts,

Amazed by the coercive animal force
Lying buried within me,
Which you alone have engaged,
Persuaded me to unleash, made me accept

As a natural coeval in two people's sharing.
I acquiesce with complete uninhibition,
Proud of being able to stir you
To such physiological epiphany.

I appreciate you, without qualification,
Except to say, lady,
That whatever it is you intuit about me,
I accept . . . I accept, *nolo contendere*.

My expectations for us, if you ask me
Point-blank, are unfocused;
In fact, I refuse to predict our future,
For fear of aggrieving resident gods,

Who might, at this hour, be eavesdropping
On my speculative revelries.
Rather, I would like to ponder the prospect
Of you and I dying joined tightly

In naked embrace, key and lock
Fitted smoothly to each other's honed lobes,
Until love's golden gates open,
In wild, silent, lubricous flowing,

Disclosing such erotic ecstasies
As no mere humans have known or dreamed,
You and I sealed eternally
In deadbolt closeness, safe as chosen angels.

9/22/81 — [3] (02622)

"PROSECUTORS WILL BE VIOLATED"

Oblivious to, and usually fully confused
In, matters pertaining to the public misuse
Of his private reputation,
Abuse of laws protecting his printed verse
From piracy and plagiarism,
And naive to adversarial recourse
Through threat of suit, he retreats, to brood.

Wandering beyond common purlieus,
Where those who spend their days
Pondering Hammurabian ways
To extract tooth for tooth languish,
Squandering entire lifetimes, in the pursuit of lucre
And power, he contemplates his next move, in solitude,
Strokes potential poems

Floating nebulously in the surrounding altitudes,
Hoping to entice them into disrobing,
Disclosing the muse-beautiful shapes they own,
If only their existence can be made known.
Never has he lamented those souls
Who have appropriated his books of poetry
And published them under their own pseudonyms

Or spoken for him, through the media,
Quoting from his private diaries,
Stolen years ago, or received degrees
And awards he neglectfully declined,
For the furious commitment to retaining his privacy.
On the contrary, his predictable, noncommittal responses
Have encouraged scalawags and carpetbaggers.

Now that the Nobel Prize committee
Has drawn its august conclusion,
Proclaiming his name, across the entire universe,
As the one chosen for verse,
And having had his refusal to appear in Stockholm
Emphatically refused by the powers that be,
His own country's presidency,

He prepares to be photographed in a tuxedo
Loaned him by his editor's brother,
To go three thousand miles for supper,
Medal, certificate and to participate in a series of handshakes
And applause from audiences eager to see
The elusive and enigmatic stranger
Who has consistently shunned publicity and adulation.

As the jet's droning engines
Soothe him over the ocean, he lapses into song,
Scribbling sibilant lyrics into his notebook,
Whose soft, off-rhyming harmonies
*

Coalesce into variations on a theme he might read,
Title as his acceptance speech.
Suddenly, his pen transcends conscious formulation,

Begins to enact the ineffable translation of angels
Repeating God's ancient preambles.
He watches the ink deploy itself in syllables,
Until the plane touches down
And time advances him, mystically, to the podium,
From which he delivers his stichomythic prosody
To a rapt and awestruck assemblage.

Later, surrounded by gawking, garrulous crowds,
Anesthetized by their inordinate attentions,
He endures the ordeal with a smile,
With equanimity equal to that of a seasoned actor,
And, politely, with unrehearsed modesty,
Excuses himself for having caused such fuss
Over what has always been a natural act,

A simple, utterly inexplicable gift
Bequeathed him at age five,
When, so he's been repeatedly told by his mother,
He read aloud, then recited,
Book I of Milton's *Paradise Lost*, in its entirety.
(At seven years, he fully memorized
The Odyssey and Wordsworth's *The Prelude*.)

At last, the solicitudes, introductions concluded,
He returns to his estate in nature,
The cabin along Derby's verdant Housatonic,
Where he's resided, in quiet anonymity, forty years,
Without being spied on
Or having his pipe and books purloined
From the porch he may have briefly vacated,

The retreat where he no longer finds peace,
For the curious souls seeking artifacts,
Tatters of his privacy. Too soon, too late,
He discovers he's a freak, anomaly,
A complete stranger to his former way of living,
Who goes to bed in fear
And wakes in dread of being found dead

By local authorities, whose postmortem will indicate
Death by human sacrifice,
Cannibalistic perversions perpetrated by neighbors
Ever anxious to prove his brain size
And penis and little toes
Not all that different from theirs, in fact,
Actually a tad less in aggregate weight.

These days, they come to his grave, stricken,
In contrition, grateful for his legacy,
His heart's prodigious verse,
And they linger on the epitaph, emblazoned in stone,
And marvel and shake their heads,
In docile resignation, pondering the inscrutable paradox:
"PROSECUTORS WILL BE VIOLATED."

9/23/81   (02623)

Keeper of the Keys: Willy Sypher

Like an equestrian with a display
Of medals, ribbons, and trophies,
He has his motel keys,
Stolen methodically each time he stays
On the road and leaves,
As he arrived, anonymously as a ghost.

His collection has grown,
Over the past few decades,
Like bounding sheep and leaping gazelles
Or lizards or flying fish,
Eerie, weird, approximating perversity,
For the degree of his uprootedness.

He can't satisfactorily explain
Why his activities have increased
As his sales volume
Has decreased consistently, each year,
Causing the keys to multiply —
Fifty roaches at a time, from a single egg —

Keys fastened to plastic tags
With return-mailing information
*

Emblazoned across their faces;
Solitary keys stamped, unevenly,
With three- or two-digit numbers,
Cryptic, medieval, inscrutable;

Keys previously rubbed and nudged
By thousands of other sweaty fingers,
Dropped like cigarette butts, unthinkingly,
Into myriad linty pockets,
Used to unlock the same door
He presently cajoles and forces open,

To gain admittance, this evening,
For ephemeral sleep in a sleazy bed,
Whose sheets still show traces
Of one's menstruation, another's orgasm,
Torn in two corners,
For having tried to outlast repeated washings;

All keys, all doors, alike,
His individual experience identical,
So that he himself has actually become
A skeleton key, a master key
Capable of opening whole days, weeks,
Unlatching his life a night at a time.

Tonight, he stares at his shaking fingers
Signing the register, notices them
Fumbling around the keyhole
Before he inserts his soul
Into the aged whore's shriveled vagina,
Comes inside dryly, limp, impotent as a corpse.

9/24/81 (02385)

A Public Official Relinquishes His Incumbency

Today is everybody's new fiscal year,
Everyone's but mine.
For me, nothing seems changed.
Future and past are the same senile brain,
Impoverished by confusion,
Wallowing in spiritless bankruptcy,
*

Displaying a slovenly vagrancy
Symptomatic of mismanagement and embezzlement,
Filibustering to keep its very blood flowing.

At midnight last night,
My bicameral dreams turned to nightmare,
Failed to appropriate funds
For the business of the bodily processes
To continue uninterrupted.
All agencies ceased functioning
Except hallucination and pernicious paranoia,
Which continue like frog legs twitching
Long after electrocution.

Everywhere I gaze,
Vision is shattered china — a plate
Knocked off of a table —
Or an hourglass giving way at the neck.
Neither faces nor places
My known identity has previously frequented
Register certain images.
Even symbolic logic fails to explain
This deadly cessation overwhelming me today.

And as I vacate my office
Before dawn presages a new administration,
I allow my eyes a final sweep
Of my life's abandoned memorabilia, and I weep:
Faded framed photographs,
My books, my resigned wife,
Two children groping for explanation
Why their daddy is so homeless, gone,
And my gone, disappointed soul.

Now, another inessential sun
Spiders stealthily up the horizon's threads,
Suspends itself invisibly above me,
As if waiting to ascertain the way my vague shadow
Will veer, before deciding my fate.
This day marks the fiscal start
Of my heart's retirement from public life
And assumption of private practice
With the firm of Silent, Decayed, Buried, and Brodsky.

10/1/81 — [1] (05774)

Mistress Mississippi [Δ]

Traveling south is the singing, tinkling chimes
My eyes' inner ears and outer eye
Celebrate
While listening, while driving the highway,
Down,
Narrowing the miasmic miles, by hours,
To minutes, inches, an infinitesimal distance
Finally separating you and me
From all that accreted lonely desire and silence
We've allowed to infiltrate the lacunae
Infusing our clandestine relationship.

Going ever southerly is Sikeston,
Blytheville,
Memphis's "Old Bridge," spanning from Arkansas
To Tennessee, now Oxford, now Jackson —
Fantasy's landing, which your silhouette fills
With the mythohistorical image
Of a lace-frilled, brocaded plantation maiden,
A moon-white Melanie, fragile of voice and lilt,
Slender, delicate shape,
A roundelay whose whisperous music
Is my veins' juice. Mississippi is you,

A waiting lady,
Not naiad, vestal virgin, or muse,
Rather palpable, pedestaled, naked evocation,
Fuguelike, elusive, dream-seeming
Yet real as the ecstasy
Your lips translate for your seething body
Each time we achieve
A perfectly timed spiraling of simultaneous climax.
I and you, my sensual Delta belle,
Child of my deft conception,
Will accomplish our own sweet ruination and doom.

Although intuiting this too poignantly,
My intellect refuses
To reverse the heart's direction,
Chooses, instead, to let itself suffer the future,
A volitionless choice, really,
Since profligacy and Old Testament prophecy
*

Are so ambiguously interwoven
As to permit, nay encourage, indecision, at times.
Now, I arrive. The South is my anointing.
I, a paltry Isaac, sacrifice myself to your keeping.
Lady, annihilate me gently!

10/1/81 — [2] (00154)

Running Scared ^Δ

Suddenly, rising before my vision,
Loblollies,
By now become quite familiar sights,
Sentinels, martinets at attention,
Invite me to press ahead.

Without suspecting the nature of my quest,
They accept my presence.
I'm not even certain they realize
My license plates
Display an anomalous "Show-Me" slogan

Or that my status as interloper
Makes me a questionable alien.
They let me pass unapprehended,
Without creating unnecessary paranoia or strain.
Hurricane Creek, Arkabutla Lake,

Senatobia flash, fade;
The Batesville-Oxford exit materializes,
Dissolves. All the way to Jackson,
The noncommittal pines,
Lining both sides of I-55,

Hover like trained circus bears
Standing in line, on their hind legs,
Their nubby limbs tentative paws
Balancing their vast weight
In the precarious backwash and sky-breeze.

Restively, I project my thoughts
On diversionary screens
(Such as sipping Chablis with you, lady,
*

In naked midnight revelry),
To keep fear's monkey off my back,

Let my fancy stray
From crowded metaphoric fields,
Where it frequently delights in picking images
To make into a bouquet
It might place in a vase-shaped poem,

Quash all chance for my imagination
To glue transmuted reality
Into loblolly bears
Capable of mutilating my courage,
Chasing me out of this state of mind,

Through which I drive to find you.
Only after dusk's shadow
Locks the pines in penumbral cages
Do I relax. Someday, I'll relate
How close I came to quitting the quest.

10/1/81 — [3] (00151)

[The sweetest music dissipates.] †

The sweetest music dissipates.
My ears wilt like rose petals;
The senses desiccate like browning pine needles

10/1/81 — [4] (08084)

[I enter your house, not a stranger] ∆

I enter your house, not a stranger
Yet strangely new to your accouterment,
The unaccountable and the inscrutable artifacts
Gathered from Sri Lanka, India,
Juan-les-Pins. Why you've chosen me
On whom to lavish your passion I won't know
Until time has translated itself a dozen ways
And the autumnal days, spent in ruminative solitude,
Disclose their universal secrets.

For now, I accept this gift, your sharing,
As an angelic bequest. Your kisses,
The mad rhapsodies of our lovemaking,
The music we set loose through the bloodstream —
All precious gems in the diadem we wear
(Our sharing) in this illicit relationship
Of our making. I accept you, now,
Without doubts, devoid of self-conscious guilt,
And I am willing to set you free,

Whenever the heart cries out, in desolation,
Realizing gravity calls us,
As it does all terrestrial objects, graveward,
To relinquish our hold on the ineffable,
The impalpable. Tonight, while I still hold you
In heated embrace, let us sport us,
Transcend the sweetest metaphysical liquefactions,
And defy time, hold this night back.
Let us pass through the fire,

Singed, scarred, yet unmarked,
For the darkness that hides us inside the light
Emanating from our eyes. Let us survive
Trials that would turn the future to cinders,
Kindle the past, in a last-minute attempt
To rescue all that has been irrevocably jettisoned
And forever lost to the winds of chaos.
Now then, lady, take me to bed,
Gentle me, tender me with your friendship,

Your energized sensibility. I love you
For seeing in me a poet
Who might speak, might sing, your volcanoes
And geysers, might shout your tides
And galactic disturbances, might reiterate
The seismic desires your heart causes
Each time you seek to touch another.
Tonight, I will myself into your sweet keeping,
A creature seeking total appreciation.

10/1–2/81 — [5] on 10/1 (00155)

[Mustard and turnip greens,] †

Mustard and turnip greens,
Collards and poke,
Jerusalem artichokes and cucumbers
Float in the aura of your lips' garden
            I harvest

10/2?/81   (08272)

Wind Devils ᐃ

Both my eyes are wind devils
Spinning northerly
Over a continuous field,
From which my retreating memory
Has gleaned your supplest harvest,

A desiccated desolation
Whose fanning tornadic dust
Blinds vision,
Turns my invisible grief to muddy furrows,
As I try to see my way clear.

These disturbances are neither metaphors
Nor wholly optical distortions
Caused by day's dissolve into twilight,
As I drive farther from you,
Rather mortal waterspouts

Rising preternaturally
From each eye's outbound tide,
Phenomenal occurrences
Resulting from abruptly changing pressures
My heated heart, freezing

In natural reaction to sadness —
Our predetermined parting —
Inevitably postulates.
As the miles accrue,
I watch your shimmering image refuse to focus,

Through the tunneling funnels,
Until, suddenly, I am one
*

With the twin sinister wind devils,
Their fierce motion mine,
My vertiginous spirit just more debris

Being precariously ferried along,
In arbitrary dispersion.
Slowly, home closes in on chaos.
The eyes' wildness slakes,
Changes from banshee screams to shouts to silence,

Finally plays out entirely. Soon,
Lukewarm routine will bathe and soothe
My irises and bloodshot whites.
The field, an erased slate,
Will lie fallow until our next seeding.

10/3/81 — [1] (00180)

A Universal Speck

I fly into the dragon's eye —
A tiny sliver of universal metal filing
Worn, torn, and thrown
From time's friction wheel.

Just now, from this frightening height,
I can hear the creature
Scratching raw its Cyclopean eye,
With blunted claws.

The noise is a locomotive
Crashing down a vast chasm.
I cringe. It rages like a hurricane
Engulfing everything in its path.

My entrapment lasts a lifetime.
Suddenly, the giant's tear ducts
Release a flooding river. I slide
Out of hiding, over the lid, in plain sight.

With nowhere to escape his terrible gaze,
I stand in a fighting crouch,
Like David, glaring into his hoary eye,
Threatening to annihilate him with my bare fists.

Suddenly, the vicious creature subsides,
And I am left in silence,
Aware that this brush with death
Is only a poet's omen, a visionary's insight.

10/3/81 — [2] (05775)

Goldenrods ^Δ

This day is Jackson.
The entire afternoon is named [Jane Rule],
In celebration of the lady
Whose eyes, with a slight flirtatious wink,
Transform me and all things in nature
Into intimations of love.

Through its striated recesses,
So autumnally luminous, its garden,
Extending endlessly along the Natchez Trace,
We chase our shadows,
Trying to make them converge,
Engulf us in wonderment,

Until all motion ceases, in a field
Just off the highway,
A field filled with goldenrods
So yellow even the sun
Can't compete, a field which dapples us
With natural completeness,

Awakens us to the creatureliness we possess,
Makes October riot our faces
With graceful smiles, bathes our skin,
In liquid softness,
To shimmering. We photograph each other
Against the crowded flowering,

Trying, together, to disappear
By becoming one of those arrested moments
And somehow enter the spectrum
Eternity projects with its soft prism.
Even now, as I am borne forth,
That glory-washed light

Compels me back to you,
As in a vortical, daydreamy déjà vu —
Two stems growing side by side
Amidst millions, your green eyes
Supple leaves, our vibrant, teeming love
Yellowness too yellow to fade.

10/5/81 — [1] (00172)

[A lusty breeze] ^Δ

A lusty breeze
Brushes sequins from the elegant trees,
Sends them skittering, in shadowy retreat,
Across the earth's floor.
A coronation is in session,
This Octobering, a celebration of the senses,
Attended by the entire community:
Those who dance,
Those who sway or stand
In reverential attitudes
Age bequeaths its patriarchs and matriarchs,
And those who only compose.

Beneath all this frenzied activity,
A poet sits captivated
By the ecstasy decay engenders as it nears the abyss,
Witnessing the inevitable coming undone
Of all things sundered by time;
Listening to the sounds shadows make
Scratching the ground, dry leaves evoke
Rolling head over heels,
In unpredictable degrees of dismay and consternation,
Before settling in for the winter;
Savoring the leaves' free-floating female aromas —
Nature's final menstruation.

He realizes his own private visions
Are mere approximations,
Imaginative hypotheses for the phenomenal change
Occurring before his eyes.
He knows his words lack depth and dimension
*

Required to register prismatic gradations
In hue and intensity,
Enlighten potential strangers to his experience.
His testimony, although not phony in its intention,
Suffers from negative capability
And faulty insight into the inscrutable ways of Elohim.
Suspended disbelief has ever been his weak suit.

Yet for all his inadequacies,
A certain reflective potential lets him get
Beyond his bodily processes,
Allows him, occasionally, to transcend his equivocal greeds
And petty passions and focus on those objects
Exploding with godly extravagance.
Just now, he knows he's in the procreative throes
Of universal upheaval. Composing poetry
May be his one hope of translating death
Into an atom, essence, element
Capable of sustaining life
By denying silence its annihilating stroke.

10/5/81 — [2] (00268)

Song of Soaring

Having been shoved away
From the portable corridor,
Its most viable tie to civilized life,
The sleek, slender jet whines slightly,
Like a tiger cub,
Moans, slowly, into sympathetic vibration.

Cabin lights wince once.
A vague bell signals, in approbation,
That all systems are engaged for ignition.
Erogenous nozzles, placed overhead,
At regular intervals, spray cool air,
In simultaneous climax,

And the plane begins to inch away from its terminal —
One of myriad fall leaves
Shimmering on its limb, the runway,
*

Preparing to enter the first vagrant breeze,
Exit on the next slipstream,
And disappear through the sky's needle-eye.

Now, soaring translates all my timorousness
Into wishes filled with piety
And quiet atonement. Hopes of surviving this flight
Wing toward the sun's source.
How miraculously the singing voice inside me
Knows the notes of my uncomposed fugue!

Time is a sacred wind instrument,
A silver flute accompanying my movement,
With the smoothest, most soothing music
Any human ever heard.
I relax as it cruises past my ears
Without using itself up,

Satisfied that if this is the essence
Which buoys spheres, the entire cosmos,
I need not fear abrupt deviations
Or spinning out of preassigned ellipse,
Losing axial rotation.
My fate, today, is the flute God plays,

Whose ancient reverberations
Commit my spirit, if not my resistant flesh,
To air. The lyrics I hear and write
Share me with silent ears and lips and eyes.
Distant whispers invite my reply —
The poet, leaf, notes being blown slowly home.

10/8/81 (05776)

Shopping the Line

After last night's Wagnerian operatics,
The ocean is repentant,
Or seemingly so, in its calm obedience.

It is Sunday. The watery surface
Is a piece of silver lamé
Loosely stretched over a display table,

For inspection by the Purveyor's clients.
My eyes appraise the day's fabric,
Draw back slightly from its bright glints,

Then focus on other swatches
Being offered from the same book of seasons:
Tattersall, dotted with dragonflies,

Clothing this steamy-hot ten o'clock;
Hound's-tooth check,
Composed of empty-masted sailboats

Slowly making their way out of sight,
Under motorized power;
Bathers walking the beach singly, in pairs,

Forming coarse or smooth waves
Out of their warp-and-woof preoccupations,
From which imagination might choose

One design, this morning,
To cut and sew into a robe
Memory might take home and wear — holy raiment.

10/11/81   (01025)

[For two days and nights straight,] ^Δ

For two days and nights straight,
The wind has raged —
An unofficial typhoon, a cyclone, hurricane.
We have registered its vicissitudes,
In consternation, frustration over lack
Of beach amusements with which to entertain our children,
Respect for its force,
And our overwhelming helplessness
In changing fate, with man-made dictates.

The air is abuzz with sand grits,
Inhuman bees, fleas, gnats, and dragonflies,
Rising off the beach, with each gust.
Trees and shrubs cease being stately palms,
Euonymus, sea grapes.
*

They gasp in the tattering, relentless wind.
Even clouds, redefining themselves, continuously,
In the sky's kaleidoscope,
Can't gain firm purchase above the purposeless earth.

Meanwhile, we remind ourselves that a vacation
Should conform to no rigid preconceptions,
Rather resolve itself one discovery after another.
Being here, regardless of conditions,
Away, by ourselves, should be sufficient release
To allow our weary spirits rejuvenation.
God might march armies against us,
To occupy our habitable husks,
And still we should revel in our irresponsibility.

10/15/81   (00267)

Sand Crab ^Δ

How could it be, this Sunday morning,
That with the greater myriad seascape
Flailing sailboats, busily, in the offshore breeze
And the sky aglitter with wheeling gulls,
The beach bikini-littered,
In officially sanctioned pseudonudity,
I should sense my eyes inordinately absorbed
By the antics of such a curious creature
Digging in the sand below the patio of my private resort?

Why should my focus,
Tightened down to a fine, microcosmic tune,
Exclude the entire universe,
Save for a solitary, elusive, inscrutable crab,
Exiting its hole, flinging handfuls of sand
Adroitly over its shoulder
(Loosely speaking, phylogenetically, that is),
Then, scrutinizing its terrain for moving intruders,
Skittering sideways, out of sight, to dig anew?

Why have I remained so preoccupied
With its methodical routine
That, for nearly three hours, I've stayed here,
*

Leaning over the railing, fascinated,
Peering down at this prehistoric entity?
Perhaps it has nothing to do with the crab itself
Or its habits, rather the simple fact
That it's been years since I've been distracted
From familiar images, asked to reflect on the adventitious.

10/18/81   (05777)

Evolution

Morning light brings me to my senses,
Awakens me, abruptly,
To the fading nocturnality of sleep phases
My eyes have just left behind
To seek refuge beyond Lethe's wet lips.

Io invites me to taste liquors
Dripping irresistibly from tree-tongues
Speaking the sweetest eulogies,
Singing themselves through cool autumnalities,
Into death-erections, time-climaxes,

Orgasms tinged plum and ocher,
Burgundy and cucumber and pumpkin hues.
My nostrils sip from the eyes' snifters,
Then get crazy,
My breathing filled with erratic, dazzle-dizzy beats,

Whose arrhythmic caesuras
Reflect moon-tides, blood-flooding in veins
Rooted in air and earth and flesh.
Suddenly, my own waking
Turns to wizened inspiration.

My transmogrified eyes
Enter the aroma fallen leaves exude
In their various stages of sacred decay.
Fortunately, poets, like dinosaurs and volcanoes,
Require a thousand thousand years to disappear.

10/20/81 — [1] (05778)

A Curse on My Father's Successors ^Δ

To this day, sterility fills my nostrils.
My ears still echo painfully,
From the fear treachery instills in those
Who must succumb to the arrogant dictates
Petty men require to reinforce misguided notions
Of human grandeur and success.

How I ever escaped pre-Nazi Poland,
With my genitalia intact,
Avoided capture at the merciless hands of administrators
Dedicated to draconian force,
Goyaesque grotesquery, and the horrors of war
Waged in the name of free competition, I'll never know.

Even now, whenever I near the city,
My nerves tauten;
The stomach goes into numbing peristalsis;
My courage falters briefly,
As I pass the office my father abdicated
Unwittingly to his close associate, Brutus . . .

Or was it Iago, Judas? Memory forgets,
At some deeply seated psychic behest
Energized for my sole protection.
Yet time arrests my best intentions,
Reminds me of that season
When that blessed man was flung into limbo,

By fate's arbitrary and impersonal determination.
To this very moment,
His visage lingers like a dust storm
Stippled with flying debris
The size of dying cows, henhouses, tires.
His silhouette, in profile, is a razor

Cutting slivers off my myopic eyes.
Crying only underscores the horrible grief
His undeserved termination nurtures.
Each occasion that arises
By which I come in to the city
Causes renewed recrimination and animosity.

Now, I head southerly, homeward,
Having made my appearance
Just long enough to affix my signature to documents
Without which the universe could not survive.
My brief obligation accomplished,
I spit backward, not waiting to hear the splatter.

10/20/81 — [2] (00862)

Our Town: An Acrid Approximation △

They gather in motley disarray,
As usual, every weekday,
At the Capital Café — merchants, purveyors,
Proprietors, independent operators,
Various derelicts collectively considered businessmen
By their own kind. They gather
Like bees thrumming garrulously about a comb,
Conceiving new absolutes,
Final say-sos, obligatory encomiums
On presidential policies, sandlot baseball,
Town-hall politics . . . like pigeons and squirrels
Leaping from vulgarity to calumniation,
As though each laugh and guffaw were a limb, a ledge . . .
Like chimpanzees discovering sexual mechanisms
For the first time, oblivious to embarrassment
Public exposure creates. They prate and stomp,
Bang, slap, grasp the table, in oratorical attitudes
Redolent of Cotton Mather, Menachem Begin,
And Huey Long. Later, when I come downtown,
To patronize the office supply,
Ye Olde Jewelry Shoppe, Butternut Flowers,
The barber, grocer, druggist,
And make a return, for credit, at our Gambles franchise,
I can't dissociate the image of each face
Imprinted from myriad early a.m.'s
We've spent, in isolate and inviolable contiguity,
Within the Capital Café,
Where I, too, go regularly to compose myself
Into potential strophes,
Forge poems in morning's metaphorical cauldron.
I see, smiling behind their counters,
*

Squirrels, pigeons, chimpanzees, bees,
Their visages, anyway, mounted atop clothed shoulders
Of the town's venerable patricians —
Giza Sphinxes each, half man, half beast,
Whose dichotomies reflect
Not the traditional apposition of head and heart,
Spirit and flesh, rather creature genus,
Each a distinct species within the same venal kingdom.
With taciturn economy, we exchange words
And money for services and goods rendered,
Then quit our necessary intercourse,
Knowing we must both coexist for survival —
Transplanted poet
And homegrown boy made good,
Coevals in a community too slowly expanding
For distinctions in idiosyncrasy
And artistic sensibility to go unnoticed.
For now, we have achieved a tenuous balance;
We're at impasse. We realize
That if there were a viable way for them to eradicate me
Without disturbing, to a small degree, the town's balance of trade,
Me to indict them in my poetry
Without valid criticism citing inordinate cynicism,
We would each accomplish the other's demise.
Coexistence is society's solution
For keeping perfection from reaching fruition.
They gather; I come to write.
The days are layers of the semi-opaque window
Through which we stare,
Witnessing our lives parade in costumed review,
Layers growing brittle, peeling away,
Occasionally revealing our trivial shapes
Changing though changeless, mutations moving toward Sheol,
Waiting to accommodate all our voices simultaneously.

10/22/81 (00583)

The Necromancer

This morning is a silver chaos,
Whose cacophonous welter beckons me enter
And be sundered. I submit,
*

A helpless victim of self-induced indecision,
Fearing that to resist the road's abracadabra
Might be to set in motion immediate annihilation.

A silvery, somnolent saturnalia
Slants across vision,
Like a million magicians' sword-points
Penetrating a fancifully decorated sarcophagus
In which fate has placed my soul.
I am both illusionist and his illusion,

Manipulating delusion, proving truth false,
Fractionating expectations,
Emerging from my perforated shell healthy,
Having survived apparent extinction well enough
To be proclaimed fit for the next trick:
Complete disappearance of my eye-dentity.

The rain on my windshield
Sets up a mystically repetitious prestidigitation,
Whose echolalia bespells me,
Lulls me into too convenient complacency.
Death is a wily creature,
Who plays possum at safety's feet.

Hoping to exit this argent dilemma,
I drive on, blindly,
Through a debris of darts, knives, and tomahawks
Hurtling out of the streaked nimbus.
My raw, taut nerves cringe
As I press ahead, trying to locate a rabbit,

The right card, matching halves
Of the severed body of my willing imagination,
Beyond the horizon's gray, shimmering mirage.
But arrival fails to materialize.
All my artifices fail.
Only the miles perform on cue, change shape,

Become hours transmuting into afternoon
Evolving into another sleepless night
In transit — a road show with no ending,
On whose stage I do my routine:
The Great Floto, waving my word-wand
Before audiences filled with sightless deaf-mutes.

10/26/81 — [1] (03486)

Generation Gap [Δ]

Gray, wet, cold, and filled with forgetting,
This late October morning
Marks the fourth birthday of my boy, Troika,
Who remains warm and joyous at home,
Content to investigate and rediscover gifts
He received Sunday, at his official celebration,
While I drive south,
Questing a birth of my own to commemorate.

Now, reconciled to the distress
Isolation always impresses on my transient psyche,
I enter quiescent brooding
As though swimming through oblique seas
Completely submerged for eternities
And realize that my years
Are an exact extension of ten times his.
Just a single zero distinguishes our ages,

Yet the physical distance separating us
And our spiritual directions
Make all the difference. He owns time.
Fate is his ally, while for me,
It's somehow more closely aligned with accident
And circumstantial convergence.
Already, my westerly sun is setting.
Queen East holds him gently between her breasts,

Feeding him the sweetest, warmest milk
The moon ever released
From her tumescent glands. I reflect
How, ten years hence,
When my boy has reached adolescence,
Begun to scale puberty,
I will have endured a prostate operation,
Survived a triple bypass,

Filed for Chapter 11 twice, and failed
To be invited to disclose my ego
On *The Dick Cavett Show*, be photographed
For front-cover exposure on the *Saturday Review*,
As the latest Nobel Prize–winning poet.
Sitting here, behind the compliant wheel,
*

My car guiding me willy-nilly,
I see my life extending, hurtling down,

As if my spirit were an unattached feather
Fluttering earthward, from a hawk
Diving furiously, out of a high, gray sky,
Talons-first, onto the back of a rabbit.
Suddenly, I glance up. The bothered sky
Opens abruptly, emitting a jubilant radiance,
Reminding me of my mission:
I'm on my way to my second childhood.

10/26/81 — [2] (01456)

In Defense of Physical Manifestations ^Δ

From the outermost extremities,
Where the distinct edges of both antipodes
Rub noiselessly against eternity, we come,

Converging on each other in a furied rush,
Our urgent passions cyclones,
Locomotives closing, on the same express track.

The location of our fated clandestination
Has no latitude or azimuth,
Rather is measured in fiery degrees

That vary the place, in our mutual heart,
Coincident with the erratic beat
Our sympathetic imaginations generate

Every time either of us contemplates our separation.
Such sweet release is both rhyme
And divine reason for this distanced longing

You, mistress, and I, your poet,
Conceive as strophe, caesura, and closure
Whenever we awaken the universe with our singing.

Now, we blend our voices again,
In seminal harmony, remembering the words
Deleted from Genesis, repeating them

(An orgasmic catechism),
Letting them connect us to our godhead,
Through physical epiphanies — the body's cosmic poetry.

10/26/81 — [3] (00179)

Sky-Robes

The sky is alive with precious flecks —
Diamond dust blown over cooling glass
Backed by black velvet.
Peering into this vast mirror,
I see my own psyche
Reflected as myriad clustered nebulae,
My tininess magnified a thousand thousand times.

Nearer to earth, murmurous chirping crickets
Weave night's shroud, out of afternoon's faded fabric,
With their reiterating legs. The garment,
Sequined with stars and vague, shadowy leaves
Not yet unstitched in brusque November winds,
Fits itself about my naked spirit.
Never before have I worn such celestial raiment

Or taken such fastidious pride in my appearance.
Tonight, as if just born,
I cross October's stage, strutting, prancing —
A dancing, lambent flame
Balancing on a candle's self-generating tip,
A baby, universal savior, a poet
Alive for the first time, now, tonight, forever.

10/27/81 — [1] (03577)

Exhortation in Praise of Spontaneity ^Δ

Lady, I'm so pleasured
That you believe in me as you say.
My response to you is just this: I'm happy,
Glad, because I promise you, lady,
*

I wouldn't expend such precious energy
Spewing a ruse on you,
Weaving a spider's net to heave over a tired fly
Or other unsuspecting victim,

Because what I do with my time is essential
To the ordered rotation of the planets,
The harmonious conjunctions of fates,
The viable operation and maintenance of my poet-soul.
And, lady, there just ain't enough time
To squander even the slightest integer
On dissimulation or fabrication, making impressions
Just for their own selfish sakes.

My purpose is ever to fashion, from truth, illusion,
To contrive, transmute, fantasize,
And make more palpable, reality,
Transcend pain and depravity, via metaphor,
Teach the hinged door to revolve,
Forecast unpredictable meteorological vicissitudes,
With absolute precision, convince death
To focus on ghosts rather than mortal hosts.

Lady, take me as I am, or reject me
On the premise that you can't stand hyperbole
As a way of life, the standard
By which Shakespearean and Faulknerian excellence
Is achieved and maintained. If you vote yea
To my outrageous articulations and scandalous fantasies,
I shall expose you to words breathing worlds.
Otherwise, you and I will die from natural causes

Before either of us ever discovers why fate
Collaborates so amicably, with human psyches,
In creating Korans, Rig-Vedas, Upanishads, *Absalom,
Absalom!*s, and *Paradise Lost*s. For now, I beseech you,
Be patient with my seemingly strange ways.
Wait while I conceive my "Ode: Intimations of Immortality,"
In this bar. Don't force me to cease, pay,
Race home, to sleep, each of us, in separate beds.

10/27/81 — [2] (00161)

Cosmic Consolations ^Δ

Leaving you, this glorious morning,
Presents an incongruous dilemma:
I, we, know I must go,
Even though staying one day more
Might pose no monumental distress to the universe.

Perhaps this reaving
Is the only protection beautiful people possess
Against satiety. Just as God
Wrested perfection from bone and flesh,
So He shaped yawns, sleep, death, decay

As hiatuses placed predictably
Between dreams and doings, failings and success,
Ancient and succeeding civilizations,
Making reincarnation the exceptional rule,
Renewal of the spirit a foregone conclusion.

So, lady, for now, then, anyway,
You and I must not fret,
Rather forget dejection, delight in the prospect
That the future has reserved places between the spaces
And will notify us as we converge.

10/29/81 — [1] (00178)

Even the Highway Is My Crucifix ^Δ

Even now, the voracious miles devour the hours,
The hours memory,
On my inexorable exodus northward, home.

Bailey's Woods, through which you traipsed,
I ran, to challenge my manhood
And commune with Faulkner's lingering echoes,

Sinks into dusky retrograde, like a reluctant sun
Descending into a velvet crevasse.
Rowan Oak shimmers yet, though vaguely,

In its Hellenic, antebellum elegance,
A green-and-white bouquet
Wilting, by the minute, in my eyes' grip.

Oxford itself, where you and I rendezvoused
Two nights and days,
Browsed within the drowsing coverts

Of the unobtrusive cemetery on the Ole Miss campus,
Consecrated to those who died in '62,
From wounds at Shiloh,

And where, later, we taught our lonely souls
To translate silences, transpose unspoken notions,
Into love poems

That might illuminate the cold room
We chose to hold the shared strophes
Our tight-woven bodies composed . . .

The elusive mirage
I pursued, with euphoric exuberance,
All the way south out of time

And finally arrested long enough to penetrate . . .
Has now completely unshimmered me.
The distance between it and my existence

Is an optical delusion so wide
That vision refuses even to ponder its inaccessibility.
The dream slips back into cool disenchantment.

I chill. My sallow, sweaty flesh
Manifests the tired spirit's death.
Nothing is left except to bury myself

In my life's solutidinous waking work, writing,
And daily obligations casketing my fate
And pray for occasional exhumations.

10/29/81 — [2] (03539)

Rummaging in the Attic △

Bailey's Woods is a magical Victorian attic
Punctuated with myriad irregularly placed windows,
Crisscrossed with protruding beams
And rafters angling toward cathedraled eaves,
Sweeping galleries, pinnacled turrets,

A miraculous catchall
Stuffed with fabulous bric-a-brac,
Relics, from past decades and generations,
Decomposing in various stages of oxidation,
A space suffused with dust-mote ghosts,

Buzzing insects, tiny creatures
Left unmolested for seasons,
In the serenity engendered by few human intrusions.
Only occasional daydreamers
Come to repose, lose themselves, for moments,

Before descending, by ascending,
Into the outside universe,
Where time's punctual ukase
Precludes accidental discoveries, reverie, forgetting,
Aery observations, rarefied insights.

Bailey's Woods is the secret place
To which I escape, my safest retreat
Whenever the need occurs
To climb the highest peak in my cosmos
And survey the terrain for enemies,

Or return to confirm that certain special memories,
Stuffed in nooks, on shelves,
Are intact. Just yesterday, in fact,
I came upstairs, to look for nothing particularly,
And found you, browsing in the shadows.

10/29/81 — [3] (00069)

Arrested $^\Delta$

I

This Monday morning, a warm drizzle
Or slow soul-mist
Rolls over our tiny community.

Gazing out of the Capital Café's plate glass,
At the rain-mottled courthouse,
Which sits as stolid as a rhino in zoo display,

My eyes skitter between tumid drops,
Unscathed. Vision remains dry.
Insight is an adroit athlete

Avoiding obstacles whose fluid discontinuity
Makes second-guessing irrelevant.
Despite the lack of set patterns

Or possibly because of their unpredictability,
What I reach with my seeing
And what I eventually retrieve

Are two quite dissimilar images.
In fact, traces of the original
Always dissolve in the intervening shimmer.

II

Suddenly, I hear a bailiff's "Oyez, oyez,"
A judge's unimpassioned sentence,
And see a condemned man rising from his seat,

Escorted, by a matched pair
Of sheriff's oxen, out the double doors,
Down the streaked stairs,

To the street, across from where I've malingered,
Trying to keep from getting wet.
As I stare, recognition connects me

With the scraggly vagabond
Being taken one block north, on foot,
To a cell in the county jail.

My eyes glaze with the slow grief
Running down his neck and face.
For a moment, the drizzle imprisons us both.

11/2/81   (00582)

Life Everlasting

Sweet Jesus, I'm off again,
Drawn to my life's lodestone, the road,
Caught in this fluid nexus,
Pressing ahead, with unquestioning obeisance,
*

As though my questing were destiny's
Foregone conclusion
Instead of a fated odyssey,
The wayfaring Jew's abnegation of place,
Destination, and mortality,
St. Jerome and Moses sojourning in exile.

Jesus, this wilderness gets cold at night,
Arid by day. Sun and moon
Are both my children and forebears.
I wear them in the skullcap
Between my legs — a scraggly pair of gonads
Enlarging and contracting with the tides.
My parchment flesh
Is a sacred Coptic text, the stars' cabala,
Containing ancient secrets of the people
God chose, then smote, in the beginning.

My own codices proclaim me
Descendant of Priam, Ishmael, Hagar, Ahab, and Cain.
Driving dead-ending highways,
Going nowhere, over and over,
I placate Lares, ghosts, Eumenides, and saints,
By paying with tokens of my poet-soul,
At tollgates maintained by the State of Grace,
In the Land of Thanatos.
Gaining safe passage, I arrive alive,
Exempt from death's sensual temptations, forever.

11/9/81 — [1] (00861)

Takes Its Toll

Having completed his delivery,
Received signed carbon copies in triplicate,
Willy races hastily away,
In his all-purpose station wagon,
Takes to the road, heading southwesterly,
Hoping to arrive at his next destination,
Columbia's only family-owned budget motel,
Before the listing sun is totally scuttled
In the cold ocean toward which he floats,
Comatose, this late afternoon.

His slowly groping vision absorbs the silence
Through which he passes,
Quietude pervaded by preemptive winter —
Brittle, unpicked cornstalks,
Stubble, raw fields, whose disced furrows
Are scabs, cicatrices, and scars,
Trees ravaged, shivering arthritically
In the bitter, freezing winds
Raging across the empty Illinois prairie
He traverses as twilight disappears

And night emerges from storm clouds
Forming on the horizon. Willy watches,
Not apprehensively,
Rather with a boredom informed of wisdom.
He's made similar trips
At least three hundred times,
Without mishap. Soon, he'll see
The JB Bridge, enter Missouri,
Aim into the vectored slipstream
Intuition uses to guide his gone spirit

Toward warm, convenient harbors,
Safe, familiar way stations
Shimmering out there, in the limitless invisibility.
Now, he awakens from his vague daze,
Into the waning dusk, strains to reaccommodate,
Positions himself differently,
Braces for the remaining hundred miles,
By straightening his back, stretching his legs.
Suddenly, cramps in his calf and neck
Throw two nooses around his brain.

He doubles over, in excruciating immobility,
As his car plunges across the median,
Into the opposite flow, and explodes
Like a grenade. Momentarily, the sky ignites
In a spectacular, sizzling girandole
Composed of crackling flesh, gasoline, metal.
As fast as it erupted,
Night reshapes itself around the opening, closes,
And the road Willy Sypher has known so long
Buries his memory beneath its concrete groan.

11/9/81 — [2] (02384)

A Nocturne

The crepuscular sky
Is a wide piece of mottled sheet metal
Corroding before my eyes,
Decomposing into terra-cotta rust
As it metamorphoses slowly into ore.

Before me, I see night accreting,
Rising from the horizon,
A jagged cordillera piling high
From metallic dust
Sifting through the parallax, into blackness.

Soon, only scraps of a moon and stars,
Sparking in faradic magnitudes,
Will remain, for gazers to speculate
On how a solid plate of polished parabolas,
Strapped to the planet's back,

Created afternoon's brilliant rays
From a solitary flame,
Magnified day's illumination
By acting as a catalyst
For gas changing to vapor turning to celestial illumination.

11/9/81 — [3] (05779)

Dreaded Silence

Silence pervades the petty pace
This place creates inside my echoing psyche.
Each phrase my tongue formulates
Makes a few unanswered circles,
Before fading into the petrified fissures of my brain.
Even the music, programmed to exude spontaneity,
Drifts off on the smoke-ocean's waves

And disappears with all my hopes of fashioning poetry
From this lonely ambience. Quietude
Is my unravished bride, a virgin prostitute,
My muse, whose deaf-mute afflictions
Disqualify her from partaking of my persuasions.
*

I sit in imaginary sands,
An abandoned Sphinx spewing stranded answers

To personal enigmas, unable to listen to my own words,
For fear I might recognize myself
As the laureate the years have subjugated to failure
After such a celebrated youth.
Tonight, I can't even translate my name,
From sacred cabalistic formulations
Emanating behind my eyes, let alone decipher

Rhyme-chimes striking the cosmic tympanum
Separating my outer ear
From God's inner reverberations.
Silence is a malicious rumor
Condemning me to stuttering epilepsy,
Rendering my talent a womb
Doomed to deliver, stillborn, all my conclusions and dreams.

11/9/81 — [4] (02625)

The Salesman Performs His Own Last Rites

All the way out I-70,
He counted the accumulating miles and hours
As though they meant something consequential
In the sequential order of the aging universe,
Rather than just being more senseless data
His digital odometer might neatly record and display,
At the press of a stray finger,

Whenever fancy or wayward whim dictated release
From concentration, contemplation,
In which his eye and brain were engaged.
And as he went ever westward,
Gaining distance on his forgettable past,
The sky kept descending, changing costumes,
Disguising itself as something elfin, tantalizing,

Until he no longer realized his ship was drifting,
Leaving the safe harbor inside the reef,
Entering the leeward drift,
Being drawn subtly into the pernicious sea
*

Floated with finned monsters and right whales,
Creatures of outsized proportions
And designs decidedly not of his comprehension.

Soon, he sensed, by sheer intuition,
He'd veered too far from shore to exist
As he had in his pure state of maternal bliss.
Suddenly, time and space, measured by integers
Illuminated in green diodes, warned him of danger,
Yet stopping, reversing forward motion,
Was impossible; he'd passed the point of no return.

Within a matter of fears, night blinded him.
Setting his instruments on automatic pilot,
He let his hands go limp on the wheel,
His eyes cease focusing on the centerline.
He'd never been lost before,
Abandoned, on his own, alone with his thoughts,
Accosted by dream-demons at night,

While driving out from his home, to alien cities
Beyond familiar extremities,
Never been required to calculate his own survival,
Navigate death's shoals,
Arrive at a strange port, after dark,
Park, bed down in foreign quarters.
Now, before him, flickering lights dimmed and brightened,

Invited him to exit each passing cloverleaf.
Finally, he managed to slow,
Creep off the road, roll to an awkward stop,
And haul his minimal gear indoors,
Where all he was asked to do was sign his name,
Address, and license-plate number on a card,
Before being assigned a room in which to sleep the night.

Next morning, dazed, on waking from sunlight
Breaking through the open drapes, he rose from bed
Without the slightest recognition of where
And when he'd died or why
Intimations of his demise had coerced him to leave,
Like an aged American Indian or Eskimo,
Range beyond his known reaches, to the unknown, and submit, alone.

11/9/81 — [5] (02626)

The Alchemist

I fly, fleet as a phantom,
Through this Midwest terrain,
Toward Tipton, then reverse my circuit,
Returning, tonight, to Columbia, to eat, sleep,
Entertain my lonely soul
During the hours between both perfunctory needs,
Quoting poetry I've neither seen nor heard

Yet memorized preternaturally,
Urverses my solitudinous heart
Churns out, into the bloodstream, with nervous breathing,
Purging oblique, vague thoughts, with fresh Chablis,
Each time the dry lips require a fix,
Freeing word-notes, strophes, cadences
Flexible as sleek snakes slithering in the sun.

Such habits, I realize, lead to intemperance,
Solipsistic, antisocial tendencies,
Introspection — abstractions with tragic consequences,
Especially for writers like me,
Who eschew pleasure-seeking and immediate gratification,
For the subtler self-discoveries
Available to those willing to float nonexistent oceans,

Fly with wax wings, traverse highways,
In vehicles without tires, toward shores, horizons,
Distant Cíbolas known only to navigators,
Pilots, drivers daring to drown, soar,
Course beyond memory's threshold,
Vision's scope, fancy's tantalizing mirage,
Those willing to take their own lives seriously,

Without fear of dying, confront suicide
As though it were just one more egregious chimera
Needing annihilation
In the most expeditious and economical way.
Such passions, I realize,
Are anathematic to active, tactile spirits
Too busy with the intricacies of self-aggrandizement

To squander energy listening to ephemeral rhymes
Time might wish to weave about their eyes
*

And inner ears; too blind to heed universal music
That spellbinds the planets, keeps them aligned,
Ensures day night's surcease,
Night day's release, God's ordered performance;
Too certain of their own perfectibility.

Yet this is precisely what I do best.
In my sedentariness, I confess everything,
Without the apologies or guilt
Usually considered essential
In redressing the apparent disparity between dream
And reality. I always allow myself
The benefit of the doubt,

Quote from my soul, with epicurean wholeheartedness,
Record the onion in its skin,
Undressing it layer by translucent layer,
Until I become the metaphor, the naked truth,
At once both less and more
Than the sum of whatever, at any given moment,
I'm about to become: the poem itself.

11/10/81   (02627)

Time-and-Motion Analysis

I take to the road again,
This quick, crisp morning,
Set the vehicle's cruise control, sit back,
And let myself partake of my exodus,
Relaxed. My exile, expatriation,
My wilderness sojourn in this Midwest,
Has kept me far too long from my destiny:
Illuminating, with painstaking accuracy,
In limner's strokes,
My secret soul's book of seasons.

My aggrieved heart begs release,
Craves solitude, days untainted by voices —
Human multitudes —
Shouting praises to themselves and golden calves.
My diluted blood must be renewed soon,
Pumped and filtered through sky,
*

Stream, dirt, shoot, and root,
While I am left to my wiles,
Undirected, to write and read and recite verse,
Sieving eternity's sluice, prospecting for truths.

This hour's drive has allowed my juices to revive,
Run, with alacrity, through the sun's lungs.
For a few moments,
My easily entranced fancy
Almost achieved enlightenment.
Now, the factory looms just ahead,
Beckoning me resume my time studies,
Record data, fashion job descriptions,
Calculate new rates on unprofitable operations —
The poetry of a middle-aged failure.

11/11/81 — [1] (05780)

Migrant Farmer

It seems strange to cast seeds
In a bar, glean, from vagrancy, faces,
Songs that glued youth to exuberance,
Deeds wrought from super feats of strength
Achieved, preternaturally, in crises,
Athletic contests, loves lost and forgotten —
Such a strange place to harvest dreams.

Yet the man who furrows his land,
Husbands its desolate acres,
With infinite delicacy and thoroughness,
Plants his entire life by hand,
One tiny word at a time, can't be concerned
With geographical irregularities, vicissitudes
Occasioned by climatic changes during the moon's phases,

Nor does he have energy to squander
Worrying about impressions neighbors might draw
Witnessing him, all hours, all seasons,
Pacing, in moody solitude, over his fields,
Waiting and praying for, exhorting his crops to mature,
Reach retrievable levels deemed acceptable
By those his intuition knows must judge his expertise.

His task, that of farming the heart's terrains,
Goes on seven days a week,
Regardless where destiny takes him
And fate allocates homesteads, watering holes
Where, momentarily, he might cease his migrant ways,
Set down roots, rest from his journeys,
And survey the lay of his endless labors.

He is his own soul's poet, the only one
Who controls crops seething in his fertile loam,
Growing profuse as moon-fruit, honey in combs.
Just now, the bar closes. He leaves,
To seek newer territories, arable soil,
Frontiers so rich in potential image and metaphor,
He can't resist his itch to keep wandering.

11/11/81 — [2] (02574)

The Man Who Conceived Himself God

Whenever I leave home, on extended trips
To unknown zones,
My desperate, festering, questioning heart
Begins to grow agitated. Consternation
And angst drive me to caffeine, mornings,
For increased exhilaration, followed by Chablis, nights,
To smooth off the raw edges.

I resort to composing poetry, in lonely moments,
When focusing on barmaids and waitresses
Half my age — oceanids, naiads, other sirens —
Drives my vibrant psyche crazy as goats
Scaling Grenoble's severest slopes.
I grow melancholic, pretending my own children
Are "home," in my motel room, waiting for me

To return from my obligatory nightly vigil
On Mount Helicon, no matter the bar's name.
But I know better. I'm a failure,
Whose familial status is AWOL —
"Absent without leave" — a sneaky bastard
Who's used his sacrosanct vocation as an excuse
To justify frequent leaves away from his family.

It's not difficult to understand why both kids
Defy me when I return, spurn me
Each time I announce my next exodus,
Why they pay so little attention to me when I arrive,
On Friday night, to spend the weekend with them,
Before departing, again, for regions
Beyond their comprehension and empathic sensibilities.

But it's completely unfathomable that my wife
Ignores such selfish behavior on my part.
I can't imagine her failure to see
Our separation as a fact of life
Caused by our mutual actions.
She refuses to acknowledge our status.
I could cry that we've arrived at such a state,

On account of my intractable impatience
With my ambition. I've failed
To achieve celebrity in my chosen vocation, poetry,
Which has caused me uneasiness, shame,
Infamous behavior among my peers and colleagues.
Now, I sit here, so very isolated,
Trying to decipher the strange sensations deriving from Chablis

I've been imbibing, these last three hours,
Without appreciable accomplishments.
Suddenly, I realize my inebriated condition
Has rendered me a useless vagabond, derelict,
A family man without a family, a father
Relieved of his most sacred responsibilities,
Husband singled out by eunuch death, to survive his sins.

Asked to finish my drink and settle the tab,
I proposition the fair-haired lady, Lucy Rogers,
Who has pandered to my eccentricities all evening.
Although only eighteen, a waitress of inconsequential credentials,
She will have to serve as executrix of my estate,
No matter how dilapidated and diminished
From its former eloquence and elegant delicacy.

To her, I shall soon bequeath all my inheritance.
The bed we'll share shall bear the weight
My incredible intellect requires
*

Despite its unenviable desolation. She shall become
The silent partner in my depredation,
Recipient of my importunate, vasectomized semen,
Expecting to be the receptacle of genius,

While I realize my lust generates barren seeds.
We leave together, my vagabond silhouette
Embracing her lithe, blond body.
Together, we project the perfection of impersonality.
Together, we head home,
To her rented apartment, to recreate ourselves,
Consummation approximating the soul's desecration.

Without her seeing, I weep while smiling,
Remembering my own frail wife
And two rarely amused children I once made,
Trying to recollect my location
And the reason why, originally, I went AWOL,
Why I climbed the fence and ran
From the only man I ever had a chance of becoming: myself.

Now, we repose in wet, silky nakedness.
I fondle her pubic hair,
Roll my palms over her supple breasts,
Stroke her neck, braid her sinuous hair in my fingers,
So that she realizes I appreciate her femaleness.
She discovers my penis with her lips,
My toes with her lubricious tongue. I cringe devotedly,

Before languishing into a half-sleep
She interprets as ecstasy I'm experiencing
Autonomically. Yet she can't know my imagination
Has strayed, no longer concentrates on her pelvis,
Cervix, her erogenous places,
Rather deviates, contemplates my wife's lips,
Her gentle tensions, her ministrations,

That slender, elongated effigy that possesses her vessel,
Forever recalling a Modigliani
And a Domenikos Theotokopoulos — El Greco.
I stir in bed, unable to satisfy her lust.
She lies quietly on her pillow,
As I cry, evoking my boy and girl,
Grieving their absence, praying for deliverance from the pain

I've wrought on my ongoing shame.
Abruptly, I rise from the rimpled sheets, dress, and run
Into the cold, lonely night. Lights hide me
Under their penumbras. I rush toward safety,
Flying home on the most convenient cloud,
The nearest dream, hoping to reach safe lee
Before storms swarm the ocean like demons.

Suddenly, I see my children, touch them,
Hear them breathing. Having finally arrived,
I promise myself and my wife I'll never again
Uproot myself, lose touch with life, leave,
Surrender my intellect and gonads to the flux
In which destruction by gratuitous fucking occurs
Whenever simple poets posit themselves as God.

11/11/81 — [3] (02575)

Held Accountable

An eerie, sunlit silence
Permeates the countryside through which I drive.
Ahead, a sulfurous haze
Washes the horizon, obscures blue vapors.
Covering both sides of Highway 40,
Frost casts stray glints
Over grass, empty trees, stalks —
A catch of sea fish squirming in a vast net.

Suddenly, I stop the image-making process,
The scanning, asking myself to explain
And substantiate its choice of metaphor —
In other words, what the fuck
Fish squiggling in a net have to do
With this inestimably uninteresting Midwest,
In which fate asks me to survive,
Exacting taxes — my poems — on my existence.

Caught up short, my imagination
Shrugs its shoulders. Its face goes flush,
With embarrassed evasiveness,
As it tries to recapitulate, erase its offering,
Substitute a more germane alternative.
*

My eyes scoff at the words on the page,
Water, laugh caustically,
As if the very thought of caught fish

Being lifted from this land, on a hoist,
Were a Kafkaesque absurdity
Worthy of being turned into fiction or,
For that matter, captured in poetic fashion,
If for no other reason
Than to stand, forever, as a classic example
Of textual misapplication,
Perverse exaggeration of literary technique

Not leading to a desired effect,
Rather ordaining a potentially serious work
To crucial distraction, flatulence,
Ultimate critical disapprobation of the worst kind.
When I look up from my musings,
Try again to transmute the landscape
Into something other than
An exact checklist of its constituents,

My offended fancy resists artistic twitching,
Balks at the notion of tantalizing my spirit
To derive satisfying analogues from nature.
In fact, I can't even see the land
And its myriad objects, for an inordinate glare
Refracting, dead ahead, off the macadam,
Forcing me to concentrate all my energies
On the physically boring task at hand: staying alive.

11/12/81 (05417)

[Even as I enter the Capital Café,] ^Δ

Even as I enter the Capital Café,
This frost-tinged morning
Expanding, with sunshine, like raging atoms
In a reactor's uranium-fueled core,

I bring with me vestigial premonitions
Rendering this November day,
So filled with potential celebration, suspect,
An opaque vessel floated with evil omens.

I trust neither the prediction of sixty degrees
For afternoon's zenith
Nor these prelatic townspeople,
Meeting, in boisterous synod, at the table

Reserved for them by unspoken agreement,
Who, at this hour, are heated
In ethical dialectics diametrically flying out
From every mimetically wired mouth,

Finally converging on a common topic:
The eschatological numerology
Attributable to Friday the thirteenth.
Tongue in cheek, each makes his facetious aside,
Does public penance, with a wink,

While silently reminding himself
Of the consequences inherent in such fate-tauntings.
I listen, with deferential bemusement,
As they exhaust the subject, thinking how each,

By having voiced his superstitious reservations,
Has made himself visible to demons,
Destiny changers, gods, gorgons,
Spectral essences patrolling these lower remote regions,

Vulnerable to acts of God
And other seemingly gratuitous catastrophes.
Suddenly, I shove aside breakfast,
Steaming on its plate, dispatch the remaining coffee,

In a protracted, painful gulp,
Pay the check, up front, and run into the street,
Like Lot's wife gazing back, over her shoulder,
At burning Sodom and Gomorrah,

Racing to escape the imminent explosion
My paranoia predicts will occur within minutes.
All day, I wait for confirmation.
Insomnia sits vigil with me all night,

Accompanies me, next morning, into the café,
Where, already, the prelates
Have settled on a debate of enormous importance:
Who's going to pay for today's coffee round.

11/13/81 (00581)

Carrying Five Lines

He flies past the squint-eyed shops
Lining East Columbia,
Which, with its identical twin, Liberty,
Running parallel, one block over,
Forms the "heart of Farmington,"

And veers to the right, due east,
Speeds by two schools,
St. Joseph Catholic and St. Paul Lutheran,
Snoozing through their parochial routines.
Within seconds, he approaches the intersection

Connecting city with countryside,
Resists, bears witness
That the persistent traffic has abated,
Then presses on, submitting volition
To Monday's wide, silent time warp.

Freedom is both release and constriction,
Vista opening into distant vista
Teeming with shimmering images
Never seen from quite this perspective
Yet invisible to the naked eye,

Immutable within the changing landscape
Each season arrogates to itself.
He hesitates, squirms in his seat,
Peers into the unimpassioned space separating him
From his inscrutable fate.

Transports rip past his weaving vehicle,
Blasting its windshield with grit.
It shudders and stutters in the backdrafts,
Like straw caught in a smokestack,
Frequently sheers off onto the raw shoulder,

Awakening him to periodic realizations he is lost,
Rushing headlong toward chaos,
Without the proper visa, in retreat
From parasites chasing their own tails
In ever-widening diameters.

Cautiously, he edges the front tires
Out onto the highway,
*

Resumes the mesmerizing ride toward silence,
Doomed to communicate with his mute intuition
All week, until late Friday evening,

When the familiar intersection materializes again,
Tenuously reconnects his memory and fatigued being
With the two schools, shops, his home away from his "home" —
The road — sound sleep, the identity he owns
When not questing whom he was meant to represent.

11/16/81 — [1] (02383)

[My boy, Troika, and I,] †

My boy, Troika, and I,
We sit side by side,
Even when he

11/16/81 — [2] (08270)

Roads Lined with Wind-Trees △

For Jan, Trilogy, and Troika,
*   my blessed trinity*

"I was going to say that I wanted to go home,
but I don't know where that is anymore."
"Stop looking outside yourself."

Vague strains sing me awake,
Redeem silence, this interminable drive south,
From brooding and fatigue.
My heart mimes the melody,
Creating an unsuspected convergence —
Blood stirring from otherworldly stimuli.

Edging ever farther from home,
I close the distance separating loneliness
From those who have saved me
Suffering cosmic desolation,
By listening to and memorizing the breeze
Streaming past my speeding contours,

As I envision my boy, Troika, and girl, Trilogy,
Behind the voices inside the wind.
Their breathless cadences and measures
Inspire me to such sweet forgetfulness,
Dislocation ceases seizing me,
Disturbing equilibrium. I surface

As if from a dead deep-sea sleep,
I, my spirit, a vibrating diapason
Spiraling along a double-helix highway,
Traversing an endless clef,
Back and forth, gaining momentum,
Recreating myself, through replication,

Every mile I've strayed since leaving home
To seek the source of metaphor.
I realize, now, the force behind my quest
Has been you, blessed wife,
My mission to bring you time-rhymes
From my reclusive soul,

Musical souvenirs from fugues
And pilgrimages to the heart's Wailing Wall,
My brain's Bailey's Woods,
Ancient sands where Moses roamed.
For you, Jan, and our children alone,
I pluck poems from wind-trees along roads I compose.

11/16/81 — [3] (00136)

Hanging Out the Wash △

Although I pass in seconds,
My fleet eyes see her entire life
Arrested in that singularly echoing struggle:
Her fat, black body,
Clad in peach tatters, stretching, forever,
Against a full-throated wind,
Trying mightily to pin a thin white sheet
To a line, keep it from blowing
Out of her grip, with her tangled in it,

Fearing, perhaps, her own disappearance,
Possibly cursing, under her scent,
*

The additional insult to her burdensome work,
Most likely slightly sighing
Before summoning, from unthinking,
Just enough energy
To gyve it, retrieve other wet pieces,
Let them dry before sunset.
I can almost smell the freshness of her poverty.

11/16/81 — [4] (00044)

Time's Harvest △

Whining combines, grinding in tandem,
Pillage the fields,
Wrest their precious golden pleasures
Before casting them aside
As dust and stubble specters,
Vaporous surrogates,
Crones, widows moaning ineluctably,
Begging November winds
To vindicate them of their twin stigmata,
Barrenness and old age.
The land recoils, in shame, from its desuetude.

Now, across the broad Delta and as deep,
A ubiquitous conflagration
Of smoldering, black-smoking shrouds
Rises above flames
Articulating shrill, crying voices.
Soon, no trace of harvest
Will mar the terrain;
Seeds will burst, from silence, from earth —
Maidens in petticoats, silk hose,
Lacy pinafores, dancing the Maypole,
Braiding the sun's slanting rays, in their hands.

11/16–17 & 11/20/81 — [5] on 11/16 & [1] on 11/17 (00033)

Elegy South △

Today, I bear witness to the Delta's
Mid-November interment.
*

Almost nothing remains
Of scraggly-tufted cotton plants,
Plowed under recently,
Except puffs missed, first, by picker,
Disk, in its turn. Soybean fields
Sink back into forgetting
Even as planters prepare
To tear open the closed layers, for wheat,
Even as the burned remains of early grain
Smolder yet, in other fields.

Everywhere, emptiness pervades the landscape.
Whether sleeping between seasons
Or resting briefly, catching their breath
Before accepting alternative crops,
These fields have achieved a majestic quiescence,
Submitting to revocable death.
And their dying provides my life
With another reminder
That eternity is constantly at work,
Turning out newer circles,
Wider cycles. Today, my elegy
Reincorporates me with the earth's origin.

11/17/81 — [2] (00974)

Reverend Whitfield's Apostasy ^Δ

Just yesterday,
I lay on my back,
On a quilt nature had made
From brittle leaves of the ancient Osage orange
That borders Bailey's Woods,
Gazing at its myriad black, barky branches,
Redolent of tarantula legs,
Not in fear, rather amazement
That my relaxed apparatus
Might isolate and extract, from the abstract,
Such an ominously concrete image cluster,
To fluster my moment's rest.

Yet the longer I stared,
The more sharply focused my paranoia grew,
*

As though I were an interloper at Rowan Oak,
Not a votary come in humbleness,
And this tree
Had caught its unsuspecting trespasser in its web
And was ready to bite my silence,
Paralyze and consume me in my own juices.

Today, curiosity has returned me to the spot
Where I died. On the ground
Below the green-blooming Osage orange,
An impression of my shadowy remains
Still recalls me to the spot
Where, once, I came and dreamed and prayed
That Addie would sneak from the coverts
Before I'd run back into the woods,
Back to my family,
                    back, back,
Back to my heart's empty grave,
Without staying to see if she'd ever come.

11/19/81 — [1] (00051)

Doom Cloud

For miles before it and I arrived,
Collided, with terrific friction,
It weltered and moiled
From ground to sky,
Wider than the entire horizon it obliterated.

Then its enormous gray head shattered,
A natural grenade
Splattering wet shrapnel across its path.
Before my aghast eyes,
The highway slithered away like a snake,

Its slickness too fast for me to follow.
Night at high noon —
An untimely Armageddon
Too soon obscuring my destination —
Forced me off to one side,

As prodigal souls across the median
Hastened to outchase its specter,
*

Racing to overtake them
Even as it moved easterly, across the state.
Long after it faded, abated, I waited there,

As though possibly it were playing possum,
Baiting me out of hiding,
To pounce again on my pusillanimity.
When I finally did resume,
Something other than time had changed.

Whatever had intruded
Lingered before me all afternoon —
An impenetrable gloom, a pervasive haze.
Maybe I'd witnessed the universe
Entering the first stage of its last earthly phase.

11/19/81 — [2] (03589)

Sleight of Hand

Having left Oxford at eight o'clock,
In seventy-degree ambrosia,
And journeyed nearly six hours,
Three hundred miles,
Without a solitary stop in between,
I break at Perryville,
Exit and park on the McDonald's lot,
Intending to get coffee, urinate, stretch,
In whichever order
My knotted body deems most propitious
To its ongoing activities.

The shock to my system,
On my stepping from the car, in rolled sleeves,
Shirt undone three buttons,
Is so unexpectedly severe, abrupt, cold,
I cringe. My skin instantly metamorphoses
Into goose pimples.
Even before I reach the restroom door,
My penis speaks first,
Begins leaking on the floor.
I almost fear the prospect
Of pouring more liquid into my gut.

Once on the road again,
Rejuvenated by having spent ten minutes
Indulging my taste for caffeine,
I still refuse to believe
My eyes could have watched the magician
So closely, kept focusing
On his hand that held the sun,
Without seeing him make it disappear
Behind the sky's shining scrim curtain,
Catching him rearranging the mirrors,
To reflect, in my perfect surprise, his natural legerdemain.

11/19/81 — [3] (03498)

[If ever the principal draftsmen and architects] †

If ever the principal draftsmen and architects
Who conceived, executed,
And reveled in their creation of the first Greek temple
Could have survived to see the facsimile
Dominating Farmington's downtown square,
They would have convulsed themselves to death, by laughter

11/23/81 — [1] (01388)

[Breakfast at the Capital is not exactly] △

Breakfast at the Capital is not exactly
Schrafts, the Palm Court,
Or, for that matter, grabbing, on the run,
A wrapped danish, black coffee
Sloshing inside its capped plastic container
And burning fingers fiercely,
All the way up Avenue of the Americas,
Up the elevator, to an office
In the Burlington Building, to purchase piece goods.

In fact, the total lack of electricity,
Sophisticated intellect and dress,
Neurotic ambitiousness,
So starkly juxtaposed in my experiential eye,
Attest to the axiomatic hypothesis
That man can adapt to dung heaps and castles,
*

Develop characteristics specially fitted
For existence on noncontiguous islands,
Mind-spits, or archipelagian atolls.

Yesterday, a Puerto Rican waitress,
Cursing the universe defined by the tiny space
Behind the counter confining her daily slavery
To taking orders, serving dishes, humoring cooks,
Clearing dirty plates, returning servile complaints,
In Spanish, with acrimonious civility,
Transmuting propositions into sign language,
Thumb-biting, middle-finger exercises, lips
Visibly articulating silent "Fuck you"s,

Spilled eggs on my shirt, down my pant legs,
And, without apologizing, shoved a pack of napkins
In my general direction, before spinning back
Toward the grill, to retrieve more orders.
Today, the young lady serving breakfast
At the Capital Café engages
In pleasant solicitudes, admonishes me
To let her know if I need anything,
If the coffee is hot enough, the toast warm,

Whether the ham chunks are sufficiently lean
(She assures me she's told the cook,
Personally, I requested all fat be cut away
Before making my meat and cheese omelet).
A fish out of water am I, a king,
A giant in a Swiftian land,
To whose shores Zephyrus has exiled my vessel,
Tied down my oversize ego,
Taken my surprised spirit in tow, remanded me

To the custody of my own heart's intuitions,
And released my spirit to muses
Starved for the creative excesses of a poet,
Businessman turned artist —
Such a queer, eerie transmogrification
For one such as Lemuel Quixote.
Yet this Midwestern Laputa,
This pre-Judeo-Christian, Moorish Iberia,
Suits my uprootedness just fine.

11/23–24/81 — [2] on 11/23 & [1] on 11/24   (00580)

Going Cold

No matter how hard I stare
At the blue-ruled page,
My barren imagination
Can't make it yield up, from invisibility,
Its moon-fruit. On such occasions,

Trying to pluck poems drooping from trees
Lining the eyes' driveways
Leading to their crystal palaces
Is like squeezing Paleozoic rocks
To rescue trilobites from extinction

Or pressing coal to coax diamonds out of hiding,
By main strength.
Today, the entrance to the word-maze
Remains inscrutable,
Refuses to admit my addicted soul.

Suddenly, I resurrect, from forgetting,
That sad face of the lady
Escaped from the state hospital,
One snow-blown November night,
Who stood at my front door,

In thin pajamas, her feet bare,
Her numb, shivering lips and skin blue,
Imploring me to take her to Florida,
Anyplace except "home." Suddenly, I know
How cold is having no place to go, all alone.

11/24/81 — [2] (05460)

Stargazers

For Jan,
after sixteen years

Mesmeric scintillas fill me with exultation.
They emanate from you, Lady Magic,
Whose Zuider Zee eyes
Not only buoy my deep-blue gaze
But reflect my echoing pleasure's ecstasy.

Sparking splinters spin through space
As we chase the dots
Our affections postulate as stars,
Connecting them each time we touch, kiss,
Making visible our private constellations.

Like opposing electrodes spitting zigzag bolts,
We energize the sky's poles,
Whenever we climax simultaneously,
White, wet fire
Fusing our bodies, with celestial glue.

Somewhere up ahead,
A narrow, floating lens slows, opens,
Waiting for us to catch up, enter its focus,
And be possessed of timelessness.
Eye to eye, we arrest the future.

11/24/81 — [3] (02029)

Thanksgiving 1981 ^Δ

I

Just one day to go
Before tomorrow. Both our children
Know it's palpable as snow on the air,
This chilled November morning.
They're imbued with pilgrim iconography.

Their psyches are bee-busy,
Gathering symbols, myths, history,
Flying in and out of anecdote and legend,
Pollinating apocrypha and truth,
With identical enthusiasm,

Processing John Smith, Pocahontas,
Massasoit, Miles Standish in the same breath
With Kermit the Frog and Snuffleupagus,
Simulating the fabled gobbler's screeching,
With outrageous delight,

While scribbling squiggly silhouettes
Of combs, wattles, feathers, beaks,
Clawed feet varying in toes,
*

From one to three to eight,
On books, woodwork, leading edges of dreams.

II

Tomorrow, quite early,
We'll take to the road,
Our windwagon loaded with Rockwellian hopes
For adventure, sentimental gentleness,
Potential snow flurries,

And arrive in time to share festivities
Yet engendering from the table
At my parents' home, in Ladue,
Our extended family converging in noisy joy,
To partake of the Lord's cornucopia,

Before being washed back, into private seas,
By Lethe's ebbing tides,
Our homeward vessels riding high,
For peace pipes, tomahawks, turkeys left behind
To disappear beneath Christmas glitter.

And tomorrow will seem like yesterday,
Shimmering with excitement,
Except for a different set of myths
The children will already be memorizing,
Worshiping as if their heritage depended on it.

11/25–26/81   (02028)

Pyrrhic Victories

Yesterday's Thanksgiving festivity
Was a Pyrrhic victory
For those doomed to maintain disciplines
Regardless of long weekends
Or federally designated holidays.

Hiatuses, moratoriums, quiescences
Fail to let them catch their breath,
Ascertain latitude and azimuth and date,
Locate their next direction,
Exit the amazing labyrinth,

Through whose Queen of Hearts' tart-gardens
They race, chased by shadows
Of their own making, who pressure themselves
To retrieve, from the creative urge,
A fresco, poem, Golden Gate Bridge,

To substantiate their existences,
By allowing others to look, to see,
Hear, and listen, to walk across the abyss
And disappear into their own vision,
Pyrrhic victories, always,

Since those rejoicing in artifice and alchemy
Know nothing *is* that is or seems,
But dream-stuff, possibility,
Nor do their labors achieve endings.
Each completion is another tentative beginning,

A rainbow, birch, a cosmic catapult
Bending down to earth,
To grace them, fling their waiting spirits,
Hurl their purged selves skyward.
They rest, who incessantly quest after essences.

11/27/81   (02087)

A Solitary Lemming △

The café is abnormally quiet, this a.m.
Possibly, the unabating rain
Has kept breakfast regulars closer to home
Or distracted their gregarious instincts,
Diverted them, earlier, to their shops.

Whatever the case, my coffee tastes better,
For subdued cant,
Diminished cigarette haze,
Which usually rises into the grease-laden air,
Billowing with portentous storm clouds.

No matter the weather, I arrive,
Each and every morning, directly from sleep,
To slip persistent demons
*

Who refuse to be seen in public with me,
For fear of being recognized.

Thank God for paradoxes. Here, I'm safe,
Able, amidst multitudes,
To perpetuate my life's mission,
Write my cabala, without raising suspicions
I might be indicting them from within.

Indeed, I'm most severe on myself,
Demanding more from the language
Than it may wish to relinquish to strange ears,
Begging metaphors and humbler images
To materialize and thrive in this desiccated Eden

I plow and tend. Just now,
Outdoors, the rain changes to a deluge,
Threatening to wash clean
All traces of humanity from sidewalks,
Pigeons from the eaves, delivery trucks from streets.

Against the plate glass,
Strident silvery streaks tap, tap,
Shiver the resonant windows —
Oversize tympanums magnifying their tapping,
Distracting me from the task at hand.

My pen ceases purging itself, preternaturally.
Even my eyes focus outside,
Where ghosts have gathered. They're stoning me.
When I look around, the café is empty.
Alone, I prepare to enter Monday and drown.

11/30/81   (00579)

Metapoetics ^Δ

Departing is a preposterous preoccupation,
Which possesses me,
Torments my psyche to write while driving,
Record my soul's emotional poetics
For no known reason
Except to leave pieces of my hobo spirit behind,

That others might read me alive,
Exhume my loneliness
From its anonymity, my bones' former shape
From the ashes I've scattered
Across ten thousand notebook pages
(My mechanically numbered days),

Guess the delicate hue of my flesh,
From restive metaphorics,
Lyrical sinuosities, and measured involutions
I've used to scratch my signature,
In resonating echoes,
A solitary line at a time, letter by letter

By fastidiously etched letter,
Whenever I set out to find my stray shadow
Along my heart's myriad highways,
Poking through castoff litter,
Sifting glittering glass
For the merest trace of my wayward identity,

Writing myself awake,
Quoting myself asleep, at home and away,
A cloud, vapor, silence itself,
Teaching its lips to whisper, scream,
Recite wind-songs across eternity's long baffles,
To vector me home someday,

Eons from now, when, having traveled
To the horizon's thinnest edges,
I'll turn within my grave,
Prepared for resurrection, and leave again,
Driving the sky, wide, deep, and high,
In quest of that most precious poem of all: life.

12/1/81   (05781)

[My words converged, this early morning,]

My words converged, this early morning,
Leaving sleep, with my shadow,
At the exact hour my imagination awakened
And began groping, in the dark, for its robe.

They spoke, at first, in broken cadences,
Stuttering to form verses, strophes
By which the silence might recognize their voice,
Admit fancy into its 6 a.m.

Yet not until the throat's fluting
And the tongue, continually reshaped
To conform to every sound the air might desire,
Had been amply lubricated with coffee,

Wafered with dry toast
(An ascetic's natural breaking of fast),
Could mind and sentiment coalesce,
Conspire in celebrating sunlight

And pinching one's skin, touching the chin,
With quizzical finger, before beginning
To investigate the words' design,
Sift the nuggets they'd sieved from sleep's sluice.

Not until the spinning drum within the brain
Gained sufficient momentum
Could silhouettes that illusion projects as dreams
Dematerialize from the screen

And actual people emerge,
Speaking their own indissoluble words,
Rejecting, through negative natural selection,
The crucial terms of negotiable peace:

The acceptance of ideological biases,
Respect for life, survival
At any cost. Not until then
Did I realize how precarious was my tenure,

How impermanent my purchase on this earth,
Into which I'd awakened,
How mistaken my words had been
In asserting their independence,

Assuming they would find responsive minds,
Sympathetic spirits
Capable of listening and contributing
New ways for saying the same old things.

But now, the only singing voices
Shimmering the air are imaginary whispers,
Distant gods and goddesses kissing,
Insinuating, into my ears, lyrical possibilities.

I sit alone in this boisterous café,
Challenging myself
To transcend my limitation just long enough
To retrieve a piece, a speck, of eternity.

12/2/81   (00578)

[At 7:16 a.m.,] ^Δ

At 7:16 a.m.,
I bellow at my daughter, Trilogy,
Who's wallowing, like a hippo,
In her pool of drowsing half-sleep,

Knead her, like bread dough on a table,
To awaken her for school.
She rouses with a baby-bear growl,
Eschews getting dressed, eating breakfast,

Taking vitamins, especially
The oversize, unsweetened C,
Brushing teeth, having Daddy chauffeur her,
With his litany of silliness and song,

The entire four minutes it takes
From our back porch to the front door
Of St. Paul's Lutheran,
Which this hybrid of Hebrew and Catholic attends

Without bias, undisturbed
By her poor performance at morning prayers,
Her failure to memorize and recite
Key passages relating to Jesus and His Bible,

Instead euphoric within that tiny classroom,
Whose confines contain treasures of Solomon's mines:
Smiles, radiant eyes,
Words, numbers, the universe, eternity.

Somehow, we arrive
At one minute to eight, saved again
From the ignominy tardiness denotes
In the whole panoply of Christian deportment.

I wish my precious second-grader
A great good day,
Jubilation of the spirit: "May you learn
More about yourself and the world."

We kiss, hug through our bulky jackets.
She slams the door on my remorse,
Scrambles up the stairs, disappears into my despair,
As I inch away and enter the day.

12/3/81   (01457)

Prairie Town — Jacksonville, Illinois: Looking West, Along Morton ^Δ

Even from where I sit,
In this many-eyed, franchised anomaly,
Situated like property in a tent city
On the fringes of an old gold-rush boom town,
Resisting the impulse to order
An all-American "Prairie Breakfast,"
The "#3"
("2 Golden Brown Hot Cakes,
Ham, Bacon, or Sausage,
One Egg, Any Style,
Syrup and Butter"),
For only $2.17, this Sunday morning,
Listening uneasily to the wobbly music,
Waiting for the solitary waitress,
Wearing Saturday night's reprobate fatigue
All over her seaweed clothing and face . . .
Even from here, I can still see
Occasional spaces between each crematorium
(Sizzlin' Stockade, a.k.a. Bergen-Belsen;
Hardee's, McDonald's, Burger King,
In place of Dachau, Auschwitz, Treblinka),
Detect cornstalk stubble
*

Sticking up through the black, plowed loam,
Whose future is more dubious now
Than it ever was,
As the invading hordes,
With corporate offices in Anaheim, Fargo, Peoria,
Queue up for the last available lots,
On which to construct their false-fronted sideshows.
I can survey, both ways,
Only a small portion of Jacksonville's business loop,
From where I sit with coffee,
Gazing, in lonely amazement, at the vast change
That, in a mere fifteen years,
Has claimed its inalienable rights
To secure a claim on the American Dream
Of feeding the hungry, the poor.

12/6/81   (02086)

Near Helicon ^Δ

Seated in this booth,
Primed to survey distant terrains
From my perch atop the earth, I wait,
Pen poised, in midair,
Like the axis of my spinning imagination,
Anxious to see words materialize from worlds
Otherly, netherish, and surreal,

Whirling suns and moons
Inching, centripetally, toward a metaphor-core
Whose aesthetic gravitational field
Will glue all visions, prophecies, foreknowledge
Into a solitary revolving sphere,
A poem, whisper of the original Whisper
Arising out of the miasmic cooling.

But the process refuses to accomplish itself.
Creation is an exercise in patience,
Lacking all virtue.
The page remains unchanged,
For my concentration, my ruminative gazing,
And the men at the next table,
Whom I'd hoped to indict poetically,

Continue their racial vituperations unscathed,
Purging themselves, with outrage,
Of the curse worked by black athletes
Dominating Sunday-afternoon TV,
Determining, finally, that all "niggers" are ignorant,
Even professional football players.
"They ain't no different from a trained bird dog";

"Every last one of 'em's the same,
Under them painted helmets: dumb apes
Runnin' like hell, to escape their own shadows."
My ears pulsate, but my brain
Fails to translate this stimuli into images
Sufficiently objectified
To evoke a measured response. I grow tense,

Knowing the world at large has outnumbered me,
Once again defeated me
At my vocation of arresting truth
Before it dissolves into base human components —
Hypocrisy, self-delusion, lies —
Alchemizing the donkey's bray into song,
The snake's bite into a kiss, exonerating myself.

12/7/81   (00577)

Dozing Off ^Δ

Driving south, this shimmering December morn,
My head droops
Like a man-high sunflower.

Solitude is the hitchhiker
I picked up, miles back,
Praying conversation might keep me awake,

But my eyes still refuse to make contact
With his uncommunicative face,
As the highway lullabies us strangers

Into the mantra of whining tires on concrete.
Gradually, I submit to drowsiness,
Sink deep and deeper

Into the incantatory ululation
The road whispers to its wayward navigators
While luring their souls away from home.

Suddenly, time and distance
Relinquish their holds, unloose me.
I come uncocooned, exit this dead mood,

Which has imprisoned me two hundred miles,
Confiscated, from memory,
The preceding four hours. I breathe in,

Suspire. Relief snaps my neck erect.
Ahead, I detect the river
Connecting Arkansas with Tennessee.

Instinctively, I speed up,
Ecstatic to be arriving intact, back again,
From the land where shades masquerade as sunflowers.

12/9/81 — [1] (03499)

The Seven Senses

For Jan,
with devotion and adoration

Jesus, how breezy my heart would be,
How drafty its venous corridors,
Were it not for thoughts of you, wife,
That flood my blood, engorge the cells
Whenever I leave you at home.

How unsavory my pleasures would be,
How bland to the taste buds,
When I'm on the road, gone for the week,
Were it not for your tongue's impression, woman,
Memorized by my tender flesh and eyes.

How opaque my poetic visions would be,
How hazy and impenetrable hope
For new images and antique insights,
Were it not for your crystal facets, Jan,
Lighting my kaleidoscope, from within.

How acrid my sweat and semen would be,
How lacking in your sweet perfume,
Were it not for the joy we exude, my precious,
When, in bed, our noses explode
With the blessed aroma of our undressed zones.

How uninspired my ideas would be,
How vapid my imagination,
Were it not for excitement you evoke, muse,
By refusing to disclose what's inside.
Shared secrets bear dry seeds.

How rough to the touch I would be,
How ungentle touching others,
Were it not for you soothing my skin, lover,
With emollients forming fountains you coax
From ambergris oceans below my soul.

And how quiet our lives would be,
How impervious to outside stimuli,
Were it not for Troika and Trilogy Maya, lady.
They unite and unify us,
By amplifying God's silence, to audible love.

12/9/81 — [2] (02085)

Homeward Looking ^Δ

Oxford is another night away from home.
It's my wiry hair,
Silhouetted, like a crown of thorns,
Across the page I fill with loneliness.

It's my blank heart's blinkless stare,
Sharing the smoky, opaque air
With fifty other pairs of groping eyes,
Trying to achieve the Phoenix's transcendency,

Through mediocre poetry flowing slowly
From my dissociated brain.
Oxford is the green light on my Gatsbyed youth's dock,
Flashing, erratically, in middle age,

Faulknerian emanations I still crave
Despite premature senility
And an irretrievable innocence.
Oxford is a princely frog

That leaps each time I reach
To touch its shimmering shape,
An unclothed toad, Mississippi nobility,
My lonely soul's Christian pseudonym.

12/10–11/81 — [1] on 12/11   (00037)

Navigating a Brain-Rain

At first, my ears merely discern
A thumping and scratching,
Chasing back and forth across the glass.

Soon, clawless paws
And soft pads materialize on the windshield,
As if myriad invisible animals

Had leaped from the sky
And landed on my tender lenses
Without disturbing vision,

Rather redefining the welter
Before and behind my eyes.
Suddenly, it's raining dogs and cats.

Tentative and cautious, I drive home,
Hoping not to be gnawed to the bone
Or clawed blind but to survive my own inventions.

12/11/81 — [2]   (03599)

[Dear Mr. and Mrs. Claus,] †

Dear Mr. and Mrs. Claus,
    My brother, Troika, and me
Are writing you, this Christmas, 'cause
    We thought you'd want to see

What gifts we'd like to have you bring
To our house, in Farmington.
I, Trilogy, more than anything,
Would like to get a Talking Barbie, fun

12/11/81 — [3] (04303)

Supermen [Δ]

They know Jimmy Olsen's name,
Lois Lane's, Clark Kent's, Otis's,
And Lex Luthor's like their own,
Can recapitulate and predict,
Through repetition and clairvoyant déjà vu,
Every incident and cataclysmic event,
Moment by moment,
Throughout the two-and-a-half-hour movie.

They revel in the phenomenal heroics
Of baby Kal-El (lifting a Model T
By the bumper, outrunning a passenger train),
Titter and giggle at the naive reporter
Who has "eyes" for Miss Lane,
Saves her from a careening helicopter,
Reverses the planet's direction, to divert fate,
Keep her from dying in an earthquake.

What most amazes me
Is their rapt attentiveness to the pay-TV
And the happiness they afford
In making me their co-conspirator,
By snuggling close, holding my hands,
Both slightly frightened
By the awe-inspiring derring-do
Superman provides. They're pillowed on each side of me,

As though, no matter the fragile line
Between fantasy and real life,
I will be their final, omnipotent arbiter,
Absolve them of all obligations
To defend themselves against malevolence
Or werewolves and Draculas
Lurking just beyond the door.
Mine is the role of Supreme Neutralizer.

By 9:30, my two droopy-eyed urchins
Acquiesce to covers and lullabies,
Without a litany of sleep-prolonging requests
Or hastily made-up questions,
My boy proudly wearing his cape
And red-S-shield pajama top,
My girl whispering, through her yawning lips,
"I love you, Super Dude!"

12/11/81 — [4] (01458)

Drafting

I'm not ten miles out from Farmington,
Yet my eyes and head ache,
From a sun so treacherous,
This December morn,
I'm forced to pull up short, park,
Order Sanka in a Styrofoam cup,
From a horsy, gum-chewing waitress.

As I leave the lot,
Reenter the main-traveled highway,
The container begins to leak
From an imperceptible fissure halfway below
Its steaming surface.
Like a seal balancing a ball
While nudging, on its belly, across a stage,

I change positions uneasily,
Awkwardly shift the cup
From lips to rug, trying to consume enough
To make it quit. Finally, I pull over,
Splash most of it to the shoulder.
A truck speeding past
Blows the liquid back on my pants and boots.

Within miles, I recognize the vehicle:
A black flatbed with side racks,
Transporting a single camelback casket
Conspicuously stippled in bronze,
Surrounded by two-by-four support boards,
Pulleys, straps, ratchets, tents, and tarps —
Eerie Piranesian apparatus.

For more than forty-five minutes,
I drive in its draft,
Being drawn along effortlessly, in silence,
As though my car's engine were off,
The tires perfectly balanced
To maintain frictionless freewheeling forever,
Its direction and destination my own.

Suddenly, its right taillight blinks.
I pass the truck,
Making its entry toward the weigh-station scale,
And, as I hurtle north along this concrete Acheron,
Gaze over and see my own face,
Reflecting off my right-side window,
Superimposed on the sinister black cab.

12/14/81 (05782)

Witnessing the Spirit's Death

From black, through orange and lavender,
To swirled blue-gray,
I pass from hue to chalky hue,
Registering dawn's changes
As gradations of my spirit's awakening.

I'm gone again, a phrenetic wren,
A tideless navigator,
Sightless visionary, Tiresias in disguise.
Mine are the eyes of Dr. Eckleburg,
Swinging on rusty hinges, in typhoon season.

Something premonitory, this morning,
Although I know not what, disturbs my journey —
A murkiness to the sun, possibly,
Like a bloody glob in the yolk of an egg
Cracked into a smoking skillet,

Perhaps the spectral headlights
Of the eastbound traffic,
Lingering ineffectually as ice cubes
Set on a hot stove,
Suggesting an endless funeral procession.

Whatever the cause,
My frightened psyche refuses to quit yawning.
The eyes behind my eyes
Manufacture nightmares, in broad daylight,
As I pass from minute to minute to hour,

Like the teeth attached to a watch's escape wheel,
Slipping in and out of their anchor.
My breath fails to keep pace
With the heart's adrenalized beating.
The bladder screams to extinguish its own fire.

Suddenly, noon and evening begin spinning.
My shadow passes from day to day,
Breaking invisible seals
That have maintained vacuum within the mazy caves
Breathing connects and keeps inflated.

Finally, the silence grows so violent
I can hear myself expiring,
Feel death's stethoscope pressed to my chest,
As I'm rolled away on a stretcher,
Pronounced DOA.

12/15/81   (05783)

Seeking Asylum in Silence

I

Amber lights glisten off the crystal wineglass.
My eyes listen to its visible whispers,
Lifting vaporously into my ears.

The Chablis mirror into which I peer shimmers,
Echoes reflections of distant voices
Wishing to kiss my lips. My tongue translates the rim,

Tastes tinges of sweet, paradisiacal nectar,
Then speaks gentle litanies, in deference to pleasure.
Instantaneous rhapsodies dizzy my brain,

As mirages lift off the undulating ichor
That has transported my spirit
Beyond limits of human hearing, to Kubla's Xanadu.

II

Tonight, blown so totally off course
On this intoxicated ocean,
I begin to see my own reflection's timbre.

The image of my loneliness, floating naked,
Shatters the glass my cold hand holds,
As though it were eternity's only shrill note.

Slowly, my senses adjust to the self-destruction
Isolation imposes on my soul.
In a moment of madness, I swallow my pride,

Listen to the tide inside the glass disappear,
Drowning my poet's meek vision,
In the eyes' ears, and witness silence rise from the vortex.

12/16/81 — [1] (02576)

Guest Speaker

Who among you has ever been sieged
By a swarm of enraged bees while picnicking,
Molested by a band of piratical thieves
As you relaxed on a remote beach,
Or had your common identity
Mistaken for that of an international spy,
On an ordinary trip abroad
To consummate a basic trade agreement, for the State Department,
With a World War II enemy
Who, just a few years before, owed reparations
Inconceivable for their incalculability
In terms of damages perpetrated in honor of Hirohito's name —
Premeditated murder, suicidal genocide?

I ask you, you intellectual bastards,
Who among you has ever had to confront pressure,
Defend your vulnerable flesh
Or your country's ideological emblem against anarchists,
Leftists, insurrectionists like Mizmoon, Cujo,
And Patty Hearst, foreigners from within the system,
Who would sunder Crocker National,
*

Bank of America, with a Molotov cocktail
Or Thompson submachine gun bought from army surplus?
Would any of you out there
Dare put your own lives on the line,
To defend the slender fabric
With which freedom is forever reweaving itself?

Would you? Would you? Have you?
I ask you, people,
Who among you has ever had to remove your clothes,
Stand naked, dehumanized to the bone,
To prove your commitment to personal beliefs,
Free speech, unadulterated love?
Think about it before you answer,
You sycophants, slaves to what others think!
My suspicion is that not one among you
Has ever stripped for Auschwitz's Zyklon B showers,
Enlisted for Vietnam, undrugged,
Worn the Shroud of Turin for an hour,
Or bowed before Schongauer's *Dance of Death*!

You must be squirming in your seats, by now,
Asking yourselves why I was invited
To read to you my flimsy, fragile verse.
Most likely, you've already decided
You certainly don't need me to agitate you,
Alter your predetermined visions
Of the good life. Let me reassure you,
You needn't feel embarrassment on my behalf.
I've come, tonight, to testify, to play Lucifer's advocate,
Beg you question your own motives
For avoiding testy introspections, heady speculations.
My chief purpose is to make you realize
Life is all it's cracked up to be and less.

12/16/81 — [2] (02666)

Winter's First Storm

The sky is so bright, early this morning,
As I take to the highway again,
One would never suspect the temperature
*

Just outside my ice-crusted glass
Is twenty below zero,
Factored for wind chill, or that, last night,
A demon-driven blizzard
Besieged the entire Midwest,

Were it not for myriad scattered vehicles
Cantilevered, in antic stasis,
Over ditches, strewn, in precipitous disarray,
About medians, fields, streets,
On cloverleafs, like hobos
Snoozing, in drunken stupors,
Within the shabby purlieus of a huge Hooverville . . .
Were it not for the white shroud,

Whose seam — this glistening road
Stitched with slickness — I follow, for hours,
With fastidious caution, hoping,
At some point on my homeward route,
To reach its terminus, crawl out
From under the sheet, and begin freewheeling
Without fear of being stranded,
Freezing, disappearing in statistical anonymity . . .

Were it not for the conspicuous absence
Of passenger-car traffic. In fact,
Only tractor-trailers,
A few foolish souls like me,
And snowplow crews are out, moving as though
This were just another sunny, blue day,
Not a rickety bridge spanning the abyss
Beneath which River Styx rushes.

12/17/81 (05784)

Ice Storm ^Δ

Our second storm came shortly on the heels
Of winter's first snow.
This time, it took the form of a spider
Spinning the sky. By morning,
Every sidewalk, rooftop, street
*

Was a treacherous, glistening thread
In its net. Whoever among us
Dared out on foot, in vehicle,
Quickly discovered himself,
Underpinnings slipping out, trapped, tripping,
Sliding, unpredictably, through stop signs,
Into curbs, ditches, the day a lair
Congested with unsuspecting victims
Sharing inconvenience, embarrassment,
And a fundamental terror for phenomenal creatures
Capable of elevating the most basic tasks
To vital importance,
Reducing crucial human events
To ludicrous, futile exercises in maintaining decorum.
All afternoon,
Ice-spiders rappelled earthward,
Over the sides of crystallizing clouds,
While we treaded lightly,
Trying to avoid their dread bites.

12/21–23/81 — [1] on 12/22 (04700)

[Already, we've seen snow and ice] †

Already, we've seen snow and ice
Invade our private territories,
Experienced subtle and blatant inconveniences
Occasioned by the moon's

12/22/81 — [2] (04699)

A Christmas Day Hymn △

For my mother and my father

Joyously we gather, this morning,
In an atmosphere of demonstrative love,
To celebrate the unification of a family.

Few are the occasions, anymore,
And fewer, yet, future convocations,
As the nucleus continues to fractionate,

Its atoms' atoms proliferating
Into regions remote from the original core,
Formed by mother and father,

And deterioration and attrition
Begin their winnowing. This afternoon,
We gather to celebrate togetherness,

Proclaim our gratitude to YHWH,
For His having sanctified our tiny cluster,
Nurturing us with gentleness, in peace,

Allowing our intellects to flourish,
Our hearts to take nourishment, strengthen,
Our psyches to orbit on course.

No matter the name
Or justification for this ritualed holiday,
Mankind's glory and grandeur

Soar inside the microcosm Brodsky.
Tonight, we fly, as one, toward God,
In loving resurrection.

12/22/81 — [3] (02084)

[If youth is wasted on the young,] †

If youth is wasted on the young,
As some say when tongue-tied
Or grown forgetful in middle age,

12/24/81 — [1] (09005)

[I've listened to too many symphonies]

I've listened to too many symphonies
Moving through innuendos
And cued, ghostlike fugues
Not to recognize when music
Is building toward crescendo,

Heard too many solemn High Masses
And Low Church sermons
*

Laced with evasive fables and allegories
Not to realize when words
Are rising toward homiletic climax.

With such deft formal education
And decades of secular training,
I am yet at a loss to explain
Why, when my brain is versifying,
I fail to notice the embryonic metaphor

Forming in utero, growing
Toward parturition, being born,
Why, until first cries,
My ears can't hear children inside.
Perhaps the surprise keeps us alive.

12/24/81 — [2] (05785)

A Belated Gift ^Δ

From my venue in this snug booth,
In the Capital Café,
Looking streetward, through plate glass,
At the vacant courthouse,
This quiet morning after Christ's nativity,
My mystified eyes swoop upward
And stop where roof and sky converge.

Pigeons roosting in murmurous ubiquity,
About two inches apart,
Along all four edges
Of the pseudoparapeted cornice,
Transport my stupefied gaze to amazement,
Stimulate my image-making apparatus
To visual apotheosis.

Suddenly, that bland Greek facsimile
Is an Erechtheum ornamented, in gorgeous profusion,
With caryatids, a European cathedral
Surmounted with intricate Gothic spires
Lifting, in stony slenderness, to God,
A German greeting card from Victoria's era,
Laced with delicate, papery crenelations.

I blink. Statuesque goddesses,
Slim pinnacles, embossed designs
Dissolve, like ice, in my warm eyes.
When they refocus, no pigeons appear;
Rather, a tooled crown materializes,
Its jeweled points shimmering in the sun —
A Christmas gift I forgot to open.

12/26/81 (00576)

Son of the Ex-Boss

All is gone from this world of light.
His absence is slight
To those brand new to the sales force,
This season, mildly obvious to the men
Who've been with the company
Ten years. To me, the vacuum he's created
Is so pervasive that even death
Could hardly change the ache
My heart senses, today.

But things change,
The world perdures, everything goes on,
I realize, looking around the room,
Focusing on the rapt faces
Listening to enthusiastic presentations of slacks,
Suits, sportscoats — their "intrinsic values."
Neither individual key figures
Nor "standards of the industry," ambitions
And dreams stand immutably, unassailed.

These ragmen must accept the prevailing breeze,
Acquiesce out of necessity.
Except for basic health insurance,
Commission is their sole fringe benefit.
Integrity gives way to dissimulation,
Diplomacy to vindictiveness and autocracy.
But not for me!
Refusing to accept desecration, I quit.
My dad's shadow is too much with me.

12/29/81 (02382)

Too Many Irons in the Fire: A Valedictory

In certain few, fleet flights of clairvoyance,
I see my destiny
Resolving out of nightmarish miasma,
Along with unidentified myriads:
Branding irons glowing white, gleaming prophetically.

The fire in which each rests
Is a vast eye, fate's sun, perhaps,
Continuously kindled by Lucifer's sycophants,
Bleeding heat so ferociously
No mortal can grip a handle, extricate his identity,

Without risking permanent disfigurement,
Going blind. I certainly can't.
There was a time when all my irons
Were tipped with dreams my ego would brand
On every object in the universe,

Proclaiming dominion over creatures and ideas,
In reckless ecstasy,
As if omnipotence and omniscience
Were twin ministers in the trinity I completed
By believing youth was invincible.

Now, the irons fuse.
We look on, with tremulous bemusement,
Wondering how long it will take
Before our common destiny loses its temper
And melts into fluid shapelessness.

1/2/82   (05786)

Prizefight ^Δ

The pandemonious morning
Is a howling, shouting crowd.
The wind and I are prizefighters
In a ring the size of the entire outdoors.
No matter what corner
Offers me brief respite from the fracas,
As I traverse the four sidewalks
*

Surrounding their stony courthouse
And head toward the Capital Café,
I can't evade my opponent's jabs
Or slip his quick combinations.

We cease, momentarily,
As I wait for traffic to pass, abate,
The new round to be announced.
One minute is too brief
For the fatigued lungs to reteach themselves
The essentials of regular breathing.
I cross the street, on the run,
And am met, head-on, by an uppercut
To the face. My eyes and nose bleed water;
Vision goes out of focus. I reel,
Stumble on the curb, fall to the concrete.

The blurred audience stares through glass ropes
Separating their heated raucousness
From my frozen shadow. Slowly,
Slowly, vague subterranean instincts
Bring me to my knees.
Entering the café, groping for a coffee cup,
I sense my opponent still boasting,
Gloved hands thrusting upward,
In victorious exultation. When I look out,
Snowflakes have begun to fall —
Confetti thrown for the day's first defeat.

1/4/82 (00575)

Paean to Joshua Lionel Cowen ^Δ

Myth and ritual,
Streamlined to fit into our minuscule attic
And pivoting on slick-spinning wheels
Clicking rhythmically over sticks
Glistening silvery, from repetitious passage,
Fascinate us, children and adults simul-
Taneously transfixed.

Each evening, we ascend stairs,
To magical yards and depots,
*

Where dreams are the cargo we load
And ship to distant destinations
Ten feet away and fantasies the manifests
We routinely deliver
By rotating the humming transformer's handle.

Order and the almost total control
Over acts of God,
Cataclysm through human ineptitude,
Make our retreat
So appealing and inexpressibly necessary.
Together, briefly anyway,
We approximate omniscience.

As master builders,
Engineers expert in the artifice of transportation,
We become the occasion
To which our imaginations rise, each night.
Apotheosis is riding, for free,
Those colossal trains,
Singing their song electric. O ye eidolons!

1/5/82   (01459)

Word-Falls ^Δ

Still, my words spill like cascading waters,
Grazing, glancing, striking directly,
Breaking apart on crags
Lining my stratified imagination.

They crash to the basin,
Whose constantly stirred surface
Is an earthly turmoil, and begin searching
For shapes abandoned in the rainbow space,

That place, vacuum, between original creation
And practical or poetic application,
Through whose half-moon halo
Mysticism and artifice separately leap,

Coalesce, transfiguring themselves
Into restless souls questing new vessels
For their individual expression.
They flounder in the fast flow below,

Metaphors and lowly disoriented images
Treading, frenetically, in vortices
And eddying currents in the middle, close into shore,
Swollen hyperboles, emaciated phrases and idioms,

Victims of a hundred plummeting *Titanics*,
Hoping, somehow, to quit drifting,
Be sighted and picked up in time,
Out of the lonely, rolling pool of their brief existence.

Slowly, a courageous, fortunate few
Manage to be ferried downstream,
Escape the devastating straits nearer the basin.
They wade in the brain's shallows,

Taking strength, in measured reverberations,
From distant beating deep inland.
As days evaporate, some are absorbed by the soil;
Others enter the air, singing,

Every survivor a grain, a winged particle
Of the original call creation sent racing
Toward my imagination's falls,
A poem suffering the endless resurrection of my liquid voice.

1/6/82 (05787)

Just "Desserts"

Weariness stalks him as infamy a charlatan.
He's an aging athlete,
For whom the most routine calisthenics
Are pain raised to the nth power
And eating the only exercise
His distended gut still gets on a regular basis.

Whether peering in the mirror
Or overhearing his own slow thoughts
Unfolding from old bolts of cloth,
He knows that for all he's gained
In flab, he's lost.
Mens sana in corpore sano no longer translates.

Cheez-Its, beer, grease-glistening chicken
And fish, heaping helpings of TV —
*

Life's sedentary pleasures,
Gathered greedily, husbanded, and guarded over
By the king of kings, Sleep,
Keep him fit for the Feast of All Ghosts,

Held, in limbo, by Temptation and Slovenliness,
In hallowed celebration of fellows fallow,
Who, having risen from shallow graves,
The self's physical cell,
Will never quite forgive the resurrected flesh
For its damnable imperfection.

1/7/82   (05788)

The Battle of the Books: Ancients vs. Moderns △

As I approach the Capital Café's glass doors,
This unconscionably cold morning,
When the illuminated temperature/time sign,
Angling out from the bank,
At the four-way intersection across the street,
Like an unflinching hitchhiker,
Reads nine degrees,
At three minutes before eight, the rooster sun,
Brooding over this little city
As though each downtown edifice were a hen,
Flies into my eyes, flapping and scratching.

I enter the café, blinded momentarily;
Only my brain remains sighted.
Images of mythical Icarus flying sunward,
Albrecht Dürer's heathens,
Rained on, by sparks from a Biblical sun,
For persecuting St. Catherine,
And the echo of a name, Theodore G. Bilbo,
That has no associational correlative
In my streaming consciousness,
Assail my imagination.
Slowly, vision refocuses me on my location.

Ears and eyes accommodate, simultaneously,
To the persiflage rising,
From the adjacent table, like body odors,
*

And to the quasi-familiar faces
Behind the fiats, admonitions, epithets,
And phrases containing denigrating allusions
To "separate-but-equal treatment for niggers,"
Lesser yet for the invidious Jew.
"Mongrelization! That's what you've got
In St. Louis. Thank God
We ain't got none of them bastards here!"

My eyes wince, ears cringe,
As the conversation advances,
In blatant undulations,
From a peroration on the white man's burden
To physical characteristics,
Rising to raucous climax as the master
Of ceremonies, duly self-appointed, demonstrates
"Thick lips" of "Hait-ians" he saw
In his war days, by pinching his bloated cheeks.
"They'd swing through the coconut trees,
Like brush apes and monkeys — naked niggers!"

Suddenly, the coffee I've been swilling,
To warm my viscera, turns acidic.
My thawing thoughts,
Having all fallen into the proper slots,
Accomplish their process. I realize, now,
Why two of the three images
Surfaced into existence: obviously,
They were meant to buffer my senses, my intellect,
From imminent collision, distract me
From my own fate, by making me recall alternatives.
There's no escaping one's appointed hour.

1/8/82 — [1] (00574)

Dr. Zhivago

A dinner gift
for my Lara, Jan

I wish
Julie Christie
Were my mistress, and I
Yuri Zhivago,

That I might make my passions
Bow to poetry,
Be married to both, without ceremony —
A noble vocation.

Oh, let me
Write my cold self alive
And melt, forever,
Into the soul's Varykino.

1/8/82 — [2] (02083)

Kyrie eleison

Assassinations are in fashion, this generation.
Civilization's imminent collapse
Has less to do
With atomic, neutron, and cobalt proliferation
Than basic ideological confusion
Over which humans should rule
And by what sets of religious, political,
Sexual, and/or militaristic predilections.

It's become academic,
Tautologically impossible to predict,
A rhetorical exercise in finalities,
Whose fundamental question, after all,
Is "Who really matters?"
Perhaps history and her coeval, fate,
Mandated with keeping secrets,
Flatter themselves in having our answers,

Without realizing how anachronistic
Their clairvoyance essentially is.
"Who knows what the future will bring?"
Is such a fatuous slogan anyway.
Alternatives and resolutions
Are the most useful tools we have.
Now is hourly. Only the heart knows
How to tell its own time

And choose exemplars and arbiters
Whose names won't change
*

To sounds like "Judas" and "Brutus" and "R.
Milhous Nixon"
When making peaceful entreaties
To leaders of all peoples.
We must pray for us.
To hesitate is to assassinate hope. *Kyrie eleison!*

1/9/82 (05789)

Frozen Pipes

I don't know what made me doze again,
After waking from a nightmarish premonition
Of frozen pipes broken between the walls.
Perhaps it was a frenzied sense of helplessness,
Especially after I'd found all faucets
Speaking the same sibilant syllables
And exasperating non sequiturs.

Even though TV
Predicted the cold would reach a new low,
Fifteen degrees below zero,
We never dreamed, last evening,
On sliding into our inviolable sheets,
That such remote devastation
Might ever immediately impinge on our sanctum.

Yet by 3 a.m.,
Having spent my most prolific speculations
On specious scientific theories
Of hydraulics, as I skulked, in robe and boots,
Between basement and bathroom, for clues,
Trying to hold off using the toilet, too,
I finally surrendered to both instincts,

Before returning to bed
To give to my frightened wife an admonition
And an irrefutable truth:
"Whatever you do,
Don't use the stool. I just did.
We're screwed!
Come daylight, we'll have the devil to pay!"

1/11/82 (05459)

Willy *in vincoli*

Since his retirement,
The Capital Café has become the mecca
Toward which he daily directs
His deliberate crusades. Paradoxically,
For more than four decades,
He never once set foot in here
During the week. In fact,
The road, which owned his total allegiance,
Kept him away from Farmington,
His home, so relentlessly,
His waking and sleeping lives became reversed.
Only in dreaming could he take responsibility
For his growing family's successes and travail,
While, through years of days,
He drove in a funk, numb to everything
Beyond his three-tiered frame of reference:
Speedometer, centerline,
And onrushing environment,
Whose tornadic eye, filled with swirling simulacra —
Telephone poles, road signs,
Five-star communities, clouds,
Fields of corn, sorghum, soybeans,
Milo, rice, cotton, and apple trees,
Sun and moon
Sliding, like slugs, up and down myriad horizons,
Across wide, innocuous skies —
Never ceased to stimulate his mind to fantasize,
Out of his own mundane routines,
Noble deeds of godly design.

Since his retirement,
He's not quite been able to accommodate to the stasis
That small talk and false camaraderie,
Undulating from mouth to ear to mouth,
Around a table, help create
In those who've never known the pleasure
Of going places, alone,
Floating, for days, on soundless oceans,
To reach the imagination's Baffin Bay,
Patagonia, and Tasmania.
Yet he realizes the Capital Café
*

Is the last earthly outpost on his journey.
He prays old age will accept him gracefully.

1/12/82 (02381)

Artisan ^Δ

Only faith in my vocation's siren song
Could tease me awake,
Lure me from home,
This snowy morning,
To take up pen, again, in the Capital Café,
And without the slightest guarantee
I'll be paid a day's wages,
Come day's end,
When taking stock, transcribing my notebook entries
Into typed forms, filing them away,
For later revision and, ultimately, public inspection.

Yet how could I ever dare refuse?
Daily renascence
Is such a natural way
To bring the imagination's brainchildren
Into this world, from the other.
What remorse and ignominy would result
From promoting stillbirth or abortion
Just for the sake of a few brief eons
Of additional dream-sleep,
I can only guess, since never
Have I indulged relaxation to excess

Or rested on the efficacy of past metaphors
Arrested in creation's heat.
Rather, it has always been my aim
To forge portages
Between uncharted lakes and name them
With the energies expended
Connecting two newly discovered entities,
Each poem a passage between hidden thoughts.
Just now, I sit stiff-necked,
My cold toes calling inordinate attention
To themselves, my pen yet poised

To penetrate the empty air
Separating brain from page,
Perform its skills without hesitation.
Outside, the slow-falling snow
Seems to have reversed its direction.
It's all blowing skyward,
Toward the invisible source of an inchoate sun.
Suddenly, the day I hold is a moist white rose,
More than compensatory reward
For a poet whose devotion to composing the unknown
Is a labor of love, growth.

1/13/82 (00573)

Eskimo Love

A fantasy for Jan

By the time we get into bed,
On nights like this,
When thirty-two degrees would seem Mediterranean

And brain-batteries are drained of energy,
For cranking dream machines,
And antifreeze is too low in the bones

To dare let the hands and legs
Inch from their nesty retreats, alone,
For fear of being buried in an avalanche of sheets,

And when the very notion
Of going after romantic apotheosis,
Let alone attempting hasty coitus,

If just for the sake of saying no to nature,
Refusing to submit to sleep's slope,
Without so much as a groan,

Seems outrageous to the outraged soul . . .
It's then that we summon up,
From the caves of myth and memory,

Courage to transcend our unaccommodating grave.
We rush from bed simultaneously,
Illuminate the room, run, naked, to the shower,

Lie down and luxuriate
In the steamy flow from its volcanic spout,
Copulating for hours and hours and hours.

1/14/82 (04175)

Self-Reflexives

For James G. "Jim" Watson

My poems are almost always demotic,
Self-reflexive little fellows,
Parodic whimpers and groans
That celebrate man's explainable grandeur,
His fractionated loneliness.
They mock me, personally,
Their host, conduit, amanuensis, medium,
For reading the mystical, crystal cosmos
Inside whose translucent plenum men fumble,
Weightless, despite gravity,
Blind to visions, though endowed with eyes,
Ignorant and superstitious of dying,
Despite extrasensory intellects
Leaders of the tribe profess to possess,
Occasionally courageous, faithful, kind.

Once, my poems rode out, credulously,
On white-winged steeds,
To rectify imperfections in the queen's fiefdom,
Set the record straight,
Among policymakers in the Campo Vaccino,
Redeem unregenerate souls
From their devil-holds,
Redirect the reprobate, the mendacious,
The hungry, unclothed masses, to art's feet,
By blowing my mellifluous Pan flute,
From whose sensual, slender tubes
I used to tease the sweetest soothing notes,
Believing in the efficacy of music
To harmonize every terrestrial destiny
With its celestial coeval.

For years, now, however,
Neither private nor popular approbation
Has offered me a heeltap
For having brought to my craft
A high degree of freedom
From academic claptrap and patent dishonesty.
Yet if they never completely outdistance
Their voracious narcissism,
Introspective, convoluted syntax,
Pomposities of diction, mixed metaphors,
My poems will still satisfy my ideal
Of living literature: each breathes,
Leaves its readers believing a human being,
Not God, once lived and died
Inside its body, trying to translate the ineffable.

1/16/82 (02082)

The Arctic Heart

When it's this cold,
Even passages piercing the nose contract,
In fierce reaction to freezing fire
Driving, like spears, toward the lungs.

The heart grows wary.
Inspiration no longer seems
Quite as salutary or easy for the throat
To accommodate as it did indoors.

Mechanisms stutter,
Abruptly readjust to the decreased flow
Of incoming molecules,
To outgoing waste escaping, hysterically,

Like air from a child's unknotted balloon.
Suddenly, in broad daylight,
My raw-edged shadow stalking me
Like a beggar beseeching alms,

My body reenacts the spastic ritual
Of drowning swimmers,
Toxic-asphyxia victims, cancer patients
Gasping their last inhalation.

It and I are ripped apart,
In stark pain. Just prior to absorption
By time and silence, the imagination
Records our separation,

As we ascend those twin Kilimanjaros.
We're most alive when closest to dying
In poetry's high throes —
The frozen soul's radiant moment.

1/18/82 (05790)

Her First Bunking Party ^Δ

As the day drew closer, then nigh,
And the appointed hour arrived
To deliver Trilogy, sleeping bag, and dolls
Unto the keeping of others,

We could sense her anxiety rising —
A cotillion queen on coronation night,
Uncertain of balancing her curtsy
And gracefully taking her crown.

Her nervous verbal discourtesies
Only encouraged us to extend clemency.
All week, we worried eye to eye,
Without ever having to shape our concern

Into words. Something premonitory,
Traumatic, kept me at work
Long past quitting time,
That afternoon.

Perhaps fear for her safety
Had brought my ostrich tendencies
To the surface, caused me
To bury my consternation in corporate papers,

Catapulted me to bed very early,
Complaining of headache and chills.
Regardless, each minute between 9:00
And 11:15, waiting for the phone to ring,

Was a tooth on nightmare's cog,
Whose exasperatingly minuscule movements
Proved too painful a mantra
For my brain to use in bringing sleep to bay.

Suddenly, the bell's shrill clangor,
Penetrating the cold air, broke the spell
Suspending me, like a living mummy,
Between sheets. I jumped, lunged for the receiver,

And, naked to my bony emotions,
Listened to her frightened, quavering voice
Crying, sobbing hysterically,
Imploring me to come get her.

Soon, she was back in her own bed,
Familiar pillows for her head,
Quilt for her soft, fetal shape,
Fast asleep behind the resonant echo

Her tiny supplicant's words
Left repousséd on my relieved sensibility:
"I love you, Dad.
I love you a thousand thousand!"

1/19/82 (02081)

On Heroes and Heroines

Why is it that so few lives
Collide with greatness, light eternal flames
They carry past occasional grandstands,
Scratch their fragile, intricate signatures
In computerized cuneiform
(Wisdom captured, in clay, for the ages),
And, instead of dying, crystallize
In the stratospheric ice floe,
Shatter into faceted matter,
Illuminating the lower reaches of paradise?

Possibly, philosophers and social scientists
Will continue to espouse outmoded theories
Of hero worship, great men,
*

Or attribute all mortal success
To providence, predestination, timing, accident,
Lady Luck, circumstance.
Perhaps they'll lobby in Congress,
Pray, from pews, to the new stars,
For future messiahs, newer crucifixions,
Without realizing greatness is an illusion

Perpetuated by doomsayers and dreamers
To justify their very existence as purveyors of "truth."
History and myth have common origins;
Their differences are not mutually exclusive.
It's a matter of who fills top positions
At any given moment in the planet's spin
And how their administration is perceived by leaders
Blind to the cosmic dust behind them,
The silent, screaming, leviathan tidal wave
Stalking them from phantom space.

For me, those who qualify
As exemplars of godliness wear no epaulets,
Bear no official titles,
Carry no political burdens on their shoulders,
Rather share smiles
Despite financial "tights," headaches,
Make modesty their daily charity.
Of my apology for yesterday's forgotten tip,
My waitress says, "It's OK, hon.
It's peoples bein' nice that matters — like you!"

1/20/82 (00572)

Between Snows ^Δ

We leave the house, together,
Trilogy and I,
And, tasting the weather, simultaneously agree
"It's like spring, today."

"Why did you say that, my girl?"
"Oh, I don't know . . .
The wet . . . the birds chirping, I guess.
How about you, Dude?"

"It's my heart imagining itself elsewhere,
Remembering scented sounds,
Old friends of consequence,
Whose eloquence echoes a gentler time."

Our expressions hover in midair,
Like mourning doves pairing off for flight,
Reflections connecting generations
Separated not by years,

Experience, or sensitivity but poetry —
A dad and his second-grade daughter
Caught between thoughts,
Trying doors to a common lexicon.

1/21/82 (01460)

Of Fishes and Fishers

I strike out, in a blind funk,
Exchanging home
For the concrete road's abstract unknowns,

A mind-blown sailor set adrift,
Rabid Ahab
Triangulating the stars, to locate the great whale

Floating the invisible moon's currents,
Hoping to harpoon its silhouette
Breaching the horizon,

Lingering, in midvision, at twilight,
Before disappearing, again,
Into the inscrutable *noche oscura*.

Driving alone, I scrutinize the abyss,
Ever just up ahead,
As if from a swaying crow's-nest,

My eight eyes measuring the distance
For aberrations, narrowing,
Threatened by death's square edge.

No colossal image of *spiritus mundi*
Materializes, outside,
Against which to gauge inner wisdom.

I settle back, in tedious acquiescence,
Fate's hapless factotum,
My own soul's lonely outcast,

Plying these sea lanes, roads,
Going nowhere
Over and over and over, in antic panic,

Fishing for mystical answers to physical existence —
A minnow, diatom,
Strained daily through Leviathan's baleen.

1/26/82 — [1] (05791)

Painting Himself into a Corner

The land he traverses is amber, tan,
And tawny beige — doom-shades
From a Pieter Breughel scape
Deftly superimposed, as cataracts,
On his mind's twin eyes, desolate impastos
Irregularly splayed on fancy's canvas.

Even ice-clotted ponds out there,
Beyond his spectral fleeing,
Exchange places with his vision.
Rubbing his lids, he cuts his fingers
On jagged chunks, smears the horizon,
Toward which he rushes, blood-rust.

Suddenly, he speeds across the river,
Which, until now,
Has given him a sense of depth perspective,
Lent direction to his painterly word-sketch,
In temporal terms. The bridge's plane
Breaks his imagistic thought-train,

Sets up reverberations along his bones,
Detonates claustrophobias.
He's in no-man's-land, and he knows it,
By the way the painting he's made
Has framed him behind shadowy spans.
He's inescapably contained by his creation.

1/26/82 — [2] (05792)

Sonne-set

Afternoon softens in the sun's crucible.
The horizon bends at its center,
Droops gently at the edges of vision.
My living spirit enters the sky voluntarily,
Like bubbling gold filling a mold,
Slowly solidifying into a Brancusi idol
So beautifully smooth to God's touch, I die
Into the very moment of my own immolation,
My westerly drive sheer apotheosis,
Emotional high inside external ecstasy,
Mind-blown sobriety on a routine crusade.

I pause, caught in twilight's shattering,
One star in the far, cold night,
A luminescent speck, an incarnation
Rising inside my two unfocused eyes,
Peering down, through the great Eye,
Onto the moon's lunatic shadow,
Which finally recognizes me
Behind my elusive mask — a human intruder,
Trying to penetrate the supernatural portal,
Arrive, intact, at the sun's source,
And learn how to burn, immortal and whole.

1/26/82 — [3]   (05793)

Franz ^Δ

His ears are always whisperous with fear —
Wasps chasing each other's flutter,
In and out and in their nest,
And out again and again, and in and in.

He is insectile, frightened by his own voice
Screaming, in dark closets,
Pleas of innocence for imaginary crimes:
Patricide, child molestation,

Wife beating, masturbatory celibacy,
And incest. He weeps at his helplessness
In defending himself against charges
Levied, in the state's lower appellate courts,

By apprentices, in fact, actually law students
Doing their internships, as it were,
On human guinea pigs — misfortunates
Brought before the Grand Inquisitor's court,

To be taunted. Frightened by his own rage,
He's a screeching gibbon, in a zoo cage,
Being gawked at by well-paid Peeping Toms
Hoping to locate a telltale clue

To his undisclosed identity — a tic,
Word-slur, Freudian slip of the flicking tongue,
Any convenient parapraxis
To which they might neatly fit their psychoanalyses

Without jeopardizing their precious reputations.
He exists in constant trepidation,
Nightmaring scenarios in which he's arrested,
One fine morning, by two Cyclopes,

Traduced (whatever, he's not yet determined,
This specific, disturbing verb means),
And trundled off to an internment camp,
To lose his freedom forever.

He lives in fear, from year to year,
Yet never has he been reproached
For turning in his insurance appraisals late,
Nor has he been nonconforming in protocol;

Rather, his behavior has always been circumspect,
Absolutely without distinction
In a negative vein. In truth, his anxiety
May be completely fabricated, unfounded,
The result of collective, compensatory cultural guilt.

Indeed, being a pre–World War II Jew,
The youthful Kafka just may have intuited
The Apocalypse, before tuberculosis
Could save him from the indignities of Treblinka, Dachau,
    and Auschwitz.

1/26/82 — [4] (02577)

Trooper Breen, Car 279, Missouri Highway Patrol, Boone County, Meets Mr. Ladue

Closing in on his destination,
He loses patience, begins to exceed the speed
Decreed legal and safe by the state legislature,

Forgets his prudence. The gauge reaches sixty,
Seventy, seventy-five.
He realizes, in an instant, he's immortal,

Exempt from accident, arbitrary fate,
The Israelites' plight.
Velocity is the only legitimate destination,

And he's predestined to achieve the ultimate,
The infinite, the absolute,
In a godly sense, the maximum allowed,

In earthly terms. But the Speedgun
Clocks him, at Columbia's outskirts,
Doing eighty-eight,

On Trooper Breen's digital display.
He instantly becomes a prime violator,
Perpetrator of a crime

Worthy of computerization.
Swirling, circling red lights
Bring him to his senses, abruptly suspend his odyssey,
On the shoulder of a crumbling I-70,

Just in time to avoid extinction
Either singly or at the expense of innocents.
He pleads guilty,
Tacit as a caged bat, docile,

In fact ingratiating to the officer,
Actually appreciative for his sudden apprehension,
Without which his immediate annihilation
Might have been copy for the local obituary section.

Embarrassed at having to accompany the young man
In uniform and felt hat
To his car, parked obtrusively behind his own,
And prove his credentials,

Hear them repeated over police-band radio,
He accepts his flagrant violation
As part of the cost of doing business,
Resigns himself to the ignominy, rests easy,

Realizing both the damage and the restitution
Are as simple to fix as peeling bills from his wallet,
Suborning the Speedgun, the computer,
And Trooper Breen, with a supreme bribe,

Accomplished by greed. Soon, too soon,
He's on his way again,
Speeding hellbent for election,

Confirmed in his immortality, a lonely soul,
Exempt from destiny, purged,
Fast on his track, absolved of normal morality.

1/26/82 — [5] (02578)

Dinner in the Boxcars

Unequivocally, the epitome
Of Midamerica
Is Super Bowl XVI.

I sit in a booth
In Katy Station, listening to three girls,
Posing as college-aged,

Elaborating on high-school choir,
Driver's ed,
And their most recent unconsummated dates,

Clinking glasses,
Clanking plates, toasting rich boys
Willing to take them to France,

Japan, or Auschwitz,
To view the grassy knolls
Where, once, boxcars stopped

And naked bodies emerged,
Gracefully as broken souls, without knowing.
They laugh in awkward cadences,

While I linger across from them,
Witnessing their innocence,
Hoping they'll each meet Mr. Perfect,

Liberate one inhibited ovum,
Perhaps two,
Worthy of children, and leave her mark

On Midamerica —
Boy and girl windup toys,
Who will, one day, find their way here,

To proclaim their own individuality,
And produce progeny
And who, thirty years from now,

Will celebrate and hallow their parents' youth,
By recalling Super Bowl XVI
And the goal-line stand

Against Pete Johnson,
Which made all the difference for them.
In reverence, they'll also recall

How their mothers and fathers
Used to gather here, in booths
In converted boxcars, for supper and drinks,

Instead of as a prelude to Zyklon B extinction,
College sweethearts
Congregating in mating rituals, born to succeed

At meeting Mr. Izod Gucci Levi,
The proud scions of Midwestern forebears,
Inheritors of Super Bowl XVI.

1/26/82 — [6] (02579)

Katy Station's Stained-Glass Fanlights

I

Shapes, until this moment, entombed
In stained-glass fanlights
Illuminating the smoke-choked room
In which I sit sipping cool Chablis,

Begin to ripple, slip sideways,
Like rainbow-fish breaking from prisms
Beneath oceans filled with my dream-visions.
We collide inside the sliding sun.

I become the quality of light,
Essence of blue, red, tangerine, amber,
Frangible hues floating in air,
Brilliant dust motes, honeybees

Arrested, evanescently, at twilight's apogee,
A speck, formed by our converging energies,
Reveling in reckless ecstasy,
A heron among rarefied herons, soaring.

II

This glory-born moment glows with roses,
Whose unfolding calyxes and corollas
Seize me, a petal at a time.
My senses buckle under such efflorescence,

Surrender to the metamorphic alchemy
Engendered by my intense inventiveness
And self-induced fugues.
Goblins dance nimbly on my eyelids.

In this mystical house of the setting sun,
To which I come, occasionally,
Seeking repose from the known world,
Which owns my spirit, my flexible bones,

I am absolved of conventional morality,
Allowed to indulge my soul, for hours,
In powerful drowsiness, sweet amnesias,
Picking flowers from the paradisiacal air.

1/27/82 — [1] (02097)

Interregnum: After Sylvia

Had she decided to stay alive
Instead of pursuing, giving up,
The ghost, committing suicide,
*

Sivvy might have outgrown her temporal credentials,
Ascended poetry's throne, in her time,
Been besieged by attendants and sycophants.

As it was and is and will be,
Within the posthumous gossamer
Of her elusive legacy,
She defies positive logical identification.
Her words, transcending autobiography,
Are shimmering enigmas suspended from the "real world."

Her dazzling verse,
Despite its oft unfeminine perversity,
Renders her queen of exquisite and exegetical imagery,
That country, dominion, paradise
In which those who prematurely decease survive
Immortally. She lives, who died by the word's sword.

1/27/82 — [2] (02580)

Men-strual Cycles

Approximately once a month,
For two or three evenings in a row,
With undeviating determination,
He frequents Katy Station's lounge,
Overindulges his stultified libido, on Chablis.

There, he presses, soothes his muse, with dizziness,
Induces lexical visions, records, in his notebook,
Metaphors abounding in the life-force
Surrounding his corporeal aura,
In order to accumulate proof
That even in disappearance, his spirit rages,

Refuses to be diminished, discouraged,
By the sinister ministers of Christian love and commerce.
With his committed written words,
He dares proclaim his voice,
Make it heard above the jackal-cackling din,
Celebrates the universal, through his unique verse.

His silent bulk cuts a strange profile
Out of the animated gestalt,
*

A Jesus-anomaly not looking for apostles,
Merely trying to survive himself,
Outlast the past, which chases him
In the guise of vivid memories of wife and children,

Until the hour when he lifts his head
From the notebook pages and discovers he's alone,
Floating among the amber ceiling bulbs
And the frozen music — a sea anemone,
A coral, sand, shells, cold,
Silence itself, undulating bones,

Without the slightest notion of his present location
Or the least circuitous way home,
To his motel. He performs this ritual
Once a month, his verse
A blood-rush gushing from the heart and brain,
The scourge a fecundity.

1/28/82   (02581)

Willy Joins the Road Show

Fate would have it, he groused,
That they'd stick him in the outermost cubicle
Of the two-hundred-room motel,
On the coldest night of this fractious winter,
Causing him either to shiver or shrivel
Because of the heater's faulty thermostat,
Which had two settings: OFF and FULL BLAST.

In fact, even the leaking faucet,
Hot water that never kept its promise,
The mattress that sagged in the center,
Like a foundered nag, a radio
Whose voices, bleeding from hidden arteries in the wall,
Never did completely scab over,
And the snowy TV would have been bearable

Had not all of Pandemonium's inhabitants
Reserved every other room,
To convene and parade up and down the halls
The entire night, purveying their wares,
*

With lithographed posters, brochures,
Blinking signs — brokers, booking agents,
Promoters for hell's shows,

The whole hissing abyssful of inebriated demons,
Gorgons, even the great Zagan
And Beelzebub, selling their souls zealously,
Within the sleazy maze of open rooms,
To promote all-lady mud wrestling,
Demolition derbies, freak shows
Replete with midgets, three-headed snakes,

"Penis Lady" and "Full-Breasted Man,"
Circuses and rodeos, vocal groups
Specializing in country-and-western gospel pop/rock,
The full range of wholesome family entertainments.
He might have survived, even found sleep,
If not solace, had the snake charmer,
In 143,

Not seen him sneaking toward the soda machine
And invited him in for a drink,
Had her intriguing, sequined costume,
Cut to the navel, not got the better of him,
Had she not bespelled him out of his basket,
With her fantastically deft lips and tongue,
Come-pelled such beautiful notes from his flute.

1/29/82   (02380)

New Snow ^Δ

Little did we dream,
Though our dreaming encompassed Byzantium,
Nineveh, and Bethlehem,
We'd awaken to such rich Russian drifts,

That so much snow could slip through,
Elude sleep's sentries,
Position itself with such ubiquity
That even our yawns would freeze with awe.

Nor did we dream we'd get dressed,
Rush outside, to touch, taste,
*

Hurl ourselves, headfirst,
In mystical bursts, at God's feet

And keep falling into the sky,
Alice-shapes cultivating hallucinations,
Sundogs chasing their moony tails
Through ice-crystal rings within rings,

Singing, all the way wet to the bone,
Anthems to childhood —
Four explorers gathering, from waking,
Handfuls of the dream, to take to sleep.

1/31 & 2/2/82 (02079)

Trinitarians ^Δ

A hat trick, a turkey, trinity, troika,
A trilogy — by whatever synonym,
A threnody of winter grief,
These three snows
Besieging us within the same week.

Not even Sisyphean,
This absurd routine of listening to news,
For storm warnings, travelers' advisories,
Of digging out, driving to grocery stores
To buy survival from depleted shelves,

Rather Promethean,
Rock-bound beneath the taloned hours
Glowering over our growing argumentativeness,
Waiting to eat us alive
After we've picked each other apart,

Possibly not even Greek at all,
This white cataclysm
Testing our wits and resourcefulness,
But Judeo-Christian,
A Passion Week of humanistic crucifixions.

2/4/82 (05794)

[I never realized how cold]

I never realized how cold
One degree could be
Nor just how tenaciously
My creative juices might resist freezing,
Until early today, on leaving my house,
To breakfast at the Capital Café
And scribble poetries in my notebook.

Although the car started,
Its thin, tortured report made me cringe.
My fingers, contacting the wheel,
Felt as brittle as beetle husks.
Breath, bypassing the constricted nostrils,
Created its own tornado.
Vision was a sequence of crystallized indecisions

Leading safely, somehow, to my retreat
Downtown, across from the courthouse.
Shaping my hands around the coffee cup,
Like a potter, I drank its heat
Without sipping, waited for my wrists and tips
To twitch, thaw, remember their mission.
But they refused to let loose.

For more than forty-five minutes,
Warmth flowed back into my bones and senses.
Then, transfixed, I watched the pen
Assume its familiar angle of attack,
Between thumb and index,
And, as if changing the thaw to water, water to ink,
Rethink, in a single heated flourish, the universe.

2/6/82   (00571)

The Surprise ^Δ

For snowbound Jan;
condolences

On my leaving, this snowed-in morning,
She, who too well knows
The resignation of staying home all day,
*

All week, and, now,
Unbelievable as it may seem,
A fortnight, with two children,
Entreats me to bring her a surprise.

I recoil egocentrically,
Mumbling something about the hazards
Of venturing out, myself a martyr,
Our link between survival and extinction.
As I think about it, now,
Her request seems meager fee
For such extravagant freedom.

Yet, quickly forgetting, I revel in routines
That, any time other than winter,
Would already have sundered my equanimity:
Answering neglected letters
From imaginary lovers and patrons,
Completing unfinished symphonies,
Revising "Ozymandias" and "Byzantium."

All afternoon, I luxuriate
In my cozy office on the square,
I, my own best enemy,
Relaxing unself-consciously,
Oblivious to existence beyond this cosmos,
Whose changeless hours I rearrange
As though they were oceans.

Unnoticed, snow-laden dusk
Has filled the white silence. I look up
From my book, abandon Gulliver to his exigencies,
And call to inform my wife
I'll be right home. Her soft crying
Catches me by complete surprise.
Suddenly, I realize just what to bring her.

2/9/82   (02096)

Becoming Mundane

Seven below
Could be the coldest I've ever known,
Certainly the most extreme in memory.

Even more disconcerting
Is my inability to light in a warm spot,
Find a seat where hands and feet,

Not just my thick middle,
Might keep from freezing, a place
With heated floors, quick-closing door,

In which to sip coffee, listen to scuttlebutt
Crisscrossing country synapses
Or review sales for snowy February

(In the Capital Café or at my factory office)
Without lapsing into distraction,
Chasing daydreams across beaches

Stretching from Treasure Island to Crab Key,
My svelte surrogate
Escorting Honey Ryder and Pussy Galore

Into a deliquescing Mediterranean sun.
Unarguably, the consequences
Of this persistent phenomenon are disturbing.

But worst of all
Are symptoms presaging pernicious senility,
Which I seem, lately, to manifest,

Focusing so totally on the weather.
Preoccupied by forecasts, records,
I've let the temporal get the best of my poetics.

2/10/82 (00570)

Where Snow Comes From ^Δ

This whorled morning,
A vision escapes on a vagrant yawn,
Soars toward the storm's eye.

I, a mind-blown stowaway,
Ride inside its equine belly, into the sky,
Penetrating gray vapors,

And arrive just the other side of Thebes,
At Eden's gates, whose outskirts,
Burgeoning fields, verdant lawns,

Trees drooping with tumescent fruit
Shimmer in Orient light. Reapers and gleaners
Go back and forth along rows,

Connecting eternity with Earth,
Woven as if by cosmic spiders,
Harvesting manna in the gold-flecked glow,

Whose excess dust sifts into my vision,
Coalescing to vapor, flakes.
Suddenly, I know where snow originates.

2/12–13/82 (05795)

In Search of Maidens to Save

The notion of taking permanent leave
Goes both ways,
Along the brain's striated dendrites,
Clockwise and counter,
Whose horizontal circularity reminds me
Of Don Quixote's "forward" motion,
A steam locomotive's spinning beginnings.

Each sallying out I precipitate,
In noble guise,
Visor raised level with the horizon,
Armor pristine, turns to rout.
Rain rusts the hinges. Guttersnipes
Wilt my tilting lance —
A dandelion plucked with rough hands.

Defeated, my doleful spirit retreats
To its cork-lined broom closet,
Where, in Proustian solitude,
It might sort through profuse *libros de caballerías*
And find the one penned by Alonso Quijano,
That I might end my life
Knowing what I meant by "broken heart."

2/16/82 (05796)

All in a Fog

The shimmer through which I drive
Envelops my shadowless passage,
In oceanic pervasiveness.
Raw, taut fog abducts vision.
My eyes tread salty water,
Grab for directional straws,
Drown from exhaustion.

By the time I reach the downtown office,
My spirit has decomposed.
Head to toe, I'm unrecognizable to my cohorts.
Between home and here,
I've suffered a sea change, resigned,
My nine-to-five purposes reassigned.
Now, I work for eternity.

2/17/82   (05797)

[Man is a paltry thing.] ^Δ

Man is a paltry thing.
The songs he sings
Are death-moth wing dust
Sifting abyssward, with each flight.

Dirges emerge
From beauty's tenderest urgings,
Whose sepulchral lyrics
Burn eternally, in earthly urns —

Ears seared by what they hear.

2/20/82   (02080)

Safeguarding Freedoms

I

My words resist disposition,
Refuse sequestration by silence,
Abjure senility and forgetting,
Which attach themselves to the belly of dendrites,
Like parasites leeching sharks.

Quite contrarily, they fight, daily,
Nightmarish tidal waves
Minute by second rising, in cabriole shapes,
To strike: ancient snakes
Spitting suggestions of quitting, in my face,

Venomous evocations
Torturing the senses into ambitionless stupors,
Un-nerving the words,
Debriefing the paltry child inside each —
Creativity's holdout against extinction.

II

Uniformed in my blueprints,
My images engage enemies, in vicious melees.
Some collapse from combat fatigue;
Others discover retreat, surrender, defection;
A few scale metaphorical Mount Suribachis,

Take similed San Juan Hills,
Raise verse-flags,
Whose stripes rhyme their beating hearts alive
And stars punctuate caesuras
Their heroic breathing requires.

These patriotic soul-diers, my brave words,
Not only discourage invasion
And occupation by ideological regimes
Disguised in freedom's poetic rhetoric,
They safeguard man's last great hope: you and me.

2/24/82   (05798)

Lion Day ^Δ

Although my solo trajectory
Is forty-seven miles into its morning orbit,
Their echoes connect me with home:
"It's a lion day, today, Daddy,"
Trilogy sings, stepping outside.
"That's nice," I reply absent-mindedly.
As I drive her to school, she teaches me
The essential dichotomy
Between lion and lamb days.
*

Even now, the raging wind,
Buffeting my car sideways, at will,
Restates her apothegmatic eloquence,
And I wish the highway were a placid sky.

Now, amidst the welter,
I hear my boy Troika's voice
Whispering in an earpiece
I held poised, telling me,
"I sleeped too long, Daddy,"
Whose bittersweet implications
Grow even clearer with each mile.
"'Boy' awakened, went downstairs.
He came back up to my bedroom, crying,
'Daddy's taken Trilogy.
Who's going to give me my vitama C?'"
My mind flinches at my wife's narration,
Despite knowing I told him, over the phone,

Before leaving, "I love you
So, so much." I cringe
With undeniable guilt, for the sin
Of actually having forgotten him,
In my haste, in my self-imposed haste
To make the great unknown
Beyond my cosmos take notice of me,
Mark my unfathomed depths,
Record my passing, with reverential awe.
On this lion day,
I'm caught in freedom's throes,
Dying to abort my mission, return home,
Reverse and postpone countdown indefinitely.

3/2/82 — [1] (01461)

Illusionist

He lives, comfortably,
Inside his own interpretation of the universe,
A syllogistic Merlin
Capable of alchemizing words into solutions,
With involuntary, chiming terza rima,
A sorcerer's apprentice
*

Forcing his way into the lexicon,
With a few metaphorical hocus-pocuses
And a flourish or two of his lingual sword —

Houdini Alighieri,
Master of extrication from *mea culpas*,
Of illusionary excuses
For not having to posit definitive explanations
For his verbal tricks,
A wizard of shimmering mystifications
Exempt from scientific proof,
Whose very existence is tautological evidence
That he is his only truth

And time, as interlocutor,
Is the prestidigitator on high,
To whom he owes his final allegiance,
Ecstasy's source, that Elohimic force
That tells his spells which syllables to trill
And which to explode into full-throated soul-poems.

3/2/82 — [2] (03497)

Watching Myself Watching Myself Being Passed

A beige, hearse-shaped station wagon
Goes too slowly by,
Lingers, on my left side,
Like insects copulating above the highway.

Out of my eye's corner, I notice a face
Staring my way. My gaze
Attaches to its strained focusing,
Trying to ascertain its bemusement.

Abruptly, the beige car thrusts ahead,
As if chased by specters.
Through the back glass,
Into its rearview mirror, I see his eyes,

Penetrating to the weird conspiracy
Their fearful peering elicits in me.
Suddenly, I recognize his furrowed brow
And shrouded eyes as my own.

3/2/82 — [3] (03567)

Dr. Eckleburg Takes to the Road

From the first grudging mile,
Through mile three-thirty-three,
Every billboard and filling station
Was a cliché tattooed to my eyes' biceps.

Vision was a paltry diorama
Strewn with human refuse,
An endlessly scattered scrap heap,
Acne on the land's neglected face.

Even Dr. Eckleburg's resigned gaze
Would have withered, his weathered lids
Shutting tightly, to abolish the blight
My passage could not deny,

Heading south, through Missouri,
Into Tennessee, Arkansas, and Mississippi.
Unrelieved, I passed Greasy Corner,
Hughes, Brickeys, and Soudan,

Each moment, more closely approaching
My first destination, West Helena,
A rest station amidst flagrant desolation,
Where I might eat and chase sleep

Before resuming my quest for the Golden Fleece.
Finally, I arrived, fatigued,
Dissolving into a noxious asphyxia
Issuing from the fertilizer plant beside the river.

No Goshen, this mid-Sheol
(Halfway between home and the Gulf,
Home and de León's ocean), toward which I'd pressed,
A home, I guess, for those souls

With only one incarnation
And no resources to barter for another,
Until they discover Eden,
Pristine and unpolluted — a clean start.

Tomorrow, when I wake,
Perhaps I will have dreamed myself
A new life or at least
New eyes, through which to view the old one.

3/2/82 — [4] (03578)

Outshouting

The hour is too loud, now,
Too *now*. The hollering surrounding me
Dissolves into innocuous footnotes
Appended, inoffensively, to the senses' Shakespeare,
Chaucer, Spenser,
Unfolding slowly out of this morass,
Insinuating my brash verse into a din
Raucous, insolent, lubricious.

My shouting, within this converted warehouse,
Is innocent impudence raised to the nth power.
I'm a brave sailor standing watch
Aboard a cork bobbing in a tidal wave,
A sentinel manning every inch
Along Castel Sant'Angelo's parapets,
A soldier firing tracer bullets at the enemy,
In broad daylight.

A shape cradled within its own flimsy nimbus,
I yet accept my conscious destiny
As that of poet, one who must write,
Regardless of energy, hope, state of grace, location,
In order to hymn immortality,
Succeed in knowing that only by denying silence
Its right to life might I die
Having had the last word, the last word first.

3/5/82 (03579)

The Tall Convict [Δ]

On my trip home, up I-55,
I pass a stretch of the Tallahatchie River
Running under the highway
And watch it disappear, in my rearview mirror,
Like a silver sliver slithering skyward,
Through a Flemish landscape painting,
Meandering into silent depth.

Again gazing frontally,
I sense myself afloat on this road
*

Banked by pines three rows deep,
As though that river's perpendicularity
Had merged with this concrete Old Man
And were now flowing vertically,
Toward its own focal point on the horizon.

My eyes appropriate the mind's urgency
To be borne on the current,
This murky morning I flee Mississippi,
Uncertain if it will carry me safely upstream
Or deposit me down here,
A victim of my own dubious fluidity,
A convict afraid of drowning in my freedom.

3/6/82   (00046)

Feeding Time

Cut loose, my viperine visage
Clears the cluttered city,
Heads west, digesting the gristly images
My eyes zealously consumed
As I crawled, on my belly, through the sprawl.

Clock shops, tae kwon do studios,
Ethnic restaurants, grocery stores, car lots
Formed a collective, unwary rodent
Sparking my insatiable appetite to excitement,
Gaudy and incautious, announcing itself

As though no known fate
Could crumple or tarnish its sleek shape.
Even now, as I slither away,
My gastric juices crash and swirl
All that glass and plastic into pap,

Within my imagination's gut.
Like a glacier, the whole glut descends,
Dissolving, visibly, in a lump,
Until distance and forgetting assimilate memory
And my spastic, constricting intellect relaxes.

3/9/82 — [1] (05799)

Stirrings in the Attic

Sometimes, I worry
That the poems scurrying in my woodwork
Aren't mice searching after mind-cheese
But termites surfeited on their own gluttony,
Escaping decayed basement beams
Before abject collapse
Traps them in billowy debris.

Sometimes, I disguise myself as silence,
To determine whether their measures
Are diaphanous beating wings
Or feet skittering across the brain's flooring.
Even then, their elusive music
Refuses absolute attribution; their source
Remains inscrutable to my doubting ears.

Always, my chief fear persists,
That in their abundant subterfuge,
The years will convince me that one creature
Is superior to the other.
Indeed, neither is capable of rendering verse
Worth rat shit, tunnel-runs;
Rather, the poems are squirrels stashing nuts in my attic.

3/9/82 — [2] (02582)

King Willy

His entire life has been a series of arrivals and leavings.
An itinerant sensibility
Beats beneath his crumpled-cotton demeanor
And the pilled-polyester seat of his soul.

Although each motel is radically distinct,
Each sleazy room he occupies
Stinks of a similar perfume: pubic reek,
Which sets free his hallucinations,

In which he becomes ruler, whose ineluctable powers
Are legendary throughout the cosmos.
In fact, the solitary cubic illusion
That acts as a catalyst for his onanistic tendencies

Lends credence, in its daily-maintained neatness,
To his belief in regal predestination.
King Willy installs himself on a new throne
Nightly, dreams of naked maidens

Urinating and defecating
All over his flabby belly and legs, in ecstasy,
Dreams of seeing his stubby penis take wing,
Like a fabulous Pegasus,

And soar into a Zoroastrian sea of earthly delights.
Yet he goes to bed alone,
Submits meekly to sleep, plays perfect possum
Amidst hovering *Nacht*mares,

And awakens before daybreak, each morning,
To stake out the enemy,
Lying in wait, just beyond the window.
Coffee, black, brings his senses back to polyester

And cotton, occasionally to vestigial double-knit,
As he gathers up stray accouterment:
Toothbrush, aftershave, shoes
Huddled in corners, like useless retainers or slaves.

Soon, he's out on the highway again,
Aiming toward Tipton, Boonville, Fayette.
His mood is unpredictably euphoric,
As though he's been visited by a miracle,

Not merely spent another evening
Away from home. Keyed up,
Shimmering, in anticipation of presenting his line
Of fine trousers to the men's buyer

For Feinstein's Clothiers, whose "open to buy,"
Its upper limit, might yield him,
For six hours' labor and an out-of-pocket lunch,
A ninety-five-dollar commission, just might,

Providing he can interest the man in his newest offering:
Watch pockets, double pleats,
Back flap — the latest in Manhattan fashions,
For this Midwest fiefdom, his territorial dominion.

3/9/82 — [3] (02583)

Watched Over

I

The distance between being missed
And resisting reminiscence is measured in discipline,
Volition, wishing it such.

Living oblivious to childish innocences,
Kisses committed to memory
As examples of immortal poetry,

Sleeping in grotesque motels (Chimeras' nests)
Instead of under a family roof
Are the price I pay for my wayward quest —

Jason chasing Harpies and visions,
In hope that the Golden Fleece
Will be more than a sorcerer's lunatic caprice.

II

Suddenly, my resolve to create and arrest truth
By flicking the universal tuning fork,
With my omniscient whispers,

And listening to it drift softly aloft,
In Whitmanesque prisms of limitless song,
Loses its feverish pitch.

Possibly, the sweet, aphrodisiacal Chablis
Has weakened me. In the shimmering stained glass
Fanlighting this antique station,

I see three shapes, three people,
Three blessed halos, shepherding my loneliness.
I cease writing, stare up, crying.

3/10/82 — [1] (02584)

38

Something mesmeric in the very numerals
Shimmers like hummingbird wings.
A mystical essence,
*

Consisting of trinity and infinity
When one says the number three
And twists the eight sideways (∞),
Rises to my eyes' surface
And drowns me, in silent crying.

Tonight, far from your sleeping shape,
I breathe you awake,
Pedestal you, in contemplation.
Greek, Renaissance, modern,
You, lady, are time.
The oldest winds haloing the earth,
Deepest dirt deposits,
Share your elemental presence.

You are creation's synecdoche,
That golden gleam
Streaming out of the eye of Elohim.
Neither demeanor nor poetry
Expresses my appreciation satisfactorily,
Yet I let you know,
Lest whatever better angels I possess
Accuse me of abject neglect.

Relying, at the outset, on intellect,
To commemorate your aging,
And artifice, to arrest my praises,
I now resort to simple prayer:
Jan, may you, at thirty-eight,
And our two beautiful children
Be my earthly trinity
And I your source of infinite sacrifice.

3/10/82 — [2] (02669)

The Jettisoning Begins

Lately, my peripatetics seem to describe
A new sense of omission in life.
Curiously, each sallying out
Is characterized by forgetful neglect.
On each of my last three trips,
I've left toothbrush, electric shaver,
*

Dress shirts, respectively,
Found myself slightly inconvenienced,
Socially self-conscious,
My routines somewhat upset, if briefly,
By uncommon ineptitude.

I can still recall trying to apologize
For my hobo's two-day growth,
Hide incipient halitosis, body odor,
Behind spit-shined shoes,
Cologne, wool-blend trousers,
Excuse myself, with risible nonchalance,
For such obviously unintentional inconsistencies.
Of course, people understand. All agree
That I take myself much too seriously,
And yet, relief is short-lived,
Unappeasing to my skeptical sensibility,

Which already has begun to suspect senility,
Something fishy, on the fritz,
Deep within the twin spinning gyros
That balance my hemispheres, a shift, of sorts,
Conspiring, with outside dybbuks,
To distort vision, confuse ratiocination,
Overload the decision-making apparatus,
Until all my resolve to leave home collapses —
A scruffy Quijano, in his broom closet,
Doomed to stasis, crazy behavior, insomnia,
Nightmarish phobias, in which roaches

The size of hippos descend from the cracked ceiling
And enter his bleeding nose, to wallow.
O ye sinister eidolons!
I know, now, something is going on
Beyond my control. Perhaps my recent forgetfulness
Is merely the inchoate manifestation
Of a fantasy slowly overtaking me,
In which Lethe is calling me home,
One object at a time. Soon, I guess,
My hair will begin thinning; then memory,
Ambition, energy will abandon me.

Right now, my best chance for survival
Is to heed each omission,
*

Consider every lapse,
To see if I might discern a divine pattern
In the dissolution. Perhaps by anticipating the worst,
I might temporarily circumvent death,
Outlast its earthly blasts,
Half-naked, disguised as an Auschwitz cat.
Strange, I can't even remember, now,
Why I've set down these thoughts.
Surely the reason is buried in my verse.

3/11/82 (02585)

Of Fishes and Bears: An Elegy △

For Max J. Lorber,
"Muggs,"
the Bull of the Woods

So distant, this moment,
From the Wisconsin of my summertide,
Where his manly full-flowering bespelled me,
Yet so close, now that I know
Muggs has departed, I grow serene,
Draw nearer his gone spirit,
As memories call me home.

I'm alone again, a boy of ten,
A lost, awkward, chubby bear cub
Scurrying, nervously, over sandy paths
Birch-dappled, tangled in ferns and sumacs,
Searching for his voice,
Echoing still from the Big House hill,
His silhouette filling the rec hall . . .

A cub wading Lake Nebagamon,
Tonguing its ripples to slake my thirst,
Hoping to see him rise from the silence —
A muskellunge breaching the surface,
Arrested, forever, in the dripping sunset's net,
Trying, even in death, to outbest perfection,
That gesture his epitaph and apogee.

3/17/82 (00018)

Brailling the Sun ^Δ

I squint into the sun's glinting eye.
Ten thousand visions,
Like sparks spit from striking flints,
Issue through the abyss.
Images leap the vast, echoing chasm
In which tradition sleeps.

Of a sudden, Dante and Cervantes
Rise from silence,
Reciting the Bible's unspoken prose
And rhyming psalms,
Left drying in cuneiform blocks
And forgotten during the Exodus.

My eyes float in bubbling humors,
Whose fire steadily crackles from inside
And under the skull simultaneously.
Spontaneity is the mind's only liberation.
The horizon is my cabala;
I am its exegetical scholar, its scribe,

Trying, with my tiny, incisive penpoint,
To lift God's myriad vision
From just beneath His eye's lid
And translate its insight
Into music sung by deaf-mutes,
Wisdom seen by poets, lovers, and dreamers.

3/23/82 — [1] (03496)

Intimations of Immortality, in Spring ^Δ

> *For Louis Dollarhide,*
> *whose* Of Art and Artists *beguiled me*

The entire horizon is a green-dripping abstract,
Each bud and node
A broken tube leaving oily smudges
My eyes can almost touch, for their fresh impastos.

As I drive south, hour by hour,
The canvas seems to complete its own design,
*

Deus ex machina.
My arrival goes unnoticed, for its totality.

Everything in Oxford is in riot —
Magnolias, crape myrtles, cedars, and cypresses —
Except me. My conception
And execution are yet questionable, at best.

I await a painterly inspiration
To sketch me into existence,
Locate my place in the green-dripping abstract,
That I might begin setting.

Drying requires such a protracted transition
Between dying and living again.

3/23/82 — [2] (03580)

An Old Road Peddler Grows Sullen, over Supper

The desolation evoked when he's away from home
Is exacerbated, today,
By his having to stay in this sleazy motel —
And worse, on her birthday.

Supper for one, in this smoky restaurant,
As he gazes, through plate glass,
At the massive grain and rice elevators
Buttressing the river, is paltry alternative

To a celebration consecrated with candles,
Cake, and dazzle-giddy children
Spilling over with excitement for their mother,
On her special occasion.

"Alone" is too severe a sentence
For this well-intentioned road peddler,
Who never dreamed
Fate would rearrange his personal freedom

To such a disruptive degree,
Take him so far away
From twin destinations he never imagined
Having to leave behind: affluence and family.

Yet his aloneness owns him completely.
Only the innocuous beefsteak
And flaccid baked potato, on his plate,
Distract him from sullen monotony.

Solitude wears a shabby disguise.
He too-well knows
Delusions of this variety seldom last an entire supper,
Realizes the missed birthday he conceived

And, earlier, retrieved from his murky memory
Is more than forty years cold,
That, even then, he couldn't redeem himself,
For having squandered so precious a moment.

Now, he cowers behind a palsied coffee cup,
Aching to return to his room, phone home,
But home is his daily-assigned nowhere
And the road his only known next of kin.

3/23/82 — [3] (04174)

Gone Fishing [Δ]

Going slowly over the Helena bridge,
I hold my breath,
Speculate on the temperature of the water below,
Hallucinate, momentarily,
That agitated gars and oversize channel cats
Are chewing my accidental body,
Then enter the Magnolia State, unnoticed.

For miles, the highway I drive
Rolls out, down an aisle,
Like a white wedding runner,
Toward the nave of the Delta's cathedral.
I am the bridegroom, about to surrender
To the sweetest lady, Mississippi.
Suddenly, a black man with poles over his shoulder,
His wife straggling behind him,

Carrying a newborn, their five other children
Following like baby ducks,
All navigating road's edge imperturbably,
*

Shatter my dreamy vision,
Thrust me back to fact,
Locate me in one of nature's desolations.
Our passing is a mild acid

Etching my sensitive brain-plates,
Leaving prominent ridges on my compassion.
Those scraggly, cornrowed girls,
Nappy-headed boys,
Translate me into tight-throated focus
On my own two well-dressed children,
Safely home, in school.

As I hasten toward my destination,
To avoid missing business engagements
So essential to my financial position,
Those eight souls
Reverse their hold over my pious insights.
They'll catch freedom's limit today;
I'll not get the slightest bite.

3/24/82 — [1] (00056)

The Profligate △

Pac-Man's agitated martinets
Parade beneath the glass
Separating me from the programmed diode display,
In this raucous drinking place.

I try to locate my dissociated soul,
Amidst the buxom college ladies
Sauntering in and out, try to decide
What my base intentions might be.

I am neither waiting for nor anticipating
Anyone I might have met before
Or some as-yet-unknown acquaintance;
In truth, I'd prefer purchasing a whore,

To occupy and defuse my inordinate energy.
Instead, I consume two half-carafes
Of chilled Chablis and engage
A garrulous law student in inane conversation,

Endure his antic improvisations,
As he notches martini after dry martini,
On his increasingly sedentary butt.
My ears assimilate Willie Nelson,

Conway Twitty, Kenny Rogers, and Barbara
Mandrell, the darling of the college circuit,
Even in the least "country,"
Most pretentiously sophisticated center of the Confederacy,

Ole Miss. I gaze about the room,
Amused by the awkward foreplay
The species *Homo sapiens* can invent,
And sink back into my own private delusions,

Speculating on the nature of today's law students,
Wishing to copulate with a female intellect
Capable of containing my most outrageous hallucinations,
Willing to endure my dissipations,

For the rare occasion when brilliance might erupt
In seismic plumes. Just now,
I rise, grope for the men's room, disappear,
Hoping to recover my equilibrium.

In the hall, I encounter an old helpmate,
Who pinches my butt. I stutter,
Rush to appropriate her vulnerability,
And whisk her off to the Alumni House,

Where I'm spending the night. She acquiesces.
And as they say, the rest is history,
Except, now, I live in Oxford and teach
And fuck anyone, to vindicate my failure.

3/24/82 — [2] (03581)

Cloven-Hoofed Goat △

They flock to this place, the Warehouse,
To get tipsy, crocked, wasted,
Go home, in a totally devastated craziness,
With anyone willing to pay attention.

I, a pariah, witness the continuous charade,
The parade of vestal virgins
*

Submitting themselves, as nocturnal oblations,
To the most propitious accidental gods,

Knowing that the ultimate result
Is infatuation, pregnancy, and marriage —
A mildly shameful education,
By which procreation perpetuates itself.

As I sit here, witnessing the influx,
Intimations of the goat-footed satyr predominate.
I begin to doubt my efficacy
As a writer, lover, sipper of chilled Chablis.

Suddenly, three wayward females
Confront me and force me to identify myself.
The Dali-stache has piqued them.
My gold-rims and seaweed hair

Intrigue them, bring them to my knees,
Begging to be admitted into my private domain.
Slowly, I lower the drawbridge,
Raise the portcullis. They hesitate,

Then enter. The wine grows sweeter,
Thicker. My words slur,
In vertiginous circles, as we step closer
To that moment when two will go,

Leaving only us two to maneuver
Toward conclusive confusion
Neither will refuse — a perfect excuse
To submit our impersonal souls to review

By a stranger. Gazing into her eyes,
I see a gargoyle, with my features,
Leaning out, leering at me,
Its flicking adder's tongue lacerating my face.

3/24–25/82 — [3] on 3/24 (03582)

Road Games

Out of sheer boredom,
My eyes concentrate on the highway,
Counting each seam in the concrete,
*

As it rushes up, hovers,
Then disappears, in static relapse,
Somewhere miles, hours, back of my passage.

Matters of how long it might have taken
How many faceless men
To survey, grade, lay steel-rod mesh
Over meticulously rolled base,
And pour mix every so many feet
Don't even occur to me, in my numbness.

Rather, my mind, like a child
Piling blocks to the sky,
Tries to see how high it can count
Before the slightest distraction
Topples its tenuous concatenation
And scatters the digits into dizzying abstraction.

At one juncture, the number exceeds
Eight hundred fifty-three.
Twice, I'm unable to reach thirteen,
For the agonizing eyestrain.
Finally, I abandon this amusement, for a newer one:
Shaking myself awake at crucial intervals.

3/25/82 (03598)

April's Fool

I awaken, to this sunny April 1,
Out of a raspy somnambulism,
As a feckless dust speck
Lifting into the bedroom's eddying air,
In tentative search of spectacles,
Through whose ground glass
Vision might pass from forgetting,
Into terrains recognizable and inviting and mild.

My eyes fly outside,
Where spring is leaking sweet greens.
They taste its menstrual, saline sensuality,
As, in hasty unawareness,
Sight submits to cerebral transformations,
*

Swallowing the radio's news capsules whole,
Engaging embattled traffic,
Resigned to impatient rage.

Soon, arrival at work de-energizes the senses.
Losing, completely,
What minuscule tinge of individuality
They might have retrieved from last evening's sleep,
My eyes surrender. The acoustic tiles
Protruding from the heart's ceiling
Envelop me. Every dissonant breath,
Cacophonous distraction, penetrates to the spine,

Pits neural sheathing throughout the body,
Denying my mind its escape routes.
The uninventive sensibility mires,
Refuses, ultimately, to move off dead center.
Beyond the window behind my cluttered desk,
April cavorts, whose blooming is a ruse.
She can't fool me. My eyes know death's shape
Inside and out, naked or clothed.

4/1/82   (05800)

Botticelli's *Birth of Venus*

For my special deity, Jan

A perfect convergence of poised voices
Hovers before me,
Whispering noiseless mermaiden words.
Their softly filigreed syllables
Set the air, containing daydreams, rippling
With the sweetest concentricities,
Each wave a billet-doux
Delivered me, merely by thinking of you,
As I wade, slowly, into the ocean
Poetry stretches, from breath to breath,
Toward your delicate shell.
Suddenly, we are the closure creation opens
In telling itself alive.
In the distance, Noah's rainbow
Rises from the mist our literary kissing inspires.

4/5/82   (04173)

An Apologia at Passover and Easter

Passover and Easter
Vie for primogeniture in the universal *now*.
I, for one, couldn't give a damn
Which comes first or gets more exposure.

Whether a person celebrates escape
From Egyptian bondage, promulgates salvation,
Through crucifixion and resurrection,
Or aborts diseased fetuses is a matter of degree.

In fact, my wife, a nonpracticing Catholic,
And I, a Jew in name, benign, lax,
Euphemistically obtuse in "keeping the faith,"
Have two hybrid children,

Scions of cross-fertilized seeds,
Humanistic cuttings growing, vigorously,
Through narrow-minded slits
In southern Missouri's briar-thicket Bible Belt.

Rather than considering ourselves atheists,
Doubting Thomases, agnostics
Exempt from testifying, being baptized,
Taking communion, having our baby circumcised,

We've reveled in being independent of ritual.
Our myths are daily events,
Our prayers evocations of love
For one greater than us.

Neither Easter nor Passover need occur
To make us appreciate freedom.
All week, walking, eating, talking, sleeping,
We've worshiped each other.

4/9/82   (02078)

Change of Hands ^Δ

Superimposed over the business name,
BEST FURNITURE,
On a thirty-foot-high sign
Standing guard at the building's entrance,
Is the slogan **JESUS IS LORD**.

Across the cinder-block facade,
Surmounting aluminum-framed plate glass,
Is emblazoned, in stoical, bold, plastic roman,
CALVARY TEMPLE,
A not-altogether-eye-catching name

By which to snare highway drivers
Out of their daydreams, tingle desires
For impulse-buy merchandise —
Off-price sofas, love seats,
Breakfast-room sets

Of vinyl, Formica, and Taiwanese chrome,
Knockoff Italian designer lamps —
On view, not two months ago,
In the county's most spacious showcase . . .
A name not redolent of what used to be inside.

Then again, the church's intentions,
No matter the conspicuous location
Among RV lot,
Auction barn, Ford showroom and service,
Datsun dealership, farm-implement distributor,

And the glut of off-brand gas stations,
Must be, precisely, to be seen
By indirection, anomaly, paradox,
In emulation of Christ —
A lamb among lions, believer amidst heathens.

Yet as I pass, my vehicle's shadow
Scratching the temple's glass,
My thoughts get caught on a burr.
Gazing within, I see people praying
And realize another franchise has taken hold.

4/16/82 — [1] (05458)

Going Out with a Bang

Why rely on myocardial infarction,
When a garden-variety climax,
On a gentle Chablis high,
Can allow us to thrive while dying,
*

In the Elizabethan sense? I, for one,
Intend to discover the benefits
Of coming undone while under my lover
's influence. Tonight, our hearts,
Beating hyperkinetically,
Will explode in their cargo holds.
On hands and knees, we'll grope, passionately,
To gather up New Orleans,
Between our toes, Sri Lanka, in our fingers,
As our vessel drifts off Bay St. Louis,
Waiting for a wayward wind
To wish us toward the horizon, stars,
New Albion of the Cedars.

I cease my reverie, turn my head,
To discern which direction
The sky has taken, running from us.
The sounds reaching me
Speak, in cryptic Sanskrit, sinister refrains.
Suddenly, my taxed heart succumbs
To attack; my spirit drains from its veins;
My will to survive collapses like a limestone cliff
In torrential rains. Death surfaces,
Spectral and white. Twilight diminishes
To a dim nimbus. Resigned, I submit.
The unknown calls me by my initials,
As though we were old friends.
Maybe we're related by birth, after all.

4/16/82 — [2] (04172)

Incarnations of a Prospector

> *For Mark Buell,*
> *who prospects for solitude*

Strangely, his awakening locates him
Midway between Tempe
And Oblivion, roaming, naked, on horseback,
An inconspicuous interloper
Within the remote Superstition Mountains,
Neither lost nor searching,
Rather remanded, of his own blown volition,
*

To spend his remaining energies
Surviving outside time,
Hoping only to return to his constituent elements,
Conscious of each minute alteration,
Celebrating his bones' transmogrification
From their stately skeletal dome
To a more permanent earthly home,
Beneath the ageless saguaros.

As he goes, the cooling air thins to cloud.
He climbs down, kneels beside his horse,
Grabs a chunk of twilight
From the funneling sun, then stumbles,
As if someone kicked him in the temples.
Suddenly, neither animal nor man
Stands, in puny relief, against the sky.
Dying comes as such silent surprise,
He never even realizes he's dematerialized,
Taken leave of his naked psyche.
His spirit reunites with its distant spirit.
As he awakens from sleep's deep dream,
His echo is just catching up
With his death wish. He gets to his feet,
Remounts, heads for Tempe, to bathe, shave, dress.

4/21/82 — [1] (05801)

The Incivilities of Civil Law

If, indeed, the Supreme Court
Can award
Three hundred thousand dollars
To families of the few isolated victims
Of toxic-shock syndrome,
Caused, decidedly, by Procter & Gamble's
Rely tampons,

Then why in the fuck
Won't even the lowest court in the land
Hand down a judgment
Against a lady who, wittingly or otherwise,
Passes the clap
*

To a fairly reliable family man
Just trying to get a little, on the side?

4/21/82 — [2] (05802)

Through a Glass Clearly

Suffering an infection, I abstain, tonight,
From tasting the red-grape libation
My palate has grown to savor.
I remain tide-bound, landlocked at my table,
Contemplating myriad bubbles
Rising, in the clear vessel, from 7UP,
Like souls, in a Dürer engraving,
Racing toward the empyrean
Or ants crossing, in single file, vertically,
A wide lawn. Occasionally,
My gaze lifts from this strange and nervous action
Occurring within the faceted container,
To survey, in unmistakably flat fact,

The gathering, which, lacking gentle distortion
And a fantasied benefit of the doubt
Engendered by slight inebriation,
Fails to approximate knights at round tables,
Crowned queens and kings on thrones,
In a royal great-hall,
Rather, shabby college jocks,
Ladies on the make, lawyers, city planners,
Liberated divorcés,
Crowded into a renovated railroad station,
Shouting their guts out, whispering confidences
And climactic profundities, spewing obscenities,
And all to a similar conclusion: to be identified.

I sip my effervescent liquid
And swallow the dissatisfying truth of my situation:
I'm Ishmael without his *Pequod*,
Bacchus denied his godly vine,
A wino, finally,
Who at least can admit to himself
He only finds society viable
When seen through rosé-colored glasses.

4/21/82 — [3] (02586)

Erudition

Why do so many phony assholes,
Wearing robes of Plato, Socrates, and Homer,
With arrogant, authoritarian airs,
As though they were Shrouds of Turin,
Flourish in college communities, on campuses,
And nowhere else,
With such severe academic concentration?

Could it have to do, possibly,
With the mirage-shape of knowledge, fact, logic,
After which these pretenders to the throne quest,
Bowing, on wobbly knees,
Even in their most assertive pontifications
And/or with the inherent threat
Of being found not quite omniscient?

Once a decade, they whisper servile apologias
To God, their wives, students.
But the years wash them ashore, on desert isles,
Where, unable to reevaluate favorite books,
Interpret, anew, truths of their youth,
Appreciate native creativity, mortal resourcefulness,
They die a silent, violent disillusionment.

So why, then, do so many phony assholes,
Certainly brilliant enough to read graffiti
Between the lines, pursue such flatulent vocations?
Why indeed?, I, a teacher of literature
Classic and modern, science, business, law,
Medicine, and ethics, ask myself. Why?
Ignorance, of course!

4/21/82 — [4] (02587)

Troika's Dad, the Pants Peddler ^Δ

As I set out, this early April a.m.,
To service my route,
Regret from last night's call to my wife
Burrows yet, like a blind creature, through memory.

I feel the earth beneath my gentle grief
Rising, giving way,
Slowing my forward momentum.
I hear his tears, in her shimmering voice,

As though she were retelling it now,
Through the tires' ceaseless whine
Over the road from Columbia to Moberly, Mo.,
And I know too well the dilemma and its etiology.

Even now, I can see Mr. Boy
Fetused beneath his sheets,
Waiting for me to lullaby him beyond the demons,
His shredded blanket the earth's umbilical cord.

I hear his puny plaint,
His anguished sobbing, on being told
That his daddy will be gone two days:
"I'll just have to stay up all night, then, crying."

And as I drive north, this morning,
To do my sleight of hand
With fabric swatch cards and sample garments,
At stores I've called on forever,

The happy-go-lucky abracadabra
In my charlatan's mien refuses my coaxing.
Today, I can't even make sadness disappear,
Let alone cause Troika to materialize.

4/22/82 — [1] (01462)

A Failure to Exorcise Demons

The longer he sits, in listless abstraction,
Trying to locate the sun's core,
In the stained-glass fanlights entrancing him,
The stronger grows his fascination
With dissolution. Soon, his eyes melt
Like candles abandoned by gambolers
Ranting in drunken stupors. They drip images
A metaphor at a time,
Which fall to the paper below his pensive shape
And rearrange themselves, line by line,
*

In tiny, rhyming, cursive word-chimes,
Which he refers to as "poetic visions."

As he examines the splatterings, for godly signs,
His mind buckles. He's aware
Of something behind him, a force
Leaning over his shoulder,
Trying to read what his eyes have written,
Share his private insights.
He slows breathing to a cryogenic sleep,
To see if he might recognize his eavesdropper
By his heartbeat. Suddenly, his blood thins;
His skin goes cold as eels. Death flickers
Like a snake's tongue, strikes. From his wax ashes,
Beelzebub beckons him home.

4/22/82 — [2] (02588)

Hallucinating Himself Home

Heading home,
This late Friday afternoon,
Over I-70, going easterly,
Like a bubble flowing through a maze of tubing
Screwing a million other bubbles,
Under pressure, in one direction,
Toward a preconceived destination,
I, Willy Sypher,
Join the reckless procession of dispossessed waifs,
Hoping to arrive safely,
After having been out on the road all week.

Kansas City, Columbia, St. Louis
Might just as well be Cracow, Curaçao,
Kowloon, Gibraltar, Cap d'Antibes,
For my abstracted gaze.
As I soar through Erebus,
All my mind's gauges registering EMPTY,
Silence ignites my visions,
Propels me past my stalled imagination,
Toward the last exit before Nowhere,
Telling me to go straight, ahead,
Not veer. I miss the abyss by inches,

Braking frantically
Just before reaching Hell's Gate Bridge,
And wait to be hit from the rear.
But the silence firing my ears and eyes dies.
My senses escape with their priorities
Only slightly singed. I tremble
As if I were a recent accident's
Hit-and-run victim rather than survivor
Of my own capacious hallucinations.
Suddenly, I see my wife at the porch door,
Waving me home — Willy Sypher, once more!

4/23/82 — [1] (02379)

Whitmanesque Confession [Δ]

Winging homeward,
I sing myself to sleep,
Inside a wakeful minstrelsy,
Whose dream-anesthesia delivers me to fantasy.

Such sweet, complete release
Relieves me of demons. I am new,
A fetus conceiving progeny,
A speck in the Region of Ethers,

Whirling toward pre-Creation,
Hurling memory forward, to the source
Where event and forgetting conspire
To hide under history's eyelid.

I sing myself mystical. I, an eidolon,
Suddenly realize why driving
Is my medium: the miles are wisdom
My tires speak and my ears translate

Into blinks my eyes synchronize
With rearview-mirror years just beyond hearing.
The blurring trees are my ethos,
Telephone poles my mythopoeic cadences and caesuras.

The only repose I've known,
In middle-aging, has engendered from the road,
Whose sensual femininity
Has yielded to my hobo notions of freedom,

Without requiring credentials.
Under her gentle, tender persuasion,
I break into raging song, my voice
Blown across the land, like a lingering kiss.

Whether this trip be my last
Or just another measure in my wide drive
From birth, through verse, to silence,
I revel in evanescent ecstasy.

Why else, every conceivable chance I get,
Would I abandon the most pressing necessity
And set out, tightly gripping the wheel,
Notebook on the seat beside me, pen between my teeth?

4/23/82 — [2] (05803)

[How do the birds fly so effortlessly,] †

How do the birds fly so effortlessly,
Through spring rains,
Without sliding, missing their purchases,
Skidding, sideways, into mean objects?
Perhaps nature's silver

4/26/82 — [1] (08424)

Contemplating a Break

A sullen, brooding gloom,
Rising from the warm spring morning,
This late April, pervades my pupils,
Precludes escape. Its cohesive rain
Forms bars too elongated to transcend
By inventing creative leaps of faith,
Bars too narrowly spaced to slip through,
In slender, demented asides,
Just by saying out the sleekest metaphor
Making a break from its cell,
Deep in the wellsprings beneath the brain's Elba.

All day, my nostrils taste incarceration,
A sense not totally offensive
*

And yet burdensome for my quiet eyes,
Groping to intuit familiar shapes
In the distorted screen
Shimmering between them and the gray horizon —
Twin beams sweeping the distance,
To locate a distressed vessel,
Guide it safely into port, dismantle this storm,
Then board the off-course ship
And steer toward tomorrow's green, glistening shore.

4/26/82 — [2] (05804)

Post-Giraffic ^Δ

It all began so innocently,
His transformation.
There were the basic stock-in-trade
Barnyard animals:
Cows, pigs, sheep, with their appropriate voices
Easily mimicked and mimed with delight.

Then came the slightly more exotic:
Hippos, giraffes, zebras, leopards,
And the fabled snakes,
Eliciting, each in its own slithering,
Spotted, striped, elongated, and wallowing way,
The embodiment of God's mysteries.

And all this prior to Troika's
Antediluvian potty-trained days,
When his passion for things Seuss-like,
Such as Enormous Enormances,
Fluff-muffled Truffles, and, occasionally,
Spotted Atrociouses, roamed his imagination.

Exactly which trauma, gift,
Or accidental fate flew low enough
To attract his fancy,
Distract his startled curiosity from the absurd
And commonplace and attach them to the extinct,
No matter the raging anachronism,

Remains unfathomable. Suffice it to say
That one fine day,
*

Troika the Boy "put away childish things,"
In favor of greater concerns:
Jurassic and Cretaceous stegosaurs and thunder lizards,
Glowering saurians of every dimension.

Too soon, he'd gathered a herd
So terrifying in its collective Taiwanese hide,
Its stuffed, iconographic realness,
They mastered the house, his eating, his dreams —
Diplodocus, Bronty, Terry the Dactyl,
Stego the Plated Beast, Triceratops —

And we, his silent progenitors,
Even his amazed older sister, Trilogy,
Just stood by,
As he began to sing his cosmos awake,
Rearrange the contours of his mind's terrains
To accommodate these outsize monstrosities:

Fossils, bones, vivid pictures
Portraying predators in the act of seeking food
(Plants or meat meaningless,
For the gleaming teeth at the focal center of each),
Serpentlike necks and tails
Disappearing beyond the edge of the page,

On into a kind of credible infinity.
All these images filled him so,
That when he'd screech, flap his wings,
Leap from a convenient chair or table,
We'd cringe, retreat, knowing we'd succumb
To his intolerable will to survive.

And this endured, as an era,
A few million years,
In child-time, indeed
Nearly a quarter of his complete existence,
He, who, at four, has mastered phylogeny's corridors,
Exited the labyrinth intact,

Cooling off, or so it seems lately,
Moving toward a newer evolutionary trend,
In which fascination is born alive,
Mammalian, while retaining
Some of the saurians' disproportionate characteristics,
Fastening on whales, especially the blue,

Which, his Little Golden Book volume assures him,
At one hundred feet in length,
Outclasses the largest of prehistoric species
("Yes, Boy, that means the dinos!"),
Finding sufficiently weird
That massive creature, with its baleen "moustache,"

The narwhal, with its ten-foot tooth,
The sperm and beluga, the killer too,
Which, curiously, lets people ride its back,
In captivity, and the cute porpoises and dolphins,
A crew gregarious, garrulous,
Whose ability to communicate by beeping,

Breathe through blowholes,
Breach the surface gracefully as ballerinas
Leaping, staggers him with something —
A shimmering reality, perhaps —
Commensurate with his sense of wonderment.
And if he wants and has the guts, he might actually touch it.

4/28/82 — [1] (01463)

Committed

Finally, the chemicals have rebelled,
Which no amount of foretelling
Or assertive preventives,
Working, unwittingly, at cross-purposes,
Could more than delay, distract, dilute.

They've risen in a ghastly tranquillity,
Infused her brain
Like an oil slick sifting to the surface,
Above a wrecked plane. She floats
On an ocean whose name, her own, she's forgotten,

In a desolation watched over
By trained psychiatric nurses, doctors,
And a marriage counselor. Twice each week,
She phones home (she only remembers
Speaking to the dial tone).

High alternates, daily,
With low blood pressure, both vying
For the final chance to dismantle her heartbeat.
Tachycardia breaks the monotony
Her silent screaming produces,

As she shuffles from sleep to eating,
Shower to bathroom, and back,
Through the endlessly gloomy routine
Of assimilated drugs: pills,
Tablets, shots, oral mixtures — a pharmacopoeia

Calculated to make her "better,"
She a product, a compound, a formula
So newly reconstituted,
No one, including her,
Knows just what shelf life she has.

4/28/82 — [2] (05805)

Equestrian Peddler

Willy mounts his nag,
The aging, oxidized Ford station wagon
His company leases a month at a time,
As if uncertain of its, or his, perpetuity,
And sets out to peddle soft goods,
Main-street store to emporium and mall,
Alternating states (Missouri, Illinois,
Arkansas), depending on which break in the dike
Needs plugging. A master of timely excuses,
Impromptu reconciliations, rebates and allowances
Due to order-processing mistakes,
Late shipments, payments withheld,
He performs his shuttle diplomacy without complaint,
In addition to making biannual selling treks
Ten weeks wide at a crack. Willy Sypher,
"Regional Director" for Acme-Zenith Trousers,
A company man down to *his* trousers,
Who eats and breathes orders and invoices
And dreams fabrics, casts, patterns, and hand,
In his transient sleep, a messianic man,
*

Who transforms boredom of road travel
And empty nights in sleazy motels
Into a Homeric quest
For a better definition of fettered freedom,
A man accepting his limited access to choice,
By driving the highways
Connecting one day to the next, night
To dawn, mapping his location year after year,
Decade by decade — Willy the Magnificent,
Known, far and wide, for his accent
And always-right-up-to-date Hebraicisms.
Willy, conquering hero, spurs his nag.
An enclave in Far Thessaly
Requires his personal attention today.
Delaying, even for hours,
Could make all the difference in his position.
He rushes to make it by lunchtime
(Drinks and steak usually mollify
The most irate buyer). He speeds up,
Arrives just as his man is leaving the store,
In heated camaraderie
With his dread competitor, Nate Lieberman,
Of Sackowitz and Putzel Slacks of America, Inc.
All the way home,
Willy wears his boots backwards, in the stirrups.

4/30/82 — [1] (02378)

Ennui

All day, a mean ennui has chased me,
Triggered a self-induced hypnosis
So persuasive,
Funereal hallucinations, compellingly true,
Have nearly driven me insane,
Within this driving machine.

Breathing has been a series of hyper-
Ventilations, and dying so imminent,
The silence riding beside me
Has gone stale as diminishing air inside a casket,
Assumed a mustiness
Redolent of dusty attics.

A fanatical sense of decay accompanies me,
On my journey from airport
To psychiatric ward, to deliver a nosegay
To sick Susie, to factory outlet store
And back home, tracking in a great, wide circle
That encapsulates my paltry brain's circumference.

Now that I'm forty-one,
Escaping mordant boredom
No longer seems so mandatory or quintessential.
The questions of when to rest,
How to relax, take on adverbial importance.
Postponing urgencies worries me less.

Yet these retreats do little
To relieve the pressure in my veins,
Change the way my eyes read road signs
Along this floating highway —
Strange creatures taunting me
In ten-by-thirty-foot dyslexic boldface.

Suddenly, the four-lane concrete plays out.
I cringe, realizing the trip's culmination
Signals the beginning of time,
The end of suspended promises and compromises.
Dying into life frightens me,
Because it takes so damn long to terminate.

4/30/82 — [2] (05806)

In the Name of All That's Sacred ^Δ

For our blessed
Lady Jan

We three Bedouins,
Trilogy, Troika, and their dad, "Dude,"
Pack our tents, toys, books
And take to the highway,
Our destination their mother, my mistress,
Wife, five days distant from our hearts.

They sit in the wagon's facing jump seats,
Locked in docile entertainments
*

Impenetrable to my occasional gazes
In the rearview mirror.
She hones conscientiousness,
On her math workbook; Boy doodles,

His Magic Slate Paper Saver
An amazing tabula rasa
He commits to forgetting
Merely by lifting its acetate page,
As whim and philosophical impasse dictate.
Transporting, I'm transported.

Soon, our olfactories awaken us
To a new presence: St. Louis —
Broadway, Arsenal, Gravois, the brewery,
And, shadowing us like a rumor,
The hangdog river, Mississippi;
To our left, the Gateway rainbow.

Within minutes of clearing the bridge,
The nostrils relax. Plowed fields
Relieve the trammeled eyes
Of having to sieve the jagged skyline
For a design in this human Hooverville.
Illinois welcomes three ebullient spirits.

As we go north, the open land
Discloses an imposing passivity.
My children call up drowsy daydreaming.
Genies rise, on both sides,
From fog still dripping from the hazy horizon.
Echoes of Lincoln bring us to Springfield,

Where we linger for lunch,
Stretch our disheveled bones and thoughts,
Before pressing ahead,
Toward Naperville — four hours away
From that reunion we've painfully postponed, all week,
Thinking into existence.

Suddenly, time and our drive coalesce,
Resolve their lengthy differences,
Conclude. Our arrival is their celebration.
Squeezing each of us, weepy, their momma screams.
*

No matter where, when whole,
Our family is home. Our Bedouin souls begin the unloading.

5/4/82 (01464)

Keeper of the Word-Hoard △

I am the words I say.
They define my ascending declensions,
Identify my person and case.
Ablatives and datives place me
In accusative apposition to nominative
And genitive faces resembling me —
Hearing's multiple mirrors,
Reflecting an incestuous relationship
In which mating synonyms and antonyms
Escape my lubricous tongue,
Creating new confusions born of accident,
Which I label poetry.

Words I say out
Are the only known link with my thinking.
They alone connect my breathing
With that passion lacking which life itself
Would be a fatuous gesture . . . passion
And the dream of naming eternity
A metaphor at a time, forevermore.
As Creator and Speaker of Fiats and Decrees,
I am ever seeking new worlds
To shape from words, celestial firmaments
To arrest from verbal ethers —
A god in search of godly purpose on earth.

5/11/82 — [1] (05807)

Alternatives

Carbon monoxide
Burns my eyes, fries the lids to crisps,
Turns my lungs inside out,
Like dirty socks ripped from feet.

My sharp curse words slur in the heat.
Vision goes blurry as a migraine.
My groin seethes, without release,
As the traffic backs up, then stops completely,

Forcing me, with clenched fists, screwed lips,
To cage up my raging frustration.
The nerves, like pacing black jaguars,
Scratch at the brain's bars,

Lacerate my patience, create scabs
That continue to discharge
Long after my car reassumes its speed,
Leaves the city's catacombs behind.

All the way home,
Breathing is a purgation, a labored attempt
To rid the body of waste and pollutants —
Spiritual dialysis —

Whose ultimate results, seventy miles later,
Produce a smile, kiss,
A protracted embrace with my wife.
I sigh, realizing the compromise we made,

When deciding to take up residence
So far away from civilization,
Ten years ago, has proved wise.
At least here, dying only occurs once.

5/11/82 — [2] (05808)

Trilogy Is Eight, Today ^Δ

On our brief drive to school, this morning,
I break into formulaic song,
My five-year refrain:
"Here we go, we're on our way,
We're on our way to school, today,
To sing and dance and play all day
And have a very good time!"
The ritual signals peace in the kingdom.

"How did you grow so old so soon?"
I ask, knowing my question
*

Requires neither fanciful answer
Nor speculation calculated to satisfy the skeptic
Thriving inside both of us. And yet
Her voiceless shrug suggests a dozen theories.
Her dazzling, proud eyes
Contain ageless wisdom of the sisters *how* and *why*.

"On my next birthday,
I'd like to decide how old to be,
Say, ten or forty-two,
So that I could catch up with you, Dude,
And stay that way all year."
Her fragile laughter arrests past and future,
On her lips, as I kiss her good-bye,
Sadly witnessing today disappear forever.

5/13/82 (01465)

Yearnings of a Taciturn Man ^Δ

I wait, in a booth at the Capital Café,
For two fried eggs, over hard,
And dry white toast
To materialize from the spitting grill,
As I sip from a perpetual cup of coffee,
Like an emperor drunk on his power.
I needn't even raise a finger,
Just turn, and one of three ladies-in-waiting
Runs to my beck, with steaming ichor.

There's no illusion to my suzerainty.
My enormous influence
Extends to the outer boundaries of this dominion,
Camouflaged in water-stained, flaking wallpaper
Laced with faded fleurs-de-lis,
Whose sky is a suspended ceiling
Floating with fifty migrainous cool-white suns,
Grease clouds, vents, and grids —
Mosaics owing their design to abject neglect.

If not by name, at least on sight,
I recognize potential adversaries, ancient enemies,
And those owing allegiance to my eccentricity
*

Congregated at tables, in specious debate,
And nod . . . frequently, I nod,
To dispel the numinous belief that my high position
Requires isolation, that deaf-mutes
Are exempt from preemptory yearnings
To communicate, as well as rule, by the seat of the soul.

5/14/82   (00569)

Monday Morning: Coming Alive

All weekend,
I've been leaning into a mean wind.
Now, Monday morning's calm
Leaves me unable to balance my shadow,
Maladroit in the simplest steps.
I am a sober drunk,
Whose inebriated spirit
Can't even clear its throat
Without calling attention to its presence
Among the quick and conscientious
Ambitiously kicking out from the gate
Like three-year-old colts
Racing after the working world's
Mythical Triple Crown: wealth, power,
And immortal health.

My swivel seat squeaks loudly,
Throughout the frenzied office. I apologize
To the ceiling and floor,
For my unavoidable obtrusiveness,
As I restraighten Friday's finished business,
For the tenth time,
Waiting for today's first order from the field
To be phoned in, then sent down
To accounting, for credit check. I wait,
Concentrating on the vague cameo profiles
Floating beneath my fingernails,
Hoping to recognize someone, a gentle muse,
With whom memory might communicate.

Soon, my dense brain clears.
The intoxicated spirit regains its equilibrium.
*

By noon, I'm juggling cancellations,
Articulating excuses, arranging extensions
On delayed shipments, as though born to the vocation.
By five, I'm glorious Pegasus, soaring!

5/17/82   (05809)

In Search of Lost Citizenship Papers

Radiating out from the epicenter
Of my ever-changing psyche,
Equidistant from nowhere, everywhere,
Tremors claw across my forehead
Like freighters plying the equator,
Playing themselves out
Like straight lines finally bending into infinity,
Electric gestures galvanized into flickers,
Forgetting spreading
Throughout the brain's mass,
Metastasizing as it consumes the fragile cyto-
Plasm, distorts the elastic heart's arteries
To arrhythmic groaning. I grasp my temples.
The eyes cringe as though my fingers
Might seize them, squeeze sight from them
Like wringing blood from turnips.
No sounds or images materialize.
Resignation lifts my weak hands high,
As if giving the world a victory sign.
Just now, I can't remember why
I even bothered trying to recall who
And where I've been before this moment,
Going west, toward dusk.
Maybe it was just death requesting of me
Proper identification
Before issuing my necessary passport.

5/27/82   (00860)

Willy Loses His Sense of Direction

Blinking rapidly,
I actually slow the windshield wipers
*

To stroboscopic strokes,
From flowing, arcing motions
Repeatedly erasing and reshaping vision,
To conform to rain-blurred miles
Piled high with drooping, tumescent trees
And splotched concrete. Through the spaces,
My eyes grope for and glean pieces of the whole:
Clover tufts, purple and white, and weeds
Wagging at roadside, predators
Lighting and scurrying, lighting and scurrying,
As rabbit, turtle, bird, and dog guts
Turn into jet-black crows.
My pupils scan left to right, dilate, contract,
As if focus were a facile matter
Of homing in on a specific object
Rather than deciding which fraction
Might yield the most fascinating insight.
Suddenly, my own gold-rimmed profile
Floats into my scope. I pause,
Do a double take, concentrate.
The strange handlebar mustache, large bulb nose,
Brillo hair haloing my brain-container
Cause me consternation. It seems
I don't know, or at least can't place, the face
In the rearview landscape.
At once, even the concrete and the shale bluffs
Abandon my memory. Their location,
Relative to my relative position,
Might be a foliated lunar plain
Or a stage set from a Tom Mix movie.
Who is viewing what, where, is of the essence,
If I'm to decide when my arrival
Is at hand, my journey concluded.
For now, my hands clutch the wheel,
Hoping desperately
The fingertips might elicit, from its vibrations,
Familiar scintillas,
Intuit an appropriate direction to take.
My eyes submit to spirits
Hovering about this speeding wagon,
Screaming feebly to be detected, ferried home,
On invisible slipstreams,
*

And go slowly blind, as the gray horizon
Descends, like a fragrance,
To coerce my body's gravitational field.
Outside powers transmute two hours
Into twenty centuries. When the numbness passes,
I step out, through the whale's mustache,
A nomadic, mad Jonah,
And announce myself to Feinstein the clothier,
My third customer of the day.

5/28/82 (02377)

Hearing the Music of the Spheres

June's cool music,
Shimmering from morning's moist lips,
Captures my imagination, captures me,
Transmutes my confinement into free verse.
I sing in the air's cosmic key.
Neither sound nor its counterpart, friction,
Possesses my ears; rather, it's my song's pure stretching
Toward inexpressible arpeggios
Floating between sky and my vision's threshold,
That zone, godly yet effable,
Where inspiration is distilled, from its essence,
Into figments accessible to the human ear.

In the distance, I hear myself forming chords.
I touch my throat.
Guttural strumming ripples off my fingertips,
Like plucked guitar strings
Setting tones along a fleshy neck ringing.
Slowly, my senses accommodate to the melody
They translate from the glistening skin,
Recognizing, in my subtle humming,
An accompaniment to the sun's rumble.
Suddenly, I locate myself,
An unformed note in morning's score,
Waiting for my own coda to recompose me.

6/1/82 — [1] (03495)

Neuroses

I own no phobias
Except those whose dangerous contents
And warning messages are disclosed
On a label pasted, conspicuously, across my brain.

Almost always, when I reach for a bottle
Filled with volatile grains,
To alleviate tertiary pains in the neck,
Eyestrain, I forget to read the precautions

Memory flashes on experience's screen.
Just today, suffering begs me
Seek relief from the fear
Of chimeras peering at me from the rearview mirror,

As I drive south, wired,
Seven large cups of unadulterated coffee
Igniting and crackling across the axons,
Like St. Vitus's dance.

But the neuroses won't leave me alone,
In my solitude. Vague faces,
Grotesque death masks, plaster casts,
And wax facsimiles resembling my mustached profile

Jeer like gargoyles and poltergeists,
Challenging me to retaliate,
Stick out my tongue,
Smudge them into extinction, with my thumb.

Abruptly, I twist the mirror aside,
Causing my curious eyes
To concentrate on the anonymous desolation
Rushing up to me innocuously.

Briefly, order reshapes my perspective.
The sinuous road smoothes out,
Straightens. Tranquillity lulls me into dreams.
For a while, I almost believe

No phobias ever arose, this morning,
To disrupt my fragile aspirations
Of reaching the end of my life alive.
For a moment, I almost think

I might arrive free of parasites,
Hosting no ghosts, but, then, I know
Even death provides no escape
From a moribund mind. Of this I am living proof.

6/1/82 — [2] (03597)

Willy's Day of Reckoning ^Δ

He's spent nearly fifty years of his life
Behind myriad steering wheels,
Driving highways and back roads,
In company-owned station wagons and vans,
Through blown snow, tornadoes, rain,
And glorious, sun-dreamed days.

Now that he's seventy-two, they're all saying
He's outstayed his usefulness,
Despite the fact that he's still capable
Of servicing eighty-eight accounts in three states,
Yet able to tote five sample cases
From car to buyer's office and back again,

Sometimes six times
In a stint protracted twelve or fourteen hours,
On his marathon campaigns,
Occasioned, of late, by outrageously high
Gas, motel, and meal rates —
Fifty-dollar days, when he's not obliged to entertain.

This afternoon, Willy will have to travel
To 1128 Washington Avenue,
St. Louis, Mo., the sacred home office,
To and from which he has sent his orders,
Received confirmations, paychecks,
Weekly updated stock sheets,

For more than forty-five years.
He'll arrive not prior to 3:30,
As instructed by typed memo
Dictated by the son of the founder's son,
Twenty-one-year-old Julius Gottshalk III,
Youngest graduate of Harvard Business School.

All the way up to St. Louis, Willy's cold hands
Grow colder, as though wrapped in dry ice.
Sweat drains uncontrollably
From his armpits, forms half-moon stains
On his freshly pressed dress shirt.
He licks his lips as if posing for a picture,

Smoothes his eyebrows, mustache, bow tie,
Combs the thin hair haloing his pate,
Then takes the parking ticket
From the attendant, in his shaking hand,
Not aware, until this moment,
His own moment is nigh.

Standing alone, in the rear hallway,
He sighs, then enters the well-lighted office,
Weaves toward the front,
Where the receptionist waves him to a seat,
To await his Maker's earthly surrogate.
He hesitates, then bolts unresignedly.

6/1/82 — [3] (02376)

Killer Sun △

As I exit Memphis, pressing toward Oxford,
The killer sun,
Skimming noon's shallows, in search of prey,
Spies my movements, swims my way,
Bites me to squinting.
My eyes bleed crow's-feet, go blurry,
As if death and darkness had abruptly converged.
Feet and hands freeze.
Pine trees lining I-55
Become a gray cordillera,
Beneath whose shadow I run, in plain sight
Of the insanely circling sun,
Wondering why I've been singled out,
Condemned to surrender to an enemy
I've never seen, let alone offended.

I pass Hurricane Creek;
The Tallahatchie River disappears rapidly.
*

Soon, the Batesville turnoff looms.
I veer, head east,
A maimed spirit hoping to reach shore
Before nothing of me remains
In Mississippi
Except this early morning's promise
To my wife (I'd be very careful),
Resonating in her surviving memories,
And the vaguely brave gesture
I made to myself, on leaving,
To be wary of staring down adversaries
Even if I might wipe them, from view,
With a solitary salute.

6/1/82 — [4] (03501)

A Devotee of the Southern Way of Making Love [Δ]

My delayed return to this oasis
Was neither calculated nor accidental
But occasioned by insomnious fates,
Who've busied me writing splendid praises
To Faulkner, nature, Balnibarbi,
Kept me deskbound,
Gyved to a squeaky swivel seat in my office,
Spinning around, for hours,
Like a human orrery,
Mystically drawn to my own thoughts' lodestone.

At home, I've ventured far —
Without measuring my trips in harbors reached,
Great Walls traced from end to start,
Matterhorns scaled, fjords and gorges avoided,
Portentous abysses wished into nonexistence —
Just by conjuring my expectations
Into replacing fact with fictions,
Positing possibility as the shared denominator
For people willing to build reality,
Like castles and cathedrals, ten stones a year.

Here, I'm obliged to take politeness
And decorum at face value. Nothing is
*

Except as it appears, in this Mississippi Eden,
Where Naiads and Oceanides
Assault my lusty sensibilities just by speaking,
Walking across the lawn, in bare feet,
Stretching credibility, with distressed jeans.
What seems mere amenity *is*, unequivocally.
Yet how nice to be treated with respect,
Not need invent subliminal reasons

For surrendering to the most convenient appetites,
Indulging taboos, renouncing ageless guilt,
Setting aside the imagination,
For the sake of undreamed pleasures
Immediately satisfied. When at Ole Miss,
I suspend disbelief, not only willingly
But with eagerness, for a lovely smile,
Fingertips whispering kisses on my lips.
All the enchanted kingdoms I might elicit
Can't approximate a Southern lady making herself naked.

6/1–2/82 — [5] on 6/1 (00158)

Log-Thoughts South △

Not even 8 a.m.,
Yet my tanks have been fueled
With liquid-cool caffeine,
Its quickened mixture leaned out,
Into a smooth, fusion-induced brain-spray,
To make certain alertness accompanies me
On this next leg of the odyssey.

I leave Oxford, Mississippi, for West Helena,
Arkansas, with cargo from the Holy Land,
Farmington, Mo., where the pants I transport
Were manufactured and loaded,
To be bartered for universal exchange
In one of five outlet stores
I, a glorified delivery boy, oversee.

The red-clay excrescences fade,
As I range westward,
Toward Old Man. The planted land
*

Lets me pass unmolested,
My carpetbagger persuasion
Adumbrated by a decidedly Hebraic strain
Not as blatant to the fates

As to my own ill-at-ease feelings.
Possibly, my fears are unfounded. Yet
Why tempt providence,
By announcing my cut-rate presence,
With full-page-newspaper-ad campaigns?
Instead, I'll make my stop,
Inquire about bad checks, sales, profits,

Then get back on the road,
Heading northerly, home, at sixty-five,
All the way up I-55, to Highway 32,
Three hundred thirty miles from *right now*,
Without the slightest doubt
About not having stayed to partake
Of the genteel amenities proffered absentee landlords.

Just ahead,
The bridge rises through heat-shimmer.
Within minutes, I'll unload my goods
And repack the car's hold with garments
Too defective to be sold, even by me,
Merchant of distress, purveyor to the depressed,
Expert in determining the "perfect" price.

Then, refueled with steaming java,
I'll take off, filling out my log, on the run,
With impressions and thoughts
My children might someday read to their own,
To remind them of their grandfather,
A man with three college degrees,
Who remained a slave to his ancestors' wandering ways.

6/3/82 — [1] (00073)

Tête-à-tête

What a fine and private day this is
For dreaming while driving home.
*

The afternoon is so faultlessly unintruded,
I easily tune out enemies, dubieties,
Notes come due on impulses spent,
Unmaterialized Yukon strikes,
The past's flashes in the pan,
Improprieties, committed under the influence
Of youthful exuberance or pure impetuousness,
That discriminate against no age group.

I revel in my three-times-two hours,
Luxuriate in my insularity,
Free to ruminate over old misgivings,
Recycle misappropriated priorities,
Give possibility new life
Merely by moving a few mind-rooks
Into positions where, disguised as intuition,
They might anticipate fate's disguises
And capture their adversaries,
Without a fight, just by thinking ahead.

As I go, twilight invites me out
For an early nightcap. She toasts the sun,
With a heeltap from her glass slipper.
I kiss my fingertips as they fall away
From my face, realizing that, soon,
My own journey will have been run
And I will have come full circle, home,
Somewhat wiser
And slightly more humble, I hope,
For having had this audience with his majesty, myself.

6/3/82 — [2] (03596)

Freeing Genies ^Δ

Last evening,
We four cavorted, colloquially,
Through twilight's deepest recesses,
Our sequestration from the warring world complete,
We inviolable, lightheaded, and giddy
In our directionless quest for fireflies
Incandescing erratically as a city skyline
Glimpsed from the distance.

As a family, collectively,
Repeating summer rituals, to our greedy delight,
Beholden to no one,
We connected dots hovering in the soft air,
Until their invisible lines,
Disclosing love's precious shape,
Helped define the passion dazzling,
And golden happiness flashing, within each of us.

6/8/82 — [1] (01466)

Katy Muse

This sweet retreat welcomes me home,
Accepts me
As the lonely son of someone's mother
Somewhere.
She smothers me in soft intimacies and lights,
Seducing me, immediately,
With her celebrated cool-Chablis philter,
Beneath whose persuasion,
She too well knows from other occasions
When I've come in, off the road,
Ragged as a cinder-stoned hobo,
My better senses will submit
To my weaker tendencies, inebriation.
She knows me as her peddler poet,
The guy who can translate his silence, from pyrite,
Into stained-glass strophes,
Metaphors relaxed and occasionally amazing,
For their angular chanticleer dream-notes,
A seller of men's pants by day
(Irregulars and grade A's, in the same spiel),
By twilight a solitary weaver of words,
Shy, taciturn, intimidated
By the world beyond these protective confines
Watched over by Katy Muse,

In fact atavistic,
The throwback road-peddler poet's
Own phonetic conception of his societal role,
The heartland's bard,
*

Supporting his passion for lyrical verses
And essential compressions,
By professing the gospel of providence,
Supplying cut-rate merchandise
To department-store and outlet buyers
Hungry to satisfy a hungrier public,
Provide a few additional turns in a season.
Keep them begging — that's the credo
She most easily recognizes, who knows me
As a frequenter of her peaceful abode,
Where, to her alone,
I've confided my unreconcilable schizophrenia.
Tonight, I would like to delight
In abstaining from writing fitful diatribes,
Rather indulge in Shakespearean flights
And soar beyond this four-cornered cloister,
Toward *forever*,
Forget, for an entire evening,
Why I was chosen to be both psalmist and salesman
Simultaneously, throughout my life.

6/8/82 — [2] (02589)

Age Is Wasted on the Young

Why, with so many potential starts,
Does the heart,
So often in an erratic flash-flood impulse,
Latch onto a mate
Just to save itself from temporary loneliness,
Then spend the rest of its natural life in cloistral regret?

Why do the passions seem to black out
Whenever they approach a female
In sandals and skintight T-shirt and jeans,
With breast-length tresses, a lady, nymph,
Naiad, dressed in doe-sleek flesh,
Whose silky pubes beg for gentle violation?

Why was Eve surrogated in so many, many guises,
Meant to tease and seduce,
Bring young men to their knees,
Not in contrition but in lusty concupiscence,
*

To covet venally, crave beyond all belief,
Only to contract diseases, on first and unutterably naive contact?

I, a sinner of renown and devout commitment,
Refuse to speculate on why snakes
And Eve-eggs seem to make contact fortuitously,
Taste of the most rakishly sweet gluts,
Then waste away on each other's love.
I have no idea why desire dies

Or, for that matter, what causes decay
In the most stable associations.
All I know absolutely
Is that both sexes are Rabelaisian when let loose
To seek their own levels of eroticism.
Of this I am perfectly certain,

Because I have witnessed children
Fitted for their wedding rings by God himself,
Only to discover that it means nothing
When the exotic bosom is bared
And the strange penis is unleashed from its lair.
I declare a moratorium on unfaithfulness.

Dear Lord, grant each of us amnesty,
Else we shall fail, as sensible adults,
To procreate as families, perform responsibly our roles
As parents reverent and mindful of offspring and spouse.
I proclaim a halt to all eyeballing,
Lest youth sunder society without even trying.

Let the nubile lady flourish, her song resound,
Her telltale smell permeate the air,
And may she find ample companionship,
Needed stimulation, and teaching. For those of us
Already past basic inane placation,
May we perform up to our passion and beyond,

That scions we consign to this universe,
Through natural release, be nothing less than the best
We, in our most creative moments,
Can conceive, not the whorish prophecy
We, in our lust, may carelessly cause
While traveling in Sodom, Rotterdam, and Gomorrah.

6/8/82 — [3] (02590)

For Annie Ruh, Violinist Extraordinaire

So far from home, so totally alone,
I almost don't know
Who owns me or whom I own,
In this oblique flight
From my origins. I die, for lack of companionship.
Not wife or children or parents
Still alive, although aged,
Console me, register the slightest tremor
On the sophisticated gadgetry. I fly by the seat
Of my soul, my paltry soul,
Through an endless emporium of strange faces.

Why was I singled out to fly solo,
Experiment with Milton's verse,
Converse with wayward devils and saints?
And for what purpose? Perhaps my mission
Was not merely to witness one-megaton bombs
Explode on unprepared Hiroshimas and Nagasakis
But to listen to electric violins
Awaken lazy souls drowsing on Mount Helicon.
Tonight, I stare into an alien crowd
And question my presence
Among presences not quite settled into the mode.

The violin, attached to a million volts,
Drives through my skull.
I die and rise and shiver on the strings
She touches and bows. I am a pizzicato note
Floating through the air, with a hair trigger,
Ready to fire. Why was I chosen
To spout, through my blowhole,
Like a right whale and lift, like a Wyoming geyser,
Into the horizon, where I might hang,
Suspended in endless arrest?
Maybe my destiny was meant to end on your fingertips.

6/8/82 — [4] (02591)

[Tonight, a serene, peaceful feeling]

Tonight, a serene, peaceful feeling
Overflows me, like foam
*

Rising, slowly, over the rim of a stein
Filled too enthusiastically with soft gold.

I sip from evening's vessel,
Imbibe its cool, liquescent scents —
Mystic tone-poems
Dripping from twilight's violet lips and eyes —

Then grow inebriated,
Contemplating each pieced mosaic in the sky's cathedral,
And enter the earth's mind
As though chosen to complete some godly design.

By the time my senses finally free me,
Night has fully descended.
It and I, previously unknown to each other,
Will seek a mutually desired libation.

6/9/82   (02232)

Tipton's "Hidden" Treasures ^Δ

The Midwest, through which I drive,
This too-cool June dusk,
Pressing toward Columbia, before sunset,
Is at rest. Wet fescue
Laced with goldenrod, strafed by barn swallows
In jagged flight, collecting insects,
Sets my olfactories on edge.
Its rank, sweet seething is dream-semen
Fertilizing my paradisiacal eyes with memories.

Rabbits emerging from the thick grass
At road's shoulder, red-winged blackbirds
Perched atop its drooping tassels,
"Mushrats" and possums
Flattened, occasionally, along the winding macadam,
Skunks, their faint traces
Staining the fecund air, and grazing cows,
Myriad and stolid, remember my passing face
From summers, decades, generations ago.

I, too, this peaceful evening,
Vaguely recall being through here before,
On other journeys from waking,
*

Toward sleep, traversing this desolate road
One strut, strophe, foot at a time,
On my way from poem, home,
To poem again, along the circumference
Of the dome my geodesic imagination measures,
Which shelters me from hell-stones.

As God's paltry emissary in the gentle emptiness,
I record existing conditions,
Make certain His work remains untrammeled
By civilized usurpations.
Satisfied, tonight, I write my final line,
Then freeze — off to my right,
In a Cyclone-fenced clearing,
Three white missiles, cleaving to slanted gantries,
Hold the entire horizon at bay.

6/11/82 — [1] (00122)

Tempus Is *Fugit*ing

Why is it, now I'm grown,
My parents have so little time
To lavish, on my acts, their undivided attention,

Ply me with outsize kudos
For the same petty accomplishments
That used to gain their spontaneous praise?

Maybe it's not that I've aged
Or that they've changed so radically;
Rather, they're making clocks differently today,

Eliminating the minute and hour hands,
Keeping only the sweep-second,
Which none of us can see.

6/11/82 — [2] (05810)

[The less geopolitical mess]

The less geopolitical mess
We attempt to redress, these days, the better.
*

Even malicious deceits and lies
Regarding arms treaties and talks of peace
Serve a fated purpose:
Our best intentions antagonize adversaries
And allies alike.

Each evening, before sleep,
I reach deep into prayer's well,
Retrieve a relevant dream to accompany me home,
Then draw the sheets over my eyes,
Hide from low-flying specters —
Death's reconnaissance vessels —
And wake into morning's hell-storm.

6/18/82 (05811)

The Man Who Could Do Anything

For Saul,
with love,
Father's Day 1982

This cool June afternoon,
I sequester myself outdoors,
Set free my restive, poetic spirit,
That it might forage, reconnoiter,
Then, retrieving a piece of the ancient order
That formed youth's core, lead me home,
Through years grown unruly
As shrubs fused into a solid clump
Beneath steamy honeysuckle.

I see you, through their dense vines,
Dad,
Hacking weeds, with a dull scythe,
In the backyard of our new white manse.
I, age ten, stand just behind you,
Believing your swipes
At the far margin of eight untamed acres
Might actually discourage nature,
Contain her throbbing intransigence.

Even now, I can still envision
Your severe concentration, a thorn-crown
*

Fitted to your brow,
And I wonder how, then, it could have been otherwise,
Because to this day, Dad,
I still believe
If you decided to engage a hundred enemies at once,
You'd sunder them with reason,
Then send them running, with your love.

6/19/82   (02077)

Lay Herpetologist

This 7:30 highway
Is a three-headed viper,
Whose blind, wild striking at the haze
And inconsistent weaving and sliding
In and out, like leather strands
Inexorably forming morning's lanyard,
Spit fear into commuters
Trying to fathom how to cross its path,
Mollify the maddened serpent,
Arrive at work without being stricken
Or driven out of their minds permanently.

By the time I pass, on my way home,
The three empty lanes
Disclose no traces of the fracas
That occurred earlier — no bloodstains,
Fractured glass, scattered metal,
Derelict vehicles marring the shoulder.
Instead, emboldened by open stretches,
I press ahead,
Oblivious to potential disaster,
Unafraid of three-headed metaphors
Lurking in afternoon's rush-hour traffic-grass.

6/22/82   (05812)

Sales Meeting: Spring '83

Sleepiness hypnotizes my eyes, this morning.
I try, self-consciously,
*

To keep from releasing conspicuous yawns,
Allowing my wavering head
To droop, too long, in sideways attitude,
Disclose my disaffection for either soft shoulders
Or classic men's tailored clothing.
Not worsteds,
Polyester in Dacron-, rayon-, or nylon-blended weaves,
Or natural combed cottons excite me.

I drowse through the entire presentation,
Remarking hardly at all
The myriad testimonials to "intrinsic value,"
"Sell-through capacity," and "viability" of the line.
My mind tires, expires, and submits to burial
Beneath self-aggrandizing hype
Calculated to stimulate the salesmen in attendance
To mystic apotheosis,
Mythic ethers in which each envisions himself
As a prophet of profits.

My overriding focus is on the serving table,
Just behind this showroom's partition,
A Monet-pond floated with danishes and doughnuts
Instead of lily pads,
Flanked by twin gurgling coffee urns
(Abutments of a painterly Japanese bridge),
Whose vague aroma seizes my dormant mentality,
Awakens me to my latent potential
For reshaping malaise into myriad Givernys —
This blind poet's brush-stroke oases.

6/28/82 (02375)

Total Eclipse △

For Janny — Diana

Through steamy July's midnight leaves,
You, in blue negligee,
And I, completely naked, stand on the patio,
Holding hands,
And observe the full moon succumb, by degrees,
To the earth's umbra.
*

Even the naked eye can see it
Slowly metamorphosing from yellow-gold to black
And back, like a swarm of grass-
Hoppers passing across a wheat field
Three hours wide.

Slugs, coursing, like oceangoing boats,
Over concrete moats
Separating our castle from West Columbia
And the rest of the universe,
Distract our focus. Then, bleary-eyed
Yet amazed, we gaze skyward
And remind ourselves, again,
That time is one continuous motion, not sequential,
And effacement a temporary phase
In the overall design.
We proclaim our momentariness divine.

7/6/82 (00109)

Marking Time

I swim, in a dim nimbus,
Through morning's rain-gray layers,
Trying to mark my aging depression's extent,
Record today's location
In relation to last year's place in the flow.

Now that I'm forty-one,
Perspectives and flexibility atrophy.
The mind tightens its blinders,
Responds not with elastic, imaginative alacrity,
Rather from habit, under pressure

Above and below the oil slick
In whose sticky prism I float
Like a stag beetle squirming belly up.
It happened so fast,
I haven't yet fathomed the depth of my depravity.

Daily, on waking, I dive into life,
Frightened of drowning on the way down
Or learning, on returning to the surface,
*

There is no bottom,
Dying indefinitely, a day at a time.

7/7/82 (00859)

Fancy's Flight ^Δ

Under painless pressure,
Within the belly of a flying machine,
I subject my desolate self to the elements.

Although, until today,
They've known me only by my prophetic echoes,
Theban ethers accept my poetic presence

As palpable evidence of my faith in heavenly possession.
Climbing so close to the Source,
Soaring this high, in timeless suspension,

My writing composes itself.
Neither mind nor fingers collaborate.
Only my eyes, reading to lips

Reciting to ears hearing familiar meters
Splayed across my page,
Attest to the efficacy of my most recent arrest.

7/9/82 (05813)

Heading Home

For two weeks and two days,
I've laid waste all my faculties —
A renegade from needs, duties, reading,
No slave to decision-making tactics
And politic strategies, a patient convalescing
From a disease without etiology or symptoms:
Dynamic fatigue.

How convenient for me, to time
My nervous breakdown
With the annual lull-in-July-business vacation.
*

Who could possibly have foreordained
Such a propitious convergence of body and fate?
Thank God for small favors,
Sparing me the embarrassment of a public collapse.

Now, as I fly home,
Yawns, like swarming grasshoppers
Consuming the sky, with their insatiable appetites,
Obliterate vision and memory.
The sheer fear of resuming routines,
Relinquishing the heroic nomenclature of being alone,
Owing nothing to anyone, aggrieves me.

Suspicious, I listen to the landing gear
And flaps unwind on their mechanisms,
As if, in their cryptic voices,
I might discern the universal secret to continuity,
Harmony, and change.
Only the whisper of concrete massaging rubber
Speaks to me — home again, home!

7/25/82 (05814)

Boon Hogganbeck

The fog through which I drive,
This beguiled morning,
Is my white madness. We see eye to eye,
At the blind epicenter,
Where outside pressures, decency,
Reason, logic, traces of compassion, even,
Engage my inner desires
To inflict evil in a shameless display,
Whose baseness derives from lust,
That pure, unrestrained quantity the heart seeks
At its dourest hour.

Hyperventilation bespells me
One sense at a time, until nothing,
Save intuition's paltry groping,
Remains to guide my highway straight
Toward whatever destination
Middle age might single out from myriad roads
*

Leading Rome-ward, home.
Suddenly, the fog lifts. I emerge
From my sullen thoughts. Just ahead,
The city's spires and domes
Shimmer against the belly of the fiery spider,

Suspended, in waiting, within its rays,
For today's unsuspecting victim.
Quickly, I slow, turn, head back
From where I came.
All day, I sit under a plum tree
On my front lawn,
Witnessing its small, hard fruit
Being plucked abruptly by blue jays and thrushes
Oblivious to my innocuous proximity,
Wishing secretly
To reach out, from my numbness, and squeeze their necks.

7/27/82 (03562)

Voices Within Fortune Cookies

> *Pray for what you want, but*
> *work for the things you need.*
> — Chinese fortune

The distance and degree
Between want and need is so thin
A pin can't pry them apart.
My heart realizes what time it is,
And why, but is a paltry arbiter
Of all that keeps it beating.
Even my eyes refuse to intuit, through vision,
The scene in which Gethsemane
Assimilates my fleeing spirit, forces me
To accept deterministic circumstances
As the be-all of creativity.

I stall, lapse, fall into lethargy's thrall,
Victim and sacrificial lamb,
Desiring to race, naked, through my baseness,
Like a frustrated fox
Chased by its own barking shadow,
*

A transitory shadow owned by no one
Particularly,
A pasted crepe-paper effigy
Glued to my own ancient kindergarten window,
Wasting away, fading in the sun's splatter,
So that black and white metamorphose into gray.

My nerve ends jangle.
St. Vitus's dance reaches the bloodstream,
Screams. Its voices sputter like flames
Snuffed by an aged lamplighter
Leaning into oblivion. I die for the third time
Tonight, dreaming of an ocean-suicide,
In which I might achieve transmogrification.
Oh, to be an anemone
Or jellyfish strangling in its own tentacles,
Floating seaward, freely, toward the horizon,
Toward tomorrow, today, forever.

8/2/82 — [1] (03494)

Jogging Bailey's Woods ^Δ

I own this morning,
Through whose sultry fumes I course,
On fleet feet. Mine may not be winged,
Yet they approximate the mercurial,
Traversing Bailey's Woods.
My entire body absorbs the jolts,
Compensates for exposed roots
Too old to still grab hold a sandy purchase.

This woods accepts my human intrusion,
Knowing I come, in humbleness,
To offer my groans and sweat and agony,
For the sake of proving nothing
Other than that my aging spirit might endure
Despite the bones' brittleness,
The muscles' extravagant suppleness
Decaying in plain sight of the bemused ego.

Soon, Rowan Oak materializes.
I emerge, dripping like dirge sounds
*

From a French Renaissance cathedral, spent,
The sensibilities wilted, my heart exploding,
So that even the solitude
Refuses to relinquish its code, show me
How to penetrate the silence,
Enter the bird-chirping stirring in the sturdy cedars.

I cry out loud, from relief,
Shake the perspiration from my face,
Clear vision, view the great Greek edifice,
Hoping no one will be home
To accuse me of trespassing,
Make me aware that I don't belong here,
In this sweet Southern retreat.
No windows or doors creak;

No trees whisper. Cautiously, I move
About the house,
Caught, in its halo, like a moth
About a kerosene lamp,
Walking out the pain in my heavy legs,
Until dizziness equals the heat
And feeling ceases to be a factor.
I realize the people who lived in this place

Have long since departed
And that I am so totally alone,
My shadow has no difficulty distinguishing me
From among the others
Projected, backward, from the stately cedars
Lining the driveway. Suddenly, I shudder,
Wondering what has brought me
To this climax, and in broad daylight.

Perhaps something my spirit demands,
A confrontation, trial by fire,
Has drawn me to this dappled location,
In humbleness, to kneel and pray
That, someday, I too,
My voice, at least, might reach beyond the limens
Of normal expectations
And speak, just once, the Faulknerian tongue.

8/2/82 — [2] (03534)

Strangulation ^Δ

Kudzu is a radical manifestation
My imagination can't efface
No matter how concentrated my gaze inward.
In every direction,
I see green-seething Piranesian chains,
Sense their impending threat,
As I drive westerly, into a wet fog.

Suddenly, vision is engulfed,
Cancelled. I strain
Just to keep the median
In my eyes' grasp. The Delta materializes.
Knee-high cotton, dragonflies
Admit me into their keeping,
As though I'd never died before.

8/3 & 9/30/82 — [2] (03515)

Tours de Force ^Δ

From Jefferson,
The reverse-threaded nut
At the center of Yoknapatawpha's hub,
They flow outward,
Along their own spokes, toward the sun's rim

And over, just as originally they came,
Ferried back, privately,
To time's origins,
On emotion indigenous to his fictive abyss,
Which he mythicized, from mere words, into a world.

Hitched to their own mystic spirits' team,
They return to truths
Whose accents they immediately recognize
And whose actions recall their paltry heritage —
Inhabitants of Lascaux's groping.

One holds a broken narcissus;
Another boasts a bolted spotted pony;
A third drags a fish, on a rope, in the dirt —
*

Fluid illusions, to whose turbulent currents
Each submits his hopes and drowns.

8/7/82 (03522)

Taking a Bad Fall ^Δ

Occasionally, even familiar locations
Grow indistinct. Energy
Suspended in memory's dense Bailey's Woods
Dissipates. The muscles go weak.
The body's best intentions betray the brain,
Whose sustained demands
Send complaints ranging the entire nerve-work.

Sunrays slanting across the eyes' screen,
In deep-green shafts,
Distract focus from the rooted path,
Leaving the feet to grope
As though both legs were blind men's canes.
Suddenly, one foot catches
On an intractable snag, buckles.

Earth rushes up to arrest motion,
Crush the body like gravel.
Pain reigns supreme, as the broken shape,
Inutterably disgusted, scutters,
Within the frustrated nimbus of its defeat,
Back home, to be fitted for crutches.
The limping spirit submits to the woods' shrill will.

8/8/82 (03532)

The Wandering Jew Returns

Arriving home,
Unutterably alone, bereft even of memory,
I read the sky's mind.
It already knows my time, to the eon.
Article by expensive garment,
I disrobe, flounder
Beneath breathing mimosas and blooming magnolias,
*

Calling out to distant Cassiopeia and Betelgeuse,
As though we know each other
On a first-name basis.
Calling, waiting, drifting, listening, hoping,
I scan the suspended stars,
For the slightest palpitation.
No audible reverberations float earthward.
Only my somnolent shadow
Recognizes my dream-weary ratiocinations,
Recalls the shape which confirms my youthful music,
That beautiful confluence of juices and abstracts,
Essences, humors, and fleshly cells
Composing the human being that God,
In His irrepressible hope, supposed I might be
If only the earth's poetry
Would erupt from my bones, bury the universe
Under its molten word-flow.

Now, I scurry from penumbral plums and dogwoods
To sinister pines,
Hoping to find the person I left behind,
A fortnight ago,
Keeping watch for the enemy —
Millenniums inexorably advancing on my hour,
To devour my grandiose moment.
Home is nowhere, no one,
Nothing other than a Saturn ring,
A blistering nebula
In whose disoriented lacunae I float, alone,
A singular, wingless luna moth
Cut from cosmic cloth,
A construction-paper *fin de siècle* effigy
Hanging from an Oscar Wilde sky,
Caught in an Aubrey Beardsley silhouette.

Hush! Hush! He's home again,
Who has wandered beyond Asia Minor,
Touched Atlantis and Cíbola,
Flown over ancient Constantinople,
And orbited the moon. The magnolias and mimosas
Know him by his solar odor.
They've seen this soldier once before,
When, to the trumpeter's tattoo, he left, forever,
*

To do battle with the rapacious aggressor, death,
And submit, without knowing when or how,
To his pervasive persuasion,
Trying to defend wife and children against the unknown.
Now, Valhalla laments his surrender,
As he commits his soul to irrevocable suspension
Among future generations — symbol of eternal uprootedness,
Moses climbing Mount Sinai, to die alive.

8/12 & 8/19/82 —[1] (02202)

Wrangling with the Nemesis

I sit outdoors, bum-legged,
Listening to the birds' persistent chitterings,
Wishing some great passion might revive my spirit,
Absolve me of my solipsistic gloom.

Such cool evenings in August
Almost never arrive,
To relieve our seething days of their humidity
Or release us, on biwinged dreams,

To soar o'er the ramparts of infinity,
Where poets, bridge builders, and pilots connect shores
In the normal course of an eon's span.
Tonight, I join the chorus

Singing the katydids' rhythmic villanelle;
My heart reverberates
To the cicadas' swelling knell.
Peering into the pewter dusk,

I watch for familiar objects, designs
Etched against the soft sun,
Wobbling into the crevasse between Earth and oblivion,
Hoping to take the hobo's bow, now,

But through the screened-in porch,
My wife's slow, low-pitched obbligato
Wafts toward me,
Forces me back from the abyss, into her feminine tenderness.

8/14/82 (05457)

A Road Peddler's Lament [Δ]

A lump constricts his soul's throat,
This parochial 6 a.m.,
As he tiptoes from the bedroom
In which they sleep,
Within the safety of their dreaming naiveté.
His shadow outdistances the house,
Retreats obliquely,
In a Midwesterly direction,
Toward ramshackle gates
Containing a landscape his remaining days
Divide into sprawling feudal estates.

His fate portends him as neither hero nor victim,
Rather suzerain without vassals,
Warlord conscriptless,
Bereft of geographic reckoning,
In desperate quest of a heritage to conquer —
An unkempt emperor,
Circling back to his children (nestled safely
Beneath soft sheets,
Innocence filling their slumber with sweet visions),
In hope, at week's end, of making amends
For having abandoned them for his empty dreams.

8/18/82 — [1] (02088)

Day's Tripper

Once again,
In this Midwestern city on the plain, Columbia,
Seated in Katy Station's bar,
Where, close by, long ago,
Locomotives puffed and lurched varnishes into berths
Beneath Victorian canopied eaves
And wrinkled, twinkle-happy people disembarked,
Entered these dark bowels,
And waited for family to retrieve them and their cargo,
I relax after my day's journey,
Ruminating over the distance traveled since dawn,

Since century's turn.
Katy's stained-glass greens, reds, and blues
*

Pulverize my eyes' rods and cones.
I repose inside a slow, blown zone of emotion.
Color blindness afflicts every idea
Effervescing, in silence,
Within the diminishing circumference time describes
About the inner perimeter of my wineglass.
Exploding dust motes,
Loaded with clickety-clack factories
And shabby backyards, capture my imagination.

Suddenly, I'm being jostled, rhythmically,
Atop an overstuffed plush seat,
A magic carpet transporting my spirit from here
To the farthest reaches freedom permits
The mind's spontaneous probing to go,
In quest of new frontiers. I hear the whistle
Scribbling signatures on the night air,
Announcing its superiority to all it races past,
In its raspy penetration
Of the sumac-and-cedar unknown. I sleep,
Believing in destinations,

Waking to the sweet, supine surprise of safe arrival,
A bit gritty
But none the worse for wear, nervous
Yet thrilled by the prospect of being greeted by family,
At a prearranged terminal,
Instead of merely sitting here,
Staring into a stained-glass Chablis parallax, alone,
Within the refurbished purlieus of this ghostly station,
Waiting for any soul to recognize me
As my generation's passenger, dying to be transported home,
In a two-horse brougham, to the place I once decried.

8/18/82 — [2] (02592)

Saying No, Again

For Bob Hamblin,
who introduced me
to Ernest Becker's The Denial of Death

So many times
I've tried to measure the height my shadow casts,
*

Without arriving at a definitive size,
That now, when the occasion presents itself,
My psyche refuses to undertake the delicate task,
Fearing scholastic censure
From those specializing in mythic proportions
And heroic dimensions. It declines to climb Sinai,
Areopagus, Helicon,
Lie in wait for my slow-approaching shadow
To scale the summit
And stretch out under an inadequate sun
As it spreads itself over all of Athens, Tyre,
The Roman Empire.

Something immobilizing there is,
In calibrating heroics, that explodes the hemispheres,
Obliterates human grasp.
I prefer to regard creativity
As a form of immortality from which "the worm at the core"
Is excluded, by virtue of fruit
Unchewable by gods and humans alike.
I no longer participate in mock trials
In which the mind defines genius,
By placing calipers about a Petrarchan sonnet,
Or deciphers various Rosettas
And identifies Stones of Scone, by blind touch.
Whatever I write is sufficient inspiration
To ignite the cosmic fire, deny fate its due.

8/18/82 — [3] (02593)

Under the Stars

Such wondrous chatter
Pervades this star-watched patio,
Crowded by college students bemused by music
Concocted by students communing, in harmony,
For pleasure's sake alone.

I relax in the dark August outdoors,
Mesmerized not by sounds
But fingers weaving webs along strings
Electrified, vibrating to Delta blues,
Presley, Beatles, the latest reggae,

While I, so totally isolated from youth,
Pretend to comprehend the rhythms
By which these gathered bones speak and move,
When, in fact, I accept the eclectic renditions,
With suppressed boredom.

Oh, to be twenty years young again,
To smoke dope,
Get drunk, without remorse,
Fuck the nearest, most convenient cunt
Seething within the prescribed limit of exhibitionism.

Twenty years too late,
I sit outside, under an indulgent galaxy,
Hoping to have some untried naiad
Approach me with an invitation to dance,
And end the night in bed, with a princess.

8/18/82 — [4] (02594)

"The Worm at the Core"

Certainly, if invisible at first,
"The worm at the core" burrows forth,
Squirming, inaudibly, toward the surface,
Past bones, floating lymph nodes,
Cardiovascular apparatus,
Lower and upper intestines.

It breaks the peritoneum as if it were an untried hymen,
Emerging, initially, as an inauspicious flu,
Accompanied by slight mucous and urethral excretions
At the mouth and penis,
Minimal arthritic inflexibility
Of the maxillae, patellae, and ankle joints.

Gradually inflaming,
It widens into a full-fledged virus,
Whose new strain remains unisolated,
Nameless, a radical threat to the passive masses,
Too consumed with and thralled by their own narcissism
To regard, as threat, its potential spread.

The flesh cracks. The worried muscles weary,
As they hurry through paces
*

Accomplished with mindless expertise, not long ago,
Fumbling for excuses, stumbling to keep up,
Initiate and recover from basic motions
Aimed at defeating stasis, beating inertia at its game.

Not so suddenly, the body submits.
They diagnose the malaise as pernicious depression
Aggravated by organismic psychoviral fatigue,
A very strange case indeed,
Whose etiology derives not wholly from disease
Or mental deterioration,

Rather both and neither — very strange.
A deranged physiology, perhaps.
The country's leading specialists
Violently agree and disagree on the obvious,
Without settling on proper treatment. They argue
Over their quintessential credentials.

Meanwhile, the body persists in dying.
The slimy worm bloats on life,
A measly crumb at a time, day by day,
Until, like the pest of Pharaoh's fabled blight,
It consumes seven times seven years,
In one final, silent, stinging bite.

8/19/82 — [2] (02595)

An Eye for an Eye

Even the ugliest, most hapless lassie
Displays, occasionally, a shapely leg-curve,
A smile capable of disguising the truth of God's abuse
And seeming misogyny.

I, a frequenter of casual drinking spas,
Like Columbia's Katy Station,
Can vouch for the wayward calf, breast, mouth
Of exceptional quality. Youth's brief extreme,

Which manifests itself as sweat-beaded wineglass,
Mascara highlighting the otherwise flaccid eye,
That urgent aroma lovemaking exacerbates
And pleasure perpetuates for its own sake,

Is on the make so transitorily
That when it does show,
There's no mistaking its primordial intent:
To taste of the apple's voluptuous, fleshy essence.

There is that time, in every lassie's life,
Though evanescent,
When magic metamorphoses the commonplace
To fairy dust and the little cinder-lady

Attends her one and only extravaganza,
Meets Prince Not-So-Charming, in the flesh,
And is bespelled forever,
Saving her from the disgrace of physical isolation.

Tonight, as I scan Katy's lounge,
My eyes spy many likely maidens,
Any one of whom might easily excite me
Despite her wens and flab,

Minimal life-webs she relentlessly retells
As though trying to squeeze blood
From proverbial turnips, and make me completely satisfied
Just by submitting to my lonely requirements.

Yet we are all such aliens,
Who frequent this place for the same reasons,
So alone,
That our needs war against each other

Rather than read similar scorecards,
Perceive inadequacies as deformities
Common to Helen and Beatrice and Dulcinea.
Beauty, or pulchritude, as the Romans would say,

May not be more than skin-deep
To the myriad Narcissuses our society breeds,
Yet it is the superfluity
Truth glues to its mousetraps,

To lure its fleshiest victims to slaughter,
Separate those who would worship love
From those who would make a truce with the gods
By taking the not-quite-perfect goddess for a wife.

Tonight, I am quite confident
I could blindly choose any of these special ladies
*

For my helpmate and find contentedness,
Providing she could overlook my shortcoming: infertility.

8/19/82 — [3] (02596)

Boxcars △

If, despite my own delusions,
Pretensions toward immortality,
It's actually been decided already,
Then let me die in a boxcar hurtling east,
Not pressing toward Auschwitz or Treblinka
But rattling behind a shimmying diesel
Bound for Altoona and Horseshoe Curve,
In Pennsylvania,
Where, for the first and last times,
My youth grasped for myths
Commensurate with its capacity for wonderment
And suspended disbelief,
Those distant fixed markers, along the track
Between St. Louis and Manhattan,
Whose Dopplered apotheosis
Always assured me my dad and I
Were making progress toward a destination
Punched on a printed ticket.

Let my dying be recorded on the side
Of a boxcar flying easterly, toward God.
Let it read "Radioactive,"
"Inflammable," "Extreme Caution,"
That my life, even in demise, shall be considered
Volatile. Let death transport my spirit,
From here to eternity's golden depot,
As though I were God's precious cargo,
Worthy of a presidential suite
Rather than a hobo's hasty burial beside the track
In some remote Hooverville.
Let me go headlong over the abyss,
Inside rolling stock with hotboxes sparking,
So that Charon's darkness
Will flicker with my passing. Let me die
Inside a boxcar bound for paradise.

8/19/82 — [4] (00095)

Bodily Functions

Words, like a benign sneeze
Unable to assert itself,
Tease me with tip-of-the-tongue notions
Not quite flowing as speech.

Already, I've driven seventy-five miles
Without getting down
A single stroke
Or solitary strophe — the cursive curse.

Slowly, the road becomes an ocean.
I, a bobbing cork,
Float toward a shore called home,
Absorbing wave vibrations,

Recording analogues just below the surface,
Swimming symbols,
Shimmering images, not exposed to air,
Flowing in their own deep currents.

Abruptly, I disappear,
As a mature sneeze
Takes me whole, explodes, full-blown,
As poem. Relief is so complete!

8/20/82 (02076)

[Over the years,] †

Over the years,
My salient growth, though introspective,
Has been conspicuously outward.
No longer can I disguise my corpulence

8/21/82 — [1] (04835)

The Birds and the Trees △

Today, at ease with everything
That formerly chimeraed me with doubts
*

About succeeding at surviving my inadequacies,
I relax outdoors,
Surrender my senses to extravagant soaring forces
Pervading August.
An anabasis is in progress. I am sparrows,
Robins, the occasional mourning dove,
Claiming the air and trees as their Constantinople.
What a rush, to be possessed
Without possessing another's spoken-for soul!

This breezy afternoon,
I exult in just being a co-conspirator,
Sharing the sun's voluptuous touch,
Appearing to move and articulate without strings,
As I seek out my heritage,
Recognizing, in the shapes of redbuds, mimosas, oaks,
My own seasoned irregularities.
Their precarious outreaching
Reminds me of my own frangibility.
I imagine, in their simplicities, myriad ambiguities
Inherent in our godliness.

At peace with all creatures, coeval and alien,
In harmony with ideologies
Inimical and aligned with my universal insight,
I submit my spirit, unequivocally,
To the Grand Inquisitor.
Whatever His decision as to the appositeness
Of my petition to live forever
Rather than relinquish my position
Two score years from now, I will abide by it.
But if I must expire, let me fly home,
From tree to tree, on the winged backs of my singing words.

8/21/82 — [2] (02075)

Coleus

Beet reds, lime greens, purples, and bloods,
Washed over coleus leaves,
As though by a van Gogh ex machina,
Growing in the bed buffering me from Earth's square edge,
*

Invite my eyes to scrutinize their hues,
Touch each subtle nuance
A millimeter at a time, like myriad ants
Spanning their membranous shapes.

I finger each tie-dyed design
As if tangibility might allow my mind
To appropriate the godliness of precious manifestations
Without having to die. I am ravished
By the extravagance of their variegations,
Relieved to be trespassing free of bees,
So unintimidated and alone,
In this ocean-sea's farthest reaches, which I call backyard.

For what reason the Great Painter chose
To mix His pigments to such sportive degrees of fancy,
I shall never know.
My concern isn't centered in metaphysical speculation,
Except as it helps locate me more closely
Within the soul of the whole of eternity.
In these capriciously tinctured coleus leaves,
I see myself. No two moments resemble each other.

8/26/82 — [1] (02074)

Breezes, Birds, and Bees ^Δ

How soft and sweet and sleepy the breezes are,
This August afternoon,
When bees seem to float in endless hovering
And birds etch the empty air,
With operatic posturing. Their pastoral songs
Belong to a long-ago effluvium
Suffused with denimed pioneers, hearty souls
Willing to partake of Creation's slow unfolding,
If for no other reason
Than that their heritage resembled the parched earth,
Not concrete apartments, tarred streets.

I listen too intently; that's my basest fault.
There's not much room, in my conception of the universe,
For mistaken hopes or misleading dreams.
Today's notions of heroics are grossly limited,
*

Not even whimpers but knowing silences
Splayed, like dim shadows,
Across Biafran faces, unspoken grotesqueries
Imagined by the boxcar people huddled in the dark stench
Of their endless captivity by the Aryan Pharaoh.
Therefore, the least imaginative bird call,
Alliterative breeze, bee-fluttering

Excites me to life's schizophrenias,
Paroles my sensibilities from their fetid incarceration
In musty penitentiaries below the soul.
Today, for some unexplained reason,
I revel in just being here,
An evanescent trespasser, a Bedouin pitching tent
On the desolate sands his existence describes,
In its lunatic orbiting. In writing,
I signify my pledge to remain faithful
To the breezes, the bees, and the birds.
They alone inspire me to exercise my freedom to fly.

8/26/82 — [2] (00135)

Il penseroso and L'allegro

I

I sit outside,
Listening to incipient crickets ring twilight,
With their silvery litanies —
Day's rhythmic halo and coda.

I am simultaneous man — here and hearing,
Alone and lonesome inside my quietude,
A brooding music whose notes
Sing of sleep even as I lie awake.

Everywhere, paradoxes share the air
With my escaping breath.
Why I, not the lilacs or mimosas,
Am concerned with beauty, dying, leaving behind

Legacies and monuments to my earthly design,
Rather than just being,
*

Is my enigma, time's riddle.
Let me be pinks, purples, ravished by bees.

II

Now, I course from night, toward twilight,
Over one of a thousand dream-bridges
Spanning Bunyan's slough,
And choose, cautiously, the westerly exit,

Sixty-five years wide,
To my appointed climax. My speed
Is ambition's by-product, my earthly waste
Radioactivity measured in cosmic lives.

Birds' chirpings load the air to exploding,
This glorious morning.
Although I can't understand their translations —
Orient verses with lunar feet —

I'm grateful for gifts possessed:
Consciousness of death's restive presence
And a blessed faith that human rage
Will vitiate the reaper's rapacious ways.

9/5–6/82 (05456)

Perseus Subdued

I leave sleep's stupor
Like steam lifting off a pond,
Twilight vapors taking human shape,
As if a sculptor's hands
Were formulating, from moist clay,
Divine designs. My last yawn
Is the climax that breaks the umbilical connection
Between night and the new day.

Morning's fog,
Through which I drive tentatively,
Is the primordial mist
I've so recently visited. Up ahead,
Just beyond the gray horizon,
*

Looms the abyss. Miasmic haze,
Sulfurous and purple,
Burns my eyes, even from this distance.

Suddenly, innocence becomes wisdom,
Not the fabled snake molting
But the chary chameleon
Blending into the earth's skin,
To hide from Krakens, Gorgons, and Chimeras.
I squirm, turn stony,
As though Medusa has seduced my verse.
The city savors its latest victim.

9/7/82 (05815)

Off Again, On Again

Off again,
On a moment's notice,
Packing the last minute's afterthought,
A haphazard ingathering of scattered effects
From Dagwood Bumstead's closet,
Jack Benny's protracted sight gags,
My own natural grab bag
Of metaphysical tricks: whimsical notions,
Capricious, idiosyncratic fancies,
Delusions I might be Vasco de Gama,
Martin Frobisher, Cristóbal himself,
Setting sail south,
Out of time, reach, rescue by patrons,
At God's mercy, determined to succeed
In the same single charge,
No matter how many days, decades, it may take
Just to set my course,
Cross the equator, throw anchor overboard,
Into tepid sands, and stand naked,
The warm wisteria-scented air my flag,
Claiming myself, in my own name,
Emperor of Now and Then
And All Days Remaining . . . off again,
This scintillating September morning,
Without a solitary clue
*

As to my direction or the location of my soul's polestar.
Anyone's guess owns me,
As I go, a poet hoping to sight land
Before my metaphors wash me ashore,
On an atoll at the head of a falls
At the farthest edge of an ocean
Cosmo-nautical miles from nowhere,
Where the rest of my life might be spent
Lamenting the roar of the earth
As it soars in its orbit,
Interminably spinning.
Off again, today; I'm off,
My slender "magical pen" the arrow
Floating in my compass. Just now,
It seems to be holding steady,
As I hit I-55
And aim toward Memphis, Oxford, and beyond,
The arrow a wand, divining rod,
The rod become leading edge of a single wing
Buoying my flying mind,
The wing a sail billowing in the singing wind
My meters create inside the slipstream
Breezing by my ears. Suddenly, I hear a voice
Calling my vessel home.
Before I know it, I've arrived,
My drive's conclusion my lines' climax.

9/8/82 — [1] (03583)

Members of the Cast

I steal from our sheets, at twilight,
Sneak, barefoot, across the rug,
Softly as a black leopard
Stalking its own shadow beneath an ivory moon,
Leave you sleeping in our room,
Escape, beneath your uneven breathing,
Like the soul of a spirit recently deceased
Exiting its vessel, then stretch,
As my moving silence parts the stale air
Hovering, like penitents at matins,
In the hallway at the head of the stairs.

All morning, into afternoon's haze,
I've chastised myself
For having taken such pains
To keep from waking you, ask why
I wasn't compelled to pause,
Linger above your delicate fetal shape,
Run my fingers through your hair,
Kiss your twitching lids, grasp your gaunt hip
(Protruding, under the sheet, like a cliff)
As if to hold on for my precarious existence,
And say my "God be with you" in person.

Perhaps my urgent retreat
Was foreordained, in secret, by jinns
Bent on accomplishing my disappearance
Or mythological witch-muses
Conspiring to abduct and seduce me with philters
Before the sun could intercede
And regenerate, with reason, my subdued senses.
More likely, sentenced to exile,
For my fundamental lack of spontaneity and passion,
I was reenacting my best scene:
Romeo fleeing his lover's deathbed.

9/8/82 — [2] (03584)

Working the Promised Land ^Δ

Having arrived at the Marion junction,
Just prior to West Memphis,
Down I-55,
I turn right, westerly,
On Highway 40, then proceed
Sixteen miles, to the Hughes turnoff,
From which point my disappearance begins.

Traversing one leg of the triangle
Connecting me with Forrest City and Marianna,
Beneath a ninety-two-degree haze, I squint,
More from shame than eyestrain,
Glimpsing hovels, canted and ramshackle,
That might be hencoops
Hammered together in a hurricane

Rather than houses, twenty by twenty,
Built from odds and ends
Gathered by resourceful blacks,
To accommodate their paltry needs —
The South's neo-Cubism,
Adapted to the *nada*-soul's Dada-body.
Suddenly, I pass Greasy Corner,

Population 24, then enter Hughes
And stop to buy Brach's lemon drops
At Lock's Food Center,
Squatting, innocuously, at road's edge,
Behind which the town's one cop
Waits all day long to make his obligatory arrest.
Close by, the high-school band

Adds insult to the injurious air,
Practicing for Friday night's football game.
Just out of town, a paving crew,
All black save its supervisor,
Tries to revive tired shoulders. I slow
To the alternating iridescent red flags.
Bloodshot eyes remark my air-conditioned insularity,

With blinkless gazes generations wide.
Something primordial about this land
Frightens me.
Perhaps it's the somnolence of growing things,
Their lackadaisical silence,
That reminds me time
Keeps a completely different beat down here —

It's always late or much too premature,
Delayed or hasty, in any case.
Or maybe it's just that cotton and beans
Decline to be slaves to a clock.
Whatever, I sense myself captive,
In this hellish Delta,
A rag-selling carpetbagger out of my element

Yet forced to interlope in territory
Fertile for surplus and irregular merchandise.
Soon, I'll arrive in West Helena,
Stay the night in a motel,
*

Make my morning rounds, return home empty,
Then strike out with another wagonload —
Next time, for Mississippi.

9/8/82 — [3] (03506)

West Helena's West Side [△]

They are a gregarious breed,
These inhabitants of West Helena's "Shantyville":
Children, whose toys are each other,
Scantily garbed in torn shorts and shirts,
Barefooted, the girls with cornrowed coifs,
Their rowdy counterparts close-cropped, nappy,
All playing jump rope, swatting pebbles,
Whose trophies are smiles, laughter;
The women socializing like parakeets and cockatiels
Set free in a pet store,
Gossiping from hovel to hovel, porch to front door,
In their rickrack canvassing,
From 6:00 a.m. to sunset; the men,
Youthful and aged, sedentary as circus bears,
Jocularly squabbling, almost falling asleep
Between drawled dialogues, all oblivious
To the highway's squall, paralleling their interplay.

This community, whose combined income
Might equal that of one Ladue family,
Has an integrity paradoxically cemented
By its very poverty, a shoddiness so long endured,
Whose symbols are tumble-down porches,
Drooping, corrugated-tin roofs,
Yards strewn with rusted cars, gamecocks
And hens, rubber tires,
Fires spewing gaseous effluvia
All seasons, especially in hundred-degree heat,
That none notices anyone else
As a disgrace to the neighborhood, not keeping pace
With the local gentry. Even the churches,
Profoundly and quintessentially Baptist,
Leave everything to be desired, for appearance's sake,
Are indistinguishable from the grocery store
And open-pit-barbecue shack, two doors up.

This area, no more than ten square blocks,
These blacks, so closely interwoven,
Provide me with no sociological microcosm
Or cross section. My mind finds no consolation
In drawing easy academic or pseudoscientific conclusions;
Rather, instead of refusing to accept their existence,
For lack of empathy or imagination,
My blind compassion is aroused. Abruptly,
I leave the highway, turn up North Baringo,
And drive through the heart of the West Side.
I, with Missouri license plates,
Fancy late-model station wagon,
Make myself naked as an Auschwitz prisoner
Standing in plain view of a thousand camp ladies.
All eyes peer in at me, peer in,
Leering at the anomalous caged creature I've become:
Captive Gulliver in anxious Lilliput.

I turn back and forth, down the peopled streets,
Lost in a maze, frightened
Despite the colossal docility pervading this place,
Trying to locate an opening, escape.
Five minutes protract into five years.
Black children, teenagers, women and men,
Fat and emaciated, tattered, slovenly, happy,
Flash past me like shadows on a Praxinoscope reel.
I seem to be standing still,
Rotating, without spinning, on a revolving axle,
Fixed in a fluid suspension,
Until, accidentally, the highway materializes,
Spewing me, once again, into the speeding milieu,
Which refuses to see and acknowledge
West Helena's West Side.
I drive easterly, toward Oxford,
Knowing only that I won't arrive in my original guise.

9/8/82 — [4] (03527)

Earthly Rewards ^Δ

Leaving Helena,
I cross the bridge, a wide anxiety,
*

And traverse the twelve-mile Delta stretch,
The first leg of the zigzag
That will take me south, to Clarksdale,
Then east, through Marks and Batesville,
On into Oxford.

I play Randy Newman music,
Volume turned up all the way,
On the tape deck, to get in the mood.
Haunting refrains commemorating "Kingfish,"
Rednecks, Birmingham
And satiric pieces about "Keepin' the niggers down"
Grate up, down, and around my spine,

Remind me I'm an intruder in this land,
Come, uninvited, to the university
Forty miles from Jefferson,
To wile away a night, playing poet,
With notebook, pen, wine,
And a slightly careless arrogance and insularity
Befitting the self-imposed bohemian image

I must have read about, in youth, and memorized
(That unstudied derring-do
Hemingway, in his San Fermín phase,
Fitzgerald, at the Plaza, exemplified),
Trying to sculpt, from wet-clay days,
With words and licentiousness,
A shape resembling Michelangelo's *David*,

Failing to achieve such noble stature and pose,
For lack of spontaneity,
Rather sitting on my fat ass, all evening,
Swigging chilled Chablis
Poured from half-carafes repeatedly drawn
And charged to a large tab,
Staring at the seductive coed face

Of every Caddy Compson in the place
Where I've cast my lot —
The Warehouse, in Oxford — to write my odes
To mankind, womanhood, love
(Angelic, courtly, pastoral, and physical),
Melancholic politics, age and youth,
Day and night, life and its coeval, death,

Without any definable priority.
And as the pages fill
With my swill-brained, soaring metaphors,
Brilliant visions, and occasional lyrical riffs,
I realize that a writer's life
Is, of necessity, a matter of sacrificing action,
For a little thought, a bit of scribbling,

And a whole shit-pot load of being lonely,
No matter the spirit's geography.
Before I know it, one o'clock and I
Are the only patrons left in the bar.
I pay, weave my car to the Alumni House,
Read the note taped to my door —
"I'm waiting . . . my place, Temple" — and leave in haste.

9/9/82 — [1] (00162)

Extravagant Fancies of an H.M.S. *Bounty* Deck Hand [Δ]

Oxford is the last stop on my fun run
From Farmington
To the outer reaches of freedom's elasticity.
Two nights on the road,
And my flagging soul snaps back home.
Fly and return,
Stay awhile, then escape again:
The formulaic refrain
My blood has sung so many years
It no longer needs to rehearse
Before performing entertainments, spontaneously,
To crowds of one or less.

Tonight, as I sit here with a half-carafe
Of platinum-tinged Chablis,
Fashioning thoughts from my tarot pack,
Vague Vieux Carré hallucinations
Silhouette my blurred visions, with possibilities
Never before conceived by me.
Just what if I didn't return,
If I set sail, instead, for some distant Pitcairn isle,
*

To unloose new issue,
In total isolation, outside the adversarial world,
Create an original language
Dependent not on phonics but touching,

Build a hut, to satisfy my erotic fantasies
And radically unfulfilled lusts from the other world,
Under whose thatch roof
Creatures evocative in their slender femaleness
Might reclaim me from fumbling,
A harem consisting of supple, naked ladies,
Whose single objective would be to discover me,
Head to head to ten toes,
Over and over, night after night,
Allow me to remember my animal origins,
Cast off my cerebral vestiges,
Arouse in me celestial bodiliness I'd forgotten?

Suddenly, I shudder.
A draft of cold air from the galvanized duct
Hits me in the neck. The wine,
By now my confidante, leaves my face.
I go invisible as a polar bear in snow,
Slowly grow swollen, within my inebriation,
Both omnipotent and ignorant of my location,
Suspecting only that I've dropped anchor
Not on some exotic island but in Oxford,
From where I'll have to reckon a course, in the morning,
If I'm to arrive home, by sundown,
To escort my wife to the annual chamber-of-commerce banquet.

9/9/82 — [2] (00166)

Polar Poet ^Δ

The imperative to create, from silence, sounds,
Compound nothingness
Into fragments of potential spoken words and verses,
Disturbs me so deeply
That whenever I find myself without company,
I tend to invent entire universes,
Worlds peopled with such absurd Joseph K.'s,
*

No one other than the Creator
Would ever recognize my spawn, for the disguises
In which I cloak their fictitiousness.

What a strange vocation I was doled out,
To do overtime, rhyming souls
Who were never born before they met me,
Let alone dreamed of being released
From the unknown. I was deeded lands
On which only a poet might survive,
By his sheer expertise in extracting sustenance
From the sheer precipitous cliffs,
Devising divine designs from the columnar tumble
Of snow descending from their heights.

I climb out of my hibernal den,
To make of my endless days
A home framed and roofed with the poems I write,
Whose metaphors and imagistic symbols
Are the shingles and siding that hide me
Securely inside the pleasure dome I erect
From fluff, from nothingness. I yawn,
Stretch, paw the ground,
Scratch the sky, trying to locate my shadow,
On the slow floe moving oceanward,

A primordial polar bear
Lumbering home, lonely and totally alone,
Who knows only that if he is to reach shore,
He'll have to endure the arctic cold
For decades on end, resist his critics,
Persist in leaving his paw prints in the ice,
Hoping they'll show up at night,
Beneath the midnight sun,
To attest he once passed here,
Laid claim to the cosmos before his words became Earth.

9/9/82 — [3] (03595)

Legacies [Δ]

Shiloh, Corinth, Brices Cross Roads
Echo in my veins, as I flee Oxford
*

And head home. Once more,
Those names resonate out of an old order
Yet proclaimed preeminent
By every Ole Miss Johnny Reb
In polo shirt and rouge-cheeked coed
Wearing Ralph Lauren blouse and shorts.

They parade before me like brigades
Practicing to enter a fracas
Only days away: handsome law students,
Elegantly mannered, soft-spoken ladies-to-be,
Whose greatest efforts will be spent
In defense of spendthrift sentiments,
Divorcements, penchants for Kentucky bourbon,
Mexican tequila, Mississippi white lightning.

Even now, through Tennessee,
Into Arkansas, coursing north, toward Missouri,
I both envy and lament the generations,
Past and present, whose heritage —
Whatever skeletons rattle in their closets,
Swords clatter in rusty scabbards —
Cements them, black and white alike,
In an elemental sense of place, to the future.

I have only myself to claim and blame.

9/10/82 — [1] (03541)

Silkscreen

For my dearest Jan,
this love-print

Jan, your life and mine
Used to be superimposed silkscreens,
Whose chiaroscuroed edges registered,
Disclosing a single silver wing,
Buoying an invisible fuselage
Shaped like a dove's godly body, to the visionary eye.

From this distance of days away,
I see through the diaphanous design,
To the image-core, suffused with our lonely hearts.
*

The soaring form is a knife,
Whose leading edge bleeds black sadness,
Like rain, over a white sun.

Driving home, I can only wonder
What hallucination, optical illusion, or life-lie
Might intervene to transmute the shape
Our abstract lives have assumed,
Retrieving the single silver wing
From the knife's black-bleeding leading edge,

And bring the silkscreen back into focus.
I can only wonder and hope
That, once more, we will soar as one,
Serenely corporeal, so high against the sky
We might see our wide love
Bending, like a flying rainbow, across our days.

9/10/82 — [2] (02072)

Cartographer

He flies out, mile by mile by mile,
His driver's pilot-log
So crammed with scribbled entries
(E.T.A.'s,
Destinations, cargo manifests),
Its rubbed covers won't stay shut —
A *Domesday Book* bulging with lyric-data
Compiled at His behest,
Who, alone, may wish, at some future date,
To make him accountable to the chapter and verse
Of fate's untimely imposition on his forward progress.

And as he goes over roads foreboding and lonely,
Occasionally soaring
Within the thin-walled insularity of thoughts
Verging on poetry, for their free-verse meters
Engendered by freewheeling speed
His machine (a lighter-than-air
Type D–Rigid mind-ship) achieves,
He realizes why his destiny has kept him
So serenely preoccupied
*

With recording every measure of his psychic quest:
He's God's Prince Henry, charting the skies.

9/14/82 — [1] (05816)

Called Away Suddenly

Incautiously, he makes his morning rounds,
Over slick roads
Pumiced, to perilous luster,
By successive thunderstorms. From Farmington
To New Athens, across the JB Bridge,
Then back, and on out to Columbia,
He's watched over, by spacious rainbows.

Three stops before lunch,
To promote folded towels, masking tape,
Ninety-six-roll-per-case
Single-ply, facial-quality toilet tissue,
Thirty-weight kraft paper,
Bowl and wet-mop disinfectants,
Corrugated cartons, and perforated poly bags,

Take their toll. He quits at 1:00,
To eat smorgasbord and contemplate his failure
To consummate a satisfactory commission sale
With his oldest, most reliable users.
His plate is an overstuffed sofa
Tufted with butter beans, fried chicken,
Bread pudding sweating sweet sauce.

Willy Nelson's melancholic plaints,
Like odors wafting from a distant kitchen,
Permeate the room, accompany his crunching,
Divert him, briefly,
From his own woes, to those of the fictive protagonist,
Who's just lost his "angel"
To another, as a result of neglect and lust.

Suddenly, between bites of corn and limas,
He realizes he, too, has a wife
Who, most likely, is, at this moment, home,
Watching soap operas on TV,
*

And who, for the past two decades,
Has known his every move and location,
Monday through Friday, fifty weeks a year,

A wife he neither sees,
Except as a weekend phantasm,
Nor really knows, other than as a body
Accessible to him on an "at-once,
In-stock basis,"
His private, prepaid drop shipment
Waiting, on the dock, for his arrival.

From the adjoining bar,
Drunken "fuck you"s and "shit"s and "goddamn"s
Fracture his trance. In an instant,
He bolts from the table, pays, and pulls away
From the restaurant, with tires squealing.
Hours later, he rings his front doorbell,
Clutching a Tuesday bouquet of Talisman roses.

9/14/82 — [2] (02374)

Incarnations of the Pawnbroker [Δ]

How can a soul roam so far, alone,
Without engaging another —
A hobo, even — in the most fundamental conversation,
Somewhere along the road, in a bar
Or nameless graveyard, while eating cheese
And cold hotdogs? How can a spirit,
No matter how wayward and dissociated,
Fail to make contact
With at least his own shadow, if not a kindred waif
On the Spanish Stairs, along Haight-Ashbury,
In Katy Station, hidden away in mid-Missouri?

I, the liberated guy my youthful psyche
Always dreamed of becoming,
Almost to the total exclusion of goals consistent with growing
(Grades, girls, golden gewgaws and baubles,
And clever gadgets), ask myself
These painful questions, hoping to resolve the dilemma
In which my private essence,
*

So temperamentally independent, from the beginning,
Now wallows.
Sitting here, alone, bereft, invisible,
I listen for the slightest feather falling from heaven,

Praying Milton's archangel Michael
Might whisper, in my ear,
Intimations of God's nearness, His commiseration
For my solifidian diffidence. Any answer
Which might help provide a justification for my plight
Is welcome, tonight, by any presence.
I shall make every allowance,
Forget precision tolerances I've defined to differentiate friends
From potential enemies, accept the sleaziest whore
As my confidante, toast the first person
Who will share this table with my lonesomeness.

To this day, I can't remember my name
Or birth date or race, those basic credentials
Which engender identity. I, having misplaced my face
In fate's burning furnaces,
Intuit, from a singular, sinister detail —
A solitary tattooed serial number just above my left wrist —
The possibility that for almost forty years,
I might have been only my own ghost,
Roaming back toward Russia, Poland, Vienna,
Schleswig-Holstein, to reunite with my truncated soul,
So abruptly dismissed by one man's misappropriation of history.

9/14/82 — [3] (02597)

In Irons, at Katy Station

This station is such a strange, mystical place —
Static yet absolutely alive
Inside my imagination — whose caboose,
Neutered of its rolling gear
And sitting flush with the floor (a dead fixture
In which college kids who've never ridden a train
Can share beers or hard-liquor mixes),
Still moves, from side to raucous side,
Along track my mind sets with ties
And gyves with golden spikes . . .
*

Whose light is Canaletto's, Monet's, on sunny days,
When it seems to hover, shimmer,
Float, inside these otherwise dim interiors,
Like sand, in the twilight sky,
Radiating pink, orange, and purple prismatics . . .
Whose doors and windows and bearing-wall vaults
Are derivations of Piranesi's *carceri* decors.

I marvel at such a strange, mystical place,
Whose aura can, at once, disorient
And comfort me, this oasis so unlikely,
For its Victorian echoes amidst Midwestern chic,
Yet so accessible, if for no other reason
Than that the heartland's arteries are so accommodating
To foreign bodies. I, for one,
An Ishmael of the main-traveled highways,
Know the importance of having a home away from home.
For me, particularly, this curious little lounge,
In Columbia, Mo., provides respite from the cold and heat.
I frequent this way station frequently,
Whenever my road peddler's odyssey
Casts me in this direction.
I, a very contemporary Windwagon Smith,
Tack back and forth,
Trying, like shit, to hit this calm, once a month, and stall.

9/14/82 — [4] (02598)

High-School Sweetheart

He passes from one incarnation to another,
Each time he frequents the bar at Katy Station.
Tonight, he spies, at the table across from his,
A facsimile of his high-school sweetheart,
Julie Bregman — a petite lady in sandals,
Ethnic curls, profound frown
Redolent of intellectual poise and certain savoir-faire
Gained from having done time in Montmartre cafés
And London pubs where Dylan Thomas grubbed.

She reminds him of his ancient flame —
That girl who knew so much about Anaïs Nin
*

And Stephen Crane and Walt Whitman,
The Greeks, French Decadents, of the *fin de siècle*,
And Oscar Wilde —
Whose clitoris required vigorous stimulation
At least every other weekend,
In the coverts of her parent's country-club estate,
Late Saturday night, after the Fortnightly.

So often, during the past decade,
He's thought about her,
That absolutely serious dedication, to existentialism
And oral sex, she possessed,
Who, at twenty, abdicated her feudal position
At Northwestern, to marry a movie producer,
For a chance at everlasting fame —
Barbra Streisand's Katie, in *The Way We Were*.
Oh, how he's wondered where she might be now,

That high-school girl who grew too fast
For her classmates, desired to escape the sentimentality
Of proms and graduations.
Now, after more than twenty years
And a wife and two children he's abandoned,
For irreconcilable differences, as the law decided,
He's reminded of those late-night drives
Into the moon-dappled country, where they discovered
Their sensual zones and came and came

And came, all over each other's expensive clothes,
Those evenings away from the gang,
Places surreptitiously ferreted out,
For the sake of experiencing each other's capacities,
Pleasures possessed mutually,
Those incredible days when both of them thrilled
To their subtle tolerances.
Tonight, he looks at the table, at the lady
Across from him, and wonders where she might be —

Julie, that premature lady
From Ladue High, who could gaze at him
Like a coquettish Mona Lisa
And undo all his poise, dismantle him, without notice.
He focuses on her precocious twenty-year-old features
And begins to cry, realizing, unequivocally,
*

That she is no more, in fact hasn't existed,
For two decades, as the dream he prayed might materialize,
Which was stillborn when he went to Yale, in '59.

9/14/82 — [5] (02599)

Turkey Truck ^Δ

Caught behind a speeding turkey truck
On Highway 63, going north, toward Moberly,
Discouraged from passing, for the traffic
Heading into Columbia, from the hinterlands,
I continued to cringe, the next thirty miles,
As white feathers peeled off,
Striking hood, windshield, my eyes,
Like a December blizzard,

And all the while, those white phantoms —
Scraggly-plumed birds
Stuffed in crates piled six high
Times perhaps twenty rows deep,
On each side — remained hypnotized
By their sixty-mile-an-hour ride.
Never did the feathers quit flying,
Though the snow changed to gardenia petals

Momentarily, then back to dirty feathers,
As I finally closed the gap,
To scrutinize victims in sinister cages,
Creatures forced to squat, on stiff legs,
Unable to stand, stretch, change positions,
Tiny, pink, lizardlike heads
Silent from fright, their lackluster caisson
Conveying my plucked spirit to the abyss, this gray day.

9/15/82 — [1] (00858)

Trapping Moles

My words are slow on the uptake,
Intractable, need to be backed out of their holes,
Like star-nosed moles.

I tamp the ground, my notebook's paper,
With a divining rod, my pen,
To let the land sense my presence,

My eyes focused intently,
Waiting for the first fissure to appear in the white earth.
A stirring occurs beneath the surface,

A tentative upsurge of dirt.
The displacement of space makes me aware
That my quarry is on the alert, poised for escape.

Impatient, I thrust my tamper
Deep into my raised conscious,
Hoping to strike the invisible creature through the heart,

Retrieve the metaphor's entire shape, intact,
From the black depths, on pen's end.
But I miss. It's not where I imagined,

Is, rather, safe in an ancillary tunnel of its labyrinth,
Dug for just such occasions,
When the mind is pressed to surrender its phantoms,

Hand over its brainchild to the enemy,
Man. Disgusted,
I — a vanquished poet —

Throw down my ineffectual stick,
Knowing I'll be returning home without trophy,
Worse, cursed by the urge to return.

9/15/82 — [2] (02600)

The Birth of Venus

There's something about twilight's hues,
Shimmering in this place,
Soothing my importunate muse, subduing her
To subtle nuances of acute hallucinations,
That won't let me refuse choosing Katy Station
As my rendezvous with fate, when I'm on the road.

Perhaps its soft, golden shadows
Are those cast by bees pollinating paradisiacal blooms.
*

Possibly, they are God-flowers
Leaking cosmic semen throughout the universe
Or earthly nuggets being sieved by my poet's mind,
From its rickety, slow-flowing sluice.

Maybe this light is the oft-alluded-to music of the spheres.
Only once before have I seen such beauty:
The pastel illumination of the belly
Of a Botticelli nude has moved me to tears.
Just now, I see you, blessed wife,
Coming toward me, out of the hazy fanlight.

9/15/82 — [3] (02601)

Darwinian Intimations

Coming across country, from Fortuna,
Through Tipton and Bunceton,
Heading north, along the richest stretch
Of Midwestern corn, soybeans, and milo,
Toward Boonville, where I-70
Intersects Highway 5, I beg leave of my eyes,
That I might retrieve essences by the roadside,
To record in my pitching ship's log
And transport home, on my *Beagle*'s last voyage.

Not quite biologist or anthropologist
But rather seeker of unique visions,
Curious objects, oddities,
Linkages between unrealized spirits,
Kindred images, seemingly unrelated traits
In species as disparate as man
And animal, I frequently chart these seas,
In search of new Tortugas
Located within Missouri's rural archipelago.

Today, beneath a Bermudan blue sky,
I gather in black-eyed Susans
And goldenrods, growing in frenzied profusion,
To compare their registrations and spendthrift hues.
I take into account myriad ponds
Dappling the cow- and tractor-dotted fields,
Concrete silos rising, like Gothic cathedrals,
*

In this heartland Provence,
And last-minute butterflies, swallows, and larks,

As part of the larger lifelong study
I've been conducting, with variations
On themes: myself in relation to the world,
And inherited characteristics of my forebears
I possess and manifest
In the strangest ways, from day to day.
These outward emblems in nature
Attract me back to my protozoan origins,
Just by reminding me

That all things animate and otherwise
Have a basis: we share the same location in space
And time, if only for moments,
In the spinning planet's scintillating span.
I am brother to the cow and grass,
Flower and tree, house, hill, and horizon,
Child of the sun and moon,
Conceived within morning's and evening's womb,
Father of the expanding universe,

By virtue of my precious, God-wrought bequest,
Imagination. With it,
Informed by His Word, I can speak to the stone,
Translate the wind into ancient hymns,
Record my aloneness as substantive metaphors
That repeat, in unmetered poetry,
The glorious nomenclatures of the inarticulate soul.
Were I deprived of retrieving essences,
My entire means of survival would be direly jeopardized.

9/16/82 — [1] (05416)

Images, Symbols, and Signs

As I pass through Kingdom City,
On my homeward trek,
My eyes register outrage, scream uncle,
In their feeble attempt to be engaged and to read
Every pervasive road sign and billboard
And plastic-lettered or hand-painted shop logo
Reaching out like a screeching eagle's beak and claws.

I pause, longer than caution permits,
To stare at a life-size horse
Surmounting a Western-wear store
Abutting a strip mall
Bedecked, at its ends, with an Exxon insignia,
Vaulting fifty feet into the sky,
And gold Siamese-twin arches in a gesture of copulation.

Further down the highway, I'm beseeched to purchase
Factory-outlet kitchen glasses, fireworks,
Men's dress slacks, insulation batts,
Beef jerky, and country-cured hams and turkeys.
Not to be outdone, a small sign shouts,
"Minnows Worms Catfish Crickets,"
To the unemployed, retired, and recently fired

Wishing to drown in their disillusionment
Vicariously. Finally, I stop to refuel
My one machine and jettison waste from my other.
The rank odor of ancient motor oil
And grease, permeating the station,
Awakens me as though I were a surgery patient
Surfacing from anesthesia.

Bombarded by brand names, on cans,
Bottles, tin containers, cardboard boxes,
For candies, liquid tire patches,
Gas treatments, cigars, sodas, prophylactics,
I realize there's no escape,
Save one, from the endless fusillade of images,
Symbols, shapes, graphic-art work, cartoons,

The miscellanea and trivia and ageless ephemera
By which the civilized world
Continues to run naked across its own Vegas stage.
Suddenly, leaving the key in my parked car,
I tear off my shirt,
Throw it to the ground, and bolt, like a frightened cow,
Into a nearby meadow,

To find, for a few moments, eternal solace
Beneath end-of-September's plenteous sun,
Then run down narrow, mazy paths —
A flustered, nimble-toed bovine —
*

Until, out of breath, I come to a raucous halt,
Before an irregular board nailed to an oak,
And slowly read "No Trespassers — Keep Out."

9/16/82 — [2] (05415)

Seeking Help

My wife and I,
Like halves of a fractionating atom, fly out of the house,
One north, the other south,
In urgent silence, denied of lip rituals
Or a good-bye's common courtesy,
Rushing elsewhere, in haste,
To find the identical blind psychiatrist
Who resides at both ends of love's continuum
And tell him all the life-lies
We've cribbed, since high school, on our mind's cuffs,
Unleash black dogs,
Collapse the dam holding back flood-mud
Twenty-five fathomless years deep,
All for the sake of saying it
Out loud,
Shouting down the Theban cathedrals,
Routing out the rats,
Long accustomed to nesting in the catacombs
And castles we built by hand,

All for the sake of articulating it,
Our paltry desperation,
The future's unsoothing disillusionment,
Those human truths
(Base and petty cruelty, greed, selfishness)
Which we've woven into our tapestry so precisely,
Over the past decade,
No one without a trained eye
Might ever even notice them as imperfections
In the design. We head out,
Toward opposite poles of the same lodestone,
Knowing only that our fierce need
To speak the unspeakable
*

Must be broached, even if secret promises,
Briefly disclosed, are forever breached,
All for the sake of naming each other
Co-conspirators in the plot
To overthrow love and, we hope, in the process,
Receiving immunity from newer persecutions.

9/21/82 (04171)

Metaphysical Inquisitions

In this incipient autumn
Of my forty-second year,
The adjectives "gorgeous" and "glorious"
Seem more than adequate as modifiers
For my mood. At first glimpse
And on hearing them recited by my miming lips,
They appear sufficiently descriptive,
Perfectly suited
To the intellect connecting eyes, ears, and lips to their hemispheres.

But as I scan the limestone cliffs,
Seething with draped watercress
Cascading from wet-yellow flanks,
Gaze out across fog-laden valleys
Along both sides of the highway,
Trace the horizon, for migrating shapes,
And register summer's trees
Just entering cool-hued maturity,
My heart knows these words are unsatisfactory.

This gorgeous morning may be pied,
Glory-torn, and ornamented in natural piety,
Hopkins-like and Wordsworthian,
Simultaneously.
It might even be that my senses
Can actually intuit, from the sun and wind,
Their own location within the whole,
Share in God's heritage.
Yet where is the soul who can transcend head and flesh and survive?

9/24/82 — [1] (05817)

An Autumnal

The nights slowly grow colder.
The old white Gothic manse shivers,
Suspires in shorter breaths,
Fills, each dawn, with a chill
That afternoon suns less successfully reverse,
As September-crisp days
Give way to October's brittle vapors.

This morning, descending the stairs,
I can't distinguish the floorboards' creaking
From snapping, cracking joints and tendons
In my bare feet,
Nor am I able to slake the freeze
Racing up my bones,
Through the mazy space between them and their flesh.

What a strange, vague shape
My naked body casts
In mirrors I pass, on my way to the bathroom.
In this nexus between dream and dawn,
The demon who's driven me
Doesn't seem to recognize his reflection.
To me, he's pale and frail, a trifle frightened.

9/24/82 — [2] (02071)

Imminences

Sugar maples, dogwoods, and sumacs
Are the first to be seared in autumn's cautery.
Their dapple-dazzling hues,
Fusing natural, evolutionary russets,
Tawny beiges, fawns, ecrus, and golds
With ecclesiastical crimsons and purples,
Swirl around my eyes like cosmic nebulae
Seen through a spectrometer.

Once again, September's ending
Invites me to delight in its giddy climacteric,
*

Share its filling up and spill
As though its colors were a whitewater river
Shimmering toward precipice and falls,
Or grains in a revolving kaleidoscope,
Ghosts taking off their clothes,
Rather than leaves abandoning photosynthetic tropisms.

I've arrived slightly early, this time.
The heart's party
Has not got into full swing; guests are yet lingering,
Confused, perhaps, by the vacillating weather.
None knows quite how to dress,
When warm afternoons refuse to cool down
And chill mornings assume the moon's ivory glow.
My Host and I stand alone, for a moment,

Before His urgent revelers,
In garish capes, ruffled silk shirts,
Velvety ties,
Isadora-scarves, and hand-painted lace,
Sequined and beaded extravagantly,
Break down October's door,
Sunder us, in riotous and blundering drunkenness,
As they move past midnight, toward moribundity.

Both of us have seen monarchs migrating,
Spiders caught up, everywhere,
In last-minute thoughts and conundrums,
Mud daubers and other wasps
Boarding up the world around them,
Squirrels being feverishly acquisitive,
Just for preservation's sake,
Turtles crossing concrete Phlegethons, to escape fate.

We read the impending season's oracles
Not without grieving,
Knowing the soul's *loci dei* and *hominis* are one
And the same, and briefly discuss
The possibility of arresting the present,
Transcending the inevitable. For Him, yes!
For me, the dying leaves
Afford the closest, most vicarious insight into paradise.

9/29/82 — [1] (05818)

Backlash $^\Delta$

Lands which less than three weeks ago
Were crowded with cotton plants
Dripping liquid fluff
Now either are disked into furrowed oblivion
Or, having been picked clean,
Resemble potter's fields
Littered with victims of attrition — brittle stalks —
Arthritic cripples shivering in the heated breeze.

Only the soybean crops
Strut and flaunt their stuff, like peacocks,
In this end-of-Septembering season,
Below Hayti, Caruthersville,
On down toward Braggadocio, Memphis.
Even these, usually green as watercress,
Seem to have been drenched in urine,
By a mythic Swiftian colossus.

As my tired eyes rotate southerly,
My spirit begins to unwind,
Leaving memory behind, with two children and a wife,
To protect it from parasitical spores,
Jettisoning reason and intellect,
To better prepare myself for superstition and bigotry,
Resistance to the new crop I've come to introduce:
White slaves from Detroit, Boston, and Ladue.

9/29/82 — [2] (03526)

Outsmarted $^\Delta$

For Mister Boy,
his fifth birthday,
10/26/82

"You be circles; I'll be X's,"
The little fella asserts from his perch
On the lowest of three back-porch steps.
I readily acquiesce,
Realizing that to be asked by my four-year-old
Is tantamount to being invited to play
With Her Majesty, Miss Muse, herself.

Firmly, he abrades the gray concrete,
With an irregularly shaped stone
He's just dug from the coleus garden.
His scratches render a white crossbones
In the upper-right corner,
As if to announce "BEWARE" of his powerful prowess.
I borrow the rock, from his proffered palm,

And, with feigned certainty,
Place my first O, below his mark,
Showing I own no fear or doubts
About the outcome of our contest.
With celerity, he grabs the makeshift chalk
And emblazons, at the shape's heart,
His second hallmark.

Furtively, I seize the rock again
And, in mock high seriousness,
Let my entire body
Descend on the middle box of the top row,
Next to his original choice,
Pretending, with silent, solemn resolve,
My symbol will stop his progress.

He grabs the flint from my hand
And enters his final sign,
In the bottom square at the opposite end,
Exactly diagonal to the top.
Gouging a line through all three,
He makes a victory shout so loud
His mother runs out of the kitchen,

To join in his celebration.
Meanwhile, I sit on the stoop,
Dramatically protracting my frustration
And disgust at being beaten so handily.
Soon, like an ardent cave artist,
He crosses two parallel vertical lines
With two side-by-side horizontals

And, assigning X's to me, this time,
Draws his first circle, in the upper right,
Just as he did last go-round.
*

Enormously confident, I accept the rock
And mark the spot at dead center.
As we exchange stones and gazes, I know he knows
I know he's going to win again.

9/29/82 — [3] (01467)

Going to a Colloquium at Ole Miss [△]

A celebration, twenty years to the day,
in honor of James Meredith,
who was admitted to the University of Mississippi,
as its first black student, on September 30, 1962

Up as far as Hayti and Sikeston,
The northernmost zone for growing cotton,
Crops have already been harvested.
Down here, below West Helena, Arkansas,
Going southerly, toward Clarksdale,
Greenville, the entire Delta
Is awash with white polka dots —
An October snow, in the upper eighties.

And as I go, bolls broken wide open,
In furrowed rows
Pressing in on both sides of the highway,
Remind me of popcorn, in a green dish,
I'd like to snatch in my fingers
And nibble, repeating so, to satiety.
But the Mississippi salt on my lips stings,
As my imagined snack metamorphoses.

Each fluffy puff, innocuously drooping,
Becomes a Klansman
Beneath a sheet, amidst leafy coverts.
Frightened by agoraphobic misgivings,
I increase my speed, aim eastward,
Hoping to elude this White Citizens' Council,
Reach Oxford intact, in time
To hear James Meredith fulminate on black supremacy.

9/30/82 — [1] (03512)

Implacable Impasse ^Δ

So strange. It's so strange
How so much has changed so little,
In so few ways
Nobody can put his finger on or touch, these days,
With a divining rod's twin tines,
Intellect and emotion. Twenty years have elapsed,
Yet black students at Ole Miss
Maintain that ingrained low profile
No amount of administrative rhetoric and cant
Proclaiming "affirmative action"
Can disenchant from the old Colonial tyrannies,
Handed down not an eye for an eye,
Rather inequity for deprivation, welt for silence.

Sad. It's so terribly tragic
To see white coeds and their cotillion beaus
Coming and going, coming, coming
Without even knowing the "Michelangelo poet,"
Let alone the trauma of both '62s —
Neither Shiloh nor Meredith
Fits into their neat schemes for law school
And marriage into positioned riches,
With clothes and cars and cosmetics
Posing the most radical challenges and threats
To their growth, success, both races intermingled
Yet neither realizing what goals need to be set
And met to perpetuate the soul of a dying society.

10/1/82 — [1] (03529)

A Chance Encounter ^Δ

Last evening, in Fulton Chapel,
On the Ole Miss campus, filled, to capacity,
With blacks and whites and national news media
Brandishing video equipment
Instead of the National Guard bearing M-1's,
Tear-gas canisters, and night sticks,
I witnessed history's not completely inconspicuous demise.

A score of years rolled up behind a podium,
In the guise of a retiring, slightly fuller figure
Of the student youth who, at twenty-nine,
Defied an entire society entrenched in its White Citizens' Councils,
A bewhiskered man chanting in damning staccato,
Not strident, yet uncompromising,
In his desire to effect black reunification, in Africa,

And basic rights and decencies still unheeded,
According to his heart, at the University of Mississippi
And in America — equalities still rampantly abnegated,
As exemplified by ratios, facts, statistics,
In every profession across this disenfranchised land.
I witnessed half the audience exit
As he concluded and a panel of black graduates began,

The predominantly white dispersion
Not even lingering to add their applause,
Their flight disappointment's overt manifestation.
They'd come, I suspect, like spectators to an auto race,
Anticipating catastrophe.
Even as I listened, I couldn't help asking myself
What he was doing now,

Whose education had entitled him to life's riches,
Why, living in Jackson,
These past years, in uncontroversial seclusion,
He'd satisfied himself with owning a bar and tree farm,
Remarried, begun another family.
Not that I faulted him;
Rather, I apprehended his acquiescence to the establishment,

In a land singularly deplorable for its poverty.
Yet I was sad, nonetheless,
Watching this soul, who had asserted himself
With such courage, in 1962,
For the sake of abjuring second-class citizenship.
And as I sat attentively,
My eyes and throat choked with invisible tears.

Later, back in the lobby of the Alumni House,
Where both of us had accommodations,
I introduced myself, explained my presumptuousness
By saying he'd spoken for me, in those days,
*

When we were of college age,
That my admiration for his actions at that time
Persisted yet. I was so glad

To get to tell him so,
Though we each seemed not anachronistic
But slightly anomalous, amidst students
Who'd grown up in integrated schools, never known
(And so, regarded all our reminiscences as foolish)
The vituperations of a Ross Barnett,
Orval Faubus, James Eastland, or George Wallace.

As we exhausted our large small talk,
I handed him a copy of *Three Years in Mississippi*,
Asking if he might inscribe his book to me.
Reading his script, back in my room —
"For L. D. Brodsky / To Our Future /
J. H. Meredith / Sept 30, 1982" —
I knew our future was already history.

10/1/82 — [2] (03528)

[The courthouse does not squat obliviously,] †

The courthouse does not squat obliviously,
In its gray, amorphous concreteness,
Rather sways, as echoes,
Resonating from the makeshift stage
Between Square Books and the city hall,
Pelt its east wall — a cappella gospel,
Delta blues, Choctaw chanting

10/2/82 (04357)

The Circus: Between Stops ∆

Having driven, four hours,
Without a solitary rhythmic phrase or metaphor
Breaking through my lethargy,
To anoint this trip,
I slip into a depressive fit. Narcolepsy
Threatens me with sabotage.

Expediently, I veer off, at the next exit,
Evacuate ship, at a roadside shop,
To get a grip on myself, sip soda
From a cold can I press to my temples,
As I rest before setting out again.
My forehead throbs like a turbine.

With my having more than two hours yet to go,
The dread of boredom acts as a whip backing me,
A scraggly, drugged lion, into a corner,
Onto a pedestal. Sitting on my haunches,
I pray for a thought-hoop
Through which the fates might command me to leap,

So that I might keep my sanity,
While being careful not to get singed
By synaptic fires dancing around its rim.
Suddenly, the performance ends. I roar
As the metaphor dissolves into my two children,
Rushing, from the porch door, toward my car.

10/3/82   (03568)

Morte d'Arthur ^Δ

Just to sit outdoors,
Amidst last-minute swifts
And barn swallows, monarchs, spiders, and hornets,
Entranced by fall's circumstantial pomp,
Whose deep-throated organ chords
Are russet and orange, burnished purple and gold,
Is sufficient reward for a gypsy
Who's strayed too often, wandered off alone
Without marking his location in the cosmos.

My eyes tire from the penetrant scrutiny
The senses require of me,
This October twilight, when dying leaves,
Browning pine needles abdicate their regal thrones.
Yet the evanescent splendor
Glory's hour manifests is indeed Wordsworthy.
And so I try to write eternity
*

In my meager script, transliterate God's voice
Into audible verse,

By describing the visible, the aural, and olfactory.
Suddenly, I get up from my spot
Beside the ancient slave shack
By the cistern beneath defoliating redbuds
Shading the garden, which recently hosted dusty millers
And coleuses in such flamboyant profusion,
One might have mistaken them for royal courtesans.
I follow my boy, Troika, on his odyssey
Across our yard's Ionian unknown, to Tyre,

Witness, in silence, my five-year-old's wonderment
As he bastes himself with leaves,
Hastens to the pine tree's base,
Where he submits his entire being to its needley apron,
Rushes off again,
To investigate holes dug, in the thick grass,
By snakes, moles, bumblebees,
Pull onion clumps, smell their sweet tang,
Then runs to catch a languid butterfly

Left behind, in the frenetic migration south.
I witness his total commitment
To all that is occurring in this urgent interlude
And wish I might enter the season's plunge,
Achieve ecstasy, reach Xanadu
As one ready for anointment, baptizing,
Knighthood, under my lionhearted son's
Sacred coat of arms. And yet,
He is only my fortunate scion, not my destiny.

I leave him to his childish fancies,
Content myself with winter's whispering intimations,
Realizing that the gypsy in me
Must neither retreat from nor be complacent about
My marginal, inessential victories over old age,
Rather accept whatever consolations
I might isolate from inchoate transformations,
Knowing death is a manipulative barbarian,
Who invades each of us, regardless of our allegiances.

10/5/82 (05455)

The Birthmark

At my conception,
Time left its birthmark on me.
My body, newly emergent,
Was tinged with invisible syllables,
Whose inscrutable, flesh-hued registers,
The genes' blueprint,
Would, for an indeterminate span,
Manifest themselves and recede unpredictably,

Not as construable splotch,
Grotesque discoloration, or excrescence
But as a vague tingling
Engendering insatiable urges to scratch,
Pinch the skin past pain, to numbness —
Poison ivy of the imagination,
Which no analgesic could mollify,
Psychic herpes, without etiology.

Only after these many decades
Have my eyes finally trained themselves
To translate sensations into symbols,
Abstracts into definitive shapes.
In my eightieth year, the original dust and clay,
Resettled, hardened,
Highlight my birthmark's cuneiform.
The smell of its coalescing etched letters spells "death."

10/6–7/82 (05819)

Adopting Orphans [△]

Words surge to day's surface,
From metaphor's core,
A torrid birth from cosmic rock
Churned to magma,
In the earth's brain, pushed upward,
Under staggering force,
Erupting past dark strata,
Medieval forgetting,
From a source out of time,
Before primordial forests and swamps,
*

Even beyond reach
Of God's collective, unconscious omniscience,
An urgent convergence of words,
A phonic convocation,
Whose thrust is neither blunt nor oblique,
Rather conceived
(The words suspended yet,
By multiple umbilical cords, from the world's fundus)
To penetrate the planet's rough crust,
Be heard as many voices
In unison, beseeching anyone
To take them home, cradle them in a poem,
And listen while their cries
Grow lyrical and wise in the years' ears.

10/14/82 — [1] (05820)

Horses of the Same Color

Fever has ripped the reins of this vehicle —
My four-wheeled steed, Rosinante —
From my enfeebled grasp
And sent it careening from side to side,
Cutting a swath in the concrete highway,
Like a rodeo bronco
Whirlpooling within its own folding clumsiness.

Neither spectator nor participant
In limbo's swirl,
I, attached to Pegasus by fingertips
Desperately gripping its swishing tail and mane,
Trail behind, training remaining energy
On groping like a blind gopher
Going toward an opening in its shadow.

I yield to the freewheeling motion,
Hoping I'll not be thrown,
That I'll arrive home intact,
Be allowed to sleep a thousand drowsy hours
Without encountering unicorns, centaurs,
Three-toed ponies
Stampeding feverishly over my dreams.

10/14–15/82 — [2] on 10/14 (05821)

[Something erudite, esoteric, absurd] ‡

Something erudite, esoteric, absurd
Informs precise shadows
Driving off redbuds, mimosas, oak trees,
In increasingly extravagant cantilevers,
As afternoon screws through westerly climes,
Toward frigid destinations.
Outside, I approximate ancestral phantoms,
By flying obliquely into time's eye,
Intercepting sunrays
Cascading, angularly, from paradise.
I enter their *locus dei*,
In midstride, penetrating to the center,
Where the stuff of shadows, dreams, memory, insight
Engenders universal metaphors.

This cold, crepuscular occasion
Has chosen to show me these afternoon shadows
Are not mere accidents of refraction
Or optical delusions,
Rather my coevals, swirling circles,
Cast by night's carbon arcs,
Trying to find a common, superimposed focus,
Dancers engaging in pas de deux,
Antipodes closing fast (airships,
Titanic icebergs). Now, the shadows liquefy.
Slowly, I float away from my mooring —
A straw caught up in its own motion,
On thoughts fraught with sharp edges;
A dark ocean

10/16 & 10/18/82 (05454)

Remembering Eden

Curiously, the only trees untouched
By October's providential censer
Are those close-huddled novitiates in Eckert's Orchard.

They are all at vespers, as I pass,
Shivering in green robes,
Beads, from their expiations, strewn at their feet.

Their endless rows remind me of penitents
Kneeling in crowded cathedral aisles,
Surrendering their spirits to Eucharistic ecumenism,

Beneath a 360-degree clerestory
Of stained-glass trees
Circumscribing their sacred space.

Perhaps these defenseless innocents
Haven't yet intuited communion is ritual,
A provisional myth, an act of faith,

Not a fact of nature, lowercase truth.
Maybe this isolated congregation,
Transfixed by the wind's scriptural whispering,

Refuses to acknowledge incipient dwindling
Ubiquitous among its kin. Most likely,
These eight-year-old apple trees,

Many still clutching rosaries, in their flexible limbs,
Can't bear the notion of letting go,
Prostituting their foliage, for a few gaudy moments,

Prior to accepting nakedness. As I drive west,
My restless memory almost recalls
When hope was once green

And the poet in me clung to its boughs,
Giddy, defiant, profuse, devout,
A flourishing worshiper of eternal perfection,

Determined to prolong virtue.
But I weep, wondering how long it will be
Before this orchard tastes its own forbidden fruit.

10/20/82 — [1] (05822)

[He passes, through October's glorious corridor,]

He passes, through October's glorious corridor,
With amazing alacrity,
A phantom sworn to return to his origin
By fleeing it with feverish determination.

His eyes recognize spectral ephemera,
Without sending it forward for permanent recording.
Leaves preening in sugar baths
Fail to reach ciphering apparatuses.

Eighteen wheelers, in snorting hordes,
Ransacking the concrete prairies he uses,
Blow by him, nudge his vehicle aside
As though his speed were slow motion,

Ferrying their suspect cargoes
Toward destinations he'll never reach,
For his urgent impatience. He's being chased
By a nameless, inscrutable force

That refuses to disclose its insignia
And critical specifications — whether fiendish machine,
Invisible telekinetic creature,
Or flesh-and-bone beast or human is a total enigma.

Yet he speculates his severe fear
Is no mere hallucinatory fugue,
Rather adjunctive to his running away
From something, toward its incontrovertible opposite.

If only he could stop long enough
To pick up a hitchhiker,
He might locate his position, adjust headings.
As it is, he drives by dead reckoning,

Praying his direction hasn't deviated so greatly
That reaching home will be complicated
By irretrievable warps in time.
Suddenly, just up ahead,

The entire environment rages. Blinking lights
Make the bright day wince.
He brakes abruptly, swerves, stops on the shoulder,
And cringes as he watches, transfixed,

Two oversize cranes
Delicately extricating, from its grave,
An overturned petroleum tanker,
Liquid and steam ominously streaking from crumpled seams.

Instantly, he recognizes his contorted shape
Lodged, impossibly, within the twisted cab,
Feels his life rising, soaring
Along an endless strip of twilit horizon.

10/20–21/82 — [2] on 10/20 (05823)

Watching for Snakes, in the Forest ^Δ

This late-October early a.m.,
The Capital Café bristles
With born-again-Christian apologetics and rhetoric.
Snide asides from the Apostles' table,
Positioned farthest back, near the kitchen,
Slither across the smoky air,
Like "ground slides" escaping detection,
Before they lunge. Their fangs
Bite the Baptist persuasion's tough hide,
Scratch the Jews' sumptuous presumptuousness
By focusing on Begin's nose, Dayan's eye patch,
Cause necrosis to set in
Among the few Catholics who've remained in the community
Despite perpetual autos-da-fé
Calculated, through social exclusionary strategies,
By the "right" people, to expunge the "Irish scourge."

Meanwhile, I sit listening, in a nearby booth,
Not so much stupefied
As frightened by the White Citizens' Council diction
Lifting in lofty circles as if a pagan god
Had blown smoke rings, from a cigarette,
More from boredom than complacency.
Suddenly, I notice some of them
Watching me scribbling strophes on paper,
Then sense their pious silence
Scrutinizing my statuesque, Job-like pose
As though preparing a dynamite charge.
Hastily, I pack my notebook in a tattered attaché
And nudge not past their table
But a nest of rattlesnakes,
Waiting for their coiled shapes to strike,
Subdue the troubadour passing through.

10/22/82 (00568)

Ministering to the Fish [△]

Having decided, after more than a month
Of bribes, cajoling, draconian threats,
That there was no other solution
To Trilogy's disinclination
For changing, biweekly, its water,
We prepared to bury her half-alive fish,
In a brief Sunday-afternoon ceremony,
Out back. I had forced the issue
To this infelicitous conclusion,
Fulminating, in scientific argot, about salmonella.
She acquiesced past the hoeing,
Right up to the moment
Whose wretched, pragmatic truth
Seemed so perniciously inhuman, cruel,
Once the cold bowl in my icy palms
Awakened me to the deed
I was not only initiating
But coercing my eight-year-old daughter
To witness, condone, and assist in perpetrating.
Abruptly, I declined to complete the act,
Instead led the procession back to the patio,
Where she and I shared in cleaning stones,
Scrubbing the filmy glass,
Refurbishing the plastic anemone and seaweed,
Father, fish, and daughter participants
In a secular baptism, ordained to receive grace
For at least another half-week.

10/25/82 — [1] (00686)

Quarterly Board Meeting

Having reviewed balance sheets
Neatly accordioned in blue folders,
Distributed, around the mahogany table,
To all officers on the board,
Concluding with requests to pursue capital expenditures,
For the next two quarters,
And offering a studied prognosis on profit prospects
In this precarious economy,
*

We sigh, close briefcases,
On undisclosed potential cancellations and bankruptcies,
And leave the austere offices, on a high note,
Absolved of direct accountability, for three months.

The six of us compose the chief executive core
For a St. Louis–based clothing corporation,
A wholly owned subsidiary,
Whose parent company, Abraham Zion,
Is one of the top hundred conglomerates in the country.
Crowded in the CEO's Toronado,
We pass the baseball stadium,
City hall, whose shape resembles Versailles,
Remark DeLorean's recent debacle,
The PLO, getting laid
Anywhere, but not in town,
And reassure ourselves we deserve our salaries,

By enumerating differences from firms
Who've recently filed Chapter 11s,
For lack of adequate operating capital
To pay their creditors. "Shrinkage,"
"Dissipation," "attrition" — each of us
Seems to be able to freely supply synonyms
For the predicament we've been witnessing,
The past three years.
We're different, we reassure each other,
Over martinis; people *need* our products,
Especially three-piece suits from China
And our Czechoslovakian corduroy sportscoats,

Garments of Korean and Taiwanese silk, Burmese madras,
Harris Tweeds from Perth.
We have competition, we know,
Detractors among vendors, union sewers,
And the ILGWU
Main office, in New York City,
Which has frequently threatened not to negotiate,
Let alone renew, the next contract.
By 2:00, we arrive back in the office,
Just in time to review Abraham Zion's
Latest stock listing, smoke,
Swallow our Cambridge Diets, before heading home.

10/25/82 — [2] (02373)

The Last Movement

This late-October early morning is a scherzo
The Lord has orchestrated
From disparate scores, a ceaseless reiteration
Consisting of diminished-seventh seasons,
A month of Sundays scaling the treble clef,
Reaching our eyes' ears, today,
In quick, crisp wind-trills,
Pizzicati tripping from the sky's violins,
Oboe and flute notes
Lifting off the leaves' soft-lipped fluttering.

We listen to its themes kissing earth,
Seeking gentle recapitulations,
Finding sweet sequestration
At the base of the yielding brain,
Screeching, occasionally, into silence,
As off-key and cacophony
Blend into harmonious overtones,
Before inflating the entire outdoors
With its capricious, golden-horned solo — the Lord's coda.

10/27/82 (05453)

Dissolution

8 a.m.
Is a painful resolution to waking.
Such activities have always flustered me,
Foreordained lethargy and indolence,
Continual doses of cough medicine,
Whenever the shape lying in bed,
Beside my rising shadow,
Fails to stir, its breathing erratic,
Even as I dress, fumble in dimness, disappear.

It's then I realize
How coeval in depth, if not degree,
Sleep and death are, that two people,
Man and wife, once devoted souls,
Can lie side by side,
Between the same sheets,
*

Six feet deep in separate dreams,
Sharing the wide silence,
And allow themselves to be buried alive.

I die, each morning I wake,
My hollow gaze the bouquet I place on our grave.

10/28/82 (04170)

Costumes

Busily trivializing this golden October,
Day by hour by minute,
In systematic declension,
As though my protean business endeavors
Were somehow Mosaical,
Never stopping, not even in sleep,
To assess the significance of necessities
Such as rushing from one engagement to another,
Keeping topped vast stock lists
Consisting of pocketing and waistband trim,
Buttons, toilet tissue, disinfectants,
Issues of the moment — a sea never the same
Yet changeless in its aggregate —
I've neglected to invest my best efforts,
Have squandered my energy's tendency
To renew itself, endlessly,
Just by letting the gentle sensibilities
Controlling slower motions focus me
On those so close the most casual notice
Is capable of awakening disparate souls
To this golden October's potential
For letting us forget pettiness,
Cease self-deceits, betrayals,
Concentrate on each other's faces, graces,
Comparatively basic needs to share,
Be touched, submit to love's insufficiencies.
Today, I take off my mask,
Go door to door, naked,
Hoping no one will recognize the seminal me —
It's Halloween!

10/30/82 (05824)

["Indian moon," my little fella named it.] †

"Indian moon," my little fella named it.
My little fella caught first glimpse,
As its shimmering pink

11/1/82 — [1] (08310)

Hayride Halloween ‡

At dusk, we wove away from town,
Found our destination,
At the end of the county-highway maze
Outlined on our hand-printed map,
Just as the Magician's legerdemain
Exchanged pastel sun for pink Indian-summer moon
Skittering between half-empty trees.

Outsize stumps fiercely blazing,
Encircled by hay bales
Supporting shapes not quite recognizable,
For the spark-laced twilight, drew us to the campfire,
Invited us to repose, cast our lots
With hot dogs affixed to green sticks,
In frivolous crucifixions.

Against the firefly glitter
Stirred by occasional breezes escaping the mild evening,
The irregularly shaped house rose,
A formidable reminder of man's presence
In this undespoiled expanse,
And the tumescent moon danced a gavotte.
We were at peace with the outdoors.

Soon, two new John Deere tractors,
Like paired Ming dogs,
Assailed the quietude, with raucous snorts;

11/1/82 — [2] (05452)

On the Lamb

I met a man, the other day.
His soul was white as fleece,
*

And every time he'd kneel to pray,
He'd smear his face with grease.

I followed him to church, at nine.
His prayers were black and blue,
And when he reached to sip the wine,
He spilled it down his shoe.

The priest withdrew his sacrament;
His eyes were wide as a ghost's.
The man had come to save face, repent,
But failed to savor the Host.

The man I met so long ago,
Mary's little lamb,
Led me out of town, and so
I moved from Bethlehem.

11/2/82 — [1] (05825)

Even Chickens Fly

Leaving New Athens,
Passing through the countryside,
To Waterloo, Illinois,
Crossing the JB Bridge, into Missouri,
I diligently record tractors,
Chickens, ponds, cows, autumnal trees —
Shapes filling my eyes like corpses caskets.

Their bones rattle in my brain's chambers,
Where age stores its legacies.
I can actually hear those fowls and cows
Scratching and kicking the earth
Above my numbness, this somnolent day.
My dazed spirit's flesh
Shrivels beneath the heat of memory's flame.

Time cauterizes its painful wound.
The stiff chickens levitate,
Rise, from their rigor mortis,
Inside my eyes, fly high into the sky,
Whose horizon, until just now,
Was the earth's surface, keeping me buried
Within the confines of my six-foot-deep mind.

Now, as I drive home,
My westerly perspective widens,
Focuses tightly on cranes, barges,
The bridge, cars, train tracks, planes,
Far below my soaring. Momentarily,
I slow to let my shadow close the gap,
Then flap my wings and, drifting, disappear.

11/2/82 — [2] (05414)

Beyond Halloween

Pumpkins flourishing within orange shimmers;
Huge Indian-summer moons,
Haloed by iridescent ice crystals,
Rolling through pink eccentrics;
Hawks wheeling in high-diving spirals —
These circularities, signs of time unwinding,
Are talismans whose purpose is to alert me
To my own divestiture,
The loosening of too-tight springs,
My inexorable spinning away from my beginnings.

I accept these precious measures
Not so much as admonitions,
Rather as promises of continuity, scintillating reminders
That Halloween both presages doom
And foreordains the future, through whose mild climes
Birds of paradise swoop,
Moons spew ivory seeds,
Causing naked maidens to ripen from pumpkins,
And I, a hoofed man-goat, race,
Reveling, gloating, eluding my gone soul's ghost.

11/2/82 — [3] (05413)

November 2, 1982

In the olden days, local prohibitions
Made it mandatory, when polls were open,
To close the doors of every saloon.
Otherwise, no one of age, seemingly,
*

Would avail himself of his responsibility
To cast a vote, or if so,
It would too often be a straight ticket
In favor of John Barleycorn and his cronies,
Jack Daniel's and Jim Beam.

In those times, one could not be too sure
Frances Willard or Carrie Nation
Wasn't waiting outside, in a dark alley,
With hatchet raised to scourge the demon rum
From their Victorian empyrean,
Or that others from the Woman's Christian Temperance Union
Might not be lurking in the purlieus,
To report back to disconcerted brides-to-be
And abstemious wives. So the saloons would close.

But why, in 1982,
Citizens still heed such an anachronistic ordinance,
Especially when everyone realizes
The franchise is just an irreligious litany
And social drinking may, indeed, be
One of the few civil duties
To which people should owe allegiance,
Is beyond belief. Yet, at 6:30,
I sit in Katy Station's lounge, alone

Except for a bartender polishing brass,
Rewiping glasses, brandy snifters,
And a Stepford-wife waitress
Praying to the popcorn machine,
Manicuring her cuticles, with a match pack.
Listening to Leon Russell,
Sipping opaque soda,
I try to couch a Constitutional amendment
That will free all indigents of their dependency.

11/2/82 — [4] (02602)

Manny Bernstein

He spends his daze
Trying to find a way out of his rage,
Which spans the lapses his memory suspends
*

Via its intricate fail-safe apparatus,
Plumbing his numbness,
Groping for hope, as he leaps, precariously,
From ice floe to ice floe,
In his brain's archipelago.

A pelagic fellow, though no Ishmael
Or Ahab, rather paltry, shameless nomad
Hawking goatskin tatters
As actual fragments of Joseph's coat,
Moses' robe, the Carpenter's Turin shroud,
He goes from pothole to pothole,
In a seedy Midwest cosmos
Whose map he knows like the back of his penis.

Like Ahab, he chides the fates,
For having relegated him to such a degenerate chase
After the lack of all color.
Mosaically, he climbs Mount Sinai nightly,
To be excoriated for having condoned anomie and lust
Among his pagan flock.
A lackluster Joseph flaunting his hues,
He flies from tribe to tribe,

Trying to find an opening in their closed societies,
Which entice him with loose women,
Liberal spirits, angel dust,
Just for a chance to buy his exotic promotions,
Carried across deserts and oceans:
Nostrums, beads, occult talismans, codices.
A haphazard bastard
Seeking a luckless fuck among his people,

By which he might perpetuate his namesake,
Claim temporary suzerainty over death,
Despite questionable matrimony,
He leaps, from ice floe to floe,
Across entire Negevs,
Pressing to exit the metaphysical maze
That both contains and sustains him,
Peddling garments, verse, charms, sinecures.

As the daze heightens, widens,
He realizes his persuasiveness fails to convince people
*

He is the King of kings.
Indeed, he seizes himself by the gallbladder,
Squeezes his balls. There's no escape.
He's Manny Bernstein,
Purveyor of costume jewelry for discerning women
And, for girls, titillating negligees.

11/3/82 (02603)

[Dear Lord,] †

Dear Lord,
  Please hear my discordant metaphors

11/4/82 — [1] (08309)

Bardic Apostle

Afternoon and I dissolve, simultaneously,
Into the cow-strewn twilight,
Whose dripping orange washes the countryside,
Circumscribing Tipton, in celestial hues.
My eyes are baptized; they go blind,
In the sun's blazing fountain.
Trialed by fire and water, I choose to die
On this Midwestern pyre,
Not by being burned alive but singed
In the sweetest diminishment,
The world's diurnal interment,
Not by drowning, either,
Rather being trapped beneath the surface of my astonishment,
Amidst this oceanic dusk.

Death in this peaceable kingdom is not demise
Or retreat; instead, it's a welcome friend
Disguised as sigh, silent gaze,
Awed loneliness so crowded with wonderment
No flaws show on the horizon's rim and dome,
Below which I sit, proclaiming toasts,
Singing hosannas
To the highest Host, the One,
Whose ghost follows and guides the poet in me
*

As I come and go as I dare and please,
To share my visionary images
With suns, stars, cows, barn swallows, farms,
Not caring whether others read my verse
Or even remember I was His earthly emissary.

11/4/82 — [2] (02604)

The Duelists

We take to the road,
You and I, in opposite inspirations,
Like duelists standing back to back,
For twenty years,
Before stepping off ten paces,
Then whirling to face each other,
Detonate our emotions' smokeless charges,
Blasts the fates disregard as frivolous.

Two crack sharpshooters,
We know neither will miss the mark,
Each other's heart, with invisible hollow-tips
From our private arsenals. All day,
The distance between us increases.
Twilight is the anointed turning point,
That oblique hour we'll start home,
From our separate destinations.

Not yet arrived, I yet tremble.
My brain's base sparks.
The eyes triple-focus your errant shape,
Imagining my spirit being blown away,
Through a hole in my spine,
As, on seeing me for the first time
Since last night,
You fire, "Why are you late?"

11/12/82 (04169)

[I rummage, this gray, drizzle-dreary day,]

I rummage, this gray, drizzle-dreary day,
Through memory's camelback trunks.
*

The eyes' fingers sift vestiges of us
Laid in mothballs long years ago:
Wheat jeans, long-sleeve paisley shirt,
Crocheted tablecloth pinched in, variously,
To approximate a Victorian wedding gown;
Fleet, dual-cowl phaetons,
Sixteen-cylinder Pierce-Arrows, Packards,
Boat-tail speedsters, Cords, Duesenbergs,
Which once transported my sporty imagination
To the eight corners of seventh heaven;
Kamchatka and Kodiak bears,
Siberian tigers, Russell's vipers,
Undulants, rhinopotamuses,
Pentaceratopses, diplodocuses,
Ornitholestes; phantasms, mares, jinns,
Imperturbable manifestations
That once formulated a great myelin sheath
About my tiny psyche's God-cord.
Now, those scintillating excitations are the drizzle,
Whose gray grief is a faded arras
Hanging in a dim Vatican I pace interminably,
Mumbling wayward cantos,
Not so much lonely as mind-blown, empty,
Whose old vows (*mens sana in corpore sano,
Semper fidelis*) mock even memory,
With their temperamental echoes, I a blind poet
Resigned to the monastery old age maintains
For those who leave life prematurely,
To be embalmed in mist, mummified in fog,
As I have, this morning, while rummaging
For something to place in my grave — this poem.

11/19/82 — [1] (04168)

Twyla's Own Language

Each balletic step, leap, twist,
Trim, nimble-limbed trope
Twyla articulates
Is a belletristic syllable in a dialogue
The eyes delight in listening to,
As they participate, vicariously, from a distance,
In her conversation with Terpsichore.

Her feet are the sonneteer's rhyme scheme,
That fluid, loose-jointed troubadour's mime
Gods recite in amorous languishment.
I scan the spaces she abandons, as her dance
Perpetuates itself independently of her body,
And try to memorize each corporeal word
Her bones never reprise.

But my senses can't quite master
The language she dances.
Translation requires, for catalyst, a Rosetta stone,
To negotiate the distance between trance
And fantasy. As yet,
I'm unable to answer, with my verse,
Her flirtatious invitation to celebrate.

11/19/82 — [2] (05826)

Looking Backward, 2002

So programmed are we to know ourselves,
Yet so fleet is the eon we're bequeathed,
In which to complete our oblique symmetries,
Spew atavistic disquisitions
Relative to relativity, relevance, and revelation,
Discover love's dispenser-vended ravishments
And adversarial reprisals,
That when we finally achieve prime-time status,
Our scripts read like Hirohito notes of surrender.

Old notions of traditional male and female roles
Crumble, under sundering modernity.
Men scrabble to hold their own,
In matrimony's traveling mud-wrestling show.
Women collect the ossified remains of their ancient rib,
Throw them on the growing bone pile,
And, forgetting their sacred origin,
Set fire to memory, inhale forgetting
As though it were a dazzling draft of Colombian gold.

Ah, but the suffering is such painless distraction.
In fact, everyone benefits
From dissolution except the children
*

Eve and Adam have unloosed, in Edenic innocence,
Who, of necessity, are left to feed their own ravenous psyches,
Forever after, each sad expulsion,
Pick up their parents' fractured dreams,
And fashion, from airy imagination,
The intended shape of the last, lost generation.

11/24/82   (04167)

The Day After Thanksgiving

This drizzle-dreary morning
Is Thanksgiving's eulogy, a weary hymn
To those golden, heroic hopes
We limned, around the bounteous table, yesterday,
Two innocent children, their youthful parents,
Recalling deeds not from experience or memory,
Rather by psychic requirement to create
Outsize myths, reinforce freedom's possibility
At all odds, arrogate, to ourselves, travail,
Without surviving entire oceans
Or owing allegiance to senile queens and kings.

This slow, gray, grieving day,
We and society will demonstrate our appreciation,
By causing the GNP to increase,
Bartering, borrowing, placing, in layaway,
Largess, gewgaws, gaudy baubles,
Scrimshaws and gimcracks,
Neiman Marcus one-of-a-kind items
For the Mr./Mrs./Miss John Smith,
Miles Standish, Governor Winthrop, of our remote colonies,
Suspecting, in our collective hearts,
This ritualed folly may be our only nexus to the past.

11/26/82   (05827)

Creative-Writing Instructor ‡

In his Monday-night writing class,
He rehearses diverse techniques,
*

Stylistic elements, strategies, by which creativity
Might be relieved of its mystique,
Brought down to street level,
Not only professed but practiced
By those whose only exposure to Madame Bovary,
Meursault, Joseph K., and Holden Caulfield
Engenders from xeroxed excerpts
He injudiciously infringes on, from reserve copies,
And distributes to eager students
Anxious to isolate and dissect the vital organs
In modern literature's awesome body.
He oversees each delicate operation
With patience and conscientious prodding,
Accepting his obligation to instruct and delight,
Alternating occasional tongue-in-cheek witticisms
With professional aplomb. As writer-in-residence,
Master of artifice, poet at large, illusionist,
Midwife of the inconceivable and the unspoken,
He's most concerned with reliability,
Cause-and-effect plausibility,
Authenticity and fraudulence in thought and misdeed,
How to resolve that glaring enigma
With which Fitzgerald tantalizes his reader:
If Gatsby represents everything Carraway scorns,
How can he turn out "all right at the end"?
Who's pulling whose leg, in East and West Egg,
Remains at the locus of his focus,
As he records his own hopes and dreams,
Through poems he floats —
Boats beating on, against the current —
And grows noticeably older, each Monday night,
As the tedium despair and failure breed
Metastasizes in his tired, unsurprised eyes,
Praying, that, just once,
Someone will submit "Bartleby the Scrivener,"
"In the Penal Colony," "A Clean, Well-Lighted Place,"
To ravish him with beauty, just once,
Before his unprepossessing existence
Stiffens into tragedy's death-mask effigy
And is remembered not as that of a poet, not an iota

11/30/82   (05828)

Twilight — Midnight — Sunrise

One slumberous, penumbral two o'clock,
He awakened asweat,
His chilled flesh plastic wrap
Stretched taut over a bone-china bowl
Holding a lifetime's leftovers.

When he drew back the sheets,
Peered through his sheer skin, into the container,
Where his vitals lay sleeping yet,
He realized why he'd arisen
So empty and dreamless.

There, lodged between spine and flaccid penis,
Palpitating like a pacing caged tiger,
Was death's globular octopus,
Its pulpy body suspended, like a webbed spider,
At the center of its slender tentacles.

Yet when he tried to isolate the pain
That had recalled him from silence,
All that remained of the elusive phantasm
Was a slight, spasmodic, necrotic spot on his hip,
As if his belly had been kissed by a lit welding tip.

And each following evening, at the same mystical hour,
For three months to the day,
He would arise to observe the progress of his dreams,
Then masturbate, ejaculate red semen,
Hoping to expel the demons, notice a change in his fate,

Until, one night, his bodily magma escaped,
Through the suppurated crater in his side.
When he awakened, his cold robes were dust,
His dust caravels floating home, to the sun.

12/1/82 (04166)

Filing a Flight Plan △

As I sit behind this vibrating wheel,
My flying is confined to highway vectors
*

Separating sere earth from puce sky.
The horizon is Ghiberti's prize doors,
Keats's Greek vase
Seen sideways, as in sleep,
Whose elusive revolving confuses vision,
A Byzantine frieze
Engendering myriad dubious perspectives.

I, Tiresias, an eyeless pilot,
Cruise IFR,
Buoyed by the wind's singing wings,
Oblivious to ice, lightning,
Cosmic possibilities of being stopped in midflight.
I, a fearless seer peering into the gloom,
Rely on my own inspired capacity for hope,
To locate my soul's glide slope,
Find runway's end, and elide into silence.

12/9/82 — [1] (03523)

Keats's Urn-Turning Lovers ^Δ

For my loving Jan

I leave my sweet wife sleeping sweetly,
Gracefully embracing her pillow
As though it were sacred space
Relegated to Eve and her soul mate,
Undulating among seaweed,
In quest of dreams to arrest from their beds,
In her head's deep grottoes,
And thread into a necklace
To be worn between her naked breasts.

Hours from this empty hour,
I'll reflect on my neglectfulness,
Having failed to caress her,
Express, with a soft kiss
Pressed indelibly to her twitching lips,
My uneasiness and regret in leaving home,
Not waking her, begging her keep me
Beneath the sheets, beg me stay
Within her sacred space, forever begging.

12/9/82 — [2] (00146)

Autobiographia Literaria ^Δ

Whether it's the foot-wide floorboards,
Seamed with rope, exposed roof beams
And square-timber supports,
Ceiling fans, antique chandeliers
Converted from kerosene to incandescent filaments,
Or stained glass casting soft rose,
Amber, purple, green, violet, and cobalt blue,
My shadow knows it's in familiar surroundings,
Welcomes blessed anonymity.

Perhaps the chilled, platinum-tinged, hexagonal glass,
Caressing Mouton-Cadet, half-filled
Continually,
Is the stimulus memory requires to allay anxieties
Arising whenever I range too distantly,
Relocate my soul briefly,
In hopes of finding my jettisoned past
Shimmering in whispers and half-lights and innocent faces —
Byzantine mosaics affixed to Oxford's temple walls.

Whatever the case, this place accepts me
Sans questions, explanations,
Justifications for my peculiar behavior,
Even though it appears I,
A middle-aged businessman from St. Louis,
Out of state, anyway,
Keep strange company with a Doppelgänger,
Who exchanges vested suit, dress shirt
For a poet's jeans, work shirt, and boots, on a moment's notice.

Here in this godforsaken desolation,
Where linger traces of the great scribe,
My spirit comes alive. I write verse
As if my life depended on it,
Knowing I'll die without a reasonable expectation
For success, suspecting, all the while,
Creation is merely a pretense for surviving the night
By my self's self,
That soul, within the whole, that craves posterity

Without all the preposterous protocol and notoriety
Attendant Nobel Prize recipients
*

Yet rejects celebrity, in favor of abject neglect,
For its unchallenged possibility of posthumous redemption.
Suddenly, I realize why I've come so far
Just to expose my lonely parts
To the darkling elements: it's my outsize ego
Craving exercise, desiring to stretch its hawk wings
Over zones unflown since the falconer died.

12/9/82 — [3] (03518)

Rep for the Mid-South ^Δ

From Smitty's, just off the square,
The hub, I exit Oxford,
Unceremoniously following South Lamar —
Silk Stocking Avenue —
Past High Victorian house after Gothic house,
Then out onto Highway 6, heading due west,
Toward Clarksdale and Helena, Arkansas.

Neither the gray day nor its rain
Diminishes my urgency to escape;
Rather, it creates a dialogue
In which ratiocination can speak, mile by mile,
As December's increasing desolation
Awakens me to pervasive emptiness
Both without and within:

Silent ginning companies,
Surrounded by cotton wagons stuck, in the mud,
Like degenerates in gutters;
Implement firms, their lots glutted
With factory-new Case tractors, Deere pickers;
Motels crying for stray salesmen,
Like desperate Loreleis;

White "public" schools, privately funded, once,
To keep the universe harmonious, equal
Yet separate, now abandoned,
Due to the Supreme Court's ukase to bus students;
Spayed fields, soggy as graves hastily dug
By retreating armies. Just recording it
Gives me fits, disturbs my equanimity.

Lafayette, Panola, Quitman counties
Disappear, in listing retrograde,
Like three torpedoed ships in the wartime Pacific.
Soon, I'm traveling north, on Highway 61,
Through Coahoma County, on a rutted road
Paralleling the Delta and Old Man,
Going too slowly, being passed

By all manner of vehicles, this nasty morning,
And not really knowing or caring why
I've assigned myself this task of escaping,
Let alone asking from what, to whom.
Yet my actions are my passport;
My itinerary varies from day to day,
Depending upon the emptiness of my best intentions.

12/10/82 — [1] (03514)

Abnegating Fate ^Δ

I see this cold, rain-gray Delta day
As if through a handkerchief:
Oncoming vehicles slide in and out of focus,
Like motifs in a concerto newly premiered;
Their headlights are fear-filled eyes
Peering out of a moonlit cypress swamp.

On both sides of the highway
Separating West Helena from Oxford,
Defunct gins, sloggy fields,
Stalks feebly waving missed cotton tufts
Like tattered truce flags
Appropriate what little remains of daylight,

Making my journey an inward trek
Into the heart of a glacier
Whose whiteness drives men berserk.
Slowly, as I go, the opening closes;
Twilight changes to groping,
Groping to total surrender.

I pull off, onto the stony shoulder,
To pass the hours dozing,
*

Between disruptive hallucinatory interludes.
All-night trucks, spewing water-waves,
Shiver my bones, with their primitive moaning,
Capsize what few peaceful dreams I have.

Morning never arrives.
Instead, a translucent shimmer issues forth,
From my yawn. Dawn is sleep's sneeze.
I stretch, resume my journey
As though rain never detained me nor fog
Ever caused me to postpone my own funeral.

12/10/82 — [2] (03509)

A Latter-Day de León ᐃ

It's five o'clock, Friday afternoon,
And while I should be just arriving home
From the factory, to celebrate, with wife and children,
Another week completed and remunerated,
I find myself stranded down here, in Oxford,
Mississippi, getting blitzed sipping Chablis
By the half-carafe, disintegrating innocuously,
Like Ozymandias in time's silent, sandy ossuary,
Integers and figments, every eon.

What attracts and keeps me attached to this town
Is neither theological nor mystical,
Although both diversions might prove cathartic
For my travel-weary head and heart.
Instead, the compelling spell
Is my desire to discover, in this oasis,
An elixir to counteract bodily stasis,
Relieve me of the responsibility of aging,
Release me from going crazy growing staid.

Perhaps by exposing myself to youth's music,
Getting high, vicariously,
On coke, beer, ludes, whiskey straight, life,
Being blown away by such myriad beauty
As no Helen ever dreamed,
On the most unprepossessing of coed visages,
Following the mountain's upward girding
Down into the Happy Valley,

I, a shattered Rasselas,
Might undo, in one night, the damage done
Pursuing, all these years, a suitable calling,
Decent epitaph to incise on my stone.
Possibly, the blond, tight-jeaned,
Taut-titted, submissive lady of eighteen or twenty,
Whispering sibilant, liquescent pruriences in my red ear,
Holds the secret to my freedom,
In her indiscreet and profoundly unsound evocations.

I, twice her age, listen to her delicate tongue
Lick my brain, burning to be born again,
Between her wet, white lips,
Eclipsing eternity, inside her flying sails,
Running wing and wing, in a timeless breeze.
Suddenly, in frenzied dalliance,
She sees through my inebriation, to friends across the room,
And slips from me. I pray for a tornado
To blow my old bones back home forever.

12/10/82 — [3]   (00164)

Apologia pro vitae suae

*For Trilogy and Troika,
at Christmas*

Wherever I peer, poinsettia plants
Sneer at me
Indignantly,
For my having failed, at this late date,
To procure a tree for my blessed Trilogy
And Troika, two glory-born children,
Representing both genders majestically.

Why I've not taken them out in the country,
To cut a spruce
Or fir, of their choosing, from the forest,
Eludes me. With Christmas upon us,
I've blatantly neglected my fatherly duty
To honor its mystical rites,
Perpetuate its time-bound superstitiousness.

Something suspect there must be
About Christianity's most splendid myth
That makes me hesitate, remonstrate, each year,
Before quashing the temptation
To forgo the entire ritual.
Perhaps the fear of being called Scrooge,
Accused of misanthropy, looms too large.

Regardless, a Jew married to a Catholic
Has a tortuous path to master,
Especially when he can almost see himself clear
To accept the Resurrection and Eucharist
And she can handle the Seder, at Passover.
In a situation such as this, it's a pity
Our most potent substitute is humanism.

12/10/82 — [4] (04165)

[He envies, to maddening distraction,]

He envies, to maddening distraction,
Those whose virtuoso music
He surrenders to, five miles deep,
Beneath the car radio's Vesuvian core,
Hoping to be consumed
In its myriad magmatic, incantatory voices,
Noisy word-wings soaring toward him
As he flees his own paltry chorus,
Shadows chasing shadows across the states
Through which he guides his loneliness,
Coevals to the unmapped end,
Failing to locate, there,
Inspiration's headwaters,
Where, in purple-surfaced pools
Festooned with watercress edged with baby's-breath,
He might baptize his mind,
Find tranquillity, in the earth's ripples,
Let his tongue sip God's liquescent essence,
Appropriate His cosmic pulse.

Days materialize and dissipate,
In dismaying retrograde, taking with them
*

Whatever mythical overtones he might have made
By placating gratuitous fates
With concupiscent music from his bodily lute.
He strays, a crosswind his silent songs,
Lost in their own confused maze,
He an uncelebrated maker of verse,
Incapable even of weeping,
When the spirit almost moves him
To reach for improbable registers he knew
Before the music divorced his soul.

12/14/82   (05829)

In the Scuppers, with a Hose-Pipe On

Dizziness, like a whale breaching spectacularly,
Rises, spewing gaseous effluvia
Above the rolling ocean lane I navigate,
Changing vision from a passive act
To an active task. I squint, shake my head
As though it were a thermometer being snapped
To bring down its mercury bead.
Yawns foreshorten the horizon,
Pattern my drowsiness, like periodic road signs —
The mind's Burma-Shave ads,
Lining imagination's unkempt edges.

Exhortations to attendant gods
Have no effect on my aim.
The vehicle weaves across the center line,
Lurches, shamefully, off both shoulders,
Just misses hitting cars I pass,
As instinct alone controls my forward motion.
Soon, the leviathan dives,
Two useless harpoons dangling near its flukes.
Faint and sweaty-cold,
I feel myself drawn under, by its suction,
Whirling in its swirling turbulence, drowning.

12/15/82 — [1]   (05830)

Nepotism, Sinecures, and Honorary Positions

Yes, I guess I'm impressed,
But then, what less should one expect
Than perfection,
From His Excellency,
Especially with his reputation for being the best
At clandestine quests?

Of course, just because he succeeds
In keeping his duplicitous deeds
Secret
Doesn't mean I shouldn't begin proceedings,
Post public decrees,
To expose his treacherous lechery.

His background is black as bat wings,
Twice as rife as hippo shit.
He's left no potential stone unturned,
No cherry unpicked,
Bastardized every wife and maiden in the kingdom,
With spurious flourishes of hurried unconcern.

How do I, the prosecuting attorney,
Possess such privileged information
About the quintessential sins he's committed,
All these years, beneath the disguise
His nobility provides? It's quite simple, actually:
He and I are the same guy.

12/15/82 — [2] (05831)

Faulkner's Unravished Brides of Quietness ^Δ

Meta, Ruth, Joan, Else, Jean:
He needed them,
Each in her ordered place
Within his disoriented middle-aging,
Parenthesized, all, by Estelle,
Who, moving through endless dispassions
He created and embellished
When distracted by bills, wills, movie scripts,
Bad back, inebriated blackouts,
*

Nonetheless kept the lock stitch from unraveling
Completely, wearing, both of them,
Independently, the same tattered fabric
They'd drafted as teenagers
And would lie buried beneath, in St. Peter's.

He needed them, to slake the solitude
His demon-laced sullenness
Imposed, inwardly, from within frontiers
He never fully tamed,
Claiming, briefly, fragments of landscapes
Contiguous to desolations
Claiming his brooding moods as their landlord . . .
Needed them, to allow himself freedom
To expose his deeply disguised sentimentality,
His gardenia-petaled gentleness,
Close in on love's ever-shifting simulacra,
Its romantic obbligatos
He may have so long ago imbibed from Keats,
Hold time's quicksilver sands,
Kiss her/their soft hands, toes,
Lips, breasts, sweet, ambrosial cunts.
He needed them, to be whole
Momentarily, to control, wildly, those moments
When poetry and prose would fuse rapidly,
Then slowly come undone,
In the most ecstatic sundering of flesh
And emotions — two sets of bones
Directed heavenward, like cathedral spires.
He needed them, each, as lover,
Quintessence of a pedestaled Greek goddess,
Daughter and mother
Entwined in a kind of blessed incestuousness
He alone could both justify
And not excuse, he the sole proprietor
Of his own soul's Holy Roman Empire,
Existing in a timeless sequestration
Transfiguring mistress/wife/mother
Into living visions, real dreams,
By grafting his rib onto motley skeletons,
Letting passion seal the natural seams.
He needed them not as female embodiments
Or as anodynes but, finally, as secret sharers
*

In the outsize genius he'd been bequeathed,
That they might let him forget,
Occasionally,
The pestiferous sibilances of green horseflies
Dive-bombing the landfill
Just behind the fence his gentility had built
To keep prying eyes
From scrutinizing, passing judgments on his dominion,
And remind him, now and again,
How sublimely he might aspire
To freeing those two amorous prisoners on the urn,
Reshaping them in eternal embrace,
Before breaking the mold, feeling the clay turn brittle and cold.

12/16/82 — [1] (03553)

Prometheus Bound

Raw, primitive sounds,
Filtering through chrome-trimmed Peavey speakers
Man-tall and extravagant, confound me,
Command my allegiance.

I'm bound, to this barstool, like Prometheus,
Waiting to have my heart eaten out
By the sweetest harpy
Swooping low on whiskey vapors, wheeling.

Two doomed, beautifully plumed spirits
Wrangling on the rocks, we'd be,
Connected to earth and sky, simultaneously,
By our treacherous lovemaking,

Creatures casting rapturous silhouettes
Against a red-dripping sun
Rising, in a prairie-grass-fire haze,
On a flooding, blood-rush crest,

Whose music would sing the singed bones awake,
Bring all the raucous sounds down
To whispers — feathers twisting
From wings disappearing into the distant shimmer.

Suddenly, I stir, squirm in my swivel seat,
Weaving precariously, in the high air,
*

Trying to keep from crashing to the waves below,
Cursing the fates, with slurred words,

Who would bereave me for such deprecations.
Caressing, in oblique silence,
The last lady on earth, Dana, the waitress
Who asks to take me home with her,

I apologize for my inebriation, accept her charity,
Beg to share her strange favors,
Realizing even defrocked gods
Need appreciation, a female human to care.

12/16/82 — [2] (01344)

On the Passing of Laureates

His sodden, puffy face
Is a flour-and-water-paste effigy,
A plaster-of-Paris cast, a death mask,
An exact, if flaccid, facsimile of that visage
He feared, all those years prior to dying,
In his chimeraed nightmares,
Would possess him, subjugate his imagination
To menial tasks: copying, memorizing, reciting
The Rig-Veda, *I Ching*, Upanishads

Rather than harmonizing his destiny
With original cantos and villanelles,
Which, in halcyon, supple days, he created,
With indefatigable unself-consciousness.
Now, supine and silent,
A dissipated artificiality betraying his face,
With eternal gloom and a stare
So demonically brooding
As to scare his embalmer, pallbearers,

Demigods hovering nearby, in wait,
To dismantle and transport his cold soul,
He reposes within the stasis
Of ultimate mortal horizontality,
Just another anticlimactic closure
From one of his obligatory elegies,
Lacking metaphor, image, symbol,
*

An émigré leaving behind his edifice,
For succeeding laureates to inhabit or raze.

12/17/82 — [1] (05832)

Getting Our Tree [Δ]

We'd postponed, until the last week,
Selecting a Christmas tree,
Feared, possibly, creating too much hype
Prematurely,
Creating a keyed-up condition
From which none of us might recover
Enough to properly sanctify the holiday,
With reverence and austerity.

When, finally, we did decide to venture out,
Scout a suitable icon
Of Scotch pine or Minnesota fir,
To accommodate our metaphors and ornaments,
Contain our blinking visions,
There seemed, for quite a while, that night,
Not the slightest chance we'd find one.
All lots were empty, stands unmanned.

Our bewildered children began to accuse us,
With their worried, nervous discouragement,
Their urgent refusals to let us
Quit driving, resume, on the morrow, our search,
Of having failed them,
So anxious were they to get underway.
Then, after we'd circumnavigated our floating island
Three times, without success,

Both children, simultaneously,
Spied a solitary tree, leaning, obliquely,
Off to one side of a filling station,
And screamed — a blessed revelation,
For a mere seventeen dollars,
A miraculous manifestation, at that,
One which fit atop our station wagon
Compactly, without scratching the paint.

Making routine unique,
We'd redeemed ourselves unwittingly,
Elevated our casual stature, to omnipotent heights,
Fashioned, through gratuitous accident,
Peaceful, reasonably understandable magic.
And for a fleet eon, that evening,
Each of us became an extension of Genesis,
Innocents absolved of fear and trembling.

12/17/82 — [2] (01468)

One-Room School ^Δ

I leave, at home, three sleeping souls
Scribbling, on dreams' blackboards,
Tantalizing aphorisms
And scandalous, self-actualizing half-truths
They dare not express in waking,
For fear of paring too close to the bone.

Their teacher, master, and mentor,
I've excused myself early, this morning,
To tend to last-minute Christmas chores
Before we leave town, for the holidays.
I've commended them not to their wiles
But to writing "I love you, Dude"

Two thousand times each,
In soft breathing's chalky script,
Knowing I hold little sway
Over my students' gentle disobedience,
Whose gray-swirling obscurities
Translate this season into scintillas,

Unique glitter-wishes, darkling sparks
Prefiguring the Nativity —
Two blessed blond-haired cherubs
And seraph Jan marking time
Until dawn-light's revelation
Illuminates their one-room universe and they rise,

To find me sipping coffee at the table,
Waiting to grade them,
*

Sticker kisses and smiles to their dim eyes.
Soon, we'll dismiss, take with us
Clean slates, new instruction sheets,
Multiply, by four, the day's unrecorded glories.

12/20/82 (01469)

Trilogy Solos ^Δ

We'd always speculated
That her illnesses concurrent with my trips
Were self-induced, her temperamental fugues
Set pieces impressed for the occasion,
A spitting cat's fear, fight, and hate.

Yet my wife and I
Were always loath to accept that these manifestations
Were signs of loneliness in our little girl,
Trilogy,
Or that a creature so innocent might actually grieve

Her daddy's reiterating three-day
And weeklong forays into the wilderness.
Rather, we chose to see her histrionics
As manipulative tactics of a child actress —
Little Orphan Shirley in the flesh.

But now that two nights have passed
Without my sitting at bed's edge,
Listening to her read, repeat prayers,
Feeling her lips kissing me on the cheek,
And having witnessed two dawns

Issue in gray rains,
Through which I haven't driven her
To the Capital Café, for breakfast,
Then on to school, by 8:00,
I've begun to understand all those tantrums,

And even though I know her location,
Am certain she's safe from catastrophe,
With her grandparents, in Florida, this week
Between Christmas and New Year's,
The remorse I feel is of divorce and more: death.

12/27/82 (01470)

Disappearing Acts

Sunrise is a bright-red velvet rose
Unfolding, magically,
From one end of God's open-ended wand.

No matter how many dawns have enchanted me,
In my brief sequence,
This most recent trick supersedes all the rest,

In its illusionary perfection. Possibly, frost,
Rendering my windshield translucent,
Creating hesitation, guesswork,

Has transmuted vision to arbitrary images.
Maybe it's the army of twenty-two degrees
That has brainwashed my view,

Changed imagination's threshold for change,
Made blind faith desirable
As a surrogate for knowing destinations precisely.

Whatever the case,
This last day of this passing year,
Transmogrifying fast, before my eyes,

As heated drafts, from inside vents, wash the glass,
Consign its dazzling designs
To reality's forgetting, like senile dementia,

Will linger as blessed legerdemain
I briefly engaged, on my drive to the horizon,
To see the Sorcerer about acquiring a wand.

12/31/82   (05833)

[He rises, robotically, from his bed,]

He rises, robotically, from his bed,
Exclusive of wife,
Who, for five years, has sequestered herself
Within the solitude of a valetudinarian's convalescence,
And dresses in mismatched socks,
Too-tight shoes, polyester trousers,
Work shirt disintegrating from excessive bleach,
And leaves, each morning, each season,
For the Capital Café.

He has rendezvoused in this seedy place,
Among magi, disciples, apostles,
Ever since his wife
Cremated her soul, five years ago,
Nested, forever, beneath her sheets,
In clammy black ashes,
A cataleptic not yet forty,
Commended to the rut she's worn, so deeply,
Between waking and sleep.

In the beginning, he pretended the ambience
Was conducive to his verse.
After all, hadn't he admonished himself
It wouldn't be easy, squeezing turnips dry,
Riding foundered Rocinantes,
Outlasting winter's scurrilous blasts,
Missouri's July humidity, Hades-heat,
Ignoring the damnable slander people invent,
Who have nothing better to do with their insensitivity?

And for a few years,
As though it took recognition and vision
Time to refocus the doom they'd engaged,
By moving from St. Louis to this small town,
They actually discovered an illusionary bliss,
Among the ubiquitous desolation.
The bulb inside which the two of them burned —
Twin incandescent filaments
Illuminated by their self-generating love —

Had not yet flickered, dimmed,
Diminished into cold, blind silence.
Then two children materialized,
Each birth unscrewing the light, a few turns,
Until, by degrees, he and his lady awakened,
One fine day,
To discover themselves dispossessed of Eden,
Condemned to wayward straying,
Sentenced to fending off plagues, solitarily.

That was when she volunteered her spirit to bed,
He began frequenting the café
(Instead of ministering to her, tending their kids),
Spending entire weeks amnesiacally,
*

Hiking to the outskirts of his feckless intellect,
While seated, to salvage, from their ruins,
Through verse so painfully personal
That each syllabled line became a snake's spine
Constricting his mind, signs of former life,

Anything to metaphorize connubial existence
They'd once shared, before their descent from grace,
Arrest, even fleetingly, love's faded anthem.
Today, the curious who pilgrimage to his small town
Seek out the Capital Café,
To glimpse him writing, in his favorite booth,
Linger, in their cars, before the house,
On whose sweeping porch he reads, all summer,
A few daring enough to trespass,

Steal his books, pens, wineglasses,
Presume to ring the bell, take his mail from the box,
Photograph the Gothic extravaganza
They all know still sepulchers the famous writer's
Vegetable wife.
Oblivious, intransigent, he refuses interviews,
Continues, in isolated frenzy,
To write paeans to the lady he's fatally neglected,
Hoping, before he dies, to write large his wrong.

1/4–5/83 — [1] on 1/5   (04164)

Don Jewan of Malta

For nine days,
We've shuffled past obligations and compromises,
Sluffing off routine duties,
Slogging through mud-puddle mazes
Designed, by sadistic queens and eunuch potentates,
To neuter the best suitors,
Divest them of their most ambitious concupiscences.

And we've barely survived society's trial
By nakedness,
We three, posing as a sacred trinity,
A ménage à trois
Dedicated to the three-persons-in-One theory
*

Of creation, conceptionally speaking,
Camille, Miriam, and I,

Two married ladies, refugees
From marriage's war-torn boredom, and I,
Flying off to Spain,
Lying on the beach, at Alicante,
Fornicating, like snakes, beneath the blazing sun,
A once-a-month indulgence,
For a Tenorio like me, on the run

From a hundred and one friendly suggestions
That I cease my philandering,
Take a respectable job, wed, have kids,
Settle down, forever,
Become fidelity's cuckold,
Dying to a ripe old age —
Not I! Never!

Tomorrow, we'll get dressed again,
After nine days, fly home,
To the silence propriety requires of us,
And I'll resume
My guise as proprietor of a beauty salon
In Ladue, "manned" by an all-gay crew,
Which provides me perfect cover.

While today's last, least hours remain,
I'll make my stand, in bed,
Extracting the most exacting pleasure
From every writhing, moaning pelvic contraction
And labial action. If I must ride,
Let it ever be bareback,
Astride sun and moon, across the horizon.

1/5/83 — [2] (00857)

[Sparrows tear frosty morning's air,]

Sparrows tear frosty morning's air,
Like pairs of scissors snipping fabric,
So frenzied, severe.
The cold cloth parts to the passage
*

Of those who dare not cease their peripatetics
From cistern to tree to patio
And back to the barn's eaves,
Disappearing beneath its corrugated-sheet roof,
Momentarily,
Before again cutting the glistening sky in two,
In myriad motley tatters.
Vision shatters, goes hungry,
Trying, from scattered pieces, to reassemble the pattern —
Sparrows scavenging for scraps
To sew into scarves to wear about their throats.

1/6/83 (05451)

Mystic Dissolution

In the crowded solitude
This speeding vehicle engenders about me,
I dissolve. My psyche pulls loose from its roots,
Like an aborting fetus. No pain,
Rather amniotic peacefulness, attends my spirit,
As day assimilates my ideas,
Absorbs my juices, appropriates my emotions,
Transmutes energy into poetry,

Until whatever shape I inhabited
On leaving home, earlier,
Totally dissipates,
Turns into perpetually burning flames
Illuminating the highway my words pave,
Traveling skyward,

Until flames and verse become the conversation
Angels engage in, translating my soul.

1/7/83 — [1] (05834)

Willy Takes an Unscheduled Inventory

After a ten-hour workday
And 170 miles logged already,
Seventy yet to go,
*

I head homeward,
This late Friday afternoon,
As twilight overtakes the swollen sky,
Crowded with snow-laden clouds.

My wagon is a manumitted slave.
It no longer labors
Beneath the weight of irregular pants,
Surplus suits and sportscoats,
Being transported, from warehouse
To outlet store,
Like biodegradable waste.

Suddenly, my bedraggled spirit squirms in its seat,
Like an ameba next to heat,
While the forlorn and desperate caterwauling
Of my chattering conscience
Calls out to me,
To take an on-the-spot check of my stock.
Apparently, something is missing.

By degrees, I isolate the shortage:
It's my naked heart, exposing me to its loneliness.
If only there were someone
Waiting, at week's end,
To embrace my undressed soul,
Robe me in love's crushed velvet and plush,
Proclaim me benevolent emperor of old clothes!

1/7/83 — [2] (02372)

Trance-Dance

As I drive easterly, out of sight,
Lovely lady night
Eases my entry into day's void,
By engaging in the most pleasing striptease
She's ever displayed.
I shift positions frequently,
As if my seat were an active crater
Disturbed by the earth's fire-breathing beast.

By degrees, my senses awaken,
Grow erect,
*

As pen probes, presses delicately over
My notebook's previously unmolested membrane,
Making direct connection
Between brain and the erotic object at hand.

The darkness begins undressing.
First comes its satin skirt,
Exposing layers of diaphanous taffeta
Tinged orange and mauve.
Next, having lain on horizon's stage,
Dangling her legs over the edge,
As though hoping to be transgressed,
Yanked into the audience below,

She commences completing her slow, total disrobing:
Off come the starlike pasties, from her breasts,
The sequined G-string,
Concealing the last vestiges of her secret soul,
That black hole
Through which, each dusk, her life expresses itself.

Suddenly, I'm flooded with pastel light.
Morning distracts my passion.
The pen that has kept me captive, at its ends,
Bending my attention to its center,
Refuses to function, goes flaccid.
When I gaze upward again,
The only trace of that lovely lady
Is a single iridescent, moon-shaped earring,

Suspended in space. No doubt,
She snared it on the velvet curtain
Separating firmaments,
While outracing her sustained applause.
I break from my trance, reach for that crescent,
Am left with a handful of glitter, as she retrieves it, too.

1/10/83 — [1] (03493)

To the Four Corners and Back

For Lady Jan

In one evening, without leaving our bed,
I traveled to Sumatra, Jakarta,
*

Obscure Indonesian tribal islands,
On a cruise ship bound out of Liverpool;

Lingered while Itzhak Perlman
Interviewed Leontyne Price,
Laurel, Mississippi's, favorite soprano,
Who, a few spliced minutes later,

Would sing two distinctly virtuosic arias,
With the Boston Pops Orchestra,
Under the mystical guest direction
Of Seiji Ozawa;

Eventually entered Washington, D.C.
(Its cable-TV institutions
Under siege by Lex Luthor
And his three criminal companions from Krypton),

Hesitating to see if Superman,
Recently enfeebled by his appropriating apparatus
To satisfy his lust for Lois Lane,
Would gainsay earthly appetites,

Favor truth, justice, and the American way,
Over concupiscence, or not.
But unexcited by either climax,
I moved on, again,

This time to my wife,
Resting quietly beside me, to my right,
Nestling inside the refuge
My silent eyes usually provide

When their attention enters outer dimensions.
For eons, we touched,
Then accompanied each other home,
Through the straits of our deep, immediate breathing.

1/10/83 — [2] (02070)

Crucifishion

Despite all the elusive metaphors
He'd ever fished for, in the Great Abyss,
Caught on his brain-hook,
*

Almost brought up to vessel's edge,
Then accidentally lost,
To slippery, jerking fate-quirks,
He'd never really netted a complete shape

But rather dragged onto imagination's deck,
At the end of his magic pen's gaff,
Phosphorescent approximations
Of shimmering, great-flying leviathans,
Ichthyosaurs, marlins, narwhals
Persisting, beyond vision's misty focus,
As finned rainbows twisting in dripping halos.

Today would be different.
The lure, which, for three nights straight,
He'd stayed awake designing, with dream beads,
Phoenix feathers, poets' hopes,
And hooks contrived of tyrannosaurs' teeth,
Was now ready for baiting. Unflinching,
He slashed the barbs through his wrists, and cast.

1/15/83   (00103)

Bespelling the Speller ^Δ

Each ritualed Wednesday morning,
During the school season,
Trilogy and I say out a new rosary.
Joyously, we rehearse
Spelling words that bespell her,
With their "miscellaneous" variations
Emanating from the same sounds,
"Foreign" orthographic mutations
Requiring memorization, not logic

Or studied guesswork. I coach her,
Suggest tricks,
As with "physician," whose middle,
Most difficult, part is, like his patient,
"Sic" (*sic*). She prints the letters
Across a quicksand napkin
That gathers around her penpoint, at each twist,
Then waits for my next selections:
"Snore"; "corn"; "sore"; "foreign"; "scarlet."

She scribbles, between bites of crisp bacon,
Egg, jellied toast. I tip my coffee
To liquid lips Demosthenes would envy,
Emblazon, across her sacred scroll,
"Wow" and "100 percent."
At her behest, I finalize my grades,
With perfection's exclamation points,
Then send her out into the world,
To respell "Treaty of Versailles" and "League of Nations."

1/19/83   (01471)

Throwing Snowballs

They're not even flakes,
Though their cascading shapes resemble snow,
But goose feathers coming unloosed
From day's gray flesh,
Slipping between interstices in cages
Zooming through the landscape, like Shinkansens,
Blurring my view, while illuminating the soul,
As though the entire sky were astir with spirits
Swirling in Tiepolo whirlpools.

Having deposited my child at her school's white stoop,
I linger close by the playground,
To assimilate antic, ephemeral gestures
Escaping Currier & Ives kids.
My hot hands, gripping the wheel,
Turn cold, get wet,
As memory presses forgetting into snowballs
Packed and thrown
At the exposed necks of youth's unsuspecting mates.

Too soon, I abandon my fantasies
To duties looming just past 9 a.m.,
Determine to refocus my priorities, over coffee,
At the Capital Café. I pause at the door,
Unwilling to relegate my instincts to reason
Just to placate fate and destiny.
Standing in the street, I grab a handful of feathers
And hurl its serried shape at the courthouse,
Which frowns and glares at my slight derring-do.

1/21/83   (00567)

Willy: A Punctual Man

A doom-laden luminescence
Makes manifest its presence, this day,
As I enter the internal maze
Placed before me, in the third circle
My escape circumscribes
About the outer radius of my innermost freedom.

As I go, my shadow leans into the wind
Velocity sets astir
With burning chert and chalcedony flecks,
Turning like a crazy tin vane,
As if somehow to determine the direction
From which God's whisper emanates.

My portentous fortune collides with flakes,
Five miles north. An albino demon
Catches me, beneath its netted snow-ropes,
Neglects my credentials,
With painful disdain. I scream my name:
"I'm Willy, you bastard!

"Willy Sypher, asshole! Let me go!
I'm in a hurry, have no time
For being detained or forced to explain why
My exemptions have precedence,
How, I obtained, in the first place,
My official pass to unauthorized locations."

Nothing I say can change fate's mind.
Its preordained ways
Weigh on my progress, like rain-soaked clay
Suffocating me, in my grave.
Slowly, the cold snow melts around my bones.
My brain drains away, as slush,

Along both sides of the highway
On which I set out, earlier this morning,
In search of untrammeled passage
To the Lesser Blefuscan Spice Isles.
My pulse conjoins with the silence abounding,
Transports my spirit, on breath-wings, home.

Below me, headlights blink,
Sink into shimmering mist,
*

Disappear within the tears my flying eyes drip,
As they rise, through vision, into His whispers,
Whose vectors energize me, in specific directions,
Until I arrive, on time, for my meeting.

1/25/83 — [1] (02371)

Third-Quarter Report

Accounts receivable,
Gross and pretax-net profits,
Terms, turns, surplus reserves
Against cancellations, abrupt bankruptcies,
And the classic — liabilities versus assets —
Whose pedestrian assessment is the bottom line,
Separating failure from success,
Black ink from bad blood . . .
All these measurements,
Serving to determine his destiny,
Resolve themselves around a walnut table,
Beneath the crusty scrutiny of stewards,
Entrusted with the Grail, the sacred scrolls,
Whose accusative yawns, coughs, tics
Are acquiescence or disapprobation,
Depending on the hour, a toothache, lust,
Or alcoholic insatiety.
His tides are tied to their collective moon,
His ocean's rising or falling
Obedient to their salty review of his business acumen,
Every three months.
Today, the figures presage doom.
He may drown in the boardroom's gloom,
When he presents his current reports.
Yet he's ready. Now that he's forty-two,
Change is in order. He can accept defeat.
His resignation would be no extreme,
Rather sweet, sorely needed release.
After the reading of the meeting's minutes is concluded,
A quorum recorded, he slips out the door
And bolts into Washington Avenue,
Where, poised in the center,
Between the street's speeding two-way traffic,
*

He waits briefly, hesitates,
Then commits himself to his suicidal tendencies,
Flinging his deeds, headlong,
Into the *DNR*'s front-page streamer —
The most sensational leap of his entire life.

1/25/83 — [2] (02370)

Wayward Willy

Instead of tapering off, with his aging,
His trips proliferate
Almost as if in reverse ratio
To acceptable expectations.

Yesterday, it was a brief passage,
150 miles deep,
To St. Louis and back;
Today, it's New Athens to Columbia,

An intermediate stretch, a milk run,
Three hundred miles wide,
Across two states,
In his station wagon, weighted with cargo.

Tomorrow, he'll be the bumbler bee,
Pollinating lilacs and honeysucklers,
As he buzzes between Salisbury and Tipton,
Both in the same day,

For brief consultations with his trustees
(Those sweet ladies
Who manage outlet stores he oversees
For corporate headquarters),

And lights just long enough, in each small town,
To have breakfast and lunch,
In the Stamen and Pistil Café,
Review stock, discuss sales,

Ads, items for return, bad checks,
Before circling back to the hive,
His drone's room a cell
In Columbia's Honeycomb Motel,

Where, for ten years, now, or more,
He's thrived, weeks at a time,
While faithfully making his routine rounds,
In quest of his destiny's destinations, unquestioningly.

By Friday night, he'll be done,
Head home, in the dark, for Farmington,
Four hours and forty-five minutes
Distant from his farthest stop,

Then spend the weekend with his wife
And children, recuperating,
Suspended in a docile somnambulism,
Acquiescent, undemanding, obtuse,

A brainwashed POW
All too accommodating to their demands,
Until Sunday evening,
When, once again, his fever will surge —

The highway's siren song
Winnowing through his blood and bones,
Piquing him to sleepless importunacy —
And Mistress Monday will beckon him follow her out.

1/26/83 — [1] (02369)

The Acknowledged Legislators of the World

The disturbing thing about words written,
Even if not placed in print,
Is that they render relatively permanent
Otherwise ephemeral simulacra,
Record forgettable memories,
Regrettable as well as delicately wrought expressions,
What socks ghosts in the closet wore,
Gossip and papal confessions
Better left whispered among gods,
Unimaginable expletives, the ineffable.

Once published, truths and half-truths
Achieve cardinal priority, lose distinction.
Retractions and apologias
*

Only reinforce the spurious and the specious,
Fuel incredulity,
Underscoring exaggeration, making sensational
The least monumental cliché,
Showcasing the grossest human anatomy,
By dissecting greed and venal behavior.
Lies, in ermine robes, assume the throne.

Veracity cowers, bows to its knees,
All too frequently,
Before those rulers who would cast aspersions
On dogs, the disabled, dreamers.
Only poets and their readers can save us
From our own worst perfection,
By describing not what has been or is,
Rather staking claim to phrases
Worded to nurture interpretation,
Encourage metaphoric legerdemain.

1/26/83 — [2] (05835)

In My Bereavement

For my own blessed Jan,
on learning of the dissolution
of Shelley and Roger

My heart moans like a rabbit
With one bloody leg in a rusted trap.
My ears hear their own raging pulse,
Above the universal din,
Distinguish their body's thin bones, sinews
Rubbing against each other,
Like static, on a radio dial,
Filling gaps between stations. Suddenly, I know
I alone own my own aloneness.

No more than days ago,
She and I sat chatting before the hearth,
Sipping, slowly, sweet Chablis,
Our silence inspired by the crackling logs,
The two of us mesmerized
By embers exploding within the fireplace —
*

Lightning bugs igniting a July sky, in January.
We even toasted the quietude
Our insularity not only provided but engendered.

Now, I'm dying, a victim of that silence
We tried, in our radical privacy,
To be deserving of, by worshiping together,
Outside society's pale,
Living on the fringes, within the limits of this preserve.
How was I, in my neglectfulness, to guess
That I would be the one to trespass,
Transgress against my wife,
By denying her the basic right to possess my heart?

My heart is a mild, meek child
Crying out, in the primal wilderness,
For that which it has abruptly surrendered: its freedom.
I haven't the slightest idea why
My wife has decided to leave me,
Lest it be failure to make good my promise
To compromise my outsize ego,
Share, with her, whatever dreams she might devise
Along the trap line we vowed to walk together,

Forever,
That time five years back,
When both of us were new to each other
And attuned to the promises of multiplying
Our divided lives, within the confines marriage defines.
Now, my dying is so loud
I can't hear myself crying, for the bleeding.
How, dear God, might I extricate my leg,
Save this union from dismemberment?

I beg you, Savior of all mankind,
Please permit me one apology.
Allow me to confess and, in doing so,
Absolve myself of my gross indifference,
With this promise: dearest wife,
From this day forth, in blessed perpetuity,
I shall pedestal you,
Profess my ineluctable deference to your preferences,
Cherish your presence as the essence of my destiny.

1/26/83 — [3] (02501)

Keeping the Covenant ^Δ

For Charlotte and Saul,
my mother and father

I am heir to my parents' heritage.
I share their awareness
That decency need not be worked at,
Simply create its own environment,
By its mere existence, and that loving others
Is not an effort made
But a pleasant mutual discovery engaged in,
Each time people converge.

Why, at times, I'm so strident,
I can't answer,
Even to my wife, whose concern is tantamount
To fear that her husband may be going crazy.
Yet I can never forget my regret
Over having failed to assimilate
My most precious inheritance: selflessness.
I require the presence of things, to define my essence.

Lately, it's occurred to me
That I'm the beneficiary, for better or best,
Of my ancestors' fetish for saying out praises,
To every stray waif and beggar,
Just for the sake of perpetuating blessedness
And mercy, as worshiped and preserved
By tiny human beings
Reaching skyward, for confirmation and purpose.

It appears that no matter where I go,
My shadow and voice conspire,
Recreating the shape of my loving parents
Promenading, hand in hand, along a Kiev esplanade,
Speaking, with equal facility, to strangers and friends.
I am the keeper of their keepers' promises
Never to neglect or forget their sacred covenant.
The poems I recite are those on the stones Moses broke.

1/26/83 — [4] (02502)

Grabbing All the Gusto

Having concluded their set,
The relatively anonymous duo breaks,
Retires to opposite sides of the room, to mingle
Amidst the raucous crowd,
Whose group has reserved, for three days,
The motel, *en bloc*.

These people (rock stars,
Demolition derbyists, fair persons)
Come, once a year, to book their shows,
Make their sensational promotions known
To the few who've not been initiated,
Like me, for one, who has just begun

To understand the cosmic import
Of all this midnight carnival cavorting
And exorbitant, exhibitionistic misbehavior
By adults in pointed boots and Stetson hats,
Formulating mile-a-minute expletives
While pinching passing waitresses and playing with themselves —

An outrageous mix, macho and arrogant,
Perpetuated by men bent on exploitation,
Spotlighting human freaks, showcasing anomalies.
I gasp and wheeze between breaths;
Contagion breeds in this smoky opium den.
The two players reconvene,

Assume electric piano and guitar, synthesizer,
Fill the room with music
Poured from soup cans, dripping
From the tips of invisible peppermint sticks,
Whose lyrics are the most hip
Country-and-western syrup in the business.

The creatures from the blue zoo lagoon stir,
Rouse themselves from the slime,
Abandon, for the moment, their beers,
To submit their shadows to antic dance,
Disappear into the quick mist, as the sounds
Surround them like vapor rising from a haunted swamp.

I lean too far to the left,
Slip from my barstool,
*

Out of sight, wet, to the flesh, with wine.
An unexpected hand grabs for mine,
Clings. I rise into the most beatific face,
A shape straight out of my dreams.

Awakening, abruptly, into my previous fate,
I recognize, at the ends of my fingers,
Velma, mid-Missouri's
Three-hundred-pound mud-wrestling queen,
Inviting me to a tag-team match —
Best three out of five falls, no time limit. I accept.

1/26/83 — [5] (01355)

Jumping Freights

Shimmering reflections of the barn-red caboose,
Off on its own private siding,
In this dim Katy Station lounge,
Hover on the surface through which my eyes dive.
I, like a bindle stiff,
Try to grab hold of its iron safety railing
And disappear behind the rising exhaust —
Sulfurous cinders and smoke —
Spreading out across the wine-blotter sky
My imagination supplies,
As I sit here, by myself, tonight.

Yet no matter how close I come
To catching its fleet mirage, freedom's dream,
The essence of mortal escape from pedestrian ways,
It gets lost in the whale-white steam
Lifting, like vaporous fevers, off my forehead,
As sweet Chablis reaches deep into my brain,
To liberate concrete images caged there,
Unleash visions of sleek silver passenger trains
Forging ahead, at great speed,
Through scenic national-forest gorges,
Past steep sierras, ravines, precipitous cliffs.

Suddenly, I recall, precisely,
My wife and children and myself
Riding high inside the cupola of a caboose,
*

On the Sunday-running Gold Coast Railroad,
Whose entire five miles, backward,
Forward and back,
Behind a rickety locomotive,
Were fired by Fort Lauderdale, Florida, volunteers
Desiring to recreate and savor the past,
And the ecstasy our bones knew, in those moments,
Going absolutely nowhere,

All afternoon,
Fast as our cast-iron imaginations
Could spin their driving wheels, along tracks
No longer fit to transport anything,
Lest it be fantasies.
Oh, how we reveled,
My exuberant five-year-old boy,
His sister, Trilogy, Janny, and me,
Clackety-clacking, in spectacular abandon,
Fashioning, from mere nostalgia,
Prismatic revelations of old golden days,

Swaying over decayed sleepers,
Rusty, pitted rails running perpendicular
To the airport's major runway,
Mimicking its once-proud whistle, with pride.
But that was last year.
Now, sitting here, peering into the wineglass,
Distant yet queerly near,
By reason of this barn-red caboose,
Occupying space in Katy Station's waiting room,
I lament my inability to jump the freight
Racing through my yards, tonight.

1/27/83 — [1] (02503)

Voyeur extraordinaire

Two tables away,
I witness the spit-shined shit:
Cigarette fitted between his manicured fingers,
Wrist watch calibrated in fourteen-karat Piaget
Or Rolex — I can't say for certain,
From this vantage, yet
*

He's a spiffy graduate nonetheless,
Who, most probably, as summer flunky,
Clerked for Abner Jablanow,
Supreme Court justice
From the Thirty-third District.

Right now, he's completely committed,
Between suave yawns, subtle winks,
Shiftings in his seat, reorderings
Of her Bloody Marys, his martinis (extra dry),
To subverting his date's best intentions,
Suborning her most inhibited erotic desires,
While I, in work shirt, jeans,
Dirty boots, hallucinate,
Superimposing my own lonely soul
On their tête-à-tête, masturbating in public,
For lack of more satisfactory alternatives.

Sitting here, I run my fingers
Swiftly through her hair, imagine her naked,
Beneath silk sheets, her milky flesh
Glistening beneath my slim, sinewy body,
Her clitoris palpitating between my lips,
While he, her suitor, sweats
Before being kicked, headlong, into a death-pit
At Auschwitz. Now, I am her victor,
Despite my negligible position:
Voyeur, heuristic fictionist, poet of the lonely.
I dominate her completely, with my distant vision.

1/27/83 — [2] (02504)

Blitzed Desiderata

He had run his patience's course,
Forced the issue, pressured himself
To a point beyond which existence existed
As nothing except habit, surrendered ambition,
So that only his own loneliness mattered.

Then, at that juncture
Where caring passed into neglectfulness,
He undressed, ran, absolutely naked,
Through the music room,
Where drunks played easy-to-get

And high-school pompom girls, in short shorts,
Serving drinks, pirouetted,
Through dooms of smoky gloom,
Before his sustained pagan refrains,
And blew his primal shofar,

Whose resonant strains
Called, from distant hills, all lost sheep
And rutting swine,
Bovines, equines, reptiles,
And every disgusting, lusting creature in between,

Unloosed his pagan nature,
So that he tried to rape every dame
And wayward lady that passed through,
Offering each his shepherd's staff,
His palpitating God-rod,

Or any other manifestation within his province
To will or conjure or produce,
By waving his bare magical wand,
His succulent fuck-stick.
And as he ran through the crowd,

The spectral image of the proverbial jaybird,
He heard his own voice
Chastising his blatant amorality,
Never once realizing
That his exaggerated actions were actually appropriate,

His nudity neither crude nor obtuse,
Rather to be applauded by those
Still flaunting their clothes,
Pretending innuendos translated into tendencies
Capable of sating subtle lusts.

Now, chameleon night transmogrifies,
Defies logic, in its disguises,
Rises to dawn's occasion,
The dividing sun a glowing mitosis,
Its essence exploding in rosy permutations,

While he penetrates sleep, enters dreams,
Surrenders his mares to day,
*

As waking catapults him into *now*,
Now into a confrontation with his own nakedness,
Nakedness into speculation

That, in only moments,
He'll take his own life,
For lack of spectacles more exciting,
Submit his spirit to God's prostitute, for keeping,
Mimicking mythic Biblical rituals as he dies.

1/27/83 — [3] (02368)

Between Reincarnations

Just past noon,
He mounts his winged steed, Ganymede,
And spurring it in the flanks,
Whipping its mane, with his reins,
He forces the creature to erupt,
Take flight abruptly.

Within a matter of flaps,
Both beast and rider assault the sky,
Glide into soaring orbit,
Their two shapes fused into one shadow,
Which eclipses the sun
As they pass between it and the invisible moon,

On their journey to his destiny's depot.
Arriving inside an eye-blink,
He presents his credentials to the keeper,
Stables his fabled Ganymede,
Then enters evening like a star borrowing light,
Silence speaking to galaxies,

Where sleep bathes him in emollients
Extracted from celestial vestal breasts,
The sweetest milk ever expressed.
All these years, he's waited
For his soul to superimpose this dream
Over death, postpone reality indefinitely.

1/28/83 — [1] (05836)

Prologue to a Barnyard Book of Verse [Δ]

If a thousand cows meowed
As a thousand sows bowwowed,
We might see the fiercest melee ever fought
Between cloven-hoofed pussies
And screw-tail doggies.

Feline, canine, swine, bovine —
Who could imagine such docile creatures
Creating mayhem,
Condoning pandemonium,
Just for the sake of sating a cliché?

On the contrary, I suspect
That if a slew of beeves mewed
As a few pork bellies barked,
Whoever was in earshot
Would chortle, snort, and guffaw nonstop,

Until the cows came home,
The dogs lay down with fleas,
The cats chased their shadows, up a tree,
And the hogs turned their purses inside out.

1/28/83 — [2] (05837)

Blown into a Snow Zone

As I leave town, this Friday morning,
The horizon behind me
Glowing like the halo containing an infected wound,
The moon riding high, as a watchdog,
In the crow's-nest, atop the mainmast
Of a listing ghost ship
Floating nowhere, in circles, interminably,
I sense doom looming, up the highway,
Like a typhoon spawning in sea grottoes.

Yet as I proceed,
6:30 gradually relinquishes its primacy,
Takes a backseat to waking dreams
*

Continuously unwinding from accreting miles.
Heading easterly, into the surfacing sun,
I'm neither crazed Ahab nor bungling Icarus
Driving into day's eye,
Flying toward Leviathan's blowhole,
Trying to reach the sweet oil in the case,

But Willy the road peddler,
Hoping to rise above it,
Dive in, be swallowed alive,
Survive inside its cosmic testes,
Revel in ecstasy, forever, without being devastated.
But the breaching creature falls back,
Into a solar ocean-haze black with snow.
All afternoon, I follow it down,
Drowning on my own misthrown harpoon's barbs.

2/4/83 — [1] (02367)

Happy Hour

In this college-town lounge,
Youth, in all its elusive permutations,
Passes before my stupefied perusal. I muse
How identically each male is dressed,
In blue jeans, jogging shoes or boots,
Flannel shirt, oxford button-down,
Or, from nine to one, a V-neck sweater.

This peacock species differs imperceptibly,
Only in facial hair,
That single distinguishing idiosyncrasy
Dictated by whim, emulative heroic image,
Divine design (those with a Moses
Or Christ complex), appreciated, reinforced
Not by their girlfriends, wives, blind dates

But their own chauvinistic compatriots.
Amazement keeps me in my seat,
Makes reordering Chablis a sweet divertissement,
As I pass over the boys in men's gaits,
Concentrate on the women,
*

Who seem to swim just beneath the current,
When, in truth, they provide the bedrock

On which each tedious, inebriated conversation
Whirlpools. My gaze centers on them
Not collectively,
Rather on one, intensely, then on another,
Until I can almost feel the secret revulsion
Each keeps hidden, the prescient fear
Of having been relegated to the bone heap prematurely.

What a rush, to realize
I'm actually capable of empathizing with another soul,
No matter that she's a stranger,
Protagonist of a decidedly opposite sex.
These modern victims, unknown heroines,
Blow me out of my complacency, arrest my spirit,
Thrust me into a confrontation with my heart.

Suddenly, I know, or think so, anyway,
How second-class citizens
Identify themselves: all they have to do is listen,
Permit themselves the indiscretion
Of listening to the bullshit lifting from lips
That, in private, promise them life,
Liberty, and the pursuit of labial eroticism,

And be assured that their well-intentioned swains
Are Kickapoo Indian Juice guys,
Brooklyn Bridge promoters,
Freeloaders, flimflam men,
Wolfsheims, Shylocks, dubious Houdinis, Nixons,
Fixing everything, from the World Series
And Super Bowl to their own nefarious marriages.

In desperation, I sit back, collapse,
Sip my sweet Chablis, and weep for our coevals,
Realizing females don't even have a chance
Against testosterone,
Let alone the arrogant bones
That support the skeletons of shallow stallions
Who gallop, loud and raucous, down private paths.

2/4/83 — [2] (02505)

Katy Station, Friday Night

Little bodies, big fig trees,
Females reeling, in easy-wheeling feelings,
Over plains, like eagles peeling off,
Corsairs down-diving,
Against Zeros, ladies homing in on their mates . . .

This place is a strafing zone, Bikini,
An atoll where the latest weapons
Are unleashed against unsuspecting enemies:
Boys and girls of college age and older,
Pairing off, in combative actions,

Ph.D. candidates,
Computer programmers, lawyers, nurses,
Human-resources persons, waitresses,
Aerobic-dance instructors,
Land developers, poets, profligates,

Each with a special interest to defend,
Against pretenders to the throne.
I sit unnoticed, slightly comatose,
For repeated Chablis I've ordered,
Hoping to end the evening as I began — drunk,

Alone, unmolested by the free ladies
Who frequent this place, frequently,
In search of trim, slick-haired bodies,
Exciting one-night fucks,
Stimulating hallucinatory suck-offs —

And praying to escape this Friday-night maelstrom
Before the volcano's lid blows,
Half a mountainside explodes,
And Columbia, Mo., is buried under Pompeii's ash . . .
Naked whores, kitchen pots, and all.

Witnessing this pagan rite,
I'm appalled by the base nature,
The bowing to sacred cows, golden phalluses.
Now, the night winds dissipate;
Hounds, in the distance, bay.

I allow myself five minutes
In which to pay my check, find my coat,
*

Wave good-bye to vague acquaintances
I made as the night slipped away.
In a flurry, I gather my belongings

And disappear from the grinning din.
After grabbing notebook, pen, glasses,
I bolt from this smoky Golgotha,
Race the car's cold motor, head home,
As the sun offers itself up — a brand-new religion.

2/4/83 — [3] (02506)

The Last Train Home

All last evening, he listened volitionlessly,
Not heeding weather predictions,
Not caring less what the morrow might bring,
For inebriated pleasurings
He busied himself with, at Katy Station.

Of greater consequence, by far,
Was the need to locate himself, along the tracks
His imagination had lain,
Forty-one years broad, across his geography.
And on a handcar, he went out,

Rolling, slowly, back and forth,
Inspecting old roadbed,
The rotted ties, rusted connectors and spikes,
Cracked rails, over which his entire life
Had journeyed, in style,

And trying to isolate dangerously neglected sections
In need of immediate repair,
Areas no longer passable, for collapses,
Geologic variations, stops from youth,
Early manhood, last year,

Now obsolete, for recent changes in his design.
All evening, he traversed memory,
Making at least a dozen round trips,
Before quitting, in utter frustration.
Just before going to bed,

He noticed, from his steamy motel window,
The snow beginning to winnow
Yet entered sleep as though tomorrow
Were another postponement
To be relegated to his present forgetfulness.

Now, running, at thirty miles per hour,
Through blinding whiteness,
Groping, constantly,
For a constantly closing opening in the snow,
He heads home, castigating himself, relentlessly,

For having spent last night
Traveling into his past,
Lapsing, for relaxed, empty stretches, into reverie,
Not taking to the road,
On first mention of impending travelers' advisories.

With all his heart, he wishes, this moment,
He were spaciously ensconced
In twin converted roomettes, on the *Super Chief*,
Which his parents, sister, and he, for two days, once,
Occupied, from Kansas City to Los Angeles.

Realizing such irrelevant fantasies
Can't dismantle the present,
Resurrect history, or help predict the next seconds,
Which he gathers in, one by one,
Driving home, alone,

He knows ghosts are watching through the snow-smoke
Issuing from his brain's piston chambers,
Valve casings, dashpots, boiler stack,
As he guides his locomotive, for the last time,
Toward today's noisy scrap yards.

2/5/83 (05838)

Trial by Water

Instead of filling to the brim,
With days flowing into decades
Shimmering with wisdom's translucent prisms,
*

His spirit's basin drains perceptibly;
Even stagnating molecules disappear.

The vessel that once maintained liquid voices
Can't contain its own dwindling,
For invisible fissures
And still more traceable breaks in the skin
Ineffectually sealing his brain.

Just now, inundation begins.
Drowning sounds its low, Gregorian moan,
As it sucks, from the bones, marrow it mixes with earth,
To plug the leaks permanently —
A workable dissolution, at least.

2/8/83 (05839)

Roger

The sad little fly
Has finally ceased the mad spinning, on its back.
Its brittle wings can't sing it home,
For weight agony and loneliness have added
To the narrow marrow containers
Beneath its iridescent flesh.
Its dying spirit, like an ice-glazed twig,
Has stiffened, cracked, snapped.

2/15 & 2/17/83 (05840)

Biblical Cliffs

The granite strata through which I pass,
This too-warm Wednesday morning
Midway into February,
Expose their shattered patterns.
In them, I see my own anfractuousness,
Envision irregular designs
Beneath my well-seamed flesh.

As I meander up the highway,
Unreleased from sleep's keeping,
*

Drowsy as a drugged streetwalker,
And repeatedly smooth through jagged ravines —
Debris left by blasting crews,
Scars inflicted, viciously, by humans,
On nature's supplely muscled belly and chest —

My senses detect uneasy queasiness
Welling from the depths
Below the psyche's bastion,
Almost as though an unknown volcano
Were set to explode.
Whatever precipitousness
Is closing in on me, I don't know,

Lest it be fate's Red Sea,
Paralleling the highway I navigate,
Previously held back
By these chiseled cliffs,
Within whose shadowy banks I flee.
Suddenly, the sky is opaque, arterial.
My heartbeat drowns beneath its closing waters.

2/16/83 — [1] (00856)

Wishy-Washy Admonitions

Fuck with drugs, bud,
You're gonna suck hind dug
On the rutting she-serpent's gut!

Fella, stay strung out,
You'll pickle your brain, in brine,
Turn to seaweed, in kelp beds,

Feed, finally and forever,
On pelagic idiot-sin-cress-ies
And irrelevant delicacies from the nevermind!

You'll go blind, guy,
Trying to find every interloper
And trespasser hiding behind giant squids,

Avoid being taken prisoner,
By agents, officers, of the netherwaters,
Escape paranoia's slimy tentacles!

Take my advice, boy:
Toying with speed leads the incontinent and greedy
To giddy depths! Avoid that shit

Or start preparing yourself, today,
For the cosmic bends, Mr. Fish!
You'll enter hell belly up!

2/16/83 — [2] (05841)

Blue-Moody Fugue

In this public room,
I assume an attitude of subdued seclusion.
My entire body is subsumed
Beneath afternoon's pervasive domination.

Bones, ideas, sight, touch, dreams
Submit to the languorous light
Dripping, like honey from a tilted jar,
Into this lounge; they mimic its sweet accents.

My disappearance goes unnoticed
By those around me,
Too busy weaving themselves
With silken syllables to heed my golden silence.

The covenants they create exclude me.
No matter, clauses and riders I conceive
Guarantee my exclusivity,
Shield me against eviction,

Regardless of acts of God, cataclysm,
Forced entry, eminent domain.
For the immediate future, I'm safe in this place,
So far away from home,

Free to enter into any agreement I deem appropriate
To relativity's well-being,
Distort order, postpone necessities,
Arrogate amoralities to my own needs,

In the name of the great god Poetry.
Even now, although drowsiness
Threatens to dismay the initial inspiration
Already forming within my brain's furnaces,

My inclination is to surrender my senses, completely,
To the twilight, that they might write verse
Worthy of my outsize ambitions,
Transpose the light into paradisiacal keys,

Whose music will illuminate my metered spheres,
Flood my solitudinous galaxy,
With mellifluous tones so fragile and compelling
I'll not be able to avoid their spell,

Rather will rise from my lethargy,
Leap like a nocturnal feline on the prowl,
And yowl at the gibbous moon
Sliding through the night sky,

Behind the streaked window I've appropriated.
Just now, I look up,
Realizing that I am the poem itself,
The frangible planet orbiting my soul's Son,

The one witness to my own blessed dissolution.
Suddenly, the glass rejects my passage.
Vision refracts, backs up.
I can't penetrate my own distractive face,

Glaring at me. The hours growl at me.
Sweet inebriation sours.
I realize my stay has overextended itself.
The end is at hand. I surrender to the glands, and sleep.

2/16/83 — [3] (02507)

Mr. No-Name Poet

Lost, displaced, by whatever name
A commonplace waif,
Dissociated tatterdemalion,
Whose modest denomination among the angels
Bears no relation
To anything resembling Miltonic hierarchy,
Rather Satan's lowly principality,

I proclaim myself, celebrate my soul,
By composing poetry
*

No man can readily penetrate
Yet each, with assiduous energy, can comprehend.
I announce my presence aloud,
At publicized readings, through vitae sent
To universities desiring magicians

And public exhibitionists, for private occasions,
And by essays and poems,
Printed beneath my pseudonym, presented
To waiting audiences hooked on my papal edicts.
Why I've arrived at such an elevated station,
I can't say, for certain,
Let alone affirm, except to emphatically assert

That persons involved in academic consortia
And pedagogic rhetoric
Have persistently requested my appearance
At their gatherings, commencements,
Regents' board meetings.
Each day, I suspect, three requests,
At least, beg me come to speak my speech,

Before such-and-such reverential sodality
Or sacrosanct society,
On topics ranging from rampant herpes
To the urgency of protecting endangered species,
Such as Galápagos turtles and American bison.
I decline, by refusing to look at my mail,
Answer my phone, open the door, for every bell,

Yet regret each missed opportunity
To declaim against bigotry,
Whether racial, religious, or geopolitical.
I remain isolated in my own emotional doldrums,
Hoping to enter, while remaining aloof from,
The universal arena,
Desiring to die, bloodied by my own sword only.

2/16/83 — [4] (02508)

Three Nuns

In the booth in the boxcar I've been assigned,
In the refined restaurant
*

In the town where, frequently, I spend the night,
I sit across from a trinity of nuns
Fully robed. I can't imagine them
Ever having been children,
Let alone possessing breasts, cunts,
Knowing the ecstasy of orgasm, pregnancy,
Enduring amniocentesis, episiotomy,
Cursing, laughing, donning a bikini,
Attending a beach party, getting stoned.

Hearing them whisper their sacred whispers
Re priest So-and-So, Mother Superior,
Sister Such-and-Such, Father Vis-à-Vis,
I grasp, sensually, each boiled shrimp,
Revel in peeling away its shell,
As though I were performing
A perfectly earthly eucharistic feast,
Expiating sin, a layer at a time,
Until arriving at the mystical body,
Eating with pleasure denied those people
Robotically consuming trout, across from me,

Proclaiming themselves transcendent,
By virtue of their vows of abstinence.
I see them, in my peripheral vision,
While pondering my roast beef,
Remarking the strange juxtaposition we occasion —
These ladies of the Church,
Inebriated poet, in the flesh.
Suddenly, I experience a revelation:
We're all of the same cloth,
At once above and beneath society,
God's ministers, trying to coexist.

And yet, and yet,
What of my expletives, their circumincessions?
How can I justify the discrepancies
Between our behavior? They're so strict,
Disciplined, strait-laced;
I am a reprobate goat.
And yet, and yet, I compose godly poetry,
While they debate, rhetorically,
Metaphoric essences, fabulistic aesthetics.
*

Eschatologically, who can say
One persuasion takes precedence over the other?

2/16/83 — [5] (02509)

Disenchanted

The windshield wipers —
Flutes playing in tandem —
Keep time for my meandering,
Register the highway's syncopations,
Signifying, repeatedly,
My states of mental alertness and fatigue.

With each arpeggio, they briefly erase
Pernicious fog-beads
Colliding with my onrush,
Out of an opaque sky
Stretching down,
Enveloping the road, like a giant snake-bag.

My ophidian bones and brain suffocate.
Neither music nor poetry
Lifts, mystically, from the trance
My somnolent spirit inhabits.
I coil inside morning's white silence,
Uncharmed.

2/17/83 (05842)

Miscellaneous Man

Dissident, infidel, libertine, gypsy, sham,
A damnable example of ambiguities,
Since, above all,
He's one of the sweetest family men
To descend a rubber tree —
An adult baby chimpanzee,
Whose wife and children smother him, capriciously,
In loving, touching whimsy.
Why, then, his stupendous apostasy?

Those who've met him and known him intimately
Just once,
*

Whenever he's ventured from his nuclear group,
Entered and penetrated
Anonymity's slender, polygamous cunt,
From the front, via back roads,
Have only met a phantom,
Known a ghost, slept with bones alone,
Hosted, for a moment, the road's echo.

In fact, he's been missing in action,
These last ten years.
His disappearance has never been reported
To the authorities, by his wife,
From mortal fear he might be discovered alive,
Dying from an undiagnosed virus
Or unidentifiable spore,
Being gnawed by the worm at his spirit's core,
Suffering the dread malaise anomie.

Why, finally, have he and his mate nurtured the ruse,
Abused their mutual self-respect,
With subterfuge, lying, unfulfilled promises,
All these desolate years?
Their barrenness is the iceberg's apex.
They are heirs apparent
To their own Dark Ages' futile estate.
Once again, he takes flight,
Before daylight can question his intentions,

Bending with the sun's rays, as they attenuate,
In a daze suspended,
His destination a function of unadulterated instinct.
Debased, aimless, questless, he digresses,
Pressing ever ahead, in all directions,
On his steeplechase toward Nowhere,
Everywhere.
His accidental existence yet defies defeat.
Resurrection requires all his energy.

2/23/83 — [1] (04163)

Space Shuttle

He is a piece of the cosmic miscellany,
An anonymous phenomenon,
*

Spiritus incognitus,
Drifting naked, in the space his eclipse creates,
As his brief clay shape wobbles, precariously,
Through the Gates of Hades,
His twin spinning formations resembling amebas,
Not flaming meteors.

Spun loose,

He soars off course, at screaming speeds,
Burning, illuminating,
A white, hot-glowing soul-coal
Floating, like a diamond-faceted satellite,
In its own blind orbit,
A shabby navigator whose asbestos scales
Fend off the fires of reentry
Yet who can't land, for faulty telemetry.

Days change to decades, in the same time
Dreams tarnish, hopes fade.
His apparatus is so bluntly calibrated,
Only cataclysmic aberrations register on his gauges.
Forever assumes a palpable immediacy,
As his one-man flight continues as planned,
Unscrubbed, all systems go.
Not even he knows his shuttle's slope.

2/23/83 — [2] (02510)

The First Feathered Bird on Earth

Each morning, I slip out of a wizened yawn,
Into freshly pressed flesh,
And dress in archaeopteryx feathers and claws.

What a fine, mad, prehistoric ritual I precipitate,
Day out, day in, systematically,
Just to remind myself continuity exists

Despite collective forgetfulness.
The difficulty is not in waking,
Rather in rising, beside whom, in what room,

Since sleep's destination
Is so incalculable when the spirit is ripped,
The soul cut loose from its moorings.

Every day is a clichéd "new beginning,"
Another way to celebrate the self,
A Renaissance antique yet recent,

The Biblical reenactment of Jurassic vestiges.
I am, simultaneously,
Styracosaurus and Billy Dee Diana Holiday,

A creature crude and wild,
The meek, mild seed seeking a female garden
In which to settle and germinate.

My dreams are poems floating to the ground,
Like brittle leaves waving good-bye
To trees who've nurtured their spontaneities.

Just now, the sullen soul stalls,
In mid-flight,
Craves white wine, on which to float its ship,

Extend its oceanic limits,
That it might outdistance sweet Madeira,
Reach Plymouth Rock, without mishap,

Propagate a colony consisting of metaphors,
Brainchildren dressed as caesuras
And classical villanelles.

I invite intrusions such as these
Into my secluded ruminations,
Welcome Hester Prynne,

That she might reaffirm my heart's predilection
For amoral mortality,
Cora Tull, to renew my aversion to hypocrisy.

None comes to my literary rescue,
As I sit here, in the middle of nowhere,
Swilling Swiss Colony Chablis, by the carafe,

Waiting for some frantic revelation
To grace my perceptions, trace its footprints
In the sand, make me understand

That waking is a very precarious undertaking,
At best, an effort definitely worth making,
If one desires to stay a step ahead of death.

2/23/83 — [3] (02511)

Willy's Thousand-and-First Vow

Once again, this gray morning,
Perfunctory leave-taking sunders him.
His dazed spirit dresses in yesterday's rags,
Packs its scanty possessions,
In a brown, gusseted IGA bag,
Pays cash,
Then disappears in the rickrack
Of the highway's rain-slick slipstream,
Screaming silent manifestoes
Against waking and sleep, freedom and routine.

And as he weaves down the concrete flume,
Like a balky log in a series,
His spirit assumes a wizened appearance.
Its covering loosens, pulls away,
Exposing myriad vermiculations,
Labyrinthine tunnels
Just under its crusty surface,
A spongy, inessential crumbling at its core,
As if, for decades, undetected,
Thieves had been embezzling Solomon's stores.

Today's link fastens his past to tomorrow,
In a choker that constricts his throat.
Through the drizzle's grim glimmer,
He sees the continuous *now*
Devouring him, mile by hour by day,
Without even a hint of a finish line
Within the horizon's elusively diminishing design.
Convincingly, he vows his next stop,
At Finkel's Men's Shop, will be *the* end . . .
Until tomorrow, at ten o'clock.

2/24/83 (02366)

Sprung Loose, on Sunday

Having feasted on Sunday brunch, in the city,
My precious family and I disperse,
In opposite directions — dandelion seeds
Seized by alternating breezes,
*

Set adrift, by our own volition,
To seek separate destinies, for an entire week.

Trilogy, Troika, and my wife, Jan,
Band together, in blessed trinity, against aliens,
Like Madonna and twins
Huddled within a *futuro*-cubistic Cimabue,
Whose ornate frame — my gold-leaf prayers for them —
Haloes them inviolably.

They head home, to our game preserve,
Where there's safety in sanctity
And familiar placenames.
I defy the numbers, drive west, on my own,
Not quite free
Yet succumbing to wanderlust, arbitrarily,

For the sake of staking claim
To whatever remains of my mind's dwindling frontiers.
This blessed afternoon,
I cruise, headlong, toward the edge,
Where my Continental Divide widens into years
Galloping like wild, snorting stallions
Cavorting, unbridled, across a sky-pasture.

The journey is its own justification.
My burned-up energy
Provides a worthy return on its expenditure,
By virtue of what I'm learning
About solitude. The search is the Zen.
It alone engenders further searches

Into the dense hemispheres,
Where lunacy shares its lair with beauty
And the muse sprawls naked,
In the imagination's tall grass,
Waiting, like Lilith, for brainchildren
To pass, from abstraction, into poetic corruptibility.

Just now, I indulge my senses to their extremities,
Scream, exultantly, to cows and trees
Beyond reach, sing the sleeping awake,
In roadside cemeteries,
Make promises to myself (which, first chance,
Each and every one, I'll break),

That I might be reminded of my heritage:
I'm the chimera-guy, Wizard of Flimflam,
Zoroastrian bastard, Diaspora Willy,
Disaster Joe, of the *Holocaust Show*,
A poet who knows it's time to collect his personae
And get the hell home.

2/27/83 (02069)

Unloading, at a Sacrifice

This trip is significantly different
From all the others he's taken,
These past ten years.
They were strictly made for business,
Out of definite necessity,
Not with intellectual prerequisites,
Rather set, programmed to the last detail,
Predestination at its human best,
Deus en machina,
Down to a fine, routine design,
With every base covered,
From the same Ramada-Holiday-Johnson Inn,

Same room 116,
To the same Katy Station restaurant and menu
And college-town lounge,
With the same leggy barmaid
Supplying his need for chilled Chablis,
All evening, at the nod of a finger,
A wink, mind-think,
As he'd stare at both prominent zones,
Highlighted, invariably, by Lycra tights,
Invite her into his night-flight,
No matter where he was
Or when.

Yet this trip is significantly different.
He's just been dismissed,
For failing to book adequate business
In the dried-up Sinai
He's religiously serviced, thirty-five years.
At least they might have waited
Till he arrived home,
*

Got off the road, to let him know
They'd decided to let him go.
Dusk, five hundred miles distant
From the nearest commiserating wife,
Is a rather infelicitous limbo.

Suddenly, he's cut free.
His psyche bleeds from its spirit's main arteries.
Fear attacks the escaping oxygen;
Breathing hyperventilates
Erratically as an out-of-time tractor engine.
Slowly, even his focus on the steering wheel
Diminishes to brief views
Beyond the windshield, whose tinted glass
Provides a Praxinoscope reel of his life.
The violent spinning begins.
Now, loudness, fire, pain, silence —
His final promotional offering is a complete success!

2/28/83 — [1] (02365)

Regrinding Lenses

This Monday-morning sun is a grinding wheel,
Whose abrasive pumice,
Biting into my lids and pupils,
Is creating such vicious friction,
Vision spins off its main focus on the road,
In scintillating grits,
Each spitting out a dissociated image:

Here, a brindled cow, fencing, hedgerows,
Billboards, phantom transports;
There, a ghost town on a narrow strip
(A blocked artery of America's obsolete heart)
Paralleling, in echoless isolation, the highway,
And myriad farms teetering, obstinately,
On bankruptcy's sere lunar fields.

Somewhere among these reflections,
My brain proclaims, am I,
Or my fleet, peregrine shadow —
At least I pray so.
Otherwise, all this insight
*

The sun's fiery honing is supposed to create
Would render separation without registration,

And I would be just one more fleck
In the prismatic spectrum,
A feckless consciousness
Without the necessary requisites to effect change.
Let my imagination identify me,
Within the design, assign me a shape,
A place in the universal pecking order,

That I might presuppose a destination
For my flight across the horizon.
Let me realign all these elements,
Stare directly through them,
Into the eye at the sun's epicenter,
Without going blind.
Ah, there's where clarification originates!

2/28/83 — [2] (02068)

A Modest Proclamation, for the Record

Flying south, on Highway 69,
Out of Pittsburg, Kansas, toward Tulsa,
I set this down —
Let me set this down, in my ship's log:
A man can sink to depths
He'd not believe possible
And still not drown,
Can sink beneath the surface sounds
Resonating, like whale bleeps, from his cries,
Those poetic manifestoes
Proclaiming his paltry ego's fragile hopes,
And continue swimming, miraculously,
In the terrific whirlpool his stasis creates,
He a smooth, chromeplated ball-bearing
Spinning in, centripetally,
From a roulette wheel's outermost halo.

Let it be known I set this down,
March 2,
Anno Domini 1983:
A man can even withstand failure,
*

See through self-delusion,
Lose not only his ambition but memory,
Grow senescent prematurely,
Yet persist in projecting a positive image
Against the cosmic scrim curtain,
Since all these crises, collectively,
Are definitely lesser evils
Than death.
Set this down: less is greater,
When one is weighing fool's gold,
An ounce of U-235
Better, by God, than a pound of plutonium.

3/2/83 (05843)

The Route to Auschwitz-Birkenau $^\Delta$

I leave sweet Tulsa asleep,
Head east,
Past Harvard and Yale Avenues, toward Joplin,
Over rain-spumy I-244.

Soon, I approach the tollbooth,
Take my punched, perforated card,
From a human semaphore,
Then enter the Will Rogers Turnpike.

My phantom sampan rolls, uncontrollably,
Through low spots in the road.
Bow and stern pitch forward
And back, forward and back,

Like the outside escapement
On a porcelain-faced Ansonia mantel clock,
Trough to crest, trough, crest, trough,
In vertiginous progression,

Until my restive intestines mutiny,
In one collective gesture.
I swerve off, onto the slick shoulder, skid,
Retch breakfast, out the open door.

As I lean over the sill plate, wet torrents
Pelt my bare arms and neck.
I can't retract into my protective shell,
Because nausea overwhelms me

Like a geyser. I linger, as if bespelled,
In an attitude of stupefaction,
Waiting for the pain in my gut
To unloosen its grip on my brain.

Extended minutes later,
I resume my trip, drenched to the skin,
Cold as a molding bread loaf
In its knotted, sweating plastic envelope.

Past Claremore, Big Cabin,
Vinita, Afton, Miami,
All the way to the state line, I drive,
As if into a hurricane's eye,

Without relief. Suddenly, I shudder.
Shivering sets my teeth
In sympathy with stuttering, muttering speech
My tongue tries to release, under its breath,

Unsuccessfully. Fever scales my walls,
Falls, safely, to all fours,
Crawls over my entire forehead,
My flesh, like leaking corrosive chemicals,

Until even vision is a gratuitous suicidal act.
By the time I arrive home,
Nothing remains
By which my wife and children might identify me,

Except the silver watch on my left wrist,
Gold bracelet on my right.
They slide them from my bones, set them aside,
Before dumping me into bed.

3/4/83 — [1] (00855)

A Mystical Pit Stop

I wheel past "America's Greatest
Exotic Animal Paradise,"
Without the slightest hesitation.
A mild skeptic, I need to take a leak
So desperately,
The only diversionary tactic imaginable,
*

To postpone the inevitable,
Is speculating on what bizarre creatures
Might be grazing there, slithering,
Bounding from limb to limb, perching,
Crouching, sleeping on their backs, swimming,
Climbing, squawking, fornicating,
In absolutely graphic lack of modesty:
Tasmanian kudus, unicorns,
Black and green leaping lizards,
A three-breasted cockatoo,
Martian centaurs,
Gorgons from Borneo, chimeras,
Mares from the cratered Plains of Schizophrenia,
A pink-winged Spotted Atrocious,
From the Seussian gorge above Peruvia,
California, a matched pair
Of Loch Ness Playboy bunnies,
Prairie dogs, parietal frogs,
A colony of medulla oblongatas,
And two Medusa-like Portuguese jellies.

Suddenly, laughter overtakes me,
While I gaze into the rearview mirror,
Comes alongside,
Motions me to pull off the road,
As though arresting, ticketing, my forward motion.
I obey, out of instinct,
Not fright. When I do so, control goes.
Before I can exit the car,
My tan polyester pants,
Like cosmic litmus paper, change shades,
Across the entire fly,
Down both thighs.
I invoke the most convenient deities,
Repeating, "Christ!" "Shit!" "Vishnu!"
And then "Christ!" and "Shit!" again,
As if imploring them with ritual
Might somehow make the stains disappear.

When I gaze up, out of my hazy funk,
I see a colossal buffalo
Surmounting a billboard in a nearby field,
As though riding it bareback,
The copy below screaming, in block letters,
*

**"EXOTIC ANIMAL PARADISE —
TURN AROUND — YOU'VE PASSED US!"**
Abruptly, I jump into my vehicle,
Gas it to the next junction,
And, exiting, turn back, west,
Toward the flag-bedecked main gate,
Pay, park, search, surreptitiously,
For a "comfort station,"
Locate, instead, a Harp-Twanging Snarp
Making otherworldly music.
By the time I leave, my pants have dried clean.

3/4/83 — [2] (05412)

The State of the Art

Delano, Fitzgerald, Milhous, Baines,
Jimmy, Gerry, Ronnie, Harry, and Ike —
History's most recently decanonized saints,
Whose names have come to stand for indecision,
Ambitions, and vanity with a capital *V*.
Hail to the chiefs!
Their nicknames read like Mr. Blackwell's list
Of this half-century's best-dressed hobos,
Picks of the glittering litters.
Their deeds are last week's theater stubs,
Bus transfers, moth-eaten dreams.

Where are the saviors, heroes, martyrs,
The spirit's gleaming religious leaders —
Not necessarily Martin Luther King,
Gandhi, Buddha, Muhammad,
Jesus, Moses Maimonides,
Rather just the humble poet,
Homegrown Whitman, Wordsworth, Frost,
A modern Dante, perhaps, or Homer?
No one would mind, I think,
If he spoke Aborigine, wrote Farsi,
So long as his song was original.

We lapse into a continuous poppied drowse,
Content to sip from our own images,
Which ripple on the surface, beneath our blurred gaze
*

Into the universal wine cup
Someone keeps filling, keeps filling
Each time we turn to converse with deities
Passing between Arcady and Earth.
And little do we notice the room spinning,
Sun and moon closing the gap,
Diana and her lover — curs eternally stuck —
As the tottering urn slows, stops, shatters.

3/10/83 (05844)

A Mother-Goosed Rhyme

Simple Simon met a hymen,
On the way to Jamaica.
He begged for a mango cake.
She sliced, for him, her pie, man.

3/13/83 — [1] (05845)

Jamaica

Afternoon curls up, beneath streaked clouds,
Like a sheet of parchment
Crowding heat. Now, sweet rum-breezes,
Weaving through palm fronds,
Fan the torrid West Indies.
Ocho Rios is a glowing scroll
Composed of dazed souls washed ashore,
Onto this volcanic landfall, centuries before,
In British slave-trade frigates,

And those cast here, now, off Montego Bay flights,
Met by Japanese vans
And transported to local "resorts,"
Each day, ad (packaged) infinitum.
Sipping planter's punch,
On the hotel's patio,
We can almost read their ancient and recent defeats,
In our own hopes, rising, ashen,
From travel posters and brochures we used to kindle our dreams.

3/13/83 — [2] (05846)

Jamaica-Bound

For Jan,
who asked for this gift

My lady and I
Have sailed into West Indian latitudes,
Moored at Ocho Rios, Jamaica,
For a week's retreat from desperation,
And begun to surrender to the sun's persuasion.

Our blood runs with less urgency,
Spurns superfluous turns and moves,
Eschews wasted energy
Whether awake or sleeping, yet the spirit flirts
With its own uninhibited capriciousness,

As time redefines itself as liquescence,
The wayward fragrance of bougainvilleas and hibiscuses,
The taste of strange rum elixirs,
Aromatic, black-textured sex
Hovering just above native flesh.

We tell the hour by our appetites,
Fashion, from flapping palm fronds
And quick, crisp calypso cadences,
Our own rhythmic myths. Our kissing eyes
Are reminders of all we've left behind.

By week's end, we may need a vacation
From such exquisite languishment.
Right now, the indolence we share
Seems only fair recompense,
For two stray renegades,

Who, reaching Jamaica,
On their way back home to themselves,
Have stayed long enough to find, in time,
Their inarticulate passion's former eloquence,
The sublime rhymes of hearts on a lark.

3/16/83 (04162)

Break-Fast ^Δ

"Gone and back! Gone and back!"
The Capital Café's bleached waitress
Remarks my absence, remarks my return,
With coffee and water offerings and a smile.

For a week, my wife and I took breakfast
Outdoors, beside the Caribbean Sea,
Leisurely repast
Attended by trained Jamaican blacks

Arranged in residual Victorian classes:
Busboys in white, waiters wearing red,
Maître d' designated by blue uniform —
Precision martinets

Changing guard, three times a day,
For British, American, Canadian visitors,
Carrying Blue Mountain brew, in one hand,
Cream, in the other, placing too many spoons

Sideways, on the freshly pressed cloth,
More glasses and various-sized plates
Than we'd ever use to portion out croissants,
Mangoes, star apples, gooseberries.

Squirming over tape-mended leatherette,
Staring down at the viscid remains
Of biscuits and gravy, smoked ham, on the chipped plate,
Now out through the rippled windows

Fronting Liberty Street and the courthouse,
Focusing on this typical mid-Missouri,
End-of-March snowfall
Trapping crocuses, tulips, forsythias, in freeze frame,

I know, in my heart, my spirit is home.
Fragility, delicacy, sunshine
Have abandoned ship, somewhere in the West Indies,
Left me to tack back, in crude winds

Devoid of female spices, hibiscus scents,
Heated-breeze-screeching ferns and palm trees.
*

The sea my dreams sail, this morning,
Is a dried-up memory. They freeze, on its white shore.

3/21/83 (00566)

The Physics of Love

For Jan,
at thirty-nine

The whole notion of epiphany, apotheosis,
Is rolled up in a Marvell ball
Called love,
Screaming toward us, seizing our eyes,
Gathering up our lives, in its forward motion.

We neither object to nor encourage
The blessed volitionlessness of our magnetics
But, rather, blindly worship vital dynamics
That shape, from space, poetic tropes
In which we clothe our naked hopes and dreams.

Curiosity, delight, sensual wonderment
Are placebos low-flying deities prescribe,
To placate our primal needs,
While treating us with paradisiacal elixirs,
To free our earthly senses.

As one sum, we two have become indivisible
By all attractive numbers.
Uniquely, we've discovered *the* formula:
Tenderness squared, multiplied by trust,
Equals time to its highest power, eternity.

3/23/83 (00106)

Brain-Taint

The nightmare I leave, in jettisoning sleep,
Is a prerelease penitentiary
Littered with loitering men and women
Engaged in unsavory sex,
A den of seething snakes, Barbary pirates,
A blighted patch of psoriatic flesh
*

Flaking outward, from its core,
Toward my Cyclopean eye, which itches, twitches.

Reprobates and vipers, sick tissue, convicts
Converge on my early blur,
Disturb waking's smooth surface,
Like a slingshotful of Goliath-stones
Thrown at a cress-festooned pool
Or high against the forehead of a poet
Unused to witnessing Vesuvius erupt,
Spewing human magma, lava, ash over his dreams.

I rise from my terraqueous bed of stones,
Scale crumbled Atlantis,
Grope for clothing, to hide my invisible bones,
And probe the chiaroscuro, for an opening.
But they, the naked elements,
Refuse to unhand me.
My ravaged shadow enters day,
Dragging me along, in a tawny body bag.

3/24/83 — [1] (05847)

Buck Private Willy Sypher

All Willy's wars have been fought,
He realizes, now,
In demilitarized zones, no-man's-lands.
Whether in police action
Or full-scale "retaliatory" aggression,
He's enlisted, for each fracas,
As a conscientious objector,
Even defected twice,
Once to Toronto, once to Stockholm,
Without ever being detected by authorities
Charged with seizing his spirit,
Searching his soul, for illegal hopes,
Sub rosa dreams,
Signs of potential permanent subversion,
Court-martialing his reactionary heart.

He knows, now, those adversaries
Against whom he's waged his battles:
*

Chronic back pain he's fought,
In saggy motel beds, night to night;
Cataracted obscurity,
Peering through the tinted windshield
Of the half-track he's maneuvered,
From mirage-like mom-and-pop shop to factory outlet,
In the Rommel-desert of his twilit campaign;
Loneliness, boredom, inescapable rage,
As if he were shackled to the floor of a Kafka-cave,
Beneath a clepsydric stalactite
Dripping memories of dead lovers and friends;
Obesity, emphysema, caffeine nerves,
Varicose veins, specters paranoiac and hallucinatory.

He's defended against entire armies
Of competitors deploying garment arsenals
More sophisticated than his,
Who have harder-hitting, farther-reaching impacts
On sales and profit margins,
And more efficient means for resupplying
Depleting stocks. He's died a thousand
Embarrassments, in trenches he's shoveled out
With feeble-tipped excuses for late deliveries,
Substitutions, blatant defects,
Buried himself beneath ineffectual restitutions.
He has met the enemy,
And he is, indeed, theirs, immitigably.
Tonight, he'll post his final dispatch from the field:
"Gone AWOL — Willy S."

3/24/83 — [2] (02364)

Eliotics

Eating peaches, rolling trouser cuffs,
Parting hair, in the middle,
Daring to take a stand, start a scene
Or two . . . bullshit! Bull . . . shit!
All that precious literary stuff,
Academic fluff, contrivance, artifice,
Useless Prufrockian allusion,
Is so artificial, pompous, and contemptibly abstruse,

To the forty-two-year-old guy
With wife and three kids,
Who's lost his job on the assembly line,
Overnight, and to the black teenager
Who's even bored breaking windows,
Robbing vending machines,
And to ladies being paid fourth-class wages,
With prurient insults as perks,

That if, in fact, poets are supposed to be
The world's unacknowledged legislators,
Perhaps it's best we neglect this wisdom,
Let it remain epigrammatically unclichéd,
Except among students of literature and linguistics,
Who languish, in classrooms and coffee lounges,
Xeroxing, cribbing, paraphrasing, citing sources,
Mass-producing original dissertations, to order.

And as for daring to eat a peach,
Streak across a trafficked street,
Disturb the universe, stuff a telephone booth,
Crosley, or automatic dryer, with attendant fools,
Even inscribe the entire Lord's Prayer
Within the perimeter of Emmett Kelly's dot,
I'd like to believe its all ancillary, anyway,
Compared to caring for caring others comparing.

3/24/83 — [3] (05848)

A Break in the Routine

Last night, he misplaced his glasses,
Spent anxious, grave, speculative misgivings
Straining his brain's retentiveness,
Tracing his maze, backward and forward,
From bathroom, where he last recalled sitting,
Viewing *Vogue, People, U.S. Health*,
To his bed, which he'd meticulously arranged
With love's accouterment.

Ranging, repeatedly, upstairs and down,
Like a supplicant genuflecting,
Growing increasingly sullen, he finally resorted
*

To begging his wife for help,
Actually insisting on her participation,
As if a brash, emphatic exhortation
Might lace his helplessness,
Hide his suspicion that senescence had set in.

Within less than a two-minute search,
She discovered his gold-rimmed spectacles
Resting, inertly as a dead bird on its back,
Undisturbed, where he'd set them, on the sheets,
During his fastidious preparations.
His relief, her brief victory recorded,
They receded, immediately,
Into their love's classical Greek tedium.

3/24/83 — [4] (02512)

The Sorcerers

Some people simply are bequeathed more energy
Than their genes can contain
Or were equipped, at birth, to maintain.

I sit cattywampus from a loud couple
Screaming, raucously, at middle age,
Like a pair of mad Ming dogs,

Here in an otherwise sedate Thursday-night
Katy Station lounge,
And listen, like a distant father confessor,

To her "fuck"s, his "cunt"s and "shit"s,
Her hyperbolized "asshole"s
And extravagant "pissed off" expletives,

Disbelieving the degree of their dysfunction.
Never have I been witness
To such perversity. Every third word

Is a witch's curse, a scourge
Gathered in from Biblical discouragements,
To describe a Pharaoh's blights.

Their obscenity rivals Hitlerian rhetoric —
A heightened medieval fright
Delivered at the Reichstag, to Wagnerian opera.

They eye me, eying them mesmerized.
Suddenly, I realize they're plotting against me,
As if I'm a saboteur, voyeur

They've been ordered to dematerialize.
I look down, to avoid their crazy gazes,
And wait for snake fangs to paralyze my brain.

3/24/83 — [5] (02513)

Good-Luck Pennies

How strange! All day long,
The change in my work-shirt breast pocket
Has continued to slip away,
Fall out, on the street, down on the counter,
Through an imperceptible opening,
Located somewhere in the universe,
Providing me with endless opportunities
For finding "lucky pennies."

Each time I spy a glistening copper
And reach down (at no small expense,
For my extensive girth)
To retrieve, symbolically, the worthless coin,
I praise my good fortune,
Not suspecting my dishabille is the reason
For my repeated providence,
A cost recovered without exorbitant recompense.

As day is deposited in night's repository
And my pocket continues to empty,
I realize good fortune is purely accidental.
Its superstitious rituals,
Such as locating wayward pennies in gutters,
Are as far-fetched as commoners marrying British princes.
Now, I rub Lincoln's bust,
As though it were a magical touchstone,

Hoping to liberate a golden genie or dybbuk,
From night's prestidigitation.
No white rabbits or phoenixes arise,
No fires ignite, no occult hoaxes occur,
*

By which I might judge my own charmed existence.
To my dire disillusionment,
My fingers, groping inside my right breast pocket,
Discover a hole. Suddenly, I know luck's secret.

3/24/83 — [6] (02514)

'Round Midnight

I have, categorically, fallen in love
Two hundred forty-two times,
In my all-too-brief lifetime,
And still not exhausted every possibility
For bringing to mutual fruition
The blessed Kama Sutra.

Having satisfied fifty-nine positions,
With eighty-two prostitutes,
Fourteen high-school cheerleaders,
And three serious sorority ladies,
I can say, categorically, that scholastics
Are passé without radical sex.

The more I question, the less I guess
About, arbitrariness.
The greater the largess I inherit
From the collective unconscious,
The smaller my destiny, categorically,
In cosmic measurements. I reject excess,

Despite my psychic tendency to exaggerate
Blessed, celestial concupiscence.
Categorically, I assert my independence
From the senses, while confessing innocence
Of naked female flesh.
Arrested in Keatsian poetics, I regress.

Tonight, I ply my flimflam profession,
By persuading the young lady
Serving drinks to meet me, after hours,
For a baptism, of sorts, categorically,
No sordid tryst, rather charismatic affair
Between tortoise and hare.

At the stroke of twelve, we revive, categorically,
Slide into each other's embrace,
Beneath time's silence, converge on eternity,
Hoping to find, in each other's urgency,
An attraction neither spurious nor boring,

Rather torrid, extraordinarily memorable.
But the clapper striking the hour
Never ceases. It traps us in our magic,
Refuses to release us from basic lovemaking.
At daybreak, we awaken to our strangeness
And leave, in haste, by separate lives.

3/24/83 — [7] (02515)

A Pre-Easter Resurrection, in Thirty-Three Lines

I leave Columbia, heading north,
Toward Moberly, Salisbury,
Listening to Ronnie Milsap,
Melissa Manchester. My eyes pan
Both sides of the highway, this morning,
As if feeding their appetite for detritus:
Dead possums; tractors, boats, cars
Stranded on macadam lots,
In the stalled economy's no-man's-land.
A garbage truck enters the traffic,
From a side street, like a bull walrus
Rolling up on a zoo pool's lip.
Ten cars abruptly halt,
Lumber impatiently, for the next five miles,
Waiting for an open stretch, to pass.

Suddenly, the land is fences, cows,
Empty trees, ponds, sheet-metal silos,
Lean-to feeders, propane tanks,
White-clapboard farmhouses.
Wispy spits of smoke fleeing chimneys
Take my gaze upward.
My eyes are doves zigzagging at random,
Spirits flying through blue space,
On their way to nameless destinations,
*

Before the day slips between history's pages
And is forgotten. Mine is a celebration,
No matter its silence, its private nature.
In the naming, I proclaim the moment;
In the moment, my coordinates fix my location;
In the location, at its core, I live;

And in living does the flame burn,
Which alone lights the way home,
For the soaring heart, in its evolutionary revelations.

3/25/83 — [1] (05411)

Suffering a Reversal

Just south of Moberly, Highway 63,
My fleet station wagon approaches,
Then overtakes, a one-horse buggy
Slowing to exit the route.
Throwbacks to another century,
Such as this Amish anomaly, rarely obtrude,
And when they do,
I'm usually too bemused to collect souvenirs.

As I pass the enclosed rig,
Its spokes seem to reverse their motion, stop.
No driver appears on the seat,
Open to the cold air, for lack of side curtains.

Suddenly, I wonder whether hallucination
May have stupefied reason,
Suffused fatigue, with shimmering simulacra,
Transported metaphor through time,
Fixated, in my tricked vision,
Historic images,
Forced my distorted perception to see *now*
Through yesterday's prophetic eyes.

Ten miles down the road,
I'm still stymied. Perhaps the phantom buggy
And ragged dray nag never existed.
Maybe today happened eighty years ago.

3/25/83 — [2] (05410)

An Exotic Species

He swims in a pelagic morass
Three parts chaos,
One half the remaining half
Finned phantasms, succubi, chimeras, and mares,
The other a galaxy of last-minute humans
Lying on history's coral bottom,
Embedded in dreaming's sargasso.

Peering out, into triple-thick,
Polarized, bifocal bigotries
That his visitors train on him,
Peering in, continuously,
Through his printed verse, he hovers, shimmers,
Alternating between delicate blue angelfish
And spiny, toxic lionfish.

His images and visions glimmer dizzily at them,
Without their recognition.
They glare at his strange poses.
His antic tropes share a common demotion
They ascribe to creatures exotic,
Foreboding, unpredictable.
Agape, they know not what they excoriate

Yet rap their fingers against the glass,
As if to shatter his concentration,
Frighten him into abrupt disappearance.
Year after year, his books appear.
The critics usually come at feeding time,
To applaud his bubbles, witness him assimilating crumbs
Sifting down from an invisible source above.

Although he's grown older,
His wisdom mystifies. The economy of his rhythms
Inspires them to giddiness.
Oblivious to their patronizing commendations,
He swims outside the limits
Within which they've tried to confine him
All his life — a fish out of water.

3/29/83 (05849)

The Death of a Road Peddler

He leaves home, this rainy morning,
Takes to the highway,
In search of appropriate adverbial
Or adjectival modifiers
By which to identify his identity,
Among the blurred attitudes
With whom he slept and awakened.

Day's swarming fog is a Pharaoh-blight,
Through whose misty visibility he drives,
Blindly following nervous taillights
Leading his desperate mind nowhere
Conclusively, going, just going,
His gone spirit clawing the red beams —
Pieces of seaweed in a bleak ocean.

And as he climbs the concrete ladder,
Each mile another rung,
Billboards dripping their smears
Like parrots screaming through rain forests,
His vision stoned by wash spewed back
From tractor-trailers he passes,
Intuition begins spinning, at the same speed.

He can almost call out
What, almost, he can see, through the density.
He temporizes, tries to suppress insight,
But the immense emptiness
Absorbs him, through its pores.
Gradually arriving at when, where, and why
He died, he realizes, too, how and as whom.

3/30/83 — [1] (02363)

United We Fall, Divided We Stood

Sanctimonious clones
Weave through our most recent generation,
Like termites tunneling in beams
Supporting the pleasure dome we've inherited.

Neither hedonism
Nor narcissistic tendencies per se
Can account for the weakening, from dry rot,
In society's main foundations;

Rather, a general malaise, lassitude,
Speaking "professionally,"
Has overtaken, outmoded us,
A sophisticated contagion, if you will,

That goes by the generic acronym
"DP" (data processing).
It's a case of contraindications,
A wholesale phasing-out, a plague.

Even state-of-the-art conventional wisdom
Remains its own cliché,
When gauged against such staggering capacities
To ingest megabytes,

Eliminate current methods, technologies,
Entire lexicons and encyclopedias,
In a matter of keystrokes and seconds.
Ah, and with what voraciousness

It complains, on sating itself
(An endless surfeit),
While the sanctimonious clones
Phone each other their congratulations,

Overseas, from one room to the next,
In their own homes,
Applaud their continual "improvements,"
"Perfections," "advancements,"

The bottom line always the highest priority:
"Utilizing more fully";
"Saving time, human resources, money";
"Storing more, retrieving more" —

Aphorisms incised in the public psyche.
Silence, privacy, uniqueness
Are credos relegated to immediate antiquity —
Scientia est omnia!

And the only person, agency, authority
From whom I can hide,
Anymore, is myself.
Even my schizophrenia can be programmed,

My unconceived verse
Brought up, on a scope,
By anyone entrusted with my imagination's code.
Catastrophe always seems to draw us closer.

3/30/83 — [2] (05850)

Blanking Out

In this very public lounge,
On this very Wednesday, late afternoon,
I seat myself off in a corner,
At my very own cast-iron-base table,
Beside the stranded Katy caboose,
Beneath its amber yard-light,
Place my gold-rimmed readers before me,
Their case open for business,
With three magical Bic pens,
And a glass filled, to shimmering, with Chablis,
And wait for inspiration to displace fatigue.

The blue-ruled notebook I've brought along
Is an ancient scroll,
Containing my scriptural rituals,
An incunabulum printed on goat vellum,
An extremely early German Bible,
Whose genealogies record my heritage,
The Apocrypha and Pentateuch, in one volume,
My golden *Doomsday Book*,
Mother Goose translated, by Dr. Seuss,
Into the world's smoothest hallucinatory verse.
Gradually, my pen begins to add to the contents.

In this amniotic halo, my imagination swims,
Releasing confounded images,
From nests, webs, crevices, fissures, lacunae
Grown over with stagnant brain-cress.
Dim guilt dissolves.
*

Antique sins and recent neglectfulness dissipate,
As the soothing fluid infiltrates the languid hemispheres.
In the near distance, a plaintive saxophone
Massages the ears' clitorises;
They take their sweet, wet time climaxing,
As my waking fears are transposed into sleep-notes.

When I gaze up, from the cryptic script
Crosshatching the page I've just constructed,
The room has filled with animated faces,
Whose antic gestures suggest Reginald Marsh.
Even Dave Brubeck and Stan Kenton
Have abandoned their pervasive signatures,
For frenetic improvisations neither jazz nor classical,
Rather pre-Beatles cheek-to-cheek
From the postadolescent fifties,
Out of which I emerged, like a giant alligator,
From St. Louis's sewer system.

Equanimity, on this very Wednesday,
Loses its cool. Seated in the corner,
Hunched over my open notebook,
An empty wineglass standing sentinel
Beside spare pens, extra spectacles,
I realize how foolish my visage must appear.
What a strange creature sits here,
Among all these vibrant people
Eagerly engaged in verbal foreplay.
What an utter fool,
Dedicated to hermetic verse — his singular purpose.

Abruptly, I gather my accouterment,
Settle my tab, and rush from this renovated station.
Heading out, into the cold March night,
Sweating like a gymnast or boxer
Having recently competed against an adversary,
I enter the unfamiliar environs,
Notebook in hand, knowing, only by rote,
The way back to my motel. Once in the room,
I, a fat, naked monk, again open the book,
To the empty page on which I concentrated, three hours —
Today's Rosetta stone, forever blank.

3/30/83 — [3] (02516)

Charlie Cagle, Pornographer Emeritus

I met a man, once,
A professor of semiotics, rhetoric, and linguistics,
Actually, who, though he claimed
To possess an avowed distaste for bagels and lox,
Could devour cream cheese
By the hour, the pound, the box

And who, for an encore,
Could boast having written eighty-three
Pornographic novels,
Which ran the commissioned gamut,
From S and M and sodomy to basic sixty-nine
And hard-core homosexuality.

Oh, how I admired his versatility.
What a guy, that Charlie Cagle,
Even if I never really did discover,
Until long after my invitation to his campus,
To read my poetry, chat with students,
That his colleagues considered him an obtuse fag.

What a guy! Even now, I shiver,
A poet who, through sweat of his Semitic brow,
Has penned and had published,
By accredited presses, fifteen books of verse,
Trying to imagine anyone,
Let alone Charlie Cagle the Lonely,

Fashioning, from lusty, prurient scratch,
So many perverted words, to order,
Such a canon of airport paperbacks,
At 750 bucks a trick,
Over a ten-year period,
Just to supplement an untenured academic's salary.

Not often, but every now and again,
When I'm away from my blessed family,
Bent on writing another chapter
For the Great American Trauma
Or trying to compose another "Byzantium,"
I focus on Charlie Cagle, the bagel hater,

And smile, envisioning him "pigging out,"
As they say, on the campus,
*

On Sally Cream Cheese,
The apotheosis of all his prepubescent dreams,
Eating out, chowing down
On, his fantasies. I laugh aloud,

Contemplating all that wasted talent,
That incredible, squandered, underpaid erudition,
Languishing at Jezebel State,
Where, no doubt, he yet teaches, to eat,
Since, as he confessed to me,
He'd simply quit turning out fictive trash,

In whose creation he'd so delighted,
For its ability to distract him from his own celibacy,
Because, glutted with submissions,
His publishers had offered only 350 dollars
As an advance on his eighty-fourth novel,
Dr. Bagel Unlox the Secret to a Box of Teenage Cream Cheese.

3/30/83 — [4] (02517)

On the Road, at Passover ^Δ

For Trilogy and Troika,
doves on the wing

Where are my children, tonight?
Sweet Troika and Trilogy,
Where may you be, my blessed progeny?
God, how your absence devastates me!
My distance from you, our silence,
Is a pack of screaming Tanganyikan banshees.
I can't stand the absoluteness of our separation.

Whenever I'm gone from you two,
My thoughts are ragged beggars
Scavenging the urgent crowds, for handouts
That infrequently materialize.
Your faces, in my abstracted gaze,
Are the occasional coppers that drop into my hat,
By accident or as patronizing gratuities.

You, boy, nearly five,
And you, my sweetest daughter, at eight,
Break my desolate peddler's heart.
*

Here I lie, in this sagging motel bed,
So far from home,
A peregrine obliged to moor in foreign ports,
Four nights a week,

As you share your lullaby, your prayers,
With just one half of the pair
That brought you into this timely existence.
Oh, how I despair,
Trying to justify my impoverishment,
Reason why I have been singled out
To ply this wilderness, by myself,

While you're so busy growing up,
By yourselves.
Dearest offspring, boy and girl of mine,
Please realize destiny provides its victims
Few choices, fewer petitions and appeals
To higher divinations. I am what they were:
A goddamn improvident peddler!

Perhaps, one day, when you're both grown
And have children of your own,
You'll know, I hope to a lesser degree,
The awful, impotent emptiness
That sometimes descends on parents
When they realize they're unable
To keep from repeating their own parents' inadequacies,

And you'll forgive me my gross oversights,
The inexcusable neglect I've shown you,
These formative years. God knows
I'd change my lot, in a moment,
If only Job and Moses could shed their clothes,
Wear giddy, indolent Pharaoh's robes.
Children, I love you as God does.

3/30/83 — [5]   (02518)

Alzheimer's Poet

Words, verdant tropes, slender measures,
Growing skyward, in bright profusion,
Seasons past,
*

Erode from the cortical surface, like topsoil
In fields fallowed from neglect
Or by decree. I survey, from the edge,
Nature's phenomenon,

Gazing, abstractedly, at scraggly weeds,
Clover, onion clumps, dandelion galaxies
Crowding out the old rows,
Where growing poetry
Sang the wind, ignited sun and moon,
Scented my endless prairies, with aphrodisiacs
Sweeter than Jamaican mangoes.

My numb ears discern, in the distance,
A gate, on rusted hinges,
Complaining, occasionally, from disuse.
No larks or barn swallows dart
Above this otherwise voiceless desolation.
Suddenly, the silence recognizes my presence
Leaning against the painless barbs,

Invites me in, to walk its gutted ruts.
As I approach its opening,
The rasping gate ceases its tedious whimper,
Speaks to me, in whispers
I once whispered, planting each syllable
By hand, furrow by furrow, on my knees,
In blessed, measured reverence.

Despite the shabby, uneven turf,
My feet assume the ancient earth's rhythm,
Leave behind, each forward step,
A familiar echo of flowing meters
Blown from thrown seeds grown ripe.
All day, I pace, sleeping, the night, outside —
An old sower harvesting his memories.

3/31/83 — [1] (05851)

Aging Paleontologist

Formidable creatures that once inhabited my dreams
Are no longer extant.
*

Perhaps a shower of midlife comets
And meteors entered my outer spheres
And made the clear, thin air
Dense and impure. Possibly, they blocked rays
Emanating from the source of all purpose,
Caused dreaming's magnificent beasts
To weaken, decrease in size,
Rely on more modest prospects, to survive
Their altered environment.

Even primordial nightmares
Pose no threat to my equanimity;
Only postdiluvian species infest their jungles,
Bayous, woods, and swamps:
Chameleons, snakes, worms, turtles, crocodiles.
Nothing outsize or enigmatic remains,
From my early days, when every venture out
Was a new threat and challenge
And curiosity could be sated
By discovering strange phenomena, at every turn
Of phrase. Today, I stand at the edge,

Peering into youth's tarpits,
Wishing I knew a way to exhume giants
Who used to roam my imagination at will.
Every fossil I come upon
Is a metaphor too brittle to remove intact.

3/31/83 — [2] (05852)

A Post-Easter Resurrection

As I enter the café,
A vaguely strange, empty voice petitions me,
Inquires, facetiously,
Whether my shadowy somnambulism
Is a waking state or sleep's perpetuation.

I respond as though peering back at Earth.
My wobbly answer is a light-year
Lapsing 7.8 minutes,
From cortical hemisphere to the nearest ear.
My next closest revelation

Will be four years late, this morning,
If it arrives at all.
My drowsy brain is a swirling vortex
Suspended in skull space,
Whose nightmarish miasma is a lava flow

In slowing slow motion; molten thoughts
Turn cold, on leaving their crater.
I am sky and ground simultaneously,
Erupting banked image-showers,
Raining dry ideas

Down onto the ruled page by my coffee,
Below me, on the rectangle
Circumscribing my entire universe.
Suddenly, accouterment floating in vision's ocean
Becomes continental landmasses:

Amber, patterned ashtray is Africa,
Pepper shaker Australia;
Asia and Europe are water glass
And coffee cup, saucered on a soiled napkin;
Clumped silverware is the Americas,

And I am Prince Henry of Farmington,
No Renaissance genius weighing anchor,
This first day after Easter,
Or latter-day saint
Or martyr but a humble navigator,

Trying to pass, safely, through the straits
Defined by Simile and Metaphor,
Without breaking up on reefs
Surrounding Cliché Bay
Or luffing, indefinitely, in the Sea of Tedium.

Previously a mere meager Sunday poet,
I realize cartographic skills
Dormant in me until this hour.
Possibly, I'll spend my world-without-end
Mapping Dreaming's undiscovered keys,

Redrawing obsolete dimensions
Previously attributed to Fantasy's inlets and coves,
*

Straightening curves, rounding off squares.
Abruptly, I arise from my booth, fly from the café,
And enter the sunny day, empty-handed.

4/4/83 (05853)

Cracow Now ^Δ

Defeated, exiled, indefensibly committed,
Those dispensable souls
Relegated to the ghetto in Cracow:
Bankers, Talmudic scholars, grocers, musicians,
Strict, disciplined family men,
Whose reverential Leahs, Rachels, Miriams
Bore, in pride, brilliant children —
Now ghosts guiding wheelbarrows,
Filled with bedsheets and pillows,
From cultured sanctums to cluttered hovels,
The metamorphosis of three centuries,
Accomplished in months: Jew to lice to typhus.
The Madagascar Plan,
An abstract Max Beckmann canvas
Gessoed over with troops invading snowy Russia —
Hitler's untimely gluttony,
Bringing to a too-swift, irreversible conclusion
The Final Solution, for the fragile tribes
Confined to reservations bearing names
Neither Linnaeus nor Darwin could have contrived,
Varieties of the Venus's-flytrap:
Auschwitz, Treblinka, Belzec,
Chelmno, Majdanek, Sobibor.
Merely writing their bleak syllables makes me weep.
Each is a puff of coughing stench
Escaping crematory stacks
Punctuating the skylines comprising my verse,
Each a caesura too frequently repeated.

This morning, forty years down the road,
The measures of my sanity fade into the cacophony.
Today, I, too, as messenger for the dispossessed,
Wearing a *J* on my brain-band,
*

Push my worldly belongings — paltry words —
In a rickety wheelbarrow, across the years,
Toward precarious lodging in *your* ears' ghetto.

4/8/83 (00084)

Jugiter novus

April is my future in its pubescence.
Trees just budding
Are teenage females
Shyly noticing "peach fuzz" glowing on their legs,
Lips, and arms, and jocks, in locker rooms,
Boasting newly acquired "tassels."

What astounding discoveries,
These monumental ephemeralities,
A recent season each, a climacteric,
The passing of civilizations, in a generation,
Daily, change and stasis
Adversaries, in perpetual disagreement,

Whose dialectic is both nadir and zenith
Of life and death, simultaneously,
Every step ahead progenitor of its own retreat.
Even as I go south,
I sense my soul's shadows,
Oblique memories, flying back up the road,

Refusing to share in the terrible pains
Growing inherently demands
From soldiers, crusaders, bedouins, builders,
Blackguards, and poets.
I pause, my eyes caught up in net-hues —
Tyrian purples of early redbuds,

Adolescent mauves, tawny beiges,
A sporadic stippling of white dogwoods —
Lingering, finally, on soft greens
Everywhere seething, breaking open,
Leaking, spewing, bathing me in their newness.
I am, today, tomorrow's ancestor and scion.

4/9/83 (05854)

The Untimely Affliction of an O'Neill Poet

His fingers are icicles,
Static suspensions
Incapable of radiating the brain's emanations,
Wands bereft of magical abracadabras,
Jaws of an autopen
Frozen, permanently, on the ghostly space
Where, once, his trope-stick danced.

He can't imagine what might have caused
Such white frigidity,
Brought about poor circulation,
Or fathom the metaphorical etiology
Of his blood's distress.
He's had adequate rest, lately,
No social pressures, business disasters.

In fact, just last week,
Convinced of posterity's beckoning nod,
On the strength of recent magazine acceptances,
He ordered a word processor,
To assist his acquiescent muse,
In initiating new clues to intractable sophistries,
Spare him creativity's fundamental tedium.

Now, faced with this perplexing crisis,
Unable to write, make verse issue
From his stiffly gripped pen,
He tries to decide what, next, to attempt.
Slowly, he slumps over his desk,
Knowing, in one perpetual moment,
The inutterable hopelessness his stroke forebodes.

4/12/83 — [1] (05855)

Making One's Mark

Ignorance is a well-lubricated slug,
Whose scintillating tracks
Flash, a hundred suns loud.

Under its own persuasive intoxication,
It slides over words so eloquent,
Meaning is lost between its lines.

Byzantine thoughts arise, shimmer,
Are squeezed dry and left behind.
Ambiguity crisscrosses ambivalence.

Paradox bisects irony,
Until those close enough to focus on the whole
Notice there's no design to the flow.

In fact, it manifests a disturbing drift,
As if bent on luring the senses
Into a dense smoke screen,

A clear obfuscation, leaving no traces,
Save the scintillating tracks
Burnished across the eyes inside the deceived and the stupefied.

4/12/83 — [2] (05856)

Baptismal Rite

The morning's voice is serene and tranquil,
Shaded in synonymous nuance,
As if my ears might actually distinguish
The murmurous greening, everywhere yawning,
From redbuds' purple-pink singing,
Strophe and antistrophe
Reiterating, between dogwoods and forsythias,
From responsive readings
Proceeding among sparrows, robins, and jays.

There's a blending of all spring things,
This gentle, April-scented day,
That begs my senses awaken,
Leave off their self-centering,
Come to a complete stop,
Suspend their tensions, in the momentary alembic,
And surrender to the cleansing.
At first tentatively, then with eagerness,
I enter my eyes, immerse myself completely,

Until seeing and hearing become the voice
Speaking the earth's sweetest secrets I breathe.

4/13/83 — [1] (05857)

A Gift of Time ^Δ

Driving I-55, south,
I weave the tedious hours into a lanyard
With which to gift my mistress,
Mississippi, on greeting her,
Later this April-rainy afternoon.

I braid the subtly changing strands,
With an artificer's nimble-handed precision,
Alternating green with silver,
Silver with green, in dizzy, crisscrossing sequence,
Whose susurration is the music of uprootedness.

The rain's varying rhythmic densities,
Pelting windshield, rising from the tires,
Shimmering amidst the vernal hues
Filling the distant landscape,
As I cruise past Sikeston, toward Memphis,

Rather than confusing vision,
Appear to enhance the necromantic design,
Defining itself mile by mile by mile.
The lanyard expands lengthwise,
As if on divine consignment to me, God's artisan.

Hour after arachnid hour,
It continues to devour my concentration.
The closer I get to Oxford,
The more complete becomes my woven creation,
The greater grows my anticipation

Of knotting and clipping its superfluous residue,
Cauterizing it into a seamless silver-green necklace
I'll slip over my naked lady's head.
Suddenly, I glimpse her emerging from the woods.
She already knows what I've brought her.

4/13/83 — [2] (00153)

Blown off Course ^Δ

Navigational cruise control engaged,
Radar, sonar, occasional radio music
Suffusing my hemispheres as I sail south,
*

Past Luxora, Victoria, Osceola,
Under a moody, tornado-frustrated sky,

I begin to quiver and twitch,
As if every nerve were a halyard
Drawn typhoon-taut,
Poised to deliver a massive whiplash
To my sparrow heart.

A sharp-edged lightning barb
Scratches a permanent scar across my cornea,
Startles me out of my drowsiness.
My ship veers off course,
Into the murky waves buffeting sea lanes,

Then rights itself, returns to its channel
As though by ghostly divination.
Sporadic rain intensifies,
Transforms into a continuous deluge, shreds my sheets
Like shot pocking Yankee flags.

For the next half-hour,
My vessel remains inextricably fixed
In a petroleum tanker's backwashing draft.
I'm unable to pass, for crosshatched vision.
My lungs breathe its diesel reek,

Fight to prevent hyperventilation,
By sending my brain chasing lunatic hallucinations.
Lepanto, Jericho, West Memphis flicker,
Retreat phosphorescently.
Now, without reason, I head westerly,

Toward Hughes, Forrest City, Marianna,
Neither escaping from nor embracing demons,
Rather permanently off course, lost at sea,
Tied to the mast, gasping, about to drown —
Ishmael up to his neck in misdirection.

4/13/83 — [3] (03507)

In Flood Time ^Δ

Crossing the bridge at Helena, Arkansas,
I see, beneath me,
*

The ink blotter it spans,
Oozing out, beyond both banks, perniciously,
As though someone had spilled an entire sky
Of India-ink or sepia nightmares into its channel.

For miles on end,
Fields bordering Old Man glisten.
Water malingers, ubiquitously, in creeks, gullies,
Runoffs. Last year's furrows
Are mere finger-paint smears
On the murky Delta's unearthly surface.

This mid-April, this mid-South
Is no place to be contemplating planting.
In fact, its intractable flatness rejects the thought,
With seditious viciousness.
Far beneath, the great cloaca
Refuses to absorb and funnel one more sedimentary ton.

And yet, as I drive toward Clarksdale,
Turn east, in the direction of Oxford,
Mississippi, I realize the land,
Like its vassals,
Hasn't a chance at either succeeding or failing,
By its own plan or hand.

It, they must pray and wait
For May, when, by God's grace,
Irrigation will have run its course,
Scratched its inky signature across every deed,
Marking all old debts "PAID,"
Persuading Demeter to accept the new season's seeds.

Passing through this extended bayou,
I'm reminded of the Mariner's curse: to drown in thirst.
Here, the reverse obtains:
Earth, earth, everywhere earth;
Not a clod to turn! Worse,
Rain's in the forecast, and sporadic flash flooding.

4/14/83 — [1] (03508)

Admiration for the Man Who Admired Faulkner ^Δ

Decay infiltrates my nostrils —
That pervasive reek of cancerous flesh
Being eaten from the inside out. I wince,
Gasp for precious breath,
While trying to perpetuate amenities,
Not stifle conversation about chief surgeons,
Catheters, chemotherapy. My replies
Die in their own choking silence.

On visiting Oxford eight years ago,
We'd come, first, to meet him.
Then, the house and porch
Were antiseptic, pristine, and quaint.
He, by then curator of Rowan Oak,
Spoke anecdotally of his famous former neighbor;
His wife applauded his recitation.
We were enchanted. It was all so spotless.

I squirm as his wife applauds medical anecdotes
She's heard three dozen times, recently,
Refusing to intrude, to factualize
A piece of intended truth the drugs distort
Or cue a forgotten line or two.
The screens are pushed out, curtains torn;
Dust has accumulated.
A shabby pallor has invested the house, with gloom.

That first trip, my wife and I
Were untainted, too, with our six-month-old girl, Trilogy.
They delighted so,
Knowing we'd journeyed that distance,
To appreciate, linger over, appropriate their heritage,
By wishing to visit their folk hero's domain.
He reveled in showing us the home,
With legerdemain, as though he owned it himself.

Before I go, he invites me back
To the converted bedroom
That stores his books, files, artifacts —
*

His thirty-five years of academic desiderata.
I pause before his most treasured possession
And stare at the austere portrait of the writer
He admires, reciting the inscription for him,
Which Faulkner once penned, in black ink, on the mat.

* * *

Two days ago, I received word,
From someone at the university, that he had died,
Two weeks prior. Even now, I see him,
Inviting us in, eight years ago,
My wife and child and me, mere strangers
In that moment only. Now, I cry
For the man I grew, over time, to admire
Not just for his admiration of the writer I've also admired.

4/14–15/83 — [2] on 4/14 & [3] on 4/15   (03521)

Seeking a Change of Venue ^Δ

Halfway through April,
This country's trees have awakened from sleep,
Begun their greening. Glens, forests are peacocks
Haughtily preening dogwood dazzlements,
Stipple-dappling the eye pink and white.

Only somnolent kudzu,
Barely perceptible, for its charcoal drapes
Clinging thinly to the landscape,
Like Louisiana Spanish moss,
Has failed to assume blooming tumescence.

As I head toward Memphis, from Oxford,
Metaphor transports my sordid spirit
Through a series of hallucinatory orbits,
Each circling the same core:
Northern Mississippi.

I am, in various earthly guises,
Jewel and Lucius, Henry, Quentin and Joe,
And sixteen-year-old Ike.
I am, at forty-two, an adolescent
Lacking requisites necessary to set myself free

Yet needing prescience, humor, and courageousness,
To find my way into,
Not out of, the darkling woods,
Locate truth's numinous luminosity,
Looming, like giant stallions and bears, in the gloom.

For too many decades already,
My psyche has refused to do blood rites,
Neglected tribal sacrifices,
Conspired, with society, to hide in its soft folds,
Like chlamydia undetected by its host.

I've paraded naked, fully clothed,
In broad daylight, gone by two names
Simultaneously —
Benbow/Bond — an intellectual moron
Groping for a solution to my own ambiguity,

A nexus from the edge, into the depths,
Where growing up and focusing in
Converge on intuition
And loving someone other than self
Becomes the heart's single passion and purpose.

I've pondered these bleak and dire requirements
Entirely too long,
Without being able to reconcile or conclude
Their seeming irresoluteness.
Perhaps this is why I drive to Mississippi,

With such frequency: to ask its phantoms
To judge me without the harsh partiality
I display in sentencing myself,
Have them praise my reprobate soul,
Accept my meager profligate's ego, without provisos.

4/15/83 — [1] (03543)

Wisteria ^Δ

As I approach the "Missouri State Line" sign,
Just miles beyond Blytheville,
Three hours north of Oxford,
My eyes focus, proximately,
Not on the great white segmented worm
Stretching out endlessly ahead

But on the purple, wilted sprig of wisteria
Perched on the dashboard —
Ghostly Mississippi I picked, yesterday,
While visiting Rowan Oak,
Loitering beneath its formal cedars,
Leaning against random magnolias and dogwoods,

Beguiled by mid-April's crystal twilight
Slipping past evergreen boughs
Scratching the sky's glassy fenestration.
I lift the twig, inhale its thick-dripping, sickly liquors,
Through sinus ducts leading to brain vents.
Emily Grierson appears in the mirage before me,

Not a gray-haired, wizened, haggish spinster
But ravishing mistress in gay brocades,
Waving to me even as her diaphanous shape
Continues to diminish into a past
Whose future never seems to arrive,
No matter how much faster I drive.

Perhaps we met, last evening,
Dined with nothing save wine and candle-flicker
Separating our penetrating gazes,
Then made our strangers' nakedness
Shameless friends, for ages.
Maybe the too-sweet ethers vex my memory.

Unused to such perplexing dilemmas, I weary,
Wondering whether, by a reversal of fate's worm-screw,
I actually might have died, last night,
Or if, instead, the highway I drive, now,
Could be the wedding bed
Mississippi's succubus sleeps in, by day.

4/15/83 — [2] (02067)

One Out of Six Million

At what point he entered the void,
Became the point,
Eviscerated all antecedent penetrations
Refuses public scrutiny,
Loses itself, in diffusive philo-syllogisms.

His invisibility, this too-sunny morning,
Is nowhere more apparent
Than in the words he tries to set free,
To bribe immortality, with diamonds —
Hide-and-seek victims, bound for Gross-Rosen,

His mind's Cracovian *Aktionen* expose,
In word-scourges imposed on his ghettoed dignity.
His deloused poems huddle naked,
Waiting for Teutonic razors
To shave their pubic hair and armpits,

Render them fit for pyres and crematories,
From whose putrescent stench
No phoenixes will rise nor survivors' cries
Be recycled into rhyme-lives . . .
Ah, but not until they've defied time,

One lacerating syllable after another,
Albeit with stuttering mutters
From articulating Zyklon B showers . . .
Not until their verses are buried alive,
In mass chasms fluting the air, like salt domes.

He stares directly into the homicidal sun.
In a last lucid flash,
His flesh and bones, blistered, blasted, atomized,
Pass back through the void,
Rejoin youth's jubilant, cultivated voices,

As though no *shtetl*, ghetto,
Or Holocaust ever erupted from daymares.
Suddenly, he sees himself atop Mount Sinai,
On his knees, piecing together the shattered tablets,
Reciting his own stone-poems, to the Philistines.

4/19/83 (00088)

[Willy has driven this highway] [†]

Willy has driven this highway

4/28/83 — [1] (08595)

Seduced by April's Lesbians

Reaching out to seize vision, by its rods and cones,
From nature's spacious grots
Along both sides of the highway
My eyes drive, redbuds,
Vibrantly fuchsia, muted lavender, mauve,
Growing like deep-sea corals,
Arrest my forward motion,
Slow my bones, in hasty escape
From terra cognita, to mime-time.

Like tiny, imitation plants of Chinese jade,
Each leaf fastened and wired, by hand,
These extravagant cantilevers
Lean toward my passing vehicle,
Distract me, by their brittle shimmering.
Unable to maintain concentration,
I stop on the shoulder, flow into the frame.
As I near, the sheer purple smear
Dissolves into dotted blossoms — God's pointillism.

For moments, hours, eons, indeterminate equivalents,
I stand among lissome redbuds,
Snapping twigs, sniffing sweet fragrances,
Drowsing, in soporific exultation
Adumbrated by my own ineffable adoration
For April's graceful ladies,
Who are possessed of lacy salaciousness.
Suddenly envious, lusty, I undress, run naked,
An incarnation of their lesbian possessiveness.

4/28/83 — [2] (05858)

The Fate of Nations, Their Industry and
   People

After all these years
Of boasting a favorable balance of trade,
Why have you voluntarily opted
To lift our hearts' mutually agreed-upon embargo,
Dispense with every restriction?

Why have you consented to permit foreigners
To intervene, compete, with cheap innuendos,
Artificial subsidies and incentives,
Calculated to capture, temporarily,
Market shares glaringly precarious,

Within a system we perfected,
Then let grow slumberous and inefficient,
For haphazard practices
We complacently perpetuated, from neglect
And a gradual relaxation of standards, for personal satisfaction?

Why have you resorted to breaking price,
Compromising privacy, passion, and lasting gratitude,
Allowed outside parties to bargain for your heart,
Even though the tarnish on our dreams
Might have been wiped clean?

Now that we've set the dates, placed ads
For our "Going Out of Business" sale,
Consigned our lares and penates
To public liquidation,
Refused to impose minimums on willed memories,

The apparent reason for the reversal surfaces:
It seems I, not you,
Refused to interpret and reevaluate our need
To stay ahead of the amortization schedules
We vowed to honor, at the outset,

By frequently updating the intellect's apparatus,
Tightening the body's slackening tolerances.
Too late, I realize why
You finally agreed to entertain new resources:
It was time to phase out my obsolete designs.

4/28/83 — [3] (04161)

Miasmic Chiasmas

All these years,
Despite his seer's insights,
He's not realized, until this crisis,
*

That the mirror into whose surface he peers
Is the paper on which he writes verse
His uncertain cursive nurtures,
In successive drafts curiosity erases
And replaces, a line at a time,
Across the reflective face he now recognizes
Not as God's but as his own.

No wonder the object he fixes
Has always appeared so inexplicable.
He's never learned to reverse its flow,
Right its upside-down images,
Focus all edges, angles, contours, wedges
Contained by and containing
Imagination's silver-flecked retinas.
Today, composing his own epitaph,
He's finally seen himself complete, in the glass,
Watching it change, from paper, to stone.

5/2/83   (02098)

Between Seasons $^\Delta$

Even Willy, whose major preoccupation,
These forty years,
Has consisted of road-peddling closeouts,
For Acme-Zenith Clothing,
Of St. Louis, Mo., can't concentrate,
Train his tactical strategies on retail merchants
He's faithfully served for decades
And with whom, today, he has appointments to keep,
In Moberly and Jefferson City.

He can't focus on wholesale surplus,
Broken and odd lots, overstocks,
Off-priced seconds, can't cope with smiling
While writing fill-in orders
For three-piece banker's- and business-stripe suits,
Navy, tan, brown, and gray
Brass-button blazers, basic dress slacks
In 100 percent–polyester Madison fabrication —
Tin lizzies of the menswear industry.

It's not that there's no more gold to be mined
From played-out shafts;
Rather, between seasons,
Twice each year, he gets restive.
He can almost sense callow oats,
Sown in youth's Festus, Tipton, Salisbury,
St. Joe, Dexter, Cape Girardeau,
Trying to grow in his fallowness,
Distract him from habit's calling, in need of weeding.

With summer merchandise paid for,
Crowding store floors, selling through,
And fall's bookings put to bed,
This lush May rounds-making for reorders
Never fails to take its toll on Willy.
Something about leaves unfolding,
Tumid, juicy grasses exploding,
Sucking in the sun's yellow-green fulgence,
Primes his plump, slovenly body for love.

Sometimes, it's the college females
He can't help ogling, in Kirksville, Columbia,
Whose naturally casual voluptuousness
Awakens his carnal fantasies,
Causes barnacles to loosen their hold
On the base of his brain's scuttled scow.
At other times, like this morning,
It takes little more than mellow warmth
To trigger his desires for reincarnation,

Another go-round, a Second Coming,
As, not exactly in jest, he puts it,
Testing the depths of his suppressed intellect
Whenever being the entertaining guest,
Made to play Captain Queeg, Shylock,
On B.P.O.E. stages,
Troubadour to every rube audience,
Whose caterwauling curtain calls he observes
With obliquely obsequious bows,

Knowing, finally, as he's known, always,
That in the beginning, fate assigned him
One of her lesser destinies,
*

Mandated that in the celestial pantheon,
He, Willy Sypher, would be made to endure
Ordinariness,
In Semitic resignation
Not so much to history's fickle penchant for holocausts
But, a cut above, mere bigotry,

Hoping someday to transcend, through ambition,
Routine that wombs, in sweet numbness,
His unremarkable genealogy, and knowing, finally,
That at about this same impasse, twice yearly,
Each crisp fall, concupiscent spring,
He'll be required to assess his attributes,
Question his blessed necessariness,
And renew his faith in peddling raiment
As a way to the kingdom, the Kingdom.

5/4/83 — [1] (00083)

[Who has ever shared another's solitude?]

Who has ever shared another's solitude?
I ask you, point-blank
(Whatever that ancient saw implies,
Or is it "denotes"?).
No matter the adequate, the satisfactory, phrase,
I must apologize for coming to you
In such a miasma, doldrum, funk, as I do —
A crusty pedagogue,
Who's too long had belletristic concerns,
Instead of stew-in-the-pot,
Dewey-infused pragmatic absolutism,
Rolling around in his stately-pleasure-dome head.

I come to you, naked, begging absolution,
For having ravaged you with useless poetry,
Metaphorical rhetoric,
Conceits, hyperboles, cosmic paeans to your beauty,
God, lesser deities, and earthly heroes
And (oh, don't let me neglect them)
Heroines: Clara Barton, Carrie Nation,
And, to be sure, Jane Fonda
And her eclectic, electric, aerobic horseman.
*

I come to you, in your disillusionment,
Unable to excuse myself for having failed to tame
My raging chimeras, keep them at bay.

Now, you and I sleep in separate bedrooms,
See psychiatrists regularly,
Visit Sri Lanka, Oxford, Skagway,
Ocho Rios, on a moment's whim,
After scavenging the Sunday paper's travel section,
For a salutary nexus to Panacea.
We share each other's passion for solitude,
Enter the radio's classical station
As if wading into an endless ocean,
And drown in our profound unhappiness.
Why we persist in loving one another
Is destiny's guess. Our separation would devastate the universe.

5/4/83 — [2] (02519)

Objects Oppositely Attracted Positively Repel

My drives are tied to right and left hemispheres,
Not the spine's primal base,
To dreams, fantasies, fugues, hallucinations
(A brain-typhoon uprooting my psyche,
At right angles to reason),
Not a libido-rain
Fanning, instead of slaking, burning bushes,
Perpetual flames, upstart brush fires
Igniting, erratically, across my heart's dry plain.

I am metaphor-crazed,
Not a sex maniac, purveyor of pleasures
Oral, anal — erotically provocative.
My desires are neither easily aroused
Nor surfeited by drowsy fornication,
Lascivious carousing, devouring, by the hour,
Kiwis and nectarines dangling from clitoris trees.
To nurture them requires eternities.
One word is worth five million sperms.

Yet all my life, I've speculated on why,
When chromosomes were divided,
*

Originally, I was meted out
Only sufficient X's, Y's, and Z's
To permit me two corporeal issue,
Little bodily spontaneity, even less
Physical prowess, why my destiny
Was to copulate with goddesses,
Procreate tropes and strophes, sire poems,

Not be allotted
More easily achieved goals,
Realizable and felicitous ambitions, needs
An individual might satisfy
Without first acquiring specialized degrees
In fable, myth, parable.
As it stands, I am what I *am*,
A poetry man dancing on quicksand,
Shouting apologies as I drown in your disillusionment.

5/14/83 — [1] (04160)

Guilty Until Proven Innocent ^Δ

A red-winged blackbird
Lifts, precipitously, from a soggy field
Contiguous to vision's periphery,
Swoops into view, level with my windshield,
Shimmers before being sucked back miraculously,
Just as my fleet vehicle slices, in two,
Its uncompleted flight pattern.

I cringe at this averted collision,
As if witnessing, firsthand,
The *Hindenburg* mooring at Hades' cracking stack
Or the *Titanic* slipping into pelagic oblivion,
Before reminding myself history's sentries
Only guard the front and rear portcullises
Of time's fortress, not its interior.

Although neither ponderable nor prophetic,
This near miss persists fifty miles.
That fate considered implicating me in murder
Places me in the quizzical position
Of having to compose this brief,
*

In my own defense, against a felony
I never even intended to commit.

5/14/83 — [2] (00098)

Going to Oversee a Store Closing

For Faye Wallace

Listen . . . listen . . . it's in the distance,
Invisible yet persistent,
As I near Memphis, slowly approach Hughes,
Press toward West Helena. A low moaning
Sets up its vector. I adjust my compass
And home in on its ululating frequency.

There it goes again. Can't you hear it?
The wind's soliloquy? Death's breath?
Or is it my sluggish blood,
Shooting, through constricted vascular passages,
Toward the heart's Charybdis?
Maybe it's the Dark Prince's hissing sibilance.

Whatever that sound, those cloyed voices,
The noise grows to pandemonium's shrill,
As I close in on my destination.
For weeks, I've been dreading this confrontation
With those gentle people
Who've worked for me, these seven years.

Suddenly, I can smell their swelling chest-rattles
Wafting, as if from a dank, dung-infested cave,
In my direction — that unmistakable odor
The flesh articulates, on its way graveward.
They're lamenting my arrival.
I am fire, pestilence, famine; their knelling is my plague.

5/14/83 — [3] (02362)

Out of Desperation

Saturday evening, in an empty restaurant
Three hundred thirty-three miles
*

South of home, alone,
Sipping Chablis, listening as Don McLean's voice,
Drifting through recessed speakers,
Is sliced by wood-slatted brass ceiling fans,
He tries to imagine himself elsewhere,
Unsuccessfully. He's definitely
Situated in West Helena, Arkansas, for the night.

Waiting for a Kansas City strip steak
(Very rare), baked potato
(No sour cream; butter on the side),
He reprises the Biblical nature of his visitation:
The nearly seven good years
His business has flourished in this community,
To be followed by who knows how many lean ones,
Now that he's arrived to dismantle the name
They've labored, tooth and nail, to build.

Previously, all his experience
As manager of outlet stores, for Acme-Zenith Clothing,
Was gleaned in the service of progress,
Not backsliding, deterioration.
He takes this "cutting of losses,"
As the front office has termed it, in their memo
To their board of directors, personally —
A blemish on his professional integrity,
Misdirection of his efforts.

"A matter of numbers," they relayed to him.
He sips, from his third sweaty glass,
The sweet nectars that, by now,
Have begun to eviscerate his aching heart,
Deaden his memory of the many trips he's made,
Christmases celebrated with his staff,
Congratulatory phone conversations
(On rainy, snowy, or humid days)
Filled with praises for exceeding sales highs.

Supper materializes and disappears,
Without his physical acknowledgment. He touches nothing,
Rather calls, brusquely, for another wine,
Then another, and a sixth,
Until the music emanating from the connecting bar
Nets his depressive spirit, magnetizes him,
*

With its blatant laughter. He changes places casually,
Steers toward a corner seat, beside a lady
Who gives him a clearing to land.

They share their collective desolation like old pros.
She rehearses her worldly dissatisfactions.
He mumbles something about failure,
Which she misconstrues for deprivations
And duties she can provide. Her hand on his pant leg,
Smoothing and resmoothing, persuades him
She is a person of her word.
They stay until the band cases its instruments,
Then navigate the threadbare carpet

Complicating the otherwise straight path to his room.
She leads the way, feels for his key,
Holds open the door, for his tangled torso
To penetrate, then enters all but naked,
Before he can even extricate his left hand from its cuff.
When he awakens beside strange, sagging breasts,
A flabby body garnished in pubic hair,
Past the bellybutton, he starts,
Aware that he's erred amnesiacally.

The wake-up call resurrects him from death.
She stirs, rolls slowly over,
Gentles him into erection,
With steady stroking. He falls back, submits,
As though today had dawned years ago,
Without credentials or history.
He performs his best oral sex on her,
Then suggests they shower, dress, separate,
That he might complete his appointed task:

To conduct final inventory, load unsold goods
Into his station wagon, say good-byes,
Depart without disclosing his guilt.
Time telescopes him binocularly,
Until the highway he drives home
Swallows him, in its fine focus.
For three hundred thirty-three miles,
He ponders the demise not only of his outlet store
But his morals — family man that he was.

5/14/83 — [4] (02361)

Inundation $^\Delta$

This Sunday, on which I leave West Helena,
Take to the highway home,
Marks May's exact midpoint.
Such lush puberty touches my eyes first:
Magnolias, weeping willows, spireas —
Anomalies so green,
One might never fathom
The weird stirrings at their submerged feet.

But the fields are turbulent,
Many of them murky oceans and seas,
After this incontinent season's flash floods.
Even undulant acres of rice
Are frustrated, unable to hold seed.
One more storm, and the entire Delta
May dissolve into primordial swamplands
Fit for wading stegosaurs and diplodocuses.

Driving east, out of Marianna,
I see trailers, tractors, shacks, churches
Floating on the earth's surface,
Like toys in stagnant bathtub water.
I pass Soudan, enter Hughes,
Reach Highway 40, then turn north, up I-55,
Trying to let forgetting dry the wetness
From memory. The trickling persists.

How curious to have witnessed all these fields
So glutted with rain,
One could almost fish them, with bamboo poles,
Especially when, tangibly, I can recall
These same lands, last July and August,
Begging for precious precipitation,
Dehydrating, shriveling beneath the scald,
Like slugs sprinkled with salt.

5/15/83 — [1] (02066)

May Stocktaking $^\Delta$

Snakes dispossessed of their nests prematurely,
Levees tested, fire ants let loose,
*

Fields backed up, like clogged sewers,
With sediment, sludge, silt,
Entire commercial districts desolate, on Saturday —

The mid-South winces under such oppressiveness.
About the only businesses flourishing
Are fishing, with crickets and minnows
On bamboo sticks, and church,
With Baptist emphasis on the Baptist persuasion.

All other preoccupations, professions, hobbies
Take secondary and tertiary places,
In this season-oriented civilization,
Where livelihood and survival are measured, alike,
In bushels or bales per acre, inches of rainfall.

Still, despite modern suppressive techniques,
The land's most exportable commodity
Remains bigotry. Neither cotton nor beans
Can encroach, supplant its hold over a market
Dominated by "traditional values and morality."

Not even Wendy's, McDonald's, herpes,
The carpetbagging chicken Colonel,
Food stamps, Social Security, boll weevils,
Or mandatory retirement for the dead
Can compete with dyed-in-the-khaki black skin.

Negroes prove, daily, by acts and deeds,
That there actually are levels of poverty,
Degrees of squalor, classes among the classless,
Nuances, shades, hues, gradations
To be distinguished, within the all-black rainbow.

One generation after the next
Is born mortgaged, repossessed,
Auctioned into Egypt, emancipated.
On hands and knees, each crawls toward the Jordan,
Canaan, and Beulahland,

Without escaping farther than Helena, Clarksdale,
Marks, Ruleville, Hughes, and Soudan.
Although June planting, July blooms, August harvest
Cancel all debts, blur distinctions,
Inspire respect, through September's end,

When white men reinvent God's covenant,
Interpret Scripture, to exculpate themselves,
Blame society's ills on the Ethiop,
This May, the earth seems oddly concerned,
As though it knows the rains are not going to abate.

5/15/83 — [2] (03510)

Flying Swine

Colossal, white-gleaming, red-striped machines,
Retreating from glorious airborne soaring,
Congregate, between flights,
At this concrete, cantilevered, kerosene-cloyed beacon,
Like very pink, squealing piglets
Seeking feeding, at convenient, omnipotent teats.

Nearby, barrows and gilts, boars and sows,
Exotic breeds intermixed, not too proud
To be seen eating out of the same trough —
L-1011s, DC-9s
And -10s, 747 jumbo jets,
Wide-bodied, stout-bellied, snub-snouted.

At varying intervals, with minimal disturbance,
They nourish, fill themselves, to bursting,
Then lumber away from Earth,
Scurrying about the pen, over paths
Densely worn, while the piglets race, play, leap,
Occasionally, achieving the grace of flying machines.

5/25/83 (05859)

Lines Composed Beside the River Coln,
at Bibury

For Jan,
my companion in travels

Listening to the crisp-whispering Coln
Trip past the creeper-covered Swan Hotel,
Under a cloud-plied Bibury sky
*

The dimming Gloucestershire sun
Scroll-saws into gingerbread,
To adorn vision's twin mantelpieces,
I shimmer. Inspiration and exhalation
Seem so serenely medieval,
In this built-stone-by-stone weavers' village.

I have come by way of bustling London,
Through densely trampled Windsor,
Spent far too few hours
Musing on drowsy Christ Church's meadows,
Staring into Balliol's and Merton's courtyards,
Lost in belletristic relics
On display at the Bodleian: Shelley's guitar,
Looking glass, cherubic portrait, and manuscripts;
Shakespeare's First Folio; the Magna Carta.

My journey has taken me into the Cotswolds,
Via Woodstock, Bladon, and Broadway,
To Stratford-upon-Avon,
Where, yet, the bard has the last word first,
From his burial church to preserved birthplace.
My senses have swelled, with delicate smells
Of lilac, wisteria, horse chestnut,
Whose lavender, fuchsia, and white hues
Pollinate my voluptuous sleep, with lush dreaming.

I have even climbed an insane spiral,
To the top of Guy's Tower,
Where, for a fleet hour, as castle guard,
I surveyed Warwick's sheep-strewn scape,
Without sighting invading armies,
Before descending, with my dizziness intact,
To its peacocks, greens-kept lawns,
Beauchamp staterooms, then drove away,
Past Leycester Hospital, by the town's West Gate.

And yet, for all my leisurely peripatetics,
Only now, sitting outside,
By the slender, trout-crowded Coln,
Gazing, vacantly, at the roadside sign
Posting Cirencester six miles distant,
Have I begun to hear England running in my veins.
*

I am the Wye, Avon, majestical Thames,
Circulating through New Jerusalem.
Her blood and mine ebb together, heavenward.

6/1/83 (05860)

Lacock

In this tiny Wiltshire village at Lacock,
Nestled in the misted hills
Between Chippenham and Melksham,
Where Queen Silence reigns,
Beyond history's interregnum,
We visit eleventh-century St. Cyriac
And Fox Talbot's abbey,
Walking, in awe, amnesiacally,
Amidst paths thick with white cow parsley.

Later, we submit our tired spirits
And weary bodies to the care of innkeepers,
At the Sign of the Angel,
A canting, half-timbered, sagging, slate-roofed
Wool-merchant's house. Enchanted,
We slip, fast, through the dank chill,
Over creaking floorboards, into bed,
Steadily draw up five hundred years,
About our heads, and let England's dead souls awaken.

6/3/83 (05861)

[There is, about this secluded purlieus,] †

There is, about this secluded purlieus,
A certain placidity
I've nowhere else in my travels achieved.

Birds seem undisturbed;
They reiterate concertos and sonatas

6/4/83 (05862)

By the Avon, at Salisbury, Being Bespelled

By the banks of the Avon, at Salisbury, I sit,
Partaking of an idyllic scape
So anachronistic,
No listener of mine ever would incline
To believe my vivid description,

And yet it does exist, all of it,
Every word a prismatic surrogate, I swear,
Each a paltry articulation of visions,
Calculated to set dust motes to music,
Imprison picturesque images.

Gliding straight, then bending,
Obliquely, to my right, beneath St. Nicholas Bridge,
The River Avon awakens my senses
To my own dynamic silence.
Its swift current mirrors my reverberant intellect.

Directly across, on the opposite sedgy margin,
A pen preens atop her mounded nest;
Downstream, a cob floats in this direction,
Slows, before me, goes to the other side,
Satisfied I mean no molestation.

All along the banks, mallard drakes and ducks
Revel in their leisurely feeding.
Occasionally, they flutter out of and above the meadow,
Quacking mimetically, flying frenetically,
For ten feet, before splashing down.

Unshorn sheep grazing, an occasional horse
Fill my imagination, with this living pastoral
Dominated by the cathedral spire,
Rising above the trees. No Turner
Or mesmerized Constable ever recorded more

Than I, in this enchanted hour, have fixed,
With my eyes' quill. Still,
Something remains unfocused, uncomposed,
Its spell illusory and unbroken:
A touch of the truth, momentarily spoken.

6/7?/83 (05863)

The Pilgrim Returns

Leaving Heathrow, achieving assigned altitude,
37,000 feet above the Atlantic,
Our jet cruises westerly, toward Gander,
Newfoundland. Suddenly, it drops
Through two air pockets, minutes apart,
Like a pair of suicide boots
Tossed, successively, from a wide sky-bridge.

"No cause for alarm,"
Our sanctified pilot recites, chapter and verse,
From a standardized flight breviary,
To his frightened, huddled congregation,
Even as I, his wholly committed disciple,
Conjure screeching archaeopteryxes
And winged chimeras driving us out of the air.

Eucharistic peanuts and drinks are hurriedly served,
As if conceived to distract and soothe
Fractious nerves, elicit sweet forgetting,
Precipitate Morpheo-Christian myths,
To mitigate, with visions of afterlife,
Thoughts of dying agonizingly, "just in case,"
At least, in the balance, to preserve the common peace.

Three hours into our sweep,
Microwaved haute cuisine ("pardon our plastic")
Substitutes for traditional popcorn and candy,
For those who've purchased headsets,
For the latest Paul Newman movie, *The Verdict*,
While the philistines are cursed to languish
Through a tedious crossing of the time zones.

Except for the parentheses occasioned by landing, now,
And takeoff, seven hours earlier
(With one exception, and that,
Although resembling a Holbein Dance of Death,
Not filled with leaking O-rings,
Turbines "making metal," seizing precipitously,
Things scientifically technical),

This trip has concluded without incident.
In fact, our smooth passage
*

Has revivified my long-abandoned belief in miracles,
Faith in acts ineffable and unseen,
Destiny's consequential covenants.
Indeed, I've already decided to partake, again,
In next year's crusade to New Jerusalem.

6/8/83 — [1] (05864)

Not Returning Together

Having spent two weeks touring England
And flown seven hours, together, from Heathrow,
We've just parted company,
You to stay in Manhattan, six days,
I fleeing, alone, to yet another gate, beyond customs —
Yet another jet,
To St. Louis, this time,
South of which, by still a few hours more,
Our two children will be waiting up, in their beds,
Listening, beneath the cricket-whispers,
For my tires to crunch the driveway gravel.

Now, musing out, through the fuselage window,
Along the silvery, triangular span,
Past its reverberating, circular turbine,
Into the misty distance forever expanding,
Down, at the turkey-stitched earth-quilt,
I'm suddenly reminded not how man and machine
Rely, completely, on each other,
To maintain straight and level flight,
Rather how the alliance you and I have fused
Requires neither physical presence
Nor codified rules to keep its equilibrium intact.

And yet as home vectors my bones,
I can't deny my heart its disconsolateness.
Missing you is a grievance
I, who greatly appreciate freedom, must tolerate,
And distance aggravates the pain.
You have been my heart's mascot and lover,
I your dependable friend.
For a time, possibly even a lifetime,
*

We must fend for ourselves,
Until, again, our family is reunited,
Each of us joined, again, in secular blessedness.

6/8/83 — [2] (04159)

Willy v. Willy: A Paternity Suit

On leaving, for the week,
I, a wifeless waif, vagrant Willy,
Entrust my two fluid children
Into the custody of a loving country family,
With whom they'll commune, say grace, at supper,
Fish for bluegill and bass, at the pond,
Play with geese, turkeys, sheep.

A widower neither by fate nor choice
Yet bereft nonetheless,
By nature of my mate's determination
To resume her premotherhood profession,
Slip, as of late, into freedom's sleek gait,
I persist in hackneyed rituals
My trade has obliged me to observe.

Each mile of cloud-scribbled sky
My wren-eyes scrutinize, as I drive west,
Recognizes my fleet shadow
Stretching out along the highway.
This mirage-clotted space has owned me,
Thirty-five years. We speak a language
Characterized by melancholy and despair.

Tonight, silence, laced with cold Chablis,
Naked beneath diaphanous veils
Crocheted from cigarette smoke and whiskey fumes,
Will try to seduce me, as usual,
And, knowing my weakness for excess
And sensual gluttony, easily succeed
In reducing me to lonely, onanistic dreams.

When I awaken, tomorrow morning,
In that all-too-familiar strange motel,
Coffee, juice, and newspaper
*

Will be waiting outside my door,
Like faithful Dalmatians. I'll shower, dress,
Check the mirror, for recognition,
Then set out again,

This time without manifest insecurities
Or doubts about my capacity to inspire disbelievers,
Project the universal necessity
My product line has achieved.
By the morrow, I shall have effectively erased
All traces of sad-faced resignation
Those precious, gesturing children bequeathed me.

I evoke forgetting so completely, anymore,
I might be a ceaselessly receding sea,
Whose ebb erodes evanescent shores, wipes them clean.
Soon, the kids will grow, go.
No one will be waiting to remember me
To them, confirm their paternity, my heritage,
Remind me dying is a daily absolution.

6/13/83 — [1] (02360)

[Lately, the ragged demons] †

Lately, the ragged demons
Have restricted my sleep to only three dreams
Per evening — leitmotifs
That, until recently, reiterated fantasies
In which a shape possessed of heroic stature,
My youth's approximation,

6/13/83 — [2] (08760)

Waiting for Connecting Trains, at Katy Station △

Stranded at the far tip
Of this insular peninsula inhabited by demons,
I scream. Twilight shivers
As though a frigid blast had passed low
Or cat claws had scratched its back to bleeding,
*

Below the fog that curls and whirls like waves
Weaving into shore, from deep marine grottoes.

Somehow, Cracow and Auschwitz invest my visions
With dim, stimulating intimidation. My screaming
Translates itself into shrill dreams
History's *Juden* endured, whose sacrifices
Hardly mattered except as stench sullying the air —
Obliterated spirits assuming transcendence,
Through involuntary, premature "retirement. "

Sitting here, in this public place,
Katy Station,
That vast disgrace shames me. I cry aloud,
Oblivious to the taut-titted cabaret ladies
And studly boy/man industrialists,
Resembling, in their proletarian arrogance,
Grosz caricatures instead of Midwestern students.

My crying is muffled by the stationary boxcars,
In which customers take repast leisurely;
I imagine the train flying toward Hades' depot,
Clacking, madly, over shattered rails
Fashioned from gold fillings and wedding rings
And laid on sleepers made of bones.
Lemon and salt drip from my eyes, to my fish.

Eating is a tribulation of enormous discomfort.
Never would I have dreamed,
On taking a seat, two hours ago,
That the dishes put before me
Would take on Egyptian significance,
Become a Seder, of a sort, for an assimilated renegade
Who never embraced Orthodoxy, in a synagogue,

Or even Reform worship,
Amidst the affluent hypocrisies of suburban America —
Let alone figured in the Final Solution —
Rather chose to remain a poet/ghost,
Hymning his own uninformed Kol Nidres,
From bunker to pogrom, desert to slum to ghetto,
Along his own lonely, self-imposed diaspora.

Twilight dissolves into stained-glass fanlights.
I am left stranded on its shore,
*

In my drunken twitching, like a bridged whale,
Sick to putrefaction. Trying to float myself
In a final glass of ice-cold Chablis,
Escape to open sea, I pass out.
My dying is an omen of the dread death lurking.

6/13/83 — [3] (00192)

Prelude to a Little Night Music

Although it's not yet late enough
For traditional lovemaking, Katy Station
Remains enigmatically sedate.
Perhaps this phenomenon owes its existence
To the summer-school session in Columbia, Mo.
Whatever truth is in vogue, I only know
That this quietude, unusual though it be,
Provides me with welcome surcease from crowds
Thronging city streets, whorehouses,
High-school tracks, movie theaters.

Each year, it seems to grow
More and more insupportable — the earth,
I mean, of course — less able to sustain life,
With any semblance of decency.
True, the zoo and Muny Opera and Chrysler plant,
MX missiles, Nixon's tapes, and endangered species,
Such as pandas, nuns, and married couples,
Remain protected by incumbent legislators
Seeking reelection. But the trick
Is ever in telling the magician from his "magic."

Tonight, I sit outdoors, on the brick patio
Moating this old depot.
Blue yet lingers above mid-Missouri;
It casts a pewter hue over my aloneness.
Listening to distant sounds twitching in my ears,
Like northern lights in a crisp Wisconsin night,
I look up from my placid vantage,
To assess the nearness of potential intruders,
And realize each whisper is a star
Just flickering into ignition, calling vision home.

6/13/83 — [4] (02521)

The Self-Made Son of a Self-Made Man ^Δ

Never have human hopes been more grandiose
Or dreams extremely "curiouser"
Than those evoked by the exalted potentate,
Hyman Ben-Maimonides,
Supreme ruler of the Wholly Blown Empire,
Which he alone administers by the seat of his pants,
While surmounting his throne, in the W.C.

With very little luck and a modicum of respect,
Hyman might have mastered himself
As well as the conquering of demesnes, provinces,
City-states, and principalities. Indeed,
Hyman could have changed fate,
Had he chosen to remain a devoted son,
Spend earthly eternity in suburbia, with his family,

Rather than retreating to the country,
Eschewing affluence,
Refusing to assume responsibility for an inheritance
Funded, mutually, in trusted perpetuity,
By his father, Solomon L. Maimonides,
Who accumulated his corporate fortune
In oil, stocks, land, gold, and, originally, pants —

Slacks/trousers/britches, knickers, jodhpurs,
Made to order (contracted, after the fact),
In the grim, dim dust of his Houston Street loft —
A self-made man, purveyor of needs
As well as panaceas . . . ah, but not his son,
Hyman, who, after too many seasons
Beside the pool at the Patimkins' country club,

Succumbed to the inexcusable miscalculation
Of allowing assimilation to pervert his intellect,
With just enough education
To make him stray, forever, from pecuniary pursuits,
Bring him to his knees, in undeviating obeisance
To words instead of deeds,
Poems too precious to be measured in common marketplaces.

When, exactly, his worship began,
He can't recall. Most likely, it occurred
*

On his graduating high school, that Y in the road,
Where he turned, permanently, to the left,
Took to reading, pondering, criticizing,
Writing adolescent verse, instead of apprenticing
To his dad, the self-made Baruch,

And fancied himself a splendid ascetic,
A scholar/poet in the mold of John Donne,
Milton, Swift. As a graduate student,
He conceived himself Shelley and Keats.
Later still, his admiration fixed
On Kafka, Camus, and Faulkner. He'd be a fictionist,
Like them. "What nobility of purpose!"

He'd frequently murmur, as a wife lighted,
Then flew away, his children grew,
Under another man's roof,
His mother outdistanced, by a decade,
The old ragman, then died . . .
While Hyman still writes a novel, each year,
Dreaming one will appear in print, someday.

6/14–15/83 — [1] on 6/15   (02522)

Fleet Summer Showers

In every direction except directly above,
The five-o'clock sky is cobalt.
Overhead, charcoal-hued smudges
Unloose, briefly, rain trudging like tortoises
Down a dry highway.

I sit outside,
Under the tongue-and-groove eave
Of this Victorian depot, listening to the drops
Splatter on tabletops, baked bricks
Hand-laid, in vertiginous zigs and zags,

Watching as the water encroaches closer, each minute,
On my pensive presence,
Poised behind open notebook,
Pen crooked, to catch the slightest shift
In its poetic dialectic.

My ears and eyes are mesmerized
By the trick the drops perform most consistently:
Casting themselves, at capricious intervals,
Unassisted, into my Chablis-brimming glass,
Like basketballs through a hoop, from thirty feet out.

Within minutes, practice is finished.
I raise my platinum-shimmering glass
To the magic of flash floods,
Brainstorms, fleet summer showers,
Which leave, in their wakes, creative awakenings.

6/15/83 — [2] (02523)

[Having seen sparks peel off a grinding wheel,] †

Having seen sparks peel off a grinding wheel,
Possibly out of a Dürer etching,
This

6/15/83 — [3] (01487)

Incarnations

Sitting out here, on this distant patio,
Sipping Chablis, at Katy Station,
At peace with the planets, in harmony with man,
On this docile Midwestern evening, in Columbia,
I try to reconstruct my genealogy.

Such aimless preoccupations
Have not always been so easily emancipated.
Only recently have my visions been able to isolate
And recreate chimeras from my past.
In Milton's day, I was a hissing bit player.

By the late eighteenth century,
Thanks to Mr. Swift, I, a revered projector,
Was elected to the Academy of Hot-Air Balloons,
One of the select few who could navigate
To Blefuscu and Laputa, blind,

Without running adrift on the Great Barrier Reef
Or arriving at Terra Incognita,
Dehydrated. For a brief spell,
Now that memory revives, I even recall
Sleeping with Johnny Keats,

At the foot of Specchi and de Sanctis's Spanish Stairs.
I was his unacknowledged lover,
For three years, before tuberculosis claimed him.
A disreputable bugger was I,
Taking advantage of that gentle boy, they claimed,

Though I knew, all along,
He had chosen me as his covert inspiration,
In those frenetic dying times.
Too bad we both couldn't have drowned
In the Bosporus — how Lycidas-like that might have been!

In modern eras, I've conspired with presidents:
Lyndon Baines, Gerry Ford, and "Tricky Dick,"
That villainous bastard of erased-tape fame.
Proud as hell am I,
To boast such an impressive record of curmudgeons.

Having discovered embodiments
Not altogether satisfying, in fact embarrassing,
To a degree, I might not again attempt,
With such agreeableness, to evoke my prior guises,
Rather might remain content to invent the present,

Create the future, by regenerating spontaneously,
Like a fly. Just now, I sit here,
Sipping sweet Chablis,
Going crazy, without my wife and children,
Knowing that being a poet is the loneliest incarnation of all.

6/15/83 — [4] (02524)

Wednesday-Night Patio Party

For Monica Jennings

Five guys tuned to three guitars,
One trap set,
*

And a single amplified voice
Jar my psyche out of its complacency,
Collide with my dying vibrations.
I respond by engaging ancient stirrings,
Remembering myself from other ages,

When the mere passing of a sandaled lady
Might cause my blood to curdle,
My sinful desires to cringe, behind their designs.
Just now, my blurred focus
Is adequate, in transporting me toward romance.
Ancient Roman days surface,
When I played Nero to a burning civilization.

I look across this patio, through the sounds,
Trying to locate uncommitted love
That might fulfill my needs.
Suddenly, Bacchus's handmaiden,
Who has, on gentle command, brought me Chablis,
By the glass, carafe, vineyard, all night,
Stands absolutely still, before me.

I freeze, contemplating her shimmering body,
As though she were Venus de Milo,
Nakedly Greek, beautiful,
Uninhibited, resurrected from time's depths,
A ready-to-wear mannequin
I might take home with me, as is, complete,
And bed, in blessed, absolutely carnal animality.

Jesus, what an unbelievably pleasing being
She has been,
Who has carried sweet Chablis to me,
This entire evening, while I've indulged my senses,
In total debauchery. I desire her
So totally — those thighs,
Whose moving nexus I've wistfully penetrated,

And breasts my lips and tongue have sucked,
Each time she's passed my table.
Now, trying to attach myself
To a passing perspective, I can't help
Again settling on my waitress. For God's sake,
She's so spectacular! Ah, now she's returned!
Lady, make yourself accessible,

That I might vibrate on my own,
Without the five guys
Possessing their three guitars, traps, solo voice,
Pray you and I might make music,
Beyond the stars, beyond the plangent moon.
Monica, it's been a thousand years
Since sonic blasts have distracted me orgasmically.

6/15/83 — [5] (02525)

Night Flight

The music screws my mind down
Fine as a microscope.
I might be van Leeuwenhoek,
Discovering, for the first time,
The magnifying glass. Ecstatic about my revelation,
Despite all my detractors
Swearing there's no way to see
To the leaf's heart, throbbing euglinids,
I probe no-man's-land,
In hope of finding harmony's sweet secret.

My ears shear away from their fuselage,
Slip, fast, into the night,
Without the ship crashing, flight aborting.
The drums and electric strings
Wing me home, despite my clumsy shape.
Flight is a lighter-than-air affair
In which the susceptible spirit engages,
That cares to share fascination.
At this late hour, only my dreaming apparatus
Responds to the music, as night harmonizes with day.

6/15/83 — [6] (02526)

Xerox City

I absorb the sounds,
Metamorphose dance into words
Obscene and sensual, desire myself alive,
*

Into realms never before orbited.
My eyes assimilate the gyrating bodies,
Blush evanescently, recover
In time to capture the memorable steps
Through which organs pass,
On their way toward orgasm —
Music squeezed to the bleeding turnip.

Who can guess the degree to which human beings
Rise, on their way down
Toward earthly paradise?
All evening, I sit outdoors,
My eyes and ears slaves to youth
Enacting their spring rites. My spirit dies
Five thousand deaths,
Wishing it could compete with agile Terpsichore
But knowing its best overture
Is a meager pinch on the ass of a passing muse.

6/15/83 — [7] (02527)

[Having driven a hundred miles, in a funk,]

Having driven a hundred miles, in a funk,
Unresponsive to the outer spheres
Immediately beyond my windshield,
I, like a Kamchatka bear
Taking days to escape hibernation,
Gradually awaken, grope for some clue
To my present location. *Nowhere*,
In every direction radiating outward,
Embraces me, like a vaguely familiar friend
I've never met. I nod quizzically,
Mumble a confused salutation,
Then confess to perpetuating a case
Of mistaken identity. Silence intercedes,
As I progress from egress to access,
Primary highway to tertiary outer drive,
Cloverleaf, cul-de-sac, circumferential,
Business bypass, until, out of gas,
My psyche stalls at a curb,
Beneath a familiar mimosa cluster,
*

Before a familiar gingerbread house,
And, standing in the doorway,
My wife waves. I nod animatedly,
As if shaking off amnesia.
How and where *nowhere* became *somewhere*
Is my sleeping secret alone.

6/16/83   (05865)

Street Cleaner ^Δ

Too early for the town's shopkeepers
And the elderly eternally sleeping, in rest homes,
Convalescing from belated death,
He wakes, takes coffee at the Capital Café,
Skims the local eight-page weekly paper,
Chats with the barber/mayor,
The chief die maker,
From the glass factory in Flat River,
Five miles away, and the blond waitress, Sue,
Who's outlasted three management changes,
In the past seven years.

Then he maneuvers through the downtown streets,
All six blocks,
Briefly amused by an Elgin street cleaner
Shifting, from curb to curb, in antic frenzy,
Like an upside-down stag beetle
Trying, mightily, to right itself.
For twenty-two miles through the country,
He can't eradicate its persistent image;
Each cow, boulder, and barn
Comes at him, jerking violently, from side to side,
Belly-brushes churning him under.

Although for the next fifty miles or so,
Going south, toward Cape Girardeau,
Sikeston, New Madrid, Hayti,
He ponders his own potential victimization
By diabolical forces
(Becoming human detritus, gratuitously,
Beneath an infernal machine controlled from Below),
And despite his visceral uneasiness
*

(Most likely from too much coffee —
Most likely), he knows his real fears
Emanate from actual loneliness.

Mist lifts, through vaporous ray-straws,
As if being sipped by a thirst-crazed sun.
He traverses Missouri, Arkansas, Tennessee, unnoticed,
Then enters Mississippi
And applies for an operator's license,
At the Benevolent Klavern of White Pariahs.
Suddenly, he's guiding the Elgin cleaner,
North and south, along Lamar,
Trying, against the bias, to sweep bigotry
From Oxford's one-way streets.
But they're too dusty, and his tanks are dry.

6/20/83 — [1] (03504)

Gentle Revolutionaries ^Δ

Last evening, the four of us
Cavorted outdoors, beyond the porch,
Weaving sparkling torches, vertically,
Through horizontal air-hoops,
Heaving volatile, exploding wads
Against the pocked concrete patio,
Igniting magical fuses connected to cones,
Rockets, Roman candles,
And three-way pinwheels
Nailed to the ancient oak's impervious bark.
Darkness was a thirteen-starred-and-striped flag.

We cavorted, Father's Day night,
As though there might be no Fourth of July
To celebrate, tightly clustered
Within the rectangle our excitement evenly pieced
With laughter and fright
And neatly stitched into asymmetry's symmetrical design.
We were, for those moments,
Inviolable, within our own Fort Sumter,
Defiant, behind our scintillating fusillades,
Man and wife, girl and boy —
A glorious nation of four, proclaiming our interdependence.

6/20/83 — [2] (01472)

Fisher Poet ^Δ

My skull is a live box,
Whose barely squirming residue,
Submerged in turbid brine,
Gives off dung-heap odors
Whenever I lift its lid and reach in
To grab a slim, swimming idea, by the fin.
Rarely do I get one on the first try.

At times, I even resort to sifting the container,
With a rhyme strainer or metaphor net,
To liberate musical bait.
Once in a great desperation,
I might even dive in
And isolate mates from the school — twin similes.

Then, to the hook on the end of my pen,
I affix the illusive lure,
Heave it overboard, into the cursive abyss,
And wait for a lunker to take hold,
Run headlong, plunge to the depths,
Surface hellbent, then breach —
A day's catch, taken from the imagination's lake.

6/21/83 (05866)

El desesperado

Abruptly, at 10:30 in the morning,
This formerly normal Thursday,
He finds himself driving south, out of the city,
Instead of routinely sitting numb,
Half-dozing, his toes cold
From too much air conditioning,
Dunning delinquent accounts, by phone,
Updating payroll folders,
Shuffling random papers
Into one of myriad plastic files on his desk,
Like an obsolete card-sorting machine.

In stupefied hindsight,
He can almost see the jagged, ripping sound
His psyche screamed, tearing away from his brain.
*

It seems like a sleek lightning streak
Cracking through his last two decades
Or a grisly hawk swooping through the mist,
Talons outreaching, to grasp his nape.
Driving south, he cries, from fright,
Amazed by the colossal, soothing silence accompanying him,
As he escapes work, place, time, identity,
His destination suicide, Canaan, *release*.

6/23/83 (02359)

Road Peddler's Ode

I focus on the trip odometer,
With rapt fascination, instead of the road,
Its precision wheels winding,
Winding miles onto their shaft,
Beginning with white tenths, at the far right,
Spinning infinitely faster,
In metered calibrations that fascinate,
Fascinate my apparatus, this a.m. —
Brain, tires, timing chain, axles, gears
Revolving in concert, evolving my spirit,
On a crash passage toward madness.

10.3, 38.8,
101.1 — the agitated miles fly by,
Like medieval specters resurrected from caves
Spiked shut with handwrought bigotries.
I watch them changing guises
But don't recognize faces, as I pass them.
Featureless trees, suburban tract-necropolises
Connected like a herd of circus elephants,
Billboards, filling stations, churches,
Satellite banks, car lots, fast-food beaneries —
They recognize, inescapably, my essential abandonment.

Morning widens.
The circling ciphers repeat the tedious lyrics
Of their siren song: a muted ululation
Inviolable and prolonged,
Whose perpetual drone inscribes drowsiness
Across my mind. Suddenly, I awaken,
*

A sedentary Sisyphus, courting daymares,
And suspect that my actual destination
Has never existed, rather that the road itself
Is the lunacy I was doomed, generations ago,
To roll, up the years, down the decades.

6/27/83 — [1] (02358)

Between Grief and Nothing

Gray, green, amber, and tan hues fuse,
Then separate, repeatedly,
Into rain clouds, fields of beans, corn,
And undulant wheat, and sedge,
Mowed by crews, withering at road's edge.

For a decade, I've driven to New Athens
And returned rejuvenated,
Composed incarnations, in my book of seasons —
Odes, aubades, villanelles,
By which to celebrate my dapple-dazzlement.

Now, as I leave for the last time,
Cross the Kaskaskia,
Heading west, toward the Mississippi River,
A shiver scales my fleshly Everest,
From toes to sweat-wet forehead.

The close, feverish humidity slips off my lungs,
As if they've been waxed; breathing beads up.
Under these conditions,
Even if only as poetic gesture,
Death is far better than regretting, forever.

6/27/83 — [2] (05409)

Pharaonic Curse: Megalopolis

Traveling into the city, by car,
I pass through a zone
Shrouded by mist lifting, hysterically,
In low-swirling whirlpools,
*

As though a lonely apotheosis of the Apocalypse
Had chosen to waylay me
Or, somehow, a necromancer had distracted me,
Caused my ship to veer off course,
Orbit primordial Jupiter,
Trapped in the interstices between two of its moons —
Stygian visions rising from morning's miasma.

For miles, I drive lightheaded,
Blind as an owl minus its dormant wisdom,
In fact, frightened by the persistent mist
Refusing to dissipate despite an insistent sun
Shredding Earth's flesh, with its claw-tipped rays.
Whether omen, oracle, or vagary
Is sifting up from the wellsprings of paranoia,
I know only that no overcast
Has ever lasted seventy-five miles
Nor polluted haze, like an extended plague of locusts,
Swarmed my imagination, so far away.

6/28/83 — [1] (00854)

Spring '84 Sales Meeting: Presentation of the Tailored-Suit Line ^Δ

"Sales-help, in retailing, these days, is grievous.
That's why, guys,
We take such pains making our buttonhole,
Lapel, and pocket treatment.
Garments must *sell themselves*, in today's market!

"Fellas, we're talking intrinsic value,
Quality for the price: bluffed edges,
Contrasting red-piped lining,
On our soft-shouldered-silhouette suit —
The classic, center-vented, six-inch drop.

"Also, gentlemen, our double-breasted model,
With semisoft shoulders, side vents,
Full lining, sixteenth-of-an-inch edge-stitching,
And peaked lapels with buttonhole,
Is the finest buy in the entire industry.

"Acme-Zenith provides a *complete fashion statement*!
Now, you schmeichlers, without further ado,
Get the fuck out — yesterday!
Sell hell out of this line!
Our shit's the best in the business, by God!"

6/28/83 — [2] (02065)

Our Credo, Spring '84 △

"Whether you're promoting cottons
With wash-and-wear profile,
In pinfeather, poplin, or seersucker,

"100 percent–polyester vested units
(CVP* or CP**)
From our extensive textured-stretch collection,

"Or worsteds and wool-blend tropicals,
In stripes, basic solids, tick weaves,
Mixture and windowpane plaids,

"Be certain your customer knows our suits
Are strictly class actions
And that Acme-Zenith Clothing, of St. Louis,

"Is an equal-opportunity manufacturer.
We're not picky who shops our line
Or buys, provided they pay on terms — net thirty."

*Coat-Vest-Pant
**Coat-Pant

6/28/83 — [3] (02357)

[Century-old companies file for bankruptcy.] †

Century-old companies file for bankruptcy.
Widebody jets
Miscalculate runways, come to rest,
Belly-deep, in myriad Tokyo Bays,
Like wading brachiosaurs.
*

Marriage, as an institution, is obsolete,
While divorce, at epidemic proportions,
Is practiced, zealously, by all faiths.
Conventional wisdom has reached

6/28/83 — [4] (06134)

[I leave Farmington, at 5:55.] ^Δ

I leave Farmington, at 5:55.
Everywhere, low-lying mists
Slither and hiss close to the grass,
Like swarming vipers in a primordial bayou.

Sun and moon — Capulet and Montague crests
Hung from invisible hammer beams
Bracing the sky's parallel clerestories —
Pantomime destiny's doomed daily litany,

Which I've tried, these two gone decades,
To unmemorize, physically jettison,
Through road travel. They remind me
My intellect and its foe, passion, yet feud.

How, after these many mute uprootings,
Solitude and loneliness hold sway
Over looming lunacy is an enigma
Metaphor, symbol, or fact can't deduce.

I know only that this latest trip,
Emanating from inchoate Earth's dark forest,
Started before my heart's first breath.
Even death can't reckon the destination.

7/1/83 — [1] (00030)

You Can't Go Back, Exactly ^Δ

For Frank Sachs

A slightly different ritual, this flight
To Duluth — being chauffeured, just southeast,
Into Wisconsin's northernmost reaches.
*

How I recall youth's odysseys
From St. Louis, on the Gulf, Mobile & Ohio's
Sleek red-and-maroon *Abraham Lincoln*,
To Chicago's Union Station,
Taxiing to LaSalle Street Station,
For the Soo Line run to Hillcrest, beyond night,
Playing cards, in gritty berths, traipsing aisles,
Being lullabied to sleep, by the clacking tracks.

Going back twenty-six years later,
In khaki slacks, blue blazer, tie,
Invited to "Explore Creativity" with campers and staff,
For their "Trails Forward" program,
Returning as a celebrated poet, not a boy,
I can't avoid trying to measure, in metaphor,
The gap between today's absolute precision
And that agreeably fatiguing unpredictableness
We reveled in, who, amidst the fifties,
Could still watch towns dissolving,
The world revolving, through a train window's praxinoscope.

7/1/83 — [2] (00019)

[Pine cones and chipmunks,] †

Pine cones and chipmunks,
Two immutable symbols of this beautiful Wisconsin

From every perspective, the lake predominates.
The entire town consists of two streets,
Forming a navigable T,
Whose top, trailing down to the municipal dock,
Boasts Bridge's Tavern

7/1/83 — [3] (01486)

Hiatus ∆

My six-day escape to Wisconsin's North Woods
Fades into shade, shape, scent of Norway pines,
Diminishes to a faint, crisp brain saturation,
In which memory and forgetting collide.

The immemorial prestidigitation continues.
Chipmunks, children, canoes, the lake
Metamorphose. At forest's edge,
A boy emerges. His aged surrogate hikes home.

7/6/83 (00020)

The Motion of Heavenly Bodies ^Δ

Poetic rotation is the only motion his psyche knows,
Whose twin spinning dynamos,
Both swirling hemispheres,
Go from stasis to full speed,
Sleeping to complete dream,
Without shifting gears, without moving,
Simply by focusing on the road
That transports his soul, from home, Home,
Along reiterating free-verse lines
His abstract passage concretely casts —
Energies orbiting Energy, in endlessly bending song.

7/11/83 (00137)

Viewing the Pageant

Having already made four calls, in two states,
He decides to stay, overnight, in St. Louis,
On its outskirts, at the King Bros. Motel,
Where, suspended within the television's crackling glow,
Like a low-circling moth
About a coal-oil lamp,
And forgoing his evening meal,
He sits, transfixed, in rigid mystification,
As eighty ladies fuel his unused juices,
With frenzied lust, fuse truth and fantasy
Into hallucinatory delusions
In which, by turns, he, Willy Sypher,
Assumes the roles of Romeo, Cyrano, Lothario,
Sheik, prince, impresario extraordinaire,
Courting Miss Universe to distant Xanadus.

Now, morning's haze erases his visions,
Like rain washing incisions from sandstone grave markers.
Leaving town by 8:00,
He can almost feel himself being worn away,
In the highway's staccato bellows action.
Last night's briefly emancipated identity
Has dispossessed his imagination.
Not even an insightful Oedipus or suspecting Quixote,
He knows the road peddler's curse.
Yet as he goes ahead, westerly,
He throws his focus into the rearview glass,
As though a gently moaning echo
Might overtake him, show him the way home,
To his wife and two children,
Who died so long ago, keeping his vigil.

7/12/83 — [1] (02356)

The Empress of Popcorn

From a distant corner within this subdued lounge,
I peer through anonymity, spying,
Watching her mix salt, oil, pearl-like kernels,
Pour the ingredients into her "three witches" cauldron,
Bespell the red-lit, glass-sided apparatus,
Reminiscent of an Amsterdam whorehouse,
Into a slowly climaxing orgasm.

Focusing on her filly legs, her slender, bending ass,
That brazen gesture suffused with concentration
And haphazardness and envisioning us naked as natives
Bathing beneath a cascading Jamaican falls,
I fail to witness her perfunctory actions:
Filling baskets, with napkins,
Lapses occasioned by raised eyebrows and fingers

Requesting one waiting tray after the next,
Crowded with sweaty glasses of Chablis
Or vessels extravagantly hued
With red, orange, cream, and green fluids.
Yet when I return from my fantasy,
Gaze across the space separating me
From the frenetic popcorn maker, from her, us,

Nothing remains save the vaguely European light,
Redolent of a pre-Nazi cabaret's,
Shimmering, laserlike, within its chrome cage,
Illuminating a perverse ejaculation:
Blood-ripe orchids, chewable parachutes
Blooming from a sky-pot, permeating the room,
With the numbing stench of cum doomed to miscue.

7/12/83 — [2] (02528)

Calibrating My Days

For Michael Keene

Not a fortnight ago,
We huddled around a tempestuously fanned fire,
At Lake Superior's southernmost shore,
On what remains of eroded Sage's Beach,
Stood with hands jammed into down jackets,
Hoods drawn tight, against the force
Roaring in off July's five-foot waves,
While memory's eyes,
Like children catching fireflies, in vented jars,
Arrested the soundlessly reiterating rocket flashes
Each successive multiple blast
Scattered into the darkling space separating Duluth
From our vantage, ten miles away.

Tonight, isolated from my northern companions,
Within this mid-Missouri bar
Loading with artificial, stained-glass twilight,
Clad in sandals, sport shirt, shorts,
Anesthetized by Chablis vapors,
I gasp and sputter, from cigarette smoke
Cluttering the opaque air,
Memorize each match-flash exploding the space
Separating my psyche from the amorphous *Zeitgeist*
Suffusing Katy Station and its passengers, loitering
As though ordained, by the High Priestess of Blefuscu,
To discuss nothing spontaneous or private,
And I question why epochs are measured in fire or ice.

7/13/83 (02529)

Willy: Fisher of Men ^Δ

I set out from my Jefferson City motel,
Heading home, this soiled a.m.,
Gnawed to the bone, like a pig carcass
Thrown into the Amazon,
By store owners and their cloned gofers;

Heading home, via Holts Summit,
New Bloomfield, Fulton,
Arriving, finally, at Kingdom City,
(A far cry from paradise or earthly Canaan),
Where I veer onto Highway 70;

Heading home, with my week's meager catch
Of endorsed, bona fide orders,
Written net thirty and confirmed by the buyer
(Feeding out next April's line, this July,
Is like catching man-eaters, by hand!);

Heading home, to my apartment, on Waterman,
At DeBaliviere, its halls reeking ghetto recipes —
Eternally simmering fish,
Matzo-ball broth, chicken necks.
I bite my lip, savor their Sabbath tastes,

Give thanks that the Red Sea parted,
Trying to remember that, though neither poet
Nor upside-down Itzhak Perlman,
I'm no Auschwitz statistic, either,
Or bone-smolder seething over Polish soil,

Rather Acme-Zenith's Midwest rep,
The *best* and *only* for forty years,
Who can yet sell hell out of a suit
Missing its sleeves and lapels,
Slacks lacking zipper and back pockets,

And who, at sixty, can still swallow, whole,
Easy as egg in my beer,
Piranha and jewfish, alike!
All I beg is, when convenient,
They be served kosher — preferably filleted!

7/15/83 (00080)

A Toss of the Coin

Driving south, out of the city,
This hell-fired July,
When the heat is breathing's nemesis
And persistent brain fevers
Oscillate across retinal screens,
Like erratic bleeps on a fetal monitor,

I try to decide whether, indeed,
Dying and living, under these conditions,
Might not depend on a coin
Fate has tossed, for me to call.
All day, I wait, with open palm,
Hoping time hasn't worn both sides smooth.

7/22/83 (05868)

Moon's-Day Morning

Heading west, out of St. Louis,
Behind my rain-stippled windshield,
Whose wetness, after fifteen straight days
Of hundred-degree heat, is an augury of blessed release,

I approach the north-south interchange,
Green-and-white signs, screeching like macaws,
Coalescing, slowly, within the dull glow
Of my caffeine-starved brain: Memphis/Chicago.

This morning, both choice and conditioning
Slip their knots. My psyche,
Deciding to violate all former ties,
Flies by, refusing to deviate from aberration.

Thirty miles out, dense gray
Dissolves into discharged amber strands.
Despite having less than ten dollars in my pocket,
I plan my trip expansively,

Stopping only twice, all day —
Once to top my tank, with six gallons,
The other to pick up a hitchhiker, time,
Whose direction and E.T.A. are precisely mine.

7/25/83 — [1] (05869)

Obsolete Equipment

Images sift through, sink into, twin pools
His eyes provide to hemispherical computers
And are then translated onto cuneiform chips
His slipping memory still manufactures,
In its miniature, refractory-lined furnaces.

His apparatus no longer evidences speed,
As, in its youth, it could; rather,
Each fed-in whim, notion,
Takes extensive heavy-duty cycling,
Before issuing uniquely designed metaphors.

Lately, he's even experienced shutdowns
(Unexpected, if brief), the attendant pain
So grievous that, on regaining power,
To his mortification, he's felt amnesia,
Pervasive as termites, infesting his mainframe.

In fact, twice, now, twice
During the past seven days,
His entire system has been effaced,
Erased by unknown agents, his banks dispossessed
Of their blessed synaptic linkages.

Thrice, he's suffered humiliating uncertainty,
Wondering whether his mind would take wing,
His fingers again record his tongue's singing.
Lately, he spends his on-line time
Composing permutating versions of his own epitaph.

7/25/83 — [2] (05870)

Unassimilated

His existence has been a sequence of subsistence-level positions
Held for relatively brief stints,
Depending not on basic competence but temperament
And innate patience, how agreeable he's been
To commit obsequiousness and servility —
In essence, how destitute he has to become
Before succumbing to "Yes, sir," "No, ma'am,"
*

Wearing tasseled, oxblood Bass Weejuns,
Club or rep silk ties,
Baggy Brooks Brothers khaki slacks,
Reading the newspaper, voting,
Going to Yale, rowing at Henley-on-Thames,
Prostituting his simplicity, to WASPish prosperity.

He's taken spells, occasionally retreating, for a decade,
Behind beard, boots, work shirt,
And wheat jeans, reciting Roethke and Plath,
To beaver-busy streams, hiking, in Wyoming hills,
Hunting deer, with bow and arrow,
Writing his own Whitmanesque prose, on the go,
Canoeing, alone, in the Quetico,
Owing no echoes to any recognizable voice,
Lest it be that of his blessed mother,
Ten years deceased,
Who always believed his exaggerated claims
Accorded him Nobel-laureate status.
He might also, inexplicably, conform, for a decade.

Even he has no concrete thumbnail sketch
Or Interpol dossier on his "true identity."
Despite all the years
Spent tracking his elusive paths, his illusive locations
Remain an enigma, to the proper authorities,
Governmental agencies, his one-time wife.
In truth, his inscrutable presence
Is threatening to the unseen hierarchy ruling the state,
In which, ostensibly, his census data is essentially recorded.
Despite communal efforts,
Willy Sypher's never quite been persuaded
Either to submit to the good of the state
Or admit he's no match for Torquemada, the Grand Inquisitor.

7/25/83 — [3] (02530)

Proposition to a Lady of Propriety

For Monica Jennings

All evening, I scrutinize her youthful ass,
Her bemused, if incidental, asides to rude drunks
*

Dying to pinch her tits, stroke her belly,
Deliver her from Pharaoh's bondage,
With their "Midwest" touch.

I calculate her nubile flesh,
Amused by the poise she employs,
Serving drinks to bores, perverts, whores,
And wonder what Londons, Lucernes, and Lisbons
I might show her, in a single soar

From this regionally exotic, if limited, lounge,
Where she works, three evenings
Each week, transporting drinks from bar
To overstuffed seats, suffering her meager check,
Demeaningly acquiescing to every man's request.

Night is a series of Chablis glasses
She brings me as though I were England's king.
I, as noble poet, decline such dubious accolades,
Concluding, with a final proposition,
That I might pleasure her,

By bedding her, happily forever after, tonight,
If only she might accept my awkward gesture.
I've actually traveled the Cotswolds,
Hardy's Dorchester, the Lake Country, Wales.
I'm qualified to fly. Come, lady; take my controls!

7/25/83 — [4] (02531)

Daddies' Girls ^Δ

I come close to crying
For all the petite Jewesses isolated in small towns,
Trying to "make a little extra change,"
Work themselves through college, serving drinks and dinners,
Excelling in local golf and tennis tournaments,
For which their fathers have coached them,
Despite class restrictions, quotas.

I almost cry, whenever encountering them —
High-heeled, sophisticated, serious —
Knowing that, despite their skill, discipline, spirit,
*

Shrill fate has relegated these ladies
To the Zyklon B showers
Even before they achieve their sweatiness,
Prove themselves before the *Führer*.

I've witnessed them, in my travels,
So stalwart, so intent,
As though centuries of blight did not exist.
Listening to them express their ambitiousness,
I squirm, wishing, somehow, to admonish them
The referees are corrupt, bigoted,
That holes in one, six-love sets

Are skewed in favor of privileged losers,
That Jewesses, no matter how adroit,
Can't win, and expertise is a sin
Punishable by life isolated in German work camps.
Tonight, I dine in silence,
Double-tip my haughty, taut-titted, Semitic-looking waitress,
Praying for her safe passage, regardless of race — amen!

7/25/83 — [5] (02532)

Contrary to Human Nature

Frequently, my leave-takings
Do not occasion a reciprocal return
Over the same known roads,
Rather stimulate my nomadic spirit,
Send me into water-strider frenzies,
From which no recovery is possible.

In mind warps such as this morning's,
My only recourse is to set gyros,
Magnetic and electrical,
And pray my eventual destination
Will correspond with destiny's best intentions.
Flight plans serve virtually no purpose,

Except to notify next of kin,
In case the pilot accidentally survives,
A nonoption for those who actively pursue
Extinction, through suicide.
*

Heading home, I recognize my meditative limitations,
Accept today's mandate: to stay alive.

7/26/83 (00853)

Limbo Now ^Δ

For faithful, patient Jan

Fleeing Farmington, this Friday morning,
I cut across the countryside,
Plumb-lining swerving Highway 32.
Whether my urgency engenders from nervousness,
Worry, or guilt, on leaving home again,
After such recent excursions to Ocho Rios,
Europe, and Wisconsin, is unassayable.
Doubtless, the elements conspire against my heart,
Whose wayward pilgrim peregrinations
Defy disciplined belief in traditional achievements
And ethical destinations — amen!

Instead, I keep to the road, to myself,
Alone and inaccessible except to a gratuitous few,
Who know only my disguises.
Even my children fail to recognize their daddy
Clad in tatterdemalion poet-clothes,
On his returning from remote regions,
Satchel brimming with Diaspora verses
Flowing in de Tocqueville meters, Whitman feet.
Nor does my wife alter her tired demeanor
When I enter the door,
Like a prisoner of war recently freed.

Neither petty insights nor trite conversations
Hold sway over either of us
Anymore. Yet love, or its essence, lingers.
Yes! Yes! And we both know it,
Though its vibrant core-flames sputter,
Subterraneously, in caves we've dug out,
With hands and lips, claws and tongues,
This last, lost decade,
While we've fought to retain youth's fading tan,
Its sensual elegance, easy-reasoning omniscience,
Our reverence for Rabindranath Tagore.

What, then, is it, I frequently question,
On these incessant trips
Out from the center, bereft of my blessed children
And patient helpmate, Jan,
That keeps repelling us, causing me to flee
The single source of peaceful repose —
My sanctuarial nest, my Mosaical family?
After all this desolate time away,
I yet have no guess,
Unless uprootedness is my apprenticeship,
My destiny, I God's cosmic messenger.

7/29/83 — [1] (03556)

Willy's Southern Route ^Δ

"Scalawag," "rapscallion," "abolitionist,"
"Ragman carpetbagger" —
Apposite epithets, I've been called them all,
Time and again, with vicious derisiveness
And outspoken indignation, on trips to Mississippi,

And worse. "Nigger-loving Jew!
Who needs your kind, here in Jefferson?"
Mr. Compson yelled, last week,
From his hardware-store porch, on the square,
As I approached Klein's Dry Goods, for an order.

Whether it's the two gold caps, my nose
Not quite patrician, for its hook,
Just below the bridge, my vested suit,
Even in July's booking season,
Or "ACME-ZENITH — ST. LOUIS" stenciled on my cases,

I can't say for certain.
Whatever, their eyes, like rusted knives,
Cleave a raspy path to me,
With indecent, too-shrill obscenities and threats,
As I walk the sidewalks, cross the streets.

Spit just misses hitting me,
As I pass their somnolent, buzzard-huddled bodies,
Squatting on splintered benches
*

About the courthouse. In abject silence,
My outraged class-consciousness disintegrates.

I'm neither Moses nor the Nazarene among zealots
But Willy Sypher, Midwest sales rep,
Schlepping seconds and overstocks,
Slightly out of my element,
Trying to make a killing, without being crucified,

Hoping to buy time, selling on time,
Despite inimical racial and religious odds.
Thank God for small favors —
All my competitors, whether based in New Orleans
Or Bremen, Georgia, are second-class, too.

God only knows, there's no room,
In the magnolia, mockingbird, and julep code,
For another Jew, even if Ku Kluxers
Have to wear trousers under their robes.
And who knows? Theirs may come from Klein's, too!

7/29/83 — [2] (00079)

A Renewal of Faith △

In my fleet vehicle, tracking south,
I whisper past the highway sign
Proclaiming Wilson and Lepanto,
Cruise through viaduct uprights,
And approach, minute by mile, belle Memphis,
Unnoticed, as of yet, an unknown specter
Hurling, recklessly, toward the river.

Whether seeking absolution,
In Beulahland's sacred baptismal stream,
Or on a crusade to a Canaan south of Eden
Remains for me to ascertain.
Already, my flesh has begun to quiver and itch,
As if I were slipping, naked, in quicksand
And unable to scream for assistance.

Tyronza and Jericho remind me
I'm yet enslaved by Arkansas,
*

May not reach Mississippi for another hour.
Regardless, my heart has faith
You'll be waiting, in Bailey's Woods, William,
To anoint my buoyant spirit,
As I jog, joyously, through the humid, fluid gloom.

7/29/83 — [3] (00149)

The Warehouse, Friday Night ^Δ

The smooth, cool, nubile wine I sip
Slides smoothly down my throat,
Into my dry brain. Wilted mind-vines inflate.
Wisterias, honeysuckles, crape myrtles, magnolias,
Lilacs, and rose of Sharons glisten,
Grow profuse, in my imagination's formal gardens,
While I sit back, witnessing a Chablis-rain —
Libation inspired by ripe grapes
Plucked, squeezed, and fermented at my estate —
Rejuvenate a desolate crescent
I converted to a cemetery, metaphors ago.

This civilization, where I've come to rest,
Friday night, July 29,
Is Mississippi, neither Indian nor Scotch-Irish
But homogeneous collegiate male,
Suckling, leisurely, America's supple breasts.
Every day, in this red-clay plain,
Named "Oxford," with a modicum of satiric wit,
Is Friday night, "showtime,"
Roy Scheider popping uppers, getting laid,
For the sake of saving face, with an avowed feminist,
La belle dame sans merci.

Tonight, for the select-few Orthodox sects,
The Sabbath begins; for my lonely spirit,
An absolutely indescribable renegade hybrid,
This evening marks the end's onset,
The beginning of physical apocalypse,
In which the spirit will be lost, in a cosmic blizzard
Emanating from wine showers beyond the moon.
Just now, I quit my philosophic musing,
*

Concentrate on the incontestably beautiful face
Surmounting the perfectly shallow lady
Imbibing, smoking, posing for me, across the way,

And die a thousand deaths, in a solitary sigh,
Imagining myself twenty again,
Fucking my brains into flowering Judas trees,
Wandering Jews, birds-of-paradise —
Ole Miss cunts born, bred, and dressed
For one reason, undeniably:
To procreate, in unadulterated mental slumber
(Having children their Grail quest and only raison d'être,
Their effete men their only encumbrance).
I accept her fleshly wink, her nod,
As my invitation. Tomorrow, we'll be old friends, intimate.

7/29/83 — [4] (00163)

It Was the Summer of the Snakes, and She Ran △

It was the summer of the snakes,
And she ran, naked, down University Avenue
Instead of pacing herself through Bailey's Woods,
Ran, with palpitating nipples and thighs,
As if to escape invisible, lacerating fangs,
Accepting companionship of strangers,
Content to be gazed upon,
Undone by salacious, straining eyes,
Brain-raped, every step she'd take.

It was the summer of the snakes,
And she ran past the Ramey-Memory House,
Buie Museum, to South Lamar,
Left, left again, around the courthouse,
A stark, crazed, winged singing shape.
Malign eyes, glaring behind drapes,
Store-glass bordering the square, doors ajar,
Porch supports, arrested her fleshly ecstasy,
With a collective, accusatory stare.

It was the summer of the snakes,
And she ran for her life, from herself,
*

Toward the pool in St. Peter's Cemetery,
Where, long ago, floating in ooze,
She'd climbed up out of youth's slime,
Entered and, simultaneously, was penetrated
By the great elongated viper, time,
Who became her seducer, judge, future executioner,
She his bemused and dutiful concubine.

It was the summer of the snakes,
And she ran, in a trance,
Her cadence a transcendent manifestation
Of her first earthly fantasy,
A demon-driven dance of death.
Returning to the nest, bare toes hissing
On the shifting path on a moccasin's back,
Past Oxford and Mississippi, skyward,
She ran, and she ran, and she ran.

8/6/83 (00170)

Amicable Separation

Cut loose from the domestic noose,
Mistakenly taken for dead,
When, in fact, the heart yet palpitates,
The feverish lungs murmur imperceptibly,
I submit my day-sweaty flesh to the slab.
My soul demurs, preferring to remain with its body,
Like a forlorn possum standing in the dark, interminably,
Beside the still-warm carcass of its mate,
Annihilated by a hit-and-run drunk.

What tenuous breath-bond connects me
To this plot, my earthly birthplace, you —
That tie memory yet nurtures with occasional laughter
And tears — I can't determine, with certainty.
Something about our years shared
Has toughened the fibers, made my vertebrae
Impervious to the hangman's abrupt thrust.
Even now, dissolving into twilight,
Our shadows huddle side by side, in the keening silence.

8/15/83 — [1] (04158)

Katy's Tatterdemalion

Arterial crimsons, deep venous blues,
Amber tans and tawny beiges
Approximating gradations of fleshly hues
Pulsate through stained-glass fanlights
Paralleling Katy Station's Tuscan-red brick stringcourse
And land, haphazardly, within the glimmering shimmer
Spinning wooden blades agitate,
As they swirl static cigarette smoke and whiskey odors,
In an emphatically undiminishing listlessness.

The crazy blades take in and evacuate colors
As though they were amebas and protozoans
Being fed gratuitous food particles
Instead of fascinating prismatic pulsations
Meant to stimulate my imagination's rods and cones.
I sit here, blitzed on sweet, chilled Chablis,
Mind-blown by the blizzard
Assaulting me, this otherwise dreary-weary
Lord Jim afternoon,

And focus on dust motes, anonymous faces,
Receiving sensations as though I ruled kingdoms,
Owned South African diamond mines,
Clipped coupons bequeathed by Gould, Fisk,
And old "Gold Spike" himself, Leland Stanford,
Rather than owning up to the alias of displaced waif
Unable to conceive, let alone determine,
My most immediate destination,
Upon leaving this place — a tatterdemalion,

A basic bum, with a college education,
Drowsing here, now, numb as a monk
Cloistered within the shabby, meager isolation
His seedy order evokes,
Who, with capacity for neither scandal
Nor fantasy, must settle for quotidian heresies,
An upper-Ladue hobo, a William Burroughs
So dissatisfied with leisure and privilege,
He must emigrate to Mexico City and Tangier,

Just to show those who set prevailing protocol
That coke and heroin can succeed
*

When everything ethical
Fails to elicit a spontaneous response.
Twilight intercedes. The fans cease.
Dust motes die, behind fading colorations,
Like butterflies sliding into sleepy quiescence.
I slump into my padded red-leather seat,
A nomad trapped in night's net.

8/15/83 — [2] (02533)

The Man on the Lawn, in His Pajamas

Just after the unregenerative rain,
I leave behind youth's Ladue mansion,
My spirit's true birthplace,
Looming, in Monday morning's humid womb,
Like a perfectly white cruise ship
Adrift in a pale-blue lagoon,
And set out for Jefferson City, the capital,
Where my destination will end, day begin.

But all the way out, I see him,
Substance or shade, spectral simulacrum.
Visions of him roaming the front lawn,
Searching, stoop-shouldered, in pajamas,
Amidst the scraggly box elders
Guarding the house like ragged soldiers,
For the elusive newspaper, thrown slipshod,
Persist in my rearview mirror, two hundred miles —

Not even him, really, searching myopically,
Who, materializing in my stuporous gaze,
As I turned the corner by the garage,
Caused me to slow, stop, lower the window,
To respond stupidly to his smile,
Gentle inquiry as to where I was going,
Valedictory admonition to drive safely,
But him fixed there, so vulnerably, in his pajamas,

The man whom I'd always associated with trips,
Goings and comings, journeys to L.A.,
Pittsburgh, New York, on business,
Traveling in immaculate Hickey Freeman suits
*

Or Oxford or Schoeneman — *la crème* —
Always on the move, wishing us adieu,
In his own crisp and matter-of-fact taciturnity,
That glamorous ragman with no stitches showing,

And always with a gift, on his returnings
(Madame Alexander dolls, from FAO Schwarz,
For little sister, another electric accessory
To complement my Lionel setup),
Who, at seventy-five, no longer calibrates his days
In dates with bankers, lawyers, brokers
To be consulted, controlled, set into motion, for him,

Rather in watched-pot hours to outlast,
Bodily functions to monitor,
Fidgeting and pettiness and forgetting to govern
Despite his still being able to perpetuate his routine,
By dressing, going to his desk (in his basement, now),
Professing, to the silence, his hunches,
Best intentions, investing yet, by phone,
Years and months and days collapsed into seconds.

Heading west, through an inevitable opening
In destiny's needle-eye, I suddenly realize
That I am my father, he is I
As I was most accustomed to seeing him,
And the blessed, perpetual evolution
That recycles each of us, according to its own needs,
Has merely shifted our positions, temporarily,
Along the road connecting the capital with the kingdom.

8/22/83 — [1] (05871)

Premonitions ^Δ

All day, the baleful, black-tattered wind
Has reversed directions. By degrees,
It's assumed the disguise of a demonic banshee
Screaming down a blistered sky;
A Ming dog foaming at the teeth and gums,
Biting, blindly, at poles, eaves, plastic signs;
An accidentally escaped mental patient
Clawing his way back to celled safety.

Now, afternoon accedes to night's force.
The wide, lightning-riddled horizon
Is a Krupp muzzle, an erupting volcano's crater
Seen from the earth's core, upward.
Ashen debris pocks plate glass,
Corrugated sides of prefabricated buildings,
Chrome car grilles. Quiescent bones,
Moldering six feet below, grow restive,

As though the rabid universe were bent on retribution
And, at any moment, might call
The margin agreed upon by all investors
In death's short-term glamour-stock offering.
Yet the inevitable apocalypse delays,
Defuses its ultimate threat,
Somehow contains its horrific pestilential fury,
For another occasion, while each of us,

Assessing his own unique potential for selfishness,
Petty human cruelty,
And destruction, proceeds, in nature's cessation,
To annihilate every blessed dream
Mankind might have hoped to achieve.
Relieved of final extinction's consequences,
Assured that the diabolical wind is a charlatan,
We got to bed, believing Dewey has gained the presidency.

8/22/83 — [2] (02534)

The "Dude" Introduces His Boy, Troika, to Katy Station △

For beloved Troika the Boy

A week ago, Friday night,
My five-year-old boy, Troika, and I
Visited this disreputable college-town lounge,
That he might see a "real-life" caboose
(Though parted from its trucks)
Revealed in all its barn-red glory
Despite its having come to retirement, on a siding
Decidedly devoted to those more concerned with consuming booze
Than either hauling freight or traveling miles
To exotic L.A. or Tucumcari, New Mexico.

We traveled, by road, from Jefferson City,
Just the little guy and his dad,
Far enough to sit high atop the raucous bar,
In the stationary caboose's cupola, as though keeping sentinel
Over a hundred-car freight
Instead of mindless human faces
Bobbing, among their own kind, on bad tracks.
He actually believed this station was an operating depot
Rather than a ghost of the McCoy,
Renovated, by an enterprising Jew, to recapture nostalgia,

Make a more-than-successful return
On investment — my boy so overjoyous,
Amidst the amber, aquamarine, and scarlet running hues
Discharging from "borrowed" yard-lights
From the Illinois Central and Duluth, Missabe & Iron Range,
That no one could ever convince him
What he was witnessing was for mere show —
And I, his father, participated in the dissimulation,
Knowing that the last Pennsy *Spirit of St. Louis*,
Santa Fe *Super Chief*,

And Soo Line from Chicago's LaSalle Street Station,
To Milwaukee, Solon Springs, and Hillcrest,
Quit running too many years ago
To remember with clarity. I perpetuated the ruse,
That my one son might appreciate the heritage
His father had enjoyed so deeply
And, beyond youth, muse on the once-removed déjà vu
Engendered by computer quiz games,
Remind his children that, once, the trains ran
From Katy Station, that they ran, once.

8/22/83 — [3] (02535)

Foregone Illusions ^Δ

People who live in glass caskets
Shouldn't throw bones,
Not even their own,
Unless they expect to be found hiding,
Alone, above ground,
As though fulfilling a cultural decree:
Public sacrificial sepulture.

Funereal eulogies permeate the air,
With choking putrescence. The stench
Blends all hues into one:
Carcinogenic black.
The earth grows top-heavy,
With skeletal levitation,
Wobbles awry, begins to drift,

Split. A godly energy
Locks it into spinning orbit, releases
Its hold, the final minute,
Before apocalypse can succeed
In annihilating man's dreams
For immortality. The drowsy populace
Repeats its prayers, prepares for sleep.

8/23/83 (02536)

The Floating of Davy Jones's Bones

Adrift within his solitudinous addiction to words,
Rhetoric intricately engendered
Of an intense compulsion to push the language
Beyond existing Faulknerian outposts,
Metaphors forged on Lucifer's anvil,
To fit Persephone's high-strutting stallions,
He grips, tightly, his psyche's gunwales,
Tries to maintain balance,
As the word-pool sucks him into its slow undertow.

Poet, no matter how vociferously he demurs,
Is his profession, avocation, curse.
Tropes draw him out of his deepest pools,
Like water striders pacing vertiginously,
Luring, to twilight's surface, an ancient trout
Who has not tasted the sky, in decades.
Ancestral visions, contemporary images
Keep his eyes glued to varihued spoons
Rippling dappled afternoon. He strikes

Whenever the spirit possesses his ears.
Ultimately, it's to the sound of phenomena
*

That he responds: avalanches, tidal waves,
Hummingbird wings singing above mimosa blooms,
Jupiter's moons shifting positions,
Slugs making their undeviable way to China,
Elephants and possums lamenting a mate's death —
Things defying detection by imaginations
Tightwire slim. He strikes,

Realizing time, compressed to its essence,
Yields the most effective poetics,
Knowing death is devious bait, at best.
Just now, phosphorescent flying fishes
Leap over his bow, gracefully as ocelots.
He records their presence, in his log,
Floats adrift, in irons, solitary as a skeleton,
Waiting for a change in his deranged brain,
By which to chart a new course, escape.

Stasis refuses to give way, make room
For newer equations, reinterpretations.
His caravel seems a paltry adversary on a sea
Far too tempestuous for his gentle temperament.
By degrees, his bilge pump fails
To keep beat with the furious, intrusive meters
The water's cadence sets up,
In its awesome attempt to scan him.
Inebriated, the good ship *Poet* capsizes.

8/24/83 — [1] (02537)

Electric Incantations

Reddish reflections rip the evening to shreds.
Female harmonies expand the air,
Like humidity saturating a dry plain.

I sit back, inoffensively inebriated,
Foot tapping to the electric keyboards,
Envisioning God's naked angels masturbating,

Stroking clitoral strings,
As quavering vocal chords reverberate.
Katy Station is the devil's depot,

Receiving flown, blown souls
From every remote region, the moon's purlieus,
Exchanging deranged, for sane, minds.

Listening to the intense plaints, I unwind.
How much is due to the wine,
How much to the music makes little difference,

When related to the final relaxation
That engenders from the skewed strains,
Which my bones assimilate, my brain retains,

Long after each song diminishes
And all that remains, beyond the abrupt cessation of sound,
Is the quivering whisper of unfinished compositions

Begging completion, vindication, resurrection.
In this outdoor auditorium,
Where chords and metaphors fuse,

Memories buried in my fore-hemispheres
Clear the earth, the stars, far galaxies,
Bear my heart, on heron wings, to the very start of things.

8/24/83 — [2] (02538)

Lady Grace, Manslayer

Focusing on the angelic specter gyrating, on stage,
Under the Lucifer-lights
Fractionating my brain, to despair,

My eyes feel themselves surrendering,
Being subverted by primal stirrings,
Taken over, possessed by blatant sexuality.

Hands, head, legs, thighs, lips, breasts
Arrest me cold. Totally mesmerized
By such overt animal carnalities,

I succumb to her whole rotating soul,
Sucked into her depraved cave.
My senses reacting, like a bat's, to sound,

Not sight, I fight her off
Despite her base overtures, aimed my way.
She knows I'm unable to resist.

As I listen to her primitive vocalizations,
My muscles, nerves, sinews, vessels collapse;
Ataxia prevails; the solar plexus withers;

Hysteria enters the bloodstream, screaming.
She bleeds into the spotlights,
Heightening her spectral complexion, beneath night,

Until even the music metamorphoses,
Assumes the sky's absence of hue.
When I look up, the stage is vacant.

Where her black-skirted torso writhed
Are three microphones, on slender stands —
Fans left crucified, in her transitory wake.

8/24/83 — [3] (02539)

Sunset over an Anchored Schooner, in an Ancient Lagoon, Detained

A mellow glint, tinge of vaporous honey,
Shimmering through this room's stained-glass baffles,
Singes my silver-nitrate eyes, with images
Gathered, in ancient times, from random isles
You and I sailed to, over seas
Beyond the Hesperides' fringes.

Solitary, now, in this remote lagoon,
At anchor, within languorous afternoon's coverts,
Yet cut irretrievably loose, as if exiled to Elba,
I sip Chablis sunlight, from memory's glasses,
Until night fills up the dissipating space.
My dizzy visions liberate your naked shape from its prison.

Why I was doomed to pariahhood,
Foreordained to concatenate words into golden chains
To dangle between Héloïse's and Francesca's breasts,
Predestined to sublimate actions into metaphors,
Why I'm preoccupied with meters, cadences, rhythms, rhymes
Instead of blessed with conventional expectations,

I have yet to satisfactorily explain to the Grand Inquisitor,
Who questions me, every free occasion,
*

By waylaying my spirit when it flies the highroad,
From the City of Poetry,
Toward spontaneously unbridled irresponsibility,
Depresses my soul, with irrepressible guilt,

For having neglected my wife and children, for a muse
Impalpable, miragelike, and mystical
Rather than fleshly, immediate, fallible, impassioned.
Yet destiny has relegated my paltry being
To this pathetic impasse, whose disreputable legacy
Consists of composing poems, in isolation,

Eschewing all consequences and essences
That don't bear directly on the theoretical and sublime.
Tonight, in this remote lagoon,
Blowing out the fading twilight,
In flute notes liquescent as tea-heated honey,
I lament my wife not being beside me,

Drinking in another endless day's dithyrambs,
Our boy and girl forgetting to prayer their daddy, at dinner,
A hundred and one consecutive evenings,
And know, even as I sip afternoon's last drips,
That redesigning cytoplasmic blueprints
Is as absurd as asking Meursault to repent,

Joseph K. to drop his suit against the lower courts.
I accept my fate, sans resignation
Or acrimonious rejection. Sitting here, sipping Chablis,
I listen to the crepuscular dissolve,
Feeling my anchor's gentle tug, in this lee cove,
And screaming, to oblivion, that I won't be completely forgotten.

8/25/83 (02540)

Taking Communion

All roads lead to Pandemonium.
Morning's snarled cloverleafs,
Bumper-locked knots, maladroit flows
Reflect Lucifer's sense of humor —
No laughing matter, his cynical misanthropy.

Betrafficked, trying to circumnavigate the city,
This rain-ruined a.m.,
*

I catch myself repeating ancient rituals,
Witchcraft tactics,
Evoking superstitious incantations

Calculated to make arrested motion dissipate,
Stasis, stifling my progress,
Release its grip on freedom's vehicle,
Permit me to proceed, unimpeded,
Toward Cíbola, shimmering below Earth's halo,

That prismatic kingdom the mind designs,
With cantilevered rainbows,
And dreams construct, from convenient visions
Recorded in architectonic God-books:
Korans, Torahs, scrolls, apocalyptic codices.

Inexorably, the press dismantles itself.
I drive westward, silent, expectant,
As wet highway changes to dry
And the sky opens to receive me,
Like a ghost poised to take the Host.

9/12/83 — [1] (00852)

Doing Translations

No matter the variation in shape or implication,
Translations
Invariably rearrange the way we see objects,
Sense essences. Often, they deteriorate in our presence.

Take, for example, lyrical ballads,
Moving from English, across Teutonic tongues,
Like freight trains
Scraping through vast switching yards,

Or victims of brutal car wrecks,
Whose mutilated, blood-blasted bodies,
Nakedly isolated on alabaster slabs,
Once were unravished Keatsian brides of writhing quietude.

Yet, briefly consider Christ, if you will,
Whose common human form, when crucified,
Assumed inordinate mystical proportions,
Or Hopkins's windhover, a mere bird

Before his pied verse converted its inconsequentiality
To emblematic incarnation,
Borne forth, on soaring, singing wings,
Toward the achieve of, the mastery of the thing.

We who take the time to reclaim ancient truths,
From outmoded scrolls, Greek odes,
Freudian theories no longer espoused, benefit
From perpetual reevaluation. We survive,

Who are willing to take the time to translate
Untranslatable rhymes,
View mutilated versions of Praxiteles' psyche,
With an unbiased eye to the future.

Death is inevitable, since insatiable time
Devours us, without distinction.
Either we surrender, silently, to this irreversible process
Or learn to speak eternity's tongue.

9/12/83 — [2] (02541)

Half-Lives: Willy in Flight [Δ]

By Friday, even die-hard road peddlers
Reach apogee,
That outermost node
On their territorial ellipse, head home,
To recuperate, reacquaint themselves
With unbemused children who've grown old
In the five-day interim and wives
Disillusioned with premature widowhood.

I, at the antipode, a clothing merchant
With a notable success record
And no mean resources set in reserve,
For unforeseen reversals, collapses,
Acts of God or lesser deities,
Seem, with ever-increasing frequency,
To be heading out of town as weekends arrive,
Driving away, at the slightest caprice,

Almost as though compelled, by djinn-spells,
To keep my momentum going,
Not even allow a solitary hour to intervene
*

Between evening store closing
And next morning's ritualized door opening,
Let alone between Saturday night
And Monday's 9 a.m. onslaught.
In fact, I'm driving south, just now,

This fog-riddled Sabbath, toward Oxford,
For what reason I know not,
Unless it be to fetch effects
I might have recently neglected to bring back.
Just lately, I've noticed things missing:
Certain swatches, enthusiasm,
Sample garments, after-the-sale catharsis,
Pride, purpose, humor,

The abstract attributes, anyway,
Which, when lacking concrete application,
Leave a guy with an empty feeling inside.
Possibly, that misbegotten waitress
I awakened beside, last trip,
Neither of us recognizing each other's nakedness,
Robbed me. Perhaps that accidental lady
Is the only female my loneliness has ever known.

9/16/83 — [1] (03603)

Ritual Disappearance ^Δ

Dislocated somewhere between dawn and noon,
He wanders south, distractedly,
Vectoring in on FM 100,
Listening to Memphis's chauvinistic voice:
Steely Dan's "Deacon Blues" and Randy Newman,
Fitted in, judiciously,
Between prolix advertisements
For Mud Island and the Peabody Hotel.

He drowns in the innocuous sounds.
His minimal, infrequently conceived images
Smolder at ignition point,
Like too-tightly-packed stacks of dry leaves.
He's just not used to all this freedom,
Accruing to him, this Friday
He's embezzled from his rigid work ethic.
*

Never before has he shirked his duties,
Left town without notifying someone
Where, in an emergency, he might be reached.

What oblique, preternatural fiat
Has commanded him to abandon all moorings,
Pull out, from under his psyche,
The spare rug he always keeps
Under the rug he's forever pulling
From underneath his feet, he can't understand.
Yet, in this strange desert, Mississippi,
He fears distant voices
That shrink into their sheets as he nears Oxford.

Not habitually given to superstition, visions,
Or oracular divinations by self-ordained mystics,
He gropes, this day, for any clue
As to what might be causing him,
A mere unacknowledged poet, to flee,
Who augments his paltry teacher's salary
By novelizing formulaic pornography, to order.
Suddenly, he realizes why dying Chickasaws,
Even at forty-five, go off and hide.

9/16/83 — [2] (03503)

Awakening Sleeping Dragons [Δ]

Having just lunged through Bailey's Woods,
On my return path, emerging, from its cool coverts,
Like a steam locomotive exiting a tunnel,
I stall, fall to my wobbly knees,
Beneath a fruit tree teeming with webworms
Trapped in catatonic stupors.

Slowly, I rise, stare into their airy bag,
And breathe heated drafts,
To excite their swarming dormancy.
Like free-falling parachutists,
They begin to stir, spin, swerve, whirl,
Until the entire net is aswirl with nebulae.

Even more for having accomplished a physical act
So psychically satisfying,
*

On a Mississippi afternoon this tranquil,
I can't conceive what sadistic vagary
Could have motivated me
To commit a practical joke so perversely trivial

Or why I should have been distracted,
No matter how momentarily,
From the elation abating pain begs us celebrate
When spirit and bone fuse earth with sky.
My actions defy explanation.
I am aware a desecration has eventuated.

Spent yet recovered enough to resume jogging,
I descend, again, into the womb-woods,
Maneuvering in Rowan Oak's direction,
Hoping, simultaneously, to forget the old,
Discover a new purpose for coming here,
Run free, perfect my humanity,

Practice resurrection, in this solitude,
By extending all my fleshly thresholds.
The harder I press, as if punishing my body
For some undefinable apostasy,
The more clearly I recognize those moiling worms
As surrogates, reminders I must keep jogging.

9/16/83 — [3] (03531)

Browning and Barrett: A Meeting South ^Δ

Not until last evening
Had he ever really perceived himself effete,
A pariah, a breathing anomaly,
Or, of all things inconceivable, a liar.

Yet there he sat, in the Warehouse,
Husbanding Mouton Cadet in a sweating casket,
Writing verse, self-contained,
Oblivious to raucous sounds, from the music lounge,

Confounding the air around him,
As he tried to fire his imagination,
Like a cave man striking flints
Above wet shavings and shreds.

Seemingly locked in concentration's
Escape-proof Houdini box,
He fumbled with image-chains, rattled them,
Hoping they'd give like clover stems delicately knotted.

When he gazed up from his empty page,
She was seated in the chair
Across from him, staring into his frustration,
With laser-beam exactitude.

He squirmed, realizing, at once,
She had located him at the epicenter of a lie
He'd fabricated, earlier that afternoon,
To avoid making good his promise to dine with her.

She didn't have to say,
"You're not on the road, heading home."
Instead, she lifted his filled glass to her lips
And kissed its rim lubriciously,

Drawing him into her soft witchery.
Twenty years his junior,
Not termagant, Lorelei, or Pandora,
She was yet his bittersweet courtesan,

The one mistress who could force him
To compromise his strident resolve,
Take him to bed, despite conflicting desires
Which might predominate, like last night,

When all he really wished to do
Was compose paeans and odes
To two distant mistresses: Beatrice and Héloïse.
In moments, he felt his blood reverse its flow,

His discipline diminish to a feeble demur,
Then submit to her capricious concupiscence.
And it was accomplished.
Her victory over his spirit was complete.

When he awakened, this dawn, she was gone.
He reread her note, all the way home:
"The sonnets you inscribed inside me, last night,
Are the best I've ever read — Elizabeth."

9/17/83 — [1] (00167)

Regional Supervisor

Mistress, whore, courtesan, sheer metaphor —
The highway he drives, between dawn
And twilight, glitters with excitement,
Evokes, like new oceans
Once revealed to antique conquistadors,
Unknown worlds, remote regions,
Mirage-shrouded fantasies.

Each passage, sojourn, flight
Is a slightly surreptitious assignation,
An illicit relationship
During which he discloses his most private insights
And intuitive misgivings to the road,
Who gently strokes him,
Applies her soothing pleasures to his senses.

The entire trip to Oxford and back,
333 miles each way,
Is an unpremeditated celebration of release,
A ceremony in which sharing
Has neither boundaries nor bonds
And responsibility to each other's sensibilities
Is the coefficient of sensuality rendered times energy spent.

Arriving home, now,
Totally satisfied and renewed after his drive,
He parks, unloads the car, showers,
Applies double douses of aftershave,
Cologne, straightens his apartment,
Then begins the gourmet dinner
He'll eat, as always, by candlelight, alone.

9/17/83 — [2] (02355)

Outpatient

On this warm, autumnal Farmington morning,
He malingers in the Capital Café,
Prosaically disentangling
September-ending's suspended metaphors
And dangling participial malaises —
*

A hobo-poet, stowed away in his own rolled bag
Tied to a divining rod
Slung over his bony shoulder,
Still trying to cross the heartland's Sinai,
Without realizing his caravan
Mired here, years ago, in living quicksand.

Not like the lunatic Roman moved, by sheer beauty,
To kiss smooth the rim of his vase
Or out of dissolute solitude
Does he bite his coffee cup's rough lip,
Talk to its steaming draught,
Lifting above memory's hemispherical peripheries,
But as falconer stroking falcons,
Poised to set free blindered thoughts
Caught in tautologies,
Let them circle on verse-thermals
Soaring toward the eye of the sky's volcano.

Suddenly distracted from implacable distraction,
He gazes up. Sane focus
Identifies those loitering in adjacent booths,
Rocking on wobbly stools,
Shoeing time, to inaudible music,
Spewing sibilant philippics and jeremiads,
As kindred inmates without cells —
The Capital Café's regular, nonpaying clientele,
On leave to spend or suspend each day
In patient tranquillity,
With nothing, nothing but freedom on their hands.

9/28–29/83 (00134)

Homecoming Bonfire

Across the country, crisscrossing tradition,
This crisp, autumnal Friday night,
America pokes her makeshift sticks,
Wadded with kerosene-soaked cheesecloth,
Into the splintery interstices of hastily piled pallets
Gathered from factory loading docks,

Then waits, with restive patience, momentarily,
While the brisk evening air ignites,
*

Screams into frenzied stallions,
Their forelegs raised in kicking fright,
As though trying to break from a tight-locked stable,
Escape their own imploding confinement.

She watches voyeuristically,
As if witnessing a Joan of Arc martyrdom
Or, paradoxically, a witch-dunking
Instead of the collective celebration of courage
Her brave native sons deserve,
Who, tomorrow afternoon, will engage the enemy

Itself, in variously hued helmets and cleated shoes,
Breakaway mesh jerseys,
And super-lightweight pants,
Before thronged coliseums shouting for defeat, victory,
Requiring visceral, if not cerebral, stimulation.
She delights in the roaring flames' jagged halo,

Backs away, keeps relaxing her hold
On the frantic, gasping blaze,
As if being attacked by a repeatedly striking cobra,
While scantily clothed dancing shadows —
Amazons — continue to inspire primal chanting,
Until, by degrees, the heat consumes itself,

Night, like a vast, black silence,
Laps in, toward the circular burning island,
Snuffs it, like a candlewick, into oblivion's smolder,
And America, having fulfilled this patriotic ritual,
Dwindles, again, into domestic insularity,
Unaware of her own echoing, primitive connections.

10/10/83   (05872)

[Prepositions and indefinite articles]

Prepositions and indefinite articles
Proposition me, with subtle differences and kinships,
This dangling participial morning,
When neither familiar rhetorical syntax
Nor metaphorical sets
Stimulate memory or imagination to identify rhythms,
*

Recreate, from the collective word-hoard,
Unique concatenations called "poems."
I submit to their meretricious overtures.

All the wide road long, I drive,
Like reading an endless line from the Bible
Repeats liturgies and myths
I've heard and seen, a lifetime,
Without being able to escape their ethical pressures.
Whores, courtesans, day ladies,
Purveying marish maladies, verse-curses,
Roam the streets, with garish abandon,
Trying to distract me from my assigned passage.

My failure to concentrate is their success.
When I awaken from my narcoleptic digressions,
Review the progress of my dreams,
Recorded, neatly, in the notebook on my lap,
I realize, at once, what has happened:
In haste, I left home naked,
Entered the universe, like a new-dropped calf,
Forgot to guard against accidental impasse
Brought on by syntactical oversights.

10/11/83 — [1] (05873)

Antique Locomotives

Afternoon whispers a gentle rain, in my ears.
I, a retired engineer, whose defunct memory
Still hears distant click-clacking trucks
Skimming shimmering tracks,
Highballing all the way from St. Louis's
Market Street terminal
To Columbia's red-brick Katy Station,
Sit, reposed, within this Victorian depot.

My delight is the excitement the mind's senses engender,
Seventy-five years late,
As I imagine massive black locomotives
Scuttling through vast, endlessly open expanses,
With their varnished passenger cars
Trailing obediently behind,
*

Smell, taste, chew acrid coal smoke
Spewing through fluted stacks, like exploding firecrackers,

And witness, solitarily, from a distant hillock,
Their fleet behemoth shapes
Materializing, dominating the landscape, diminishing
Within the violent nimbus their very transience postulates.
As I peer through plate glass,
Across the refurbished brick patio
Ubiquitously puddled with warm October circles,
My drive wheels slow, going up the grade,

Whine, scream, scatter sand granules,
In an effort to gain purchase, surmount the plane,
Dominate the painful incline
Separating the past from this present hour.
They lock. Everything stops.
I slip, begin to slide backward.
All the way home, my bones resonate
With the click-clack of the slick tracks' crack express.

10/11/83 — [2] (02542)

The Sizing Up of Willy Sypher

His entire adult life
Has been an undeviable, irremediable exercise
In wandering through odorous corridors,
Sleeping in sordid, lumpy beds,
Beneath sleazy sheets,
Eating, unnoticed, in roadside cafés.

Orphaned from birth, a glorified hobo
Born with a greasy spoon in his mouth,
He's moved from peddling boiler compound
To encyclopedias to wholesale men's clothing,
Without dropping a stitch, losing his place,
A proverbial magician doing necessity's tricks,

Illusionist and artificer, whose flicking tongue
Mesmerizes, anesthetizes, dupes
Unsuspecting rubes, numbs the best
Into buying his Kickapoo Juice rhetoric
*

And bloodroot-tonic histrionics
As dogma, gospel, metaphorical Torah scripture.

Having possessed neither friends nor enemies,
Not disrespect, reverence, or enmity
For destiny, fate, chance, or circumstance,
Rather, with a degree of equanimity, perceiving his lot
As God's tabula rasa,
Upon whose glazed slate he might write his name

Ten thousand thousand times,
Just as a reminder that he's his own tribe's scribe,
He's always regarded himself fortunate,
For his sheer ability to survive in Houyhnhnmland,
Derive a weekly paycheck, for his efforts,
Shelter and feed himself, on weekends.

After all these years selling himself
To the nearest earpiece,
Closing the most propitiously commissioned deal
On whatever commodity he might be embracing
With all his heart, guts, trust, and love,
He realizes how ephemeral it all is,

How oblique and obsolete
Each newly introduced fabrication, formula, and design
Really seems, in the hierarchy time establishes
While moving him and his coevals
Toward their preordained destinations. He realizes
How insubstantial his deeds really are,

When measured against the higher rhetoric,
The conventional wisdom,
And ultimate theatrics cued by the Master Prompter.
He knows and, knowing, accepts
His sad, tragic aloneness as dues required
By the Union of Human Survivors,

In order that he might perpetuate his singular spiel,
From town to ear,
Drown his cheerless doubts, in wine and beer,
On saturnine Monday and mercurial Thursday nights,
Secure his insurance and retirement
Against the day catastrophe strikes, old age bites.

Tonight, sitting, tranquilly, in Katy Station's confines,
Contemplating Wednesday evening,
A lonely stoic, pariah, tribeless Moses,
Willy decides it's OK;
It's really not all that paltry or shabby.
He's content, finally, with his indefensible ordinariness.

10/12/83 — [1] (02543)

In the Beginning

For Linda Bader

Stranded, abandoned, suspended in a dim nimbus,
As if swallowed by a Jonah-whale
Or spider's lair, I fight to free myself,
Share the clean, un–Love Canaled air

With my own belief in posterity: the future
Untrammeled by pollutants and crude carcinogens,
Monday Night Football, *Quincy*,
The Dukes of Hazzard, *The Love Boat*, *The Muppet Show*.

All the faces in the lounge conspire against me,
As though I were a spy,
A dread pariah with a spider's deadly bite,
Capable of spreading contagion, plague,

Instead of postulating E equals mc squared,
A freaky, quiet guy with wiry hair
And an outsize nose, who spouts formulas,
Logarithms, equations, throughout the night.

I fight to free myself from preconceptions
Regarding my birth and purpose.
I am, in fact, a mere poet, making verses,
Denying spurious accounts of my absent-mindedness.

All I ever desired was to poeticize, in peace,
Oblivious to Pulitzer and Nobel prizes, unself-conscious,
As though godly gifts and public rewards
Bore no relationship to each other.

Perhaps I'll succeed in convincing myself, tonight,
That being stranded, abandoned, suspended
*

In a leviathan's belly, an arachnid's net,
Is, in fact, the beginning of wisdom, God's vision

Distilled to earthly focus, the mortal locus,
From whose epicenter all knowing emanates.
Perhaps this temporary impasse
Is Genesis trying to find its own original voice.

10/12/83 — [2] (02544)

Ahab Makes a Sighting

He's passed at least half his waking days
Adrift on concrete sea lanes,
A crazed Ahab, whose guilt
Has been the peg leg he's dragged with him, as baggage,
All these years he's peddled rags,
Knowing his children and wife
Have regarded him as shipwrecked, dead.

For weeks at a stretch, he's ridden in silence
So white that night and day
Have ceased to distinguish themselves conventionally,
By means of sun- and moon-moved zeniths,
Rather have fused into a lunatic steeplechase,
In whose blind maze he's driven,
Going nowhere, at a furious pace,

Never arriving at a charted location,
Those lands where passion and wisdom and providence
Persuade the stray spirit to anchor,
Investigate the brain's terrain,
Entertain possibilities of sleeping, all night, naked,
Staying, forever, in spontaneity's cove
While yet returning safely home.

Lately, under indescribable pressure,
His nebulous quest has lost its frenetic edge.
Whether finally realizing the fatuousness
Inherent in his ritualed traipsing
Or just naturally fatigued, he's slowed measurably.
Perhaps that ivory mass spouting on the horizon
Has quit its flight, gathered itself for attack.

10/13/83 (02354)

Autumn's Eulogy

Still, though tainted and tainting inexorably,
The leaves sing and breathe deeply,
As if filling their lungs, for the ageless sleep ahead.
They pretend act 3, scene 5,
Will not arrive or, if so, that *Exeunt omnes*,
Somehow, will leave them on stage,
To make curtain call after reprised curtsy and bow.

Season's end never did disillusion me
Or engender vexatious pathos,
Render my spirit vegetable, inept at sensing grandeur,
Appreciating majestic transfigurations;
Instead, it always brought me to my knees,
Prepared to receive natural communion,
Within the leafy, cathedraled silence of dying things.

This afternoon, sitting outside,
Inside a perspiring wineglass,
Growing increasingly inebriated on freshly cut grass,
Listening to crickets and birds perched on the abyss,
Witnessing final butterflies
Disappearing into autumn's pastel crevasse,
I submit to ever-present blessed necessities,

Realizing again, at forty-two,
As I have all the way through my aging's cycle,
That death is neither malevolent nor benign,
Rather coeval, ubiquitous,
A factor to be contended with and accepted,
Respected, for its suzerainty, its prerogatives of ukase and veto.
Seasons may end; a poet's appreciation echoes, forever.

10/15/83 (05450)

Mortis spiriti

This season's leaf-turning
Fails to burn my psyche, in its blaze,
Renew my color cells, with its hued epiphanies,
Like a pastry chef forgetting to refill bags,
*

With decorative icings.
My metaphors wilt, spill, run together
Like paints hastily mixed, applied too quickly.
Perhaps it's simply one more manifestation
Of my not seeing the trees, for the forest,
My knees or feet, for the leaves
Nestling them, in desiccated caress.

10/17/83 (05874)

Shiftings

As the great plates
Which once maintained our shiftless continents
In their perfectly fitted contiguousness
Sep-ar-ate,
The frictioned disintegration our spirits suffer
Becomes silent screeching
Too shrill for our psyches to listen to
Without weeping sympathetically.

As the crevasse between us widens, widens,
Irremediably,
The distance from which we see each other
Highlights our irregularly shaped edges,
Those formerly meshed uniquenesses
Whose seamless blending was two oceans touching,
Flowing into and through one contour —
Alien nations: Lilliput and bully Blefuscu.

And neither of us knows, though both suspect,
Omissive and commissive truancies,
Petty negligences, and delinquent forgivenesses
Set minuscule fissures in motion,
Caused divisiveness and schisms to open, like furrows,
In our Edenic heartland garden,
Grow into a spectacularly deep trench,
We kneeling on opposite sides.

Years after the original rift,
Our drifting souls yet catch a glimpse of the whole,
That blessed, chaos-shaped mass
Out of which our love evolved
And in whose embrace we totally dissolved.
*

Memories, fantasies, hallucinations torment us.
We were love's last best aspiration
For unsundered wonderment, one world.

10/20/83 — [1] (04157)

A Night in the Burying Place ^Δ

Although not unique to me,
Even by the grandest stretch of my pliant imagination,
The notion of being in a familiar location,
All evening, knowing no one,
Is, of all human sensations, the strangest,
For its evocative, womblike solitude,
A palpable déjà vu, whose immediate echoes
Connect this room (in which, sipping Mouton-Cadet,
I record whispering visions)
To the collective mother/mistress/muse
Who begot each of us who ever aspired to greatness,
Tried to create, from dust,
Dream-domes, God-ladders, space-bridges,
In clay, paint, ink, with strokes, notes,
Actually fashioned, from scattered figments, a Yeats poem;
Fra Angelico triptych; Prokofiev concerto;
Hammered Etruscan gold; sacred scrolls
Containing the Torah, Koran, Upanishads,
Dead Sea preachings; Lascaux's pictographs;
Tenth-century-B.C. Chinese pottery.

Tonight, more poignantly than on most,
I sense this nexus,
In the profoundly unrecognizable faces
Reveling about me in scattershot folly
And cloven-hoofed-goat lust. I am a gate-crasher
At my own funeral, a pallbearer
Carrying my newest verse into lonely apotheosis,
In the Warehouse, in Oxford, Mississippi.
Although I realize this place is no better
Than others, for begetting children,
I seem to gravitate to these environs frequently,
To release my earthly burdens into the air,
By burying them here, initially, in my notebook,
Letting them soar into their own ultimate orbits.
*

Yet never has the raucous crowd
Seemed so funereal as it does now,
Nor have I been so unaroused.
Perhaps this land, this place
Have served their purpose, are full, fallow, hallowed.
Tomorrow, in my car, I'll start searching
For a new plot conducive to birth.

10/20/83 — [2] (03517)

Traveling to the State Capital ^Δ

Highway 7 comes up luck's number.
This fall morning, I leave Oxford,
Not heading home but south,
Cross-country, via Water Valley, Coffeeville,
To I-55, then down toward Jackson,
Where, for two days, I'll assimilate rhetoric
Fashioned by and for professors
Who teach English or law
(Perhaps dabble at creating novels or handling cases),

While I attend a very high-class "Conference"
(With a very uppercase *C*, at that, I might add),
Calculated to promulgate harmony
Between seemingly disparate disciplines,
Whose main focus (can you imagine?)
Will be "The Law in Faulkner's Fiction."
How else might Mississippi attract teachers
From Yeshiva, Johns Hopkins, Yale,
Delaware, Georgia State, U. of Chicago?

This miraculously tranquil Sabbath a.m.,
I bob through Yalobusha County,
Whose kudzu-cascading woods,
Brilliant with hue-stippled leaves,
Myriadly punctuated by weary fields
Proudly offering up white-tufted bounty,
Distract me from the gathering at hand.
For a few hours, I actually forget my credentials,
Revel in being original to untainted Eden.

10/21/83 — [1] (03516)

Attending a Lecture ᐃ

Driving with cautious, courageous confidence,
I enter, penetrate to the center of, the state,
My psyche a surgeon guiding a scalpel
Home, to a sebaceous cyst's indurated core.

Not knowing what I'll find, on arriving,
I press ahead, down I-55, toward Jackson,
Reiterating rosary beads named Bilbo,
Barnett, and Vardaman.

Oncoming headlights
Suggest baleful weather anticipates my presence.
The bright sun falls away, into my mirrors,
Like a buffalo herd tricked over an abyss.

Gray eyes hidden in the breathing sky
Peer at my unyielding shadow,
Say nothing, with their passionless stares.
Yet measurement-taking has left me naked,

And my shadow has dissolved in the gloom
Hovering like buzzards over a steaming rabbit.
My guts shudder. Suddenly, I wonder
Why I decided to attend the Law and Southern Literature

Lecture entitled "Legal, Racial, and Moral Codes
In *Go Down, Moses* and the Snopes Trilogy,"
Especially when I, like Faulkner,
Consider myself, foremost, a failed poet.

10/21/83 — [2]   (03513)

Wind Instruments

The wind clipping past my car
Is a sloop continuously slipping its moorings,
A sleek sea gull gliding sideways,
In a ceaseless, easy soar —
The sibilant slicing sound silence sings,
Whether severing air
On the leading edge of a sculpted hull,
Feathered wing, or deliquescent echo.

The wind is my fluid buoy, my music,
Whose seminal constituents are two parts euphoria,
Three caprice, two more metaphor.
All my northerly trip home,
She transports me whisperously. I vibrate
As though my bones supported the entire sky
And my flesh, containing both,
Might inflate, lift, disappear into the cosmos.

10/22/83 (00288)

The Bell Ringer

For Jan,
this Sunday hymn

Muted church bells, hanging on frosted air
Stippled with glistening sunlight,
This breaking Sunday,
Frame a lithoed idyll by Currier & Ives.

In a drowsy nimbus, I half-listen
To their distant timbres,
Trying to envision hands gripping ropes,
Coaxing note after note into small songs,

Those devoted, monastic palms
Tugging at November-cold raw-hemp cords
As though each were connected to God's earlobe
Instead of wheels in a pigeon-sullied belfry,

Those slight, robed arms and shoulders
Pumping with hope of awakening angels
To our loneliness, this desolate Sabbath morn,
Not just going through cosmic motions.

Suddenly, like ink dripping from a tipped well,
Stillness fills spaces the bells made.
All day, my wrists and biceps ache,
As if engaged in isometrics, with the sky.

11/6/83 (02064)

Groping for Tropes

The wide, white road
Breaks open, ahead of me, continuously,
Like a tidal wave gaining momentum as it goes,

While I, vibrating atop its crest
As though saddled to a battling Appaloosa,
Scan the horizon, for landmasses,

Grasp the frothing wave's lathered mane,
To maintain equilibrium, as both vie
To stay energized in my brain's eye —

A mixed metaphor groping for a fixed position —
Horse and natural force, distortions,
Concrete abstractions of abstracted concrete

Breaking open, ahead of me, continuously,
Like a wide, white road,
As I gain momentum, going, poemward, home.

11/8/83 — [1] (03538)

[Off to my right, this impatient twilight,] ᐃ

Off to my right, this impatient twilight,
A blood-rust sun hovers in gauze,
Like a wound oozing beneath a bandage.

Wincing as if empathizing with the pained sky,
Staring too long, squinting,
Almost as if caught in its throbbing pulse,

I suddenly find myself blinded to the highway
Confining my vision to an uneven slit,
A cicatrix of a kind, a corneal scratch.

For minutes, I continue innocently waiting
For fate to hit me, from the rear,
Or maliciously slap me into a ditch,

As I fear for my very survival, this trip.
When again I can see,
Distinguish horizon between low and high,

Daylight has funneled into night's eye;
The cut has healed. All that remains
Is a violet striation, a brittle scab,

And not a trace of pain,
To remind me how vibrantly
My heart was keeping pace with the sun.

11/8/83 — [2] (03500)

Lexical Senescence ^Δ

Within their sweaty nest,
Writhing like sperm in vasectomized testes,
My restive words seethe, hyperventilate,
Swarm all over each other,
Without form or coordinated purpose,
Whose only formulations, this morning,
Are discordant metaphors, unrealized climaxes.

Potential essays, critiques, poems, plays
That once aspired to Nobel eloquence
Are stranded, in fragmented sentences, truncated ideas,
Misguided, unmodified predicates and objects,
On the tip of my brain's flaccid ballpoint tongue,
While I, like a masochistic voyeur, sit by,
Witnessing even desire die of natural causes.

11/10/83 — [1] (03536)

In Retirement ^Δ

He sits, all afternoon, on his bony ass,
In the placid, unfascinating atmosphere
That driving for long distances provides his imagination.

Unable to conjure a single winged metaphor
Worth netting, pinning,
Preserving beneath prismatic glass,

He fidgets, twists in his reclining crucifix,
Tries to count cracks in the highway,
Decipher mile markers,

Translate and assimilate billboard slogans,
Count the various states on plates
Fastened to cars he stalks and overtakes,

As he waits for lifelike thoughts to escape
From the closet in his brain's basement,
Where he stored them, in mothballs,

Those soft-floating transformations
That hovered, nearly forty summers,
Before abandoning his shores, for warmer territories —

Larva, chrysalis, butterfly.
Now, as if the cycle were complete,
He drives home, neither fluttering nor singing,

Rather, uninspired inside his moving cocoon —
A doomed collector of verse, poems,
Silently reciting old flights, from memory.

11/10/83 — [2] (03540)

The Elephant Man ^Δ

It had been so long since dreams
Had poppied sleep's uncultivated fields
That rather than being intimidated by demons
Besieging last night's equanimity,

> I actually savored the change, without complaint,
> Purposely didn't awaken, didn't stir,

As snakes, malign and innocuous,
Sprouted, like dragon teeth, in place of my fingers
And toes. One grew from my nose —
An elephant's trunk — another from my groin.

> I actually savored the change, without complaint,
> Purposely didn't awaken, didn't stir,

As booted, uniformed, blue-eyed youth,
In quick-precision goose step,
Paraded before my Reichstag reviewing booth,
Where I saluted, ranted, saluting, saluting.

> I actually savored the change, without complaint,
> Purposely didn't awaken, didn't stir,

As I flew, my stiff body the fuselage,
Arms, stretching to bed's edge, wing spars
Of the *Enola Gay*, and gave orders
To break the egg for the mushroom omelet and ate.

> I actually savored the change, without complaint,
> Purposely didn't awaken, didn't stir,

Because it had been so long since dreams
Had poppied sleep's uncultivated fields,
Since demons — or deities, either — had even tried
To awaken me from death's blessed equanimity.

11/20/83 (00266)

Reinstating Claims ^Δ

For three days, the ocean has roiled and tumbled
Like a clumsy bear at play in snow.
Today, on entering the patio, I sense
Unspoken fiats have caused total change.
The body that accompanies me, from sleep, shivers.
It's a spell, I contend. The air is crisp,
As if I were spending Thanksgiving postlude
In Plymouth, not Fort Lauderdale.
The water is preternaturally still.
What movement occupies my eyes
Formulates itself as evanescent objects
Void of evocative symbolic implications.

A Coast Guard helicopter materializes,
Flies out, from Port Everglades, in a great sweep,
Like a metallic boomerang, then disappears,
Allows the fragile, metronomic waves,
Lapping the sand, to resume cadence in my ears.
A man and his son slice the near horizon,
That spit between water and sky,
With their running — scissors splitting my concentration.
Three petroleum tankers, at anchor
Two miles out, awaiting a berth in the harbor,
*

Spewing smoke plumes from their stacks,
Might be knights gaining courage for a joust,

Right whales drowsing in obtrusive solitude,
Or just rusted boats — flotsam my scanning intellect
Temporarily isolates and annexes on paper,
To prove it can make itself useful,
Participate in the process of discovering something new
Even if there are neither pilgrims anymore
Nor unclaimed shores to stake, in freedom's name.
Perhaps, possessing the ability to connect antipodes,
Link the remotest planets to lands closest at hand,
Merely by thinking metaphoric analogues into existence,
Is my best means of conquest, the one way
To outguess, stay ahead of, forgetfulness.

11/25/83 (05875)

Tension Is the Father

> *If necessity is mother,*
> *then tension must be the father, of invention.*
> — Herr Diogenes Brodsky, F.S. (Full of Shit)

How perfectly curious,
On an end-of-November morning
This stunningly sunny,
When my mind has settled in fluid neutral,
Two hundred miles drowsy,
Suddenly to be struck by cacophonous incongruities
So apparently oxymoronic,
Echoing through my slowly rousing brain:
Galli-Curci, Patrice Lumumba.

What these names could possibly be doing,
Swimming beneath my cave-pool,
Or signifying, rising side by side,
Defies easy explanation. Inaccessible metaphors
Refuse to excuse their simultaneous appearance
Within hearing range of my imagination.
And yet despite or, more precisely expressed,
Because of their incestuous pairing,
They have revived my respect for the unexpected.

11/30/83 (05876)

Death's Messenger

As his days passed from adolescence,
Toward middle age,
Like an Athenian marathon runner,
Then beyond, penetrating the edge
Where all paths become one horizon,
A vague malaise,
With which his own maladroit rage harmonized,
Began to overtake him. Death-breaths,
Laced with unsavory anal gas,
Flesh-rot, chilled the sweat on his neck,
No matter the pace he tried to maintain.
Despite seizing lungs, hardening arteries,
Metatarsals contracting hairline fractures,
He actually managed, for a few decades,
To keep even, endure the pain.
For the last three years, sidetracked,
Confined to a wheelchair,
He's fashioned endless skeins of hemp
Into inoffensive macramé hangings,
To decorate the padded cell
In which his insane brain remains incarcerated.
A dismal bastard, always lacking the time of day,
For the severe tedium his vegetation flowers,
He escapes, cataleptically, on rare occasions,
Into the vortex of a shallow daydream,
Where he catches glimpses
Of the supple marathoner
Who used to infuse his once-sleek physique
With that haughty attitude of pseudoimmortality,
Traces of those slender, striated legs
That bore his soaring shape
Across the tape, on victory's sibilant whisper.
On days like today,
When figments refuse to coalesce
And blind silence pervades his hemispheres,
He dies step by step, without moving,
Minute by inch by twitch and heartbeat,
And each measurement is a blasphemy
Echoing fecklessly as Bishop Berkeley's tree
Crashing, repeatedly, in an uninhabited forest.

12/1/83 (05877)

La vida es sueño

Coming and going,
In and out of snow flurries
Opening and closing like moist lips
Manipulating quick kisses, he scurries,
The car abiding by his guiding hand,
Without complaint or hesitation,
Despite ice, eyefuls of slush
Hurled by eighteen-wheelers flying past
With imperturbable arrogance and nonchalance.

He is this day's waif, cliché's victim,
The mythic downy chick
Picked up in the swooping goshawk's talons,
Out of its barnyard midst,
Fate's trifle, God's providential gewgaw,
The Diaspora's displaced road-poet,
Creating, in cerebral flight, his own pogrom,
His entire route a crowded Cracow ghetto,
A crawlspace separating tomorrow from Auschwitz.

Now is already too late to plea-bargain
With the deadlocked hour
Or suborn the immediate future's magistrate,
By promising to refuse further inducements
To amass kudos and lucre,
Prostituting his talent, writing screenplays
For daytime TV and the movies.
Neither commutation nor reduced sentence
Is a viable option. He must submit.

Out inlets, in exits,
Going through openings about to close,
Coming through closures barely opening,
He deftly controls the snow,
Manages to keep to the elusive highway,
Like a pencil balancing on its tip
As it faultlessly navigates an intricate maze,
Going, going, without knowing
When the end will appear, when disappear,

Or if, miraculously, his living spirit
Might actually arrive at a destination
Beyond history's concentration camp,
*

He complete his mission safely,
Be returned to his wan-faced children and wife
In time to celebrate Christmas,
Open gifts strewn at the tree's base,
Kiss freedom's sweet, peaceful lips.
Possibly, he never even left home, for threats of snow.

12/14/83 — [1] (00851)

The Powers That Be

Accidentally rhyming "blizzard" with "wizard,"
I see myself instantaneously transfigured,
Behind my eyes' mind,
Into moon stones, vaporous as bleached bones,
Blown across my heated hemispheres,
Particles floating in a dust mote oceans wide,
Caravels, argosies, ghost ships
Slipping, whisperously, through history's grip, into oblivion.
No mere paltry human am I
But shimmering simulacrum,
Image in God's eye, silhouetted,
Whenever, at the slightest rhyme's provocation,
My imagination decides to stride free,
Strike out, stake new claims,
In the name of the poet Alfonso el Sabio.

Jesus! How can one brief snow,
Not even threatening to dethrone forward motion,
Elicit such voluptuous hyperbole,
Amazing verbal legerdemain,
Miraculous word games emblazoned on the soul?
Just knowing that, in a tight,
I might leap tall buildings, in a single bound,
Outpace speeding locos, in a single insanity,
Extricate myself from a Houdini-proof illusion,
Harpoon a white whale and survive
To parse the tale, in Ishmael-feet,
Is unbelievably reassuring, especially
For a paltry human being who yet believes
In make-believe's irrefragable capacity
To keep reality from being defeated by the enemy: itself.

12/14/83 — [2] (02607)

A Christmas Card for My Parents [Δ]

12/25/83

For slightly more than two score years,
I've tipped the cornucopia
With you, Mom and Dad, at Christmas.
We've witnessed its bounties spill into our lives,
Like tides kissing warm shores,
Exulted in the tight alliance
Our family's families have maintained,
Despite ever-widening boundaries.

Now, in my forty-third season,
My coming home seems tactically impracticable.
I've been reassigned to a distant parish.
With terrible sadness, I'll regret
Not kneeling, amidst gifts, at the tree's altar,
With brothers, sisters. You, especially,
My caring, sharing, unsparingly devoted parents,
Will I miss, this Christmas.

12/15/83 — [1] (02113)

The Fish

Just ten days left till Christmas,
Yet I sit in Katy Station,
This frigid evening, blitzed on Chablis,
Feeling bereaved, so far from home,
Avidly practicing dying in primordial silence.

Ice-olated like a fish in an air pocket
In a lake frozen-in for the winter,
I persist cryogenically, circling, occasionally,
The crystal glass's prismatic pool,
To test the breadth of my derelict soul's neglect,

Diving, to fathom at what tepid depths
My suspended inhibitions
Might float free, fins shimmering like cilia.
Dizziness occludes vision
Rather than enhancing wisdom. I languish,

A ravaged scavenger skimming the bottom,
For memories to stimulate breathing,
Keep dreams buoyant, clairvoyance alive,
In the Red Sea irrigating my days —
A fish out of water, swimming upstream.

12/15–16/83 — [2] on 12/15 & [1] on 12/16 (02608)

Death of a Backwoods Man

With two full days' accumulation of excrement
Seething in his bowels, like garden compost,
Rife with parasites, tapeworms,
He plods through his duties, in a stupor,
Muscles anesthetized, gut in such pain,
Delirium shuts off all impulses
That otherwise might have activated his brain.

What has caused his movements
To vary from their oh-so-regular routine,
He can neither ascertain nor rectify;
Rather, he chooses to endure discomfort, in silence,
For embarrassment the slightest sharing creates.
Even as fever prairie-fires his hemispheres,
He refuses to seek treatment,

Instead curses old age, for the scourge
That has laid him low, "stove him up."
Suddenly, like an erupting volcano, he explodes,
Releasing a gangrenous stream of fecal matter
That sprays underwear, pant legs,
The tattered chair in which he slumps.
He realizes, at once, his appendix has ruptured.

Alone, crumpled on the floor,
Unable to stanch the crimson flow, reach the phone,
He flounders in his own futile humiliation,
Drowns in each pint, ounce, drop, bead of blood
That splats to the base of his consciousness,
Where it pools, briefly,
Before draining memory, deeds, dreams.

12/16/83 — [2] (00850)

Booking Passage

When prose flows,
The poetry goes to pieces.
So is it when I compose strophes.
Those grandiose notions
Clot like ice floes,
Block my psyche's arteries.

There's just no room
For two boats
In the same channel simultaneously
Or space, in the brain's hold,
To contain both cargoes.
Let each vessel pass alone.

1/2/84 (01473)

Cobra and Mongoose

Aimlessness stalks, with such stealth, its prey,
Assails its victims so rapaciously,
It's almost impossible for them to assess the damage,
Calculate the extent to which they've succumbed,
Until it's too late
To do anything about rectifying the oversight,
Correcting misdirections and deflections,
Deflating compressions, or to deny their own blatant neglect.

Without realizing it, their souls are consumed,
Chewed up and spewed out, into the universe,
Like saints' bones strewn through illuminated breviaries,
Orphans left in foundling homes and bulrushes,
To be adopted by anonymity and failure,
Like newspapers set out on curbs,
For recycling into napkins and toilet paper.
Their spirits are transmogrified into doom.

Too soon, reality shows its cruel hues,
Bares its supple, tender teats,
Suggesting ambiguousness hard to square with truth.
Fact has it that spilled blood
Spells creatures killed, bodies annihilated
Beyond all reasonably dubious shadows
Emanating from the valley of the quickly dead.

There's no room for the imagination
To exhibit its Crystal Palace glass,
Perfumes extracted from white-whale cases,
Its Edison talking machines
And Sholes & Glidden typewriters,
When the Serengeti erupts,
Refuses to acknowledge death
Stalking both mongoose and cobra arbitrarily.

1/11/84 — [1] (02609)

Viewing a Gauguin Retrospective, at Katy Station

In this safe place,
So totally foregone from my conclusions,
I lie at anchor, truce flag raised,
A recluse out of the storm, inside the reef,
Tight into the lee shore.
Seclusion is my host, I its phantom guest.
Requiring, in my brief retirement,
Millennial quiescence, inutterable forgetfulness,
I hereby serve notice on all demons
And naked Polynesian maidens:
Beware, all ye who enter these gates!

1/11/84 — [2] (02610)

A Break in the Routine △

In a flash, Willy became completely savvy
As to how fast routine duties
Can deviate from set patterns
When the slightest distraction preempts instinct,
Causes thinking to stir, awaken,
Stretch imagination's contracted synapses
To restive ambitiousness.

Just this bristling, snow-stippled dawn,
Not twenty-five miles down the highway,
Driving out to make his calls
(Despite God's personal affront to his labors),
*

His intellect's dynamo, powered by caffeine rods
Run deep into his overheating core,
Already designing the day's strategies,

He came upon three seemingly fatal accidents —
Shattered vehicles littering shoulders, ravines,
Like flotsam from a sunken ship —
And never even considered stopping
To proffer assistance or at least mollify his curiosity
As to whether the victims, survivors and dead alike,
Might still be trapped inside.

So absorbed was he in memorizing his lines,
Getting right his cues, perfecting his spiel,
Determining, then reworking, a hundred times,
The sequence of his suit, slack, and sportscoat presentations,
To entice prospective buyers into placing orders
For Acme-Zenith's fall-'85 line,
He passed them by, without batting his mind's eye,

That is, until he reached his first client,
Czarlinsky's Haberdashers, late in the afternoon,
And realized, halfway through his showing,
He'd forgotten to pack all the swatches
For his worsted and wool-blend tailored clothing.
Never had this happened to Willy Sypher,
Acme-Zenith's crack rep to the Middle West.

A man not generally given to poetic flights,
Let alone fictive metaphorizing,
Willy suddenly likened himself to a victim —
Gulliver bereft in a desolate Houyhnhnmland,
Quixote marooned on an island —
Stranded by dint of his own dereliction, with only his slacks
To nourish his highly compromised sallying forth

And with no way of returning, four hundred miles,
Before Friday, since he'd made his dates well in advance,
Touting his early entrance into the marketplace
As a divine sign of his company's intention to proselytize,
Win over infidels, by selling them on the A-Z motto,
"Quality Because Of, Not Despite, Diversity."
In a day or three, Willy's apologies will become routine.

1/18/84 — [1] (02353)

Lady Snow

This snow-laced dusk has the soft hue
Of a porphyry nude statue
Backlighted with amber and alabaster incandescences.
Its nubile cast is that of pale innocence
Suspended gracefully, in haloed silhouette,
From the profiled faces of delicately carved cameos.
Moon dust touches my eyes, with the subtlest crust.

Someplace in this frigid universe,
My energized bones take wing.
The flown soul sings the brittle winds awake.
My paltry, boisterous voice screams itself home,
Cathedrals itself beneath oblivion,
As though sensing ulterior purpose
In its meager Renaissance verses.

Suddenly, I embrace night. Her female physique
Annihilates my loneliness, welcomes me back,
Within her forest. I've arrived uninvited,
A hunter whose oblique quest for stray prey
Has brought me all this way, to her purlieus,
In search of hidden virtue and ethics to church,
Before more snow closes the passes,

Cancels the search for the golden city of Cíbola.
Tonight is beauty's nude statue —
Aphrodite, Venus de Milo,
Brooke Shields seated in compliant, benign silence,
Passionless, devoid, an unindicted co-conspirator
In Michael Jackson's siege on celebrity,
On TV's American Music Awards.

Realizing I'm a latecomer on the scene,
A mere twentieth-century post-*Howl* poet,
Whose Ginsbergian visage augurs poorly
Yet whose lunacy registers positive vibes,
I accede to her spectacular energy,
As the falling snow accumulates,
Gathering, into herself, my psyche's fibers.

Finally, coming into her throbbing, lubricated vagina,
I die, a blithe spirit flying toward paradise.
*

Such precise spontaneity, planned manhood,
Hardly fits the specific requirements
Imposed on pretenders to the celestial throne.
Indeed, night is Snow Queen.
I wouldn't dare preempt her regal unpredictability.

1/18/84 — [2] (02605)

The Conventional Wisdom

Today, a strange torpor pulses through my brain,
Like current phasing, crazily,
From AC to p.m., a.m. to DC,
Draining off my most productive energies,
In its clepsydra-like alternations,
Creating a negative force field
That repels dreams, lyrical winds, beams
Emanating from pirouetting comets and shooting stars,
Rainbows, moondogs, and naked maidens.

On turn-down days such as this,
When gray lethargy insinuates every movement,
Changes its hue to suicidal blue-green,
I resign, consign my spirit to its moodiness,
And hibernate inside silence's cave.
Long ago, I assayed the futility of fighting
Dubious last-ditch battles, risking loss,
Dying despite the dignified peace achieved
And decided, at such time, to just say, "Screw it."

1/19/84 — [1] (00849)

Willy's Notion of Stewardship

Before today, the last time Willy
Had made a tour of Acme-Zenith's Tipton factory
Was a decade ago, when the company
Bused all its sales reps,
After their spring meeting, to view,
In situ, "the whole shtick,"
The sixty-six piece-rated operations
*

For their top-of-the-line men's dress slack —
Ammunition the better with which to impress
Old and prospective users of their goods, alike,
Obligatory nomenclature for all road peddlers.

After all, don't doctors, accountants, pedagogues,
And other professionals like him
Frequently subject themselves to refresher courses
In their respective fields of expertise?
Why shouldn't he be familiar with new methods
For applying waistbands, flapped back pockets?
Jesus! Computers, hydraulics, pneumatics
Aren't confined exclusively to space shuttles
And CAT scanners! Actually,
Zipper slides and stops, crotch pieces
Are every bit as critical as reentry ellipses
And sophisticated rectal and breast imaging.

With this wisdom floating through his thoughts,
Like dogma from another century,
For almost two hours, on his drive home,
By sunny Friday noon,
Willy had resolved to pay a visit to the Tipton plant,
Introduce himself to the manager,
Chew the fat, for half an hour,
View the new German, Japanese, and Italian machines,
Verse himself on pertinent facts,
Such as production capacity, in pairs per day,
Capital outlay to purchase, and payout years
To recover and justify, these exorbitant wonders.

Staying two hours,
To allow his absolute amazement to catch up
With his brain's assimilative powers,
He stooped over, stood behind,
Peered and ogled at, from across the cluttered floor,
Various humans working at breakneck urgency,
Their arms and fingers, knees and toes and legs
Speeding, twitching, manipulating fabric,
Air, daydreams through ceaselessly repeating cycles.
And as he watched, Willy began to cry,
Though no one would have noticed,
Had they focused on his presence among them.

Tears evoked by an inner sense of pride
Congealed in his eyes' crow's-feet,
Made the frenzied scene
A kind of tribal crucifixion,
A Bible tableau crowded with victims being sacrificed,
All witnessed, obliquely, by Willy,
Who had never, in his forty years,
Experienced anything approximating a revelation.
Yet today, as he sailed homeward,
He could almost see each of their hectic faces
Individually, almost hear each one
Cheering him on, to sell the hell out of his line,
Keep them in work, producing, keep them from starving.

1/19/84 — [2] (02352)

Yen Ching

Words are my
    Fortune cookies.
I break them open, every opportunity,
    With reckless expectation,
Each time hoping they'll assure me
    The future is another new poem,
The present is my cup of oolong tea.

1/20/84 (01474)

Form Follows Function

All the way in from the country,
I couldn't smother that image
Smoldering like a wide clot of pine needles
About to ignite into a brush fire,

That dirt-strewn, orange-hued Cadillac hearse,
Whale-shaped, rocket-finned, mammalian,
Stalled halfway up the Flat River exit ramp,
Beached, inadvertently, in cement shallows . . .

Couldn't drag it back into pelagic serenity,
Douse it with amniotic seas,
*

Which, while allowing it to circulate, breathe,
Might let death fuel its furnaces —

Charon's barque set adrift
Yet mired in its own fiery waterway . . .
That embarrassed vehicle, that female cuckold,
With its hood raised like a nun's habit in a razoring breeze . . .

Couldn't banish that naked anomaly from memory,
No matter how the approaching metropolis
Continued to intensify the burning in my nostrils,
Ungyve the eyes' hydrants.

Not even after amusing myself, in the city,
Slaking my craving for a glazed pastry,
Evening's tart, could I eradicate that stalled catafalque,
Puke-hued, lugubrious, cursed,

Trailed by at least twenty-five cars,
Headlights murmuring an uninspired hymn,
Beneath the strident sun, the entire procession
Littering the highway, like glittering crumpled cans.

1/25/84 (05878)

Leaving Them

Always, in youth, going away
Was the sweetest clover-scented roundelay.
No matter the season,
Leaving home was renaissance May,
A decade-long *carpe diem*,
Since I knew they would be waiting up,
Regardless what inconvenient a.m.
My quixotic and reckless ecstasies
Might appropriate from their dreamless sleep.

Going away was always only a day's bereaving,
Whether rafting from Itasca to Plaquemines Parish
Or idylling through two master's degrees,
Inside the university's womb,
Where the poet-in-embryo grew, slowly,
Toward that moment when life and I,
*

Simultaneously, would be born,
Leap into breathing, commence looking, seeing,
Envisioning, in each other,

Colossal possibilities for committing, to public memory,
More than ordinary deeds,
Reshaping myths, stubborn as dandelions,
Into deliquescent, evanescently hued clusters
Of bougainvilleas, honeysuckles, lilacs
Blooming, perpetually, in gardens
Tended, second to second, by the collective unconscious.
Always, in all ways, taking leave of my parents
Carried no grave consequences,

So long as they manipulated the weights,
Assayed my ciphers, irresponsibilities,
Gaucheries, social faux pas,
And silently compensated for my disrespectful complacency,
With their unmistakable love for me,
First child, son of their own mild spring,
Who, themselves, have aged so completely,
I sense, in each leave-taking, the wide abyss.
Inside the distance, my own lonely moaning echoes.

1/26/84 (05879)

Suffering a Head-Snake

Traversing Route 32's zigzagging trajectory,
From barren Esoterica,
Heading toward civilized Hesperides beyond Phariseeland,
I maneuver my frenzied vehicle,
Wrestle its steering wheel,
Just to keep from careening into the abyss
Paralleling both sides of the road, stay clear of debris.

I am Nemo, wriggling, frantically,
Ten feet above my vessel's deck,
A feckless piece of flotsam
Flailing to free myself from a colossal squid's
Tentacled squeeze. Breathing burns
Worse than being cremated alive.
The sea surrounding me is Dante's Stygian matrix.

Now, I'm Nemo's ghost, truth transmuted
By metaphor. My reflection
Glares back at me from the bubbling slime.
Corruption's face is grafted onto its pocked visage.
My eyes were just inside the giant squid.
What I see, this malevolent morning,
I see with brainless clarity:

The world unsorted,
Filtering through unadulterated hatred.
I am the enemy, the Hydra,
Whose hundred thousand mouths,
Nipping away at my sanity,
Are attached to undulating, serpentine stems
Emanating from my imagination,

As I try to drive across country, today,
No doubt hallucinating, to some degree,
From having drunk too much coffee,
To stay awake, not stray,
After last night's struggle with sleep's demons,
Those spitting, hooded, hissing cobras
Who mistook my shy, tiny dreams for easy prey.

2/16/84 (05880)

[Faces arrested in spontaneity's mesh]

Faces arrested in spontaneity's mesh
Are sibilant, shimmering stars
Painted on a Broadway-stage scrim curtain.
Their evanescent illusion beguiles me,
While not letting me forget
Through whose sky my imagination flies,
This histrionic evening,
When loneliness plays Juliet to my fated Romeo,
Blanche DuBois to my Stanley Kowalski.

All this hoteled world is a stage,
Over which prostitutes in gaily painted silks parade,
Capitalists, diplomats, and visitors on vacation
From Tierra del Fuego, Massillon, Ohio,
Sri Lanka, Farmington, Mo., and Kiev converge,
*

To enact minor roles, with a dramatic aside
Or swollen cosmic soliloquy
Calculated to capture the spotlight's focus,
In that moment between celebrity and dead silence.

Yet I sit, an audience of one, enraptured,
Captivated by the appearances reality assumes
Beneath proscenium floodlights,
Screaming memorized lines, from my seat,
To anyone who might listen. No one does,
As I scan the lounge, for a recognizable visage,
My wife's profile astutely glued to my performance,
Her eyes following my maladroit moves,
Approving despite their minute perception of my miscues.

She is a simulacrum, a spectral essence
Hovering at memory's peripheries,
Witness to my senility, a critic, estranged wife,
Who still sleeps beside me, nights
And days, although passion has dissipated completely.
My intellect squirms in its earthly dirt.
Anxiously, her image paces in the wings,
Waiting to upstage me,
Displace my name on the marquee.

2/23/84   (04156)

A Delay in Takeoff: Prolonged Taxiing

Rigidly buckled into the foam flotation saddle
Imagination cinches to the girth of this Pegasus
I'll ride, today, 39,000 feet deep,
Beneath gravity's outer edge,
Between mirrored abysses,
Pelagic and atmospheric firmaments,
I clutch coffee cup and pen — twin reins —
Raise them above notebook
Mounted, spread-legged, on the tray table before me,

And yank as though to coax this winged beast
Into obeying anxiety's reflexive vexations
(By my achieving equilibrium, controlling direction,
Dictating speed, pace, rhythm,
*

With the relatively easy flick of conditioned intellect
And an occasional kick in vision's flank,
To discourage whimsy's natural inclination toward laziness)
Were a measure of the flesh's dexterous poetic vectoring,
The soul's equestrian prestidigitation.

Suddenly, I set the empty cup aside,
Clip pen to my inner sportscoat pocket, thumb the tray closed,
Stow the notebook in a pouch just below,
Tighten both eyes, as my own weight
Pushes backward, like Sisyphus's stone,
Against the inclining plane of the plane's takeoff —
Rotation, lift, turnout, and climb.
How unfortunate that flying metaphors
Can't compare to heavier-than-air horses in full stride.

2/26/84 (05881)

Portrait of Painter and Poet, on a Snowy Morning △

No day fills me less with guilt,
For setting aside obligations,
Idling in soiled clothes, sipping a continuous draught of coffee,
Forgetting success and the Protestant ethic,
Than one in which I'm inspired to worship and wonderment,
By a blizzard, or is more tranquil,
For forcing me indoors, to invent my own escapes.

This morning, my six-year-old boy, Troika,
Has fashioned himself in a wizard's image.
The breakfast table on the sunporch is his easel.
Crayons, watercolors, pencils, tape,
And felt-tip pens lend, to him, omnipotence
He transposes, through brain-hand alchemy,
To multihued construction paper.

Fascination exchanges his ions for mine,
Binds mine to his, in electrolytic ecstasy,
To which our closely confined existences submit.
My senses penetrate his eyes' excitement,
As he gazes at, probes, one of his mother's fanciful paintings,
Crucified on the tongue-and-groove wall,
And apprentices to his destiny, by copying a desert scene

Replete with prickly cacti, lizards, a riverbed
Flowing through its Dead Sea geography,
Despite eternal mummification. Up, down,
His eyes climb to, then descend from, her rendering,
Like a monk ascending Giotto's campanile,
To breathe vision, borrow a few inspirations,
Bring them back, to share with his brothers.

I nurture silence, contain my curious astonishment
At his obliviousness to the raging snow,
Cascading in colossal drifts, twisting in midair,
Like snakes slithering sideways, in straight fright.
I strain to keep from snapping concatenations
His spinnerets have connected to intellect's hooks,
To lure stray prey into his head-web.

Too soon, he concludes with a flourish of hues
That brings into view a many-horned sun,
Until this instant neither gaseous red
Nor cracking like a parched quarry bank,
Its fiery pieces cascading, desertward, like meteoric snow.
"This one's for you, Dude.
Now I think I'll make a blizzard."

The distance between his shifting and my quiet respect
Promotes creativity. Behind his focus
Through porch windows, I focus on the shivering devil
And unraveling mummy he shotguns with dots.
Both of us watch them buckle under his wintry blast,
As my perspective, slowly filling with his images, widens,
Begins sifting into his picture, like tranquil snow.

2/27–28/84 (00685)

Having the First and the Last Say

Who is best known in Cloneville, Connecticut:
Dr. Seuss or Dr. No?
Few have ever paused to consider the question
Or speculated on the rumor that Pussy Galore
And Thidwick the Big-Hearted Moose
Once made skin flicks together, on Crab Key,
Or that, once, a Star-Belly Sneetch
*

Seduced Plenty O'Toole,
In a belly-dancing studio behind St. Sophia.

Nor has it ever been satisfactorily ascertained
Whether Ian Fleming and Mr. Sneelock
Were lovers traveling around the world,
With the Circus McGurkus, or just brotherly elders
The collective imagination selected
To go out, among aborigines, and proselytize,
Sing praises to the great god Sodomorrah —
Modern-day Oscar Wildes, in Bible robes,
Ghost writers of the Dead Sea Scrolls.

All that most cultured, literate people realize
Is that neither Ernst Stavro Blofeld nor the Grinch,
No matter how apocalyptic, can succeed, ultimately,
And not because fictions are artifice,
Illusion ephemeral, rather because man,
Whether evil or meek, is penultimate.
The last word, like those spoken "In the beginning,"
Adumbrates and nullifies everything in between,
And the copyright to that one has already been assigned.

3/2/84 (05882)

Donating a Library

I drive the countryside,
In my trusty traveling companion,
Its latest incarnation
An '81 Ford Country Squire station wagon,
Overloaded, today, with my books and papers
Instead of three-piece worsted suits.

Its front end rides high
As a laden oceangoing petroleum tanker
Bucking, pitching, rolling
Like Queeg's *Caine* in a screeching typhoon,
This glisteningly brilliant Tuesday morning,
Through whose troughs and crests I ply.

What a curious mission, this one,
On which I've been assigned to ferry tomes,
*

From my home, to a new location, across the state,
And oversee their disposition,
Cataloging, and shelving in a university library,
Especially since I've written them all,

I, the surviving scribe from the lost tribe,
Who, for forty years, has peddled trousers,
Suits, coats, from my car,
The Diaspora's last, gasping straw boss,
Stevedore, Eric Hoffer of the road-poets,
The original dharma bum, Moses,

Who, during all those endless sea voyages
Overland, just happened to keep a perpetual log,
Recording the imagination's attitudinal latitudes
And spontaneous longitudes, chart Juliet-stars,
And, not quite by accident,
Capture, in verse, the processional passage of generations,

Beginning with Adam and his Satan-swayed coeval.
Today, I engage in sacrifice.
My dispossession, certainly not a volitionless act,
Completes the last climacteric of my old age.
My Torahs, Korans, cabalas, Rig-Vedas,
Kama Sutras, and Upanishads will be made safe,

In the public domain, available to scholars,
Who will come to fashion their dissertations
From formulations and speculative hypotheses
And exegetical documentations
Engendered by the unpublished manuscripts I'm placing on deposit.
I no longer care about baring my soul,

Sharing my privacies, once so fastidiously guarded
From pernicious eyes and petty academic egos
That might attempt to blur my insights and visions,
With imprecise pedagogy, arrogate, to themselves,
Overviews reserved to me, by virtue of a spirit
Not nurtured behind university walls but in the desert instead.

Approaching death, with an open mind,
Has helped me redefine my position.
Today, I drive the countryside, with my manuscripts
And published books, relieved, ultimately, to know
*

That only the verse I rehearsed can be examined.
My words return with me, to our native tongue.

3/6/84 (00848)

Even the Seekers Hide

We spend so much energy
Fending off silence's tentacles,
Which would squeeze the life out of us,
Render us pulpless, isolated in necropolises
Inhabited by breathing souls,
Were it not for the fight we each wage
Who care about our gregarious heritage,
Those few, among multitudes,
Who know the poetics of dreaming,
Alone, can save their spirits
From pulling the graveyard shift, through eternity.
Yet even Einsteinian scientists,
Nonviolent seers, visionaries
Like Gandhi, Jesus, Martin Luther King,
Writers like Milton, Wordsworth, Whitman,
Are fall guys, too,
Despite their attempts to let destiny's clepsydra
Baptize them in sacred ichor,
Failures, too, for not recognizing the paradox
Inherent in their collective inventive sensibility:
That to create, from nonexistence,
Something universally unique, immune to oblivion,
Necessarily requires silence's patience and nurturing,
Since, otherwise, humans couldn't hope to hear,
Stethoscopically, the throb of God's rhythmic pulse,
Let alone dream of imitating its poetic flow.

3/7/84 (05883)

An Unaborted Distortion

This wind-torn morning,
I give birth to breech words.
They are agony's progeny,
*

With shapes distorted beyond normal description
And only cleft palates
To distinguish the pitch of their pain.
Their collective brain can't transpose ideation into metaphor,
Exchange concrete retinal images for symbols,
Transliterate God's voice into phonic melodies.

My offspring are grotesque effigies,
A hundred Mussolinis hanging upside down, naked,
For all who would stop to gawk
At their flabby appearance on this page.
They swing limp, in the air, as I read them aloud,
Mocking me, bearing the stigmas
With which my syphilitic rhythms have cursed them.
Take them from their incubator! Cut the respirator!
They'll never measure up to expectations.

3/8/84 (05884)

Welfare State

Words back up, behind my mind's cage,
Like winos and other derelicts
Lingering in line, all day,
To apply for and claim unemployment benefits.

They have neither any place to go,
These vagrants of mine,
Nor design to their wayward lives,
Who waste each spendthrift moment, on the dole,

Begging sympathetic release from meaninglessness,
By standing, like Salvation Army Santas,
On street corners my brain assigns them,
Where they mime my rhyming measures, with chimes,

Singing out my strophes to bemused passersby,
Who would toss them a few kudos,
To say they've fulfilled their day's good deed,
Promoting culture, nurturing poetry.

Still, my mendacious friars — fat little monastic liars —
Abjure societal responsibility.
They prefer to stay in fuguelike stupors,
Waiting for their chance to swell a stanza,

Reverse the surface flow in one of my verses,
Through ironic convolution, involuted paradox,
And spew precious praises
To truth, beauty, the future of the universal *now*.

They would sap my imagination's energy,
Tap my veins limp,
Were it not for punishments I've created
For getting drunk on sentimental bombast and rhetoric.

Lately, I've taken drastic measures to curb their profligacy.
I've stopped writing poems altogether,
Taken up pornographic hackwork,
In the hope of purging my craft of harmful elements.

3/9/84 (05885)

Mysterious Disappearance

This desolate black-dog day,
Dawn's rusty capstan and hawser
Draw up my chain-fixed anchors,
Suspended on each side of my ship's blunt prow.

The lids rise. Slowly, the eyes focus
Just past the nose, which parts the wave-tossed air,
Leaving no identifiable traces, in its wake,
That a vessel registered to the Brodsky Lines,

Plying life's transoceanic route, on its maiden voyage,
Collided with an iceberg,
Listed at Nowhere's epicenter,
And, emitting no distress messages, went down,

Belly up, settling into Oblivion's swollen, shifting shoals —
A wrecked derelict, whose carcass shelters
Feckless, finned swimming denizens,
Ancestral anemones, starfish, barnacles,

The whole nested, in festooned seaweed,
Far below commerce's cargoed surface,
My sad, undelivered soul
Stranded and abandoned in the gypsy currents' sandy hold.

3/20/84 —[1] (05886)

Conflict of Interest [Δ]

Trilogy awakens with a sore throat
And a fear of returning to class
After having missed, yesterday.
Mr. Boy is eager to show off Panthor
And Battle Cat, his newest acquisitions,
To the kindergarten at Jefferson Elementary.

Although she's completed her homework
And Troika's confident his Masters of the Universe complement
Is adequate to fend off all enemies
And potential cosmic adversaries he might encounter
During his three-and-a-half-hour session,
Both children guard their comments,

Let my ebullient effusiveness power the drive
From home, across town,
To the Capital Café, for pancakes and bacon
Corrupted with syrup, then on again,
To the school's entrance, where, with a delicious kiss,
I'll "dessert" them, take to the highway, for work,

Knowing I'll be stranding two precious souls,
For the next three days,
Depriving them of my mightier-than-He-Man strength,
My omniscient mastery of fractions and Latinate classifications,
Leaving them "dadless," while I set out
To practice my own strategies and tactics for survival.

3/20/84 — [2] (00684)

Jesus, You're Forty, Jan! Rejoice! Rejoice! [Δ]

I

Almost half your years have you shared with me.
At first as your superior, then your peer,
I nurtured appreciation of your fairness,
Witnessed your beauty reverse itself, turn outside in,
Like thirsty earth sipping summer rain through its roots.

II

I still remember the gentle, diffident, spindly filly
Who pranced in her art-school corral,
*

Tantalized and dared me ride her bareback,
Up the Hill, around the humanities track,
Then danced through open scapes, to taste freedom's lather,

Even as she fled heady responsibility,
By grazing in Maxwell's Plum, Yellowfingers, Friday's,
Where Ruby Tuesday and Lady Jane
Cavorted with Nureyev, Dylan, and Lester Sperling,
Arresting pleasure, on an earthly plain,

Before exchanging her Manhattan dreams, for reveries
Sculpted in studios secluded throughout Coconut Grove,
Where, on sultry evenings, sailboats tinkling in the bay
Transported her over oceans millenniums away,
Like Fred Neill echoes resonating in the breeze.

III

I yet recall the pain you exorcised, giving birth
To Trilogy and Troika, those foals
You and I collaborated in extracting from our imaginations,
To reenact, on stage, our individualistic passion plays —
Protagonistic souls full-blown, from day one.

Bless you, Janny, my precious wife,
Mistress, lover, courtesan. It matters little the priority
Or order I assign you — your titles —
Now that reaching it, you've completed forty,
Entered, volitionlessly, the first year of your fifth decade.

What counts is that you and I have stayed
Devoted to each other, prideful,
Reverential, despite fissures in our vessel,
Cast, in cold brass, while too hot, respecting one another
As though the universe would collapse with our shattering.

IV

Whatever sarcasms and petty violations we've committed
In the names of ego and self-righteousness,
Don't ever let us disintegrate. We two represent
The last pair that boarded our generation's Noah's Ark.
We must exit, at Ararat, separately, intact. We must!

3/20/84 — [3] (02114)

[Incised on his stony face was this epitaph:] †

Incised on his stony face was this epitaph:
"He died, lived awhile, in suspended adolescence,
Then was born. Everything prior,
All memory of his brief orbit,
Sifted back

3/21/84   (05764)

Prehistoric Presences

I

The highways I use, this March,
Pass through antediluvian ooze,
Whose Midwestern desolation distresses me.
In all directions, I register and arrest
Suggestions of deathly malevolence.

Somehow, I'm a vestige from an undreamed future,
An anachronism roaming, in silence,
Through an echoing necropolis
Cluttered with rusted, dilapidated skeletons,
Cenozoic herbivorous and carnivorous creatures,

Ominous even in their jagged sedentariness:
Primordial pickers, gins, seeders,
Bailers, binders, rakes, disks, gleaners.
Their very existence is sufficient stimulus
To fever my brain, with fear-flames.

II

As I head westerly, on Route 24, toward Salisbury,
An eighteen-wheeler, trailing me for miles,
Screams past, spewing noxious fumes.
Briefly awakened, in its draft, I gasp,
Choke on my recognition of its spectral shape.

Within seconds, I jettison history
As a convenient metaphor, palpably aware
A "terrible lizard," in the corrugated flesh,
Pumping ancestral blood through its lines and jets,
Has just spared me, for heftier prey.

Scared, I pull onto the shoulder, to rest,
Before pressing ahead. Five miles up,
I overtake that same truck — jackknifed,
A crimson cow straddling its saurian cab-face,
The semi's colossal, chagrin-tinged body petrified.

3/22/84 (05408)

The *Spirit of St. Louis*: Poet in Flight

Throughout my twenties, I could fly
My mind's Ryan, from New York
To Le Bourget, with just a periscope,
A rotary compass, two water canteens,
A rucksack with maps, charts, hunting knife,
A standard nine-foot steel prop
Powered by a Wright Whirlwind radial engine
(Consuming only five gallons of oil,
355 gallons of petrol), and a dream.

I could fly blind, float on treated fabric
Coated with paint, slide through the sky,
Like a sleek eagle seeking out prey,
Miles below, by isolating minute moving shadows.
So keen was insight and inspiration, then,
When passionate youth's ambitious hopes
Could override confusion gratuitously,
That breathing in and seeing past fatigue and fear
Were as easy as believing in death's indeterminacy.

Now, at twice that age of miracles, if I fly,
No matter the streamlined conveyance
Intellect might choose to transport my spirit,
Outside turbulence proves too defiant
For my brain's carefully regulated cabin pressure.
Nausea, fate's surrogate, holds sway,
While intimidation guides me in, through the fog,
On invisible frequencies, down a glide slope
Calculated to deliver me, safely, to a foregone conclusion.

3/27/84 (05887)

Of Earthly Vessels

*For my beloved dad,
on his birthday*

The vital vessel called Saul Brodsky
Is neither reliquary, filled with breathing bones,
Dreaming's fragile memories,
And shreds of faintly scented saintly robes,
Nor transparent jar on history's shelf,
Containing jellybeans gone stale;
Rather, its flexible shape,
Still resilient, from tibia to hippocampus,
Resembles living Greek statuary —
Heroic soldier, statesman, emperor, deity.

No matter the elegiac verse and biographies
Steeped in legends and lore
Lionizing his leonine demeanor and deeds,
His fleshly apotheosis cannot be diminished
By arresting it with words, photographs,
Or by arrogating to it verbal immortality.
Today, God celebrates His own reflection
In the seventy-five-year-old diamond
He's compressed from all time —
His precious vessel Saul.

4/5/84 (02115)

[Tyranny and outrage — standard brain-patterns —]

Tyranny and outrage — standard brain-patterns —
Both laid in, on the bias, atop the same bolt
Stretched, taut, along a table myriad generations long,
Forty-three years wide,
By imagination's electric-eye-guided spreading machine,
Then drilled, pinned, and cut out, on the lines,
By intuition's radically whirring circular knife,
Stack up, waiting to be numbered, piece by piece,
Back up, as life's factory line-shaft
Breaks down, under the daily crush of presser feet,
*

Needle bars, throat plates, bobbin cases,
Tension releases, failing to keep pace
With personal expectations, maintain quality standards
On garments that won't pass final exam,
Clothes sewn without pride or expertise
Necessary to transmute handwoven abstracts
Into images capable of adorning the cold senses,
In poets' robes. Today, I stumble,
Fumbling in nakedness, unable to hide behind my shame,
As tyranny and outrage stone me with epithets.
Bruised and bleeding, I lurch home,
Alone, a victim of my own hopes
To design and fashion the ragged world
Into tailored metaphors suitable for every occasion.

4/12/84 (00847)

The Poet's Bone Marrow

This mica-bright April day
Is a vibrant rainbow without colors,
A Tara hallway
Glistening with teardrop chandelier-prisms,
A terrestrial stratosphere
Flaming with pulsating sunspots.
Yet in a less aesthetic context,
More realistically speaking,
Today is the day of my spirit's extirpation,
The hour fate has appointed me,
To make my unexpected exit expectedly.

Suddenly, I recognize and can translate
Those anticipatory metaphors
That swarmed my brain, earlier this morning.
They were death-progressions,
Preludes and codas, prologues, eulogies,
And benedictions rolled into one sundering
Emanating from an opening in the sky's dilated pupil,
Strophes and antistrophes singing me home,
Trying to soften God's blow,
By begging me enter the flow, of my own volition,
Without apologizing for my life-lie.

4/18/84 — [1] (05888)

Ageless Sage

Upon realizing he'd actually completed,
Rather than just begun,
Forty-three years, embarked on forty-four,
Instead of said good-bye to forty-two . . .
At that very moment,
One day later than his natal celebration,
He refused to contain his outraged amazement,
Soared through morning's greening mist,
In quest of metaphors with which to register his complaint,
Attempt to tyrannize fate,
By intimidating its terrestrial messengers,
With his poetic rhetoric,
Persuade the cosmic decision-makers and timekeepers
To reverse their determination, return him
To his former state of graceful aging,
Whereby he alone could choose
When to become something new by growing older,
Without his being surprised into accepting a season's end,
On a rigid calendar's say-so.
All afternoon and into evening's eaves,
He etched his jet stream across the unrelenting hours,
Scrambling in search of a solitary suitable expression
On which to perch, hoot, in ululant refrain,
His unassuageable disillusionment and hurt.
And he never slept again,
His eyes wide, day and night, surveillant,
In ever-mindful anticipation of the next surprise,
He growing older and older, still older,
Without realizing time had died ages ago.

4/18/84 — [2] (05889)

Le vedute, Piranesi Style

Piranesi lurks in this crazy Katy Station.
He hangs from invisible chains of stained-glass refractions.
I gaze at recessed amber ceiling spots
Floating, on the smoothly shifting surface of my wineglass,
Like streaking northern lights
Tantalizing my frigid, wind-blurred eyes,
*

Riveted, in sweet amazement, to Sage's Beach,
On the westernmost tip of Lake Superior.

As I focus downward, into the gold-flecked crater
I hold beneath its nubile bowl, by a slender stem,
Memory transmutes the swimming hues to snow
Scattering in a globe, containing a reindeer scene,
I shook frequently, when passing through youth,
To revel, briefly, in an eight-year-old's conception of art,
Beauty, and the universe. To this dissipated day,
I can still joyously recall that innocuous fallout.

The past veers too near my present essence,
This lost late afternoon in April,
When my spirit, without trying to conspire with night
Or sleep's narcotic ethers, presses death
To awaken prematurely, take shape.
Apparitions in the glass haplessly collide,
Like protons in battery paste. The electric flow they produce
Barely illuminates my brain's incandescent filaments,

Yet my mind responds to its own shock,
As though writer's block and high voltage
Emanated from the same nightmare.
Succubus and incubus copulate, in ecstatic frenzy,
Within the navigable lanes my alcoholic ocean provides,
Like minnow mating with whale,
Snail outracing Juan Fangio's taillights.
Giambattista Piranesi snickers under his cape.

Having spent too many energies conceiving words,
Pretending to be secure, within my poetic insularity,
Imbibing chilled Chablis,
I arrive at the shadowy gate,
Where stained-glass fanlights
No longer throw off humilities, at night's knees,
Nor do the recessed *carceri* spots brighten the darkness.
Instead, reality descends like acid rain,

Dissolving my sturdy columns, crumbling, to ruins,
Appian Way villas, catacombs,
Egyptian obelisks transported, over alien waters, to Rome,
Which my imagination had hoped to preserve, for future poems.
Alone in this unequivocally out-of-place station,
*

Where, once, trains terminated and set out
And, now, only life's dropouts convene,
To settle irrelevant, inconvenient scores,

I come, once each month, to get drunk,
Fashion, from nothingness, paeans to me and dust,
Entertain obligatory innuendos from maidens-in-waiting
Wearing designer exercise outfits or jeans,
Adding, to my tab, their margaritas and stingers,
And be reminded that growing old
Is God's idea of a practical joke,
Sort of like old Piranesi dangling ropes from nowhere.

4/18/84 — [3] (02650)

Scavengers

Distinct images split, in my mind's fly-eye;
A kind of poetic mitosis occurs.
First, I try to assimilate, into day's design,
The lady hobo climbing the grassy incline
Beside the road I drive
With contemptuous disregard for the speed limit
Or the car's aerodynamics,
Hoping to arrive somewhere other
Than the destination from which I set out.
But the hobo — like a Botticellian diaphanous nude
Rising from among the waves, buoyed by a shell —
Waving her prize, shaking her bounty
(A rimpled hubcap) at the moon,
Defies proper codifying and placement in my files.

Next, halfway there, wherever that may be,
I stop at a McDonald's, off I-55,
To take coffee and a leak,
And encounter twenty terminally living people —
The Perry County Old Folks Association —
Huddled in their Thursday-morning reserved booths,
Mesmerized joyously and at ultimate peace,
Beneath the inexplicable Einsteinian permutations of bingo,
Which they accept on near-blind faith.
Suddenly, I hear my number-sequence called
*

And leave without buying coffee,
As if to avoid having to make an acceptance speech.
Back on the road, heading south, I sigh,
As if relieved of dying in public.

All afternoon, I scan the landscape,
For intruders, alien hitchhikers
Who might be trying to catch a ride with me,
Toward my destiny.
Why those old people, that female hobo
Might have interrupted my otherwise empty gaze,
Who guided them, set them on a trajectory
To collide with mine, I just can't imagine,
And yet I sense, in their dereliction,
My own disaffections. At age forty-three,
I step off the precipice, with them,
Only difference being, my spirit still flies.

4/26/84   (05890)

A Springtide Nocturne

Tinges, traces, shades, gradations of lilacs,
Redbuds, magnolias, flowering crabs,
Weeping cherries! I taste their muted hues,
Savor lavenders, pinks, purples, mauvy scents
Softly gentling spring's silky pubes,
With April's sweetest saturation.
My tongue, like a garter snake's,
Tests the mild jubilation,
For lurking aliens, lingering ecstasies
Waiting, for surprise's right instant, to leap from hiding,
Assault my membranes, with sensualities.
It listens to these tender vibrations,
Proclaimed and arrested, simultaneously, by bees,
Birds, tree limbs swaying with first leaves

breaking open.

This late-April late Friday afternoon
Is a series of visitations, crucifixions,
Resurrections, in which my simple heart participates
Like a minor Christ, a quasi-Christ,
*

Bathing in his own nonsectarian juices,
A feckless pilgrim questing the slightest pleasure
From this complex, syllogistic springtide,
In which all creatures majestical and meager
Ask why they've been born or have survived
To share another renascence.
Just now, I snap, from its supple bough,
A lilac sprig, lift it to the lilac-stippled horizon,
And watch it blend with me, inside its scent,
As it enters the endless lilac sky.

4/27/84 (05449)

Rush-Hour Convert

Not exactly Gethsemane, this lush May garden
In which I browse involuntarily,
Rather circumferential I-270,
Skirting greater St. Louis,
This early-a.m. rush hour,
Where I've slowed, nervously braking, jerking,
Weaving my obscene stream of consciousness
Into, then out of, illusory lacunae,
Trying to take advantage of transitory advantages,

Finally coming to a grudgingly halting pace,
Behind an eighteen-wheeler, whose mud flaps
Proclaim its vague provenance and destination:
"JESUS IS LORD — TRANSPORT FOR CHRIST."
Despite my efforts to disentangle the chains
With which its exhaust-fouled wash
Has manacled my brain to its moving crucifix,
Emblazoned, as if eaten away by battery acid,
Across its cavelike corrugated door,

I can't disengage my entranced imagination
From reading, repeating, memorizing, in hallucinatory litanies,
Printed slogans, glued at skewed angles of attack,
Calculated to awaken my lackluster angels
From their stuporous, snoring retreat on Philistia's shores:
"THE KING IS COMING"; "JESUS SAVES";
"EVERY KNEE SHALL BEND";
"TRUST IN THE LORD"; "CHRIST DIED FOR YOU";
"GOD IS MY PILOT — I'M ONLY THE COPILOT."

They sing to me, these magisterial anthems.
My contrite heart weeps.
Suddenly, rush hour peels away from morning,
Like a glorious robe. I witness His body,
Naked, lacerated, profusely bleeding,
And I am borne away, transported, on memory,
To a greater calling. Blindly, I reach,
Switch off the ignition,
Abandon my vehicle, in the middle of the screaming highway,

As the rabble, pelting my disappearing shadow,
With horns, expletives, and dexterous, hysterical gestures,
Is obliged, by slowing, to acknowledge my self-sacrifice.

5/8/84 — [1] (02351)

[It tends to end. Even straight lines bend,]

It tends to end. Even straight lines bend,
Eventually, in Einsteinian dimensions,
Until all friction and passion fractionate into atoms
Black as demons slowly decomposing in gaseous bogs
Leagues beneath the Dead Sea.

The end deepens endlessly,
As though it were a diamond-tipped drill bit
Chipping away Hades' layers,
Bruising hissing lizards, criminals, sinners
Bathing, leisurely, in scum-covered baptismal fonts.

It probes mother earth's lubricous labia,
In clitoral worship, hoping to return to the beginning,
When the Word held preeminence
And firmaments above and below gave way to a world
Capable of conceiving *Homo sapiens*.

Ah, birth, you paltry bastard's stepchild!
I tried to spare you my intellect's pain,
But you insisted on materializing as verse,
When I would have sentenced you to a speedy demise,
Testifying at your own dissertation's trial.

This evening, I bear witness to my soul's dissolution.
Death of the spirit is a passing fancy.
*

No one need remark, with eloquent eulogy
Or TV documentary, the assassination of a pope
Or presidential hopeful, rather record this truth:

All intentions, whether honorable, unscrupulous,
Or merely meant to record the lives of minor painters,
Are significant, to the extent of reminding us,
Twenty generations later,
That the past is as relevant as the immediate *now*;

Otherwise, the only entity that persists
Is forgetfulness itself. Slowly, my mind wilts,
Like an unrefrigerated gardenia.
My disintegration is inevitable.
The end repeats history's script.

This evening, I witness my own spirit's burial.
Delicately, I place my coffined bones in the soil,
Throw clods over the stammering voice
Still lifting out of the open grave.
Who would guess God's essence graced this death?

5/8/84 — [2] (02643)

Moby Quixote

Concrete sea lanes twenty-four feet wide
Have contained and guided his passage,
These last thirty-five years.
So little difference have the seasons made
To the maintenance of his charted voyages,
He can barely differentiate the gone decades.

He only ponders his own physical changes
Occasionally, on days such as this one,
When, in early May, the sun lulls him awake,
Makes him rely on side- and rearview mirrors
To augment his diminishing vision,
Causes him to focus, furtively, on his own features.

Heading home, from a workweek's roamings
For new sightings he might harpoon with barbed pitches
He hurls expertly, aims right to the heart,
*

With zealous devotion (selling clothing,
For Acme-Zenith of St. Louis, all these years,
Has made him Ahab of the Midwestern waters),

He slides alongside a jolting school bus,
Whose windows are antic with gesticulant hands,
Animated faces, of children being ferried from the islands,
Somewhere. Their gestures catch Willy's attention.
Distractedly, he takes the lunging, yellow-black bloat
As a whale, not boat.

In an endless moment of reckless ecstasy,
He enters his mind's wooden dory,
Suspends his imagination in its own wet depths,
With his lapsed ambitions pulling frantically on the oars,
Steering, undeviatingly, toward the great whale,
Now circling, circling, edging for position.

Suddenly, the fragile vessel shifts, shudders.
When he awakens, he's prostrate
At the base of a steep ditch, stiff but unscathed.
Slowly, he rouses to milling children
Forming a life preserver around his body,
Buoyed, almost wholly, by his own stuporous curiosity.

By degrees, disgrace overtakes his disorientation.
Realization of his deeds materializes.
Once back in his Waterman duplex,
He ponders his citation for negligent and reckless driving
And knows his thirty-five years have come atumble.
Breaching fear leers at his numbered days.

5/9/84 (02350)

Sir Galwyn of Arthgyl ^Δ

Without the slightest tip of my hat, to time,
I've arrived. Faith's leap
From Missouri, through Arkansas and Tennessee,
Into Mississippi, is performed in a wink of the eye
The artificer's mind blinks
Simply by aiming its necromancer's ink,
In legible metaphorical script, across *Doom's-Day Book* pages
My mere breathing turns, on mystically distant cue.

First to recognize my once-familiar presence
Are loblolly pines and burned-out cypress swamps
Lining I-55, which guides me home,
To Oxford. Next are the vague scent of lilacs
And even less obtrusive fragrances of magnolias,
Redbuds, dogwoods, whose pubescent foliations
Are nature's appropriations of May's naiveté.
Even I anticipate partaking of her gentle innocence.

Hernando, Senatobia, Como,
Sardis, the Tallahatchie, and Batesville
Sing me a pleasing litany, this glistening morning.
Each is a naiad, dryad, nymph, sprite
Dripping with Mississippi's lubricous semen,
Each a naked surrogate mistress
Welcoming me home, bestowing my senses with freedom
Capable of making relaxation happen.

By this evening, I'll have surrendered
To magical camphors, aphrodisiacs,
Tasted of the sweetest feminine delicacies —
A lotus-eater conspicuously lost in his exultations,
Slave to excesses so beguiling
That to refuse indulging would undo the enchantment,
Render night a shorn ewe
Rather than rabidly passionate cloven-hoofed goat.

No! No! One must never abstain
From momentary vagrancies
Or refrain from promoting spontaneous licentiousness,
Provided these occasions are discreetly infrequent.
Tonight, to libidinize my vital spirit,
I must do a dance atop a tombstone,
Consort with ghosts and courtesans,
And fornicate with Mississippi's concupiscent moon.

5/10/84   (00159)

[Day dwindles like a Chardonnay bouquet] ^Δ

Day dwindles like a Chardonnay bouquet
Escaping, behind a released cork,
Afternoon's moist, smoothly contoured neck,
*

Into lilac twilight. I sip its deliquescent essence
As if my lips, buds, brain cells
Had never tasted such fresh female fragrances —

Those rife odors of frantically growing honeysuckles,
Bee-bothered and sweet as pea pods
Sucked clean, chewed complete, or ewe teats
Throbbing between frequent manipulations of young tongues;
Redbuds, spireas, magnolias, fuchsias
Exploding into girandoles, like Fourth of July skyrockets,
Across May's horizon. Agitated by such lushness,
I grow intoxicated on Oxford's nocturnal vapors.

Suddenly, as if a slave to my own hallucinatory vagrancies,
I tear off all my clothes, run, naked,
Past the kudzu-cloyed railroad cut,
Down Old Taylor Road, toward the highway.
An alien dislocated in space, I grope my way home,
Entering pastel dusk's labial gates,

Penetrating night's densely suspended membranes,
My impregnated imagination convulsing, its heart's pulse
Subsiding to that of a hibernating bear. Eons liquidate.
The bittersweet dream-sleep
From which I awaken myself releases me from demons
Who would masturbate my baser nature,
By stroking my flaccid penis into a bloated ego,
Then crown me Exalted Imperial Wizard of Mississippi.

With every shred of nervous energy that possesses me,
I resist their oppressive threats, keep running,
As if fear were no mere pathetic fallacy made animate,
Rather existed as a definite physical nemesis
To be outdistanced despite the pain. My thighs rebel.
The flexing tendons, ligaments, muscles propelling me

Begin to hyperventilate. Night leers perniciously,
Sneers as though it knows it has its unclothed victim captured,
Snared like a scared human gyved, to Laputa's shore,
By horrifically minuscule cretins. "It's all a mistake!"
I proclaim to an oblivious gibbous moon.
"I'm innocent! Can't you see, even obliquely?
Being and being here were mere acts of God.
I had no choice! Don't you see?

"Leave me be, you fuck! I mean you no harm.
I simply strayed too far from home.
Loneliness overtook me, in the doldrums,
Three hundred thirty-three miles south,
In no-man's-land, because in a weak moment,
I allowed my poetic sensibility to spend itself

Extolling the end of a gently descending Mississippi day
Instead of remembering that poets, no matter their persuasion,
Are, foremost, spokesmen for the *now*,
Not naysayers of yesterday's obvious foibles,
Tomorrow's clairvoyants. I denigrated the present,
By defiling its preciousness. Complacence gained control over my soul,
Forced me into assuming the role of a pimp
For every immortal metaphor hitchhiking home."

Now, I languish, worshiping the lunatic moon,
Like those Mosaical infidels who praised the golden calf,
Beneath the sway of Baal,
And Mississippi is a distant fascination
That once engaged, coerced, me into idolizing its brilliance.
It fades, as its liquors ferment into white, white vinegar.

5/11/84 — [1] (03551)

[It is an evening of serene honeysuckle.] ‡ ∆

It is an evening of serene honeysuckle.
Oxford can't sleep, for the profuse sweetness
Careening across town, from the east, on sultry breezes.
These efflorescent first spring days
Annihilate their victims, with madness,
As if myriad elusive recluse spiders
Were biting themselves into frenzied senselessness.

Tonight, I wander about the shimmering square,
Barely aware of my own diminishment,
And come to sit on a moist bench below the courthouse,
Listen to distant revelry
Weaving, like sifting confetti, from the Warehouse.
No persons stir, yet next to me,
I perceive someone beckoning me speak,
Reciprocate, with nonexistent conversation

5/11–12/84 — [2] on 5/11 (00171)

[Not Bierstadt, Church, Heade, or] [†]

Not Bierstadt, Church, Heade, or

Something I've touched, today,

5/23/84 — [1] (04356)

In a Drunk Funk

In this heartland oasis, Columbia,
Toward which all highways I've ridden, today, have aimed,
I rein in my restless, spent spirit,
Stable my peripatetic senses,
Provide them with provender and libation,
Then throw open splintery, rusty-hinged gates
Giving onto undulating acres.
Between firmaments, this luminous, blue twilight,
They indulge themselves in drowsy carousing,
While my imagination loses itself in daydreaming
Generations deep, decades wide, high.

Up through time's down-spiraling stack,
The brain's flaming tongues backslide,
Enunciating their chaotically inspired fire's voice
Through inarticulate dust motes flying skyward,
Like Yeatsian salmons' motile sperm
Swimming, in frantic, antic surge,
Upstream, toward the dream's spawning beds inside the moon.
Oh, what a saintly purge,
To envision such golden greens
Melding into yellow, merging into God's blue-fluid hues!
What a majestic turnon!

Now, dusk musters the courage
To foist, on my aesthetic, its tentative splurge.
I gaze into its pastel swirling,
Like a myopic beggar peering into a stereopticon,
To see, in Kansas City's stockyards
And in St. Louis's Eads Bridge,
*

An Old Testament equivalent in 3-D.
Suddenly, I realize how inebriated I've become,
Admiring the sunset beneath Columbia's dusk,
Just how out-to-pasture I've set my steed,
After my forever-after hard-day's ride.

5/23/84 — [2] (02651)

Migrating Turtles

Although this mid-June morning
Ostensibly
Should have seemed not appreciably distinct
From the recently diminishing decade's myriad others
On which I've headed northeast,
Out of Farmington, followed Highway 8,
To Flat River and Potosi, through Steelville,
To I-44, before disappearing, forever,
Into the world's evanescently trafficked density,
It, the innocently anthropomorphic morning,
By nine, was soaring toward eighty degrees,
And the two-lane highway,
Tortuously writhing like a shot snake,
Was littered with too many squashed turtles
Not to evoke more than slight fright in me.
My eyes might have been twin video lenses
In a camera shoulder-mounted
On a war correspondent in a foreign land
Or lodestones attracting disparate images to their cores.
Whatever the case, something in the capacious air,
Rife with the vaguely sweet-sour taste of cut hay,
Seemed imminently dangerous
As I drove toward St. James
(Weaving erratically, to avoid smashing tortoises
Meandering, in pantomimic strides,
From one side to the other, without knowing why,
Let alone having even consciously decided
To try such a monumental feat,
In plain sight of freewheeling catastrophe)
And began pondering my own reasons for leaving home
Merely to exercise my option on loneliness,
*

Measure fate's depths, in miles,
Try its patience, goad death one more time,
Before arriving at my final destination,
Deciding to better my chances for immortality,
By not hiding inside my shell, on my ride to hell.

6/12/84 (05891)

[Vague, translucent shades]

Vague, translucent shades
Emanating off Father's Day, fading, fast,
Into yesterday's sand-granule basin,
Dapple regret, with shadowy guilt.

Memory's fretwork, carved by artisans
Trained in necromantic masonry,
Bears chisel marks
Similar to those which sculpted Norman tracery

From pain — that creative consciousness
Born of the disintegrated soul,
The spirit's fumbling, in history's dim cellar,
For stairs vision might ascend,

To present its reinvented self in human form,
Illuminate its ancient lacunae,
Swim, float, soar,
Then enter the eye at the core of the metaphor

Swirling, in turbulent, diffusive currents,
About our collective lives,
Battle death to the death,
In hand-to-hand transfiguring manipulations,

From which not shade, vapor, or bones
Rise from the blasted remains.
Only the verse, like Earth's first cooling,
Shrinks to the size of its foreordained orbit.

6/18/84 (05892)

Crossing the Galactic Time Zone:
Heading Home, for the Day

Rose-golden sunset flashes across my screen,
Shattering my scatterbrained passivity,
Placing my daydreaming heart on first alert.
Disturbed from my cataleptic naps,
I stir, shake like a wet dog
Drying its fur in systematic spasms,
As my senses try to ascertain their location
Beneath dusk's cascading cosmic avalanche,
To no avail. Within a matter of blinks,
My vehicle passes through the parallax
Between twilight's lacy, hand-painted scrim curtain
And night's black backdrop.
Even my memory penetrates the barrier.
Upon my arrival, nothing remains
Except brittle bones that once sustained the shape
My inflated skin maintained,
To ensure my identity and safe passage
In the land where I sojourned a lifetime, daily.
By morning, the *Doom's-Day Book*'s invisible ink,
With which history facetiously recorded my passing,
Will have dried to a fine, clear, shiny patina,
Leaving a space, between its ruled lines,
For another of fate's more celebrated disappearing acts.

6/19/84 (05893)

Discontinuing Passenger Service

In arriving, we leave each other behind.
Inaccessibility widens like twilight,
Each night, with scientific precision.
Agony's express train,
Careening through the heart's wood-trestled ravines,
Whose faraway moan, in the lifting mist,
Is that of a bull elephant grieving its mate's demise,
Pulls into fate's station exactly on time.

Its two anesthetized passengers,
Dazed from having stayed too long, together,
In the same deluxe compartment,
Head for opposite gates draining the platform,
Giving onto separate destinies,
Their only possessions their very uprootedness.
In the distance, jettisoned memories they legally annulled
Slump, wine-glutted, in tenement gutters.

6/21/84 (04155)

An Air-Conditioned Premonition

My mind's blower fan
Slipped into an elliptical wobble.
Its erratic rotation, from slow to slower,
Began to set up the most grotesque roaring,
As though there were no more bearings
To let the brain's axle spin freely
On its twin bushings — left and right hemispheres.

After my initial neglect, casual lack of concern,
I finally responded to the flames
Rapidly spreading through my burning synapses.
By the time I could climb down
Into my imagination's wire- and pipe-strewn basement,
Catastrophe had collapsed the apparatus,
Shattered, beyond repair, metaphor's data banks.

Like a tattered, hungry bum
Rummaging through a smoldering dump,
I stumbled over the rubble, hunting for a black box,
Hoping to discover my crashing heart's
Last transmission, at least accurately report
The purported "First Cause" of my disappearance
Into senility's cataclysmic abyss.

6/25/84 (05894)

Hush . . . Hush . . . He's Almost Here

Jubilantly, I clear the city's peripheries,
Outdistance its outermost crosshatched enclaves,
*

Consisting of concrete foundations shoring up hillsides,
As, once, trees did, against acid-rain erosion,

And give my visions over to twilight's sway.
At least a thousand times,
During these last fifteen years,
For no reliable reason, I've escaped to the country,

For the weekend (on whatever wayward daydream
Seemed to be thumbing southwesterly),
No matter what hour of the day, day of the week,
Wishing only to elude time's evasive cuckoo,

Who, daily, circles my pedestrian wavelengths
And nests, by night, in my Hebraic crown of thorns.
Just now, dusk suckles my nubile eyes
As though they were murmurous Brancusi breasts,

Desiring to inspire me, with my own supple excess,
While, driving southerly, out of sight,
I derive insight from the sheer flying freedom
Dying alive engenders, in my Odyssean quest

Toward no specific destination or epistemology,
Rather tending toward bending, headlong,
Into each new twilight rising from the seething abyss,
Riding swirling purple thermals — eternity's prodigal son,
   returning home.

6/27/84 (00846)

A Lost Tribe's Latter-Day Scribe

Armed only with my ubiquitous addictive fix,
Liquid caffeine-bean
(Its steam lifting, mesmerically, from Styrofoam
Seemingly molded to fit prehensile thumb
And simian forefinger), a fine-point Bic
(Braced by three digits of the opposing hand,
As if to protect my brain's left hemisphere
From being victimized by its right),
And, below that, lying in submissive grace,
Awaiting eloquent violation or violent gratification,
*

Like Anaïs Nin sketching herself into suggestive essence,
My blue-ruled notebook . . .

This familiar accouterment has provided me
With a means for encoding my secular Trinitarian beliefs,
Allowed my vows of abstinence and chastity to flourish
(Despite a natural tendency toward base complacency,
Which, daily, possesses me),
Even when the poetic life seems too "precious,"
Just by my bowing to the Scriptural Power
That pervades me with intoxicating mysteriousness.
If there be any greatness in my paltry psyche,
It must be my capacity to cajole the mediocre
Into nobility, refine, from cacophony, melody, unmask chaos,
By naming stars, insects, unborn babies.

6/28/84 — [1] (05895)

Initiating an Action, in the Southern Sector [△]

As I drive south, vision engages the enemy —
A pervasive Pleistocene haze
Slouching, amphibiously, across the vaporous horizon.

Frightened, the eyes retreat into daydreaming,
Neglect their fastidious sky-watch,
To concentrate on their interior terrain's changes.

Somewhere between Cape Girardeau and Hayti,
The crazed varnish of this sunny day
Flakes off like myriad Icarus-wings

Spiraling out of the densely particled atmosphere,
Into my viscid seas. Now, focus
Is a matter of peering into the gathering blackness,

Hoping to discern an opening
Through whose waxy fusillade I might shoot
Like a stray bullet accidentally hitting its mark

Before shattering into a drain pan at the base of the brain,
For taste's ordinary coroner to retrieve,
Autopsy, ascertain, then disseminate as public information.

Just outside Memphis, my momentum emerges,
Asserts itself over its oppressor,
Converts the blinding rain to poetic insight.

By the time I arrive in Oxford, Mississippi,
A blazing sun has melted the afternoon
Into a seething creature breathing heated blasts

From its beaded snout. Once again, I realize
The humid drought can't be far from hand.
Meanwhile, I prepare to inaugurate myself

As the most recent occupier of this vanquished land,
Knowing that although physical possession
May be nine-tenths of the law,

Only freedom to impose poetic will from within
Can prevent defection, allow the defeated
To tolerate outside intervention.

Suddenly, I collect my rhyming lines and exit,
Head home, to Farmington. There, at least,
I speak the same language as my masters.

6/28/84 — [2] (03505)

Rehearsing in Mississippi △

Having evacuated my sweet, insular purlieus
260 miles ago
And exchanged it for this seething heat,
Infused with vague psycho-hypochondriacal fears
Pecking at my peristaltic gut
Like a goose chewing buttons off the sleeve
Of a hand extended to pet its beak,
I course down I-55, below Memphis,
Toward Oxford, not knowing why I've come
Or whose necromantic prophecy I must fulfill,
Compelled to put in my silent appearance,
As though I were the earth's menstrual seed
Cycling toward fertilization,
Down its interstate tubes, doomed to abort
Or, at best, misconceive any potential poetic accretions
*

Which might accidentally attach themselves
To the ceiling of my pulpy imagination's fundus.
Swamps crowded with cypress and gum stumps
Enter consciousness, through my eyes.
Vision is inundated with moccasin-phobias
Slithering through my brain's fluted convolutions.
And even though I choose to disregard the possibility
Of lynch mobs, Nazi swastikas
As pure fantasy extinct as saurians,
My heart can't quit its involuntary fibrillating.
Something there is, about this mid-South,
That transfigures my most romantic illusions
To grotesque chimeras, who stalk me
Even as I enter their domain, in peace,
Waving my invisible truce flag.
Something would have me witness, firsthand,
My own craven ruination,
For failure to accept my exile to the spirit's Elba
As a trial by which I myself might decide
Whether my patience is sufficient
To withstand an eternity of writing verse
For recitation by the unredeemed
Or if I should just stay resigned to confinement in Hades,
Without worrying about creating paeans to angels,
Panegyrics and encomiums to saints,
Benedictions to myself, as God's earthly surrogate.

6/28/84 — [3] (03525)

Making Berth at Oxford ^Δ

This is a snug harbor into which I've purposely drifted,
Anchored ship, before slipping down the gangplank,
Swaggering into town, unnoticed by its Stepford citizens.

What's one more visitor, more or less,
When uninvited drifters endlessly descend
To pay obeisance to the sainted patron of this place —

Those inspired by what they most admire (prose poetry)
And those who know their own writing success
Has been adversely affected by the scratch

Of that little bastard, Mr. Bill, "over yonder at Oxford,"
Who, having spent his apprenticeship "Stoned,"
Exploded the very mother tongue that had blown his brains?

Actually, I've put in, this virtually deserted Thursday,
To let bids on necessary repairs to my bowsprit,
Have the foresail mended and fitted with new battens,

The main halyards replaced, by a hemp weaver,
Not go crazy, fornicate, in St. Peter's,
With the first ghost flying low enough to lay,

Whose surname might just happen to be Faulkner.
Professionally, I couldn't care less whom they worship —
White writer, "nigra," old-world Jew, nudist,

Or blind sailor like me, Tiresias.
My first and only concern is for my own survival,
Not someone else's posthumous apotheosis.

As soon as my vessel is seaworthy,
I'll set sail, again, in quest of the bleached whale,
Whose enormity besieges me, with my own seething epilepsy.

Tonight, confined to this leeward harbor,
I might as well bow, with a grace,
To base complacency, exercise my least attractive appetites,

Partake of the local "snatch," as Mr. Bill might say,
Relax, get into the indigenous sound-and-light show,
Which begins, each evening, by nine

And lingers way past dawn.
I might as well sample Oxford's exotic spices,
Since I may be laid up, here, a brief while,

Waiting for parts with which to outfit my distressed ship.
Just now, I am visited, at my table, by a creature
So innocently motivated by my silence,

I might hyperventilate. She offers me her breasts,
Her intellect. Without hesitation, I acquiesce,
Knowing local Loreleis can't resist foreign exhibitionists.

6/28/84 — [4] (00165)

On the Virtues of Being a Man of Action [△]

For my dear friend
Thomas Michael Verich

Passionate actions may neither last long
Nor reveal their perpetrator
As either possessing the quintessence of class
Or being motivated by selflessness,
Yet they certainly suggest spontaneous energy
Arrested in evanescent suspension
And focused, effectively, to accomplish the necessary climax
Between the animal in question and the object of his affections.

In layman's nomenclature, what this implies
Is that a fella with Rabelaisian appetites,
Like Bluto or Otter, of *Animal House* fame,
Either shits or gets off the pot,
No fucking around. Drunk is instant drowning
Within the *now* sex and drugs power;
Tomorrow is a dour "nown" borrowed from Shakespeare,
To maintain appearances, with no intention of repaying the neologism.

I mean, it's uninhibited exhibitionism to the max.
It's tomorrow today, right this very second,
Despite the Einsteinian time-lag inherent in straight lines
That naturally bend convention whenever mores
No longer find acceptance among younger generations
And die of spiritual attrition. It's Emmett Kelly
Sweeping dinosaur dung, just for fun,
Under the Vatican's Raffaello-cartooned Gobelins.

It's Ernest Hemingway taking that fast final leap,
Not allowing even God to be his gofer,
By pulling his own shotgun's trigger, showing Faulkner
Dignity's extreme possibilities, in the face of supreme failure,
Cerebral senility . . . Mr. Bill, already conversant with Bergson's
Stream-of-consciousness theories, spurring his horse
One too many unnecessary jumps
Before coming to rest in Byhalia, Mississippi.

There's definitely much to be said
For the perpetrator of passionate actions
Who grabs the mean-spirited bull, by its horned head,
*

Wrangling it to the ground, tying its legs,
Squeezing its balls, in a final frenzy,
To ensure its docility, keep responsibility at bay,
And delays just long enough to assess his next move,
Then risks his life, on the fixed twist of destiny's dice.

6/29/84   (03520)

Saturday-Morning Auguries ^Δ

As I drive out of Oxford, toward I-55,
Two blatant paradoxes, like Medusa-snakes,
Coil about my not-yet-awake imagination and squeeze.
The first, fused with irony, materializes,
Separates into a pair of black college-age ladies
Walking briskly against my flight.
Sporting bright-red T-shirts
Proclaiming "Ole Miss Rebels,"
Both consider themselves safe from violation.

And as I go, this summer day's other pervasive presence,
Kudzu, sends out its seething tendrils,
Juicy leaves, to take up accommodations
In my otherwise vacant psyche's eyes.
Strewn in festoons and cascading green drapes
And chains, from treetops to earth,
They resemble stalactites
Perforating tunnels in underground caves,
Through whose voluptuous illusions
My gaze passes, in hypnotized fascination.

Abruptly, kudzu and T-shirts have dissolved.
Red and green assume confusing hues,
Without contrast, beneath the mist-sifting sun,
As Mississippi becomes Tennessee,
Then Arkansas, then southeast Missouri,
And I'm home, almost emptied of memory's legacies,
Almost assimilated, again, into my 1950s
Neoconservative dream of suburbia,
Whose reasonableness would mediate all evils,
Milk dry the Medusa-snakes' venomous threats,
If not defang their bites. Yet, right now,
*

I can almost feel kudzu stalking
Those two black girls, with red "Rebels" shirts,
Walking almost carelessly toward Oxford,
From Sardis, to partake of Saturday shopping,
Almost hear it screeching as it stretches
To get hold of their carefree spirits,
Metamorphose them into mummy-trees,
Whose subtle beauty, disguised as blight,
Will nurture the procession of progressive evolution,
And I realize I never left Mississippi alive.

6/30/84 — [1]   (03537)

Kryptopterus bicirrbis

No wishy-washy fish,
The politician is *the* ultimate exhibitionist,
Who, wearing no clothes
When he swims into the public eye,
Exposes his prismatic motives to scrutiny so close,
Like gnarled toes (on feet
Shoved into shoes two sizes too tight)
Being x-rayed by an ocherous fluoroscope,
That even he can't feel when they're being seen through.

Rarely will he concede he's "out of water,"
On matters of national security,
Or that he needs his think tank cleaned,
Algae scrubbed from its brain-walls,
Fresh seaweed and snails added, to oxygenate ideas
That, otherwise, might remain torpidly submerged
On the floor of his resourcefulness,
Like colossally innocuous Plecostomuses.
Yet he'll scurry to the surface, for free feeding and breeding.

Despite minor variations, his species is characterized
By similarities that render generalizations appropriate.
For instance, in a big stink,
Each can hold his breath indefinitely
Or at least stay below till it blows over;
All dress in a basic uniform consisting of fins
And elaborate scales; they can float in one place,
*

For days, as though a convenient coma
Had interrupted the most pressing engagements.

Enfin (or is it "in fin"?), I might just add
That one can't really commend too highly,
Or be judicious enough in condemning, those
Whose greed can affect an entire school of thought
Or at least prejudice certain leaders
To remain sticks-in-the-mud, take no risks.
As a group, these transparent creatures keep their cool,
Provide those of us with private, quiet lives
Insight into their very entrails.

6/30/84 — [2] (05896)

Landlocked in a Writer's Block, Driving West

My pen enters its own slipstream,
Screams past my unintoxicated waking thoughts,
Like a postmeridian shadow its twin,
Then drafts on a sleek wind skidding west,
On its elegiac trajectory home.

Stupefied, undeniably fascinated,
My eavesdropping eyes listen to its ballpoint tongue
Whispering sibilant vocables
Into my notebook's attentive blue-ruled ears.
Its lips' script accuses me of intellectual voyeurism.

I have a history of feeble excuses I've used
In situations such as this,
When, inadvertently, my imagination's been seen
Peeping through keyholes,
To watch sensual metaphors undressing,

And been caught up short, forced to confess
Its seemingly perverse excesses,
By its heart's anti-defamation league.
Valid pretexts elude me. Pleading "poet"
Fails to mediate the heinous nature of my crime.

Carcassonne is no place to be found guilty,
Sentenced for conspiring to plagiarize images and ideas
*

Consigned to the artificer's spirit,
Not the inhibited artificer. Just now, I realize
Driving west is my punishment — death by deprivation.

7/5/84 — [1] (05897)

An Exhortation

Soar, this morning, my bindle-stiff spirit!
Let this roaring, two-handed engine you fuel
Cut a swath, twenty-five miles wide,
Across summer's primeval forest,
Like a lunar tornado or colossal reaper
Shaping cosmic fields into windrow-strings
Strung tightly on the earth's harp,
Which my fingers, fitted to their magical pen-picks,
Might set into sympathetic node with my heart,
Just by stroking them into scripted existence —
God-glyphics scored with audible metaphors.

7/5/84 — [2] (05898)

[It used to be,]

It used to be,
Not too many weeks (was it decades?) ago,
Willy could make actions happen
Without exposing the magical apparatus
Required to manipulate his prestidigitations.

He could easily create priestly illusions and motions
Capable of persuading potential opponents,
Competitors' agents disguised as gracious hosts,
That *seen* and *seem*,
Like opposed magnets, are equally attractive

When turned just enough
To circumvent conventionally accepted intrigues.
At the proverbial drop of the most convenient hat,
He could produce whatever clichéd rabbit
Might adequately satisfy the occasion at hand,

Whether ordered to appear
At a major resource's board meeting
And present swatch line and sample garments,
Cum spiel and rabbinical incantation
Celebrating the glorious gospel of ethnocentricity,

Keeping the business "in the family,"
Without spelling it out in too-obvious Yiddish,
Or required to fly to L.A., make an unexpected guest appearance
At the annual MAGIC trade show,
To provide citified buyers with a sense of the authentic

He has daily embodied, traveling for Acme-Zenith,
Between K.C., Sedalia, Columbia,
St. Louis, Springfield, Peoria, Decatur, Chicago,
And back, twice each month, for years —
Willy Sypher, epitome of *the* crack salesman,

That Dreiserian drummer,
Newest approximation of Charles Drouet,
George F. Babbitt reincarnated,
Who, whether enduring the MoPac's
Cigar-reeking parlor car

Or making his dates in a company-leased Buick Electra,
Could be counted on for a laudatory performance,
Exemplary deification of the company's products,
Regardless of his sons' perfunctory misdemeanors,
His wife's brief emotional insurrections,

And was always on the job, a *semper fidelis* guy
Trained in the ancient virtues
Of draw-against-commission, commission-on-delivery.
Today, at regional sales meetings
Held biannually at Clayton Inn, in St. Louis,

They mock his epic seriousness,
His fastidious concern for accuracy of detail
When deciding on models to be included in the new line
Or finalizing prices for the summary sheets
He'll refer to, with his customers,

As though they were Dead Sea Scrolls,
Talmudic illuminations, or cabalistic scriptures.
*

No longer do his eloquent intrusions hold sway
Nor his relevant questionings of company policy
Command the quiet approbation they once did.

In fact, his own aged dislocation,
The folds under his chin, the belly-rolls
Showing beneath his Lacoste knit shirt
Render him, despite his undeniable experience,
A dubious factor in today's financial equation for success.

He shrinks into his corpulent muteness,
At least assured, by virtue of thirty years' tenure,
A living. No longer (was it decades ago?)
Is his opinion assimilated into the decision-making
Magical apparatus called "company policy";

Rather, in today's modern pace,
His minimal input is tolerated, out of deference
To the importance his fiefdom once represented.
After all, he can't hold a proverbial candle
To the major discounters or Army PX's,

Who have made his formerly prestigious accounts
Seem paltry, by quantitative comparison.
They put up with his untimely suggestions
As though he were their doddering grandfather,
Knowing their silence is preferable to opposition.

Willy is a laughingstock,
Still trying to promote leisure suits
When hawking polyester, per se,
Is akin to selling iceboxes to eskimos,
Twentieth-century Imari vases and cloisonné jars

To experts trained in Ming Dynasty fakes.
Willy, Willy, you sad bastard!
Why have you stayed so damn long?
Who ever would have guessed
Someone as sincere as you might eventually fail

Simply by displaying such loyalty,
Who tried to accommodate those who trusted you
With their tarnished crown jewels?
Why didn't you quit in a fit of righteous indignation
Or retire to your gold-plated hunting-case watch,

Instead of hanging on long past prime time,
Deteriorating into mosquito-bite orders,
Promises demolished by cancellations of unproduced goods?
I ask you, Willy Sypher, why,
Why have you remained with Acme-Zenith,

When you might have succeeded in moving paintings,
X-rays, space rockets, or calculators
(Today, they refer to them as "computers")?
Is it that clothes are robes, robes Mosaical,
And Moses is the essence of Judaism?

Or is it conceivable that old geezers
Just possibly knew the truth
Inherent in not wavering in one's allegiances?
Whatever the case, old Willy Sypher
Yet remains on the semimonthly payroll,

Receiving a company check
Predicated upon an estimated draw against commission
On accounts sold from previous seasons.
Hopefully, if failure assails him,
It will take at least three months

Before the machine will detect his insufficiency
And determine, in its omniscience,
The efficacy of effacing him from its ranks
Or maintaining his encoded statistics,
In the bytes of its floppy-disk files.

Regardless, tomorrow is another unique day
On which Willy will go forward,
To vanquish the invisible enemy
And either succeed or be handily vanquished
By an equally unfathomable foe.

Meanwhile, Willy eagerly awaits doing battle,
For the sake of his company's glory,
With the shadowy forest-boar
Who would run him through, in gory torture,
With its bloody horns,

On the merest dare, for nothing more than hope
Of receiving credit for having smitten Willy,
The once and only king of polyester leisure suits,
*

Who achieved fame and saw it fade
In the flickering of a single decade,

Then witnessed his whole life disappear
In a solitary whispering reminiscence —
That memory of 1929,
When, with exuberance, his spirit caught fire,
Dug Solomon's mines, then died, buried alive.

7/5/84 — [3] (02644)

Outbound

Alone, out on this open road, my spirit flows
Like low tide retreating into the depths
Of the ocean's ever-receding horizon line. I drive
As though I were tomorrow's pallbearer
Trying to arrive early,
To rehearse graveside services,
Perfectly execute my own approaching demise,
Without calling attention to my own disguise.

So often have I made this trip,
From Necropolis to Farmington,
I'm not even alarmed by the unearthly speed
My vehicle achieves, freewheeling seaward;
Rather, my deteriorating spirit revels,
Celebrating the still-green surge
My escape leaves in history's wake.
Even as I disappear, my words awaken the shore.

7/9/84 (05899)

On the Demise of an Egyptian King
of the First Dynasty, in His Infancy

He's home again, home,
As though his heart never severed
Connections with its head; except, of course,
He's led the unobtrusive cortège,
Bearing his dead vessel, to its resting nest,
*

Here, where silence is measured in intervals
Between damp dripping and baking clay
And days are eternity's eye-blinks,
Washing flesh and bone, then dust, from the mystic lens
That focuses the spirit against memory's screen.
In this solitary instant, he's eoned.

What more need we say, to ornament his eulogy,
Save, "Go. God be with ye.
May peace attend thee, again and again,
As thou return to the world,
In periodic perpetuity"?

7/18/84   (05900)

The Doomsday Haze

Fleeing the Unreal City's heat inversion —
Whose toxic pollutants
Are the ultimate fallout ashes' presagement,
Their onstage, full-dress rehearsal —
Is fraught with credulity's mixed blessings.

My excitement is vitiated by anxiety,
As though in escaping, blindly, prewar Germany,
Disguised as Einstein's twin,
I might arrive safely,
In Theresienstadt's disingenuously hospitable embrace . . .

Vitiated, knowing that in going southwest,
Breaching history's shimmering surface,
Reentering the destructive element,
I am necessarily leaving behind
Wife, children, roots, reason, purpose,

The fugue itself disenfranchised,
Neutered of its freedom-engendering capabilities,
Barren, sterile, terribly tragic,
Since arriving is merely a futile conclusion
To the essential dilemma: survival of the family man.

Even now, as the haze-glazed Unreal City
Dissolves into my rearview mirror,
*

Like ice cubes in a lemonade pitcher
Sitting out on a kitchen table,
I can't seem to distance its pervasive, ocherous taint.

The sky's faded-gilt frame contains me,
In its medieval shimmer,
Rains down flaking varnish shards, on my psyche,
Like heavenly fire falling around St. Catherine.
The ancient smothering has begun.

Roadside cornflowers, caught in my wash,
Flap back, as if my speed
Were the leading edge of the apocalyptic scythe
Time wields, in its periodic weeding.
Even crows, scurrying back and forth,

In their predacious dismantling of canine carcasses
Littering my fated highway,
Seem, to me, mere death-breaths begging release,
Beneath this insatiable heat.
Suddenly, the paving plays out; dirt commences.

I enter an impenetrable dust-blizzard,
From which, even my most optimistic intuition
Suspects, no return to earth will occur
In my assigned lifetime. Gasping speaks my fear.
Disappearance translates me into syllabled caesuras.

By degrees, blight gives way to night;
Night insinuates itself into sky.
My passage through the outer ionosphere
Finally terminates, in easy orbiting.
Eternity is earthly memory circling itself reverentially.

7/23/84 (00845)

Willy's Last Season ^Δ

Now, in the last gasping furlong
Prior to his retirement,
Sixty-five-year-ancient Willy Sypher
Tries, in pixilated befuddlement, as he drives home,
To recollect the first time
*

He made the circuit from Cates Avenue,
By the dilapidated Wabash station at Delmar,
To Springfield, Bloomington, Peoria, Decatur,
And back, between Monday dawn and Friday eve.

The year itself creeps, tentatively as a cat,
Into the strewn alleyway his littered memory
Has refused, too many years, to clean
Or vacate, to allow a more orderly owner
To park his worn-out metaphors and rusting similes.
Yet he distinctly recalls traveling with his dad,
That paradoxically gentle, roaring lion
With balding pate and full beard haloing his face,
Who indulged him, with kindness, while browbeating clients,

That master of hard-sell dialectical rhetoric,
Who could gauge the wind's direction
In an absolute calm, anticipate its trajectory,
Fly, head-on, into an invisible storm,
And soar, without his customers ever realizing
He'd just flown beneath their credibility's ceiling limits,
By the seat of his britches — a born pants-man,
Who always knew his son would fill his shoes,
Assume the duties of keeping the emperor in new clothes,

Even if the monarch had a predisposition for nakedness,
Balked at being pinned, chalked, fitted
By Jews, preferred to remain insulated
In his tasteless resentment toward all tailors
Who might silhouette his bulbous shape,
With a Falstaffian grace. Willy distinctly remembers
That initial trip, during which the two of them
Could enter Meyers Brothers but not Lukeman's,
Had to stay in boardinghouses instead of hotels.

Perhaps he was eight then, or ten,
But already had he celebrated his manhood,
In conscientious apprenticeships,
Those summers and after school, snipping excess threads
From restitched seams, gimp from buttonholes,
On garments his dad contracted to have manufactured
Against bona fide orders he'd taken,
Even then dreaming of elevating himself, one day,
To president of his own company,

Creating a vertical enterprise, a conglomerate, consortium,
With him as chief executive officer,
Chairman of the coupon-clipping board,
An advisor, to presidents, on tariff and foreign-trade regulations,
Respected contributor to the *Wall Street Journal*, *Forbes*.
Now, on this last journey north, toward Peoria,
Before quitting the road, for good,
Knowing even dreams can be schlepped and bought
Off-price, he lingers, fleetingly,
On his own kingly aspirations, then forgets them forever.

7/24/84 (02349)

[This day is a chambered nautilus.] ‡

This day is a chambered nautilus.
Relaxed, having stolen away from my occupation,
I play at being caught, revel in my confinement,
As if the paradoxical revelation of being trapped
Within freedom of my own making
Is somehow the most intense punishment
I need expect from the Gratuitous Executioners,
Who calibrate the cosmic measures
To suit fate's capricious idiosyncrasies

7/25/84 (05901)

At the Head of a Cortège of One, Riding South

Its imminence shimmers within the perimeters
Limiting vision to sickly iridescent hues.
Whatever private specters skim my eyes' humors,
Like frantic water striders on a stagnant creek,
Stipple sight, fill dreaming with nightmares,
I can't isolate, name, anesthetize them,
By rearranging reality into commodious images
Capable of absorbing their pervasive weight.

They, or it, persist in distorting the scape I see.
Agents are keeping me from penetrating
*

Green corn and trees, yellow-gray sky,
Amber sedge at the white highway's black edge,
To the essence of my peripatetic loneliness,
Where reason waits to be fashioned into explanation
Just by shaking it, letting it sift
Through imagination's sieve.

The great *out there* entering my lenses
Bears absolutely no resemblance to known shapes,
Categorized objects I've grown comfortable in identifying.
Today, my God-emulating apparatus and sensibility
Fail to locate my presence
Either amidst the spired city,
Where my heart resides, or in its countryside.
Something beyond has died inside me.

7/26/84 — [1] (02116)

Labors of Love ^Δ

This southering geography through which I creep
Is, sporadically, a seething compost heap,
Noxious in its pungent degeneration,
Offensive as hell. I, a traveling bard,
Am reduced to being a gardener pretending to care
About tending this arid plot, show enthusiasm
For weeding this foul spot I'll seed
With my image clusters, flowering similes,
Variegated, byzantine, and exotic tropes.

When I set out, my intentions were far less noble
Than toiling under an end-of-July sun
So diabolical even the hemispheres shrivel,
Within the skull's bubbling cauldron,
After ten minutes' exposure to its drastic rays.
I had hoped to avoid
Rendering the role of poetic Cincinnatus again,
In this primeval desolation, dreamed of resting.
Ah, but despite myself, witness what's grown!

7/26/84 — [2] (03555)

Creating Vacuums Within Vacuums

Through dim-shimmering Tiffany-type lamps
Suspended from rafters set, in neat imprecision,
Below the roof's exposed galvanized sheeting,
I gaze into an amber universe accented in reds and greens.
Cut straight, as rectangles, trapezoids, or triangles,
Or sensuously shaped into cascading glass cabrioles
Impossible to appreciate, for their preposterous grace,
These shades recreate, in my brain,
A phantasmagorical scape reminiscent of primordial time
Preceding my most apelike antecedents,
Even before the sun had set in its orbit.

This visionary insight into distances
In which time slides out and into light beams,
Like a slalom skier weaving speed through a needle-eye,
Is the prescribed release my psyche requires,
To locate itself in the colossal space it alone occupies.
It's this wine-blizzard dizziness that excites me,
Stimulates my imagination to outstretch its pedestrian limens,
Reach for lunacies suspended by nebulous umbilical cords
Connecting them to the moon and try to pluck them
From their celestial stems. Ironically,
Only daylight's sobriety lets me harvest the stars.

7/26/84 — [3] (03519)

Night Vipers △

For Victoria Buchanan

Strange, how each day away from you
Knots up, in the pit of my gut,
At suppertime, like a viper
Trapped in a croker sack, writhing viciously,
In attempting to escape its frenzied confinement.

From lack of suitable consolation,
Each consumes itself, within the black captivity
Dusk, slithering into night, prescribes for its victims,
*

While I sit at the table, unable to swallow,
For nausea's acid etching my stomach.

Oh, lady, if only you and I
Were slender, sensuous, gentle, green-stippled tree snakes,
Silently sliding, sidewise, skyward,
Toward each other's sacred, secret heat,
We might keep infinity in undulant suspension.

7/27/84 (00173)

Vague Lady from Holly Springs ^Δ

On this too-cool, last afternoon in July,
Whose blue sky is scribbled with cumulus hieroglyphs,
I sit on a green wood-slatted bench
Behind a black wrought-iron fence
Staying traffic orbiting the gray courthouse
And, like extruding rainbows from pliant paint tubes,
Try to squeeze, out of these drooping hours,
Dreams with which to arrest your delicate, disappearing hues.

To bribe memory into reteaching me your fragrances,
I've sipped chilled Mouton Cadet, for lunch,
Shelled and eaten boiled Gulf shrimp —
The sweetest flavor my tongue has tasted
Since haloing your breasts, in caressing murmurousness.
Seeking to retrieve you, I've even lingered on visions
Dressed in see-through cotton frocks and sandals,
Crossing Oxford's streets, drifting out of my gaze.

Yet for all my artificer's persuasiveness,
Neither appetite nor imagination has provided surrogates
Capable of transubstantiating your phantom shape.
Abruptly, I flee the square, retreat, from frustration,
To my refrigerated room, to proposition sleep
Into keeping despair from intruding on my raging desire
To lie down in the eucalyptus pool
You left in my bed, at dawn, and, in your rife scent, drown.

7/31 – 8/1/84 (03607)

Skimming Mississippi's Urn ^Δ

[For Victoria Buchanan]

Surreptitiously, we leave Oxford,
Fleeing two separate identities fused
Despite our traveling toward Memphis
In vehicles bearing Missouri and Mississippi plates.
We share in a collective freedom
Our recent lovemaking licenses us to perpetuate,
As long as we continue to respect the ukase
That possession is only one-tenth of the law,
As it relates to human appreciation and passion.

Ahead, I see your white car slide in and out,
As the Tallahatchie River, Como, Senatobia
Fade into sanctuarial gray somnolence
Buffering pines, hawks, I-55
From the sun. Seeing you starts me wondering
Whether we might not be Keatsian urn-children
Stranded, indeterminately, on a cement band
Girding our life spans. Ah, but then,
On a day so premeditated, why surrender to the poetic?

8/4/84 (00168)

The Peabody ^Δ

[For Victoria Buchanan]

David Cohn may own prosaic rights to the notion
That the Delta begins in the lobby of the Peabody Hotel,
But I hold, in perpetuity, poetic title
To all Tennessee, which you deeded me, last night,
In room 1163 of that Memphis Versailles,
Where our hearts, partaking of a secular eucharist,
Consummated, with wine, matrimony of our blessed flesh.

I might as well incorporate Mississippi, too,
And name you trustee of my vast estate,
So that my recorded metaphors can be probated judiciously,
In case I predecease you. And while we're about it,
Why not just extend our claim of proprietorship,
*

To include the entire South? After all,
Who, seated in the Peabody's lobby, hasn't fathomed eternity?

8/5/84 (00169)

Margie's Parting

For Carl Petersen

What the hell was she doing there, anyway,
At eighty-six, crossing Piccadilly Circus,
Committing herself to soundless drowning
In a City of Westminster lorry's droning groan,
Letting her arthritic, wren wings
Get ripped apart like chicken bones
Between a beanstalking giant's greasy fingers?

Of course, at her absurd age,
She had no business making her annual sojourn,
A half-century deep, nothing so urgent
She couldn't have flown there by phone,
Nothing save the heart's insatiable rage
To stave off chaos,
Despite the brain's steadfast lack of cooperation.

Gone . . . gone like ghostly vapors
Or a gust erupting from the wrong direction,
Reclaiming her fragile memory scraps,
Transfiguring everything amidst its swirl except us.
Shivering yet from her grisly deliverance,
We spit expletives into the void,
Like rabble pelting witches, with invisible dust.

8/10/84 (02118)

Sunday Departures

For Jan, Trilogy, and Troika

By now, as I drive south, out of the city,
Slide past the unofficial periphery
Separating thermal inversion from country skies,
They've begun their boarding.
*

Sad, sinking, tragic premonitions coil in my gut,
As my eyes watch those three people —
My wife and two children —
Being swallowed up in the creature's mazy maw,
Until they've been seated, side by side,
In the nerves' pool of communal trepidation.
My gaze pans from highway to digital clock
Methodically as an electromagnet
Heating and cooling, opening and closing repeatedly.
Minutes and distance, simultaneously narrowing and widening,
Finally converge, collide with my heart,
Seventy-five miles downwind,
At precisely 11:05 a.m. — takeoff.
I share surge, rotation, angle of attack,
Absorb the screaming engines' roar; I soar.
My grief transforms itself into loneliness.
Suddenly, I realize (why not before this moment?)
Just how empty the kaleidoscope is
When the hand that has twisted its lens so gently
Refuses to manipulate it anymore.
I can only hope that their going away
Is but temporary, in its suspension and release,
Not a precursor of our final, forever farewell.

8/12/84 (04154)

A Better Day Ahead

The disconsolate mind retreats, reaches out,
Seeking respite, finds, instead,
A head filled with empty memories and dreams —
Abandoned locust husks, limestone caves
Washed away by streams swarming with blind frogs —
And no amount of fumbling, in broad daylight,
With the spirit's moist, crumbling match
Can reignite the candle it once held high,
Illuminating curiosity's labyrinthine passageways.

In fact, the only leitmotif left, amidst debris
Constituting senility's rubbish heap,
Is his realization of being "too late,"
A Jamesian disclaimer his dislocated soul
*

Revels in reiterating, as he navigates dawn's waters,
Sailing, with an urgent tailwind,
Toward dusk's precipitous abyss,
From whose doomed conclusion he'll leap, into sleep,
Before the next sun stirs his turbid juices.

For the remainder of this day, at least,
He must continue questing respite
From paranoid demons, pernicious chimeras
That halo his listing vessel,
If only to register his minimal physical momentum
As a measurement of his defiance of death.
Otherwise, he might just as well not rise
To seek occasional intimations of consolation
Available only to those who believe eternity is now.

8/14/84 — [1] (02119)

At Tuesday's Precipice

For Victoria Buchanan

Tuesday is such a strange stepchild.
A plague must have raged through this station,
Where trains no longer arrive or depart
And intellectual vagrants, like me, gravitate,
To settle in, for a while, behind wine, to write paeans,
Brood, in musical interludes, over time and fate,
The major epistemological abstracts,
Whose cusps, writ bold in the full moon's crow's-feet,
Conspire to recreate my most trivial insecurities,
In lunar tableaux compounded of madness and excessive passion.
Seated here, waiting for the Katy to take on water

And passengers whose destinations are located
Well beyond the twentieth century, I reinvent the Rig-Veda,
Catapult my imagination twenty centuries back,
Into a past I never occupied, just to test my powers,
Press the mind to define its limits,
Outline the edge of the precipice, in phosphorescent dye,
That, tonight, I might tightrope-walk the horizon,
Defy death's unilateral treaty with itself,
*

And find my own tracks leading through this desolation,
To that lapsed atmosphere where *forever* is here
And *now* is Tuesday eternally — my blessed stepchild.

8/14/84 — [2?] (02667)

Frau Victoria △

For Victoria Buchanan

Victoria, I miss you so systematically,
I might as easily be a Nazi storm trooper
As reticent Jew-poet churching your beauty, in verse,
Evoking your blessed essence, in compressed odes
I recite nightly, while the books burn, burn fulgently,
In the *Platz*, where my dreams turn nightmarish,
For loneliness imposed, on my bones, by your gone spirit.

For all I know, Victoria, your remote, erudite intellect
And sensual, sleek shape,
Which fit my malleable brain and aging body
With Krupp-forged precision, were vagrant traces,
Not palpable smoke rising from furnaces
Stationed at Auschwitz, Belzec, Treblinka,
Not living bones fashioned from my own.

And yet, Victoria, memory plays weird tricks on itself,
Formulates the most peculiar *jeux de mots*,
In which you and I are aligned beneath a southern sky,
Not in eclipse, rather as fused comets
Cruising past the terrestrial universe, in flaming unison,
Trying to complete our assigned orbits
Before the entire sky explodes, in Holocaust bones,

Rendering us misbegotten waifs
Destined to shadow each other, like Pyramus and Thisbe,
Adolf and Eva — Dantesque Jews,
Neither of whom owns any tribal claims to Hebraic traits,
Save those which engender from unadulterated loving.
Lady, I love you . . . *Heil* Moses, Amodeus —
Victoria, you blow my bones to sacred stones!

8/14/84 — [3?] (02668)

Bearing Grudges

Always, within that shimmering distance
Separating me from my father,
There hovered that curious admixture of his,
A witch's potion, almost,
Compounded of two parts arrogance
With one part flaming ignorance of the artistic,
His graceless incomprehension of profit
Accruing from prose and poetry written for their own sakes,
Not to make money, just to be listened to.

And underlying all our encounters,
A fundamental competitiveness usually intervened,
To proclaim the ultimate deadlock between titans,
No matter the differences in age and wisdom.
We never seemed to be willing to compromise,
Bite pride, like a bullet, quit fighting
For our own egocentric *esthétique* —
Firebrands to the end, zealots both of us.
Ah, the pity of it, the pathetic tragedy,

So that, even now, though he's been gone
Long enough for memory to have ceased complaining
About the shame of it, I can't quite forgive
Or excuse my father's abusive disrespect
For the person he nurtured, if not in his image,
As a businessman, at least as one
Conversant with sustaining the work ethic
As a purposive means to reasonably effective success —
A son, poet, longing so for his dad's words of praise.

8/15/84 (02120)

To His Distant Mistress: A Loose Persuasion, After Marvell ^Δ

Jefferson City, Missouri, and Jackson, Mississippi,
Form a wide chorus only I can sense,
This celebratory Thursday morning,
As the road I drive, no matter circuitously,
Invites me home, to your embrace,
Yet half a Spice Islands–span away.

Your whispering, distant voice
Draws me, fluidly, through the slipstream
My soft thoughts reiterate,
Alternating between these two state capitals,
Where lawyer and writer gesticulate,
Act out their briefs and poetry, in isolation.

I listen to your motions being filed, adjudicated,
Witness my verse climaxing into closure,
As we fly toward afternoon's apogee,
Arrive, simultaneously,
To resume where we concluded,
Take up the loose Memphis thread,

And weave evening into a glittering cloak
To sleep, naked, beneath,
Then share in wearing invisibly, by day,
For however long it might take
Before the thread frays
And, again, we must separate, for a duration.

Tonight, lady, time may not stand still,
But we'll sure make it stretch to keep pace!

8/16/84 — [1] (00147)

Collision Course △

Singing winds bring me home,
On whispering wings thoughts of you swing buoyantly,
Whose heather-hued plumage
Is your exquisite, naked shape
Lofting across memory's orange and pink horizon.

As I fly toward you, in metaphor's fuselage,
See you penetrate my sector,
Aboard your Brancusi-sleek sky-seal,
Inexorably converging on colliding vectors,
My increasingly unchecked recklessness crescendoes.

Soon, released from assigned holding patterns
We've both negotiated,
For the tight scheduling of migrating souls,
*

We'll make our go-around and, landing in tandem,
Soar into simultaneously climaxing silence.

8/16/84 — [2] (00148)

[A very rare and daring sharing] †

A very rare and daring sharing

My indwelling has been on
    things outwardly compelling

8/17/84 (03854)

DNA Strands

The highways I drive, daily,
Are DNA
My genes require, to ensure continuity
For the generations of images and ideas I propagate
Whenever pen mates with chaste paper.

They connect my soul's remotest regions
With places I know by heart,
Allow me freedom to explore new geographies
Without losing my way back home
To dreams, memories, and ancient déjà vus.

Their interwoven configurations,
Consisting of concrete reality reinforced with God-strands,
Contain universal truths laced with cosmic secrets,
All mine, for the cost of fuel,
The patience to let the ride satisfy time's constraints,

And the pain of knowing I've been consigned immortality,
Recording every meter of the epic road-poem
My blood, cells, bones, flesh, emotions compose
As I go from sleep to sleep,
Evolving my own ethos and mystique for traversing eternity.

8/20/84 (05902)

Postmodernist Myths Persist

Nothing stays as we dreamed it might be
Or even achieves the elegance,
Eloquence, nobility of unspoken speech,
Especially since conceiving potential discoveries
Is a capacity too few grasp
Requires reaching back into the imagination's past,
To resurrect, from forgetting, ancestral pleasures,
Time-release capsules, primal associations
Which should explode, freely, our whole lives wide.

Nothing stays, since dreaming itself
Resembles not so much illusion, artifice, mirage
As glass vacuum, in which incandescence,
But not human lucidity, illuminates the universe,
With its shimmering, filamentous intellect.
Dreaming is reality's enemy, toadish fiend,
Who succeeds in reinforcing our belief in immortality,
By whispering, in our ears, deliverance
From the mediocrity of our most bodily immediacies.

8/23/84 (05903)

Oedipal Wellsprings

This Monday morning,
My eyes' slits drip liquid
As if both were psychic wounds,
Their sensitive lenses seared by marish visions
Visited on my sinning soul,
Like a syphilitic somnambulist
Slipping past sleep's electrified barbed-wire nerves.

Seeing replicates infection.
Images are my spirit's malignancy,
Attaching themselves to Leviathan bellies
Floating in opaque depths beneath the eyes,
Where oceanic silence is the mind's blindness
And misperceived intuitions spawn
Like radioactive barnacles multiplying Hiroshima atolls.

As the sun rises, insinuates the frigid universe,
Insight twitches, throws off its scabs.
*

Overwhelmed by pain, both fragile spectroscopes,
Spinning in mad frenzy, grope for focus,
Paths affording access to familiar corridors
That might lead this broken Oedipus
Out of aloneness, toward self-recognition and inner peace, home.

8/27/84 (05904)

Death Comes to a Family Man

This crisp, early-September a.m.
Marks my drifting's inception.
The brain's hairline fissure widens,
Whose minuscule scribbling is the invisible split
Between insight and intuition,
The cosmic hyphen, galactic slash,
Differentiating godly from human firmaments.

Anagogic overtones lingering from sleep
Insinuate my ears, with snakes
Slithering, fast, through high, raspy grass . . .
Or is it the planet evolving past my shadow,
On its perpetually lubricated axle,
Synthesizing spherical music —
Death whispering its black laughter, at my back?

As I head westerly, away from wife, children,
Every known face, worshiped ritual,
Toward afternoon's oblique peripheries,
Jagged as dragons' teeth,
My eyes focus, momentarily, in the rearview glass,
As if to isolate one last familiar refraction.
Its lizard-tongue flicking, the past spits in my wake.

9/4/84 — [1] (04153)

Outpost Observers

What a positively illusive enemy distance is
To us, love, as we sit out here, at polar peripheries,
Waiting for the slightest shivering of eucalyptus,
Sandpipers' scurrying through the midnight moonspray
*

Receding, irregularly as lightning, across a beach,
To alert us to furtive intruders penetrating zones
We guard with our meagerly armed hearts.

God, how loneliness expands to measureless widths,
Within the endlessly inward-bending dimensions
Our minds invent when deprived of nourishment
Fundamental to self-perpetuating gentleness.
My sensitive skin goes hot to cold,
Sweaty, dry, wet, hot again,
Anticipating annihilation, momentarily, by bleak aliens

Bent on destroying all our best intentions
To secure the peace, in dissident kingdoms
Flourishing, chaotically, between us,
Across the horizon-wide dried riverbed
Separating us. At opposite stations,
You and I wait for Armageddon or armistice.
Either way, lady, there's no escaping truth,

By truce or placative reparations
Made, in seemingly good faith,
With enemies whose weapons are subterfuge and ruse.
If we are to survive at these extremes,
It will require complete, unceasing belief
In the magic that silent loving can generate
When, in vacuums sealed inviolably,
Humans illuminate the universe, with private lightning.

9/4/84 — [2] (04152)

His One Son's Son

As I drive west, out I-44,
City shapes go thin, like coins, on a track,
Being flattened by a speeding freight train.
While I gain momentum, sporadic construction sites,
Reminiscent of paleontological excavations,
Take on blurred registration. Cranes, dozers,
Scrapers, backhoes shimmer —
Saurians floating in Mesozoic oceans.
My eyes scour the roadside, for a safe place to rest,
Catch up with my heart's erratic pattern,
Before dreadful forces overtake paranoia.

Forty miles out, give or take occasional oases,
Whose wells contain fossil fuel
And tents display every conceivable earthly delight,
In plastic-packaged, sodium-benzoate preservation
(If only the early explorers and conquistadors
Had had such magic to sprinkle into their hogsheads!),
The landscape reclaims its original patrimony.
Except for 12 x 40' highway billboards,
A strange, taintless greenness
Elaborates a Septembering that hymeneal silence protects
From all transients. I alone seem to hear it,

With my blind eyes, as if I might be Oedipus
Groping my way home, alone.
Suddenly, the song dissolves into the sweetest aroma:
Mowed oats, cut fescue, lespedeza, rye.
Freshly tended fields fusing fecund juices
Fill all my senses, with blessed perplexity.
Nose, eyes, ears, sinuses, throat implode.
The *nowhere* everywhere surrounding my passage
Opens as though it were a colossal cocoon.
I emerge, the latest phoenix of tribal poets
Who've composed Psalms, disguised themselves as blind hobos,

To avoid premature extinction as firstborn sons
Gifted with God's cosmic idiosyncrasies and creativity . . .
Disguised themselves as ragsellers, raiment merchants,
Adept in seconds, odd lots, end pieces, and selvages —
Bedouins, nomads, bindle stiffs traveling from ghetto
To pogrom-depleted ghetto, not decade-hopping
But leaping from one century to the next, with tragic flexibility.
Yet, ever westerly they've progressed, writing accursed verses
Not to vindicate or sublimate fate,
Rather confirm their mastery over solitariness and death.
Today, I proclaim myself son of the Lord's only Son.

9/5/84 (02348)

Naming the Muse ^Δ

Already, this sixty-degree early-September morn,
As I escape, again, into freedom's routine,
*

By bequeathing my responsibilities to others,
I detect, in trees, traces of imminent metamorphosis.
Sumacs and sugar maples,
Like their pre-spring counterpart harbingers,
Crocuses and forsythias, presage the pervasive changing
Just days away, with their scarlet hues
Streaking predominantly green scapes,
Like barb wounds on a horseman's arm
Or a night sky filled with Mars stars.

Heading south, to rendezvous with noon's muse,
My fleeing spirit peers inward,
Through its terraqueous caverns, for an exit
Into hours backing up on themselves.
An orange-gray, mist-laden horizon,
Split, as if into cosmic firmaments, by a wide band
Filigreed like a lady's tricolored gold pin,
Shimmers. Its slanted rays are stalactites
Dripping from God's ceiling, into my eyes.
I've become a blind, black amphibian
Swimming in fifty feet of clear liquid confusion.

Until now, whether above ground or underneath,
My surroundings have seemed oneiric,
My psyche's location a hysterical shriek away
From Bedlam's side porch, Pandemonium's cellar door.
Yet, heading toward Memphis, Oxford, beyond,
I sense myself being transformed in the sun's warmth,
Rising from the cave, ascending day's Mount Sinai,
Being penetrated by vague benedictions
Emanating from nameless angels haloing my passage
From sleep's primal fright to freedom's source.
Suddenly, you appear before me, Victoria, undisguised.

9/6/84 — [1] (03605)

A Day at the Races [Δ]

What a felicitous shift his mind has made
With the eyes' images, this trip —
Cows and corn transformed into sorghum, beans, cotton,
In an artificer's histrionic flourish,
*

Whose deft performance, metaphoric trickery,
Goes unnoticed, though ultimately not unheard,
For undiminishing invitations for him to appear at sodalities,
Token pay-by-the-plate brunches
At local temples and synagogues, in chic coffeehouses,
Renovated, midtown Friday-night bistros,
And at campuses that pay travel expenses and board,
Offer "the standard honorarium."

This glorious morning, going at his own pace,
Liberated from all ties, spaced out,
His very arbitrariness determining his nomadic course,
He sets himself for a spell of riot.
And even though he can't quite play the odds
On day's win-and-place quinella,
He knows, by night, he will have tried to light
In a warm stable appropriate to the race he's been running
Against thoroughbred syllables and tropes,
Transmuting them into illusory music
He'll tune to a shuddering lady's victory cries.

9/6/84 — [2] (03502)

Wind Instruments ^Δ

The wind's hymns nudge these slender cedars
To gentle swaying. Each is a gospel singer
Reiterating the earth's pendulous reverberations,
Whose murmurous incantation stirs me,
This early September, to Mississippi's exultation.

My ears hear my eyes crying to be heard;
My eyes see my ears trying to fly, to soar,
Into that crystalline aura where treetops and sky
Reverse allegiances, blue air nourishes green roots.
Slowly, my own voice unites with Rowan Oak's chorus,

Enters the cloistral shimmering, in joyous reverence.
Suddenly, my senses apprehend the reason for bending,
That attitude humans, as well as trees, assume
When listening to and emulating celestial music:
My bones are pitch pipes the wind vibrates, this afternoon.

9/7/84 (03533)

Tied to Our Tides $^\Delta$

Leaving the Peabody, this wet Sunday morning,
The hissing tires spider spinnerets
Weaving Beale, Gayoso, and Union streets
Into Riverside Drive, I gaze, wistfully, at Mud Island,
Where, yesterday, we listened to three black singers
Carve niches in the sky's cathedral facade,
To contain harmonies our memories might reprise
Whenever revisiting the shrine, on the Mississippi,
In which our twin spirits were baptized.

Mesmerized, I approach the span providing I-55
Continuous passage from Tennessee, into Arkansas.
Thoughts of your recent presence and absence,
Your beautiful, futile, expressive forestalling
Of the conclusion to each communion we take,
Balk like fractious mules, for unseen snakes,
Refuse to cross the river. They would have me halt
At the bridge's dead center, regardless of cars,
Dematerialize inside the grief they inflict.

Yet three phrases you shaped from your clay bin,
Compressed into savory wafers
Our tongues might taste, let dissolve, assimilate,
Keep echoing, in baffles this impasse amplifies:
"Our bodies, being 65 percent water,
Are vessels that float on their own oceans";
"Both of us are tied to our tides";
"My dear, handsome man, come back soon!"
Crying, I quit driving, dive into your voice, drown.

9/9/84 (00183)

Transfiguring Wishes

He awakens to vague cerebrations
Occasioning themselves beyond his chamber,
Into which daylight has been seeping, for hours,
Like Appian moisture leaking, through soil
Two millenniums deep, into clammy catacombs.

His complete dislocation keeps him from rising,
Placing waferish weight on both feet,
Groping for familiar handholds,
Niches and warps, in hardwood and tiles, his toes know.
"NOWHERE" is the graffito scrawled, in dream chalk, across
     his *tabula*.

Time and gravity have released his cold bones
From their flesh wraps.
No longer does mortality dog him, with its rife odor.
Lifting the shade, he feels his own shapeless shade
Enter a hovering dust mote, explode.

Suddenly, yet with inexorable indeterminacy,
He senses himself being stretched taut across the horizon —
A nebulous Saturn ring singing infinity's vespers,
Dissolving into a silver-nitrate twilight,
Evanescent day's permanent negative: night.

9/10/84 (05905)

[By degrees, as I slide south, out of the city,]

By degrees, as I slide south, out of the city,
Coffee bought at road's edge,
From an "all-nite" posada, awakens me to the fog
Hovering just above valleys vision measures
With its transits. Until sipping the steaming draught,
I thought the thick-shifting, opaque moisture
Might be night's Poe webs wafting in the breeze
Morning's wheezing breathing was causing
Or precipitation from dripping sinuses
Leaking into the eye and brain cavities.
Real fogs terminate in sun-furnaces —
Auschwitz, Treblinka, Sobibor.
Left to their wiles, mind-bogs dissipate on their own.
Lost inside this insidiously blinding scourge,
I almost wish my spirit had never fled
Its nocturnal necropolis
Or sipped the bittersweet, acidic caffeine
The dead drink to keep their infernal alertness alive.

9/12/84 — [1] (00844)

Matriarchy [Δ]

Synaptic fireflies igniting inside my brain
Illuminate daydreaming's cave,
In which déjà vu memories drip from invisible ceilings —
History's inexorable stalactites,
Whose spectral whispers insinuate my senses.
Their glinting facets reconnect our fires.

Slowly, mind-sparks transmute me into moon-splay
Traipsing through leaves that shade your tree house,
Probing rimpled window glass, diaphanous curtains,
To reach the chamber containing your chaste fragrance,
Finally, your body, lying, naked, atop a brass bed —
Queen Diana, rife in her menstrual cycling.

I ride inside your lunar Septembering tides,
Penetrate you, on memory's breaking waves,
Attach myself, polyplike, to the reef your breathing forms,
Your lush breasts corals my dreams inhabit.
All evening, your saline bleeding, lapping, lapping,
Washes fantasies, drowns demons, purifies sleep.

Awakening at day's edge, revivified,
Just as the dim-lit image of your essence disappears
Into a sky overflowing with protean oceanic swells,
I stretch, my primal strengths multiplying,
And realize nothing can keep me from repossessing you,
Though I might have to wait for the next clear night.

9/12 — [2] & 9/18/84 (00174)

Monday-Morning Launch

Mainlined caffeine
Tries to revitalize the weekend's spent senses.
Monday morning is myocardial infarction,
Toxic shock syndrome,
The lunar side of the soul's dark night.

Five cups into flight, I feel my brain-boosters ignite,
Sending my vessel into orbit,
Reverberantly circling the inner galaxy,
Whose imperfect surface my elapsing years
Have etched with overlapping elliptical paths,

As I've passed from generational phase to phase,
Gaining altitude, ever aiming higher,
Toward the day when all fuel is used,
Engines silenced, free-floating initiated,
And I assume complete responsibility for total surrender.

For now, however, I remain at the controls,
Monitoring gauges measuring emotional intensity,
Intellectual thresholds, visual acuity,
Motor dexterity, hoping the charts at my disposal
Still show accurate locations for Scylla and Charybdis.

As I go through exploding photon blizzards,
Asteroid fields, black holes, past novas,
Relying on caffeine's leading edge,
Exhausting miraculously shimmering images,
Achieving maximum speed, Monday glides into eternity.

9/17/84   (05906)

On the Way to the Country Churchyard

The unreal city I flee
Seethes in pink, sulfurous, prehistoric mist.
Five miles out, it all fits in my rearview mirror,
Where it's suspended like an inflated blowfish
Illuminated, from within, by a flickering red candle.

And as I head south,
As if swimming through a vast, pelagic atmosphere
Consisting of low-lying fog, raw smoke,
Exhaust from myriad vehicles
Commuting from the country, in lemminglike procession,

My dim senses awaken to the essence of escape,
The nature of breaking with convention,
Drifting volitionlessly, not to avoid responsibility
But continue making daily obeisance
To gods who've forgotten how to say their prayers.

Today, my leave-taking has its basis in fact.
Yesterday afternoon, I was fired from my job.
Two days prior to that, my wife abandoned me,
For another man; my child ran away.
And last night, I committed suicide.

Now, I ask you this rhetorical question:
Why would anyone in his right mind
Ever decline to drive up front,
At the head of his own cortège, when riding behind
Provides such a shortsighted view of eternity?

9/19/84 — [1] (05907)

The Irretrievable

For too many years,
Our mutual, paltry hearts had skipped
Too many alternating beats,
Without either of us realizing how labored
Our collective breathing had become,

Until "suddenly," one day,
We awakened from our separate sides of the bed,
Suffering strangely similar spasms,
Muscular, back, abdominal, brain pains,
Spiritual ataxia's nameless malaise,

Whose etiology I might never have guessed,
Had it not been for the questions
You suggested we ask ourselves and try to answer:
"How long has it been since I've listened
To my wife listening to her husband

Listening to himself?" "How long
Since I've witnessed my husband witnessing me
Witness myself in his eyes?" For weeks,
Her Sphinx riddles refused to yield clues,
Provide significant figments, insights, disclosures.

Only last night, while she lay drowsing,
Whimpering, imperceptibly, between inhalations,
Her tiny face shaped to the pillow,
Like a pearl etched into its clammy womb,
Did I fathom the extent of her desperation

And mine, the vacuum absence imposes on the heart
When lovers let their blood, from neglect,
Forgetting, or petty rejection, cause its flow
To clog, diminish to the worm's pace,
Dissipate. Rising up on my elbow,

I reached over and, from her numbness,
Arrested my wife, in my silent, grieving embrace,
As if to administer artificial respiration.
Yet no touching, kissing, stroking of her pale features
Could retrieve her soul from that depthless sleep.

9/19/84 — [2] (04151)

Vexatious Integrations

Leaving's grievous routine afflicts me, with guilt.
It's the children's faces deflating
On learning I'm not staying home, again, today,
Won't be returning, tonight, to sleep with their mama,
My wife, these past fourteen years,
Whose dreams have undergone a recent sea change,
Failed to keep pace with crosscurrents
Constantly rearranging contours
We shaped, originally, from textured ocean beds
And hoped would never need further tending.
Leaving's incumbencies numb me, with guilt.

Yet if we accept predestination,
Even conceptually, as a mere intellectual exercise,
Believe choice and freedom are mirages
No poet has ever chased seriously,
For knowing that his art arises out of intense application
And that commitment precludes distraction,
We also must accept slavery to our disciplined ambitions
As the given in any successful equation,
All of which implies allegiance to the heart's compulsions,
Not outside, conventional persuasions
To fundamental influences — God, love, and country.

Ah, but somewhere between these lines,
Where tension burrows, like assiduous termites,
In the brain's floor joists,
A solution, no matter how imprecise, exists
For resolving counterpoised dichotomies
Head and heart perpetuate, with fierce defiance.
Perhaps, at some juncture, I can discover
How to integrate staying, with leaving;
*

Writing, with those intervening silent blocks of time;
Loving, with guarding privacies;
Driving, flying, with reinventing wheels and wings.

9/20/84 (04150)

Aubade ᐃ

[For Victoria Buchanan]

You're the best in bed/at letters,
A twentieth-century Athena,
Who insinuates my head, with your intellect,
Enlarges my heart's paltry expectations,
With physical energy and sexual adeptness
So inspirative, my blood speed
Increases tenfold, just reading your printing,
Assimilating your stimulating tropes,
Fantasizing you and me arrested in Keatsian gestures,
Locked in perpetual copulative frieze,
Despite the distance, measured in days and weeks,
Fate has had his assistant, history, regulate,
To ensure we don't disturb the frictionless spheres.

Lady, you're the best in bed/letters.
Let's make certain we keep "in touch,"
By never allowing the pet owl, on your shoulder, to drowse.

9/21/84 (00175)

Fall Callings

This fall, while I dwell in a city swollen
And swelling yet, like a pretzel in a glass of water,
Intermittent trips business requires,
With unrelenting insistence, get all mixed up
Inside my stifled, shifting, dispossessed psyche.

Each day, I awaken in a chamber
Totally unrelated to that in which my naked body
Deposited its bone-bag, the previous evening.
Vespers and matins follow and precede each other,
With antic randomness,

Their vertiginous rituals confusing civilized time.
Horrified, I hang from massive clock-hands,
Above a peopled street, abyss.
No woebegone Harold Lloyd or Robert Donat,
Dangling from *The 39* Big Ben *Steps*,

Having saved his precious guts, or society,
From dread Kaiser Wilhelm's sabotage tactics,
Rather an innocent, if anonymous, man am I,
Hoping the great escapement controlling the spheres
Won't bog down, slip its cogs, for my added weight.

As I drive southwest, my ghetto soul reconciles its tensions,
Knowing its own inchoate exile
Is God's foregone conclusion, the unspoken behest
Inherent in His covenant, and that this brittling wilderness
Is the same road Moses trod, through the scrolls, home.

9/24/84   (00843)

Rosh Hashanah for One Fallen from Grace ^Δ

Dachau-sounds resound in his numb ears,
This crisp, September-ending a.m.,
Resonate like a V-18 radial engine
Cranking a Corsair's three-bladed prop
To raucous overwinding. He winces, perceptibly,
From pain strafing his undefendable brain.
Suddenly, the blades change pitch;
Those reports metamorphose into horrific moaning.
The living dead, slowly, pitifully dying,
Fill his daymares, with scions
Crying for leniency toward their tormentors, this judgment day.

Baffled by his imagination's plea for compassion
And decency, despite fate's eagerness
To wreak reprisal, no matter how inadequate,
Revenge, for those timeless heart-crimes,
He prays, to whatever wayward messianic spirit
May prevail, that YHWH make Himself available,
Disclose His requirements for individual atonement.
Tonight, this meek man knows
*

That after the shofar blows, he'll break a smooth loaf,
Spread an apple with honey, get drunk, and weep
For unredeemed sinners, not for his own lonely soul.

9/26/84 — [1] (00842)

A Day at the Zoo: Watching the Gorillas

For Sid Selvidge

Predictable beasts. Creatures sybaritic in their habits.
Yet plagued we are, occasionally, within our species,
Two powers removed from simian ancestors,
By lunatics neither civilized constraints
Nor cultivated brains can keep from committing heinous deeds
Perpetrated against saner coevals,
Loonies who would derail trains, "Clutter" front pages,
With manifold *In Cold Blood*ed Lennons, Kennedys, and Kings
Done in, for fun, by Sons of Sam,
Rob banks, in the name of Mizmoon for the Miz-Begotten,
Fanatics, political dissidents, terrorists, guerrillas . . .

Like I said, men descended hairy primates,
Related to lowland gorillas, spider, squirrel, and snow monkeys,
Gibbons, baboons, chimpanzees performing swinging antics
In artificial-zoo-habitat limbs,
Going nowhere, all day long,
In controlled limbos orchestrated for paid visitors,
Bringing in steady revenues that provide feed
For their primal needs, onlookers to reinforce their egos,
No matter how primitive . . . not men
But de-men-ted vestiges
Expected to show diplomacy, who only know violence,

Going nowhere, in their cages, throwing their own feces
At spectators too amazed, by the inane spectacle,
To get out of the way, in time,
Deflect, by virtue of coordinated movements,
Shit hurled at them, by supposedly impersonal apes,
Or constantly replenished water splashed at them,
Who've come to ogle the docu-men-ted behavior
Of animals not at all bemused by humans peering from without,
Hoping to photograph or memorize or experience, vicariously,
*

Something unusual (a suicide, masturbation,
Passionate copulation — recognizably human traits) . . .

Hirsute crazies, innocuous in their blameless routines,
Whose day-to-day pursuits of impossible escape
Allow them to maintain their distance from crowds
Gathered to record their brief arousals, mood alterations,
Fugues, frustrations, relaxations, betrayals,
Martyrdoms, aphrodisiacal exchanges with wayward mates . . .
Predictable beasts really, as long as they're confined.
Imagine what might transpire if their trainers
Decided to set them free, let them commingle with visitors.
Perhaps no one would even realize they'd been assimilated,
For their indistinguishability.

9/26/84 — [2] (02664)

Byhalia ^Δ

What a strange name — Byhalia.
It trips off my tongue's tip,
Like so many other Mississippi/Indian appellations,
With this significant difference:
My illicit accomplice, sweet mistress,
Victoria, and I have visited this remote place
To etch, on memory's silver-nitrate plates,
His ultimate humiliation, experience this *Hölle*,
In the flesh, no matter that we've arrived
Twenty-some-odd years after his pathetic demise,
About which the public knows absolutely *nada*
Beyond the Blotner/Minter melodrama
It's been bequeathed, to lullaby its intellect's sleep,
From time anon to anonymous time.

We know, though. She and I
Have traveled here, investigated, scrutinized
The now-defunct Christian Academy,
Whose flaking paint, desolate purlieus can't disguise
The original sanitarium Dr. Wright administrated
With stern eye and his penchant for paraldehyde.
We've interviewed, informally, of course,
Relics and derelicts the town has preserved,
Who remember, twenty-some-odd years later,
*

The weird *son et lumière* effects
Emanating, nightly, from that drying-out place,
Where Cousin Jimmy brought Brother Will
And from whose now-gone gates
Their most celebrated "inmate" escaped, only to die in a ditch.

We've driven here, from Memphis, purposely,
To probe and sate, simultaneously, curiosity's needs,
Fulfill the imagination's collective requirement
That, ultimately, facts must rise above prefabricated myths
And fictions fall by the wayside, like Mr. Bill himself,
Who refused to be confined, like a laboratory rat,
In a Skinner box in Mississippi,
Opted, instead, to die like Vardaman's fish, in the dust,
"Cooked and et, cooked and et,"
Anonymous as an unsigned Elizabethan sonnet
Consigned to immortality by being included
In an anthology of Renaissance poets
And accidentally attributed to another Bill,
With whose genius and fame, curiously, his own would be equated.

We have traveled to this primordial location in northern Mississippi
To confirm its existence, acquiesce to the temptation
History places before us, to accept, without questioning,
Its faithful place in the legendary fable.
But we've resisted too-easy compliance,
Refused to believe that his genius,
No matter how wired or blitzed,
Could have submitted to such shabby physical limitations.
We know, now, why he would have summoned
His feeble energies, to resist such a dread enemy,
Destitution: even in his mind's dulling baffles,
He must have sensed the ultimate Snopes volume
And *The Reivers* yet had to be written.
He couldn't quit before destiny ditched him.

9/27/84 (03554)

Willy Sypher: A Company Man ^Δ

Friday afternoon's twilight
Isolates Willy Sypher as shadowy specter
Plying I-70 easterly, home,
*

After his week of making rounds, in mid-Missouri,
Personally servicing his customers,
Just as he's been doing these past forty years.

This isn't the first such trip
On which he's had to substitute his motel room
For the synagogue's sumptuous atmosphere,
Make do with dime-store trappings
Instead of handwrought altar and ark decorations,
Torahs cloaked in meticulously stitched silks.

In fact, yesterday, he celebrated Rosh Hashanah,
Tooting Acme-Zenith's horn,
Previewing the coming spring line's innovative offerings,
For Philistines and nonsinning clients alike.
And though he dined alone,
He toasted his God and theirs ecumenically,

Hoping atonement might be more appropriate to others
Than himself, since, objectively,
He has never considered his life irreverent.
Indeed, he regards his actions as satisfactory,
If not exemplary, at least dignified,
In their innocuous, meekly anonymous routines.

To his knowledge, no one has ever accused him
Of using others to advance his position,
Coveting another's possessions,
Or committing adultery, even in fantasies.
He's always been "a company man,"
"Mr. Reliable," "Steady-As-He-Goes Willy,"

"A real consistent asset to the operation,"
His boss recently reiterated.
Responsibility, circumspection, and success
Have attended him, just as he has courted them,
All the days of his career as a traveling salesman,
Road peddler to the grass-roots masses.

And no matter that he's had to sacrifice,
Endure lapses, forgo social activities,
For plying the outcast ways of his ancestors.
He was never asked how he might like his survival —
Astringent or with artificial sweeteners.
He learned, early, to take everything served —

Ghetto deaths, ethnic prejudice, classlessness —
Return the "favor," with diplomacy and etiquette,
To make himself inconspicuous
Whenever necessary, to deflect good fortune's coquettishness.
Tonight, in his own bed, he'll cry for Lila,
Who died giving birth to their stillborn child.

9/28/84 (02347)

Premon-hiss-ions

Though it's dark, I awaken, shake my bone bag,
As though, turning it upside down,
Thousands of Tinkertoy pieces
Might cascade to the floor. But night's restive sleep
Has had seemingly little effect on the body's cohesiveness,
And its neo-cubistic dreams,
Consisting of amebas, chimeras, demigorgons,
Hissing in pits swarming with slithering lizards,
Have failed to dismantle my Crystal Palace
Or even shatter a solitary glass pane
In the forty-three-year-old edifice.

This Monday, the crisp, first morning in October,
Acknowledges my physical presence,
Records my noisy fumbling through the house,
My leaving, fleeing the city, my disappearance,
Whose traces are erased by traffic,
Like footprints shore-washed by a working ocean.
Suddenly, I overtake my bone bag,
Jostling south, and realize why
Urgency carried me away so precipitously,
Two hours earlier: I could actually hear
My residual fears hissing, in the basement and the kitchen.

10/1/84 (05908)

Intimations of Psychic Dissolution

He lets them off at the school's front steps,
While their mother malingers in bed,
Nursing last night's sleepless phobias
*

And this morning's dread of entering a new day,
And then he subsides into his guilt.
Driving south, out of the city,
He wonders how, possibly, it could have happened
That, at forty-three, he has arrived at this impasse,
Squandering his allotted hours and weeks,
Seeking so much less than destiny,
In its infinite, if conventional, wisdom,
Has lavished on his gifted existence —
Two vivacious kids, sufficient income, a wife
Whose tasteful elegance and occasional spontaneities
His romantic overtures once enhanced.

Every free chance, he grasps at convenient excuses
To escape his present-tense omniscience,
Fast-forward his past, to predict his future,
Chooses to turn his back on the truth —
That his two-handed engine
Has suffered shattered pistons, warped rings,
Scorched cylinder heads, broken lobes
On its camshaft. His paltry soul
Can't make one more mile; it balks.
Driving south, he stalls, pulls off, onto the shoulder,
Begins weeping. All around him,
Fall's prismatic leaves shimmer in the meek breeze,
Which assimilates his tears. No vehicles pass,
During the lengthening wait for assistance.
Finally, silence fades into twilight,
Night into dying, as his disappearing spirit
Eviscerates even this morning's still-warm memories
Of letting his kids off, at the school's front steps.

10/3/84 (04149)

Hobo-Poet

The hobo-poet is addicted to the open road.
Wherever he goes, freedom accompanies him,
Parenthesizing his speeding vehicle
As though it were a Jamesian aside,
Insulating his creative juices,
From the cold, calculating distractions society would conceive,
*

Thrust at him, in the form of guilt-infused responsibility,
To impede his groping imagination's quest
For curiosity's Golden Fleece.

Whether divided interstate, back road
Lacking gravel, eroded, serpentine,
Or six-lane freeway makes little difference.
Compulsion knows no restrictions,
Save those imposed by the no-holds-barred psyche,
So driven by silence rife with meters and rhymes
The inner ear involuntarily apprehends,
That the only prohibition is quitting too soon;
Aborting the nonexistent is anathema.

Something there is about fluid movement
That unlooses the soul's reclusive hermeneutics,
Allows lapsing vision time to refocus
On rough-edged, membranous memories
Neglect conveniently sets aside or lets fall
Between forgetting's shelves and the wall
Separating its physical days from oblivion.
It produces a smooth, soothing sensation,
Whose sibilances resemble spheres rotating through space.

This contemporary nomad is older than Moses,
Closer, in bloodline, to Abraham
And perhaps brother to Isaac,
Whom God required sacrificed,
That the hobo might learn pain and fear vicariously,
Then write it, from memory, into the Torah,
Whose endlessly unwinding scroll is the open road
Comprising all roads he's traveled, travels daily, today,
Those ancient goat paths

Through Golan, Mesopotamia, Babylonia, Canaan,
No less effective, if less accessible,
Than Connecticut highways and turnpikes,
The same road, in effect,
Over which he's trekked nearly four thousand years,
Across history's constantly recivilized desert,
To this very convergence of penpoint and notebook,
On whose papery skins he inscribes his destiny,
The ink his ancestors' blood, his energy their heritage.

10/4/84 — [1] (02121)

Following the River South △

While I'm still in Missouri, my eyes light, momentarily,
Like butterflies, on the green/white sign
Proclaiming Memphis 109 miles away,
Straight down I-55.
My arteries pulsate, from brain waves
Roiling my body's entire tidal basin, with nervous energy
Diana, from her omniscient, invisible position
In this hazy southering sky, engenders at will.
Still, my heart neither hesitates nor falters,

Rather charges ahead, toward its destination,
The Peabody, which waits at river's edge,
Implacable as a pioneer settlement, to accept my arrival,
Regardless of my paltriness. As the miles diminish
And newer signs materialize, I sense the tides
Swelling inside me reaching treacherous levels,
At which anxiety attacks and hyperventilation overflow.
Suddenly, my flooding blood is the Mississippi.
Above the bridge, at high noon, the moon shudders.

10/4/84 — [2] (00150)

Mizpah △

[For Victoria Buchanan]

Genesis 31:44–49

Gray the day, and grayer still
My resonating heart's regret, on our separating
Yet again. It's almost as though endings,
Not fresh, fleet starts conjured in daydreams
Devoted to arresting illusory interludes
And allocating them to our sweet clandestine use,
Were our raison d'être. I can't stand our partings,
Especially when they're suspended in rain,
Like this persistent grieving mist, through which we drive
Out from Memphis, in opposite directions,
Diminishing our blessed interrelatedness
To Mizpah-whispers etched on vision's windshield.

Yet for some mysterious reason, this Saturday morning,
Listening to the sporadic drops
Has privileged me to translate revelation within revelation,
Arising from circle within circle,
Dispersing into light widening into light on the horizon.
In the collective voice, I hear yours beseeching,
"Let the Lord watch between me and thee."

10/6/84 (00184)

Foggy Connections

As I drive southwest, out of the city,
The fog's cylindrical white eye
(A seemingly innocuous October-morning ground cover)
Swells, contracts convulsively,
Metamorphoses, through a hundred nuances,
From gray to black — eye patch of a pirate
Whose glaring face dares me do battle.

Instinctively, I sense my foot on the gas pedal
Back off, grope for the brake.
Both palms grasp the steering wheel
As if transfixed by an unexpected electrical shock.
Thought-processes clot,
Blocking alternative defensive reactions,
Making stopping on the shoulder impossible.

Like a clenched fist, the thick fog
Hits my vehicle. Blind, dizzy, lost,
Directionless, inside this pernicious trauma,
I feel every bodily function go lax.
Sphincter, pylorus, prostate, spine, brain
Inundate me with fear's adrenal-spew fluids.
Mired, neck-deep, in memory's Auschwitz latrine,

I wade out, into morning's indeterminate trial,
Literally by the skin of my teeth.
Finally, my car, centrifugally propelling away
From the storm-source, edges into a clearing
Festooned in prismatic dazzlements,
Every register, from yellow, through orange and red,
Suspended, in sugar-cube clusters, from trees —

Benedictions, elegies disguised as dying leaves,
Whose nature, purpose, and reason
Resemble my own. They are godly embodiments,
Reenactments of the blessed sacrifice
We rehearse, all our days,
Promoting vital greening, enduring brittling.
In the eye of a storm, a morning, I've survived a season of eons.

10/8/84 (00841)

Willy's Mosaical Robe

His incessant traversing of these highways
Is a bullet shuttle's trajectory
In Missouri's colossal stitching machine —

Back and forth or zigzagging paths.
Occasionally, he selects lap seams, bar tacks —
Patterns contributing to the shape

And design his finished identity takes: a car coat
Fashioned like a Mosaical robe,
To accompany him, on his nomadic journey

Through his span, stretching from Negev's edge,
At the source of the 1940s,
To Mount Sinai's base, in the mid-eighties.

So far, he's not worn it ragged,
Misplaced it, in posadas and thieves' markets,
Or been compelled to barter, trade it

For Philistine trinkets or Babylonian harlots;
Rather, he takes it with him, as an amulet,
To ward off Goebbelses in Gobelin clothes,

Gorgons cloaked in Miltonic poetics, Nixons
Naked as babies disguising checkered pasts.
All seasons, invisible as air, he wears it,

As if its skin-thin fabric might protect him
From any penetration or precipitous shift
In temperature. Simply, it is his heritage.

10/9/84 (02346)

"Higher" Learning

These past three days,
I've had occasion to observe, firsthand,
Labyrinthine rabbit runs being actively plied
By fully tenured professors, part-time instructors,
Masters and Ph.D. creatures of habit,
Enslaved graduate and research assistants,
Administrators, secretaries, and physical-plant handymen.

Safely ensconced in university postures,
They display antics, speech patterns, elitism
That suggest Winslow Homer's one-room schoolhouse,
Which memory transliterates into Pieter Breughel's vision:
Pastoral scapes depicting bee-busy spirits
Arrested in frenzied activities,
Impasto-souls hallowed in celestially gessoed groves

Worthy of Greek as well as Flemish conception,
Arcady indistinguishable from Academe,
If crazed layers are cleaned, time frames changed,
To disclose original shapes and shadows of pedagogues
Imbued, immutably, with delusions and hubris,
Who spend their daze railing against God,
From the loftiest peaks of Mount Olympus, Ohio.

10/12 & 10/16/84 — [1] (02122)

Snake Charmer

This static-garbled afternoon,
The word-hoard rises up like a poised cobra,
Alert to an intruder in its locus,
Prepared to strike, blind its unsuspecting victim,
With death-spit, create writer's block
Behind the nonfocusing eyes,
Brain-consternation accompanied by hematoma,
Annihilating, for its subdural ferocity.

I cringe, recognizing the phantom snake as myself,
That adversary hatched from Medusa eggs
Which daymares, mating with night's Chimeras,
*

Have produced from the ancient word-curse.
Fearing permanent injuries, unhealing wounds,
I feverishly grope for a burlap croker sack
In which to throw my squirming, serpentine imagination,
Whose capture will keep me safe . . . for the moment.

10/16/84 — [2] (05909)

Morning Flight

Prop feathered, mixture lean,
Throttle locked in full accelerating position,
My ship slips through wind-seams
Invisible to the practiced eye, soars freely,
Toward morning's autumnal source,
That zone, located above scudding clouds
Below the stratospheric edge,
Where breathing metamorphoses into icy memory
And strong and weak forces give way
To cosmic geography and godly persuasion.

Rarely has man chanced to fly skies
So enhanced by silence,
The human ear can actually detect time's cogs
Clicking past its delicate anchor escapement,
Hear precision gears and meshing teeth
Revolving — frictionless spheres.
Somewhere up ahead, in that screaming blue,
Through which fate guides stray vessels home,
With autopilot vectors it alone sets up,
Is a runway waiting to translate my weight into space.

10/18/84 — [1] (05910)

A Wedding Toast

To Katie and Jeff,

May your hearts forever stay
As they are today.
May you always take each other's
Breath away.

May your interwoven spirits spin
Golden children.
May your flown souls go together,
Not alone.

And may your hearts always shine
As they do tonight,
Lady Katie, Juliet-star,
Jeffrey, glowing Romeo!

10/18/84 — [2] (02123)

Ill *penseroso* ᐃ

As I spiral south, out of the city,
My secular, molecular energies are disoriented,
For my having spent an entire weekend
Dissipating in familial nuptial revelry.
The eyes — Roman amphorae, cracked and faded,
Containing vague clues to civilizations
Long gone back to life-force —
Wince, blink, shudder, shrink, shatter into silence
The stultified brain emanates, this Monday.
Resigned to its minimal, limited earthly intuition,
That vegetable obfuscation humans inherit
And frequently assume, in their hubris, to be wisdom,
Not cosmic omniscience,
I easily mistake the pervasive malaise,
Marking my passage, as hangover,
Headache precipitated, yet, by too much liquor
Flooding suffocating blood cells,
Not as brain-snakes, chimeras who invaded my psyche
Once I opened the gates, this weekend,
Dismissed the temple sentries, to indulge their appetites,
While I was allowing my own uncertain perversities
To surface. Friday and Saturday night
Were full-mooned, lunatic. In beautiful stupors,
I ran, naked, on gravestones,
Fornicated with vital ladies
Enamored of my physical presence, recited poems
Composed spontaneously: paeans to Moses,
Elegies to Dachau, odes to the future of Jews,
*

Lebanese, Syrians, Egyptians . . . mankind,
Which, through its technological sophistication,
Has made extinction, like a cyanide tablet,
Such a viable alternative to enduring,
Trying to survive the worst conceivable doom —
Universal annihilation.
Driving out of the city, this bleary morning,
I die all former deaths
Experienced by priests, prophets, martyrs, saints —
Dagon, Draco, Savonarola, Mussolini,
Mr. Chips, Walter Mitty, the March Hare.
I am, in each of my imaginative reincarnations,
Recipient of that inevitable revelation,
Realizing eternity's vast sweep is so very brief
When measured by my unhappiness.
Why I was chosen to recreate, with syllables,
Man's heirlooms and keepsakes,
With words, his shabby accomplishments and defeats,
His chronicle, with tropes and quotations,
I shall never know or ever fully appreciate.
Suddenly, I have arrived at my destination,
That small country town where I go to hide,
Plug into my silence, defend my mentality,
Against its enemy: forgetting.
Today, after having coffee at the Capital Café,
I'm going to pen the final chapter,
The conclusion, epilogue, to my autobiography.

10/22/84 (02107)

Presentiments Come to a Highway Surveyor

The terrains of my life are defined
By measuring their distances in eye-blinks,
Windshield-wiper sweeps,
Suns repeatedly setting and rising,
Miles elapsed and registered on rotating axles,
Destinations reached,
Echoing good-byes and hellos routinely spoken,
Memories resurrected from forgetting's recesses,
Cíbolas approached and lost in mirages,
Golden Fleeces sought and found
*

In unrecoverable daydreams.
The contours of my vital spirit are defined
By the accuracy I achieve, in recording rhymes,

Since the breadth and height my heart assume
Are variable coefficients
Of the aggregate length of all roads I drive,
Through the imagination's Sinai,
Any given day, multiplied by the time it takes
To invent a poem from DNA strands
Floating in the adrenalized bloodstream
Fueling my lunatic brain.
This afternoon, heading westerly, home,
I sense both ventricles and auricles
Losing definition, slowing measurably,
As if my destiny's harbinger were cardiac arrest,
Not road fatigue overtaking my soul.

10/23/84 (02108)

An Ode to the Westerly Wind $^\Delta$

October's mid-Missouri mornings
Open slowly, day unfolding into day,
Like fading sweetheart roses
Drooping over the edge of a cut-glass vase.

Their pungent decay awakens me
To my own deliberate breathing, arouses my mentality,
Creates its own occasion for celebrating the senses,
This season of decline — God's most vital climax.

Despite His cosmic adoration of us,
Which sometimes assumes inhuman designs
And illusory, unappreciated shapes,
It's difficult to assign divine wisdom to dying things

Or justify mystical intervention
As the given, not a variable, in the providential equation.
Yet, despite euthanasia, suicide,
And irrational homicidal acts,

We must accept that how and when we leave,
Regardless the reason, aren't significant
*

Or timely, just predictable, within the scheme.
Trees, dogs, grass, streets, people,

Even mackerel-crowded seas and mushroom clouds,
Disperse, dissolve, evaporate,
And are assimilated into the cycling stream,
From whose springs unique currents surge inevitably.

10/24/84 — [1] (02109)

Carpe diem: A Nocturne

So homeless, isolated, dispossessed, in this station,
Where all worship is secular, adult-erated,
Calculated to allow pagan rites,
No matter how trivial or trite,
Their fullest public demonstration, night and afternoon,

I try to relocate my groping soul,
Draw fundamental conclusions to illusory conundrums
That have assailed me, months on end,
Decide tomorrow's destination,
With a modicum of boldness and intuitive overview.

But rumination, I realize, is a bovine gesture
That satisfies only those who read Aquinas
And Buber, quote exegetical passages, in the original,
From Kierkegaard, Nietzsche, Heidegger,
Memorized precisely to impress at faculty parties.

Never have I been one to express tendencies
Toward resolutions, intellectual absolutes.
Quite the contrary, my bent has been strictly sensual,
Which may, indeed, account for my self-centeredness
And reprobate nature. My weakness has been women —

Ladies in their shapely concrete realities,
Whose coquettishness, fragrances, slender legs and waists,
Eloquently phrased tantalizations and praises
Never fail to enchant me, with immobilizing philters,
Disturb my equanimity, cause me to stray,

Deviate from my daily orthodoxies, into waywardness,
Venial dissoluteness, assume the cloven hoof
*

Of goatish creatures from fabled bestiaries,
Become single-minded, in my defiance of isolation,
To such a degree that seeking companionship

Requires immediate satiety. I rise to the task,
Despite constraints. Tonight, as an example,
My eyes scan this noisy lounge, for beckoning courtesans
I might surfeit with witticisms and subtlety,
Settle on the youngest one in the jungle, to ravish,

Then begin the inevitable stalking,
Initiating, from room's length, my own rituals.
Within minutes, we've cut through routine,
Overcome awkwardnesses, entered into instant intimacies.
Three wineglasses into our conversation,

We realize we have so much in common
It would be heinous to deny each other mutuality.
Both of us know loneliness,
On a firsthand basis, have working relationships
With personal grief that make us seek love

From mere strangers. We agree to leave together,
Live forever, until sunrise,
In my motel room. By tomorrow night,
Both of us will have found renewed refuge from solitude,
In other towns, other beds, other vows.

Ah, but now, for now, this is all that counts.

10/24/84 — [2] (02665)

Willy Suffers a Loss of Heart △

Looking out, through feverish, opaque eyes,
Onto the drear morning's graphite drizzle,
Dismantles my already tentative spirit,
Fearing its diminished energies
Will render it grossly overpowered by adversaries
Hiding behind stations of the sun,
As day crosses the meridians. My heart agonizes,
With prospects of having to face demons
*

Disguised as buyers, merchandisers, department heads,
Even clerks and service personnel,
Drag swatch cases and sample-stuffed garment bags
In and out of the car, sell from refs
Glued to display cards, like sardines packed in tins,
Proclaim the gospel according to St. Louis,
Mo., location of Acme-Zenith Clothing Co.

As my vehicle goes north, toward Moberly,
Sliding over silvery concrete, through fog
Clawing rain-soaked fields
And neutralizing the sky, my feverish, opaque eyes
Grope for an opening in my thoughts,
Through which they might tentatively escape
Without calling undue attention to my truancy.
Suddenly, I slow, pull into Steak Palace,
Turn around, and head back onto the highway,
South, to Columbia, Ramada Inn,
Room 123,
From where I'll call all today's accounts,
Beg off, using treacherous weather as my excuse,
And, after rescheduling my visitations,
Bury myself, within the bed's safe white cave.

10/25/84 (02345)

Unexpected Awakening ^Δ

Surfacing through swirling liquefactions —
Oceans impacted with opaque, feverish dreams
Sleep has kept suppressed, too many hours —
My floating psyche collides with visions of you,
As if caught in the eye of a meteor shower.

Your Southern dialect, flecked with syllabled tongues
Slipping, sinuously, into my inner ears,
Shivers my spine, chills my flesh, with heat,
Sears desiccated head-webs, cauterizes fears
My dislocated spirit experienced, initially,
In lunging, abruptly, out of prolonged loneliness,
To answer your telephone call.

And all too suddenly, I am in day's keeping.
You, lady, mistress, mother, lover,
Though so distant, have a-proxy-mated me,
With spoken words capable of dividing my waking soul
Into coital shapes: you and I embracing inextricably.

10/26/84 (00176)

Plague: Contagion and Conflagration

Fevers siege the fleshly fortress,
Seize unwitting sentries
Stationed, complacently, at every gate tower,
Squeeze off all supplies from the outside,
With tactical comprehensiveness.

Inexorably, the body awakens to its state
Of complete subjugation:
Breathing lapses; vision shatters, blurs;
Soreness racks muscles, tendons, bones, and brain;
Dismay and melancholia flood the blood.

Sneezes, coughing, ceaselessly watering eyes
Make peace overtures and negotiable treaties
Seem mere presumptuous vagaries, to the victor,
Who, with barbarian swiftness and ease,
Has unseated and dispossessed its enemy

And sees no reason to reconsider its conquest
Or even listen to history's whispers,
Which call for it to relinquish its quitclaim
On this isolated demesne . . . at least not yet.
For a week, it will gloat, play hell

With every inch of the skeletal metaphor,
Before it orders its marauding horde on,
Toward newer metaphors.
Meanwhile, it issues a feudal ukase:
Rape, pillage, plunder, by fire, all survivors.

10/29/84 (05911)

Apparitions

Slipping into morning's mist-shroud
As though it were a straitjacket
Instead of dense fog, I head west,
Through the country, toward Potosi, Steelville.

Any day other than this — Halloween —
My sensibility might lean toward "defoliated"
As an appropriate adjective for trees
Shrinking back into their own compactness.

Today, they seem, to my eye, scruffy fowls
Littering a colossal yard,
Scraggly pea- and guinea hens, reds, bantams,
Molting disreputably,

Throwing off feathery leaves randomly,
As though making themselves naked,
At winter's onset, were a cosmic joke
Paradox has decided to play, on all its ghosts,

Instead of letting its scheduled housecleaning
Accomplish itself naturally.
Something is amiss. Just ahead,
In the middle of the road, sits an amorphous shape.

The eyes strain to distinguish the ungainly form;
The brain tries to restrain the feet,
Slow my speeding vehicle.
I veer too late. My ears blaze.

Red pulsations, like submachine guns
Firing in tandem, resonate along my spine.
My own absorbent bones assimilate the collision,
Whose shattering, snapping, collapsing of dog,

Against tie rods, bell housing, differential,
Buckle my entire cringing spirit.
Without stopping, I bury the stray in a ditch-plot,
In my rearview-mirror cemetery,

Afraid the slightest delay might disrupt
Or interfere with destiny I've meticulously rearranged
To coincide with business requirements,
Cautious not to let fate cast me to the winds,

Despite catastrophe. Arriving in Rolla,
Just in time to take my client to lunch,
I get out, glance at the front bumper, shudder.
It's wearing a gruesome mask.

10/31/84 (02344)

Reveries Thawing from the First Frost

My eyes frozen on the thermometer's calibrated face,
Focusing on its mercury bead, impacted in glass,
Highlighted against a white backing,
I'm reminded of buckshot lodged in rabbits
I killed and cleaned, then ate,
On so many occasions, in my growing season,

Those times one endless trip to the woods,
One extended traipsing across fields
Riddled with frosted furrows, brittle stubble,
Raspy stalks gnawed but missed by pickers,
One jubilant plume of crystal breath
Laced with plum schnapps, dotting blue afternoons,

One unfading anticipation of setting into flight,
Over packed snow or smooth-worn paths
Woven through briar, hedgerow, woodpiles,
A fleet creature released from its still fright,
Seeing its scut flash, as it leaped and swerved,
Losing, regaining sight of it circling back,

One prolonged, arrested breathing,
As lead and aim and hopeful guess coalesced
At the breech end of the vented-rib barrel
My Belgian-made Browning 20-gauge
Thrust against the sun's rays,
Just before I squeezed the trigger — the roar

That resonates yet, this thirty-two-degree morning,
So distant from then,
Into which I venture, tentatively,
From my rented dwelling up here in the city,
To retrieve the newspaper squatting, in a stiff wad,
Like a rabbit shot for fun and left to rot.

11/2/84 (05912)

Paean to Final Flourishes

November's countryside drowses,
Slouches toward dens, to suspend energies,
After having surfeited, all summer and fall.
Past its preening, flowering prime,
It busies itself with last-minute refinements,
To neutralize arrhythmia in the ensuing quietude,
Trims to its slender essentials,
To fend off penetrant winds,
Before entering cryogenic coma.

Strange how few of nature's inhabitants
(Certainly, roses — yet growing profusely,
In the interlude promoting cold and warm spells —
Resonating like echoes, wilting, one day,
Exploding, the next afternoon)
Seem to know or intuit
That until Indian summer finishes her danse macabre,
It's open season for objects and people
Poetic enough to rebuff death's bluff.

11/5 & 11/6/84 — [2] (05913)

Transfiguring Silence ^Δ

Traversing Highway 32 easterly, through the country,
From Farmington, this thirty-degree dawn,
I watch, from the seat in my speeding car,
Proscenium lights flood the horizon orange.
Slowly, night's curtain rises,
Inviting my excited eyes to enter, penetrate the set,
And try to assimilate the silent drama
Already in progress, at center stage.

I witness smoke lifting from chimneys,
Blown out of cows' nostrils and mouths,
Hovering above ponds, as if this familiar terrain
Were a prehistoric place pocked with volcanoes,
And I see fog, its kindred spirit,
Running smooth fingers through denuded trees,
Softly over bellies, thighs, rigid breasts
Of fields lying, frigidly, beneath the frost.

Both vapors fuse into an argentiferous net
That catches my attention, arrests it,
Enslaves my senses to the task of isolating objects,
Proclaiming them images of death and resurrection
Regrettable for their Biblical heaviness,
This majestical November morn.
I pause to question why my eyes' eye
Can't ever seem to let things just be.

What does the brain have against resting,
On the imagination's Sabbath,
Those hoped-for lapses in a poet's obsession
With wanting to best God's Creation
By executing entire worlds from words
Hurriedly gathered, fashioned piecemeal,
Incomplete and precarious as bird nests
Compressed from brittle twigs, grass, fabric tatters?

Suddenly, I awaken from a blinding orient haze
Emanating from offstage left
And discover my vehicle unexplainably heading south,
Down I-55, toward Cape Girardeau,
Away from the traveling theater-in-the-round
Whose repertorial one-act plays
Have fascinated, delighted, and distracted me, the past hour,
So totally, I've lost track of space.

I can't imagine what force might have compelled me
To take to the road, unless, of course,
You, muse, were the voice
Calling me, again, to attend the sunrise celebration
Of another lifetime within a day,
Afraid, otherwise, if I'm not writing verse,
I might, indeed, miss, by forgetting to witness,
My heart's blessed reclamation from silence.

11/6/84 — [1] (03524)

Young Willy Is Chosen to Work an Important Account [Δ]

My Dear Mississippi Kiddo:

I regret my prosaic late-night arrival in Jackson,
Before heading on for New Orleans,
In the morning, but business takes precedence,
Dictates my schedule, destination, and comportment,
Unfortunately. My best foot forward
And articulate intellect, not raw passion,
By which you best recognize and respect me,
Are expected, in order that my position
As rep to the mid-South territory,
With Acme-Zenith Clothing Co., be fully protected.

I regret leaving this note on your door,
Forcing myself to escort silence to bed,
Sleep, restively, beside loneliness,
Exit, urgently, at day's edge,
Without so much as a touch, on my face and legs,
By which to identify my strange surroundings,
Locate myself within the reassuring geography
Your fragrant emanations provide.

Ah, but then, I have to believe this abstinence
Is a discreet and necessary sacrifice.
Otherwise, how might we sustain this feverish pitch
Our illicit relationship creates,
If not for our occasional acquiescences to company demands?
After all, cake consumed without savoring
Tastes sweet only to the baker.
Besides, let's not regret wasted time.
I'll be back in less than forty-eight hours!

                         Willy — 4/17/41

11/6/84 — [3] (00075)

The Dioscuri ^Δ

Before leaving Baghdad-by-the-Gulf,
We take a final stroll through the Vieux Carré,
You at my left, streetwise, ever beside me,
Arresting *objets d'art* behind glass,
Bric-a-brac, urchins, dazed tourists, minstrels,
For my stray focus to alchemize,
*

You naming, for my delight, each street,
In its anglicized phonetics
(Toulouse, Chartres, Dauphine),
I repeating its equivalent Spanish antistrophe,
With perfectly enunciated graduate-school accent.

We complete this Saturday-afternoon ritual
By sitting down to alfresco buffet
At the Court of Two Sisters. We take pagan communion,
Indulge in a eucharist of fulgent champagne
And bagels conveying, to our palates,
The sweetest pâté de foie gras ever made —
This a prelude to Dionysian surfeit
Consisting of cheeses, kiwis, melons,
Seafood fillets and salad mixtures,
Creole and Cajun dishes steaming in stainless containers,
Pastries to dazzle a Byzantine mistress.

Now, driving out of New Orleans,
Skirting swamps twilit purple/orange,
West, on I-10, then north, to Hammond,
We retreat to separate observatories,
To record what conjunctions our planets might have assumed
Since left to their own rotations and alignments
Within galaxies we controlled before resigning
To seek apotheosis for our fragile, translucent spirits.
Going home, together, only so far,
Like shooting stars pluming side by side,
We illumine what's left of our flight, with sad, sweet stroking.

11/11/84 — [1]   (00181)

Under the River's Stern Surveillance △

Imagine all the trips we've shared,
Believing ourselves invisible,
By virtue of having stayed in oblique cities
Teeming with faces remote to themselves,
Collectively related not by heritage, mores,
Sense of place but only demographic mean,
Whose gratuitous skew has little to do with volition,
Rather cosmic neglect and indifference.

How naive we've been, accepting, on faith,
Without checking our flimsy hypotheses
Against reasonably measured, undeviating tests,
That we could hide within parentheses
Containing the human equation for anonymity.
How presumptuous we've been, to persist
Without at least tipping our intellects' hats to empiricism,
If not wisdom, in making our decisions.

The fact is, our actions have been detected from the beginning,
Whether in St. Louis, Memphis, or New Orleans.
Our clandestine intimacies have been recorded
By the River Mississippi himself,
Whose ubiquitous conscience
Infuses all of us within his ethical locus,
As though our pulsing blood were his muddy tributaries
Regulating our rhythms, keeping us from being dust.

He's seen us in all our naked posturings,
Kept watch over our crossings
From bank to bank and passages through states of mind,
Over whose domain he claims suzerainty.
He's seen us, through fluid lenses,
Sleeping in hotel rooms, beseeching a reluctant future
To embrace our unfortunate moral sacrifice,
For the privilege of sending down new roots.

How we could have missed his presence so totally,
I will never know; even if I did,
It wouldn't make significant difference,
Since you and I, lady,
In being found out, have become conscious
Of the earth's unswerving interpretation of virtue.
The waters that have witnessed fruition of our misdeeds
Shall irrigate no sacred trees.

11/11/84 — [2] (00157)

Incarnations of a Stillbirth

No thoughts explode,
This crystalline mid-November morning.
*

No trochaic meters, no spondees
Spring palpitant, creamy, from the muse-womb.
Rather, a solitary, stillborn soul
Shrivels in cranial waters,
Whose loud solitude belies the quietude
Disillusionment requires, to gestate failure
Worthy of human tragedy,

A soul so misshapen and incomplete
That had it reached term, breached, breathed,
No one would have recognized it
As having been conceived by you and me,
Lady — not the offspring of fancy,
Capriciousness, laughter, touching, loving,
Rather product of embryonic disruption,
Fatigue, decadence, chaos, dislocation
Apparently inherent in our recombinant genes.

A mutual incompatibility you and I share,
Miss Muse, has rendered this morning
A futile exercise, bereft of speculations
Either on present locations
Or destinations dotting the future's lee shore.
And as I go, the solitude engulfing me
Grows louder, so loud the eyes dilate,
As if to prohibit the least assuming metaphors
From petitioning crumbs, at their asylum gates.

11/15/84 — [1] (04148)

[All in the same day,] [†]

All in the same day,
I've spoken with my mother, wife, and mistress,
Respectively positioned in the conventional pecking order
Preordained in Judeo-Christian theology,
Whose hierarchy precludes concubines,
No matter the heart's persuasion for ladies
So beautiful and brilliant

11/15/84 — [2] (05914)

Wordsworthian Echoes

He used to believe that sleep,
Whether routinely supine or upright,
Was the only freedom he'd ever know.
Recently, however, the open road,
Over which he's flown with increasing frequency,
Has beguiled him, with her siren wiles,
Enticed him from Morphean caves,
Where, enveloped in amniotic obscurity,
He's dived through all his brain waves,
Reshaped them into St. Mark's mosaics,
On vision's REM-washed retinal walls,
Shimmering within the temple consecrating his fancy.

Today, driving out of the stifling city,
Away from his wife, two children,
Rented house, entering November's vibrancy,
He awakens to the purest liberation.
His unloosed spirit, pirouetting, invisibly,
Through dust-lit trusses and sunbeams
Supporting the gold-pinnacled dome
Sheltering his ephemeral hopes and dreams
From galactic exposure, instantaneous decay,
Is alive, for the first time since birth.
Perhaps this journey on which he's embarked
Marks the start of his return home.

11/28/84 (04147)

Willy's Icarus Complex

Not he but his seething ego,
Overrun, within his psyche's forest,
Like Mayan ruins, has leaned, frequently,
Toward shaping poetry out of road sounds,
Arresting images, fleeing his screen,
That shimmer, evanescently, in his rearview mirror,
Like water striders skittering on a pond's surface,
Before being lipped into oblivion, by skimming fish.

But he's never let mechanisms invade his cockpit,
Commandeer his crew of one,
*

Betray his brain's circuitry,
By overriding its autopilot,
Since he fears the reprisals guilt might initiate,
Persuading him back to assigned altitude,
Straight and level flight, cruising speed —
Those knowns he's grown used to, over the decades.

For what vague reason, this isolated day,
He's flying so low, between cities,
Whose frequencies and vectors keep interchanging,
On myriad fidgeting instrument faces,
He can't explain, since no location
Seems to afford his unearthly imagination
Adequate runway for landing his craft.
He senses catastrophe at hand.

Suddenly, Willy shudders. Frightened,
He awakens from an illusory hallucination,
Realizing little sister death
Has fired his eyes, singed his meninges,
Nearly subverted routine instincts, with beguilements,
By causing him to exceed fifty-five, eighty,
A hundred, almost rotate, lift, climb,
Almost parse the horizon, compose the sky.

11/29/84 (02343)

After a Long Black Lapse, Snow

With all its insides spent,
The cracking shell pulls back, into itself,
Not so much demented, schizophrenic,
As bewildered, disillusioned, sad.
The cranium that contained his ancient brain
Seems defunct — a silent crater
Perforating a benign volcano,
Whose only indications that flames once raged
Are eerie striations on mind-linings
The slow-rolling inner eyes scan,
Groping for signs symbolizing inspired life.

Slumped over a table in the Capital Café,
This snow-laced 6 a.m.,
Disengaged, within black cerebrations,
*

His pen-poised hand listless as a boiled shrimp,
He awakens, fingers recoiling instinctively,
As coffee, hastily poured by a waitress
Racing to satisfy impatient regulars,
Singes his skin out of its flexed condition,
Forces his gaze outdoors,
Then toward the empty page before him,
Filling with flakes falling from his heating cerebrum.

12/5/84   (00565)

December Phoenix

This three-degree December 7 dawn,
As I flee the snow-choked city
And slip through morning's portals,
Flying countryward, low,
To celebrate my exultant soul's exile,
Memory soars free of my body,
Climbs the orange-laced sky,
Like a raging Mitsubishi Zero
Slashing the horizon's wrists,
With its rigid wings' leading edges.

Through glistening glass
Refracting ten thousand rising suns
Funneling into the greenhouse canopy
Insulating my senses from the roar
Of flaming cylindrical outboard ports,
I simultaneously witness and execute
One of history's major oracular climacterics:
Being there, here, then, right now,
My pen that stick thrust forward, to the dash,
I crash, in one last lasting act of passion.

12/7/84   (02110)

Statue of a Fawn and Piping Satyr

The invisible, shimmering image
For which you and I posed nude, in youth,
Has been assimilated by its negative space.
*

Its once-smooth contours
Assume brittle fragility, rough tumescence.
Once-inextricable lovers, clay-born,
Disentangle vine-twined legs.
Fused hip cradles slip from fixed positions.
Flesh pressed to precious flesh,
Like a transfer on Staffordshire, comes unglued.
The statuesque midair arrest
We achieved, while the world's collective breath
Sighed in envious disbelief
Of our inviolable adoration for each other,
Loses flexibility, buoyancy,
Stutters at the top of its full-stop climb,
Stalls, falls, in pieces —
Human wreckage. Jesus, what debris!
Fingers, dreams, gold-flecked curls,
Memories, slender wrists, smiles, poems,
All unidentifiably strewn, in ruins,
Wearing Kollwitz redolences — bones on bones,
Lucifer flutes, whose netherish notes
Forever will reshape galactic winds,
To lip the posthumous coda
We should have composed for the concerto,
Celebrating romance, we never wrote,
For consuming ourselves, in fire,
Even then drying our entwined design,
In an imperceptibly fissured mold.

12/11/84 (04146)

Spider Bites

What a fine fix I finally find myself in,
Entwined, inextricably, in a complex
Whose design mystifies the spider/writer spinning it,
Even as I sit
Suspended at the center of my pendulous weave,
Trying to anticipate which prey to catch, neglect,
Which to let continue unimpeded.

Only occasionally venturing out of my complacency,
I stretch a few new guy wires
*

Around tent pegs pounded into the brain,
Above which my visions once flew.
My intentions are no longer visceral,
Their intellectual consequences, at best, dubious,
Impossible to arrest, choose, appreciate.

Even those beautiful paeans I used to commit,
Celebrating grief, love, laughter,
Languish in the web — husks of victims.
I pick at them, on dreamless nights,
As if strumming lute strings, with arthritic fingers,
Whispering cacophonies, through witch lips.
I see, now, my shadow

Conspiring, with specters in the net's eye,
To dismantle time, strand by strand,
Drag me from my trap, up and down the stile
Connecting fields, in Erebus, guarded by Cerberus.
Chaos, limbo, sleep yield to death,
Whose sticky spinnerets tickle my skin,
As it winds oblivion around my paralyzed mind.

12/12–13/84 (02652)

[Finally, every line of poetry he composed] †

Finally, every line of poetry he composed
Was obsolete before it could even reach
Creative synapse, let alone
Find temporary lodging in an ice palace
Or a hovel beside the spur track

12/17/84 (03970)

Mother's Boy

> *A Christmas gift,*
> *12/25/84*

Endlessly renewing yourself,
Whose gentleness is a turtledove
*

Floating in a golden holding pattern
Or Monet's fuchsia hues
Shimmering in a pool fluid with lily pads
Ruled over by a frog-prince,

You remain, in my paltry vision,
Unalterably magnificent,
Eden's mythic princess, Earth goddess,
Sacred Lady of the Lake.
If I, a mere poet, hyperbolize,
Recreating your immutable beauty,

It might be that I, your creation,
Have an inviolate artistic bias,
Which privileges me to lionize my lioness,
Engage, without solicitation, in panegyrics
Calculated to rearrange your heart,
Persuade you to embrace my bindle-stiff spirit

Whenever missing you renders me bereft.
Then, like now, I grope for floating doves,
Elusive Monet-hues
Capable of transforming my toad-soul
Into metaphors orbiting your violet horizon —
Seer, scribe, your devoted son.

12/20/84 (02111)

New Year's Eve Day 1984

> *For Jan,*
> *for Mr. Ladd,*
> *for Trilogy and Troika,*
> *for 628 W. Columbia,*
> *for* was

I'm so far away from everywhere,
This gray Monday,
And everyone, as, one by one by one,
Runners abdicate their positions in the race,
Collapse beside the track, in the cinders,
Gasping for precious breath,
To revivify the blood, heal scratches, abrasions.

So far ahead of the pack, invisible,
This vaporous Monday,
And inviolable, as if contained inside ruminations
Unearthly, if elegiac, I hold steady
Against silence, whose forward-thrust shadow,
Like a chorus in an echo chamber,
Strides, relentlessly, to my side, from behind.

I'm so far gone from all that was,
This rainy Monday,
And might have been, that even memory and forgetting,
Traditional enemies, join ranks,
Cross the finish line, in indistinguishable arrest —
A frieze on a Greek entablature,
Death mask surmounting a travertine sarcophagus.

So dislocated is my wayward soul,
This stray Monday,
And alone and cold and older
Than all other competitors it lopes past,
On its furious diaspora, it and I grieve.
Even the stars are so far apart
They refuse to keep and record my finishing time.

12/31/84 — [1] (04145)

Collapsing Time

The crazy basin gluts, chokes,
Backs up, above fate's insatiable cloaca,
Stutters, then frees itself momentarily,
Like a televised preacher citing Ecclesiastes
Before exhorting his invisible votaries
To mail the proof of their faith,
Posthaste. The day drains itself hourly,
At peace with a persistent rain
Shading twilight to a saturnine smudge,
As though a sidewalk caricaturist,
Dissatisfied with his rendering,
Were rubbing out an almost-familiar face.
Slowly groping through road mist,
I wend my way homeward — no plowman
*

Resurrected from Housman
Or pastoral swain or shepherd of Grasmere
Returning to my Wordsworthian en-closure
But poet in my own inchoate robe.
Nonetheless, I make for the city
And its attendant New Year's Eve revelry,
Where wife and children await me —
Mate, protector, Peck's Bereft Boy,
Who's been journeying through wet terrains
Too long not to have suffered disorientation,
Weightlessness, brain spasms, pain
Impossible to isolate, for its pervasive throb.

Perhaps, tonight, snow and ice
Might set up inside my freezing heart,
Explode my emotions, turn the blood to bergs
Breaking off, from the main glacier,
At intervals predictable enough for me to avoid being crushed,
Though not so much so
That my surviving the arctic floe
Can be managed without extreme dexterity.
Now, as I approach the somnolent outskirts,
Gray twilight decomposes into Zyklon B vapors.
I've arrived in time to take my shower,
Before dressing for the celebration
1985 and its most recent concubine
Are hosting for me, my wife, and mine: lunacy.
Tonight, our triangle,
So long stranded in static disconnectedness,
Will climax in its final solution,
Join hands, in tragic obeisance to tangents
Whose truth derives from mechanical calculations:
The time it takes glaciers, volcanoes, novas
To awaken, disintegrate, go silent
And bones to rub their own touchstones
Back to unimpacted dust motes.
Ah, here I am, neither late
Nor a moment too soon —
Abraham, come home to my Sarah and Hagar,
Ishmael and Isaac . . . come home to die,
One more night, inside my life-lie.

12/31/84 — [2] (04140)

Transporter

Unexplainably, his word-spewing apparatus
Has come unattached from its cradle.
It flaps in the backwash his dreams create
When, as they surface briefly, like breaching whales,
He tries to arrest their evanescence,
With harpoons sporting barbed verbalizations.

Thoughts fly loose, like ammonia
Leaking from a tanker rolling at high speed,
Trailing oblique steam-shapes
Those driving behind him,
Too frightened to pass, must decipher or die.

Never has he learned to control intensity,
Energy under liquid pressure,
Whose diametrical solid state, words,
Fertilizes, irrigates, nurtures flourishing emotions.
Today, his broken spigot
Emits volatile admixtures into the atmosphere:

Uncontrolled tropes, wild strophes,
Adventitious metaphors, mind-whores,
Notions too abstract for the practical world
To embrace, cohabit with comfortably,
Assimilate into its lexical hoard.
In fact, he poses no small danger, today,

Traveling southwest, toward the country,
Through sunrise, into sepulchral gray
Laden with dormant cobra-snow,
Going slowly enough to allow his mind
Freedom to compose free verse,
Weaving precipitously, unpredictably,

In order to scratch measures into his notebook-scroll,
With hope that, one day, maybe,
Someone might know that he, Abe's boy,
Willy Ishmael, traveled this road,
Transporting himself by word of mouth,
Unperturbed that no one had heard his language before.

1/2/85 (05915)

[The moon-orbited Earth] †

The moon-orbited Earth
Revolves around the static sun,
Absorbing, reflecting

1/7/85 — [1] (02716)

Spectator at the Games ᐃ

> *For my blessed Trilogy,*
> *this gift*
> *for her fifth-grade poetry notebook*

All Sunday, they played,
Making a fort, in their basement's "outer space,"
Against foes on loan from TV,
Burying themselves in cinder-block bunkers,
To outlast atomic blasts,
Neutron, plutonium, and cobalt catastrophes
Solely attributable to "pilot error."
Their arsenals ranged from conventional weaponry
To Star Wars apparatus,
Their tactics changing from practical matters,
Such as stomping a sluggish spider,
Frightened from its hibernal duct,
And persuading Dad to replace a bulb,
To plans for total destruction
Of enemies extraterrestrial and next door.

All Sunday, they played
Through lunch, past supper, into sleep,
Where, deep in dreamy lacunae,
They continued to defend their besieged fort,
Against demons from Snake Mountain,
Shades, heavy-breathing Darth Vaders,
Decepticon Leaders, Robeasts,
Grotesque, for their collective danse macabre,
Performed on tremulous REM stages.
Now, they sit at the table with me,
Sharing my paranoid Monday-morning silence,
Nibbling and picking at their breakfast,
For grade-school preoccupations.
*

Staring at their brave, blameless faces,
I sip coffee hysterically.

1/7–8/85 — [2] on 1/7 & [1] on 1/8 (02089)

Cycles

Why are we so amazed,
Gazing at snow, drifted or plowed,
Accumulating at curbs, in driveways and trees,
Along fences, on porches, above eaves,
Awaiting transformation
From myriad solid shapes, into singular liquid
Guttering into the earth's cloacae,

When we know our own bones,
Once released from flexible tension,
In which muscles and tendons have kept them warm,
Disowned by decrepit flesh,
Change from individual wetness to pervasive clay,
Before reentering the life-force,
Sustaining their chain, in perpetually mutating equations?

1/8/85 — [2] (05916)

Pyromaniac

Like second-story firemen, from the forties,
Sliding down a brass pole,
At the first half-rap of an electric clapper,

Or brigades racing across strafed runways,
To douse flaming planes, at Pearl Harbor,
My heart rudely awakens from tranquil drowse,

Into the loud, crucial hours
Catastrophe gathers, like magnetized filings,
To insulate itself against implosions,

And, stretching, stirring the silence, with yawns,
Tries to select the right direction,
Size up tragedy, on the run.

But no one is manning the panel.
Exact details are scanty, tentative,
And seemingly nothing can be done

To alleviate impending futility
Loneliness and stress have imposed on a soul
Oblivious to its own dismantling.

By the time I arrive on the scene,
The destruction is complete. Amidst debris
Is a heart charred beyond identification.

1/9/85 (04144)

Willy Declines His Hard-Earned Promotion ^Δ

Refusing to accept a promotion, assume desk duty
In Acme-Zenith's recently refurbished womb,
Adjacent to St. Louis's corporate plaza,
Just above the river's cobbled levee,
Amuse himself, late into each afternoon,
With his own networked computer scope,
On which to call up, with dazzling clairvoyance,
Whatever oblique data might be required,
Retire his former work ethos,
As though it were a house dog grown old and fat,
And lose himself in wayward daydreams,
Musing, from his window, on rising skyscrapers,
Pigeons fluttering about the courthouse dome,
Vagrants and hobos congregating in streets below,
Sales figures coming into and going out of clarity,
Just below his nose, beyond his bifocals' focus,
On accordion sheets his hands can't hold, for their bulk,

Willy sticks to familiar Midwest routes
He's traveled more than forty years,
Content to service tired merchandise buyers
Or their perpetually rehired assistants,
Drive through slush, flash floods, summer scorch,
Forgo appointments to show the line, on last-minute notice,
Condone abrogations of bonded contracts,
On orders booked, sewn, packed and held for shipment,
Overspend his monthly draw against commission.
*

After all this time on the road,
Willy's learned one thing
Even the most sublime wisdom can't impose
On those unwilling to listen to their own heartbeat:
To change horses in midstream
And not beware of Greeks bearing gifts
Is the quickest way to get a bellyful of queen-size shit
Dumped in the lap of your Acme-Zenith britches.

1/11/85 (02342)

Troika's Poems

The Rhinoceros

Dad, I hear a rhinoceros!
It might sound preposterous,
But it belongs to Seuss,
Who is a very oddball doctoros.

The Word-Bird

I have a word-bird,
Who is a winged nerd.
The other day, he asked me,
"Troika, why is my name Ferd?"

"You silly bird," I answered,
"I prefer Ferd,
Instead of Turd or Kurd,
Because you're so absurd!"

1/13/85 (09171)

Moon's Day

This past September, especially,
And even more especially in the evenings,
Just within the outer reaches
The dusk-to-dawn vapor lamp describes,
I discovered Monday morning,
*

All Mondays past and as yet unconceived,
Hiding behind the back porch's
Ornamental interstices,
In the form of a black spider
The size of a silver dollar.

Actually, its intricate tapestry
Of interconnected strands, refracting the sun,
Had attracted my attention,
One particularly brilliant afternoon,
Alerted me to its covert activities.

Each night, on arriving home, after class,
I'd pause, to speculate on its imminence,
Briefly fantasize about its progress,
Remark the desiccated wings and cases
Of gnats, daubers, houseflies
Randomly abandoned within the silken vortex,

And I'd imagine myself lost in a woods,
At midnight, without moonlight
To guide me from my hallucination,
Suddenly tripped up, in fallen trees' branches,
Tumbling down a ravine, scratched,
Knocked permanently unconscious, at the depthless bottom.
Then I'd enter the house, prepare for bed.

Now, this late December, when I pass,
There are no visible reminders.
The snow-cloaked interstices withhold their history,
Yet I still see that spider,
Black as coal, emerging from its inverted funnel,
Into its trap, grasping, in mandibles
Fast as reiterating scythes, hapless prey,
Dragging it away, back into its lair.

I see stark blackness against white,
Cast in eerie orange shades
Emanating from the mercury-vapor lamp,
Rusty, like dried blood on a pillow slip,
Dripping down my retinas,
Every Monday a.m., when I awaken,
Dress in the dark, drive to work,
And wonder if there isn't an end to this lunacy.

1/14/85 (05917)

The Fungusy Mungusy

Once, there was a humongous fungus,
Who stung us, in the bungus.
None of us could stand the pain, so
We ran inside and shouted out our lungus.

1/22 — [1] & 1/22?/85 (09169)

Sick

I have the flu. I'm home from school,
And I think I've got the pox.
I'm sick in bed,
With sixteen bruises on my head.
I might have instamatic crud
And leeches swimming in my blood.
But now that the sun's begun to shine,
I think I feel pretty fine,
And I'm going out, to have some fun!

1/22/85 — [2] (09170)

Losing It

Overnight, time-lapse vines
Collapse arteries and veins in my brain,
Which, until now, seemingly
Has grown with docile innocuousness,
Its cranial circumference,
Hemispherical density and diameter,
Proportional to half the sky's size,
Its pulsating energy and drive protean,
In appearance, unslakable.

Why, then, this morning, have my senses
Gyved me to my bed,
By my own tendons, ligaments, axons,
Like mind-vines, kudzu stalks,
Lilliputian, handwoven hemp strands
Secured, with myriad frantic confusions,
*

Across a giant's body, in wet sand?
Why am I submitting without a life-fight,
Abetting measures that heighten chances for suicide?

Can it be an aneurysm, embolism?
Has cancer set into the lymphatic mass,
Traveled to the meninges, created tumors
Rumored, throughout the system, to be malignant,
Irreversible, fatal in a matter of days,
Hours, milliseconds? Or is it "all in my mind,"
Sensory invention, vagary, fancy's mandate
To fulfill its monthly quota of madness,
Nurture problems neither psycho- nor physiological,

Rather generated cosmically,
Calculated, by the Prince of Lies, to glow,
Slowly heat up, sear belief in self
To a crisp, before incinerating all hope
For maintaining an even flow.
Just now, I find myself physically floundering,
My sheets' liquid threatening to drown me —
A prehistoric amphibian, abandoned,
Stranded in a transition too wide to survive.

1/23/85 (05918)

Secular Rabbi [Δ]

Buried somewhere in Sumerian sands,
Sinking deeper, each receding year,
Like memories submerged in Lethe,
Is my heritage, the bones of those people
Whose propitious beginnings,
Although groping, inarticulate, overzealous,
Initiated the written history
Chronicling my peripatetic trajectory from *there*, *then*,
To this resounding *now*,
From whose Mount Sinai I shout phonemes
My tongue devoutly shapes into syllables,
Caesuras, feet, strophes, codas —
God's spoken words,
Transmogrifying siliceous souls
*

I alone have been chosen to awaken,
With symbols and tropes, rhyme-music,
Those anodynes against insentient time.

Today, driving westerly, writing poetry,
Thumb and forefinger quivering
From too tight a grasp on the frenzied pen
Racing over notebook pages,
In a futile attempt to record sourceless dictation,
I sense that absolutely unexplainable mandate
Which is mine, by default, if not privilege,
To perpetuate. Only invention
Can defend men against death's incursions,
Repulse forgetting, discourage greed,
Vulgarity, insidious xenophobia.
Yet even this couldn't justify my energy,
Were it not that, by composing elegies and odes
To be placed on scrolls I create,
My role as keeper of my people's ashes fulfills itself.

1/24/85 (00840)

New Orleans Suite △

I: Transfiguring Silence

Traversing Highway 32 easterly, from Farmington,
This thirty-degree dawn,
I watch, from my speeding car,
Proscenium lights flood the horizon orange.
Slowly, night's scrim rises,
Exciting my eyes to enter, penetrate the set,
Assimilate its silent drama,
Already in progress, at center stage.

I witness shimmering smoke extend chimneys,
Bellow from cows' nostrils and mouths,
Hover above ponds pocking this place,
Like volcanoes poised to erupt.
Meanwhile, fog, its kindred spirit,
Runs smooth fingers through nude trees,
Whose sylphic bellies, thighs, breasts
Breathe rigidly, beneath the frost.

Argentiferous vapors fusing in nets
Catch, arrest my attention,
Engage my senses, in isolating objects,
Proclaiming images of death and resurrection,
Regrettable for their Biblical heaviness,
This majestical November morning.
I pause to question why
My eye can't ever just let things be.

What does the brain have against resting,
On the imagination's Sabbath,
Those hoped-for lapses in a poet's obsession
With wanting to best God's Creation
By composing words into worlds
Precarious as bird nests fashioned, hurriedly,
From brittle twigs, grass, fabric tatters,
Yet lasting as the stratosphere?

Suddenly, I awaken to an orient haze
Emanating from offstage left,
As my vehicle free-falls unexplainably south,
Down I-55,
Away from the traveling theater-in-the-round
Whose repertorial one-act plays
Have fascinated and distracted me so totally,
I've lost track of space.

I can't even guess what compelling force
Has made me take to the road again,
Unless it was you, muse,
Beckoning me to attend the sunrise celebration
Of another lifetime in a day,
Afraid, otherwise, if I'm not transcending history,
Writing verse while driving,
I might miss my heart's reclamation from silence.

II: Young Willy Services Two Major Accounts

My Dear Mississippi Kiddo:

I regret my late-night arrival in Jackson,
Before heading on for New Orleans,
But business takes precedence,
Dictates schedule, destination, comportment.
*

Best foot forward, articulate wit,
Not raw passion, are de rigueur,
If I'm to keep from risking my position
As mid-South rep
For Acme-Zenith Trouser Company, Inc.

I abhor leaving this note on your door,
Escorting silence to bed,
Sleeping, restively, beside loneliness,
Exiting, urgently, at day's edge,
Without your touch on my face and legs,
To reassure me the remote geography
Into which I awaken is safe.
Dispossessed of your fragrant emanations,
I'll enter morning, unadorned.

Ah, but then, I must believe
This abstinence is a discreet sacrifice.
How, otherwise, might we sustain
Our relationship's feverish pitch,
If not for occasional compliance with policies?
After all, cake consumed without savoring
Tastes sweet only to the baker.
Besides, let's not belabor wasted time.
I'll be back in forty-eight hours!

Willy — 11/6/84

III: Under the River's Surveillance

Imagine all the trips we've shared,
Believing ourselves invisible,
For having stayed in oblique cities
Teeming with faces remote to themselves,
Collectively related not by heritage,
Mores, sense of place but demographics,
Whose gratuitous skew has less to do with volition
Than cosmic cynicism and indifference.

How naive, accepting fate, on faith,
Assuming we could hide, yet flourish, in silence,
While working out equations for anonymity,
Without first subjecting our hypotheses
To reasonably undeviating tests.
*

How presumptuous of our intellects,
To persist without bowing to empiricism,
If not wisdom, in deducing conclusions.

The fact is, we've been detected from the outset,
In St. Louis, Memphis, New Orleans,
Our clandestine intimacies recorded
By the River Mississippi,
Whose ubiquitous conscience
Infuses all beings within his loci,
As though his muddy flooding were blood
Slowly eroding us back to dust, nothingness.

He's seen us in our naked posturings,
Kept watch over our crossings
From state through hallucinatory state,
Over whose land fantasies he claims suzerainty.
He's seen us, through fluid lenses,
In hotel rooms, importuning a reluctant future
To embrace our sacrifice to amorality,
For the privilege of sending down new roots.

How we could have missed his presence,
I may never know. Even if I learn,
It might not make significant difference,
Since you and I, lady,
Were fated, later or sooner, to be found out.
Now that his omniscience has visibled us,
We have no further reason to hide;
Rather, let's proclaim our love nature's disguise.

IV: Star-Crossed

Before leaving Baghdad-by-the-Gulf,
We stroll, again, through the Vieux Carré,
You at my left, streetwise,
Remarking, for my stray gaze to focus and alchemize,
Objets d'art, dazed tourists,
A sax player, and Ignatius J. Reilly
Vending weenies, from a plastic hotdog.
You delight me, by imitating anglicized phonetics
Natives misappropriate,
When pronouncing Toulouse, Chartres, Dauphine.
*

In silliness, I trill their Spanish equivalents,
As we locate souvenirs, for our children,
Members of our "extended family,"
Who will never even meet each other.

We complete this alfresco ritual
By partaking of Saturday buffet, on the secluded patio
At the Court of Two Sisters,
Whose eucharistic bread and wine
Consist of fulgent champagne, Mouton Cadet,
Pâté de foie gras, bagels, croissants —
Preludes to Dionysian surfeit:
Cheeses, kiwis, melons, gelatin molds,
Seafood fillets and salad plates,
Crawfish, shrimp, lobster, crab étouffée,
Beans and rice, jambalaya, gumbos,
Creole and Cajun potpourris
Steaming in stainless containers,
Pastries to dazzle a Byzantine mistress.

Now, driving out of New Orleans,
Distancing dusk's translucent puce bayous,
West, toward I-55, then north,
To Hammond, we retreat, inexorably,
To separate observatories,
Where we'll record variations, in alignment,
Our planets might have assumed
Since we forfeited control over their rotations,
Seeking apotheosis of our fluctuating souls.
Knowing we're going home, together,
Only so far, we illumine,
Like shooting stars pluming side by side,
What's left of this flight,
With the heat of our sad, sweet stroking.

1/28/85 — [1] (08909)

Decidedly Not Milton's Adam

Never one to clutter or overburden his brain,
With extraneous facts
Or epistemologically significant concerns,
*

Or strain memory, grasping for treasure
Buried in medullary quicksand,
He has generally remained content
That, in the end, destiny will get him
No matter to what extremes
He might overextend his capacities for wonderment
And discovery. Even Columbus, he reasons,
Sailed over the edge,
Regardless how persistently the argument raged
As to the nature and shape
Of the earth's circumferential abyss.

Piss on it! Who gives a royal shit?
Debating absolutes is monks' play,
Whose speculations trigger plutonium explosions
From which only junkies and fools escape,
Without mental aberrations, anyway.
Knowing we're going —
The best as well as least effectual
At navigating loopholes, blind spots,
Pipelines, black holes, typhoons —
Almost takes the guesswork out of dying,
Almost makes the stay,
If not worthwhile, acceptable,
For our not having to contend with surprises
Arising from unexpected acts of God.

That's why he's never veered too severely
From charted trade routes
Or sought shortcuts to the nearest Indies.
What a grave disappointment it would be
If he did find youth's elixir,
Then had to spend the rest of his days
Questioning what's next.

1/28/85 — [2] (02091)

["Bastards!" Willy chastises invisible fates] △

"Bastards!" Willy chastises invisible fates
Shimmering, with serrated scimitars, in the gray air —
Specters, cloud-shapes, dybbuks,
*

.

Whose imminence hinders Willy's progress,
Causes him to reassess the itinerary
He's spent the last three weeks
Piecing together, from telephone conversations
With buyers and floor merchandisers
Reluctant to allow him audience or dispensation.

"Poetic justice? Divine retribution?
That's what I want to know. Why me?
Isn't it hard enough
Trying to dump closeouts, at season's end,
Without contending with variables
Beyond my control? When it pours,
It ain't rain but slush,
Tornadoes, flash floods, mud slides.
Lady Luck's a fucker, misfortune's whore!

"Today, I'm the sucker
Who just happens to have fifty bucks
To blow on supper and a motel room,
In Rolla, Mo., where I'm being forced to hole up,
Halfway to my destination,
While this blizzard,
No more than a flaky whisper when I left,
Threatens to strand me in a ditch,
Along I-44. What a bitch!

"Drawing a livelihood, once a month,
Against commissions earned daily, by the week,
What can a guy do,
When the odds beat him to the punch,
Set up obstacles to defeat him? Complain?
No! I always try to make the best
Of a shitty situation, usually have a drink,
Take time to think things through,
Ponder the future. After a few martinis,

"It never seems to matter much
Where I am, whom I'm with (waitress, barmaid),
Whether it's midnight or noon.
Even the name of the day loses importance,
When dizziness gives way to euphoria.
Only then, I suppose, does loneliness
Let me alone, to pursue my own dreams.
*

By tonight, I should be Leland Stanford,
Stretching a railroad between the moon and outer Neptune."

1/29/85 (02341)

[Leaving town, fleeing, retreating, compulsively,] ‡

Leaving town, fleeing, retreating, compulsively,
To some place less congested,
Where, in previous incarnations, on lushy slopes,
He's encamped with grazing sheep
Or, situated next to a desert
By a frontier-crossroads, false-front venture,
Pitched his buffalo-skin tent,
To sleep within, when not prospecting for solitude,
Or, beside Nile-like confluences, built idols,
He escapes the plenipotentiary city,
Like a convict scraping up and over penitentiary walls.

Following, south, an unfamiliar river-route,
Whose trail of tears flows, raucously,
Over fractious, riffle-stirring years
Precariously dotting memory,
He steers cautiously, to avoid disappearing
From his own sight, that mirror-vision
Even Narcissus couldn't accommodate
Despite shattering its placid surface, with peering.
Adrift on I-55, he finds that neither forgetting
Nor recollection functions; one cancels the other,
Until mission and destination don't exist.

By degrees, this snow-laced desolation
Recognizes his somber procession,
Identifies his weaving auto as a celestial mass
Careening through space — Halley's comet,
Racing away from Earth,
At the rate of twenty miles per second,
Between now and May, when he will reverse directions,
Erase darkness, in pendular evanescence,
Hurling past his own shadow
Swinging, eternally, in elliptical trajectories

2/1/85 (05919)

Mind-Diamonds

For Melvin "Shorty" Cleve,
1925–1985,
and
Dolores, his loving widow

What is it, exactly,
That compels us back to dust,
To no-thing-ness,
Reacquaints our clay with the earth's crust,
Compresses bones to coal, to precious stones
Orbiting the life-force haloing the sky,
Like perpetual shooting stars?

It's exactly that! Divine compulsion
Makes us labor all our days,
Shaping, from nothingness,
A design for the impalpable essence
We hope to leave behind,
On submitting our bodies to God's execution —
Mind-diamonds reflecting His prismatic love.

2/2 & 2/6/85 — [2] (05920)

Sleepwalker

He awakens, this morning, in pain.
His delicate brain-members
(Membranes so clotted and knotted with fibroids,
They're unable to conduct ichor
That once issued volitionlessly from his spirit)
Vibrate like a jet wing
Shearing from its fuselage socket, in a wind pocket,
From excess strain and mettle fatigue.

Rising, from sweaty bedsheets,
Like a diseased leviathan breaching onto a beach
Crowded with Hemingway spectators,
He grasps his temples,
Squeezes the life out of them, in his fingers' vise.
His shrieks are those of Munch-, van Gogh-,
Kollwitz-creatures bearing, on their shoulders,
Cosmic grief made of common clay.

His meager agonies dissipate into silence
Comprising the lonely existence
In which not even ghostly participants
From childhood fly slowly, low, enough,
To be identified or approximated,
Provide him justification
For lingering, no matter evanescently,
On arrested incidents, echoes, smiling faces.

By turns, he's assimilated into the disguise
He set out, last evening,
Prior to descending into Lethean tributaries,
And enters the life-stream,
Work force, daily routine,
Leaving not the slightest ripple
On the surface where he's emerged,
To nurture suspicion he died in his sleep.

2/6/85 — [1] (00839)

Sunspots

Heading west,
He sees the fire-breathing sun,
Hiding in his mind's blind spot,
Suspended in his rearview mirror,
Trembling like a tiger's-eye pendant
Against the alabaster breasts of mistress Diana,
Heaving, with intense heat flashes,
Just up ahead, fading fast, in his gaze.

For twenty minutes' worth of miles,
He drives, enthralled,
Neurons and auto conspiring to relieve him
Of accountability for motor responses,
That he might reflect on the erection between his legs.
Is it empathy and personal identification
That have created such spontaneity,
This dawn? His taut body, reveling in silence,

Writhes, with the onrush of each new truck
Pressing easterly, off whose front bumper
Pulsing Helios glints and shimmers.
*

Or might he be exercising his lusty instincts
For unadulterated self-gratification
That comes from onanistic tendencies
Indulged in by those for whom
Loneliness and fantasy provide their only romance?

Startled and alarmed by a tractor-trailer
(Its corrugated sides, roaring wheels
Razoring the space connecting them,
Like a dermatome slivering his brain's epidural layers)
Trying, unsuccessfully, on a steep grade,
To pass his laboring vehicle,
Shuddering next to him, indefinitely,
As though both were sea lions arrested in oceanic mating,

He goes limp, cold, then frigid, with fear,
Sensing the sun has risen,
The moon disappeared, and he is all alone,
Bereft of daydreams, hallucinations,
To contend with UFO's,
Near-collisions, potential "code reds"
Up ahead, on the road he travels
Slowly, to nowhere particular,

Always hoping to discover a more commodious junction
For setting up his medicine-show tent,
Opening bulging sample cases
Loaded with displays reflecting his tastes:
Vibrators, French postcards, dildos,
Aphrodisiacs. Ah, but he's fantasizing again.
He's only Willy, he damn well knows,
Sporting dried semen on his pants.

2/12/85 — [1] (02340)

On the Efficacy of Making Metaphors

Ah, what a Canaletto afternoon,
Except that the tepid Adriatic
Is mid-Missouri snow-rippled pastures,
The too-brilliant, blinding blue sky
Tintoretto and Veronese captured
Is riffled with haze-layers
*

Portending more precipitation, and my attitude,
No matter the descending order,
Rather than euphoric, jubilant, grateful,
For passable roads, windchill factor
No longer forty below zero,
Is only moderately receptive to illusion.

In truth, whenever I envision Venice,
My senses blanch, from lingering smells
Garbage, accumulating, as in cesspools,
In canals, dank basements,
Loggias, patios, palazzi, saintly rectories,
Still triggers in memory's olfactories.
And for all that city's siren glamour,
On a sunny, innocuous mid-Missouri day
Like this pacific one,
I believe being alive, right here, now,
Equidistant from Salisbury and Tipton,
Is all the artifice I need.

2/12/85 — [2] (05407)

Cowpoke with a Slight Hebraic Accent

He comes in, off the frozen plains,
After a hard day's labors,
Into Katy's restrained afterglow.
Though it's only a refurbished railroad station
Dating from the century's first decade,
Its green and red switch lanterns,
Soft music, whisperous conversation
Among animated habitués
Assuage his raging loneliness,
Make, for his nomad's roaming, a temporary home,
In which to relax his weary bones.

If this description suffers from clichés
And vagueness of situation and place,
Not to mention, let alone neglect,
Adequate characterization,
So that its readers might not be expected
To distinguish between Owen Wister
And L. D. Brodsky,
*

Its unintentional ambiguousness
Can only be attributed to one phenomenon:
History's one-man theory,
Which unwittingly posits possibilities for repetition.

If we accept a rose is a rose, a ruse a ruse,
No more, little less,
We must also be willing to admit
The blessedness of misguided poets,
Whose myriad personae defy positive identification.
Suffice it to say that a cowboy
Did drive into Katy Station,
This late afternoon, after visiting, in Tipton,
A factory dizzily busy manufacturing men's slacks,
And, lacking companionship,
Sat down with a chilled glass of Chablis,

To pass the evening, chatting with himself,
Asking eschatological and exegetical questions
Generally reserved for Hasidic scholars
And graduate students specializing in America's
Vanishing wilderness,
Euphemistically called "Westward Expansion,"
In university-class catalogs . . .
Not a wrangler, really, but a ragman,
Who simply spent too much youth
Viewing Pancho and Cisco, Sancho and the Don,
Not to suffer from mixed-metaphor syndrome.

In fact, as Willy Sypher, road peddler,
His saddlebags always bulge with clothing swatches,
And his Ford LTD wagon
Groans whenever he loads it, to the sideboards,
With three-piece worsted suits,
Corduroy sportscoats imported from Czechoslovakia
And Poland — distant reminders of the stench
That rose from Sobibor, Chelmno, Auschwitz.
Now, he finds himself sipping straight schnapps,
In the Crooked Cross Saloon,
Katy Station's less worthy precursor,

Where the first straw-strewn boxcars
Were shoehorned with unpurged Jews
Being transmigrated beyond the wide Missouri.
*

He nurses his liquor, to give history
Time to catch up with his shadow,
Recognize him as the Lone Stranger,
Whose existence ranges thirty-five centuries,
Back to that original diasporan pariah encampment,
From which Moses ventured, seeking Canaan,
Forty years wide,
Without benefit of camel, wagon train, jet,

Yet who made possible manger, crèche,
An entire dramatis personae of lesser actors,
Who would take their places on the stage,
At Rock Ridge, into which the cowpoke eventually drove,
To confront Hedley Lamarr, in *Blazing Saddles*.
Tonight, having come in, off the frozen plains,
To wrest his weary bones from the devil's clutches,
He tilts his elbow against whiskey windmills,
Falls still, amidst the bar's animated habitués,
Before riding into the dying sunset
To avoid dispelling the myth of Midwestern clichés.

2/12/85 — [3] (02648)

Lifeblood

Gently, invisible fingers squeeze brain-tubes
Containing today's twilight hues,
Compounded of rainbow prism-chips,
Honeysuckle and lilac scents,
Caffeine buzz, fruit-bat membranes,
And vaginal juices
Taken from Matisse's bronze, nubile statues.

Beneath depression's spring-fed cave-pool,
Freezing in reason's alembic,
I await, anxiously, morning's anointing,
To see what shape and registration
My bones' poetry will assume,
Whose gait and postures my body will emulate,
What pose my groping soul will seize,

Postulating approximations of ecstasy living requires
From those celebrating breathing,
*

Second to minute to decade,
Millennium to eon, every compression and release.
Suddenly, cave gives way to daylight,
Human blood floods cranial lacunae,
And the universal red-blue cycle resumes.

2/26/85 (05921)

" LOSED FOR THE SEASON"

Returning to and leaving town
Is no profound undertaking, no crisis,
Although its rote activity
Is not without emotional echoes,
Now that my family no longer resides here.

Each face, business place
Where our children, she and I shopped,
Lingered before displays
Whose cheaply priced, meager varieties
Reminded us of Wish Book listings,

And bought groceries, last year's outfits,
Dusty medications and vitamins,
Hardware supplies, fertilizers, rakes —
All the small-town daily necessities —
Has assumed opaque disorientation, in my memory.

A reverse–déjà vu vagueness
Has infected that sixteen-year experience,
Where we settled, nested, flourished,
Creating such outsize discontinuity,
I can't even recall my existence,

Except as an intellectual exercise,
Reinforce my tragic sense of absence from time,
By calling to mind Bishop Berkeley's conundrum,
Wondering about my corporeality
If no one heard my tree fall in this forest.

Just now, using Highway 32
To bypass the business district,
More quickly reach my turnoff south,
*

I pass the ramshackle Cardinal Drive-In,
Pressed, insignificantly, between Pizza Hut

And McDonald's — proof of new affluence —
Which, in its halcyon prime, as Sonic,
Boasting waitresses on roller skates,
Intercoms on stands, for in-car ordering,
Offered the most delicious soft-serve twist.

Its plastic billboard has lost its voice.
" LOSED FOR THE SEASON"
Is the only whimper it's spoken since last Christmas.
My throat chokes on that sweet cream
We so frequently ate as an after-dinner treat.

2/27/85 (04143)

The Black Pariah

Last Saturday afternoon, the universe shuddered
As though a stratospheric tidal wave
Had passed through our galaxy,
Before playing out, beyond our magnifications.
In fact, a black convict
Escaped a Texas penal farm, stole an auto,
Was pulled over, for speeding, just below Brewer,
And shot a state highway patrolman,
Through the head, twice in the neck,

Then fled, in that hijacked car,
Toward the Farmington/Bonne Terre area,
Where his sleazy vehicle was spotted, at twilight,
Leaving Highway 67, by a back road.
All night, helicopters with high-intensity beams
Scoured forests buffering frightened communities,
For a black man traveling afoot.
By morning, roadblocks, search parties
Consisting of volunteers and off-duty law officers

Were thick as a cricket or locust plague.
Local, state, and nationwide papers,
Radio and television stations
Rose to the occasion, with spoon-fed news
*

Focusing on the tragedy. Bad enough
That a man should sacrifice his life,
In the line of duty, but to leave behind
A wife and three daughters,
Ranging from three to eleven and a half years,

Was the unconscionable, back-breaking straw
That always claims victory
Over the public's stereotypical camels,
Causes the vigilante spirit to surface
In spirits least susceptible to KKK tactics,
Makes mass hysteria flourish, like phage,
In society's petri dishes. Still,
The menace is at large, in or near Farmington,
Though Sunday and Monday have lapsed

Without a trace of that black phantom,
Grown so large, if faceless,
No one dares take out the garbage,
Park his car, in the garage, after dark.
Even the lackadaisical Capital Café is astir
With cavernous reverberations,
As an entire community unites against a scourge
Threatening each individual collectively,
Prepares to take up arms, in reprisal,

This bleak Tuesday,
When all pending felonies
Are suspended on the courthouse docket,
While every available able-bodied citizen
Defends his right to public outrage,
Forgets less serious violations of human dignity
And all petty misdemeanors
Kept breathing, between negligible and nonexistent,
On artificial-justice-support machines,

By timeserving judges, lawyers, and politicos,
Who would expire of boredom and other natural causes,
Without such massive cost overruns
Committed in the name of voter constituency
Or escalating greens fees at the country club.
Now, with sunset just hours away
And, as yet, no proclamation, from authorities,
That the "nigger cop-killer" has been caught,
The pulse of the populace quickens;

Cheeks work nervously; furtive frowns
Furrow unturned foreheads;
And all are taking bets, aloud, in crowds,
As to who'll get first and last shots
At the "nasty black bastard"
On the loose, entirely too close,
No matter where, "so long's he's alive."
Dinner is a spider's and reptile's affair,
All food bolted, swallowed whole, digested

By frantic intestinal juices refusing to quit,
Even after the last bits are consumed.
Not fatigue, sleep, or TV suffices
To nullify fear looming, neon-vivid, in the air,
Until, across all screens, through speakers,
Comes the flood of on-the-spot minicam news,
Made seconds after the fatal shooting
Of Benny Brown — black, male, twenty-five —
As he sat in a stall in the men's room

Of the Wendy's in Flat River, Missouri,
Neither deluding himself he'd eluded his pursuers
Nor regretting having killed a cop,
Father of three, rather hoping to relieve himself,
Grab a fast coffee, and try again
To penetrate the dragnet set up for him,
Probably unaware of the stratospheric tidal wave
He'd unleashed, last Saturday afternoon,
While on his way from Hades to Pandemonium.

3/5/85 (05400)

Intimations of Dante at Rowan Oak ^Δ

For close to a decade, until today,
He's tried to transmute desolate scenes,
His own routine deeds, mediocre notions,
Inadequate emotional spontaneousness,
Through poetry's enchanting medium,
Into fragile, romantic rituals
And enhance, with mythic dimension,
His own fundamentally shabby imagination,
*

By plagiarizing fully redeemed dreams
Rescued, from oblivion, by the Mississippi writer
Whose admired fiction has illuminated his fancy, since college.

For almost ten years, until today,
He's remained suspended in an alembic
Composed of theories not his own,
Committing endlessly involuted sentences and paragraphs,
Egregiously overreaching his known limits,
Hoping to make gratuitous discoveries
(Like those accidental Cíbolas, Pharaohs' lairs,
And Rosetta stones lonely searchers locate
Once every tenth generation),
Groping, unsuccessfully, to penetrate the corolla's halo,
Explode Dante's innermost rose,

And be saved the grotesque revelation
That living, basically, is no mere exercise in futility
But futility's slave raised to the third power,
The devil's surname, Boredom.
Sadly, after all these annual desert treks,
He's emerged, this fated afternoon,
At the edge of Bailey's Woods,
Where, without daring to approach,
He can see his hero's ghost precariously leaning
From porticoed Rowan Oak's upstairs porch,
Screaming, "All hope abandon, ye who enter here!"

3/6/85 (03530)

Recent Divorcé ^Δ

Although no inordinately compelling designs
Motivate or guide him,
His detached psyche, like Ichabod Crane
Racing blindly, on horseback,
Through a moonless forest, flies south,
Intuiting only that motion, not stasis,
Can save it from gravity's shear,
Keep sleep's tidal wave from reaching shore
Before he retreats inland, to higher purchase,
Where vision widens, telescopes, focuses,
*

And magnification is calibrated in integers
Calculated to disclose godly manifestations —
The aurora borealis flaming in broad daylight.

Having driven three hours, under the hood,
He finally approaches Jackson.
It shimmers him awake,
To a slightly disorienting sensation of vertiginousness.
Something about Mississippi's thin March air
Creates tight breathing, chest pains.
Automatically, he takes the Meadowbrook exit,
Turns left, crosses I-55,
Continues driving, until his destination arrives.
Suddenly, he senses why, for three days,
He's not realized his pilgrimage
Is the apotheosis of death's Passion Week.
Home, again, to his empty heart, he weeps.

3/7/85 — [1] (03552)

[I hear them. I hear them so near,] ^Δ

I hear them. I hear them so near,
My ears grow numb to the noise
Disguised as animated conversation in this place
So far away from those I hear.

I'd know their voices anywhere,
Whether in a wind tunnel, diving bell,
Or just beyond hell's perimeters,
From which emanates the most grotesque hissing and moaning.

Rarely does a parent mistake his child's cry
Or fail to recognize that plaint,
Laced with fear of being prematurely bereaved,
As emanating from his own selfishness.

Tonight, you two little orphans,
I do hear your silence. It pains me so,
Knowing my separation from you and your mother
Must yet persist, one day more,

Before we'll all exist, again,
Within shouting distance of each other,
*

Beneath the same roof,
Inside the Whitman Sampler house we worship,

Despite its effete, cliché-riddled mediocrity,
Which we rent by the month, in the city,
Whose fine schools outweigh acid rain,
Factory pollution, auto exhaust.

Just one more reversing of the circle,
And I shall have obliterated time,
Arrived, again, at that fated promontory,
Where we embraced, kissed, cried, good-byed,

Without realizing we'd die for three days,
Reenact a secular Passion Week,
Before finding refuge in each other's sweet touching.
Tonight, I have no other recourse

Than endure in this very public place,
So far away from the three of you —
Intuited voices my feverish ears isolate
From white noise arcing across the night sky.

I refuse to relinquish my choice, anyway,
Of preserving you in my loneliness,
Even if it is like freezing a woolly mammoth
In arctic ice and thawing it every other millennium.

3/7/85 — [2] (03550)

For Willie, in Oxford ‡ ∆

Finding you again, so humble and accessible,
Here in Oxford, coming slowly undone,
Within the kids' music, in a sloe gin fizz,
Amidst Billy Ocean's "Syncopation"
And "Mystery Lady," I grow wistful,
Hoping we might visit "Bill's" grave,
Press up against low-flying ghosts,
Resurrect Pete, your mascot, from silence,
At the dead center of night's core,
Mississippi's chrysalis,
And remind ourselves the heart has its eon
(Call it mini-death, if you will,
*

Or imaginative hiatus from life)
In which to fulfill its primal destiny,
Before committing itself to darkness.

Tonight, Willie, you and I have touched
And, touching, reminded each other
That some forms of self-expression
Require sketching, calligraphic swirling,
Yet others the tongue's deft precision strokes,
To articulate compassion, emotion —
The soul's passionate scratching on limestone.
Whatever significance or monument-ality
We can resurrect, tomorrow morning,
From tonight's subdued carousing,
Remains for the future to assay.
You, Willie, Yazoo City's chronicler,
And I, Missouri's perdurable Jew poet,
Have blended our dispossessedness

3/7/85 — [3] (03594)

[Exotic flocks of invisible geese and ducks,]

Exotic flocks of invisible geese and ducks,
Completing their urgent northering trajectories
Before Alberta and Skagway unthaw,
Infiltrate imagination's screen,
Dazzle me, with prismatic variations
They cast inside the sky's kaleidoscope,
Which my eyes twist, trying to assist
Their joyously buoyant tilting
And last-minute wing-tip dipping,
Wishing to participate in their nonexistence,
By visibling artifice,
Entrusting my spirit to their perpetual migration.

3/15/85 (05922)

Epithalamion

Silver rain sings spring awake —
A sibilant celebration,
*

Revelrous call to all earthly ears:
A wedding, a wedding is close at hand!
Can't you hear it, in the rain,
The syllabled rain, whose whisperous tongue
Smears everything green,
Articulates its two newest offerings,
Kathy and Roger?
Ah, from their mingled seeds
May the sweetest blossoming spring!

3/30/85 (05923)

The Relinquishment

All in white, they floated down the aisle,
She pristine, beneath lace
More delicate than that which spiders weave,
Their measured interstices,
Calibrated to harp and violin, so precise,
No eyes could detect spaces
Accumulating between their graceful steps,

Until only she remained, unperceived,
The object of a collective mirage,
Poised like a great feathered bird
On the crest of an upthrusting thermal,
Poised to dive beyond the earth's rim,
Out, alone, over *nowhere*,
For the first time,

In that zone where spirit, freedom, time
Dematerialize, rearrange dreams,
To coincide with cosmic laws,
Whose regulated rotations
Bear no relation to temporal absolutes.
She arrived before the rabbi,
Her intended beside her, imperceptibly,

Her legs twin birch trees
Shimmering in shivering March breezes.
Suddenly, spoken Hebrew broke the illusion.
She realized what she'd known
From the beginning: that, in the beginning,
*

Destiny had elected her to this calling,
To relinquish white lace, for nakedness,

Dreams, for words, lace, for aging flesh,
Pure deeds, for petty disturbances
Incited by convenient ploys in the guise of chivalry,
Manly attitudes, and courageousness.
Then it was over, irrevocably,
Once and *forever* inseparably fused,
To produce and perpetuate sublime anonymity.

4/1/85 (04142)

A Nonconforming Easter Sonnet ^Δ

For beloved Jan

Penitent is the color and penetrant scent of April,
Whose trees, not days ago,
Articulated membranous tracery,
In gray-dripping silhouettes,
Against the sky's cathedral ceiling.
Now, tumescence destinies them,
Proclaims their own essences sanctuarial,
Not as reliquaries freshly decorated with nosegays
But green-stippled steeples
Collectively vesseling the sun's messages,
Via a funnel connecting us, through them,
To the Word, alternating earthward
As syllabled light-rays and birthrights redeemed,
This Easter Sunday, so renascently green.

4/3/85 — [1] (05924)

Ahab off Course

Three days into April,
Awash in a Midwestern mistral
That fills his three-masted spirit, with misdirection,
Ahab flies wing and wing,
Slave to the drift of things, a singing child,
Who, for the night, forgoes all hope
*

He might find his own lost tribe,
Rescue it from chaos,
Which time's colossal ocean circumscribes,

And chooses, instead, to revel in this sublime freedom,
On whose glistening surface his blistered ship
Lists precipitously, from imbalanced images
Shifting in the hold of his unhinged psyche.
Going nowhere quickly,
Imperceptibly, past Atlantis, faster than sound,
He slips late afternoon's chains,
Chases twilight, over its dim rim,
Then exceeds his brain's limens,

Enters that fabled vertiginous vortex
Which dispossesses sailors
Not just of their intuition but best intentions,
While allowing those select few
To taste of God's quintessential liqueurs —
Poets like him, tied to the crow's-nest,
For whom going down with a disabled boat
Is the most courageous escape one can make
From the daily rape of life's endlessly prosaic night.

4/3/85 — [2] (02639)

Reflexivity

He spun an intricate funnel web,
From his psyche's nebulous edges,
Glorying in youth's seemingly irrepressible sun,
Privately dreaming forthcoming achievements,
Neglecting to calculate ravages time might exact
Or the impact he might have on future detractors
Envious of his accomplishments,
By perfecting state-of-the-art negative capability
Able to transcend their insensitive demands.

Yet, while designing a skeletal net about his brain,
To absorb the shock of a fall he might take,
Conceiving himself indefatigable, not fragile,
His untested body's pain threshold beyond question,
He fell prey to his own creation,
*

Mistakenly attacked his shadow as it crawled across the grass,
Below the troll-bridge his naiveté had woven,
And, like Narcissus caught in his own gaze,
Suffocated in his grotesquely inextricable twisting.

4/4/85 (02653)

[From the antipodes, you and I come,]

From the antipodes, you and I come,
Stumbling over jettisoned heritages,
Renegade Catholic, self-exiled Jew
Converging at irony's zenith,
This Good Friday afternoon,
To celebrate Passover and a crucifixion —
Two exoduses — and, tonight,
With our children possessing no religion by name,
"The Last Seder."

How coincidental, this calendared quirk,
Which would create such juxtapositions.
It's sufficiently radical to make a nonbeliever
Take faith in acts of God
And other sporadically recurring variables,
Fortuitous enough to make Gentile and Jew
Sweep their differences under the circus rug
And smile while crying,
Knowing both Moses and Jesus were clowns, too.

4/5/85 (04141)

The Visigoth ^Δ

The size of a pregnant sow
(Gender disallowed, for analogy's sake),
He throws open both glass doors —
The Capital Café's Red Sea odors part.
His Alaric-vastness asserts itself
As, on elephantine legs and feet,
He navigates toward the green-marble counter
And, like a bear balancing on a rotating ball,
Gracefully negotiating the same tight space,
*

Poises his entire weight on the stool's wafer.
His massive ass overlaps the circumference,
Like twin glaciers slipping, imperceptibly, into a bay.
Blue Big Smith bibs, like a sausage casing
Straining to contain human stuffings,
Balloon, threaten to explode,
Discharge their contents, with the very next movement.
His undershirt — a truce flag
Meant to spare stray eyes frightful disabuse —
Doesn't cover shoulders, biceps, forearms,
Which, in another time, easily, might be substituted
For those of the Colossus of Rhodes,
Miltonic Chimera, or a Dantesque demigorgon.
His adjustable, green, beaked seed cap,
Pointing backwards, over apelike hair,
Shades his neck, not a face so corpulent,
All features seem to swirl toward a vortex
(His mouth) and smudge —
God's thumbprint, pressed, from a red-ink pad,
Into his blond beard's halo.
This heroic figure, new to our community,
Who may remain a month or so,
Before assuming his next assignment,
Heads the Safeway Wrecking Co.'s crew,
Hired, by the county court,
To dismantle the old St. Francois Hotel,
Condemned, last month, for the final time,
After a rain-soaked back wall collapsed onto the street.
For now, those of us who rule the "deacon's bench"
Remain satisfied taking the backseat
To his eminence. After all, with each load,
He hauls away, amidst the bricks, rafters,
Plaster dust, at least eighty years of our heritage.
It's not always so easy, these days,
To watch history disintegrate instantaneously,
Knowing we have no adequate replacement
For the town's collective memory. For now,
We allow him his speak,
In our realization that, in a few more weeks,
The square will be one parapet less,
Progress three steps closer to sacking the past.

4/15/85 (00564)

Older Than His Years

Not so leonine, this soft spring,
Suborned by redbuds
And, especially, lilacs outrageously hued,
Whose lavender, heliotrope, fuchsia, and pink perfumes
Decorate April's seventeenth day,
My forty-fourth birthing arrives and dissipates
Like a dinner candle's tongue,
Singeing lips' finger into silence,
The instant a struck syllable touches the wick.

Is it because we refuse to add, to our calendars,
Those nine amniotic months
And two or three sensual ones prior,
Spent in love's mutually consenting apprenticeship,
That we lose an entire year,
In one telltale swoop of time's felling-scythe?
Why do diverse societies choose otherwise,
Calculate those lost measures,
When inventorying the heritage of individual existence,

And we exclude them from our evolution?
Who knows why we do computations
According to absolutely arbitrary rules,
Record spans, with one too few years?
Yet why regret either perpetual dust
Or antecedent wetness —
Conditions existing on either side of life's parentheses?
Best we accept, without question, each precious breath,
Every second, whether dying or dead.

4/18/85   (05925)

Palindrome ^Δ

Sourceless voices spitting vicious syllables
Sandblast the opaque hourglass
Separating all my past incarnations
From this calligraphic grasping — my poem,
Whose measures cast backward, inching ahead,
Filling a line at a time
(As though each were a crisp layer
Of an immense onion), slowly growing naked,
As fingers and psyche conspire in her disrobing.

I listen for specific signatures,
Oral idiosyncrasies
Which might accentuate the murmurous reverberations
Resonating my flesh and cranial base,
Set them apart from specious inventions
Constantly generated by the clepsydra/dynamo
Positioned at the end of imagination's flume.
No familiar inflections, images, dialects
Recommend themselves to my groping ears.

Suddenly, silence, like a salt sea, inundates the poem,
Evaporates. The pitted glass
Keeps insight, vision, clairvoyance at impasse,
The onion strata in a dark catacomb.
And now, alone in this vast opening,
With only this page of a greater, lost scroll
To help fix my own dislocation,
I associate those moans with the Lodz ghetto.
They're my own, my own, stuck in my throat.

4/22/85   (00086)

May Day ^Δ

This soft May Day a.m.
Is riffled and shimmering with rain-glaze,
Silent as amniotic caves.
Only occasional cars,
Weaving the square's four slick strands
Into a bracelet made of streets,
Break the peaceful tranquillity, with their sibilant swishing.

Through the Capital Café's open double doors,
My eyes exit forlorn smoke-haze
Emanating, from the back table,
Like a scrim net descending or tidal wave
Undulating shoreward, in a gray, swirling nimbus
Generated by nine innocent faces
Engaged in alternately responsive conversations.

Despite vision's discipline, my volitionless ears
Hold fixed positions against the indomitable enemy,
Desperately quiver, listening to Bob Lewis,
*

The local bank's chief executive officer,
Debate inflation's medusa-like manifestations,
With Jim Snavely, MFA claims adjuster,
And Francis Carrow, president of the savings and loan,

While Ed Knight and Denver Ratliff,
Supervisors of the city's electric-light and water companies,
Respectively, keep the faith,
Refrain from cross-pollinating the symposium.
By degrees, compounded of ignorance and indifference,
The subject shifts, as it eventually must,
To sports, recent necrologies, foreclosures, violence,

And sardonic bigotries aimed at "niggers" and "Jews,"
In no particularly predictable order,
Although, usually, the unusually loquacious reverend,
Bob Brannon, of the Presbyterian church,
Has the first and terminal words,
Between whose questionably collective parentheses
The rest — pharmacist Ron Short,

Barber Wayne Province, Chevy-Buick dealer Tom Fitz —
Assert their views edgewise,
Like knife blades thrust, obliquely, into hog brains,
Or great gray-whale penises
Groping for that delicate pudendal opening
Located, momentarily, at the farthest, darkest recess,
Where eighty thousand pounds disappear into ocean.

Soon, there's no room in here, for me.
My defenseless sensibility is wounded beyond recuperation.
Swigging coffee dregs, gathering my effects,
I pay, race from the café, north, on Liberty,
Past spirea drooping to the courthouse lawn,
And slip, almost unnoticed, into my office, assume my desk.
The city's poet is now open for business!

5/1/85 — [1] (00563)

Visiting the First Grade ‡

Although, as a dad
Visiting, all afternoon, in the classroom,
He appears not just slightly conspicuous
*

(Despite all his volitioned wishes to remain invisible,
While observing his son)
But decidedly overwhelming, if indeed acceptable,
He can't completely efface his own innocence,
Erase the strange, spatial déjà vu
Remembering his face, voice, shape to this schoolroom,

Where he, like his boy, entered the vortex,
Commenced the evolutionary celebration,
Whose end, progressive education,

5/1/85 — [2] (00683)

Happy Accidents ^Δ

My seven-year-old boy, Troika, and I,
The two "guys," out for breakfast,
By themselves, arrive at the IHOP,
This nippy Friday.
I've encouraged my son to run free,
Indulge his compulsion for blueberry pancakes.
Coffee will be my accompaniment
To his pan-dandy "fantaseeds,"
As he's accidentally transformed my word.
"My tongue slipped," he apologizes,
A laughter-laden smile widening across his face.
Automatically, he flips his place mat,
Rescues my pen from night-silence,
Not to rewrite "fantaseeds,"
"Empire Stilt Building," or "elf-a-phant,"
Subsequent aberrations his tongue has committed,
Slipping lexi-cogs while conversing with his dad,
But, instead, assume his mind's
Favorite position for executing illusions
With which to illuminate future déjà-vu rooms
He may never need ransack for images
Capable of assuaging doom-filled moods,
Commence shaping Lautrec-silhouettes
Confining his fabled "elf-a-phant,"
Whose leprechaun hat, pointed ears and shoes,
Fanciful suit popping its belly-buttons
Delight my amazed, innocent-bystander eyes.
*

By the time his short stack reaches the table,
We've already been to Mzima Springs,
Roamed the Congo, sojourned in Mozambique,
Traversed Tanzania's Serengeti plains,
And returned, safely, to our vinyl seats
In Clayton's International House of Pancakes —
My mind-traveler and his guru
(A lowly poet, in his own "write"),
For whom going to school, in a few minutes,
Composing poems and treatises
For learned journals, respectively,
Won't be afterglow, letdown, doldrums,
Rather prelude to renewed celebration,
From whose beginnings the entire rest of the day
Might effloresce, should at least seem
Blessed, in respect to alternatives.
After all, its not every decade
Aberrations of such precious, measureless pleasure
Infiltrate routine destiny,
With "elf-a-phants" and "phantaselves."

5/3/85   (00682)

Talismanic Auguries

As I flee the city, this Wednesday a.m.,
Mist lifting off valleys,
Engendered by sweet, seed-laden May,
Whose ubiquitous presence
Is the taste teeth biting podded peas retrieve,
My three-dimensional vision
Focuses on the three-quarter moon,
A disk yet shimmering between fading night's breasts,
Whose beguiling concupiscence guides me home,
Southwest by west, deftly as phage
Stealthily sliding through bones, spine, nodes.

Not gold, ivory, ocherous, or cyanic,
Its shape neither nebulous nor amorphous,
Resisting traditional description,
It magnetizes sight, taunts insight
To break its cryptic hieroglyphics,
*

Incised upon the haloing sky's Rosetta stone.
I concentrate on keeping the road even, on its reel,
Despite its continuous shifting,
As my hands wind it in, mile by mile,
But its lunatic vigilance mystifies,
Without enlightening the nature of my flight.

5/8/85 (05926)

Last Day in the Old Capital Café ‡ Δ

Outpatients, beautician, insurance and car salesmen,
Sheriff, C.P.A.,
Court clerks, and eavesdropping poet
Congregate, for the last time, inside these temple walls.
Sue seems unusually busy,
As if, after her fifteen years in the same maze,
Change, no matter how convenience-laden,
Just can't replace habit and routine,
Her spinster stepsisters.
They're moving, Bob and his crew, uptown,
Five doors down and over,
To the long-vacant location across the way.
By Monday, the Capital Café
Will face the courthouse from the north, not east,
Occupying a classier piece of real estate.
Whether it will still attract

5/10/85 (00562)

On Her Beginning Her Second Decade Δ

For my sweet Trilogy,
from her proud and loving dad

Now, Monday's child
Is just hours away from becoming eleven.
At 3:43,
She'll conclude one, commence a new, revolution.
Later this p.m.,
Her brother and mother and I
*

Will do birthday rituals, ignite wishes
With which to celebrate her longevity,
Health, wisdom, joyousness, serenity,
And love toward others and herself.
We'll bless our precious Trilogy Maya,
With sweet caresses, infectious smiles,
Whose incantatory chants will scatter demons,
Keep them eddying at destiny's edges.
Right now, my throat tightens.
I know tomorrow will arrive sooner than this afternoon.

5/13/85 — [1] (02090)

A Sour Taste in the Mouth

Fatigue distills my finest thoughts to brine,
Not wine; images decompose
To turpentine, vinegar my rhythms.
My throat chokes on sour draughts —
Socratic hemlock sipped through its stems.
As death's unquenchable thirst is paradoxically slaked,
My brain shrivels, to accommodate pain's molecules.
The cells rebel. Replication forfeits its birthright,
Until life's essence, slime, dries to sandstone
And the blasted bones, skeletally intact,
Hang, by the third vertebra, from an invisible hook,
Rattling against the breeze,
Like cosmic wind chimes,
Reminding all gone souls of their former paltriness.

5/13/85 — [2] (05927)

Three White Horses

Three F-4 Phantoms,
Flying low, over twilit St. Louis,
Groping for the right nexus, to surge upward,
Tremble the sky in two, like an isolated child
Craving attention, ripping construction paper,
In the far back of the classroom.

As I leave my house, this unawakened a.m.,
My tropistic ears bend sunward,
Whose locator arc detects an ignited rocket
Entering, downwind, upthrusting orbit.
Noise so grotesque and unabating,
Capable of rumbling bones and gonads

So far below those robotic ghosts,
Sealed in chip-guided silence
So high above my futility and abject fright,
Neutralizes all human desire I summoned,
Prior to stepping out my door,
To slay paper dragons, play Don Alonso,

Whose self-appointed knight-errantry
Just might suffice to reinstate society
With a measure of heroism, no matter whom
The cosmic joke ultimately targets.
Abruptly, a wayward emotion,
Flying high against my senses' inventive horizon,

Metamorphoses into three white horses,
Sleek, elusive Greco-Christian phantoms
Galloping across a wheat field
Completely enveloped in apocalyptic conflagration —
McDonnell jets blasting afterburners,
Wheeling, coming back around, now,

To discharge their neutron delusions, on my brain,
As I leave to assume duty's calling,
On this otherwise innocuous Tuesday morning.
Suddenly, all significance I've assigned to living
Dissipates. Neither romance nor myth
Can obliterate my premonitions,

Which, like repercussive explosions,
Erupt endlessly, as migraine shock waves.
All day, I sit behind my desk display,
Pressing keys hysterically,
Trying to call up those three F-4 Phantoms,
That I might delete them from "memory" permanently.

5/14/85 (05928)

The Poet Doubts His Immortality

All contraptions logic has appropriated
And used as collateral,
In securing leverage to maintain its celebrity,
Collapse like abused Seuss-gizmos.
This Tuesday's slate is so clean,
No stimuli can deface its patina,
Trace neurological tremors into its perfect surface.
A deaf-mute's brain stews in juices,
Like a stillborn fetus indeterminately brewing.

Silence infiltrates my tumescent cells,
Nurtures confusion. Quiescence is an ocean
Flowing where blood once circulated,
Whose blue-green sound washes memory's ears
As if to stir ancient sea creatures
Swirling beneath history's granulated detritus.
The sand neither demands answers of itself
Nor stammers with excuses or lame justifications.
Change is its only omniscience.

Traveling further southwest, by the mile,
Deeper, doubt after sinking doubt,
Higher, with each magnetic fluctuation
The eyes' tandem gyros register,
Trying to locate and fix the mind's lodestone,
I proceed blindly, hoping my arrival
Will deliver me somewhere other than at Chaos Gate.
God knows, going dead is lonely enough
Without acquiescing to fate uncomplainingly.

5/28/85 (05929)

Being Attuned

Ever so slowly,
So agonizingly slowly as not to be noticed,
The indefatigable soul ceases its groping,
Abandons hope of knowing its owner,
That ephemeral custodian of its perpetual genealogy,
Who, through mutable succession,
*

Progresses, undaunted, toward earthly perfection,
Uses evolution as his convenient excuse
To condone status-quo eschatology.

Admittedly, even if only a distant relative,
The spirit bears witness to the soul's dissolution,
As it goes through its daily gyrations,
Its invisibly diminishing spinning
Sending centrifugal ellipses, in widening orbits,
Toward the source of all motion,
Then wobbling, dropping beneath its frictioned heat,
Into gravity's bone-heap, buried in calcified silence
Oblivion sprinkles lightly over detritus.

This empty Sunday morning,
A semblance of echoes awakens me.
Whether muted bells emanating from Florentine campaniles
Or steeples lacing Fiesole,
Flute notes or birdsongs
Escaping smooth Bernoulli tubes, lubricated throats,
My dull ears refuse to differentiate,
Yet my body is vaguely aware
Something essential is astir.

Perhaps the universe is making itself ready
To welcome a new guest home
Or an old friend back, after an absence
Spent in unsuccessful quest
For terrestrial immortality.
Regardless, the whirring sensation
The parting firmaments create, in absorbing me,
Tunes my mind's tines to a cosmic pitch
At which nothingness and omnipotence synthesize.

6/2/85 (05930)

Acid Rain ^Δ

This gray, rainy a.m.
Is a beggar's baggy, raveling greatcoat,
Within whose convoluted folds I grope —
An altogether insignificant insect
Scrabbling to keep from forfeiting its protection,
*

Being stranded completely out in the open,
Absolutely open to flim-whimsy,
In the middle of a flying island,
Earthly atoll, in a universal ocean,
The isle neither Laputa nor Blefuscu,
Rather Gregor Samsa's floor . . . a spectral nexus.

Ah, there's the resonating correspondence!
This gray beggar's morning is Prague,
Kneeling at George Grosz's feet,
Poised to accept cyanide wafers,
A fascist sacrament, administered innocently,
That scratches the throat, burns the bowels,
As my beetle feet spur the imagination,
In my hope of overturning the jury's verdict,
Locating a way out of this loboto-maze,
Walking upright, naked, beneath the rain,
Without having it descend as Zyklon B vapors.

6/5/85 — [1] (00838)

One Long Road ^Δ

It's usually only on trips like this
That Willy gets wistful,
Lets Missouri's misty, May-lush valleys
And hills make him envious,
Disappointed with his meager anointment,
Eager to cancel his appointments with merchandisers
(That ubiquitous euphemism for buyers,
Clerks, trainees to whom, regardless of class
Or stature, he must genuflect, when on the road),
Change positions, assume a new skin,
Enter into negotiations with invisible stockholders,
To acquire majority interest
In whatever issue might excite his fancy at the time,
Gain control, affect decision making,
Dictate policy, on company letterhead,
Place his signature on the annual report.

It's only in dislocated moments like this
(Today, heading westerly, toward Tipton,
Past Boonville, Sedalia, Chillicothe)
*

That he agonizes, realizing he's spent a lifetime
(Not the best parts — *all* of it)
Driving, sedentary as a dazed Buddha,
Unable to stop even long enough
To pluck clusters of clover from overflowing fields
Laced with goldenrod, suck on wild onions
Yanked from soft lawns, in clumps,
Picnic beside whisperous streams, for lunch,
Unstoppling a long-necked bottle of wine
And suckling from it, like a baby sheep
At its mother's teat, eating cheese, sardines,
As, in youth, he did with his sweethearts.

Only at these few impasses,
When action and regret collide, do battle,
Decimate each other's energies,
Does he hesitate, become briefly immobilized,
Fear his base hesitations
May get the better of him, cause his questioning
To reach epidemic degrees of self-doubt,
Crowd out all resolve to accept and continue,
To revel in the *what is*, not all the *might have been*s
Wheeling in the nimbus his imagination radiates.

After all, at sixty-eight, still traveling,
Servicing Acme-Zenith's Midwest territory,
He has little valid room for complaint.
On the contrary, being grateful is his heritage,
Birthright, his singular mission.
Sinister alternatives have been his people's bane,
Throughout history's tedious cavalcade.
In fact, the Chosen of the original tribes
Were no different — all of them, to a fault,
Road-souls who would stop just long enough
To let someone bury their dead bones,
Before heading off, away from home, again.

6/5/85 — [2] (02339)

A Suspicious Nature

Swaybacked gambrel-roofed barns,
Stilled tin windmills
*

Trying to outlast rust and silence,
Torpid cows huddled, like whales in schools,
Amidst oceanic May grass
Mark his trespassing, with keen eyes.
In their pervasive mindlessness, they realize
His passage presages sinister tidings.

Is he an SBA agent or local banker
Poised to call another loan,
Foreclose on one more beleaguered farm,
A rep for an eastern manufacturing firm
Or foreign megaconsortium
Interested in erecting car plants,
Parts-receiving depots, Disneylands,
Engineer scouting nuclear-waste and missile sites?

Minutes, days, decades after his fleet shadow
Fades into the nimbus haloing this oblique space,
Where the only active sign of life is decay,
That pervasive, suspicious gaze
Inanimate and animal objects cast, naturally,
At all unfamiliar shapes and sounds
Rearranges focus, to accommodate new intruders,
Dispatch them, too, with an accusative glare.

6/5/85 — [3] (05406)

Waking Early

He slides down the city's western slope,
Through inimical fog,
Out of town, edging, urgently, toward morning.
Incoming headlighted traffic
Perforates his retinas, creates blind clots
In his mind's peripheral insight.

Suddenly, forgetting overtakes blurred vision.
Instead of sweat, fear leaks from its pores,
Forming a glaze, over his brain,
Indistinguishable from water beads
The leaking fog deposits on his windshield.
An insidious fusion, at dew point, occurs.

Physical disappearance and emotional invisibility
Collide. At implosion's core,
His collective existence atomizes.
His blasted dust radiates in arching shafts
Assuming rainbow shape and hue,
As he arrives intact, lacking only his spirit.

6/7/85 (05931)

Greater and Lesser Densities

For Bill Lane

Everywhere, saturated grass is glistering glass.
Rivers are swollen sausage casings.
Trees and roadside greenery
Shudder, in photosynthetic satiety.

A primordial aura, steamy, putrescent,
Pervades this morning — first in a week
To dawn other than bleak with rain.
Now the drying out should commence.

Yet relief is ever a matter of ironies.
We share contrarieties.
Always, grass, no matter saturated or sere,
As it has been in Florida for a month,

Is, in varying climates, more vibrant.
Our lives alternate between drought and flood,
Starvation and glut, plague and old age —
Commonplace as "a chicken in every pot."

Indeed, one man's dross is another's sauce.
Equality is a philosophical snafu,
Whose Catch-22 tendencies render it useless
Except when comparing human disparities;

Then it becomes our handiest tool
For justifying morality, religion, politics, science,
Deciding to lunch at Rax or the Polo Lounge,
Favor apartheid or desegregation in the Deep South.

Wet or dry, green, sienna, or fecal,
We proceed, from actions and ideas,
*

To immobilized silence, knowing only, finally,
We'll all arrive at the same conclusion.

6/8/85 (05932)

Postmodern Noah ^Δ

Destined to spend his days under full sail,
He navigates concrete sea lanes,
His perspective contained by an eyepiece,
Vision focused, with telescopic precision,
On minute, sporadic objects,
Whose relations to each other and him
Are devoid of design, informing pattern
Which might provide a key to his dislocation.

He floats the ocean, whose briny tides
Wash shores accreting, eroding, daily, nightly,
At dawn's and dusk's extremities.
His ship, neither *Beagle* nor *Pequod*
But phantom sampan, flies his mind's Bermuda Triangle,
Then cruises in ever-widening circles,
Until whipped, centrifugally,
Through forgetting's hypnotic straits, toward oblivion.

His entire existence has been,
As it gives all indications of continuing to be,
A destinationless voyage,
Pathetic, peripatetic exercise in reading maps,
Gazing at stars, keeping logs, sleeping in snatches,
Eating at fate's makeshift tables,
A quest, at destiny's behest, for a hospitable Ararat,
Atop which he might rest his vessel.

6/14/85 (00837)

Chelmno Rain ^Δ

No rainbows potential the morning's deluge,
Whose lightning-rifled strafing,
Cyanic, sulfurous, ocherous oozing from purple,
Might be the hue of brilliance at synapse
*

Or the universe collapsing in on itself,
Through a massive black hole.
No matter, my thoughts run naked,
Across this no-man's-zone known as loneliness.

Even though my vehicle seems clean, astringent,
Traces of fecal- and urine-stained straw
Stick to rugs, seat covers, roof liner,
Like dog hairs, dandruff.
Older destinies linger yet, in the tires' whine —
That shrill moaning rubber and water
Conspire in tuning to memory's perverse timbre,
Fate's a cappella death-chant.

This lugubrious drive, I sense my imminent arrival
At one of ten thousand Chelmnos,
Myriad Sobibors, Treblinkas, Auschwitzes
Lining, like movie sets, my mind's wet highway.
Dying is not a final take,
Merely God's hobby, avocation,
A pastime to assuage the stasis of post-Creation.
Genocide is the absence of rainbows.

6/17/85 (00094)

Oedipus

Call it grasping for straws, being at odds, loggerheads;
The fact remains unchanged: he and I
Have always seen completely eye to eye,
Without ever having agreed.
Neither has either of us acceded to the other's ideas,
Ceased conceiving adversarial strategies,
During moments hindsight labels "false peace."
The quiet hiatus in which we lie low,
When not locked in taut debate,
Is like the night air above World War II London's
Underground, heard from inside.
Ours has been a police action
Conducted in that eerie zone, between sensibilities,
Known as the demilitarized conscience,
In which neutrality is observed, at awesome cost to the nerves,
*

And into which rabbits and squirrels and small birds
Never stray, even by accident.
We've waged our campaign my entire adulthood.
Now, despite his twilight,
No glimmer of potential armistice recommends us
To mutual gentleness, compassion's friend, happiness.
Why does this indeterminate fighting,
With its unpredictable skirmishes, counteroffensive reprisals,
Continue? Could it be God's sardonic wit,
His vindictive maliciousness for original disappointment,
Or might it simply be that father and son
Remain fated to maintain their respective motivations,
The one never breaking stride, relinquishing his pride,
The younger striving, despite wounds inflicted,
To achieve victory without robbing the father of his dignity,
Stripping him of his ribbons, medals, badges?
Ah, but victories without defeats,
In which both sides survive, to fight again and again,
Ultimately lead to insidious melees neither side can win,
Stalemates that bring opponents to their knees,
Lamenting familial bloodletting,
To which they'll dedicate their energies, an entire generation.

6/20/85 (05933)

Black Hole-ocaust ^Δ

> *There are evils so deep you can drop names
> in them and never hear them hit bottom.
> Josef Mengele is one of those names.*
>   — Stefan Kanfer, *People*

Voices squirm in his tongue's loose grip,
Trying to wriggle free
Before being gyved to a final solution,
Thrown overboard,
Into a sea inhabited by predacious creatures
Finning, impatiently, at varying fathoms,
For accidentals sifting from above.

A few slip his grip, elude articulation's barb,
Slither back into silence,
Avoid bloating, being swallowed alive
*

By strange, voracious appetites
Cruising, randomly, for fashionable variations
To the same old crude new clues to the future,
Obsolete philosophies, and clichéd daydreams.

One by one by one-half by one,
The rest get sacrificed.
Plunged into the collective death-alembic,
In which all false hopes coexist,
They disappear. No echoes reach the surface.
Whatever secrets they might have possessed
Keep sifting deeper and deeper.

6/26/85 (00090)

Hazy Ratiocinations

Haze stagnating in spaces separating cities
Is a cosmic witches' brew
Consisting of acidic precipitation (carbon monoxide,
Vaporous sulfurous admixtures, coal dust)
Lifting, colliding, scattering, haphazardly, into the sky,
As toxic air humans require for survival.
Like a circus tiger leaping through a flaming hoop,
I drive this highway, with furious urgency,
Threading its ever-widening needle's eye,
Uncertain which is worse: recently vacated perch
Or floor just below my outstretched legs.

Miles, spinning on slot-machine reels,
Dissolve into green, robotic diodes
Registered on the dash clock. I measure time
By sequential degeneration my vertebrae experience,
Not mechanical or electrical impulses
Whose finely tuned calibrations
Nullify and neutralize human inexactitude.
Suddenly, I pass that axis at which rotation
Is translated into magical transportation
And concrete reshapes itself into a hazy fluid
Floating me back to crystalline origins. I've died.

7/1–2/85 (05934)

The Playwrights

For Janny,
on our anniversary,
7/8/70 – 7/8/85

Fifteen years, like the Yale Shakespeare editions
Sitting, in silent, stately gracefulness, on our shelf,
Fit neatly between us.
They contain our star-crossed passages,
Not on rag-paper fibers
But memory-pages whose leaves brittle
Unobtrusively. The spans of our twined dreams
Are sewn threads holding gathered signatures together.
Emblazoned in gold lettering, between raised bands,
Their spines record our shared divertissements —
Comedies, histories, and tragedies.

Fifteen years have been placed on reserve,
In time's library, for anyone to use,
Provided they don't remove them,
Rather consult them, on the premises, as reference tools.
They need not seek our written permission,
To sift through every line, scene, act we've penned.
Hopefully, access to our chronicle
Will yield attitudes, patterns, a design
Worth emulating. Meanwhile, we go ahead,
With our projected sixty-volume set,
Postponing, till old age, correcting and indexing our lives.

7/8/85 — [1] (04139)

Seeing Stars

Twenty-six flights high,
Eye to eye with Eero Saarinen's arch-itecture,
Witness to hundreds of thousands of people
Gathered, on eight acres of levee
Above the Mississippi, to celebrate July Fourth,
We gasp as if asphyxiated by Zyklon B,
Try to temper convenient cynicisms
Which have exempted us from the company of insects
(Swarming bees, mosquitoes, flies, ants),
While not denying our own potential complicity,
Engendered by such patriotic events.

Colossal spider mums exploding across the night,
In purple, green, sapphire, scarlet hues,
Efflorescing girandoles growing from rockets,
Floating, momentarily, before dissolving into our eyes' sky,
Awaken us from our Dark Ages
Just long enough for both of us,
Caught between myriad fade and successive flame,
To see, in each other's face, euphoria,
That giddy free-fall feeling we always achieved,
In the beginning, when I and you
Would reignite dead meteors, with sparks from our heated hearts.

7/8/85 — [2] (04138)

Earth Mother

For my mother:
seventy years become you.

How many more than seventy remain
Remains to be calibrated —
Her unfinished years. A decade,
Perhaps a half, or just days?
Neither I nor she can estimate
Just by hyperbolizing,
Resorting to clichéd sentiments, borrowed metaphors
Calculated to swell a thirsty occasion,
With vintage swill, fill still moments to satiety.

Meanwhile, seated in this oblique, remote lounge,
Dissociated not from sensibility or memory
But familiar voices, shapes, conjurations,
I shimmer, reprising a persistent vision
Witnessed only by my insistent imagination,
In which she, my mother, Charlotte,
Despite her shaking hands, bends, in gentle suspension,
Within her homegrown garden,
Scissoring sweethearts and full-blown American Beauties,

For me . . . for me, her firstborn . . .
Snipping, with deliberate precision, individual blooms
Embodying the most brilliant, yet softest, hues:
Lavender, fuchsia, coral, gull gray, blood.
*

She cuts, plucks, delicately positions each stem,
Between quivering biceps and forearm,
Cradling every flower as if it were a Mosaical child,
Destined to suffer Pharaoh's decree,
Whom she might protect with her mystical invisibility.

The vision lingers, finally surfaces as history.
Those roses are the anniversary gift
She brought my Midianite wife and me,
In a byzantine vase divided into twelve compartments.
Why, feeling so lonely from yesterday's moment
When she drove over to our rented tent, on Wydown,
And delivered her present to us, do I fuss,
Ruminate, over my blessed mother?
Is it that such love has no appropriate analogues,

Or does touching exist in some mythical conditional tense?
Maybe it's her avowed refusal to be honored
Merely for accidentally having outlasted seven decades
That confuses me, creates this ambivalence,
Which scrambles my solar plexus and cerebral cortex,
Unsettles my belief in immortality.
Tonight, I realize that, in one week, my progenitor will be seventy
And I should be placing, at her feet, this metaphorical rose,
If for no other reason than that she is the poet in me.

7/9/85 (02670)

Calling for Help

Leaning over a clean, lined notebook sheet,
Posed in momentary arrest,
As if sitting stiffly so a daguerreotype focus
Might locate him, positively, on history's negative tin,
He waits and waits, anticipating ignition,
Equating his shape, mired in stasis,
With a naked beggar selling pencils, Christmas Eve,
A deaf-mute sinking in quicksand,
A rape victim submitting to fatigue.

No poems explode his head off its shoulders
Or even smolder in synaptic recesses.
Not a single theme, motif sequence,
*

Or solitary trope trips off his articulate lips,
Pleading to be sacrificed to written mimesis.
Yet he keeps his secret discreetly,
That those in Katy Station won't suspect
He's actually speaking, into his imagination's pay phone,
In a booth in plain view of everyone, to no one at all.

7/10/85 (02645)

Courtesans

The days undress themselves,
Like myriad performing quick-change artists
Using circus mirrors, for their booths.
Mirabile dictu! Look at this one,
Meretricious as a Parisian whore,
And that one, a crystal-tiered chandelier,
And that tortoise-and-hare pair!

They dance across the stage and off,
Leaving no traces save those
Memory fails to erase, with haste, from its slate,
For occasional Hansels, adventitious Gretels
To stumble upon, by accident, gather up,
In backtracking through the imagination's labyrinth,
To the beginning, where the caterpillar chokes on his opium pipe.

No matter their flamboyance
Or progressive, suggestive flirtatiousness,
They undress with unsuppressed insouciance.
The majority of our days couldn't care less
Whether they impress, on their contemporaries or us,
Idiosyncratic, passionate tendencies.
Instead, each would prefer to die disguised as Isadora Lorelei.

7/16/85 (05935)

Traveling Home, in a Hearse

Even weaving southwesterly, against the grain,
I breathe in mid-Missouri's putrescence,
Arising, from bumper-locked vehicles,
*

Like black genies escaping myriad iridescent vials,
And can't escape the city's trace elements.
For twenty-five miles, I chew the fumes,
Ruminate on the aftertaste of the pervasive waste,
Belch the flavorless vapors, pass gas
Distending my imagination's gut to explosive pain.

No amount of driving seems to relieve the pressure.
Lingering distress spreads,
Transforms the miles to hours to daymares,
As the highway shapes my passage,
Like a potter urging into existence a clay urn
To be used exclusively for my burial.
Suddenly recognizing my journey's destination,
I press ahead, due west,
Hoping death will soothe his newest guest's nerves.

7/17/85 (05936)

Marriage

Marriage is sharing paired contrarieties,
Wearing regal gowns and robes,
Totally naked,
Taking the slightest item, least occasion,
To praise a mate not for
But despite. It's that alchemical transformation
From triteness, through beguilement, to mystique,
Beneath whose Cimabue halo
Two humans become not one
But one with the One among many,
Assuming a blessed multiplicity of fused identities,
By which to perpetuate their two tiny lives,
Fighting to survive inescapable disparities
Marriage invariably exacerbates
And defend the universe, against all enemies.

7/18/85 (04137)

Pressing the Button

Never would he have guessed or prophesied,
At 5:30 breakfast with his wife,
*

That less than two hours later,
He would be standing beside his jackknifed rig,
In the middle of a major highway,
Feverishly channeling four lanes into two,
Controlling miles of thousands,
Like an international-airline hijacker,
Presidential assassin, skyscraper arsonist,
Having single-handedly created a human chain reaction
With waste (impatience, frustration, hatred)
Radiating jagged shock waves
Through half the population of greater St. Louis,
Permanently dementing one being, with the knowledge of his
    potential.

7/22/85 (05937)

[Who let the cat back into the bag,] †

Who let the cat back into the bag,
Forgot to tattle on Dick Nixon,
Flagged down Casey Jones,
Just in time's nick, picked the right lady
In the rough-dishwater-hands
TV ad

The miles, this flight south, are inhospitable.
Their shrill garrulity discourages dialogue.
Angry with my presence,
They accuse me of intruding —
The Old South's newest *car*petbagger

7/26/85 — [1] (03492)

One Final Run △

The shape of his spirit (even the space it occupies)
Is known to paltry few, and yet,
Those who do know are amazed by its shameless nakedness.
Whether egotism or genius motivates him,
He can't keep from exposing its basic elements
To anyone who approaches, anybody at all,
As though foe and friend shared his kindred soul.

Curious, his familiar anonymity. Or is it?
Perhaps his poetry fills the familiar silhouette
College students describe,
Blithely reciting any of many classic verses,
Cause to materialize when, trying to write originally,
They evoke his mellifluous, rhythmic voice.
Their very speaking is his reincarnation.

All his adult life, he's experimented with disguises
By which he might transcend silence,
Arrest, suspend, nullify the sentence
Imposed on him before his earthly birth,
Which decreed him ineligible for fleshly consolation,
Mandated his birthright turn on fantasy,
Invention, dementia, instead of passion and love.

Tonight, sitting by himself, sipping Bolla Soave,
In distant Oxford, he wishes he had a wife, children,
A house, an indentation of his body, in a bed,
An echo his snoring might remember and occupy,
As once, when youthful fire guided him,
His ambitious spirit seeded wayward metaphors,
Procreated the most holistic rhetorical tropes.

Now, aloneness and despondency overwhelm his spirit.
Its insides collapse, implode.
He can't fathom what conceivably could have brought him back
To this brackish desolation, unless . . .
Unless fate itself is contacting, contracting him,
To attempt one final mortal redemption:
Run naked, under a Mississippi moon, at high noon.

7/26/85 — [2] (03547)

5:30 Picnic at Rowan Oak [△]

*For Jim Carothers,
my dear friend*

The clipped grounds surrounding Rowan Oak
Wither like a weary, defeated athlete,
In Mississippi's deep-breathing humidity.
We drown, who have gathered, this week, in Oxford,
To pay obeisance to His simulacrum —
*

Not that of sweet Jesus but "Billy" Faulkner,
Conspicuous in his transcendence.

Each clapboard, every foundation timber,
Brick, drainpipe, shingle, chimney, and window
Recalls his footfalls, his small, drawling voice,
As though he, not we, his priesthood,
Were shivering the earth's tympanum, with our stirring,
Our carousing, in drowsy lassitude, about the house
He named, reclaimed from desolation.

Ah, but are we committing a desecration,
By violating this tranquil serenity he abdicated in July,
Anno Domini 1962?
Who gave us the right to infiltrate his privacy,
And who ordained us his trustees,
That we might partake of his once-vibrant spirit,
By eating chicken, on his lawn, his porch, in his formal gardens,

Spawning our own paltry narcissisms
Precisely where, once, he grieved, exulted, anguished,
Over Joe Christmas, Lena Grove, Wash Jones,
Got pissed off at Sutpen's cavalier excesses,
Ike McCaslin's recalcitrant rigidity,
Guffawed till the gods themselves seemed shamed
By Cora Tull's outrageous piety?

And yet we proceed without questioning either our motives
Or his. Contrarily, we position ourselves
In convenient contradistinctions to each other,
From which vantages we might register our various ambitions,
Note one another's tedious vocations
Within academe or slightly to the left or right of life,
All of us paltry approximations of his genius,

Despite our credentialed vitae and prestigious publications,
Who have come to spend this week in Yoknapatawpha,
To touch, listen for whispers, intuit
That special humid scent, sound, twilit hue
To which he responded with such lucidity,
That we might take back that essence,
To our kin existing, surviving, on the peripheries,

Proclaim that each of us is similarly gifted,
Has the capacity to create a cosmos from sticks and bones,
*

Construct a "henhouse in a hurricane."
But the fried chicken is soggy as seaweed,
And the salad has too much mayonnaise,
And the paper cups wilt in our hands, like orchids —
A curious Eucharist, shabby communion with our Lord, Billy.

7/31/85 (03545)

Going Home ^Δ

Despite my heart's disinclination,
A gray, shapeless melancholy
Has chased me out of Oxford, this afternoon,
Sent me fleeing in such soiled, sullen sadness,
Not even familiar road-poetry
Assuages the pervasive one-on-oneness
Disaffecting the two of us, memory and me.

For a week, I've eluded anonymity,
By courting approval of others
Into whose arbitrary custody I remanded my shadow —
Academicians, mainly, whose aims and motivations
Are fundamentally inimical to mine,
Enemies of freedom and creativity,
Except as those elusive concepts fit their theses.

As I head home to an empty bed,
My empty head vanishes into thin forgetting,
Where, in a shimmering clearing
(Preternaturally clairvoyant parentheses,
In which twilight and night are identical skies),
I suddenly recognize my jettisoned soul:
Odysseus, reconciled to Ithaca's parochial vision.

8/1–2/85 (03546)

Quincunxes in Everything

I wander about these drowsing premises,
Trying to take into poetic account
Each change that might have alchemized
Since we four, an intact, sane, happy family,
Vacated this somnolent Pompeii.

I sit outside, this Friday twilight,
Listening to the cricket-whisperous sky,
Sensing rabbits peering at my presence,
From grass clipped by others assigned to my absence,
And I delight in invisible robins taking flight,

Reiterating patterns their urgent blood inherits
Even before eggs are fertilized. I sit on the patio,
Admiring a wrought-iron table I've painted
Ten times, if once, whose byzantine interlacing
Dizzies my wine-blitzed eyes,

Transfigures the apparatus through whose aperture
Vision materializes, that interface at which synapse
And brain-mosaic fuse, then relax,
Whose instantaneous incandescence
Exposes the universe beneath the most trivial petal.

Slowly, chicken breasts hissing on the grill,
Ants, rabbits, birds, crickets furiously gossiping,
Phantom voices of my two children, cathedraling a past
My wife and I fashioned from sticks and stones,
Flood intuition's ducts. I weep a ceaseless litany,

As though grieving could reverse time's mechanism,
Set Pompeii's frozen, black basalt once more flowing,
Running uphill, into heaven's moat,
From which it oozed originally,
Back to the crater's implosive, roaring core,

That we might reprise those prehistoric days,
When our girl and boy rediscovered, for us,
The essentials in even the most trivial ephemera —
Aphids, cactus and rose thorns, toads,
Snow, and lightning bugs hovering in wondrous arrest.

Just now, so totally naked,
I wander these cricket-thick premises, alone,
Listening to ghosts whose souls no longer sing
Or yet remember the songs they initiated —
Sensuous roundelays, mellifluous lullabies —

Who refuse to hum melodies, recite lyrics
We once suspended above our sleeping children's ears,
To gentle them into dreams. Sitting outdoors,
This quiet Friday night, I am reminded
That naming and claiming are very distinct suzerains,

Preoccupations of poets and gods and normal beings
Susceptible to quincuncial configurations.
Tonight, I realize that neither wine nor natural highs
Privilege individuals to insights; only loneliness
Determines who shall be first in time's line.

8/16/85   (05448)

[Already, a vaguely discernible resignation]

Already, a vaguely discernible resignation
Droops, like drowsy dog ears,
August's tumescent leaves. The trees grieve,
In silent sunlight's dappled dazzlement,
For a time not even yet arrived,
As though guided, to their stylized vision,
By my eyes peering through time —
Déjà vu hallucinations
The poetic mind imposes on inanimate objects,
For sport, divertissement,
The metaphor the "be"gin- and end-all
Of every thing and being, apotheosis in a ball
Too Marvell-ous to behold alone.

In truth, trying to focus notions into words,
At sixty-five miles per hour,
And keep body and soul in straight lines
Might be like tiptoeing across a high wire
In a gravityless vacuum.
There's just so much room for human error,
That, in both cases, freedom becomes the rule,
Exceptional digressions so commonplace,
Trees, poet's insights and overviews
Assume Elysian heights, without effort.
After all, who's to determine, absolutely,
That head and heart can't have intercourse
Or leaves can't droop in August heat,
Assume Septembering broodishness prematurely,
With or lacking external intrusion?

And why be concerned,
So long as the seasons accomplish sequentially,
Poems get set and locked into history's chase,
*

And enough people are constantly transmogrified
To substitute for those dying few
Who, naturally, seem capable of mediating both realms:
Breathing and being in touch with breathless essences
Arrested between death and time not even yet arrived?

8/17/85 (05938)

[Those of us — poets, dreamers, winos,]

Those of us — poets, dreamers, winos,
Schizophrenics — for whom shimmering images,
Not vicissitudinous daily stock quotations,
Runaway gross- and net-profit totals
Sneering from monthly business updates,
Memberships in Palm Beach and Ladue society
As the fleur-de-lis pinnacle of arrival,
Are the most estimable obsessions
Take our pleasures from gray skies,
Empty eyes, surprises disguised between lines
In books unvisited since youth.

We need no extrinsic motivation
To set the mind-flints spinning, sparking,
Illuminating the darkest baffles
Silence provides deep-sea-treasure seekers
Diving three centuries down,
To reach the intact coffers of *Nuestra Señora
De la Muerte Oscura*.
Instead, we thrive on shimmering images
Derived of Shakespearean antecedents,
Rendering, from negligibles, provocative essences,
Ultimately our most coveted possessions.

8/19/85 (05939)

Just Another Fall-Tinged Tuesday in Late August

It's all in knowing how to lose yourself,
On a fall-tinged Tuesday
*

Late in August, with its green-gold Dylan Thomas–hues
Calling, so persuasively, to follow.
Just let the psyche distract itself,
With bemusing child's-play antics and fantasies
Butterflies, crickets, birds, rabbits, and squirrels display
So unself-consciously. Forget choosing
As one of myriad choices humans elect to exercise,
In selecting freedom's pursuit.
Be tolerant of grass and trees,
Ants, sweat bees, and daddy-longlegs spiders.
Surrender to the tranquillity uncompromisingly,
As though no other commitment
Ever required so much effort on your behalf.
Perhaps then, when you least expect it,
Some stupendous incandescence might descend,
Igniting the sensibility's inventive ashes
Into music ascending from the blood's diminished flowing,
Dance spinning from an enchanted, comatose princess,
Japanese bridges connecting lily-pad Giverneys
With painterly daydreams, poetry anyone can read
Who cares about jars in Tennessee,
Red wheelbarrows beside white chickens,
Somewhere in the vicinity of Paterson, New Jersey,
Greenhouses growing Roethke-roses.
Like I say, it's all in knowing
How to lose yourself, on a fall-tinged Tuesday,
When death calls too loudly
For any of us to merely excuse it as a sonic boom
Or seismic quake in a nearby fault.
It's all in knowing how to make oneself available,
Just in case Chicken Little
Hasn't deluded herself, in fact has some basis in truth
Worth heeding, just in case she may be presaging
The end, when losing oneself
Is decidedly preferable to its most convenient alternative,
Euthanasia, simply because a creative bent,
At least Biblically, has always been
The most salutary avenue humans have had to God,
Who, over the centuries, has shown favor
To those who've tried to render Him
With a degree of originality, not herd-worship.

8/20/85 (00955)

Apocalyptic Ruminations

Now that we've gained distance from the sixties and seventies,
We can render, with scientific precision,
Obligatory pronouncements and futuristic overviews,
Dismiss, with a sigh, corrupt Nixonian politics,
Jonesian "religious" practices, Peace Corps ideologies,
Fanatical assassinations of Kennedys and blacks
(Which collapsed like the *Hindenburg* at Lakehurst,
As it shuddered into flames, above its fated mooring),
In a single, slick special-edition issue of *Life*,
Accept Veblen's "conspicuous" predictions
As having circled back home, to our psyches,
We who, having lived into our forties and fifties,
Realize dreams belong in glossy books
Framed by coffee-table glass
And that all of us are heirs to viral frenzies
And paltry enzymes, distinguishable
Not by clothing, flesh hue,
But by disillusionment, excessiveness, and trenchant anxiety.
Wiser, by far, than our antecedents,
We grope toward the nineties, with lower profiles,
Hoping to survive the darkest nightmare of our feuding souls.

8/26/85 (05940)

Coexistence ^Δ

Barn swallows soar and wheel
Above this white-gleaming Victorian manse,
Weaving metaphor-nests on end-of-August thermals,
Seeking metaphysical apotheosis,
In my wine-high poetical eye,
Searching for nothing so rarefied, actually,
Just accomplishing their birdly existence,
While I, so many fathoms below,
Mired in the *now* and *here*,
Mythicize their common existence monumentally,
By transfiguring their routine flights into odysseys.

They etch themselves, permanently, into my psyche,
Memorize my breathing, into their being,
*

Tantalize my dormant passion,
Dapple me, with their skyrobatic patterns.
Carried aloft, my dizzy vision slows,
Arcs over, in a hammerhead stall. I die,
Contemplating them. Ah, but there lies
Contention's crux.
What have *they* done to transport *my* energies?
Nothing . . . everything — simultaneous fusion.
We have become one, becoming *us*.

8/28/85 & 1/13/86 — [4] (05447)

An Autumnal Aubade [Δ]

Autumn, that not-infelicitous thief,
Hides in low-lying fog,
Edges closer, each succeeding morning,
Settles, now, my scrutiny apprises me,
As subtle reds and russets, on moist leaves
Clinging, for the remainder of their waning lives,
To flowering crab and dogwood twigs.

I pluck a sprig from each,
To accompany me on my day's trip,
Place them on the dashboard,
That vision might necessarily pass through them
Before diffusing into the accumulating future,
Coat them with memory-dust,
Preserve, intact, their russet-red registers,

Delude the riotous thief into believing
He's gotten away, clean, with all summer's loot.
But by journey's termination,
The festooned bouquet I gathered droops.
I realize that, soon, even imagination
Won't be able to mitigate brooding moodiness
Which sets in, every November,

Let alone forestall immediate regret
That, by afternoon's end,
Will have grown to seething offense.
Who, having been robbed of precious possessions,
Hasn't sensed death's intrusiveness
*

Or heard his own burning blood turning colors,
Red to russet to blue, cooling to fugitive hues?

8/29/85 (05941)

The Day After Labor Day ^Δ

The strewn shards of squirrel-cracked acorns
Render our front yard
An excavated potter's field. My dazed gaze,
Borne aloft, into mazy oak-tangles,
Gropes for evocative indications,
Knows, even before metaphors coalesce,
That autumn's pervasive hold will soon take.
Focusing vacantly, through green layers,
My eyes fix the peaked moon, between leafy openings,
Sitting, forlorn, on morning's shore,
As if it just missed the last ferry to Tiburon.

Slowly, my children's chattering footsteps
Retrieve me from empty reveries.
We three stand beneath the oak,
Arrested for seconds only,
Before forgetting transcends memory,
Renders time theirs, not mine.
I must deliver them early, this first day of school.
Even as I let them off,
I intuit the impatient moon's desperation,
As she grows imperceptibly dim,
Begging me take her aboard, in their places.

9/3/85 — [1] (00681)

The Troll

Like ocean conch and freshwater snail,
He lives inside a spiral shell
His convoluted days shape about his skeleton,
Whose flesh and brain cells,
Despite their variegation, remain undifferentiated.
Each sleep, every yawn and sigh
*

Contains the sum of all his breathing desires
To stay within the confined circumambience
He's allowed to accrete about his silence.

Grudgingly, every few decades,
He deludes himself into changing venues,
Moving his sparse possessions
To a more scientifically equipped co-op grot
Or condominimal lacuna watched over by robots,
Twenty-five hours a night,
Eight weeks a day,
To ensure his lethargy its necessary insularity,
Let him perpetuate, unintruded, his terraqueous fetishes.

Only once in all his vegetable indolence
Did he risk involvement
With another human molecule. Even then,
He entered into dialogue out of self-defense,
Arguing, with his first of thirty spouses,
About how much of his bodily house
She might reasonably expect to share
With his other twenty-nine wives,
At his demise, since he'd already chosen cremation.

To this day, he carries his castle on his back,
Fearing others might attack his rights
To occupy his own thoughts exclusively.
No motives to add to his holdings
Goad him into seeking different fortresses.
He prefers the murky moat in which he's wallowed,
The slime that's lubricated his passages,
Below the drawbridge his synapses raise and lower
Whenever he realizes it's time to slumber or eat.

9/3/85 — [2] (00836)

"Back to School"

After almost three weeks' hiatus,
Willy eagerly takes to the open road.
His station wagon sags under the strain
Placed on it by its load of Republic of China
Genuine feather-edged-glove-leather belts,
*

Cotton/poly four-in-hand clip-on ties
Clumped like bananas in bunches,
Whose clubs, dots, stripes, paisleys, ducks
Suggest the Seussian Jungles of Jorn,
And Oxford dress shirts
Sliding, in their polyethylene-package condoms,
Over the Niagara-like shoals his front seat provides,
Dividing Acme-Zenith's driver/schlepper-rep
From equivocal merchandise
He'll attempt to parcel out, all week,
At extravagant closeout/bargain prices —
Barely questionable seconds
Tediously culled from more blatantly flawed myriads,
To appear, like bacon
Gleaming beneath its cellophane window, all of a kind,
Perfectly meaty, through and through,
Both sides, inside and out,
Identically desirable despite being rinds.
Through all his years, Willy's never declined
To assist with this disreputable chore.
Twice annually, at each season's end,
He's risked humiliation, at a ½ percent commission,
Forgoing his own good name,
To dump the company's bum goods on customers
He normally services with first-line items.
Yet never has he fully adjusted
To complying with company guidelines
That would have him beguile prospective buyers,
With veiled lies; rather, he's always resorted
To allowing each to rifle his wagon, at will,
Root through his pig trough,
Choose, from Acme-Zenith's "half-truths,"
Their individual "picks of the litter,"
Until, after one week, nothing's left
Except his own soiled shirts and pants,
Which, twice, at least, he could have sold, too,
For a price.
Today marks the twenty-eighth time
Willy's sallied forth,
Into rural Missouri's "Back to School" days,
Jobbing white belts, tropical golf slacks,
Yellow, pink, and lime neckwear,
*

Short-sleeved, heather-hued dress shirts —
Imperfections all —
The fifty-sixth out-of-sync pilgrimage
Since joining the firm. But for some reason,
He can't seem to get excited.
He feels depressed. Perhaps it will pass
Before he arrives at Jefferson City Slack Outlet,
His first of three scheduled stops.
Maybe it's just his colitis acting up.
Possibly, he's miscalculated the distress
The stuff he's purveying possesses.
He hopes his associates won't associate him, personally,
With this disagreeable task,
Relegate him to his ancestral depths, for eternity.
Ah, but then, he knows,
They already did, long ago. They will again, tomorrow.

9/4/85 — [1] (02338)

[No matter how seemingly mundane,] †

No matter how seemingly mundane,
Daily activities consume his most passionate energies,
Engage his image-making apparatus,
Exclusively, in pursuit of fugitive essences and hues.
He listens, meticulously, to whispers issuing from

9/4/85 — [2] (04743)

A Toast to the Forties ∆

Wood-slatted ceiling fans
Bat the close, acrid air trapped in Katy Station,
Like voracious wing-flapping crows
Slashing a crimson rabbit rapidly losing its last race.

I sit below one's slightly wobbly rotations,
Obliquely taking my strained simile
With a vaguely superstitious grain of salt,
Casting away implications of its poetic correlation,
Like fast-food packaging,
*

Christmas wrapping. Yet as I grow relaxed,
Within this air-conditioned atmosphere,
Images of the Holocaust materialize.

Rather than envision spinning fan blades,
I sense equestrian time
Wielding his vicious scythe, victimizing innocents,
Among whose screaming multitude I writhe.

This stained-glass public place,
Where, frequently, I've wasted placid hours, imbibing wine,
Writing sonnets, passing out,
Becomes a Wagnerian railway station
Animated with latter-day decadence,
College-age Kirchner, Nolde, and Marc whispers
Redolent of anti-Semitic momentary romances,
Which sidetrack my crack passenger boxcars,

Send their swill-brained metaphors
Spilling to the hay-strewn floorboard
Of a numberless, feces-sullied, destinationless *Güterwagen*,
To whose vestibule I'm led, by a Rhine maiden, as my reservation
    comes up,

Not to be made whole or clean again, by feasting,
But cease being, desist from breathing,
Beneath the swirling, vortical vapors
Descending from ceiling fans, to my open eyes,
Like crows' claws violating this modern *Hölle*,
Where, tonight, I find myself stranded,
A stranger to trains racing, blindly, toward Bergen-Belsen —
Death's best patron, buying rounds, for the hell of it.

9/4/85 — [3] (02673)

Choosing a New Place to Die

The city I flee is stuporous.
It reels precipitously, without perceiving
Its own fatigue and dizziness —
A prizefighter weak in the knees,
Wino about to pass out in a fouled alley,
Ballerina with undetectable coronary disease —
*

A city decomposing before its own eyes,
Whose collective myopic/astigmatic blindness
Makes tunnel vision a kaleidoscope.

I flee the city, via its vena cava.
Its circulatory system
Works in reverse, jettisons pure oxygen,
Depletes its clean reserves
Faster than it can inhale carbon dioxide,
Overcome pollution debt.
It thrives on noxious fumes, waste
Laced with half-burned vapors —
Proust's teacakes floating in Love Canal.

My reasons are obvious, for fleeing
To outbound regions
Seventy-five miles beyond the epileptic city:
Breathing comes easier;
Dusk and dawn aren't emphysemic gasps
A decrepit man makes,
Grasping at life-sustaining fresh-air pockets;
Lush tomatoes, zucchinis, mushrooms
Don't blend into a monochromatic acid-rain-bow;

And ultimately, I might enjoy
A greater variety of choices
As to how, if not when, I will die.
Just now, the city I flee calls
Through memory's phonetic echoes,
Begs me return, by nightfall,
So it might excite my senses, with its Lorelei lights,
Delude me into forgetting the shimmering skyline
Is, indeed, no mirage.

9/9/85 (00835)

The Caf-fiend

Crystalline, screaming, caffeine-heightened sky
Provides my liberated psyche
Exclusive excuse for yielding to speeds
Few humans have ever reached.
My heartbeat multiplies time,
As though I were mainlining steroids,
*

Freebasing Dr. Kananga's finest San Monique
Opiates. Blown open, this autumnal morn,
Driving south, out of the moldy city,
Toward Cape Girardeau, flown,
All ties vasectomized, I escape memory,
Penetrate silence, forgetting, hope —
Zones between no-man's-land
And transcendence, within whose confines
The mind discovers the origin of metaphors,
Has free run, in God's china shop,
To select myriad exotic possibilities
To stuff into its pockets, bring back, intact,
As decoration for inchoate verse
And other rainy-decade applications.

Just now, I fly so low, so high,
Even my own radar
Fails to detect my shadow skimming the planet's rim,
Casting out, over oblivion's abyss,
With this "moving" poem,
Flowing, volitionlessly, beyond prescribed measures.
My screaming brain's furious pitch
Is indistinguishable from the whirring sounds
Of Earth turning on its frictionless galactic axle.
Perhaps returning from the universe
Shouldn't even concern me;
Rather, transforming myself from abstract to matter should.
How else do essences get back to the essentials?
But right now, *now* is forever.
At the core, from which synapses flash and leap,
Thousands of generations, into space,
I pretend my senses are normal,
The day no different from other September mornings,
Except that, from every direction, visions of my exploding solar soul
Collide inside the caffeine sky occupying my crystalline eyes.

9/12/85 (05942)

[Poems only flow]

Poems only flow
When the slow soul glows,
*

Slips past that threshold
Below which matter stays frozen.
Preheating the spirit to such speeds
Is no easy apotheosis.
Teaching vision to decode the constellations,
Dandelion seeds, geodesic domes
Requires infinite patience,
Takes generations to unfold,
In the least prepossessing human vessel.
Yet verse is the connective tissue
By which history hymns men and women
Into its endlessly evolving chanson.

9/17/85 — [1] (05943)

September Moon Through the Elms: A Nocturne

For Jan, beloved;
grateful am I
for your patience and fidelity.

Beyond this warm September evening's stir,
Where vision etches its own signature
Against the red horizon, through the sprawling limbs
The elm, a Goliath drooping from the weight of shadows,
Casts into the backlight,
My eyes catch snatches of the crescent moon
Leaning a bit too precariously to the right,
As though all cradled within its listing cornucopia
Might slide out, into the void, and disappear.

Crickets singing various chants, ululant owls,
Screams and shouts lifting from the town ballpark,
Just blocks away, prowling dogs howling
Assimilate my silence, my pliant silence,
Into their sweet autumnal litany.
Listening, I pause, occasionally,
To applaud their outrageous masquerades and charades,
Who would have me for their Pierrot,
Their resident poet, keeper of secrets.

Such pleasure abounds, in day's closing down —
Or, may I say, apotheosis?
*

By the way, where are you, forgotten lady,
Whom I just saw languishing beside youth's pool,
Where we tasted each other's nakedness?
Ah, but that was two decades ago,
Before we shaped children out of our clay,
Slipped from the moon's cradle, into the void,
Disappeared into middle-aged complacency.

That was before . . . ah, but why temporize,
Try to justify history's misbegotten ways?
Tonight, we yet survive, despite our separateness.
Sitting amidst these mellifluous crickets,
I wish not that we might be as before
But as we are, that we might yet explore
What's left of love's metaphoric Horae,
Scavenge the sky's floor, for doubloons and other moons
Repousséd with our faces, search the earth, for signs of our
    newest designs.

9/17/85 — [2] (04135)

Only at Home on the Range

He merges onto the freeway, his urge to flee
With the streaming traffic's desperate momentum
That of a plains buffalo
Stampeding, with an entire herd, over a cliff,
To keep from being consumed by fire.
As he goes south, neither staccato stops and starts
Nor sporadic rain gusts
Discourage his nervous need to escape the city,
Detoxify his imagination.

Twenty-five, fifty, seventy-seven miles
Show behind his odometer's glass,
Before he realizes breathing comes more easily.
Now, the chameleonic sky is a prairie
Dotted with thousands of buffaloes
Lazily grazing on tasseled grasses.
At the western edge of the unfenced horizon,
He recognizes, in the humped, horned shape
Drinking from his ascending gaze, himself.

9/23/85 (05944)

Willy's Lucky Horseshoe

Seeking a different exit, to flee the city,
This dewy, translucent a.m.,
Taking a new highway, heading west,
Toward morning's peripheries,
He glimpses, to his right, nestled in trees
Rapidly passing through puberty, into dissolution,
The old Webster Groves depot,
Near which he and his buddy Colin
Used to crouch in wait, with stones,
To pelt groaning Mo-Pac freights,
Dream of holding up, barefisted,
Gleaming Santa Fe passenger trains
Slowing as they approach the station,
Before threading the West's wide eye.

The vision is incandescently ephemeral,
A guttering coal-oil lamp's sputtering glow.
Yet just being able to probe recesses
Almost forty years deep,
On what, otherwise, would have been routine guard duty
His somnambulistic soul performs from memory,
Lets him know he's still breathing,
Under two-score years' rubble.
All day, making his rounds, out and in
And out again, store to emporium,
He remains euphoric. His flabby belly is taut,
Diminished gray hair a blond flattop.

Perhaps, today, he'll find a horseshoe, too,
To place over a track,
Then dash away, stay hidden under Colin's bed,
As he and his pal once did,
Waiting, within that demon-ridden Cave of Montesinos,
For fate to foreclose on their deed,
Afraid they'd made a grave mistake . . .
Waiting to pay the devil his wages,
For allowing them to play at his gaming tables.
But dinner, that night, at his friend's house,
Was just one more unimmediate conversation
About Iwo Jima, Corregidor — no derailed trains nearby.
*

The statute of limitations, on his secret, has elapsed.
Maybe it's time for another rash act.

9/26/85 — [1] (02337)

Road-sary

Under his breath, onion-pungent
From his overindulging at the luncheon salad bar
At Zeno's Truck Stop,
His tongue reiterates its well-worn litany,
Rubbing teeth as though they were beads
Emanating placenames instead of prayers.
Rolla, St. James, Cuba, Sullivan,
Union, Pacific, Eureka, St. Louis
Echo, in the cab's acrid air,
Like sins disclosed, in a confessional,
By transgressor to invisible priest,
Designations filling emotions with loneliness,
Like a child blowing bubbles inside bubbles
Drooping, not floating, into liquescent whispers,
The names an idiot's slobbering nonsense
He's listened to himself spew, a thousand times,
On trips between dawn's loading depot
And sunset's crowded terminal docks.
Why today's haul should seem such slow going,
He has no notion, unless it's the cargo —
His twitching heart — shifting positions unpredictably,
In its otherwise empty compartment.

9/26/85 — [2] (05945)

Overtaken

Racing south, against inbound highway traffic
Backed up eighteen miles,
He bites his thumb, with arrogant flair —
A Shakespearean taunt to fate,
Which, in another shape and age-space,
Might have demanded his complete subservience also.

This cold end-of-September dawn,
He applauds his great fortune
To have been assigned habit and routine
As deaf-and-dumb guardians.
He's a seeker and seizer of philistine freedoms,
A creature questing easy philosophies

To justify not his quixotic existence
But that of masses (among whom he passes
With misanthropic disdain
And specific bigotry aimed at the working class)
Who, during his four road hours, five days a week,
Curse his early retirement from life.

Speeding toward Farmington,
Where he'll do accumulated bills,
Write long-overdue letters to dead friends,
Revise a few newly scribbled verses
From cantos he composed two decades ago,
In his soundproof office/booth/cubicle,

He's seized in the gut, by gripping pain
Pulsating from butt bone to his brain-base.
Abruptly, he pulls onto the shoulder,
Shuts off the motor, sits listening to the silence
Filing past like a cortège
Whisking him away, inside his own glazed eyes.

9/30/85   (05946)

Ghost House ^Δ

Tourists with an afternoon to kill,
Bookish sorts, and the simply curious approach,
Come close, closer, to the porticoed porch,
Glimpsing their own glaring faces
In windows into which they peer, as they focus on interiors
Once inhabited by real people,
Not poltergeists, shadows their imaginations cast,
Hopeful of penetrating a mystical force field,
Entering lives hovering, yet, in the dusty stillness:
Those of Estelle, Pappy, Jill, Vic-Pic,
Sister and Bill, Buddy, too, perhaps,
*

And the ubiquitous blacks — Uncle Ned, Broadus,
Mammy Callie, Boojack, Julia.
Desirous of registering the vaguest acquaintance with this place,
Exchanging, for a particle of its rich history,
Their entire ordinary inheritances,
They negotiate the mazy shrubs, paddock,
Brick grottoes, rotting cedar fence posts
That once guided spotted Texas ponies in,
From the back pasture, to Faulkner's pen.
Some spend hasty minutes,
Others precious afternoons, capturing the illusion.
Eventually, each leaves,
Whose changes, however seemingly monumental
Or oblique, change nothing.
Not a solitary cedar, mildewing clapboard,
Canting green-slatted shutter sighs in relief.
Intact, unfazed, the neo-Greek frieze
Is assimilated into Oxford's October twilight.
Evermore a passive agent,
Rowan Oak submits to the slowly fading ages.

10/4/85   (03544)

[Oxford, Charlottesville, Baton Rouge] ‡

Oxford, Charlottesville, Baton Rouge
Are loci along an invisible circumference
His peripatetic mind connects
Whenever he gets *non compos mentis*.
His is an ever-diminishing centripetal existence,
A journey to the center of forgetting,
That black hole, at each day's end,
He frequently mistakes for serried sunset.

This morning, he penetrates the Horned Gates,
Clears the spectral city,
Escapes, along the concrete wilderness
Dotted with transports ferrying carnivals,
Missiles and tanks, corrosive waste,
Between Oklahoma, Arkansas, and Tennessee,
And flies by scruffy-faced, bloodshot-eyed hitchhikers
Squatting at roadside, hoping for a ride to sunset.

Neither amnesia nor premature Alzheimer's disease
Conspires to divert him from his intended destination.
Instead, he's certain the direction in which he heads,
He's never before reckoned.
Not even the leaves autumn has stippled
In gay stage attire engage his eyes,
Resurrect his melancholy from its dazed gaze,
Or let him refocus the widening sunset,

Toward which he drives undeviatingly,
In order to gauge his arrival.
Curiously, he checks mileage.
The reels register zero, zero, zero,
Zero, zero, as though all his road-time
Were a coefficient of nonmotion
Or his car had been suspended, by an electromagnet,
From a crane fastened to a quay along sunset

10/14/85 — [1] (05947)

Dad in His Empty Country Castle

A pint-size jack rabbit
We first saw earlier this summer,
Squirming in its crowded nest —
A bed of needles beneath the Austrian pine
Shading our ancient, canted barn/stable —
Takes frightened flight from hiding
Midst late October's drenched leaves.

Without realizing, I've violated its silence,
Almost annihilated its tiny physical right to exist
In an innocuous space it has chosen for nibbling clover,
Tender onion sprouts bunched in profuse clumps,
Munching dandelion stems . . . or is all this
One vast extension of my histrionic imagination,
Illusion nurtured by resident dryads of this abandoned place?

When I take closer focus,
It becomes humiliatingly obvious nothing remains of summer.
I discover myself marooned,
A derelict stranded in isolated inebriation,
Lonely old man bereft of wife, children, friends,
*

Inventing jack rabbits that roamed these acres,
Years ago, when all of us were just growing.

10/14/85 — [2] (04134)

Donne's "Meditation XVII": An Oblique Reprise

The Lessor of Evils is a creepy sort,
Satanic in his judicial robes
And profanely perfumed periwig, dealer in reality,
An avaricious stickler, the first of each month,
When payments on mortgaged souls come due,
A no-nonsense forecloser on overextended loans,
Note taker, a reiver's reiver,
Working just within the law's outermost limits,
To exact, on overbearing demand,
Self-interest compounded by the second.

He's neither Elizabethan Shylock nor modern Baruch
But Piers Everyman, not Babbitt either
Or rich "Rabbit" Angstrom,
Rather me and you, yours and mine,
Conspiring, through cartels, to bankrupt hell,
Dominate all bets, tables, tracks, rackets,
Stack the odds, the tarot packs,
With actions licentious, mercenary, pestilential,
Each of us a Monacan principality
Precarious as paradise, in our insular arrogance.

10/15/85 (05948)

The Dismantling

For Harriet Yeargain and Dolores Cleve

Within a summer's evanescent span
(That treacherous whitewater stretch of expanding channel,
Just before the bend portending river's plunge,
That exhilarates us with its vortices,
Whisperous, jutting V's, its rush),
We've witnessed attrition, man-made decay —
The shoreline of an entire civilization disappears.

Only the least recognizable traces give testimony
To changes wreaked on Farmington's heart:
The Ben Franklin five-and-dime
Wears, on its Gothic facade, neo-Latinate robes ("The Forum");
P. N. Hirsch has been reincarnated as Dollar General,
Whose superficial transmogrification belies progress —
Obsolescence is its own best advertisement.

Parallel to Columbia, on the square's east side,
Liberty shudders beneath Caterpillar half-tracks.
Cranes, dump trucks, backhoes groan and screech,
As Lilliputians hack at Gilded Age buildings,
Which, until almost just yesterday,
Purveyed (at Lerche's Firestone) tractor apparatus,
Springfield balloon tires, beside steel-belted radials,

Vended (at Mell's Furniture and Hardware)
Charter Oak cast-iron kitchen and parlor stoves,
Leftover '30s Roper gas ranges,
Next to microwave and convection ovens,
With pressed-wood bed- and living-room suites,
Venetian blinds, paints, kerosene lamps, mantles, sundries
Materializing, daily, from a loft fifty years deep.

Half a half-obliterated block above Washington,
Hesitantly settling into the dust, is the St. Francois Hotel,
Which once catered to Syphers and Dreiserian Drouets,
Drummers from St. Louis, Memphis, Kansas City,
Displaying, from black cases, up-to-date wares
(Calicos, buttons, lace trim, millinery),
Then became refuge for State Hospital No. 4 outpatients,

Sanctuary for the dispossessed, misbegotten,
Chronically depressed spirits among lesser mankind.
Now, on the eve of succumbing to total destruction,
Only severed drainpipes, transom frames,
Collapsed horsehair-plaster-and-lathing partitions remain —
Ephemeral perches for stray swallows, pigeons,
And curious, cursory gazes of derelict spectators.

Just two blocks to the north, on College and A,
Another crew, unanimously voted for and hired by the board,
Pokes at the shell of Farmington's first high school,
Poised to dismantle the chambered nautilus
*

One fluted classroom, convoluted corridor at a time,
Through which five generations passed,
As they grew to take their places in family trades.

Today, I document October's frenzied leaves
Being bullied, with taunts, by a warm rainstorm
Dancing ten miles away, atop Stono Mountain.
If their hysterical scattering suggested friendly rivers
Floated in youth's golden terrains (local Current,
Wisconsin's Brule, the Housatonic at Derby),
Not Styx or Lethe, I'd be ecstatic.

But I sense something amiss, on this too-warm morning,
When gusting leaves, crashing bricks, and displaced faces,
Like waters bearing my shattered spirit toward falls,
Warn of my own swiftly approaching dispersion.
Suddenly, awakening from museless stupor, I shiver.
Immersed in sadness, unable to ask, "What's next?,"
I brace for winter's onslaught.

10/18/85 — [1] (02056)

Poet Quixote Conceives His Next Sally

Landlocked by a colossal mind-block
Consisting of three parts disillusionment
On having discovered being discovered
Is of no monumental consequence,
Two portions distraction from well-wishers
And sycophants, five parts fuel
Diluted with various chemicals —
Caffeine, alcohol, sugar, and salt,
All working in chaotic opposition to each other —
He withdraws to his quixotic broom closet,
To await fate's intrusion,
Listening for his obituary to be read aloud,
By orderlies, sentries, cell guards pulling duty
Along corridors connecting thought and dreaming
With commerce being dizzily conducted
In streets just beyond hearing.

The years enveloping his deteriorating spirit
Are a convulsive snake-gut
*

Consuming its victim, in Lethean juices.
Finally, on resurrection day,
He gains the fortitude to shove back
The closet door, evacuate his melancholic cave.
To his bewilderment, he sees his intact shadow
Cast, in shameless nakedness, against the moon —
A dazed, cakewalking tatterdemalion
Thumbing his tongue, in mock-poetic reproach,
At his landlocked, mind-blocked coeval
Saddled in numbing catatonia,
Both poet and sidekick Sancho
Arrested, in cruciform eclipse, by ivory shafts
Emanating from an invisible core beyond all stars,
Two lunatics in one son of the Son,
Poised to tilt against cosmic windmills.

10/18/85 — [2] (05949)

Tennyson's Tithonus Lives

Summer grows old, overnight,
Going to bed, early October, awakening naked,
Amidst November's shiver. I, ageless Tithonus,
Record each tedious alteration the cycles register,
With curious ears, which hear their silent eyes
Crying for dwindled years
Migrating like wild geese forlorn and off course.

And I wonder why, stranded in this wilderness,
Without children and wife, by choice,
I'm still troubled, if slightly, by such fluctuations.
Perhaps certain vestigial memories
Persist from those primal times before I wished
Immortality might be mine, for a trick,
And I might slip time an elixir-of-youth Mickey,

Fix the days, in a perpetual calendar's maze.
Possibly, during this pungent season,
I simply respond, to leaves, yard rabbits and squirrels,
With heightened intensity, rise, to the resurrection
Of gentle creatures and shapes, with libidinous ego,
In my lusting to come alive, become vulnerable again,
Die holding hands with sirens and courtesans,

Gratify glands so long swollen with disuse
That just the cessation of pain is orgasmic.
Ah, what else have I,
To make everlasting survival worthwhile,
Except fantasizing? Otherwise, this bliss shits.
Tonight, let me indulge in all that might have been
Had hubris not gotten the better of my death wish.

10/22/85 (04133)

Absentee Landlord

Just this past week, he read
That by the time children reach age eighteen,
They've been exposed to, have contracted,
Vicariously enacted, eighteen thousand homicides,
Witnessed thirty thousand marital infidelities,
Lip-synced a half-million obscenities,
Via TV.

No wonder, he muses,
So few regard the future as an experimental zone
In which to bring, to fruition,
Youth's ambitious schemes, rather a Los Alamos,
On whose parched and sandy desolation
Salutary hopes for inner peace of mankind's mind
Are systematically exploded.

As day lengthens, his focus shifts
To situations closer to home.
He sees himself waving good-bye to his two kids
As they walk their dogs, on the front lawn,
Waving good-bye, a hundred thousand a.m.'s,
As if his arm, extended from the car window,
Were a sickle-bar scythe,

The scene itself one of myriad similar motifs
In a perpetually creaking praxinoscope
Depicting dad as Moses posting letters home, from Canaan,
Which contain paltry sums and promises,
Always promises to send for them
Just as soon as the Messiah arrives
And can be universally verified.

10/23/85 (04132)

[Exiting southwest, out of Gopher Prairie,]

Exiting southwest, out of Gopher Prairie,
He wrestles with questions
Resembling, in their ethical shimmering,
Old Testament angels
Announcing themselves to present and potential kings.

He deliberates on cruise missiles, skyjackings,
Lasers, Alzheimer's disease, TV,
Israeli, Egyptian, and Lebanese insurgencies,
Focuses, more concretely, on the family he's abandoning
To pursue his true vocation, poetry,

Whose mandate emanates not from passion,
Fanaticism, or unadulterated fascination
With universal perversion and perfection,
Rather from the nature of a hermetic curse
Sentencing him to eternal silence, via the written word.

As he drives, the questions grow less tendentious;
His irreconcilable answers lose stridence.
Like dry *fumé blanc*, time and miles
Conspire to dilute reason's heady juices,
Deplete memory's receptor-connector fluids.

By midday, he can no longer marshal
The many tentative explanations
He's assigned to numinous "why"s presiding over his psyche
Or resolutions to illusive "who"s, "when"s, and "how"s
Haunting him for centuries.

Curiously, this scribe from the lost tribe
Suddenly intuits the desolation
He traverses and his imminent destination,
That syllabled vault in which all words, like bones,
Return to the Word, echoing between unearthly firmaments.

10/28/85 (05950)

Halloween Prefigurations

As I descend onto I-55, from Highway 32,
My ferret eyes assimilate images,
*

Isolate the vagrant design of a displaced waif,
An aged bum wearing the human shape of morning's wino,
One hand thumbing amorphously,
The other awkwardly lugging a black suitcase
(He appears to be tugging at a bulldog,
Its teeth inextricably attached to his coat cuff).

All seventy-five miles to Cape Girardeau,
His persistent, if disinterested, plea for assistance
Distresses inner peace, clutters vision,
Keeps disturbing the air between me
And that distant merge. My neck hair bristles
As if each filament were charged with frictional electricity.
Nervously, I surface from stupor
In time to swerve, miss hitting a bird-perched carcass.

Soon, my usual coffee-break turnoff appears.
I exit, wait for traffic, before crossing.
After ordering at the fast-food drive-through,
I recross the highway, descend refreshed,
Ready to resume my trek.
As I pause to merge, my ferret eyes catch sight of,
Recognize, morning's wino, leaning into my right window,
Thumb cocked like the hammer of a loaded gun.

10/30 & 11/1/85 — [1?] (05951)

[Throughout the school, excitement crescendoes.] ‡

Throughout the school, excitement crescendoes.
Each child prepares for transfiguration.
Soon, the room will be crowded with personages:
Bluebeard, Spider-Man, Sherlock Holmes,
A two-legged pumpkin, Bolshoi prima ballerina,
Clowns, Draculas, spooks, goblins, specters.
Suddenly, the bell sounding the parade knells.
Halls, stairways, every available space overflow.
Darth Vaders, myriad Supermen, gorillas,
Tinker Bell, witches, claws, saber-toothed-tiger teeth,
Wings, halos, hobos, skeletons,
All manner of evil creature, pernicious beast

10/31/85 (01475)

Commuter's Tribulation

Almost every morning, at about the same drive,
Whether vaporous, torpid, dislocated, on waking, or lucid,
He switches on the wide-vision screen
His ubiquitous writing notebook magnifies
Through an intricately angled, kaleidoscopic mirror set
Emanating from a tiny reflector at brain's base
And enters a.m.'s microcosmic drama.

Normally, in a matter of familiar roadside scenes,
He sees his spirit release him.
Shapes swimming in dim, shimmering eye humors
Attract abstract ideas
Sifting constantly shifting thought-floors,
Like horseshoe crabs
Trying to record antecedent trilobites' tracks.

Even before day's destination names itself,
He's usually traveled eons, equidistantly,
In from his seated locus, eclipsed the moon,
In Vernean spaceships, rounded the Cape,
On frigates and clippers, descended the Grand Canyon, by mule,
Passed through the horizon, at highway's apex,
Where it connects with the sky.

But this dreary morning, as he aims south,
Driving does not achieve soaring.
Metaphors refuse him escape from concrete objects,
Notebook sheets won't exchange their silence,
For his secrets, and fantasy remains beyond reach.
Ahead, rising out of mist-shrouds,
He glimpses boredom — fortress where, daily, he makes his living.

11/1/85 — [2?] (05952)

The Rime of Ancient Willy ‡ Δ

No Eliotic measurements for Willy.
He gauges his life's seeping, its visible diminishment,
Not in cups of coffee consumed,
Cigarette butts smashed into ashtrays,
Teaspoons used to stir afternoon oolong
*

Or Darjeeling, rather in miles per diem,
Destinations reached and logged, motels stayed in,
Mom-and-pop shops stopped at and sold
Ones and twos of schlock stock,
As he tries to avoid crucifixion
While being nickel-and-dimed to death,
By buyers leveraging him with Taiwan prices,

He an innocent bystander to his own demise,
In a time when 807 programs,
Direct imports, domestic factory closings
Have undressed the proudest names in his industry.
Even today, setting out for Tipton,
Jeff City, Salisbury,
He realizes, unequivocally, Acme-Zenith is dead.
It's just a matter of seasons, now,
Before six decades of tight-knit relations
Between supplier and clients will perish,
Nearly sixty years' dedication to producing trousers,
Regarded as Pierce-Arrows, to the trade,
Will be consigned to the rag heap,
Spread with the heart's short ends, soul-selvages.

And he knows doubt's shadow intimately,
Knows that he's too old to continue
With a competitor company (there've been none,
For twenty years, in his part of the country,
And he doesn't speak Chinese, Portuguese, Polish).
At sixty-eight, he could easily retire,
Draw federal benefits, subsist "independently."
But not Willy! Not he!
Not while, yet, he has access to stock sheets
Crammed with odds-and-ends merchandise!
Not Acme-Zenith's crack disposer of goods,
Who still gets singular gratification
From writing an order! He won't quit!
Not Willy Sypher! He'd work without pay,
Before resorting to that. In fact,
He's on the road, this November 4,
Trying to peddle, "at a price,"
Pieces stores can offer as loss leaders:
Cruise-wear sale items, ten-year-old walk shorts,
Assortments in broken sizes, "high shades" —
Tangerine, banana, heliotrope, madras patches.

Ah, but just to be out on the road,
Going somewhere other than numb,
Behind a bowl of sweetened sliced peaches,
In a home watched over by midwives
Attending death's birthing
Or in a hospice redolent of Taiwanese plastic nosegays.
Willy knows he's lived too long alone,
Without dreams, comforted by mediocre hope
That when he goes out,
He'll be the best-dressed man at his own marriage,
To let specters of doom
Lull him into surrendering his fundamental resolve,
Pouring himself a carbon-monoxide highball,
Coaxing narcolepsy, with barbiturates,
Aiming for the black-belching funnel
Of an eighteen-wheeler's stack, like a Japanese kamikaze
Committing battleship hari-kari.

It's celebration, even at his age,
Passion, purpose, for their own lonely sakes,
That keep him on course, in the right lane.
And he'll move the shorts.
They'll reorder, good-naturedly denigrate him,
When he informs them there are no more,
Despite four hundred on reserve.
Could they possibly use a suitable substitute?
After all, anything at a sawbuck a dozen —
How can they lose? By week's end,
He will have decimated much of the surplus,
Commission from which just might cover expenses,
Might not. No subsidies, guarantees,
Sinecures cushion his failures — never have.
Always, he's been at home adrift,
Amidst those who go to church, in voguish robes,
In hope of avoiding drafts, catching cold
On their way to Judgment Day.
As for Willy, second-class citizenship
Has had its modest advantages, nonetheless:
Pariahs suffer fewer regrets from denial;
Trials with hung juries
And indeterminate sentences aren't discouraging;
Neither is disillusionment uprooting.
Willy Sypher, at sixty-eight,

11/4/85 (02336)

Sons of Sonnes of the Sunne

Why is it that only children and unaging poets
Notice slugs perched atop pumpkins,
Orb-webs strung under barn eaves,
Lucky pennies glistening, amidst trash, in gloomy streets,
Remember given names of inconsequential protagonists
In tedious movies, forget to exercise suspiciousness,
Even toward demondom's sleaziest fiends?

If invention, heightened perception, clairvoyance
Were only coefficients of gentleness and innocence,
And compassion a matter of philanthropy,
How easy it would be to achieve distinguishing credentials,
For admittance into the Order of Soaring!
But Seeing, Hearing, and the remaining uppercase senses
Are dependent on penetrating essences

Orbiting the earth, entering the life-force,
Composed of all gone souls
From pre-Cro-Magnon, through da Vinci and Einstein,
And the quick — me and you and our issue.
Even then, only those who locate the door
Opening onto the heavenly maze
Can hope to outgrow being children and poets, become suns.

11/11/85 (05953)

Blind Leading the Blind

> *Approaching the Reagan/Gorbachev*
> *November superpower summit talks*
> *in Vienna*

As though lumbering, across the horizon, on half-tracks,
His eyes clamor and squeak, turn on a dime
Whenever encountering sixty-degree resistance,
Barely avoid overturning,
Getting stuck in muddy gullies, abysmal ruts.
Sporadically, they gain purchase
Atop lots crowded with new and used cars,
Farm implements, heavy-construction machinery.
Unavoidably, they crush every fast-food shop,
*

Gas station, church along the obstacle course they negotiate,
Trying to escape this eerie simulation,
Into which they've irresistibly awakened, this dismal day.

But the eyes have it. There's no denying Armageddon,
Especially when retinas, exposed to space lasers,
Earth-clinging, radioactive fallout,
Can't defend themselves against instantaneous incineration,
Instead surrender to unending blindness
Emanating from sightless enemies outside and within.

11/13/85 — [1] (05954)

The Manager of Outlets Remembers *When*

Heading north, out of Rolla, toward Jeff City,
Acme-Zenith's crack manager of outlets
Can't resist a very rare backwards flash
To that time when he had just one
Freestanding store, not six, under his scrutiny.

How convenient then, merely descending stairs
To the cutting room, weaving, through piece goods
Stacked like log cabins, to the factory's far end,
To get to the eight hundred inauspicious, dim-lit square feet
(Enclosed by green bins backed with black pocketing fabric
And stuffed, in that trout-crowded stream,
To their five-tiered gills, with men's trousers)
That proclaimed themselves landlord and tenant
Of Missouri's first "Direct-from-Factory-to-You Outlet."

Coursing over tortuous Highway 63, past Vichy, Vienna,
He vaguely recalls the evolution from cigar box,
In which he kept cash tendered for polyester pants,
To computerized NCR, for his million-dollar business.
Too well he remembers the exact minute
He set out, as Windwagon Smithstein,
To explore new locations for his thriving enterprise,
Just when he selected Tipton, then Salisbury,
Jeff City, Rolla, and Poplar Bluff,

And why he never returned, from that first crusade,
To his easy, conveniently pleasing small-town routines:
*

Having become a respected cog in the company's clockworks,
He'd repeated, without realizing, the curse of his dispersed people,
Enslaved himself to chasing desert mirages.

11/13/85 — [2] (02677)

Apocalypse Then and Now, and Right Now!

Birth, copulation, death, dispersion —
The four whores of the twentieth-century apocalypse,
Who've transcended Pound, Eliot, Symons,
F. R. Leavis, F. O. Matthiessen,
Ridden herd on our most impressionable psyches,
Trammeled our fantasies, hallucinations,
Whose most daring interfaces simulate nuclear incineration.

Victims. We are those Greek Chimeras modernized,
Libidinized approximations of ghosts
Still loitering in Manhattan subways,
Waiting to be mugged, raped, shot, our perpetrators mistried,
For errors by police, lawyers, judges,
Freed, legitimized, and licensed to write books,
Like Ehrlichman, Haldeman, Dean, Saint Nixon.

Where is our location? Who are the origins we resemble?
Why do we grope for heroes to worship?
There should be hundreds from which to select,
Instead of a handful left over after purges
Among baseball players, Abscam legislators,
General Dynamics and Rockwell kickbackers,
DeLorean automakers, Miss *Penthouse* America.

Will time straighten out its curving lines,
Collide with our warped sensibilities,
Somewhere in space, or are we fated
To spend the rest of our anxieties
Praying Armageddon, unlike Halley's comet,
Will resist all the media hype and conveniently implode
Into a black hole, forget us overnight,

Not erupt like London under siege from screaming V-2 rockets
Launched from Goebbels-tongues,
Hitlerian/Mengelean rhetoric resonating from the Reichstag,
*

Above which eagles hovered, in numb frieze,
Below whose frozen moments decent people shivered,
Knowing they couldn't reverse prefigurations of Final Solutions
Or avenge Eva Braun's profane assignations?

We fumble in dimness, skimming scum from cream,
For lack of more satisfactory pastimes.
We congregate in churches, synagogues, mosques,
Buddhist shrines, Masonic temples,
Miming sacred writ, in hope of surviving lunatics
Encroaching on holy papal precincts,
And praying for absolution, salvation, freedom from subjugation

By Germanic pharaohs, American Ladue blue bloods,
Nouveau riche Jews (can you imagine the gall
Of those ball-less kikes?) recently anointed
Into the oldest fold man has ever contrived:
Bigoted parvenus. We crouch in cement bunkers,
Euphemistically called condominiums,
Attempting to elude plutonium radiation. What shrewd fools!

When will we lose or outrun or choose to deny delusions
We ourselves can defuse by simply refusing to refuse
To admit they exist? When might we outdistance confusion,
Relegate contemporary rulers to Zuul-slime,
Hire the Ghostbusters, to capture and spay Dana
The Gatekeeper, castrate Keymaster Louis,
Impeach Mr. Stay Puft Great White Hope?

Tonight, fighting to keep pace with the universal steeplechase,
We tremble, fearing immediate extinction,
As though our "fitness salads" were laced with Zyklon B
And our cardiovascular systems, having grown rancid,
Like overripe tomatoes doubling as heart attacks,
Had submitted to quad bypasses, angioplasties
Performed by society's most celebrated misfits:

MM, Clark Gable, Billy Faulkner, Brigitte Bardot —
I've known them all, without having suffered jealousy,
Penis envy, sibling rivalry, Oedipal complexes.
In the end, where conventional wisdom
Is merely an ideological analogue for "bottom line,"
Only the mathematics matters.
Whether *we* or *they* outnumber the other,

In underwater-, earth-, or sky-launched missiles —
Call them Cruise, MX, Polaris-based,
Or SDI laser-guided — is inconsequential.
Only the final explosion, which annihilates all, counts.
From that point forth, existence *is* up for grabs,
At best a return to Neanderthal birth, copulation, death,
At worst, cosmic dispersion.

11/13/85 — [3] (02672)

Small-Town Origins △

Childhood is the same small town
From which all of us came,
Before seeking more sophisticated surroundings
To domesticate our displaced spirits.

It's that vague place, in a midsummer's gaze,
We wistfully allude to, in dazed years,
As the whistle stop, named Freedom,
That youth's sleek express flew through,

Forging toward wisdom's conventional city,
To repeat Sister Carrie's disillusionment,
Or way station at Taylor, Mississippi,
Where Temple Drake prematurely detrained,

To rendezvous with her future's undoing.
Childhood is our heart's darling,
The collective fancy's silhouette
Shimmering against senility's dim scrim.

No matter how far we get,
Straying from our common circumstances,
We converge on a shared heritage,
Become heirs to, beneficiaries of, regret.

We overweigh daydreams,
Plotting escapes from bland fantasies,
Masterminding ways of recreating tree houses,
Cowboys, dolls, hide-and-seek epiphanies.

Even as fate designs personalized shrouds
To throw over our drowsy, opaque eyes,
*

We stroke blankets, suck thumbs,
And nestle death's numb, shrunken breast.

11/14/85 (00119)

The Manager of Outlets Takes a Breather

Having been out, five days, inspecting trap lines,
The manager of outlet stores,
For Acme-Zenith, heads home, Friday afternoon,
Through a diaphanous, dismal drizzle.
The city at the end of the stretch of I-70 he drives
Excites his fancy even less
Than those tiny heartland farm towns
He's left behind all week, in making his tedious rounds,
Except St. Louis is his weekend retreat,

That midstride between continuous motions,
Where he pauses, occasionally,
To collect his mail, register forwarding addresses,
The pivotal point of no return,
Both sides of which consist of alligator-filled lakes,
Quicksand, collapsed pilings
No longer supporting his precarious bridge,
Which once connected family and friends with vocation,
Source of his paltry ego's birth and death.

By six, he'll have penetrated the outskirts,
Begun maneuvering through the procession
Consisting of somnambulists, outpatients, ex-convicts
Drooping, in drowsy, groping stupors,
Toward hives, dens, lairs, stables, colonies
Inhabited with vaguely familiar helpmates
And facsimile issue. With deftness and luck,
He can expect to reach his dwelling
Reasonably intact, albeit with massive brain damage

Sustained while maintaining, with grace and courage,
Patience, under rush-hour fire.
Navigating his subdivision's tight curves,
Turning down his extended cul-de-sac,
At the precise end of which his condominium huddles
Like a buzzard perched on a rickety fence,
*

He finally spies his driveway, parks,
Hesitates slightly, before wading into the dark,
As if debating getting back in his car.

Ah, but two glasses of California Cellars later,
Followed by temple services,
Accompanied by his wife, Leah, and two children,
Itzak and Rebecca, he'll transcend depression
That, inevitably, is set loose as he unwinds —
That aftershock weeklong freedom creates.
By Sunday, he'll almost be a "new man," human,
Almost sleep through Monday morning's guillotine.

11/15/85 (02335)

Documentus devilmentibus

In youth, my heart and psyche
Formed a joint venture with Satan's crew,
Executed and had notarized an irrevocable pact,
A living trust guaranteeing total freedom,
License to perform lust,
Overindulgence of appetites — no mortal contingencies
Except the pervasive prospect of forfeiture
When flesh and intellect would intersect death,
At whatever threshold
Predetermined by the codicil
Attached to their original agreement.

Recently, coexisting has grown distasteful,
Increasingly unproductive: profits have steadily declined;
No stimuli excite hemispheres;
Once-pleasurable habits are flaccid;
Even invention, curiosity suffer oxygen debt;
And the five senses die, from satiety.
Rebuff has answered the spirit's few attempts
To renegotiate the legal document.
Frustration suggests abrogation, but cowardice
Refuses to act. Rapidly, the enterprise collapses,
Descends, shamefacedly, into the infernal abyss.

11/19/85 (05955)

The Peregrine

He flees identity, memory, destiny,
Allusive synonyms
Encapsulating present, past, future,
Fate's various incarcerations,
Located in aging's mind-prisons.
He flees silence, sanity, imagination, reason,
Trying to perform mortality's hat trick,
Grasp eternity's brass halo,
Squeeze it into a triple rainbow,
Beneath whose prismatic dazzle-facets
He might dissolve, be transfigured,
Lift out of Phoenix-ash, through Icarus-mist,
Into perpetual omniscient existence,
Equidistant from Earth, God, and his own myriad spirit.

12/4/85 (00834)

Latchkey Children ᐃ

We're up early, this Thursday morning,
Conspicuously nervous — my girl, Trilogy,
More punctual than normal,
Cleaning Basil's cage, showering, styling her hair,
Reviewing spelling words, for her test,
Troika the Boy holding close to his dad
(Knowing that, too soon, I'll have flown out of their lives),
And begging me to complete the Erector Set structure
We've been building together, all week.
Seated cross-legged, intense,
We pass, between us, tiny screwdriver, wrench,
Rivet fasteners,
Insert girders, cross-members, brackets,
And put finishing touches to our motorized culvert loader.

At best, breakfast is a satisfactory repast,
While Dad finishes packing, straps his bag,
Swills coffee, to awaken still cells.
Clipped laughter perforates the chill kitchen air.
We three share awareness of jeopardy's proximity,
Pretend my absence's duration will be only eight hours,
*

That I'll be waiting, in my red station wagon,
At Glenridge School, precisely at 3:30,
Instead of disembodied, somewhere in Gotham.
Now, all this recalled detail
Settles deeper into the indispensable *then*,
Buoying me northerly, forward, toward *where* and back,
When, again, our trinity will be intact.
Yet I question the efficacy of "quality time."

12/5/85 (00680)

Infidel

Having swallowed repast, with emphatic displeasure,
Happiness and laughter lacking,
We guide our separate identities,
Bearing identical surnames, to waiting cars
And make our impatient escapes.

My eyes trace your zigzag disappearance,
As my vehicle exceeds mach five,
Slips through memory's invisible barrier,
Into forgetting's weightlessness. My tears
Smear your sad face, in the rearview mirror.

Soon, dusk erases vision.
Indecision parallels isolation, for miles.
Instinct can't discriminate between truck stop
And motel. Chimeras, like flying fish,
Breach, crash into nightmare's ocean-sea.

Tigers leap out of misty headlights,
Sporadically scratching my irises.
My self-imposed amnesia implodes,
Consumes itself, until settling somewhere
No longer frightens my silent heart.

Even it knows the blood's diastole
Has spent its last cadences retreating from fate.
Tomorrow, I'll awaken later than usual,
Cast about, for stray reflections of the future,
And see you watching me recede.

12/11/85 (04131)

[Never has he been able to formulate a set pattern]

Never has he been able to formulate a set pattern
For shifting elements in the pecking order
His unstable thoughts daily develop.
Death of a friend, family member, client
All fall under a similar categorical case,
Nominative inconsequentially different from accusative,
Genitive and ablative silent bed partners
In dative's dark catacombs.
Weather, failure, children, millions, shelter
Carry identical atomic weights,
Genealogical classifications. He can't make distinctions.

Tonight, seated in a tufted, leather-covered chair,
In Katy Station, listening to others' whispers,
He peers, through gold-rimmed lenses,
At the nearby Christmas tree's myriad lights
And begins crying involuntarily.
He has no idea whether weeping signifies resistance
Or his quivering spirit's submission.
Rapidly, repeatedly, he jabs the tree.
Its unyielding needles cause bleeding.
For evening's remainder, he savors the pain,
As if entranced by ancient tribulations.

12/12/85 (02675)

The Glassworks

The Midwest through which I pass,
This sun-crazed 8 a.m.,
Is arrested, like Pompeii, under glaze.
Grass, trees, telephone lines, wire fences
Are fragile glass figurines
Captured in various attitudes of sway and sag.
They're so perilously rigid,
It seems the slightest twitch
Might snap, shatter, scatter their glistening brittleness.

Never have my diamond-flecked eyes
Registered such silvery vibrations,
*

Nor has my imagination scurried, so nervously,
To gather crystalline analogues
By which to savor such dazzling stimulation.
The landscape is indeed a Venetian works
Presided over by an absentee Lord
And artisans multiplying His glory,
Blowing new lumen-essences into ancient creations.

12/14/85 (05405)

Dreams Almost Close Enough to Smell

For David Morris

Somewhere, just a few dawning yawns ago,
He lost his balance, teetered precipitously,
Plunged off sanity's blunt edge,
And was snatched, halfway through free fall,
In nightmare's chimerical beak.

He landed amidst Nizzards and flying monkeys
Snapping, gnashing their saber-teeth,
Eating beetles, fish and lizard scales, bones,
Munching husks, sucking, as if from teats,
The feces and urine from mates' cloacae.

Abandoned in a perpetually desolate zone
Isolated, from the known world,
By four countries bordering his dazed state
(Dien Bien Phu, Laputa, Hiroshima, Chelmno),
He began disintegrating from the inside out.

For years, no creatures noticed his deformity,
Socially excoriated him, for his timidity.
They considered him congenitally phlegmatic
And left it at that, not worried
He might starve. They even dubbed him "Hunger Artist."

Only when his flesh began to resemble theirs,
Bubbled with pustules, scabs, oozing excrescences
Exuding the same odor of dead pests,
Did they sense his innate differences,
Realize they'd been harboring an alien.

Not until then, a few dawning yawns ago,
Did anyone press for his deportation,
Take measures to send him back
To Canaan in the Slough of Agent Orange,
Where he first sank in quicksand hallucinations.

Now, suddenly, he materializes over herbicidal skies,
Sees his shadow floating on a defoliated ocean.
Skidding, sweeping in narrowing gyres,
Memory descending, forgetting misting from the surface,
He rises, slides from bed, into a wheelchair, glides into morning.

12/17–18/85 (05956)

Winter Transfigurations

A scruffy, pinto mutt
Strays alongside the highway I ply,
Between Flat River and Potosi,
This frigid Thursday. From its innocuous position,
It threatens to invade and ravage me.
Though neither Nemesis nor Goliath,
I suffice as object for its scornful paroxysm.

What derisive, mean spirit
Might exist in that fyce's opaque brain
Can only be measured by miles, not confession.
For hours, I listen to its persistent yelping,
As if its invisible, gritty, foam-drenched tongue
Were licking my tympanums to numbness,
And am held prisoner, by its snarl-pitched bark.

Normally, the entire trip over Highway 8
Takes only minor toll on my energies.
Today, this persistent headache
Can't be misattributed. My frustration
Is occasioned by the unanticipated snowstorm
Engaging me, head-on, out of the northwest,
Howling, growling like a real son-of-a-bitch.

12/19/85 (05957)

[In this remote Midwest Bethlehem,] †

In this remote Midwest Bethlehem,
Seventy-five miles beyond the city's halo,
We partake of our own sacred celebration,
A secular feast on New Year's Eve,
We four together forever, tonight,
Shooting stars announcing our hearts' epiphany —
A mother, a father, two children

12/31/85

INDEX OF TITLES

Biographical Note

Louis Daniel Brodsky was born in St. Louis, Missouri, in 1941, where he attended St. Louis Country Day School. After earning a B.A., magna cum laude, at Yale University in 1963, he received an M.A. in English from Washington University in 1967 and an M.A. in Creative Writing from San Francisco State University the following year.

From 1968 to 1987, while continuing to write poetry, he assisted in managing a 350-person men's-clothing factory in Farmington, Missouri, and started one of the Midwest's first factory-outlet apparel chains. From 1980 to 1991, he taught English and creative writing at Mineral Area College, in nearby Flat River. Since 1987, he has lived in St. Louis and devoted himself to composing poems and short fictions. He has a daughter and a son.

Brodsky is the author of sixty volumes of poetry (five of which have been published in French by Éditions Gallimard) and twenty-three volumes of prose, including nine books of scholarship on William Faulkner and seven books of short fictions. His poems and essays have appeared in *Harper's*, *Faulkner Journal*, *Southern Review*, *Texas Quarterly*, *National Forum*, *American Scholar*, *Studies in Bibliography*, *Kansas Quarterly*, *Forum*, *Cimarron Review*, and *Literary Review*, as well as in *Ariel*, *Acumen*, *Orbis*, *New Welsh Review*, *Dalhousie Review*, and other journals. His work has also been printed in five editions of the *Anthology of Magazine Verse and Yearbook of American Poetry*.

In 2004, Brodsky's *You Can't Go Back, Exactly* won the award for best book of poetry, presented by the Center for Great Lakes Culture, at Michigan State University.

OTHER POETRY AND SHORT FICTIONS
AVAILABLE FROM TIME BEING BOOKS

YAKOV AZRIEL
In the Shadow of a Burning Bush: Poems on Exodus
Threads from a Coat of Many Colors: Poems on Genesis

EDWARD BOCCIA
No Matter How Good the Light Is: Poems by a Painter

LOUIS DANIEL BRODSKY
The Capital Café: Poems of Redneck, U.S.A.
Catchin' the Drift o' the Draft *(short fictions)*
Combing Florida's Shores: Poems of Two Lifetimes
The Complete Poems of Louis Daniel Brodsky: Volumes One–Three
Disappearing in Mississippi Latitudes: Volume Two of *A Mississippi Trilogy*
The Eleventh Lost Tribe: Poems of the Holocaust
Falling from Heaven: Holocaust Poems of a Jew and a Gentile *(Brodsky and Heyen)*
Forever, for Now: Poems for a Later Love
Four and Twenty Blackbirds Soaring
Gestapo Crows: Holocaust Poems
A Gleam in the Eye: Poems for a First Baby
Leaky Tubs *(short fictions)*
Mississippi Vistas: Volume One of *A Mississippi Trilogy*
Mistress Mississippi: Volume Three of *A Mississippi Trilogy*
Nuts to You! *(short fictions)*
Once upon a Small-Town Time: Poems of America's Heartland
Paper-Whites for Lady Jane: Poems of a Midlife Love Affair
Peddler on the Road: Days in the Life of Willy Sypher
Pigskinizations *(short fictions)*
Rated Xmas *(short fictions)*
Shadow War: A Poetic Chronicle of September 11 and Beyond, Volumes One–Five
Showdown with a Cactus: Poems Chronicling the Prickly Struggle
  Between the Forces of Dubya-ness and Enlightenment, 2003–2006
Still Wandering in the Wilderness: Poems of the Jewish Diaspora
This Here's a Merica *(short fictions)*
The Thorough Earth
Three Early Books of Poems by Louis Daniel Brodsky, 1967–1969: *The Easy
  Philosopher, "A Hard Coming of It" and Other Poems*, and *The Foul Rag-
  and-Bone Shop*
Toward the Torah, Soaring: Poems of the Renascence of Faith
A Transcendental Almanac: Poems of Nature
Voice Within the Void: Poems of *Homo supinus*
The World Waiting to Be: Poems About the Creative Process

866-840-4334
HTTP://WWW.TIMEBEING.COM

LOUIS DANIEL BRODSKY *(CONTINUED)*
Yellow Bricks *(short fictions)*
You Can't Go Back, Exactly

HARRY JAMES CARGAS *(EDITOR)*
Telling the Tale: A Tribute to Elie Wiesel on the Occasion of His 65th
  Birthday — Essays, Reflections, and Poems

JUDITH CHALMER
Out of History's Junk Jar: Poems of a Mixed Inheritance

GERALD EARLY
How the War in the Streets Is Won: Poems on the Quest of Love and Faith

GARY FINCKE
Blood Ties: Working-Class Poems

CHARLES ADÉS FISHMAN
Blood to Remember: American Poets on the Holocaust *(editor)*
Chopin's Piano

CB FOLLETT
Hold and Release

ALBERT GOLDBARTH
A Lineage of Ragpickers, Songpluckers, Elegiasts & Jewelers: Selected
  Poems of Jewish Family Life, 1973–1995

ROBERT HAMBLIN
From the Ground Up: Poems of One Southerner's Passage to Adulthood
Keeping Score: Sports Poems for Every Season

WILLIAM HEYEN
Erika: Poems of the Holocaust
Falling from Heaven: Holocaust Poems of a Jew and a Gentile *(Brodsky and Heyen)*
The Host: Selected Poems, 1965–1990
Pterodactyl Rose: Poems of Ecology
Ribbons: The Gulf War — A Poem

866-840-4334
HTTP://WWW.TIMEBEING.COM

TED HIRSCHFIELD
German Requiem: Poems of the War and the Atonement of a Third Reich Child

VIRGINIA V. JAMES HLAVSA
Waking October Leaves: Reanimations by a Small-Town Girl

RODGER KAMENETZ
The Missing Jew: New and Selected Poems
Stuck: Poems Midlife

NORBERT KRAPF
Blue-Eyed Grass: Poems of Germany
Looking for God's Country
Somewhere in Southern Indiana: Poems of Midwestern Origins

ADRIAN C. LOUIS
Blood Thirsty Savages

LEO LUKE MARCELLO
Nothing Grows in One Place Forever: Poems of a Sicilian American

GARDNER McFALL
The Pilot's Daughter

JOSEPH MEREDITH
Hunter's Moon: Poems from Boyhood to Manhood

BEN MILDER
The Good Book Also Says . . . : Numerous Humorous Poems Inspired by
  the New Testament
The Good Book Says . . . : Light Verse to Illuminate the Old Testament
Love Is Funny, Love Is Sad
What's So Funny About the Golden Years
The Zoo You Never Gnu: A Mad Menagerie of Bizarre Beasts and Birds

CHARLES MUÑOZ
Fragments of a Myth: Modern Poems on Ancient Themes

866-840-4334
HTTP://WWW.TIMEBEING.COM

MICHEAL O'SIADHAIL
The Gossamer Wall: Poems in Witness to the Holocaust

JOSEPH STANTON
A Field Guide to the Wildlife of Suburban Oʻahu
Imaginary Museum: Poems on Art

SUSAN TERRIS
Contrariwise